Professional Series

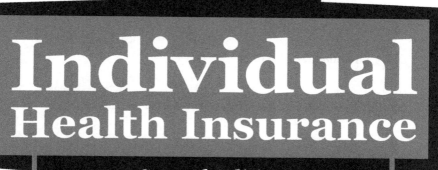

Individual Health Insurance
Second Edition

Hans K. Leida   *William F. Bluhm*

ACTEX Learning
Greenland, NH

Copyright © 2015, 2021

All rights reserved. No portion of this
book may be reproduced in any form or
by any means without the prior written
permission of the copyright owner.

Request for permission should be addressed to:
    ACTEX Learning
    P.O. Box 69
    Greenland, NH 03840

Manufactured in the United States of America

10 9 8 7 6 5 4 3 2 1

Cover Design by Jeff Melaragno

Library of Congress Control Number: 2015955666

ISBN: 978-1-62542-484-6

TABLE OF CONTENTS

Acknowledgments		v
Preface to the Second Edition		vii
About the Authors		ix
Chapter 1	Introduction	1
Chapter 2	The Products	29
Chapter 3	Policy Forms	85
Chapter 4	Managing Antiselection	109
Chapter 5	Setting Premium Rates	161
Chapter 6	Reserves and Liabilities	213
Chapter 7	Financial Reporting and Solvency	263
Chapter 8	Forecasting and Modeling	293
Chapter 9	Regulation	323
Chapter 10	Other Insurer Functions	373
Chapter 11	Managing the Business	391
Index		419
Appendix A	Section 52.7 of New York's Regulation 62	A-1
Appendix B	Report to the NAIC's A&H Working Group of the Life and Health Actuarial Task Force	B-1
Appendix C	Rate Filing Task Force Model User Hints	C-1
Appendix D	Health Insurance Reserves Model Regulation	D-1
Appendix E	Guidelines for Filing of Rates for Individual Health Insurance Forms	E-1

ACKNOWLEDGMENTS

A textbook such as this cannot really be written by one person. There is just too much knowledge needed. For this reason, in this process, I relied on the support of a number of other experts in this field to buttress my own incomplete knowledge.

First of all, my sincere thanks to Amy Pahl and Dawn Helwig. Both of them not only acted as reviewers (and caught some potentially embarrassing errors—thanks for that, too), but they also contributed specific material, even writing a few pages themselves, on the subjects of Long Term Care and Medicare Supplement. These colleagues are the people I go to myself when I have questions in those areas.

A number of others have reviewed one or more versions of the text in total, and provided valuable comments and critique. Some was hard to hear, but then I've found that the most valuable comments are always the ones that are hard to hear. These excellent reviewers include Rowen Bell, Gail Hall, Cecil Bykerk, Howard Bolnick, Rod Turner, Bob Beal, and Jim Oatman. Thank you all for taking the time and energy to help make this book worthwhile.

I am grateful for specific expertise contributed by Julia Philips, Claude Ferguson, Harvey Campbell, Darrell Spell, and Tom Wildsmith. Also, three trade associations graciously helped me (without asking anything in return other than a reference in the book); the Council on Affordable Health Insurance (CAHI), America's Health Insurance Plans (AHIP), and the Blue Cross/Blue Shield Association (BCBSA).

My thanks to those actuarial students in the Minneapolis office of Milliman who helped by working through the exercises (making sure they could be done with the information available), and even developing the spreadsheets of data for that purpose. This included Missy Gordon (who was Missy Westrom when we started this project), Dave Vnenchak, and Nick Poels.

I thank my Minneapolis colleagues for tolerating my absence as I worked on this project. I hope you will find it a worthwhile exchange.

Most of all, I want to thank my family. It led to fewer hours together, as I burrowed into my upstairs office, and I appreciate that sacrifice. Thanks for your support. Let's go on a vacation.

St. Paul, Minnesota   Bill Bluhm
March 2007

PREFACE TO THE SECOND EDITION

When Bill Bluhm asked me to write the second edition of his individual health textbook, he warned me that I didn't know how much work it was going to be. I didn't believe him at the time – I'd already done one book with my advisors in grad school – but as I found many times over the years I worked for him, Bill has a really annoying habit of being right.

When I left academia, my advisor told me I might regret it when I found myself working for "some awful boss." Happily, that wasn't what happened, though I'd be lying if I said there weren't moments when I thought back on that prophecy. In Bill, I found a mentor who valued many of the principles that had drawn me to academics in the first place, and above all a rigorous pursuit of the truth. Bill, thank you for entrusting your book to me, and I hope you are happy with the result.

As I started this project, I knew the main updates to the book would address the changes that have been and continue to be made by the Patient Protection and Affordable Care Act (ACA). Indeed, that law has touched nearly every aspect of our healthcare system, and has saturated my day-to-day practice as an actuary for the past five years.[1] This law often evokes very personal and emotional reactions in many people. I've done my best to provide an objective take on the new requirements under the law and its vast tapestry of associated regulations. They have proven to be a moving target, to say the least – imagine mowing a huge lawn, where as soon as you've finished you find it is time to start again. I can only hope the pace of change eventually slows somewhat, so that this book isn't out of date before the ink is dry.

When incorporating the new ACA material, I often faced decisions on whether to jettison older material altogether or, instead, integrate the new while retaining much of the old as well. In many cases, I chose the latter path. Some might argue the end result is more disjointed than it would be

---

[1] And, most surprisingly, earned me a citation in a U.S. Supreme Court decision (King v. Burwell).

if I'd been more ruthless in my pruning. To that, I'd counter that this book reflects the present reality of the individual major medical market, which contains a mixture of policies operating under the old rules (grandfathered and transitional plans) and the new (everything else). Understanding the history of how the market operated before the ACA is of course also important in understanding how we got where we are today.

While the updates for healthcare reform were the most extensive, I found that nearly every subject in the book was in need of at least some attention. In particular, the section on Medicare Advantage and Part D was greatly expanded. I also did my best to clarify the treatment of policy reserves in Chapter 6, because many people told me there was room for improvement in that section. Lindsy Kotecki provided invaluable help on both those efforts, for which I'm grateful.

Indeed, I could not have finished this project without the help of many people. My editor, the endlessly patient Gail Hall, was a great source of encouragement. My colleagues Bob Beal, Amy Pahl, Missy Gordon, Ashlee Borcan, Jeff Anderson, Ken Clark, Leigh Wachenheim, and Jeremy Engdahl-Johnson all provided helpful peer review of various sections of the text and suggested updates. The reviewers recruited by the publisher – Rowen Bell, Dawn Helwig, Tom Wildsmith, and Rod Turner – also provided invaluable feedback. Stan Westrom did an amazing job organizing and coordinating a small army of fact checkers in the Minneapolis office of Milliman, including Jackie Daniels, Andrew Schwarze, Stephanie Moench, Stephen Taubel, David Dobberfuhl, John Hebig, Caleb Stracke, Shawn Stender, Michael Emmert, Jeff Abbas, and Bryan Rask. Any errors that remain after all their work are mine and mine alone.

Hans Leida, July 2015

ABOUT THE AUTHORS

William F. Bluhm, recently retired as a Principal and Consulting Actuary with Milliman in Minneapolis. Bill joined that firm in 1983, when he opened the Albany office, and was in Minneapolis since 1987.

Bill spent his career in the health insurance field, working with insurers, health benefit providers, and governments. In that time, he was a frequent speaker and award-winning author. He was Principal Editor of the first six editions of the well-known and highly regarded textbook, *Group Insurance*. Many of his works have been required reading on the Society of Actuaries' exam syllabus.

Bill is a past Board Member for the Society of Actuaries, the Conference of Consulting Actuaries, and the American Academy of Actuaries, as well as Past President of the latter two. Bill was also recently awarded a Lifetime Achievement Award by his colleagues at the Conference of Consulting Actuaries. Currently Bill and his wife, Christine, run their winery, Dancing Dragonfly Winery, in St. Croix Falls, WI.

Hans K. Leida is a Principal and Consulting Actuary with Milliman. He joined the firm in 2006 after completing a PhD in mathematics at the University of Wisconsin-Madison. Hans is a Fellow of the Society of Actuaries and a Member of the American Academy of Actuaries.

Hans has a great deal of experience with group and individual commercial major medical coverage, as well as Medicare Supplement and Medicare Advantage plans. Recently, he has been helping clients navigate the changes made by the Patient Protection and Affordable Care Act's healthcare reforms. Hans is a frequent speaker and prolific writer on healthcare reform, and he is regularly quoted on that topic by the media, including in *The Wall Street Journal*, *Reuters*, *Bloomberg Businessweek*, and *Modern Healthcare*.

In 2007, Hans co-authored a paper for America's Health Insurance Plans (AHIP) on the impact of guaranteed issue and community rating laws adopted by certain states in the 1990s. That paper, which was updated in 2012, has been widely cited with the advent of federal healthcare reform, most notably by the Chief Justice of the U.S. Supreme Court in his opinion on the case regarding availability of premium subsidies in federal exchange states (*King v. Burwell*).

Hans also has significant experience with risk adjustment and predictive modeling of healthcare costs, and created the prescription drug-based risk adjuster included in the Milliman Advanced Risk Adjusters (MARA) software product. Hans lives in Minnesota with his wife Sarah and their three very active little boys, Levi, Sam, and Miles.

CHAPTER 1

INTRODUCTION

1.1 THE INDIVIDUAL HEALTH INSURANCE MARKETPLACE

HISTORY

As is true of many things that have evolved, rather than having been created or discovered, it is difficult to pinpoint the advent of **individual health (IH)** insurance. In the mid to late 1800s, there were individual accident disability policies that gradually evolved to essentially full-blown disability policies by the early 1900s. Benefits covering the cost of medical care and nursing care[1] were also introduced in the early 1900s, but were generally of limited benefit amounts and typically attached to disability policies as minor additional benefits.

The Roaring '20s (1920s) are known as a wild and crazy time, with social boundaries in many areas being bent and broken. This was also true in health insurance (which was still mostly **disability income (DI)** coverage), with major liberalizations of benefits, underwriting protections – particularly regarding overinsurance – and other policy provisions. Many of these liberalizations proved to be unwise, as there were significant losses to insurers from this source following the major economic downturn of 1929, the downturn that also marked the beginning of the Depression. A retrenchment in health insurance practices followed, and some companies exited the business. Some of those companies that had been less liberal in their policies were able to weather the storm, and continued to issue DI coverages.

---

[1] "Nursing care" in this context refers to coverage of the cost of having nurses attend the patient, either at home or in the hospital. It does not refer to today's "Nursing *home* care," or long term care.

In the mid-1930s, a new cycle of liberalization occurred. These liberalizations were more modest, and generally represented loosening of the exclusions that had previously applied. In this decade the first product that provided broad medical coverage for accidents was introduced. It was sometimes called "blanket accident" coverage, although "blanket" has at least one other meaning in an insurance context – a specific type of group coverage. The benefits included coverage for expenses of hospital, surgical, medical, and nursing care, including miscellaneous charges, when due to accidental injury.

Shortly thereafter, coverage extended to medical costs due to sickness as well. Medical expense policies were increasingly sold separately from DI (also called, at that time, "weekly indemnity") policies. Family coverage was also introduced.

Group insurance had a roughly parallel development with individual insurance, up until the 1940s when the U.S. government imposed price-wage controls that limited employers' ability to raise salaries. This created incentives for development of rich benefit plans, particularly since they were tax deductible to the employer and were not taxable as income to the employee. Individual insurance did not benefit from the same tax advantages. These strong financial incentives (in the group market) have shaped the current individual health insurance market, in that much of it has become a residual market, covering those people who, for one reason or another, are not covered under group insurance.

The group insurance marketplace had an impact on individual insurance in another way. Many group policies contained a provision that gave individual insureds the right to obtain an individual contract at such time as their group coverage ended.

In 1945, in the midst of a significant poliomyelitis epidemic, the first "specified illness" policy was introduced. This policy covered expenses for the treatment of polio, which was a high-cost illness. With the advent of the Salk and Sabin vaccines, new polio cases dropped to almost zero, and polio policies were replaced by the next generation of specified illness policies – "dread disease" policies. In these policies, payments are made, either as a flat amount or to reimburse expenses, due to diagnosis of a disease from a list specified in the policy. These typically included diphtheria, smallpox, meningitis, encephalitis, and rabies. The next generation of such policies focused on a major disease of the latter half of the 20th century – cancer.

Most recently, there is a new, emerging product worldwide, called **critical illness**. This represents the latest iteration of a specified disease policy, and seems to be much more popular internationally than in the U.S. The number of diseases included in the policy can vary from as few as three to over 100. There is substantial innovation in product design internationally, and great attention is being paid to future projections of disease incidence.[2] Regulators in the U.S. have generally been more restrictive than elsewhere. In particular, in New York specified disease policies have been prohibited for decades, as a matter of public policy.

For disability income insurance, the cycle of "liberalization followed by retrenchment" has continued to the current day. In the '60s and '70s, many liberalizations were made on policies which are renewable at the option of the policyholder, at guaranteed premium levels (**non-cancellable** or **non-can** policies). Since companies could not change premiums on major portions of their business, and since the more recent trough ('70s - '90s) in the financial cycle lasted longer than is typical, retrenchments to bring the business into the black have taken longer than expected.

This trough of profitability, and its length, was exacerbated somewhat due to a lengthening of the duration of claims experienced by the industry, combined with pricing based on previous (shorter duration) experience. As the worse experience (longer claims) emerged, companies had to strengthen their reserves to recognize the worse experience. The reserve strengthening occurred later, on existing claims from earlier policy sales, after premiums for new sales had been raised.

More recently, in light of the losses in the '80s and '90s, there has been some retrenchment in the market and the profitability of the DI business has improved. Table 1.1 shows the pattern of interest-adjusted loss ratios experienced by the carriers with the largest blocks of non-can policies from 1990 to 2013.

---

[2] SOA, *The Record*, Vol 29, No. 1, Session 60PD.

Table 1.1
Historical Statutory Interest-Adjusted Incurred Loss Ratios for Non-Can DI[3]

Year	Incurred Loss Ratio	Year	Incurred Loss Ratio
1990	67.2%	2002	76.5%
1991	68.8%	2003	73.8%
1992	73.9%	2004	72.2%
1993	76.3%	2005	65.4%
1994	85.3%	2006	70.1%
1995	89.3%	2007	65.1%
1996	90.9%	2008	58.5%
1997	87.7%	2009	63.0%
1998	85.8%	2010	60.7%
1999	78.8%	2011	64.5%
2000	71.5%	2012	65.1%
2001	73.3%	2013	61.3%

Long term care (LTC) insurance changed to a greater extent, and more quickly than DI, and promises to become even more important as the population continues to age. The majority of LTC sales are made through individual contracts. When group policies are sold, they often still look like individual coverage – the insurer issues or declines on an individual basis, although often using less stringent underwriting. The greatest changes since the early policies have come in the criteria used to determine benefit eligibility. Originally, very limited benefits were covered, because there was no accepted way to limit the potential for antiselection or abuse. As benefits became more liberal, **activities of daily living** were introduced as criteria. Today's policies have evolved to also typically include cognitive impairment among the criteria for benefit eligibility. As of 2013, there were over 7 million LTC insureds, with approximately $12 billion of premium in force.[4]

Today's policies are typically written to provide benefit payments to people who are unable to care for themselves due to: (1) an injury, such as paralysis from a car accident, (2) a chronic illness, such as arthritis, (3) an acute epi-

---

[3] *Non-Can DI: 2013 Financial Results*, by Mark Seliber, FSA, published in the Milliman's *Disability Newsletter*™.

[4] *US Individual Long-Term Care Insurance Annual Review 2013* and *US Group Long-Term Care Insurance Annual Review 2013*, published by LIMRA

sode such as a stroke, or (4) a cognitive impairment, like Alzheimer's Disease. Policies may provide coverage for one or more care settings including nursing home, assisted living facility, and/or home health care.

The previous paragraphs describe stand-alone LTC insurance; products which combine LTC insurance with life or annuity insurance, however, have grown in popularity. These products are often referred to as combination or linked products and use the death benefit or annuity value to pay LTC services should the insured/annuitant become disabled.

In medical insurance, since the 1950s there has been ongoing gradual liberalization of products. This has been true with respect to benefits, underwriting, and policy provisions. The greatest change with respect to medical benefits has probably been the liberalization of benefit limits, both overall limits and **inside limits**. (Inside limits are benefit limits applied to specific types of services, such as "doctors' office visits," or "hospital outpatient charges.") In addition, state legislatures have required insurers to either include, or offer to include, a large variety of additional policy benefits and provisions. These are often called "mandated" or "mandated make available" benefits, respectively.

By the 1960s, both **Blue Cross/Blue Shield (BCBS)** and commercial major medical products provided coverage for a wide range of hospital and medical services. In their early days, Blue Cross plans typically provided hospital coverage, and Blue Shield plans provided medical (professional services) coverage. Because Blue Cross and Blue Shield companies were typically separate companies (even when cohabiting the same location and using the same systems), they issued separate contracts, and a third contract could be written (by one of the two companies, or perhaps even by a third carrier) to provide "supplemental" coverage over the two basic policies. Sometimes the supplemental coverage included the Blue Shield coverage as well (**wraparound** coverage.) Commercial coverages often were designed to compete with these, and the products included "basic hospital," "basic medical," and "supplemental" or "miscellaneous" charges.

Basic hospital coverage would often provide first dollar inpatient care, up to a fixed number of days' hospital stay. Surgical coverage was provided according to a fee schedule included in the contract. Such fee schedules were often based on either the Society of Actuaries' table or the California Relative Value Schedule (in the 1950s - '70s). In those days (still the '60s, into the '70s), miscellaneous charges were a relatively small part of total expected cost. Since that time, many hospital and physician services that used to be included in basic covered charges have been unbundled, and are charged for separately by the providers. In addition, the practice of medicine has become much more technologically dependent, providing far more treatments that depend on expensive equipment and drugs than previously. Inside limits on miscellaneous charges soon became outdated.

One particular element of charges stands out as having started as a relatively immaterial element of claim cost, and has become quite significant: prescription drugs. In 1985, prescription drugs represented under 5% of National Health Expenditure in the United States. Two decades later, in 2005, this grew to a whopping 10.1%, of a much larger number. (The total health care cost bill per person increased 268%.)[5] Comparable figures for insured individuals show an even higher trend.

For these reasons, as well as the market attractiveness of a single policy combining all benefits, **comprehensive major medical (CMM)** emerged and became the predominant policy for covering major medical expenses. In the '90s, some HMO-type benefit provisions (co-pays rather than deductibles) were used.[6]

The latest medical policies, typically structured as a **PPO product**, combine both types of features, depending on the benefit and depending on whether benefits are being provided in network (by providers who are part of the insurer's network) or out of network. There is typically a richer set of benefits provided for in network services, and a leaner (high deductible, plus other changes) set of benefits provided for out of network benefits.

There have been a number of situations in recent decades when the U.S. federal government has intervened in the individual health insurance market to generate new coverages or products. This includes putting restrictions in the Medicare Supplement market (to stem perceived abuses in the market at that time), development of alternative delivery systems for Medicare benefits (Medicare Advantage programs), and others. Many of these are described later in this text.

---

[5] www.cms.gov
[6] Described further in Chapter 2.

When the U.S. government passed the **Health Insurance Portability and Accountability Act of 1996** (HIPAA), it had a significant impact in the individual major medical marketplace. It affected plan design, market strategies, IT policies and process, privacy practices, and others. It also affected the states, inducing significant changes in how the states regulated those policies.

An additional program began in 1998, when the U.S. created state administered programs to insure children, called the **State Children's Health Insurance Program** (SCHIP, later renamed simply **CHIP**). The federal government provided billions of dollars of matching funds for states to adopt CHIP programs. The program was initially scheduled to end in 2007; in that year it was reauthorized until 2009. In 2009 it was expanded and reauthorized until 2013, and then further extended by the **Patient Protection and Affordable Care Act (ACA)** of 2010 until 2015.

As of January 1, 2004, U.S. federal law created a new product in the marketplace – the **Health Savings Account (HSA)**. This is a combination of a self-insured account and a high deductible individual policy. Under this federal law, contributions to the self-insured account are made from pre-tax income, and accumulate tax free, provided that the account is ultimately used for such expenses. HSA products have proven to be very popular with individuals and employers, with between 15 to 20 million people enrolled in 2013.[7]

In March of 2010, the Patient Protection and Affordable Care Act introduced sweeping changes across the entire United States health care financing system, impacting Medicare, Medicaid, and commercial coverages. At the time of this writing, many key provisions of this law are still being implemented. It remains to be seen whether the law's goals of improving access to health insurance will be realized in the long run.

Key ACA features include an expansion of Medicaid in many states, a plethora of new regulatory restrictions on the commercial market, and new health insurance marketplaces called **exchanges** in each state, where low income individuals will be able to receive significant subsidies from the fed-

---

[7]Employee Benefit Research Institute Issue Brief No. 400. HSA Balances, Contributions, Distributions, and other Vital Statistics, June 2014. Retrieved August 15, 2014 from http://www.ebri.org/pdf/briefspdf/EBRI_IB_400_June14.HSAs.pdf

eral government. The law also requires individuals to obtain health insurance coverage or potentially face a penalty on their tax return. Finally, there are also significant changes to the Medicare Advantage program. More detail on all of these provisions has been included throughout this text.

The passage of the ACA came at the end of a bitter political fight, in which rate increases on individual health insurance policies in some states were used as a key lever in swaying public opinion. The practice of rescission (whereby an insurer retroactively terminates a policy based on false or omitted information on the application) became another lightning rod in the months leading up to enactment.

Due to the unexpected loss of a Senate seat, Democrats were forced to pass the law using an unusual legislative maneuver that did not allow for the typical conference committee process. The conference committee is typically where technical inconsistencies between House and Senate versions of legislation are ironed out. As a result of the way the law was passed, this legislative process was never completed, and the political climate has not allowed for subsequent technical corrections. These factors have complicated the implementation of the ACA.

After the bill was passed and signed by the president, there was still great uncertainty about whether it would be fully implemented. Although some provisions took effect almost immediately, many of the larger changes were slated to occur in 2014. Legal challenges to key portions of the law were quickly filed by opponents. Ultimately, the U.S. Supreme Court upheld the law in June of 2012, with one exception. The expansion of Medicaid, which was originally mandatory, was made optional for the states.

Additional uncertainty came with the 2012 election cycle, which could potentially have shifted the balance of power in favor of the law's opponents. This did not occur; the uncertainty created by the election and the Supreme Court case may, however, have caused some stakeholders to delay preparations for the law's implementation.

In particular, many significant pieces of state and federal regulation implementing the law were not released until after the elections took place in late 2012 and in the spring of 2013. This resulted in a race for insurers to design and price insurance products that complied with the new rules in time for deadlines in the spring of 2013. Most products to be sold on exchanges in 2014 had to be filed (that is, premium rates, policy forms, and supporting documentation had to be submitted for review by state and federal authorities) by May 3, 2013.

Throughout 2014 and 2015, legal challenges to the ACA have continued. In another near miss, the Supreme Court decided on June 25, 2015 (in King v. Burwell) to continue to allow subsidies in states that chose not to set up their own exchanges. Had the ruling gone the other way, the consequences in the 34 states without a state-based exchange could have been disastrous. The concept of antiselection, which is the subject of Chapter 4 of this text, played a significant role in the court's opinion.

According to the U.S. Census Bureau, in 2012 about 7.3% of the nonelderly population purchased individual medical insurance, compared with 58.4% covered by employer-based (group) medical insurance and 22.8% covered by Medicaid or other public coverage.[8]

Premium rates for individual health insurance vary widely by many factors, and have changed significantly over time. According to the Kaiser Family Foundation, the monthly individual health insurance premium for a single person averaged just under $150 in 2003, but varied widely by region and age:

Table 1.2

Average Monthly Single Premiums by Region and Age, January-August, 2003[9]						
Region	<18	18-24	25-34	35-44	45-64	Average
Atlantic	$ 90.91	$114.81	$132.35	$157.17	$209.06	$147.85
Mountain	103.84	9.02	117.93	132.40	193.12	135.44
New England	171.36	234.81	253.98	272.24	299.43	267.54
North Central	86.88	102.77	110.88	130.85	179.65	127.40
Pacific	104.88	107.93	123.44	152.33	210.34	143.09
South Central	89.66	87.05	99.58	125.22	182.67	123.29
Average	$ 97.03	$115.04	$130.63	$155.90	$209.86	$148.80

---

[8] U.S. Census Bureau, Current Population Survey, 2013 Annual Social and Economic Supplement, at http://www.census.gov/hhes/www/cpstables/032013/health/h01_000.htm.
[9] www.kff.org. The document calls this coverage "health insurance," but presumably means major medical coverage only. The contributing company's website, www.ehealthinsurance.com, specifies a number of other products that are technically individual health insurance, as well, including short term policies.

These premiums are derived from direct internet sales, and therefore probably represent rates that are materially lower than those in the non-internet marketplace. (This can be attributed to a number of possible reasons, including lower cost risks, lower distribution costs, and newer policy forms.) Some more recent numbers, with average annual premiums for 2009 from a study by America's Health Insurance Plans[10] (AHIP) indicate:

	Single	Family
< 18	$1,350	$2,573
18-24	$1,429	$2,967
25-29	$1,723	$3,756
30-34	$2,104	$4,512
35-39	$2,457	$5,148
40-44	$2,888	$5,736
45-49	$3,414	$6,404
50-54	$4,127	$7,331
55-59	$4,895	$8,414
60-64	$5,755	$9,952
Total	**$2,985**	**$6,328**

– or a monthly premium of $249 for individuals and $527 for families.

The initial year under the ACA regulations saw 2014 monthly premium rates that vary significantly between carriers within a state, and even more significantly from state to state. This reflects the lack of experience data available to health insurers trying to predict the number and health status of those who would sign up under guaranteed issue. The Department of Health and Human Services released marketplace premium information for the states where the Federal government is operating the health exchange. The rates displayed are for a 27 year old without any advanced premium tax credit subsidies.[11]

---

[10] America's Health Insurance Plans Center for Policy and Research, Individual Health Insurance 2009, A Comprehensive Survey of Premiums, Availability, and Benefits, October 2009. Retrieved April 9, 2014 from https://www.ahip.org/AHIPResearch/
[11] Department of Health & Human Services, Health Insurance Marketplace Premiums for 2014. Retrieved April 9, 2014 from

Table 1.3

2014 Monthly QHP Premiums by Metal Level, (Age 27 Nonsmoker, Weighted Average[1] Across Entire State)					
	Lowest States		Highest States		Average[1]
Metal Level	State	Rate	State	Rate	Rate
Gold	Arizona	$187	Alaska	$401	$240
Silver	Tennessee	155	Wyoming	324	203
Bronze	Oklahoma	114	Wyoming	286	163
Catastrophic	Kansas	87	Wyoming	259	129

[1] Weighted on county level-population under the age of 65 as projected by the Census Bureau.

Here the **metal level** refers to standardized levels of coverage introduced under the ACA (more on these in Chapter 2). If we also include the states that operated their own health exchange, Minnesota had some of the lowest rates in the country. For reference, the 2014 rates (age 27 nonsmoker) for the lowest cost gold, silver, bronze, and catastrophic plans in the Minneapolis/St. Paul area are $147, $126, $95, and $80, respectively.[12]

It is still difficult to say much about how premiums will evolve in the post-ACA markets, given that they are still generally based on experience from before the major provisions of the law took effect. Some initial studies[13] are starting to emerge.

THE PLAYERS

Most individual health markets have been characterized at some point by a relatively small number of specialty insurers. This can be attributed to a number of reasons, including limited size of the market, the need for specialized expertise, social demands, and capitalization needs. Typically, however, this market situation evolves through consolidation into a limited number of large insurers who dominate the market. It is possible that the changes under

---

http://aspe.hhs.gov/health/reports/2013/marketplacepremiums/ib_marketplace_premiums.cfm
[12] https://www.mnsure.org/
[13] See for example Kowalski, A. "The Early Impact of the Affordable Care Act." Brookings Papers on Economic Activits, Fall 2014. Retrieved 6/3/2015 from http://www.brookings.edu/about/projects/bpea/papers/2014/early-impact-affordable-care-act-state-by-state.

the ACA will induce more players to enter this market going forward. It is also possible, however, that the ACA may lead to further consolidation given the compliance burden associated with the new regulatory environment and the difficulty smaller insurers face in predicting their financial outcomes in a risk adjusted environment (more on that in Chapter 4).

Medical

The individual medical market has historically been an example of this dominance by a small number of carriers. It is a large market, albeit being dwarfed by the group medical insurance market. The dominant carriers in this market are BCBS plans. BCBS plans have historical reasons for being active in this market, either because of regulatory agreements to make coverage available under individual policies in a state, or because of their intended role in the community.

The individual health insurance market has historically struggled with how to treat individuals with preexisting medical conditions. If insurers are allowed to decline applications for coverage due to health status, then individuals with serious medical conditions may not be able to obtain coverage if they cannot obtain it from another source such as through an employer. Different states have historically taken different approaches to trying to solve this problem.

Some states have required all carriers to guarantee issue all their individual medical coverage (that is, to issue coverage, at a standard insurance rate, to everyone who applies). These states include: Maine, Massachusetts, New Jersey, New York, Vermont, and Washington. Many other states have required guaranteed issue in a more limited way, either to certain specified plans (such as in the high risk pool), or certain carriers (HMOs for a limited annual open enrollment period, or BCBS plans all year long).

Still other states (notably Connecticut, District of Columbia, Michigan, and Pennsylvania) have had an **insurer of last resort** – a particular carrier (usually the BCBS plan) was designated as the carrier to whom all residents can apply and get coverage, regardless of their insurability. This clearly leads to antiselection, and in most cases there was a quid pro quo; the insurer was provided advantages in other ways as a conceptual recompense for being insurer of last resort.

Thirty three states used a **high risk pool** to be the individual insurer of last resort. These pools are state sponsored health plans that provide coverage to certain individuals who cannot obtain coverage elsewhere. For many states, this is the mechanism by which the state provided for the group-to-individual portability required under HIPAA, described further in Chapter 9.)[14]

Starting in 2014, the ACA required individual health insurance companies in all states to guarantee to issue individual health insurance coverage to all applicants without regard for health status, adopting the approach taken by the first group of states nationwide. As we will see later, it also introduced several mechanisms to try to control the potential antiselection this may have created. As a result, states with high risk pools generally either terminated them or began winding them down starting in 2014, since those high cost members should be able to obtain coverage in the individual health insurance market (or under the Medicaid expansion).

In the past few years, a number of the large national group carriers in the U.S. (notably United Healthcare and Humana) have re-entered the individual medical market.

There have historically been two major types of players in the individual major medical market. They are distinguished from each other in various ways, but perhaps most importantly, by how they manage their blocks of individual **comprehensive major medical (CMM)** policies.

BCBS plans (depending on corporate history, philosophy, and type of license) often introduced changes in their policies by canceling the entire block of coverage, and immediately reissuing the new policy (with the new provisions) to the same policyholders. This might be called a "rollover" approach, which is notably different from the commercial insurer approach. The latter approach kept all policies in the same block, and therefore involved a significant level of pooling, especially by date of issue.

Aside from BCBS plans, who collectively have had the majority of individual health policies in force, the medical market has had a submarket of a small number of specialty commercial insurers. This is true both with respect to the CMM market and Medicare Supplement policies. It was a typical commercial insurer practice in CMM to close blocks of existing business to new issues when a new product was introduced. Most carriers

---

[14] www.naschip.org/

made a conscious choice to do this, in order to wall off, or at least ameliorate, the impact of deteriorating experience on existing business from new business rates. This sometimes led to regulatory issues, described later in the section of this chapter on public policy. Moreover, this practice will no longer be allowed going forward, as the ACA requires all blocks of individual health insurance issued by an insurance company in a state to be rated together as a single risk pool (the only exception being any policies that are **grandfathered** or **transitional** – both of which are discussed in Chapter 4).

Until recently, most managed care plans (including HMOs) steered well clear of the individual health market, issuing "direct pay" and Medicare Supplement policies when needed, but nothing else. ("Direct pay" was a term derived from the group market, where employers typically remitted premiums on behalf of employees. When individuals converted to individual policies under the conversion privilege of the group policy, they paid the insurer "directly." Later, to the extent the managed care plan opened up this block of individual policies to other sources of business, the term stayed with the block.) This was primarily because of the difficulty in making such a book of business profitable, and the very specialized expertise needed to do so.

It is possible that the ACA will renew interest in the individual market among other carriers, given the significant federal subsidies available to individuals through the exchanges. The ACA also aims to encourage new types of players to enter the market, such as **accountable care organizations** where healthcare providers share in the gains or losses under the insurance plan, and also ACA-created **CO-OPs**, a new class of cooperative insurers where the insureds own the company.

Other Coverages

Most other market segments, and notably DI, LTC, and supplemental coverages, are also dominated by a relatively small number of specialized players. In the case of DI, this occurs because it is an aging marketplace which has gone through ongoing consolidation for decades. Right now, it is estimated by LIMRA in-force/sales reports that there were at least 70 DI carriers who sold business in the 1980s and 1990s. That number has dropped substantially today, due to many companies exiting this business (and selling their inforce blocks of business to other companies), and others merging or being acquired.

LTC insurance is at the other end of the product lifetime – it is relatively young, and still evolving at a fairly fast pace. While many health insurers have developed such policies, many of them have done so only as a defensive measure in case the product "takes off." Others have tested the waters and turned away. Companies providing LTC coverage assume a different risk profile than that of most other health products because of the long projection time horizon, significant reserve build-up, and greater rating uncertainty. Some companies that still have products do not manufacture and manage the products themselves; they use turnkey products offered by reinsurers, perhaps customized only as necessary to be issued on their paper. This practice is becoming less prevalent than it was ten or twenty years ago, when the coverage was newer and the expertise less available. It is also worth noting that many LTC carriers are life insurance companies that otherwise do not participate in the health insurance marketplace.

DISTRIBUTION CHANNELS

The various coverages of individual health insurance are sold through a wide variety of distribution channels.

Managing general agents (MGAs) are producers who are authorized by an insurer to be its exclusive representative in some market segment, typically either a geographic area or a specific line of business. MGAs might conduct their own marketing activities, as well as collect premium and pay claims. An MGA will typically have a contract with an insurance company to act on their behalf by managing agents and their production. The MGA is usually paid a certain commission, a part of which goes to the writing agents. In that scheme, the MGA might determine the commission payable to the agents (rather than the insurer, as is otherwise the case). In another version, the company sets the agents' commission scale, and pays the MGA an "override" – essentially a commission added on to the writing agent's commission. MGAs will often receive marketing support from the home office, but are not employees of the company. They are usually paid by commission only.

The MGA structure occurs mostly in the commercial life and health insurance company venue. It is relatively unusual for individual health insurance to be sold by captive agents (those obliged to sell only that company's products, except in exceptional circumstances), although there are a small number of companies that have done well with this method.

Independent Marketing Organizations (IMOs) are relatively large organizations of producers who work either nationwide or in many states. They typically have a proprietary product, issued by a company with whom they have a relationship for this purpose. They may provide administrative services related to new business processing, sometimes even including underwriting. They sometimes follow a brokerage model, but sometimes, instead, just focus on producing leads.

Brokers are producers who are not employees of a company, but instead are independent agents who typically "shop around" their business. In most markets, brokers will get to know a relatively small number of insurers well, and will place most of their business with those companies. The term "Broker" usually refers to a brokerage company, rather than an individual. That brokerage company will likely employ multiple direct writing agents who do the actual selling of the insurance coverage.

Direct marketing channels of insurance are quite popular in some market segments. This might take the form of internet marketing, telemarketing (that is, by telephone), or through print, radio, or television media. In this case, there will typically not be a producer involved; the company (generally a salaried, home office employee) deals directly with the prospect in placing the insurance. *Affinity* marketing is marketing through affinity groups, an organizational structure which connects individuals who have some common characteristic. A group with strong affinity might be a state bar association, or the Society of Actuaries. A weaker affinity group might be those who have a particular credit card. Stronger affinity implies greater penetration (higher percentage of prospects who buy the coverage), and this can allow the insurer to loosen certain aspects of individual underwriting rules.

There is a wide spectrum of associations that offer individual insurance. There are professional associations (like a state or local bar association), employer associations (available to employees of a large employer), alumni associations, credit card holder associations, and many others. One well known association of senior citizens (AARP, formerly known as the American Association of Retired Persons) has become a major force in the Medicare Supplement market. There is a particular issue about such associations from the regulatory point of view, discussed in the next section.

Voluntary or **workplace insurance** is yet another distribution channel. This market is typically one where an employer "sponsors" a program, but pays none of the premium. Sponsorship generally involves allowing producers access to employees, facilitating distribution of marketing material, and allowing premiums to be payable through the employer's payroll system, called 'payroll deduction.' This arrangement could be considered a type of affinity program, with strong affinity between members. The latest evolution of this market is increasingly referred to as *private exchanges*, to distinguish them from the public exchanges discussed next. Private exchanges can be structured so as to offer a single carrier's products, or products from a variety of carriers.

Public insurance exchanges (also referred to as **marketplaces**) are a new type of distribution channel introduced under the ACA in 2014. Each state had the opportunity (and could get federal funds) to set up two online marketplaces: one for individuals and one for small group health insurance. These could either be established by a state independently (a **state-based exchange** or **SBE**) or in partnership with the federal government (a **state partnership exchange** or **SPE**). The National Association of Insurance Commissioners (**NAIC**) has promulgated a model law[15] for states that wish to establish an exchange. If a state failed to establish an exchange, the federal government established one on its behalf (a **federally facilitated exchange** or **FFE**). In 2014, there were 17 SBEs, 7 SPEs, and 27 FFEs.

The ACA exchanges are nonprofit or governmental entities that center on a website where individuals and small employers can shop for and purchase coverage. They are also supposed to verify eligibility for Medicaid coverage and enroll lower income individuals in Medicaid instead of the individual market if they are eligible. For individuals and families not eligible for Medicaid, subsidies based on their income may be available to help pay premiums and in some cases reduce cost sharing such as deductibles, copays, and coinsurance. These subsidies are only available for **qualified health plans** (**QHPs**) certified by and sold through the exchanges, and the subsidies are the main incentive for insurers to offer coverage through the exchange.

Exchanges may either allow any insurer to offer QHPs through the exchange in a **clearinghouse model** (so long as the QHPs are certified by the Exchange as meeting ACA requirements), or it may negotiate with insurers and only include selected plans using an **active purchaser model**. In

---

[15] MDL-929

either case, insurers are charged a significant fee by the exchange (the FFEs charged a fee of 3.5% of exchange premium in 2014 and 2015). The insurer must also complete the QHP application process with state and federal regulators, which is quite involved.

At the federal and state level, the initial rollout of the exchanges was anything but smooth. Technology problems resulted in frequent website crashes, causing the government to extend the initial open enrollment period deadlines and requiring manual workarounds in many cases. Ultimately, however, millions of individuals did successfully sign up for coverage (either Medicaid or commercial individual) through the exchanges.

Brokers and agents can generally assist individuals in purchasing coverage through exchanges, although they have to register with the exchange and complete certain requirements. The ACA also establishes new roles to help individuals and families successfully sign up for coverage: *navigators, in-person assisters,* and *certified application counselors.* These are generally not brokers or agents, but rather persons or organizations trained (and in some cases paid) by the exchanges to enroll people.

1.2 REGULATION

Regulation of individual health insurance in the U.S., with some exceptions, has historically been the province of state government. Insurance laws typically provide definitions of individual health insurance (under various names like "health and accident" insurance, or "accident and sickness" insurance, many of which are vestiges of a bygone era), spell out the nature of coverage, and authorize insurers of various types to issue such coverage.

Some might argue that the U.S. government's mandates regarding Medicare Supplement and the creation of Medicare Advantage plans constitute a major intrusion into state regulation. Keep in mind, however, that in both of these cases, the coverage must still meet state requirements, and can only be offered through state licensed insurers that must meet all the other state laws and regulations.

While the ACA has aimed to preserve the traditional role of the states in regulating health insurers, it introduces a significant new layer of federal regulation. In part, this is to be expected, as the law also introduces substantial federal funds into the commercial market in the form of premium and cost sharing subsidies for low income individuals. In general, however, the ACA only preempts state law when it is in conflict with the federal law, and it does not preempt it in situations where state requirements are stricter than the corresponding federal requirements. This has created a complex situation for state regulators who have found themselves tasked with implementing or monitoring compliance with federal laws and regulations. Some states have adopted state-level laws that mimicked ACA requirements in order to remove any ambiguity that state regulators had the authority to do this. This introduces a new challenge of keeping such state requirements in sync with changing federal rules.

In each state, the Insurance Commissioner(s) or Superintendent is given authority to promulgate regulations (subject to public disclosure requirements) to implement the law. Sometimes, insurers object to part or all of a regulation, and may contest it, or the Commissioner's (or his or her staff's) interpretation of the law. The legal process usually requires that the objection begin with an administrative hearing before it can be brought to court.

The boundary of what constitutes "individual health insurance" vs. group insurance is not always a clear one. There is some coverage that clearly falls within the definition, because it is issued with a freestanding, individual health insurance contract, issued to an individual or a family. Other coverage, though, which most observers would agree is substantively individual health, is provided through association groups or discretionary trusts, where there may be a group master policy (that is, a single contract between the insurer and the association) instead of individual contracts at the family level. In that case, certificates of coverage are issued to individuals and families rather than policy forms. One way of categorizing such vehicles is into three categories:

1. *Bona Fide Associations*, defined under HIPAA, which guarantee issue coverage to members.[16]

---

[16] www.ihps.org

2. *Non-Bona Fide Associations*, where membership in the association comes with the right to apply for medical coverage. In an effort to ensure such trusts are not solely for the purpose of insurance, there are some rules limiting how they must be formed and run. Despite these efforts, there is often a very close connection between the association and the insurer that sets it up, and the non-insurance benefits of the association may be minimal.
3. *Discretionary Group Trusts*, that are formed exclusively for the purpose of acquiring insurance.

Different jurisdictions handle these situations differently, and it isn't always clear what the law is in a state. (The state where a policy or certificate is "delivered or issued for delivery" generally has jurisdiction, although this may be changing.[17] This means that, where a group master policy is involved, the state of delivery of the master contract governs that contract, while the states where certificates are delivered have jurisdiction over those certificates.) Various lists, prepared by experienced compliance professionals, which purport to have comprehensive information as to which states allow or do not allow these alternative vehicles, sometimes differ widely from one another. A regulator from a particular state may often have a very different opinion about what is permitted than an insurer issuing certificates to residents of that state. Do you rely on the opinion of that regulator? The implications of the answer can be quite significant. Ultimately, such disagreements might need judicial decisions to bring them together, but those have not yet happened in all states. It would be wise, therefore, to seek reliable legal counsel in this matter, if there is any question about the validity of one of these vehicles in a given state.

The advantage to having the coverage be considered group insurance is that there is typically much less (if any) rate regulation for such a group. This is contrasted with the relatively rigorous regulation applied to individual policies in many states. However, under federal regulation implementing the ACA, "coverage that is provided to associations, but not related to employment, and sold to individuals is not considered group coverage"[18] regardless of its treatment under state law. Thus, the ability to avoid regulation through associations has become much more limited that before.

---

[17] Discussed further in Chapter 9.
[18] 45 C.F.R. § 144.102

Regulation of individual commercial medical contracts might understandably be considered schizophrenic. On one hand, Insurance Commissioners are very concerned about protecting policyholders by ensuring solvency of insurers, which argues for conservative practices. On the other hand, with respect to premium rates, the rate approval process seems designed to limit rate increases (which it often does quite well), but at the expense of product viability, and ultimately, solvency of the insurer.

The earliest draft of modern medical insurance rate regulations was something referred to as the "Chicago draft."[19] This early regulation became the basis for New York's Regulation 62,[20] and, later, the NAIC's Individual Accident and Health Rate Filing Guidelines.[21]

In the 1980s, there was considerable interest in insurance practices related to Medicare Supplement policies by the U.S. Congress. Passage of the "Baucus amendment"[22] in 1980 and OBRA[23] in 1990 brought reforms to the market that included uniformity of benefits (ten specified plans were the only ones allowed), minimum loss ratio standards, disclosure requirements, guaranteed issue at standard rates to new Medicare beneficiaries age 65 or older (for six months), and various others. These reforms are discussed in more detail in Chapter 2.

LTC insurance regulation has continued to evolve. When the policy was first introduced, there was very little data available on which rates could be based. Since LTC policies provide long-term guarantees, and no one was sure what the experience would ultimately look like, regulators were understandably cautious about restrictions on rates until experience emerged. Later, as the LTC market matured a bit, there was discussion about the need and nature of rate regulation. An LTC model regulation was adopted by the NAIC in August 2000, replacing the prior one from the 1990s. A major focus of regulators has been consumer protection and rate *stabilization* (interpreted to mean the minimization of changes in premium rates

---

[19] Schwartz, Max J. "Accident and Health Insurance Rates, Rating Plans, and Commissions," from *Examination of Insurance Companies*, prepared under the direction of Deputy Superintendent Adelbert G. Straub, Jr. (New York City: New York State Insurance Department, 1955), Vol VI, Chapter 11.
[20] 11 NYCRR 52, § 52.45 (1998) (Regulation 62)
[21] American Academy of Actuaries Rate Filing Task Force. *Report to the NAIC's A&H Working Group of the Life and Health Actuarial Task Force,* p. 9, www.actuary.org
[22] Social Security Disability Amendments of 1980. PL 96-265 (HR 3236)
[23] Omnibus Budget Reconciliation Act (OBRA) of 1986

over time), rather than the focus on lower rates themselves that often occurs in the medical markets.

Rate regulation takes a number of forms, depending on the nature of the insurer and the product. Insurance Departments typically approve the initial rates for individual policies, although they do not have that authority in all states. In some jurisdictions, the rates are considered part of the policy form, and require the same approval as the form. Required justification for those rates is spelled out in a rate regulation. This regulation also typically applies to renewal rates, in those states that regulate renewal rates. Under the ACA, the federal government now reviews insurance rate increases that occur in states that are deemed not to have an effective rate review process of their own. The federal government was not given the power to approve or disapprove increases, however, just to review them and declare publicly whether or not they are "unreasonable", although insurers with a pattern of "unreasonable" increases may be banned from the health insurance exchanges.

Some states had historically limited the extent of rate variation which can occur over one or more rating variables. This was most often a requirement of BCBS plans and HMOs, due to the historical value given to the concept of "community rating," or the intentional collapse of certain rate variables (like age and gender) which would otherwise be used. Starting in 2014, the ACA imposed a form of community rating nationwide. Among other restrictions, it strictly limited rate variation by age and prohibited rate variation by gender altogether.

In Canada, jurisdiction is split between the federal government in Ottawa and the provincial government. Most of the comments in this chapter, however, relate to the U.S. situation. This is because individual major medical coverage does not exist in Canada – it is illegal for medical providers in Canada to provide care outside of the federal system for standard benefits.

1.3 HEALTH POLICY

Over time, some attention has been paid by regulators to evaluating various solutions which might be used to solve a major challenge to individual health policymakers, the "closed block problem". This had been a long-term issue in the individual medical market, particularly in the commercial (meaning non-Blue Cross, non-HMO type carriers) portion. It is still instructive to review this history, since it provides important context for some of the changes that were implemented under the ACA. The problem was described in a 2004 American Academy of Actuaries report from the Individual Health Rate Filing Task Force (RFTF) as follows.[24]

> It is a commonly observed practice of the current individual health insurance market that an insurer will periodically "close" a block of business (meaning they will no longer issue new business in that pool of policies). There can be many reasons for closing a block of business. Regardless of why a block of business is closed, that block will typically experience claim costs rising more rapidly than would a block that was still open. If the insurer raises premiums at an equally rapid rate, policyholders may find it difficult to keep their policies in force due to the increased cost, which is a particular problem for those who have developed serious health conditions and are unable to find new policies. If the insurer does not continue to raise rates, then claims will eventually exceed premiums, and the resulting losses must be funded from some other source (such as premiums on the other blocks of business, reserves established in earlier years, or company surplus).
>
> Whether a block is open or closed, each year a substantial number of existing policyholders typically reconsider whether they should keep their existing policies in force. This process tends to be biased against the block, because standard insureds are more likely than impaired insureds to find less expensive coverage elsewhere, or to decide that the benefits they are likely to receive no longer justify the cost of coverage. As a result, lapse rates for standard insureds tend to be significantly higher than those for individuals who have become impaired. This is described as antiselection at lapse, and the cumulative impact of this over time is known as **Cumulative Antiselection (CAST)**.[25] This happens when a portion of standard policyholders (who can easily pass underwriting under another company's standards for new business) leave the closed block, resulting in a greater portion of impaired policyhold-

---

[24] American Academy of Actuaries Rate Filing Task Force. *Report to the NAIC's A&H Working Group of the Life and Health Actuarial Task Force.* (See Appendix B).
[25] Bluhm, William. "Cumulative Antiselection Theory," *Transactions of the Society of Actuaries* Volume 34, 1982.

ers (who have greater trouble finding coverage) maintaining their coverage in the closed block.

Because there are no new entrants to a closed block, experience in the closed block often worsens over time, leading to relatively large rate increases. This typically happens in cases where rate increases are based on the experience of that closed block only, rather than on multiple blocks, including currently sold business. Larger rate increases, in turn, raise the level of antiselection at lapse by further increasing the financial incentive for standard individuals to shop for more attractive prices or drop coverage. This increased antiselection leads to even higher rate increases. This process is known variously as a "premium rate spiral," "death spiral," or "antiselection spiral." In some cases, a point of equilibrium may be reached, where most of the policyholders who are inclined to change coverage have already done so, and experience and premium levels may stabilize, albeit at levels higher than would be typical for an open block of policies. In other cases, the process may continue indefinitely, leading to a situation where only the sickest policyholders remain covered, paying very high premiums, with no standard policyholders in the block to subsidize costs.

The claim costs experienced in individual insurance tend to initially be relatively low, then rise dramatically over time. This is due to the effect of initial underwriting, including possibly an initial pre-existing condition period as well as due to the CAST effect described here.

This market is very price sensitive. Insurers can charge the lowest prices by charging premium rates which mirror the increasing nature of claim costs over time. This results in relatively low initial rates, followed by sizeable rate increases. To the extent insurers follow this philosophy, the CAST effect is magnified, increasing the likelihood of an antiselection spiral.

The RFTF feels that this evolution of the marketplace, combined with the current regulatory approach, have encouraged the closed block problem. In many cases, it is very difficult for insurers to keep rates at a level adequate to cover the losses caused by this rating spiral.

For purposes of this report, this dilemma in the current marketplace is what we refer to as the "closed block problem."

The RFTF spent some time discussing the universe of potential solutions to the closed block problem, under the assumptions that external subsidies would not be available and that solutions internal to the individual market would need to be found. Ultimately, in order to organize the endeavor to a manageable size, the solutions were categorized into four representative categories: **(1) prefunding, (2) individual medical pool, (3) interblock subsidy – durational pooling, and (4) interblock subsidy – rate compression**. This categorization was made with input from the NAIC representatives, and therefore doesn't include all possible solutions – just those the NAIC felt were within the bounds of potential public policy solutions.

The prefunding approach was one where a policy's early premiums are higher than that purely called for by claim costs, and the difference is put into a reserve. That reserve is used to subsidize premiums at later durations. Leverage is gained by the fact that the early subsidies occur before most of the healthy lives have lapsed.

The individual medical pool approach is one which attacks the closed block problem by having a substandard pool, created from policyholders whose premiums rise too far beyond the going market rate. Subsidies are paid by the individual insurers from where these policyholders convert.

The two interblock subsidy methods leave the market forces as they are, but limit the extent to which rates are allowed to deteriorate, thereby forcing the company to subsidize those policyholders from another source (most likely the other individual medical policyholders.) The durational pooling model pools all policyholders beyond a given duration, and doesn't allow any further categorization of policyholders beyond that. The rate compression model limits the range of rates which could be charged to policyholders with similar demographic characteristics.

This last approach is what ultimately became law as part of the ACA: starting in 2014, individual insurance issuers are no longer allowed to charge policyholders with similar demographic characteristics different rates, with the exception of policyholders on certain grandfathered and transitional (a.k.a. "grandmothered") plans issued before the major reforms went into effect. Instead, all ACA-compliant policies in a state must be rated together as a single risk pool. Of course, the ACA's attempt at solving the closed block problem also involved significant external subsidies, in the form of tax incentives reducing the policyholders' cost of participating in the individual market, and thereby encouraging greater participation rates.

For further detail on these matters, the reader is referred to the earlier footnoted report from the American Academy of Actuaries. The model developed by that task force to study these policy solutions is included as a textbook supplement on the ACTEX website, and is described in later chapters.

The impact of the closed block phenomenon, combined with rigorous rate regulation by state insurance departments (so much so that losses were often unavoidable) caused most major commercial companies to leave the individual health market, long before most of them ultimately also left the group market. This left the commercial individual market dominated by a relatively few specialty companies – those who had been able to focus on block management sufficiently to make money at least some of the time.

Products have recently evolved in keeping with the 'consumer directed' movement, where high deductible plans are paired with tax advantaged savings accounts. Proponents of this policy believe that it will significantly help limit cost and rate increases if consumers themselves are more explicitly aware of the cost of providing their care. Health Savings Accounts (HSAs), for example, were created in 2003 by the Medicare Prescription Drug, Improvement and Modernization Act (P.L.108-173). That law allows for a personally-owned HSA account to be created out of pre-tax income, to be used for payment of qualified medical expenses, provided there is a qualified high-deductible insurance plan as part of the arrangement. Individual health insurance premiums remain non-deductible, unless the policyholder is self-employed.

It was hoped that giving the insured greater emotional ownership of the HSA and its expenses, combined with development of tools to make it feasible for the policyholder to evaluate treatment and provider choices, would result in downward pressure on costs. As of this writing, HSA plans have become quite common in both the employer and individual markets, with enrollment estimated at 15.5 to 20.4 million policyholders and their dependents.[26]

---

[26] Employee Benefit Research Institute Issue Brief, op. cit.

Of course, the many changes under the ACA have now set in motion an experiment on a much grander scale than the advent of consumer directed healthcare plans, changing the current system at a fundamental level. It will be an interesting experiment to watch.

CHAPTER 2

THE PRODUCTS

There is a wide array of products being sold in the individual health insurance market. Each of them has its own characteristics, varying from other products in many different ways. This chapter describes those characteristics, and is organized by product type. Sections 2.1 through 2.5 describe medical-type coverages, 2.6 and 2.7 describe income protection coverages, 2.8 describes long term care coverage, and 2.9 describes dental coverages.

2.1 MAJOR MEDICAL COVERAGE

The precursor of **major medical** coverage was available in the early 20th century, when a disability coverage added a provision to increase payments while someone was hospitalized. The most major changes to liberalize medical care insurance occurred in the 1930s (initially accident only) and 1940s. Major medical coverage was introduced about 1950,[1] as medical care costs became much more significant than they were previously, and it became obvious that simple coverage of only hospital costs, or only physician costs, did not adequately protect the policyholder. Major medical is distinguished from earlier coverages in that it was the first time the disparate sources of health care costs (hospital, physician, and ancillary) were combined into a common policy.

The list of health care expenditures that a policy covers are commonly called **covered services**, or **covered expenses**, and this term is typically well defined in the policy form itself. Regulators felt the need to require that a certain minimum combination of covered services should be provided if a policy was to be called "major medical," presumably under public policy aimed at either (1) preventing insurers from misleading consumers by

---

[1] *Health Insurance Provided Through Individual Policies,* Edwin L. Bartleson. Published by the Society of Actuaries, 1968.

using the name for a policy with lesser benefits, or (2) prohibiting policies which have unexpected (at least for the policyholder) holes in the benefit plan.

New York's Regulation 62, for example, requires a specific set of minimum benefit parameters that a policy must meet to be called major medical insurance.[2] (The exact wording of this part of the regulation, section 52.7, is contained in Appendix A to this text).

Once the covered services are defined for a policy, it is necessary to define how benefits are calculated from the covered services. These calculations reflect various ways in which the covered expenses are allocated between the insurer, the insured, and the provider.

Allocating some portion of the covered expense to the insured is often deemed to be good design, because it still provides some (albeit watered down) financial incentive to the insured to control costs. The portion of costs allocated to the insured is called **cost sharing**.

DEDUCTIBLES

A **deductible** is a dollar amount, specified in the policy, for which the insured is responsible before any benefits are payable. A plan with a 100% benefit after a $100 major medical deductible means that if (for example) $1,000 of covered services occurs, the first $100 of covered expense would automatically be the responsibility of the insured, and the $900 in excess would then go into the benefit calculation.

Deductibles can apply to all services under the contract, to major categories of services (like hospital inpatient charges), or to smaller categorizations. The categories might depend on where the service occurs (such as inpatient vs. outpatient vs. physician's office), whether the provider is part of the insurer's network (such as a separate deductible for inpatient stays in non-network hospitals), what kind of service it is (such as inpatient stays, ancillary services, or prescription drugs), or in other ways.

It is important to address how the deductible interacts with other aspects of the contract – in particular, provider discounts. Suppose, for example,

---

[2] 11 NYCRR 52.7

that the $1,000 claim in the previous example was for physician services, and is the retail, undiscounted charge the physician puts on the bill (commonly called **billed charges**.) If the physician is participating in the insurer's network, it is likely that the physician has agreed to abide by a payment schedule (or other discount mechanism) which might reduce that $1,000 to, for example, $700. (This figure of $700 would be called the **allowed charges** for that benefit, and is what the insurer will recognize in the benefit calculation.)

The benefit for this imaginary plan pays 100% above the deductible, so the benefit calculation subtracts the $100 deductible from the *discounted* $700 benefit, and pays the physician $600. In this case, the insurer gets the full value of the discount, and the insured must pay the undiscounted $100. This is the most common interpretation of deductibles.

Sometimes there are family deductibles that are expressed as a multiple of the individual deductible, such as 2, 2.5, or 3 times. This naturally adds somewhat to the claim cost of a major medical benefit, since there will be some families whose claims will exceed the family deductible even though the individual expenses may not exceed the individual deductible.

COINSURANCE

It is common in major medical plans that, once the deductible is satisfied, benefits above that amount are payable at a percentage (typically 75%-90%, the most common being 80%) of covered expenses. Perhaps counter-intuitively, the percentage payable by the insurer (80%) is called the **coinsurance**; the remaining portion (20%) is part of the insured's cost sharing. (This terminology is not used consistently. Some people call the 20% the coinsurance.)

In the previous example (with $1,000 of billed charges, $700 of allowed charges, and a $100 deductible), if the policy pays 80%, then the $600 of allowed charges in excess of the deductible would be payable at 80%, or $480, with the insured responsible for the remaining $120.

Most provider contracts require that the provider accept the allowed charge determination, and not seek the difference between billed and allowed charges from the insured. The practice of seeking payment from the insured for the excess of billed charges over allowed charges is known as **balance billing**.

OUT OF POCKET LIMITS

As mentioned earlier, it is generally considered a good idea to provide financial incentive to the insured to control costs, through cost sharing. Once a claim reaches a particularly large amount, however, there is usually a provision that relieves the insured of the cost of any additional covered expenses. This is often called an **out of pocket** provision, or a **stop loss** provision.

Out of pocket limits can also be considered 100% coverage once a claim trigger occurs. That trigger can be expressed either in terms of covered expense (such as $5,000) or out of pocket expenses (such as $2,000). They can also be expressed to include or exclude the deductible. If the contract is a family contract, there will often be one out of pocket limit for each individual, and a separate trigger for the family as a whole, in case no single person hits the trigger but there are numerous moderate sized claims.

MAXIMUM LIMITS

Sometimes a policy will have an overall maximum benefit payable on behalf of an individual. This limit can be expressed in terms of benefits per year (like $1 million of benefit per year), over the life of the individual (like a $2 million lifetime benefit), or both.

Overall benefit maximums were quite common early in the development of major medical policies. As time went on, the original maximums (some as low as $25,000, for example) sometimes seemed absurdly out of date, in light of modern health care costs. Those maximums continued to grow over time, to multiple millions of dollars in the 1980s and '90s.

Over time, many policies eliminated maximums. Ironically, some companies then reintroduced maximums for marketing purposes. Some marketers found that the public views a "$5 million maximum" more favorably than an "unlimited maximum." It turns out that the premium cost for such differences is quite minor, although the risk can be significant for the small insurer who happens to find the rare multi-million dollar chronic claim. (Such an insurer might have stop loss reinsurance – that is, enter into its own insurance contract with another insurer – to cover the risk of such a claim.)

Some policies that have limited lifetime maximums will have a provision that will gradually reinstate eligibility for benefits, even though the maximum had been reached. A policy might, for example, reinstate $50,000 of benefit eligibility each year, after (and despite) the lifetime maximum having been reached. This allows an insured who has previously had a catastrophic event to maintain modest amounts of coverage.

Under the ACA, major medical policies (grandfathered or not) can no longer have lifetime dollar limits on covered services deemed to be "essential health benefits." In addition, annual dollar limits on essential health benefits that previously existed had to be phased out for non-grandfathered plans by 2014.

INTERNAL LIMITS

Sometimes there are benefit limits defined in a policy that apply only to specific subsets of benefits. Today, the most common internal limits on charges for all services (rather than a single service) relate to mental and nervous benefits, substance abuse benefits, and chiropractic benefits. In addition, these benefits can also have per service limits. An outpatient mental and nervous benefit might, for example, be limited to $40 per visit, and 20 visits in a year. As in this example, the overall limit can be expressed either in dollars or in number of services.

The ACA prohibits annual dollar limits on essential health benefits; this also prohibits internal limits on those benefits that are based on a dollar value. Because the law does not prohibit limits on the number of services of a given type that are covered, however, in many cases plans replaced annual dollar limits on particular services with annual limits on the number of the services instead.

Starting in 2014 individual health insurance plans must also comply with parity requirements in the **Mental Health Parity and Addiction Equity Act of 2008 (MHPAEA)**. The details are complex, but in general the inside limits applied for mental health and substance abuse services cannot be more stringent than those applied to other services.

Some Blue Cross plans have had limits on the number of inpatient days covered per spell of illness. In the past, this was often considered equivalent to an overall maximum, since the bulk of covered charges (for very large claims) was almost inevitably due to inpatient costs. With the growing number of transplants (and their associated surgical costs), and the sometimes major costs associated with new drugs, a limit on covered inpatient days starts to look more like an internal limit.

Early in the development of major medical benefits, internal benefit limits were commonly used to limit exposure to broad categories of benefits deemed to be the greatest risk for cost, such as inpatient and outpatient hospital benefits. Such benefit designs were made without benefit of foresight of what would happen to benefit costs over time. In such cases, the hospital inpatient benefits might have been contained to a fraction of inflationary trends (with hospital inpatient benefits maxing out), while ancillary services might continue to grow because there are no internal maximums. In many cases the non-limited benefits (like ancillary services) have eventually become the major portion of benefits for the persisting book of business.

COPAYS

Cost sharing that occurs each time a service is provided is called a **copay**. Commonly, when they are used, copays apply to physician office visits (perhaps $20 per visit, for example), prescription drugs (often **tiered**, with copays varying depending on the drug prescribed, such as: $10 for generic drugs, $20 for brand name drugs on the insurer's formulary, $40 for non-formulary drugs, and $100 for high-cost specialty drugs), emergency room (such as $50 per visit), or other specific benefits. (A **formulary** is a list of drugs, promulgated by a health plan or a pharmacy benefits manager, that has member cost sharing that differs depending on how each drug is included on the formulary.)[3]

Copays came into vogue in the '70s and '80s, when HMOs first became popular.[4] HMOs tend to use copays rather than deductibles for cost sharing purposes. There are two types of services which most often use copays for cost sharing. The first type is the category of services which might be subject to over-utilization, where the insureds themselves have significant control over the usage. Examples of this include physician office visits and emergency room visits.

---

[3] *Group Insurance, Sixth Edition*, Bluhm, et al., ACTEX Publications, 2013. Chapter 9.
[4] An **HMO** is a **Health Maintenance Organization**, a type of health insurance company, typically licensed either under a specific federal law or under a unique part of the insurance or health laws of a state, characterized by hiring or contracting with the providers needed to provide comprehensive care to their members.

Another common situation where copays are used is when the administration of a benefit (most frequently the prescription drug benefit) is done separately. The administration of prescription drug benefits are typically outsourced to a **pharmacy benefits manager (PBM)**. Because the administration is done by the PBM, who doesn't have easy access to the insurer's claim records, it is difficult to coordinate claim payment calculations with other benefits, paid under other parts of the contract.

Eligibility for prescription benefits and the determination of benefits typically occur at the time the prescription is filled, and requires access to benefit information to determine cost sharing, so that the pharmacy can collect it at that time. Copay administration does not require knowledge of other benefits paid (unless they accumulate towards an out of pocket maximum); deductibles do. Since PBMs have historically been unable to access insurer benefit and claim information, there had been a compelling argument to use copays with prescription drugs, rather than deductibles that are integrated with medical coverage. Some plans, particularly high deductible plans, still have integrated deductibles today. Integrated plan designs may become more common under the ACA, since all cost sharing for essential health benefits, including prescription drugs, is required to accumulate towards an out of pocket maximum.

VARIATIONS ON A THEME – RELATED PRODUCTS

Comprehensive Major Medical Coverage

Major medical coverage originally had substantial deductibles which were intended to cause self-insurance of smaller health care costs. This was consistent with the original intent of major medical coverage to be insurance against "major" costs, rather than more frequent lower cost expenses. When adjusted to today's dollars, these sizeable deductibles were quite similar to today's high deductible, "consumer directed" policies.

Over time, a version of major medical coverage developed which was intended to cover more of the smaller expenses, and therefore had relatively small deductibles. Such deductibles were originally as small as $50 or $100. This coverage is sometimes referred to as **comprehensive major medical (CMM)** coverage.

Some carriers (particularly commercial carriers) may allow for widely customizable major medical plans, varying deductibles, coinsurance, copays, optional benefits (like maternity, accident, and critical illness), prescription drug options and copays, and so forth. These carriers try to make coverage more affordable to prospects, by allowing them to pick and choose the benefits they find most valuable in relation to cost. (Such variation will, of course, also tend to generate more antiselection, as the insureds are most likely to choose the benefits that they are most likely to actually *use*.)

Catastrophic Medical

Another variation of major medical is the **catastrophic major medical product**.[5] This product's purpose is to protect from the opposite risk addressed by CMM coverage. It is major medical coverage with very high deductibles, typically on the order of $25,000-100,000.

Catastrophic coverage is consistent with the original intent of insurance: to protect assets against infrequent, large expenses. It was sometimes purchased to roughly wrap around older policies that might have outdated overall maximums. In addition, there are some purchasers who have sufficient financial means and the desire to self-insure costs to a much higher level than is typical for others.

The ACA caps out of pocket maximums for non-grandfathered major medical policies, which will effectively prohibit catastrophic major medical products as described in this section. The highest out of pocket maximum allowed in 2014 was $6,350 for a single policy, or $12,700 for a family.

Short Term Medical

Some major medical insurers found in the past that a sizeable proportion of newly issued individual major medical policies were sold to insureds who only intended to keep their coverage in force for short periods. This led to substantial lapse rates in the first duration of policies. Each of those issued policies had a substantial investment by the insurer associated with them, due to the cost of sales, underwriting, and issuing the policy. The insurer often did not recover this investment until the policy had been in force for

---

[5] The catastrophic major medical products in this section should not be confused with the "catastrophic" plans created under the ACA, which actually provide richer coverage than the plans described here.

over a year. So when the policies lapsed before that time, even if they had no claims, the insurer suffered a loss.

In response, the **short term medical** product was developed. Early versions of this product often allowed a single guaranteed renewal, but this is no longer common. This feature has later been replaced by a product with a single limited term (typically 3, 6, 9, or 12 months). Because of the limited term, product design frequently contemplated a pre-existing condition exclusion, which is usually limited to 12 months after the policy is issued, to apply over the whole life of the policy. Because of this, individual medical underwriting for such short term policies is quite limited (typically only a few yes/no questions), which substantially reduces the cost of issuing the policy. This does somewhat complicate the claim administration process, since most claims (other than those that are obviously not pre-existing, like accidents) must be investigated for the potential that they are due to a pre-existing condition.

By having a short term medical product available, insurers can substantially reduce the first year lapse rate on their longer term products, and thereby increase the time over which they can recover the initial cost of issuing a regular individual major medical policy.

Short term policies appear to be largely exempt from the reforms introduced by the ACA. Given the ACA mandate requiring most individuals to maintain coverage throughout the year, however, it remains to be seen whether there will still be a market for these plans in the future.

Under the ACA, possession of short term medical coverage is not sufficient for an individual to avoid penalties under the individual mandate provision. (See the following "ACA Restrictions on Plan Design" section.) At the time of this writing, the ACA individual mandate does allow for a gap in coverage of less than three months without triggering a penalty. It is possible that some relatively healthy insureds will take advantage of this loophole, replacing a more costly major medical policy with a cheaper short term policy for several months each year.

High Risk Pool Plans

As mentioned in Chapter 1, states with high risk pools either terminated them or began winding them down starting in 2014, since health status underwriting was prohibited in the individual market nationwide at that time. The ACA also set up temporary high risk pools (the **Pre-Existing**

Condition Insurance Plan, or **PCIP**) in all states starting in late 2010; these also terminated in 2014.

The benefits provided by state high risk pool contracts varied by state. Most plans tended to resemble an 80% coinsurance major medical plan, with a choice of deductible and a relatively modest maximum ($350,000 to $2 million). Such plans included an intentional level of subsidy of around half the total operating costs. (This could vary significantly by state, as well as year by year within a state.) The subsidy could come as an assessment or tax on individual health insurers, all health insurers, health care providers, or from the state's general funds.[6]

Consumer Directed Plans

In the early 2000s, there was a popular evolution of individual products toward **consumer directed plans**. In product design, such plans were historically offered more often in a group context, but have now grown in size in the individual market as well.

A consumer directed plan is typically characterized by a high deductible major medical (or HMO) plan, combined with an underlying **personal spending account**. The underlying account is presented as an account owned by the insured, even when wholly or partially funded (usually in a group insurance context) by employer contributions (and therefore not taxable to the employee). The intent is that the insured will take emotional ownership of the assets in this personal account, and will be motivated to use the money efficiently. Sometimes, in a group situation, the underlying account can be notional, rather than an actual account.[7] In the individual situation, the types of accounts which are used are:

Medical Savings Accounts: These are accounts created by Congress in 1997 as a demonstration project for small group and self-employed insureds. Under this arrangement, contributions to the account are made pre-tax (being at least tax deferred), and the earnings on the account are also tax deferred. If withdrawals are used for medical expenses, they are never taxed. If they are withdrawn before age 65 without being used to pay medical expenses, the withdrawn amounts are taxable, plus are subject to a 15% penalty. At age 65, the account can be withdrawn similarly

---

[6] www.naschip.org
[7] This type of arrangement is a *Health Reimbursement Account*, or *HRA*.

to an IRA, and is taxable as withdrawn. There are limitations on the product design and contributions which must be followed. MSAs have been superseded by Health Savings Accounts, and no new MSA accounts can be opened today.

Health Savings Accounts: The Medicare Prescription Drug Improvement and Modernization Act of 2003 (Public Law 108-173) created a new type of account, called the **Health Savings Account (HSA)**. HSAs are available to individuals and to all employers, including the self-employed. The insured must be covered under a **High Deductible Health Plan (HDHP)**, and cannot be covered by any non-HDHP plan, including Medicare, or as a dependent of another family member. Required deductible minimums are lower than for MSAs, and allowed contributions are higher.

Contributions to the HSA are made pre-tax, and interest accumulations are tax-free as well. The funds must be used to pay for qualified medical expenses. The account is owned by the insured, and the insured decides how much (within the maximum limit) to put into the account. Unused amounts are carried over from year to year. The federal government has a useful information site on this subject.[8]

ACA RESTRICTIONS ON PLAN DESIGN

The ACA places a wide variety of restrictions on benefit plan design, both with respect to covered services and also with respect to member cost sharing. Several of these restrictions were noted earlier.

Since the ACA includes a mandate that all individuals (with limited exceptions) purchase health insurance, it was important to set limits on what counts as health insurance for the purpose of satisfying the mandate (so that it wasn't possible to largely avoid the mandate by buying a policy that does not provide comprehensive coverage).

A second goal of this regulation is to make it easier for consumers to compare insurance plans by partially standardizing the coverage. This should be contrasted with the regulation of Medicare Supplement plans described elsewhere in this chapter, where the plans were entirely standardized.

---

[8] http://www.treasury.gov/resource-center/faqs/Taxes/Pages/Health-Savings-Accounts.aspx

The following subsections provide more detail on how the restrictions fit together to define the "metallic" plans that were offered starting in 2014.

Essential Health Benefits

As part of the ACA, Congress required that all non-grandfathered individual and small group major medical plans cover the following ten categories of **essential health benefits (EHBs)**:

1. Ambulatory patient services;
2. emergency services;
3. hospitalization;
4. maternity and newborn care;
5. mental health and substance use disorder services, including behavioral health treatment;
6. prescription drugs;
7. rehabilitative and habilitative services and devices;
8. laboratory services;
9. preventive and wellness services and chronic disease management; and
10. pediatric services, including oral and vision care.

Individual market plans were required to cover these services starting in 2014. Prior to the ACA, it was common for several of these categories to be excluded under individual plans (or only available as a rider, subject to underwriting approval). Prime examples of this include maternity and mental health/substance abuse services.

In determining the exact list of services that must be covered within each category, the federal government required, through regulation, that each state choose a **benchmark plan** from among certain plans that existed in the state market as of March, 2010. This benchmark plan, once any missing categories of benefits were added, determined the EHBs for all plans in the state. The result is that the list of EHBs varies somewhat from state to state, creating administrative complexity for carriers operating in multiple states.

Several of the EHB categories have presented special challenges for insurers, namely **habilitative** services[9] and the pediatric vision and oral care. Habilitative services were in many cases not commonly covered by insurers, and were not always clearly defined by regulators. This made it challenging for insurers to develop pricing assumptions. Pediatric vision and dental services presented challenges to insurers who did not have contracted providers for vision hardware or dental services. This challenge was partially alleviated when the government allowed the creation of separate standalone pediatric dental plans within the Exchanges.

Actuarial Values, Metal Levels, and Cost Sharing Limits

EHB regulations set requirements as to which services must be covered by ACA-compliant plans; actuarial value (AV) and cost sharing limit requirements set boundaries on the types and levels of cost sharing insurers may impose on members for those services.

In ACA regulation, **actuarial value**[10] is the percentage of total claim costs for the plan that are expected to be paid by the insurer (rather than the enrollees) for a standard population. After considering various alternatives, the government decided to create a standard tool (the "Actuarial Value Calculator" or AVC) to measure this benchmark. All insurers must use this tool to measure their plans, or obtain a certification from an actuary if the plan cannot be measured by the tool.

While a full accounting of the various ACA limitations on cost sharing is outside the scope of this book, the major provisions applying to non-grandfathered plans (both in and out of Exchanges) are as follows. Unless otherwise noted, the requirement began in 2014.

---

[9] Habilitative services are similar to rehabilitative services, with the following difference: rehabilitative services aim to restore functions that have been lost to a patient, while habilitative services aim to help a patient gain normal functions that have never been present.

[10] Actuarial value should not be confused with the similar concept of **minimum value**. Minimum value is used in the tests that determine whether employer coverage meets minimum standards to comply with the ACA's mandate that larger employers offer affordable healthcare coverage to their employees. A full discussion of minimum value and how it differs from AV is beyond the scope of this book.

- Starting September 23, 2010, the ACA eliminated cost sharing on many preventive services, and prohibited lifetime and annual dollar limits on EHBs.
- All ACA-compliant plans[11] sold after January 1, 2014 must meet an AV **metal level** (platinum, gold, silver, and bronze). Each metal level has a set range of allowable AVs, which represent the anticipated percentage of claim costs paid by the insurer rather than the member. A silver level plan, for example, must be expected to pay between 68% and 72% of EHB claim costs (for a standard population, as measured by the AVC), with the member paying the balance through cost sharing.
- Plans must set an overall out-of-pocket maximum limit on member cost sharing for EHBs not to exceed certain published limits (the limit for 2014 was $6,350 for a single policy and $12,700 for a family policy). All cost sharing (other than cost sharing under a standalone pediatric dental policy) must accumulate to the OOP maximum.

Other Requirements

Plans that are to be certified for sale on a public Exchange must also meet a variety of other market rules. These include:
- Passing a **meaningful difference** test (to prevent insurers from monopolizing virtual "shelf space" with many very similar plans);
- Network adequacy tests;
- Tests for discriminatory service areas;
- Tests for discriminatory cost sharing; and
- Tests by the government for "outlier" premium rates.

NETWORKS

Most individual major medical insurers today have developed or contracted with one or more provider networks, either as a group or individually. A **provider network** is a collection of doctors, hospitals, and other providers, who have agreed to provide certain services for insureds of the

---

[11] Insurers can also offer certain "catastrophic" plans to individuals under age 30 or for whom buying a regular plan would be a financial hardship. While these plans aren't subject to the AV requirements, they do have prescribed benefit designs.

insurer. In return, they are provided a stream of patients and are paid according to the contracts (provider agreements).

Insurers who are geographically concentrated, like Blue Cross/Blue Shield plans and HMOs, typically build and maintain their own networks. This works well because the geographic concentration allows for efficient use of resources and personnel in managing the network.

Unless they are one of the very few jumbo national carriers, insurers whose customers are geographically diverse will typically not have enough geographic concentration in any one area to justify development of a network. Companies that fall in this category include most commercial individual major medical carriers, as opposed to Blue Cross/Blue Shield plans or HMOs.

When it is not feasible or desirable for an insurer to build a proprietary network, the other alternative usually pursued is to contract with existing **networks for hire**. These networks have been created by (usually non-insurance) companies who have invested the resources necessary to create their own networks, with the intent of renting that network to insurers. Economically, this makes sense, because the individual insurers who don't have critical mass in an area by themselves can be aggregated, and the critical mass can be found by the organizing company. The ACA includes new network adequacy requirements applicable to qualified health plans sold in the exchanges. These requirements are intended to ensure that sufficient numbers of providers of various specialties are included in the network.

PPO Products

The class of products which utilize networks are generally referred to as **Preferred Provider Organization (PPO)** products. These products typically have a dual set of benefit provisions. The first applies when the insured uses a provider from the network (hence, a **preferred provider**), the second for out of network providers.

There is usually a significant difference in the benefit levels that apply in network and out of network for a typical major medical plan. An example of such differences is shown in Tables 2.1 and 2.2. Table 2.1 shows how a PPO benefit plan might be designed if both the in network and out of network plans are structured as copay type plans. Table 2.2 shows how such a plan might be structured if both the in network and out of network plans are deductible type plans.

Table 2.1

Typical Benefits, PPO Copay Product		
	Benefit Provision	
Type of Service	In Network	Out of Network
Hospital Inpatient Stays		
Per Stay Copay	$250	$750
Physician Visit Copay	$10	$30
Hospital Outpatient		
Emergency Room Copay	$100	$200
X-Ray Copay	$15	$30
Physician		
Office Visit Copay	$10	$30
Coinsurance %	80%	70%
Out of Pocket Limit	$2,000	$7,000
Mental & Nervous, Outpatient		
Services per year	40	0
Prescription Drug Copay (Generic/Brand/Specialty)	$10/$30/$100	$10/$30/$100

Table 2.2

Typical Benefits, PPO Deductible Product		
	Benefit Provision	
Type of Service	In Network	Out of Network
Deductible	$1,000	$3,500
Coinsurance %	80%	50%
Out of Pocket Limit	$2,000	$7,000
Prescription Drug Copay (Generic/Brand/Specialty))	$10/$30/$100	$10/$30/$100

Quite often, as in this case, prescription drug benefits are provided through a separate PBM arrangement, and the benefit is subject to a copay despite all other benefits being subject to a deductible.

It is also fairly common to have in network benefits structured as a copay benefit, but out of network benefits structured as a deductible benefit, for those companies whose benefit administration system allows for this complexity. Hybrid plan designs combining features of both deductible and copay type plans for the in-network benefit are also quite common.

Copays may apply, for example, on physician office visits and prescription drugs, while a deductible, coinsurance, and out of pocket limit may apply to other services.

Measuring and Choosing Providers

Insurers who are building their own networks must choose which providers to include in their networks. A thorough discussion on this subject is beyond the scope of this text, but a few basic principles can be mentioned.

First, the insurer must decide on how restrictive the network will be. At one extreme, only the providers who meet very strict criteria might be allowed into the network. At the other extreme, the insurer might seek to have virtually all providers in the area in their network. (In some states, "any willing provider laws" will restrict the insurer's ability to prohibit participation in their network by higher cost providers.)

There has recently been a trend among some insurers to develop multiple networks, having different levels of breadth and discount. A plan might, for example, have one network with relatively fewer (and lower cost) providers, and another network with much broader but higher cost provider contracts.

Even when an insurer would like to be restrictive in building its network, it may find that it must make allowances for unusual circumstances. In rural areas, in particular, there may be a limited number of providers from which to choose, and the need to have providers in that area can (and often does) outweigh the desire for a restrictive network.

Another common challenge is that in many areas healthcare providers have consolidated into a few large systems, which often cannot be split up when building a network.

The criteria used to choose providers is typically based on a combination of practice patterns (such as quality measures, efficiency of care, adherence to treatment standards) and cost. Cost measures include the cost of the provider themselves (the most common) and other costs controlled by the provider, such as the cost of inpatient care directed by a physician. When comparing provider costs, it is common to attempt to adjust costs for the relative morbidity of the patients seen by that provider using some form of risk assessment mechanism. This is important, for example, if one provider sees an older population with more chronic medical issues while another has a relatively young and healthy patient base. There are several techniques for doing so, and this is still a developing area of practice.

Measuring and Choosing Networks

Insurers who rent networks today typically evaluate those networks mostly on the cost savings through provider discounts achieved by the network. Cost savings provided by efficient care patterns can be used, but such measures are relatively undeveloped today, especially in this market. Most larger, geographically concentrated companies (like BCBS plans or HMOs) have historically used the same networks for their individual products as they do for their group products, although this may be starting to change with respect to ACA exchange products.

The ACA has brought renewed interest in network management to the individual insurance market, since other avenues of cost management (namely underwriting) have been eliminated. Many insurers have been experimenting with very restrictive networks, and there is also renewed interest in various risk sharing arrangements between insurers and healthcare providers.

2.2 Limited Benefit Medical Coverages

Medical coverages that don't meet the comprehensive definition of major medical are typically called **limited benefit coverages**. There are a number of them in use today.

Some states have regulations that define certain plans as "limited benefit plans", even though those plans would be considered major medical coverage in other states. To save time, effort, and resources, it usually makes sense to research each potential sales state's rules in this regard, before filing the product.

Given the new restrictions on major medical plans under the ACA, there has been renewed interest in limited benefit products, since they are not subject to the new ACA rules (in particular, they are not subject to the minimum loss ratio rule which effectively caps insurer's potential profits in the major medical market).

HOSPITAL INDEMNITY PLANS

The **hospital indemnity plan (HIP)** is a plan that typically pays a flat amount per day of inpatient hospitalization. Such payments can start after a period of days (called an **elimination period**), and are often limited to a number of days of payment, such as 365.

HIP plans are often marketed through mass marketing techniques, and at one time were widely marketed through fliers included in Sunday newspapers or through the mail. They are less popular currently than in the past, possibly because the market reached a saturation point. Some insurers also found growing antiselection problems (such as one carrier who found that someone brought a stack of their brochures to a long term care ward of a local hospital.)

Because of the relatively high cost of medical underwriting, and their relatively low premium level, HIP plans usually involve no underwriting. Instead, carriers rely on pre-existing condition exclusions to avoid the worst antiselection, which would occur within the first year or two of coverage.

HIP policies can also have some additional benefit riders attached to them. Foremost of these is the **Intensive Care Unit (ICU)** benefit, which pays an added amount when the insured is in an intensive care unit.

These policies are intended to be supplemental to major medical coverage, not to replace it. The intent is not to cover the cost of care, but rather to provide a relatively small amount of income to help offset unspecified costs associated with a hospitalization, such as travel expenses or lost income.

OTHER SCHEDULED BENEFITS

Some policies are constructed of one or more (usually multiple) indemnity type benefits, each of which provides limited benefit amounts.

One version of this type of policy is one where many (or all) of the benefits are only payable if the cause of the event was accidental. Table 2.3 has a hypothetical schedule of such benefits.

Table 2.3

Hypothetical Scheduled Accident Benefit Policy	
Accidental Death & Dismemberment	$5,000
Payment per accident-caused inpatient hospital day	$30
Payment per accident-caused ICU day	$100
Payment per accident-caused Emergency Room visit	$25
Payment per month of lost work due to accident, after one week, up to 12 months	$250

Another version of a scheduled benefit policy is one under which the company has pieced together various scheduled medical payments. Such a policy might be used to help offset medical expenses, without providing the comprehensive coverage of a medical plan. Table 2.4 contains a hypothetical combination of benefits for such a policy.

Table 2.4

Hypothetical Scheduled Medical Benefit Policy	
Payment per day of hospitalization, after 1 day	$500
Additional payment per day of ICU, CCU	$250
Surgical Benefit	By Schedule, Maximum of $5,000
Emergency Room	$50
Outpatient X-Ray	$20 per x-ray
Outpatient Laboratory	$15 per test
Doctors Office Visit	$20 per visit

Sometimes such policies are limited to hospital benefits only, presumably under the belief that hospital expenses are of bigger concern to potential policyholders than physician, ancillary, and drug costs.

DREAD DISEASE AND CRITICAL ILLNESS

Some policy designs take a different approach to produce lower premium levels than major medical. They do so by providing coverage only for a specified list of medical conditions. Generically, such policies are called **dread disease** policies.

One major category of dread disease policies is that of cancer policies. In the case of a diagnosed cancer, such policies typically pay a flat amount (or charges up to that amount) for hospital confinement (inpatient days), ambulance to or from the hospital, ICU confinement, surgery, loss of time (disability income), therapies (radiation and chemo), and even a death benefit.

In recent years, a new version of the dread disease policy has become somewhat popular, particularly in countries outside North America. It is called **critical illness** coverage. A typical set of benefits for such a policy would be a lump sum benefit in the case of a heart attack, stroke, heart surgery, cancer (except skin cancer), or diagnosis of specified conditions.

Some regulators, most notably the New York State Insurance Department, have prohibited dread disease policies. One common concern from a regulatory perspective is whether consumers will fully understand the limited nature of the coverage.

2.3 GROUP CONVERSION COVERAGE

Often group medical policies contain provisions which guarantee that, when someone leaves the group and its coverage, they will be offered the opportunity to purchase an individual health insurance contract from the same insurer (or from another insurer with whom the group insurer has contracted), called a **group conversion** contract. Such provisions are typically required by state insurance law, although the existence and the details of the requirement vary by state. As of this writing, these requirements are in flux due to the changes made by the ACA.

The NAIC has a model law governing conversion policies, for those states that have adopted it. For insureds converting from basic hospital or surgical expense insurance (a coverage popular some years ago), that law requires they be offered three basic plans from which to choose. For those converting from major medical coverage, minimum benefits in the conversion policy must include a policy maximum (either per cause or lifetime) of $250,000, 80% coinsurance, and $1,000 out of pocket limit.

Group conversion policies are fairly highly regulated. Since 1986, however, the implementation of the federal law known as **COBRA**[12] has enormously lessened the importance of group conversion policies. Prior to COBRA, in many states the main vehicle that provided benefits for uninsurable persons who left their employers was the conversion contract. This resulted in substantial antiselection, with claim costs up to three or four times standard. The regulations in many states that limited premiums resulted in conversion policies often being substantially underpriced, thus requiring subsidy by other lines of business from the insurer (such as the groups from which the individual convertees originally came). In many other states, particularly in the 1980s and beyond, a major tool used to provide coverage to such former employees has been the state high risk pool. Going forward individuals will be able to purchase coverage in the individual market, since medical underwriting has been abolished.

COBRA requires that group coverage (including self-insured plans) be offered to terminating employees, for groups of size 20 or larger,[13] for a limited period of coverage. The length of the offered insurance period depends on the reason for the "qualifying event," and varies from 18 to 36 months. The insured cannot be required to pay more than 102% of the average group cost, which is substantially less than conversion premiums; post-ACA the COBRA premiums may be greater than premiums available on the exchange without underwriting, particularly for younger employees. The availability of group conversion coverage varies by state, and the requirements by state have changed in recent years. Research must be done to determine the exact rules for each state.

When an individual's COBRA coverage terminates, they are then eligible for conversion coverage. There are far fewer people buying conversion policies than there were pre-COBRA, however, since most COBRA eligible insureds only need insurance for a relatively short interim period until coverage is found under another group program, such as that provided by a new employer. Some states also have group extension laws similar to COBRA that may require a modification of the otherwise applicable COBRA requirement.

---

[12] Consolidated Omnibus Budget Reconciliation Act of 1986
[13] www.cms.gov

2.4 MEDICARE SUPPLEMENT COVERAGE

Medicare coverage in the U.S. is fairly comprehensive, providing significant coverage of inpatient and outpatient medical expenses. Coverage was expanded with the **Medicare Modernization Act of 2003 (MMA)**, adding **Medicare Part D**, which, for the first time, covers prescription drugs for Medicare recipients. However, Medicare still does not cover all of a person's medical needs.

Part A of Medicare provides payment for hospital and skilled nursing facility stays, subject to certain deductibles and copays that increase each year, and subject to a maximum on the number of days. Part B of Medicare, for which an enrollee must pay a premium, provides reimbursement for outpatient and physician expenses. These expenses are also subject to a calendar year deductible (which typically increases each year), and a percentage copay (generally 20%). In the first few years of the Medicare program, products were developed to fill in these gaps of coverage. These products, which are owned by approximately 1/5 of all Medicare enrollees, are called **Medicare Supplement**, **Medigap**, or **MedSupp** policies.

In 1980, Congress passed a law – known as the **Baucus Amendment** – which induced each state to adopt insurance laws and regulations that met Congressional minimums for Medicare Supplement policies. This law established minimum benefit standards and loss ratio requirements and governed how insurers and their agents deal with prospects and insureds in this marketplace.

A major update to the Baucus Amendment occurred with the **Omnibus Budget Reconciliation Acts (OBRA)** of 1989 and 1990. These acts further defined and standardized minimum benefits, increased the minimum loss ratio standard, and reformed physician reimbursement. With the OBRA regulations, Congress wanted to reduce the plethora of Medicare Supplement benefit designs by creating ten standardized benefit packages. It was thought that such limitation would promote greater price competition, since the benefits being compared would be identical from company to company.

Rather than specifying the benefit designs, the law called for the NAIC to define the ten basic plans for this purpose. They are included in the

Model Regulation to Implement the **NAIC Medicare Supplement Insurance Minimum Standards Model Act**, and were referred to as Plans A through J. These 10 plans have been updated three[14] times over the years. The first change came with the **Balanced Budget Act of 1997** (which added high deductible plan versions of F and J). In 2003, the MMA introduced Part D of Medicare, and required that standardized Plans H, I, and J (the only standardized plans which had drug coverage) be modified to remove all drug benefits. It also introduced two new standardized plans, K and L, which require more cost sharing on the part of the individual. In 2008, the **Medicare Improvements for Patients and Providers Act** (**MIPPA**) made several additional benefit changes. It also introduced two more new plans (Plans M and N, again with higher member cost sharing) and eliminated several plans (Plans E, H, I, and J) that had become duplicative after the various benefit changes.

The standardized plans are based on a "building block" approach, with certain benefit pieces that are "core" required to be in all plans, while other benefits are contained in some plans and not others. Table 2.5 provides a brief description of the "building block" benefits which make up the standardized plans. As described previously, some building blocks have been added or removed over the years. These are noted in the table.

---

[14] Four, if you count restrictions on use of genetic testing and information introduced by the **Genetic Information Nondiscrimination Act of 2008** (GINA).

Table 2.5
Building Blocks of Standardized Medicare Supplement Plans

	Medicare Supplement Benefit
Medicare Part A:	
Hospital Inpatient Deductible	$1,216 (in 2014), adjusted yearly
Hospital Copays (core)	¼ of the Part A deductible for each day in the hospital from day 61 to day 90
	½ of the Part A deductible for each Medicare lifetime "reserve" day (generally days 91 to 150)
Hospital "Excess" Days (core)	100% of Medicare allowable charges for hospital days beyond the reserve days (up to 365)
Skilled Nursing Facility (SNF)	1/8 of the Part A deductible for days 21-100 in a skilled nursing facility
Hospice Copays (core, added 6/1/2010)	$5 copayments for palliative drugs and 5% coinsurance for inpatient respite care
Medicare Part B:	
Part B deductible	$147 per calendar year (2014), adjusted yearly
Part B copays (core)	Generally 20% of Medicare eligible charges
Part B excess payments	The difference between the actual billed charge and the Medicare allowed charge (subject to a max, limited by law)
Prescription Drugs: (note – eliminated 1/1/2006)	
Basic benefit	50% of prescription drug charges, after a $250 deductible, subject to $1250 maximum
Extended benefit	50% of prescription drug charges, after a $250 deductible, subject to a $3000 maximum
Miscellaneous:	
Blood (core)	The first 3 pints under either Part A or B
Foreign travel	80% of billed charges for medically necessary care in a foreign country, subject to a separate $250 deductible and $50,000 lifetime limit
Preventive medical (eliminated 6/1/2010)	100% reimbursement of specified preventive services, up to $120/year
At-Home Recovery (eliminated 6/1/2010)	100% reimbursement for short-term care at home, up to $40/visit, $1600 per year

Table 2.6 shows which combination of benefits from Table 2.5 is included in each of the NAIC promulgated basic plan designs.

Table 2.6

Medicare Supplement Benefit Plans										
Benefit	Standard Plan									
	A	B	C	D	F	G	K	L	M	N
Hospital Copays & Excess Days (1)	X	X	X	X	X	X	X	X	X	X
Part B Copays	X	X	X	X	X	X	50%	75%	X	(2)
Blood	X	X	X	X	X	X	50%	75%	X	X
Hospice Copays	X	X	X	X	X	X	50%	75%	X	X
Part A Deductible		X	X	X	X	X	50%	75%	50%	X
Part B Deductible			X		X					
SNF Coinsurance			X	X	X	X	50%	75%	X	X
Part B excesses					X	X			X	X
Foreign Travel (4)			X	X	X	X			X	X

(1) Includes hospital copays in days 61-90 and 91-150 (reserve days), and hospital days in excess of reserve days (max of 365).
(2) Plan N pays 100% of the Part B coinsurance, except for a maximum $20 copayment on certain office visits and a maximum $50 copayment for certain ER visits.
(3) Plans K and L have out of pocket limits (indexed each year) after which the coverage goes to 100% on the lines labeled 50% or 75%. For 2014, the limit is $4,940 for Plan K and $2,470 for Plan L.
(4) Covers medically necessary Medicare eligible emergency care in a foreign country for 80% of billed charges subject to a $250 calendar year deductible and $50,000 lifetime maximum benefit.

In addition to the plans outlined above, a high deductible version of Plan F can be sold, where the plan does not begin paying until the person has paid $2140 (in 2014, increased annually) in out of pocket expenses.

A study by America's Health Insurance Plans (AHIP) states that:

> In 2011, most Medicare beneficiaries with a standardized Medigap policy had Plan F (51 percent). Plan C, the second most popular plan, had 14 percent of the Medigap standardized plan market.
> [...]
> High-deductible Plan F, and newer standardized Medigap plans K, L, M, and N – which contain enrollee cost-sharing requirements (co-payments, coinsurance and/or deductibles) – made up 23 percent of new Medigap purchases in 2011. Plan N, which includes cost-

sharing of up to $20 for physician office visits and up to $50 for certain emergency room visits (waived in certain circumstances), represented 18 percent of newly purchased Medigap policies in 2011 and was by far the most popular of the newer standardized plans.[15]

When Part D was introduced in 2006, existing policyholders were given the choice of keeping their MedSupp plans with prescription drug coverage and NOT enrolling in Part D, or of enrolling in Part D and having the drug benefit removed from their MedSupp plans (with a corresponding reduction in premiums). No new MedSupp plans sold can include a prescription drug benefit, however.

The OBRA regulations that created the 10 standardized plans also established a "Medicare Select" program, under which a network of preferred provider hospitals can be used to reduce the cost of a Medicare Supplement policy. With a Medicare Select policy, the preferred hospital network can waive the Part A deductible for those using the network.

When standardized plans began, insurers were not required to discontinue prior policies that were already in force. For that reason, some insurers still have some steadily shrinking blocks of "pre-standardized" business that were issued before 1991. Similarly, each subsequent set of changes has resulted in blocks of prior policies that have different benefits from policies sold today.

In addition, there are three states (Massachusetts, Minnesota, and Wisconsin), where Medicare Supplement benefits were standardized before the federal requirements; these were exempted from the federal standardization requirements.[16]

2.5 MEDICARE ADVANTAGE AND PART D PLANS

Traditional Medicare was originally enacted in 1965 as part of the Social Security Act to provide social health insurance coverage to eligible

---

[15] "Trends in Medigap Coverage and Enrollment, 2011." America's Health Insurance Plans, Center for Policy and Research, May 2012. Accessed at http://www.ahip.org/Medigap-2012.aspx

[16] www.medicare.gov

Americans aged 65 or older. Coverage was later extended to individuals under the age of 65 with disabilities.

The **Balanced Budget Act (BBA) of 1997** introduced new options for Medicare beneficiaries by allowing them to receive their Medicare benefits through a managed care plan in the private market. These plans, originally named *Medicare+Choice*, were later renamed *Medicare Advantage* under the MMA in 2003.

The MMA also introduced **Medicare Part D**, which offers prescription drug benefits to Medicare beneficiaries enrolled in Part A and/or Part B. Beneficiaries have the option to enroll in a stand-alone Part D **prescription drug plan (PDP)**, or they can choose to enroll in a Medicare Advantage (MA) plan that also covers prescription drug benefits (MA-PD plans). An entity that offers a Medicare Advantage plan is known as a **Medicare Advantage Organization (MAO)** and an entity that offers Part D plans is known as a **Medicare Part D Plan Sponsor**.

Medicare Cost plans are another form of managed care plan authorized to contract with Medicare under section 1876 of the Social Security Act.[17] Cost plans are allowed to offer coverage for Part A and Part B services, or Part B services only (they may also choose to offer Part D as an optional benefit). Many of the rules and regulations for cost plans are similar to Medicare Advantage plans, but there are differences. For example, cost plan payments are based on "reasonable" costs incurred for the Medicare-covered services they offer, including the cost of administering and operating the plan (while Medicare Advantage plans are paid risk-based capitation payments). Also unlike Medicare Advantage plans, Medicare cost plan beneficiaries are able to receive benefits under Original Medicare if they receive Medicare-covered services outside of the plan's network. CMS no longer accepts new cost plan contracts,[18] and there are plans to sunset the program entirely. A full discussion of cost plans is beyond the scope of this text.

BENEFITS

Medical coverage through a Medicare Advantage plan provides full coverage for all traditional Medicare Part A and Part B services (at a minimum), and is collectively referred to as Part C. Unlike Medicare

---

[17] http://www.ssa.gov/OP_Home/ssact/title18/1876.htm
[18] 42 CFR 417.402(b)

Supplement plans, benefit designs under Medicare Advantage plans are not standardized, and therefore vary by insurer.

In general, cost sharing under Medicare Advantage plans must be at least as generous as traditional Medicare, and are oftentimes more generous (meaning that the deductibles, coinsurance, and copayments paid by enrollees are lower on average than in traditional Medicare). It is common for Medicare Advantage plans to offer supplemental benefits in addition to those offered under traditional Medicare (e.g., eyewear, other vision benefit not covered by Medicare, and dental).

Part D plans must also offer benefits that meet minimum requirements (which are determined by CMS based on statutory requirements and called the **defined standard plan**). While insurers can offer the defined standard plan, similar to Medicare Advantage, benefit designs will vary by insurer and will oftentimes be more generous than the defined standard plan (such plans are referred to as **enhanced benefit plans**).

ENROLLMENT

There are designated times throughout the year when Medicare beneficiaries are eligible to sign up or renew a Medicare Advantage or Part D plan. These designated timeframes are called enrollment periods, and include:
- Initial enrollment period: when beneficiaries become eligible for Medicare because they turned 65 or became disabled.
- Annual open enrollment period: a period in the fall (October 15 through December 7 each year) during which currently enrolled Medicare beneficiaries can enroll or change their Medicare Advantage or Part D coverage.
- Special enrollment period: a beneficiary may qualify for an enrollment period outside of the initial or annual enrollment periods for a variety of reasons, such as a change in residence, loss of current coverage, or changes in their existing plan's contract with Medicare, among others.

Medicare Advantage plans are guaranteed issue, meaning they cannot deny coverage during a valid enrollment period due to pre-existing conditions, claim history, or other reasons, as long as the beneficiary:
- is enrolled in Medicare Part A and Part B;
- does not have **end stage renal disease** (**ESRD**);

- applies for coverage during a valid enrollment period;
- resides in the plan's service area; and
- abides to the terms of the insurance contract.

Part D plans have similar guaranteed issue requirements, except that:
- beneficiaries are eligible as long as they are enrolled in Part A, Part B, or Part C; and
- beneficiaries with ESRD are eligible.

In Part D, beneficiaries will be charged a premium penalty if they do not have Part D coverage (or alternative coverage that is certified to be at least as generous) for a period of at least 63 days any time after their initial enrollment period. Beneficiaries may also be charged a Part B late enrollment premium penalty if they are not eligible for a special enrollment period and do not sign up for Part B during their initial enrollment period (this penalty increases with each year of delay). These late enrollment penalties are designed to reduce antiselection that might otherwise occur if seniors waited to enroll in the program until they had significant health needs.

FUNDING FOR MEDICARE ADVANTAGE AND PART D

MAOs and PDPs receive capitated payments from CMS in return for taking on the financial risk of providing healthcare benefits to members covered by the plan.

CMS publishes benchmark Medicare Advantage payment rates each year that are used to determine capitation payments. The benchmark rates reflect the maximum capitation payment a Medicare Advantage plan is eligible to receive for a "standard" or risk-adjusted population.

As discussed later, each year MAOs must submit a bid including, among other things, an estimate of their cost to provide standard Medicare benefits to a standard population for the following year. If this expected cost is below the benchmark (on a risk-adjusted basis), the plan will be eligible to receive a portion of the difference between the benchmark and projected spending (known as the *savings*) in the form of a bid *rebate*. This rebate must be used to reduce the Part D portion of member premiums for MA-PD plans, or to enhance the plan's benefit offerings by either adding supplemental benefits not covered by traditional Medicare or reducing cost sharing on Medicare covered services below traditional FFS levels.

If a Medicare Advantage plan does not submit a bid below the benchmark, the plan will need to charge members a monthly premium to cover the shortfall. Plans may also choose to charge a premium in order to enhance benefit offerings when rebates will not cover the entire cost of the enhanced benefits. Premiums are community rated (cannot vary based on the health status of the member or other characteristics).

There are several ways that MAOs strive to achieve savings. Plans may, for example, require that members use contracted providers within their network. Prior authorization and care coordination strategies are often used to control utilization, and many plans implement disease management or quality control programs to improve healthcare outcomes.

CMS assigns Medicare Advantage plans a **five-star quality rating** each year, with one star representing the lowest rating and five stars representing the highest rating. Under the ACA, a Medicare Advantage plan's benchmark payment and rebate (as a percentage of savings) depends on its star rating. Plans with higher star ratings receive increased benchmark payment rates and are eligible for a larger rebate (as a percentage of savings) than plans with lower star ratings. **Bonus payments** (the difference between the plan's payment with quality rating adjustments and the plan's payment without quality rating adjustments) can have a significant impact on revenue for Medicare Advantage plans. Of course, star ratings can also have a significant marketing impact, as they are visible to consumers shopping for coverage.

Capitation payments paid to Medicare Advantage plans are adjusted to reflect the demographics and health status of the plan's enrolled population. Demographics and health status are measured on a per-member basis using a federal risk adjustment model.

Part D plans are also funded significantly by CMS, but the payment methodology is somewhat different than Medicare Advantage. PDPs are subsidized through a **direct subsidy** (monthly capitation payment per member), reinsurance, and risk corridor program. These programs result in complex cash flow issues for PDPs since they create settlements after each plan year.[19] There are also settlements associated with certain sub-

---

[19] For a more detailed discussion, see the "Medicare Part D Accounting Practice Note" prepared by the American Academy of Actuaries in April 2008, available at http://www.actuary.org/files/publications/Practice_Note_Medicare_Part_D_accounting_practice_note_april2008.pdf.

sidies given to lower income beneficiaries. Similar to Medicare Advantage, Part D direct subsidy payments are risk adjusted to reflect the demographics and health status of the plan's membership population using a federal risk adjustment model.

BID PROCESS

Each spring, MAOs and PDPs must submit a benefit package summary and **bid** to CMS. The bid is a projection of the expected per member per month cost of providing benefits to Medicare beneficiaries covered by the plan, and is used to determine the plan's capitation payments.

As described previously, MA plans that bid below the benchmark will receive a rebate (a portion of the savings) that may be used to reduce the Part D portion of member premium (for MA-PD plans) or for benefit enhancements. Plans that bid above the benchmark will receive the benchmark payment, and will need to cover the remaining revenue requirement by charging a member premium.

The bid submission and approval process is complex, and includes the following steps:

- Early in the year, CMS publishes documents outlining proposed changes to the rules for the Medicare Advantage and Part D programs for the subsequent year's bids and providing initial information related to setting capitation rates. These documents are known as the **advance notice** (of payment policies) and draft call letter.
- In early spring, CMS publishes documents containing the benchmark MA capitation rates for the upcoming year, as well as any finalized changes in the payment or risk adjustment methodology. These documents are referred to as the **announcement** (of MA capitation rates and payment policies) and the final call letter.
- The plan sponsor then prepares and submits an initial bid for each plan to CMS no later than the first Monday in June. This bid consists of a standardized bid form and supporting documentation, and must be certified by a qualified actuary.
- The bid submission is reviewed by CMS and third-party actuaries contracted by CMS during a process called **desk review**. Desk reviewers examine the bid submission and request clarification on any questions that arise. In many cases, a written response is sufficient to satisfy the reviewers' requests. In some cases, questions

may lead to changes in the bid or, in a limited number of cases, a withdrawal of the bid.
- Desk review is generally completed by late July. In early August, plan sponsors must complete a process called **rebate reallocation**. In this process, Part D bids must be adjusted once the final national average bid amounts and national average member premiums are known (based on the initial bids after any changes from desk review). In some cases, MAOs may be allowed to make minor changes to Part C bids (namely, to reallocate rebates to different benefits) during this process.
- After reallocation is complete, a second actuarial certification is required for the bid to be finalized and approved.
- After bids are approved, the plan sponsor may be subject to additional scrutiny if they are selected by CMS for a more detailed bid or financial audit.

One key difference between Part C and Part D is that Part D bids are interdependent, since the direct subsidy and member premium depend on the national average bid amount, which must be determined after bids are submitted. There are many other important considerations in bid development which are beyond the scope of this book. For just one example, a plan's strategy around low income members (who receive additional subsidies from the government for Part D) can require complex analysis.

REGULATORY ENVIRONMENT

The Medicare Advantage program was initially established with the notion that private sector plans would be able to provide Medicare benefits at a lower cost than traditional Medicare FFS through the use of care management strategies, lower administrative expenses, and other efficiencies. The federal government would retain a portion of the savings, and the remainder (that is, the bid rebate) would be used by Medicare Advantage plans to enhance benefits for beneficiaries. Over time, however, average payment rates for Medicare Advantage plans increased and eventually exceeded the cost of traditional FFS[18].

The passage of the 2010 Patient Protection and Affordable Care Act (ACA) brought a new series of changes to the Medicare Advantage program. ACA reforms focus on controlling the increase in spending and improving the quality of care. Under the ACA, there is significant downward pressure on payment rates, plans receive bonus payments based on quality ratings (as described previously in the Funding for Medicare Advantage and Part D section), and there is a minimum medical loss ratio requirement of 85% effective in 2014.[20]

There are also several new provisions of the ACA that impact the Part D program. For example, the ACA requires the current gap in coverage for Part D beneficiaries (where the member cost sharing rose to 100% for members with certain levels of drug spending) to be closed gradually over several years.

Many provisions of the ACA in the small group and individual markets parallel similar approaches taken by the federal government in implementing Medicare Advantage and Part D.[21]

A full discussion of the Medicare Advantage and Part D programs is beyond the scope of this text. Moreover, the standards and requirements for bids under these programs change every year, often significantly. It is therefore essential for any practitioner certifying bids to research and account for all necessary changes each year.

2.6 Disability Income Coverage

Individual health insurance that is intended to cover lost income due to an illness or injury is generically called **disability income (DI)** coverage. There are many variations of this basic idea, which allow such policies to be categorized in different ways.

Renewability

There are basically three categories of renewability for DI; non-cancelable, guaranteed renewable, and conditionally renewable. **Non-cancelable** (also called **non-can**, or **non-can and guaranteed renewable**) coverage is de-

---

[20] May 2014 Medicare Advantage Fact Sheet. The Henry J. Kaiser Family Foundation.
[21] For more see Leida, H. "Learning from Medicare Advantage and Part D: Lessons for the individual insurance market under ACA." Milliman, August 2013. Accessed at http://us.milliman.com/insight/2013/Learning-from-Medicare-Advantage-and-Part-D-Lessons-for-the-individual-insurance-market-under-ACA/.
For a contrasting viewpoint, see Wrobel, K. "The ACA Exchange and Medicare Part D: A Comparison of Financial Risk." Society of Actuaries *Health Watch* Issue 76, October 2014. Retrieved November 11, 2014 from
https://www.soa.org/Library/Newsletters/Health-Watch-Newsletter/2014/october/hsn-2014-iss-76.pdf.

fined as coverage which is guaranteed renewable for a guaranteed premium level. **Guaranteed renewable (GR)** policies are those where the policy is guaranteed to renew (generally to age 65) upon payment of the applicable premium, but that premium level can be changed over time. **Conditionally renewable** policies are those where there are circumstances (other than simply failing to pay the required premium) under which the insurer can refuse to renew policies. Conditionally renewable policies are sometimes referred to as **non-renewable for stated reasons only**, or **optionally renewable**.

DI coverage is generally not inflation-sensitive in the same sense that major medical coverage is. For this reason, there is relatively greater focus, both by insurers and regulators, on the initial premiums for DI coverage, since such premiums are likely to be in effect for a long period of time (perhaps even the whole policy lifetime.) The common major medical scenario of having premiums that increase annually due to claim cost increases, is non-existent in DI coverage.

LOST INCOME VS. INDEMNITY

Some DI coverage pays a flat amount per week or month. This is how DI began, and still forms a significant part of the DI marketplace. One of the drawbacks of this indemnity-type coverage is that, while the face (indemnity) amount might be carefully chosen at the time of issue of the policy, at the time a disability occurs the insured's situation might have significantly changed, and the amount insured might be excessive or deficient relative to the insured's lost income.

ELIMINATION PERIOD

It is fairly common for working people to take a few days off each year because of minor illnesses or injuries. These days off could technically be considered disabilities, since they represent lost days of work. It would be quite costly, however, to insure such disabilities from the first day of disablement. (**Disablement** is generally used to mean physical state of the individual, while **disability** is a policy-defined state of economic loss. Disablement occurs when the injury or illness first happens and results in lost time from work. Disability occurs when the policyholder meets the conditions specified in the policy, and the policy starts paying benefits.)

In response to this issue, DI insurance uses the **elimination period (EP)**. This is the period of disablement that must occur before disability payments start. This helps reduce claim costs and expenses (and thus premium), because it eliminates the frequent, small claims that would occur if payments began on day one. (In this way, it acts similarly to a deductible in major medical insurance.) In addition, if insurance immediately replaced lost wages or income, the insured would have less financial incentive to go back to work. It has, in fact, long been observed that similar populations will have significantly more people disabled on day 30 (for example) with a 0 or 7 day elimination period than with a 14 or 30 day elimination period. This is sometimes called the **elimination period effect**.

Applicants are typically offered a variety of EPs to choose from. Because of the elimination period effect, there has been a tendency in insurer offerings toward longer elimination periods over time, and the elimination of shorter EP options.

BENEFIT PERIOD

Most DI products offer a variety of **benefit periods (BPs)**, the maximum length of time for which benefits are payable, once all conditions are met. Benefit periods can (for specialty products) be as short as six months. The most common BPs are two years, five years, 10 years, and to age 65 or 70. In the late 20th century, it was somewhat common to also offer a lifetime benefit if the disability was incurred prior to a certain age, e.g., 60, but such policies have become less common now.

DEFINITION OF OCCUPATION

Benefits are typically payable if an insured is unable to perform the duties of any occupation for which they are suited by training or education. These are known generically as "any occ" products. In this situation, someone who is unable to continue in the profession they were in at the time the disability began, might still be able to function well in another occupation. For example, a brain surgeon who, through an accident, loses the function of a couple of his fingers, might be unable to continue to perform surgery. The same surgeon might be able to function quite well at another specialty or as a general practitioner, albeit at a lower income level. Under an "any occ" definition, this would not be a total disability, while it might be under an "own occ" definition. Many policies will provide for a limited period of own occ (such as two years), with an any occ definition applying thereafter.

Many insurers, mainly those who market to higher income professionals, may also offer "own occ" products to those professions, where the definition of disability is the inability to perform the functions of their own, specific occupation. If the brain surgeon discussed in the previous paragraph had an "own occ" policy, the disablement described would likely be a total disability.

There was a period of liberalization in DI policies in the 1970s and 1980s which included greater latitude in the use of own occ products. The financial losses that resulted from those liberalizations have caused a retrenchment of DI product definitions away from own occ, toward any occ and income replacement products. Over the last ten years, as DI profitability has improved, companies have been more willing to offer own occ to their higher occupation classes.

TOTAL VS. PARTIAL VS. RESIDUAL

Total disability benefits are payable if a person is fully disabled under the terms of the contract. **Partial disability** benefits were developed as a way to recognize that disability and loss of income are sometimes not black or white, 0% or 100% – that the insured may be able to perform only some of the material duties of his or her job. Insureds who suffer partial disability, usually defined in terms of lost income, can receive some benefits. The benefits are typically expressed as a percentage of total disability, and some minimum loss of income (such as 40%) is required to qualify for benefits.

Under some insurers' definitions, partial disability can be a benefit that is payable as a fixed portion of the total disability benefit, such as 50%.

Residual benefits were developed as a modification to total disability benefits where, after a person had been totally disabled for some **qualification period**, such as seven days, they could then be eligible for a benefit that was proportionate to their loss of income for some period of time. In the absence of this benefit, if the person returned to work the benefits would stop, and he or she might even need to re-satisfy the elimination period before receiving further benefits. For many years, the qualification period for residual benefits have generally been removed.

Recurring Disabilities

If a claimant recovers and disability ends, but then becomes disabled again in a short time, there can be significant differences in benefits payable, depending on whether the new disablement is considered a continuation of the first one or is a brand new one. Most notably, if it is considered a separate disability the claimant must satisfy a new elimination period, but then may be entitled to a new benefit period limit.

Sometimes it can be difficult to differentiate when a disability is a new one or a continuation of a prior one. In order to clarify this situation, insurers include provisions in their policies that fairly objectively define when a disability is a continuation of a prior one. A carrier might, for example, use the following language to differentiate when there are two disabilities:

A disability is considered a separate disability if full, partial, or residual benefits were payable for an earlier disability, are no longer payable, and either;

- the cause of the later disability is not medically related to the cause of the earlier one, and the Insured had resumed on a full-time continuous basis the principal duties of an occupation for at least 30 consecutive days; or
- the cause of the later disability is related to the cause of the earlier one, and the later disability starts at least 12 months after any full, partial, or residual benefits under this policy cease being payable for the earlier one.

There is an additional benefit to having such provisions. Imagine a claimant who is well down the road toward recovery, and wants to try going back to work. He isn't sure, however, whether he is yet able to do so. Without the recurring disabilities provision (and in the absence of a residual disability benefit), the claimant knows that by going back to work for only a single day, and it turns out to be too much for him, he will then have to satisfy a new elimination period, perhaps giving up benefits for many weeks. So, why take the risk? In this situation, it seems in the best interests of both the insurer and the claimant to allow the claimant to "give a try" at returning to work, without jeopardizing his claim status. The recurring disability provision allows this to happen.

Cost of Living Adjustments

The high rates of inflation in the late 1960s through early '80s caused many things to be reexamined. Among them was the inability of most disability policies to automatically adjust to rising incomes which accompanied that inflation. In response, there were provisions added to contracts that adjust for inflation in three different ways. Many companies have their own variations on these benefits.

The first method of adjusting for inflation is to automatically offer increased coverage to active insureds, which they then must either accept or reject. The offer is made at specified intervals. When the offer is made, some portion of the policyholder population will have become less insurable (a higher risk) while insured. Those policyholders are much more likely to accept the increased coverage than other policyholders, resulting in antiselective higher claim costs. Therefore, this coverage logically has an added cost, higher than the normal premium for the added coverage, which is charged as an additional premium for the added benefit. This benefit is often called **guaranteed insurability**, or something similar.

The second method of adjusting for inflation is to have a benefit which automatically adjusts insurance amounts over time, without action by the insured. This can be done by maintaining a fixed percentage of income, or by automatically increasing the benefit by a chosen percentage. If the benefit amount is based on income, this requires periodic financial re-underwriting (i.e., determination of the current income) of the insured, in order to accurately calculate the new benefits.

The third method of adjusting for inflation applies to the benefit payments of claimants only. Many companies offer a benefit that provides for inflationary increases in benefit payments over time. While the initial face amount may or may not vary while the policy is in force (under provisions like the first two methods), this type of benefit only applies to the face amount payable after the person becomes disabled. A policy provision might, for example, read:

> After the first 12 months of a disability, the Company will provide an indexed benefit in place of the benefit that would be payable for that month... The indexed benefit will be based on changes in a consumer price index, subject to certain limits...

Social Insurance Supplements

In the U.S., the Old Age, Survivor, and Disability Insurance program (**OASDI**, or **Social Security**) provides disability benefits to insureds who meet the law's provisions. Benefits are payable beginning in the sixth full month after disablement occurs (roughly a six month waiting period, similar to an elimination period, but during which the claim administration occurs).

The potential for **overinsurance** (insureds having comparable or greater income while disabled than they did while active, causing no financial incentives for recovery) is of great concern to insurers. For this reason, most carriers have developed provisions that integrate with payments made under Social Security. Offsets are designed so as to maintain a targeted **replacement ratio** at issue. (The replacement ratio is the percentage of pre-disability income that is replaced by disability benefits.)

In application, the basic policy is typically issued at face amounts that assume the insured will receive payments under Social Security. Optional benefits can be added (**Social Insurance Supplement**, or **SIS benefits**) which supplement the base policy with additional benefit payments that pay if a claimant is considered disabled by the insurer but not by Social Security. Under this arrangement, most insurers will require that the insured (with their help, if needed) will pursue appeals of the Social Security decision if the claimant is initially denied for OASDI benefits.

Group Wraparound Policies

Some carriers have designed policies to supplement group disability policies, by providing additional benefits to individuals in the group. In these cases, the policies may be accompanied by simplified (and perhaps somewhat relaxed) underwriting rules as well.

Waiver of Premium Provisions

Under most DI policies there are provisions that provide for the policy to remain in force, without premium payments, when the policyholder becomes disabled. Individual life and group life policies can contain this provision as well, but for life policies this is often provided as an optional benefit rider.

Waiver benefits under DI policies tend to match fairly closely to the DI benefit period. It is common, however, to sometimes have a longer elimination period than for the underlying benefits. The waiver benefit (logically) lasts no longer than the remaining premium payment period, but may also be no longer than the underlying benefit period. For example, a policy that is GR to age 65, with a five year benefit period, may limit the waiver of premium benefit to five years of premium payments as well.

2.7 BUSINESS PROTECTION COVERAGE

In section 2.6 we discussed individual disability income coverage used as an income replacement product. Disability coverage can also be used to meet specific business needs, serving a financial purpose by protecting a business against the impact of having an individual employee become disabled.

BUSINESS PURPOSE OF THE INSURANCE

These include **keyperson** insurance, which covers the value of a key person (such as a major salesman, or a small business partner) to the business. Another coverage is **disability buyout** coverage, which covers the cost of buying out a partner or owner, in the event of his or her long term disability. Finally, a coverage which is intended to simply pay the cost of keeping a business going by covering overhead expenses while the owner is disabled, is called **business overhead expense** (**BOE**). These are described further in the next section.

KEYPERSON COVERAGE

Sometimes there are individuals who are virtually indispensable to their companies, particularly small businesses. This is often the founder of the business, or a senior partner or important "rainmaker." If that person became disabled, the business might have a difficult time finding a replacement or otherwise restructuring to do without him or her. **Keyperson** coverage is sold to businesses to financially protect them against this risk. Benefits tend to be short term for this coverage (typically one to two years), lasting long enough for the insured to be replaced, if need be. There may be partial benefits, as well as a **replacement** benefit, paying an additional benefit (still within the policy maximum) after the insured's replacement has been hired. This might cover, for example, the time it takes a new senior sales executive to "learn the ropes" at the company and become financially productive.

DISABILITY BUYOUT COVERAGE

When there are multiple partners or owners of a business, they may want the ability to buy out one of their partner's ownership interest in the event that partner becomes disabled. This benefit tends to be a lump sum (or payable over a relatively short period of time), according to a buy/sell agreement which must be in effect before the disability (or sometimes before the policy is issued). It is generally only payable for total disability. A sample provision defining Total Disability for this purpose might be:

> The insured is totally disabled when unable to perform the principal duties of the regular occupation and not working in any capacity in the Business.

Elimination periods for disability buyout coverage tend to be significantly longer (one to two years) than normal DI coverage.

BUSINESS OVERHEAD EXPENSE

Small business owners sometimes purchase **business overhead expense (BOE)** coverage, to be able to continue to cover their business's overhead expenses (not including their personal income) in the event of their disability. The covered expenses for this purpose are carefully defined in the contract, and are typically offset by any business income during the benefit period. Benefit periods are typically fairly short (one to two years) for this coverage, in keeping with the short term needs for which this coverage is intended.

2.8 LONG TERM CARE COVERAGE

Long-term care (LTC) insurance offers financial pre-funding for expenses associated with care and services, skilled, custodial or personal in nature, that an individual may need in order to perform basic **activities of daily living (ADLs)** or due to cognitive impairment.

LTC is a relatively new coverage, having only been around for a few decades. Benefit definitions and coverages have been evolving in that time, as have regulations. The NAIC's LTC model regulation has not been universally adopted, and the number of states that have adopted it is still changing. As of late 2014, roughly 44 states (including the District of Columbia) have adopted the 2000 model, in whole or in part.

BENEFIT TRIGGERS

To become eligible to receive benefits under a LTC plan, the insured individual must satisfy the plan's **benefit trigger**. Benefit triggers have evolved since the early 1980s when policies generally required that an insured be confined in a hospital for at least three days and that the need for LTC services commence within two days of the hospital stay in order for plan benefits to be payable. Alternatively, a physician could certify that LTC services are needed. Plans sold since the late 1980s and early 1990s typically include benefit triggers based upon the inability to perform ADLs or the presence of a significant cognitive impairment.

ACTIVITIES OF DAILY LIVING

Minimum benefit eligibility standards (for a LTC plan to receive the same income tax treatment under the Internal Revenue Code as medical insurance policies) were established by the Health Insurance Portability and Accountability Act (HIPAA) in 1996. Under HIPAA, the benefit trigger of a tax-qualified LTC policy must be the inability to perform (without substantial assistance from another individual) at least two of six activities of daily living, or a cognitive impairment that requires substantial supervision to protect the health and safety of the insured. These conditions must be expected to continue for at least 90 days and verified by a licensed health care professional. According to the *Sixteenth Annual Long Term Care Insurance Survey* published in July 2014,[22] 99% of policies issued are now tax qualified.

The six ADLs identified by HIPAA and most commonly utilized in LTC benefit triggers are bathing, dressing, eating, toileting, maintaining continence, and transferring from bed to chair. The definition of what an in-

---

[22] www.brokerworldmag.com

sured needs to be able to do to be considered independent in any particular ADL can vary from plan to plan. Typical ADL definitions are:

Bathing – washing oneself by sponge bath or in either a tub or shower, including the task of getting into or out of the tub or shower;

Continence – the ability to maintain control of bowel and bladder function; or, when unable to do so, the ability to perform associated personal hygiene (including caring for catheter or colostomy bag);

Dressing – putting on and taking off all items of clothing and any necessary braces, fasteners or artificial limbs;

Eating – feeding oneself by getting food into the body from a receptacle (such as a plate, cup or table) or by a feeding tube or intravenously;

Toileting – getting to and from the toilet, getting on and off the toilet, and performing associated personal hygiene; and

Transferring – moving into or out of a bed, chair or wheelchair.

COGNITIVE IMPAIRMENT

Federally tax-qualified LTC plans must trigger benefits if there is a severe cognitive impairment that requires substantial supervision to protect the insured from threats to health and safety. Non-tax qualified plans must also trigger benefits based on cognitive impairment, according to the current NAIC's model regulation, but may have more liberal qualification criteria. Examples of behaviors that can be used to qualify insureds for benefits include wandering and getting lost, combativeness, inability to dress appropriately for the weather, and poor judgment in emergency situations. Insurers use a variety of tools to assess the degree of cognitive impairment including the Short Portable Mental Status Questionnaire developed at Duke University in 1978,[23] the Folstein Mini-Mental State Examination,[24] the Minnesota Cognitive Acuity Screen,[25] developed in 1999, and more recently the Enhanced Mental Skills Test,[26] developed in 2004. The focus of newer tools is identifying

---

[23] Validity Study of the Short Portable Mental Status Questionnaire for the Elderly by Smyer MA, Hofland BF, Jonas EA; J Am Geriatr Soc. 1979 Jun; 27(6):263-9
[24] www.minimental.com/
[25] 'Development and Standardization of a New Telephonic Cognitive Screening Test: the Minnesota Cognitive Acuity Screen (MCAS)' by Knopman DS, Knudson D, Yoes ME, Weiss Dj; Neuropsychiatry Neuropsychol Behav Neurol. 2000 Oct; 13(4):286-96
[26] www.lifeplansinc.com/preclaimprevention/

individuals with an early mild cognitive impairment or early dementia that previous screening tools failed to do.

ELIMINATION PERIOD

Once benefit eligibility has been triggered, most LTC plans have an elimination period, during which the insured needs to remain disabled and benefit eligible before benefits are paid. This elimination period is usually expressed in days and varies from zero to 365 days. The most common elimination periods are 30, 60, 90, and 100 days. The elimination period may be satisfied based on the number of elapsed calendar days, or only the number of days in which formal LTC services are actually received may count toward satisfying the elimination period. The purpose of this elimination period is to ensure that benefit payments are only for long-term chronic disabilities, and thereby to moderate the premium cost of the plan.

Plans may handle the elimination period requirement differently, in situations where recovery occurs prior to the end of the elimination period and a subsequent period of disability occurs. Some plans require the elimination period to be satisfied again for a second episode of care, if the first is followed by a period of more than 180 days of benefit ineligibility. Others will require that the elimination period be satisfied only once in a lifetime, even over multiple periods of disability. The elimination period may be waived for certain types of ancillary benefits, such as respite care, home modification or equipment benefits, and caregiver training benefits

TYPES OF LTC PLANS

There are three types of LTC plans, distinguished by the manner in which plan benefits are paid to the insured. These variations are described next.

Service Reimbursement Model

Under this most-popular model, the insurer reimburses the insured for the cost of LTC services, subject to fixed limits that are specified in the insured's contract and that vary by type of service received. The fixed limits can be applied on a daily, weekly, or monthly basis, depending on the particular plan purchased. A typical plan might, for example, reimburse up to $125 per day for nursing home care, $100 per day for care provided in an assisted living facility or in the insured's home, and up to

$75 per day for informal care, all subject to a total lifetime maximum reimbursement of $228,125 ($228,125 = $125/day × 365 days/yr × 5 years). Invoices and receipts from qualified LTC providers, as defined in the contract, are submitted to the insurer for review before reimbursement is authorized. Payment may be made directly to the provider, or to the insured.

Service Indemnity Model

Under the service indemnity model, a fixed benefit payment is made for any day or week that formal LTC services are received, regardless of the actual charges incurred for those services. If, for example, a plan has a $100 per day home health care benefit, the insured would receive $100 for each day he or she received home health care services, even if the cost of those services was less than $100 per day.

Disability Model

Under a disability model plan, or **cash benefit plan** as it may also be called, a predetermined benefit is paid for each day an insured is eligible for benefits, whether or not the insured is actually utilizing formal LTC services. This model is the simplest to explain and it provides the insured with maximum flexibility in how plan benefits can be utilized. The premiums under this model are generally significantly higher than the other models due to additional benefit utilization and faster benefit payout.

COVERED SERVICES

Covered services (under service reimbursement or service indemnity model plans) can range from a relatively narrow set of services to a broader, more comprehensive collection of services. Since the early 1990s, LTC plans have often provided benefits not only for care provided in a nursing home, but also benefits for home and community-based care, assisted living facility care, and informal care provided by an unlicensed or uncertified provider.

Although the definition of the types of covered services can vary from plan to plan, the following types of services are generally covered:

> Nursing Home Care – care offered in a facility that provides skilled, intermediate, or custodial care, and is either Medicare-approved as a provider of skilled nursing care services, or is state-licensed as a skilled nursing home, intermediate care facility, or a custodial care facility.

Assisted Living Facility Care – care provided in a facility that is state-licensed or certified as an **Assisted Living Facility (ALF)**. For states that do not license or certify such facilities, an ALF is a facility that meets the following minimum criteria:
- It is a group residence that maintains records for services to each resident;
- It provides services and oversight on a 24 hour a day basis; and
- It provides a combination of housing, supportive services, and personal assistance with the Activities of Daily Living.

Home and Community-Based Care – medical and non-medical services provided to ill, disabled, or infirm persons in their residences or in a community-based facility, like an adult day care center. Such services may include assistance with ADLs, homemaker services, and respite care services, and are typically provided by a home health care agency, a licensed nurse registry, or sometimes by an informal care provider.

Hospice Care – services and supplies provided through a state-licensed or certified facility or community-based program designed to provide services to the terminally ill.

Respite Care – formal, paid care provided to relieve an informal care provider.

Home modifications and equipment – services designed to allow an individual to remain at home, rather than have to be institutionalized, such as personal emergency alert systems and home modifications including the installation of wheelchair ramps or grab bars in the bathroom, and the widening of doorways.

Care Management Services – services provided by a geriatric case manager or a nurse to develop an insured's plan of care, identify local provider resources, and coordinate all necessary LTC, medical care, personal care, and social services.

ALTERNATE PLAN OF CARE

Most plans contain an **alternate plan of care (APC)** provision that allows the insurer to pay benefits for services that may not be explicitly defined or covered by the insured's contract. An APC provision offers a mechanism through which the contract continues to provide meaningful benefits even as new ways to provide LTC emerge over time. Eligibility for this benefit is based on agreement between the insurer, the policyholder, and the policyholder's doctor.

BENEFIT LIMIT

LTC plans impose limits on the amount of benefits that will be paid for any given day, week, month, or year, as well as over the entire lifetime of the insured. These limits often vary by the type of LTC service received.

Almost all plans have daily limits for institutional care (nursing home and ALF care). Although home and community-based care limits are also usually applied on a daily basis, weekly or monthly limits are becoming more common. The level of institutional care daily maximum benefit is elected by the applicant and is typically offered in $10 increments from $50 to as high as $400. The daily maximum benefit for home and community-based care is often expressed as a percentage of the institutional daily maximum. Limits for other covered services, such as caregiver training and independence support, are usually expressed as a flat dollar amount or as a fixed multiple of the institutional daily maximum benefit amount, and are applied on either an annual or a lifetime basis.

Although it is common to refer to the lifetime maximum in terms of the number of "years" of institutional benefit available, most of these limits are administered as a "pot of dollars" that is drained as benefits are utilized. Consider, for example, a plan that pays up to $100 per day in a nursing home, $75 per day for home and community-based care, and that has a 5 year lifetime benefit maximum. Expressed in dollars, the lifetime maximum would be 5 years multiplied by 365 days per year multiplied by $100 per day, or $182,500. This lifetime maximum benefit would last significantly longer than 5 years (over 15 years, in fact) if the insured only uses home health care three days a week and received a reimbursement of $75 per day.

INFLATION PROTECTION

The NAIC's LTC model regulation requires that insurers offer an option at initial sale of a policy that is at least as favorable as one of the following:

1. Automatic Inflation Protection. Under a policy with automatic inflation protection, all benefit limits increase automatically each year by a preset percentage of at least 5% on a compound basis. The premium for this increasing coverage, however, is level over time and is based upon the insured's age at issue.

2. Periodic Increase Offers. Under this approach, the insured is periodically, usually every three or five years, given the opportunity to purchase additional amounts of coverage on a guaranteed issue basis. If an insured declines one or more (in practice, usually two or three) consecutive offers, insurers may cease making these offers or require full underwriting in an effort to protect against adverse selection. The amount of each inflation offer can vary, but is typically comparable to the additional benefit available under an identical policy with 5% automatic compound inflation. If an inflation offer is accepted, the premium for the policy will increase by an amount equal to the premium for the increase in coverage, where the additional premium is based on the insured's age at the time the offer is accepted.

3. Coinsurance. With this option, the insurer covers a specified percentage of actual or reasonable charges and does not include a maximum specified indemnity amount or limit. This approach is rarely offered.

In addition to offering at least one of the above, many companies offer a lower percentage compound inflation, typically 3%, or a simple inflation option. The simple inflation option is similar to the compound inflation option, except the all benefit limits are increased on a simple rather than compound basis.

NONFORFEITURE BENEFITS

A **nonforfeiture benefit** is generally offered with individual LTC as an option, for an additional premium. A nonforfeiture benefit allows an insured who voluntarily terminates or lapses coverage to receive a reduced, paid-up benefit without having to continue to pay premiums. Nonforfeiture benefit options are not often elected, but the NAIC Long-Term Care Insurance Model Act requires that a nonforfeiture option be available to every applicant. The "Shortened Benefit Period" (SBP) is the minimum standard for a tax-qualified LTC plan as established by HIPAA, and pays the same benefits in both amount and frequency as are in effect at the time of lapse. The lifetime maximum benefit, however, is reduced to an amount equal to the sum of all premiums paid prior to lapse. The sum of the plan benefits and premiums paid to date cannot exceed the lifetime maximum benefit of the policy just prior to lapse. This benefit is usually not available until a policy has been in force for at least three years. A minimum SBP benefit of 30 times the institutional daily maximum is usually provided. Policies with a limited or fixed premium payment period have an additional alternative nonforfeiture benefit.

Plans may also include a contingent nonforfeiture benefit if an optional nonforfeiture benefit is not selected by the insured. A contingent nonforfeiture benefit is only provided to an insured if he or she lapses coverage due to a "substantial" premium increase, with the triggers for a "substantial" premium increase specified in the NAIC LTC model regulation. The nonforfeiture benefit provided is the same as the SBP benefit described earlier.

ANCILLARY PLAN FEATURES

Other plan features which may be included as a base benefit or as an option include:
- *Bed Reservation Benefit:* This benefit will continue to reimburse the insured for institutional care even if he or she needs to temporarily transfer out of the LTC facility to an acute care facility due to a medical condition. Most plans limit the bed reservation benefit to 21 days per calendar year or per hospital stay.
- *Caregiver Training* – The benefit provides training and educational programs designed to help informal caregivers obtain state licensure or certification as a home health care provider.
- *Death Benefit:* Individual LTC plans may offer an optional death benefit provision which pays a beneficiary an amount equal to a percentage of the cumulative plan premiums paid prior to the insured's death, less any plan benefits paid. The percentage paid is usually a function of the age of the insured at the time of death.
- *Spousal Riders and Discounts:* Most individual plans are available with a premium discount in the 10% to 30% range for individuals who are married. The discount can be actuarially justified by the fact that married people would have a natural live-in informal care provider, and that a married couple provides a more favorable 50% male/50% female gender mix

(at least for non-same sex couples) compared to a 30% male/70% female mix among unmarried insureds. The 50%/50% mix is more favorable because claim costs for females are higher than that of males. Some plans also include an optional spousal waiver of premium benefit, applicable when both spouses own a policy, under which the premiums for both policies would be waived if one of the spouses becomes benefit eligible.

RATE INCREASES

For various public policy reasons, the NAIC has developed a unique approach for regulating rate increases for LTC plans. LTC plans are not sold on a non-can (guaranteed premium rate) basis. The regulatory environment somewhat limits the ability of insurers to correct for rate inadequacy, however, by requiring a higher loss ratio to be applied to the portion of premiums due to rate increases after issue. Filing rate increases on LTC policies can be an unwieldy process with requirements that may vary dramatically by state. It is also not uncommon for state regulators to impose additional rate increase limitations or restrictions that are not based on LTC regulation or actuarial justification.

COMBINATION PRODUCTS

A form of LTC insurance that has been gaining popularity in recent years is in the form of a rider to a life insurance policy or an annuity policy. This form of product is often referred to as a combination product or a linked product. Both the LTC riders and the base policies must be kept inforce together. Similar to stand-alone LTC insurance, the LTC riders comply with the NAIC LTC model regulation and the Internal Revenue Code (IRC) section 7702B. Some riders comply with the IRC section 101(g) instead of 7702B and are then marketed as Chronic Illness riders, as section 101(g) does not allow them to be marketed as LTC insurance.

Most combination products first pay LTC benefits out of the policyholder's base plan values. That is, an acceleration benefit (AB) accelerates the life insurance benefit prior to death or the cash value of an annuity policy. With an acceleration benefit, the life policy face amount is reduced dollar-for-dollar by the LTC payment and a pro rata reduction applies to the cash value. Acceleration benefit options are typically 2 to 4 years (or range from 1% to 5% per year of the face amount or the annuity account value).

Some products extend the LTC coverage beyond the acceleration period after the policy value is completely depleted. This extended coverage is called **Extension of Benefits (EOB)**. EOB riders are funded by a separate premium as opposed to the policyholder's own account value. They can be one to two times the length of the acceleration benefit period. There are several variations to the EOB rider design. One design pays out EOB and AB at the same time (a coinsurance structure). A second design pays EOB after the AB is depleted (a tail design). A third design is named the pool design. Under a pool design, benefit payments are based on a maximum LTC pool amount defined at issue, which may be different from the life insurance benefit amount.

There are many similarities among LTC riders and stand-alone LTC policies in terms of benefit triggers, elimination periods, benefit periods, inflation benefits, claim payment structure, ancillary benefits, etc. The LTC riders usually offer somewhat more limited options. The LTC riders may, for example, only allow one elimination period option while the stand-alone LTC policies usually offer several options.

Chronic Illness riders under 101(g) are usually AB only. They are different from the 7702B LTC riders as most Chronic Illness riders have more restrictive requirements for qualifying for LTC benefits. Most Chronic Illness riders allow lump sum payment and require that the qualifying condition be "permanent". These riders are not subject to NAIC LTC model regulations.

2.9 Dental Coverage

While some carriers have offered individual dental policies, dental insurance is most typically a group coverage. There are two main reasons for this. The first is that dental coverage has higher frequencies of claim, and much lower cost per claim than medical coverages. This makes the insuring element (the sharing of infrequent, large costs by a pool) of this coverage less valuable. A second driver is the U.S. tax code, which creates a tax subsidy for such coverage when issued to an employer group. This subsidy doesn't exist for individual coverage.

On the other hand, the ACA has renewed interest in individual dental coverage by mandating it as an essential health benefit, at least for children.

Dental coverage is also highly susceptible to various forms of antiselection. This is only one of the unusual risks in individual dental coverage, which drive the design of the product. Each of these will now be discussed.

Dental benefits can be defined as either a scheduled amount per service (according to a specified schedule) or as a percentage of allowed charges. Often, potential services are categorized into four types of benefits. Type I is diagnostic and preventative, type II is basic services (including extractions, restorations, endodontics, periodontics, and anything not included in the other descriptions), type III is prosthetic coverage (including inlays and crowns), and type IV is orthodontia. Typical policies vary benefits by category, generally with the highest benefit for type I, and more limited benefits for types II, III, and IV.

Type IV benefits are more often absent than present in individual product plan designs, mostly due to concerns about antiselection and the somewhat voluntary nature of treatment. Costs for type IV benefits vary widely, depending on the nature of the covered population and the benefits.

One model of type I through III benefits showed roughly 30%, 40%, and 30% of covered expenses in each type, respectively – prior to member cost sharing. These do not, however, represent the proportion of final benefits, because of the relatively higher member cost sharing on type II and III services. After member cost sharing, the proportion of benefit costs to the insurer might be more like 40%, 45%, and 15% (excluding the portion of costs paid by the member).

MULTIPLE TREATMENT OPTIONS

Much more than in medical insurance, there are often multiple dental treatment options available for a given situation, sometimes including the alternative of waiting before beginning treatment. The existence of insurance coverage often has an impact on which treatment is chosen. The cost implication of these different options can be quite dramatic, and is a good example of an effect sometimes called "induced utilization," when additional utilization occurs simply because insurance is present.

This risk is typically controlled in one or both of two ways: (1) through benefit design, particularly by limiting benefits on the more costly alternative services, and (2) by requiring approval of the planned course of treatment by the insurer before treatment occurs, a process referred to as **preauthorization**.

ACCUMULATED UNTREATED CONDITIONS

Another characteristic of dental treatment that impacts the insurance risk is the ability of patients to postpone treatments, sometimes for long periods. This is particularly true when patients are aware that insurance coverage is imminent. After all, it would be human nature to ask one's dentist something like, "Can I postpone this crown for three months, since I'll have insurance coverage then?"

This issue could be addressed by trying to limit coverage of pre-existing conditions, but this is difficult to administer. Most often, individual policies will reduce initial benefits, and phase them in over a few years, to reduce the pre-issue incentive.

EXTERNAL ANTISELECTION

Most individuals have a pretty good self-perception of their own dental health, and often they are aware of specific needs for treatment. Because of this, individual dental coverage is very susceptible to antiselection by prospective insureds, who will self-select their coverage if it is worthwhile for them to do so. This requires aggressive management, aimed at limiting that potential. Even with careful management, this antiselection can increase overall claim costs for small employer groups by as much as 30% or more – individual policies would be expected to experience even greater selection effects. The available antiselection management tools have been described earlier.

PEDIATRIC DENTAL COVERAGE UNDER THE ACA

The ACA lists "pediatric services, including oral and vision care" as one of the essential health benefits required to be covered in all non-grandfathered small group and individual health plans starting in 2014. This created a significant challenge for many insurers who did not have experience administering dental coverage (or contracting with dental healthcare providers).

Regulators acknowledged this challenge in implementing regulations, and generally allow carriers to offer plans without dental coverage provided there is a standalone dental plan offered by another insurer that is also available to applicants. The rules differ slightly depending on whether the plans are offered on or off of the exchange. In many states standalone pediatric dental coverage was available in 2014.

Similar to the actuarial value rules described earlier, pediatric dental plans must meet certain benefit standards prescribed by regulation in order to be sold on the exchanges.

CHAPTER 3

POLICY FORMS

Individual health insurance coverage is provided through a contract between an insurer and the contract holder, who is usually (but not always) the primary insured. Its scope includes policies which might also cover the immediate family of the primary insured. The generic version of a policy is called a **policy form**, and is the template that is customized with individual information when each policy of that type is issued.

Group insurance was developed as a mechanism to insure groups of people simultaneously under a single contract. Many aspects otherwise found in the individual insurance process are simplified for groups, including underwriting. As long as there is a strong affinity between group members (such as all the employees of a common employer), there is less opportunity for antiselection by the individual insureds. Allowable groups are defined in each state's laws, and are composed of a number of potential types of groups, including employer/employee, associations, and others.

Individual coverage is sometimes provided through two vehicles[1] that are not individual policies: (1) a group trust policy (under which a group is formed by the insurer for purposes of providing insurance, and a trust is created to be the policyholder), and (2) an association group (where the insureds join an association that offers the insurance to its members). When there is a reference in this chapter (and elsewhere in the book) to a "policy" as the unit of individual medical insurance coverage, unless indicated otherwise, it is intended to include these other vehicles within that term. Technically, though, in these cases an individual (and his or her family, for a family policy) would enroll, typically showing evidence of insurability, as a "subscriber" to a master policy which may be a trust or association plan. In such case, the individual is provided a "certificate" indicating his or her insurance coverage, as a member covered un-

---
[1] Medicare Advantage plans provide another example of an alternative arrangement, since there the contract is between the federal government and the insurer.

der a master policy. Both these "certificates" and "policies" will be referred to as "policies."

Notwithstanding the foregoing, under the ACA and its implementing regulations,[2] federal law now generally treats major medical group trust or association group coverage sold to individuals as individual market coverage. This greatly increased the level of regulation of such arrangements.

Another foundational piece for this discussion is the question of which state has jurisdiction over a policy. The most commonly accepted answer is: the state where the policy is delivered or issued for delivery. (This is discussed further in the chapter on rate regulation.) Some states, however, have passed laws regulating all coverage of their residents, regardless of the state of delivery. Some policy forms (when allowed by the state of issue) now contain language that gives jurisdiction to where the policy form is "issued and renewed."

In the past, there were some states that accepted other states' definitions of what constituted a "group." (Other states did not.) Because of this, insurers could (and often did) issue a master group policy in a state, with the intent to populate that group with individuals who were identical to individual policyholders in most ways, including being individually solicited and underwritten. Thus, when issuing coverage to those individuals, they would issue a group certificate, which could be delivered to an individual in a different state (if allowed), but not be considered an individual contract delivered in that state. This allowed premium rate issues to be group rating decisions (which are much less regulated and less complex), and regulated by only the state of delivery of the master policy. When this mechanism first began being used, most states permitted it. Over time, though, most states prohibited it. With the implementation of the ACA, this practice is no longer allowed nationwide, as federal law now defines individual and group coverage.

---

[2] See 45 C.F.R. §150.103, definition of individual health insurance policy.

3.1 Development of a Policy Form

Development of an appropriate policy form is an important part of product development. Such a form must meet a number of important criteria.

First and foremost, the policy form must accurately describe the benefits and other policy terms which the insurer intends to offer. This is important for many reasons, but particularly because imprecise language will likely be interpreted against the insurer by regulators or courts. (These contracts are called **contracts of adhesion** by lawyers. These are contracts in which the insured is not able to help define the contract provisions, and therefore is in a "take it or leave it" situation with the insurer. Because of this, courts will interpret ambiguities in favor of the insured.)

Policy provisions are sometimes an important consideration in having a competitive product. This is particularly true in the disability income and long term care markets. Those things that the public finds most valuable are typically also the most costly, and a balance must be struck between attractive plan design and cost. For that reason, there is often an extensive internal product development process within an insurer.

At the same time, the policy form must comply with a wide array of laws and regulations that either require or prohibit a large number of provisions. In addition to these requirements, the wording of the policy form must generally also meet "readability" standards required by most state laws. This is described further later in this chapter.

Expertise Needed

Drafting of a policy form requires an interplay of many different insurance professionals. The policy design has implications for virtually all functional areas in the company.

The typical champions of a new policy design come from the company's marketing area. They are most aware of the market forces impacting the policy. It is useful to gather as much objective information as possible about competitors and their products in this process, to replace the natural tendency to rely on anecdotal impressions.

Certainly the sales force needs to have input as well, since they will be asked to sell the resulting policy. Realistic sales goals must also be incorporated into any financial projections for the product.

The actuarial area will be needed to price the product, as well as to predict how the financial results of the product will play out over time. Care must be taken to evaluate financial implications in a statutory, a GAAP, and a tax sense. Often the product development process is an iterative one, requiring ongoing modifications to actuarial pricing models. For example, "What would happen if we changed the deductible to $X, but added an emergency room copay?"

The underwriting area will want to identify any antiselective opportunities in the product design that might occur at time of issue, and make sure they are manageable. In a DI product, a new definition of "own occupation" or "income level" might require extensive evaluation of the applicant's financial history or employment duties.

The claim administration area will typically have a significant role in the product design. The role is usually one of making sure that this wonderful new benefit design that is being imagined can actually be administered for a reasonable amount of expense and in the way it was intended. Seemingly innocuous changes to a drug benefit, for example, usually administered through a **pharmacy benefits manager** (**PBM**), may not be doable within the PBM's system.

Compliance people (responsible for dealing with state Insurance Departments and, increasingly, federal regulators) are obviously critical to the process. It does no good to build a new product based on a design that turns out to be illegal or out of regulatory compliance, especially after all the effort and expense undertaken to bring the product to a state for approval. It is far better to know the lay of the land in advance of the process.

FEEDBACK LOOP

Quality improvement programs all have one important aspect in common: they have feedback loops. There is a mechanism built into the process, whereby a metric is applied to answer the question, "How did our product (or service) perform?"

Recent discussions in the actuarial community have brought the same concept to actuaries, in a framework called **The Actuarial Control Cycle**. This framework is based on a similar concept to a feedback loop, which is described in other contexts as a necessary ingredient for a quality process. Such contexts include CQI (continuous quality improvement), TQM (total quality management) and Six Sigma. The most critical element of each of these is the concept of product development as a feedback loop, depending on measurement and evaluation of the cycle as a way to improve it, rather than product development (or any other process, for that matter) being performed in one-time isolation.

This feedback loop, when applied to an ongoing line of business, can be considered a market research function with respect to external input, and a parallel function internally. It is important to build this feedback loop into the product development/management process itself, so that seeking and providing input becomes an expectation of everyone involved.

ELEMENTS OF PRODUCT DESIGN

Most products start with a *product concept* – something which distinguishes the new product from those already being offered by this insurer and competitors. It is important that the new concept be consistent with the company's strategic plan, as well as its chosen tactics to achieve that plan. A company that treats LTC coverage as an accommodation product, for example, keeping it on its shelf for an occasional sale, will treat the product development process very differently than a company that specializes in LTC.

It is a common error to assume that benefit definition is the major (or only) element of product design, but this is far from true. There are many elements to product design, including:
- A marketing plan, including peripheral (sales) material,
- A sales and commission plan,
- Special underwriting rules (if needed),
- Rate structure, relativities (by rating characteristic), level, and rate increase philosophy,
- Reserve bases,
- Special policyholder services which might be needed,
- Modifications to claim systems needed to administer the new plan,
- Policy provisions themselves,
- Related policy forms (applications, disclosure statements, riders, etc.), and
- Identification of states in which the policy will be sold, and their corresponding rules and regulations limiting product design and/or requiring special compliance practices (such as monitoring of loss ratios).

A new product's financial forecast is, of course, an important element of the decision making process. A balance must usually be found between the desired financial objectives (usually a profit target) and the desire for a competitive product design. Interestingly, some market segments (such as non-can DI) seem highly driven by product features and less by premium level, while others (such as major medical) seem very highly premium driven.

3.2 ELEMENTS OF A POLICY FORM

Readability laws, which were introduced in the 1970s, generally require that a policy form meet a minimum score of 40-50 on the Flesch readability test.[3] That test looks at the number of syllables per word and the number of words per sentence in the document. (Typically, insurance laws exempt certain words or phrases from the requirement, such as medical terminology.) A formula is applied to these two measures. In Flesch's own words: "Multiply the average sentence length by 1.015. Multiply the average word length by 84.6. Add the two numbers. Subtract this sum from 206.835. The balance is your readability score."

There are some common practices that have developed in writing policy forms which help forms meet readability tests. For example, most policies today define the insurer as "we" and the insured as "you." It is, of course, important to clearly define these terms in the contract. Otherwise there is a legal risk that the form will be interpreted differently than intended. It is helpful to read existing policy forms as a way to find useful and common practices.

Another common practice is to use capitalized words in the contract for terms that are defined in the contract. Examples of such words are described later in this section.

There are a number of major, standard elements in a policy form. We will discuss each, as well as the detailed elements contained in them. There are italicized examples provided for many of them.

---

[3] Flesch, Rudolph, (1948); "A New Readability Yardstick," *Journal of Applied Psychology*, Vol. 32, pp. 221-233

Each type of coverage requires certain provisions to be included in the policy form and has no need for others. In addition, policy forms for similar coverage issued by different companies may contain different provisions as well. Sometimes two companies will address a particular facet of the contract in two entirely different ways, with the intent of reaching the same effect.

For all these reasons, this chapter's list of provisions and policy form elements should be taken as suggestive and illustrative, but not as definitive. In drafting a policy form, it is important to have advice from professionals in all affected company areas, including sales and marketing, underwriting, actuarial, claims, administration, compliance, and legal.

FACE PAGE

This is the "front cover" of a form, which is the first thing a policyholder sees when picking up the form. The front side of the cover typically includes the following elements. Sample language is provided for many of the items.

- *Title*: There is typically a title provided at the top of the page, such as "Major Medical Policy," and possibly a very brief description of the policy.
- *Insuring Clause*: This is the provision under which the insurer promises to pay certain benefits when specified contingencies occur. This provision includes (by reference) all the other provisions and terms in the policy.
- *Consideration Clause*: This clause indicates what "consideration" (a legal term of art) the insured is giving to the insurer in return for the insurance coverage. This is virtually always the premiums payable, and might also include the insured's statements and representations in the application. This is an example of what such a clause might look like.

> *This policy is issued based on the statements and agreements in the enrollment form, the exam (if required), and any other amendment or supplements, and the payment of the required premium. Each renewal premium is payable on the due date subject to the grace period. Your rates will not change during the first 12 months this policy is in force, unless you change benefits, add or delete covered dependents, or move to another zip code.*

The consideration clause sometimes appears later in the contract.

- *Renewal Provision*: This provision indicates whether the policy is renewable, and if so, under what conditions. The NAIC has historically defined these provisions in the following way:

    o *Noncancelable* (equivalent to *Noncancelable and Guaranteed Renewable*). This is the strongest form of renewal and rate guarantee, where the insurer may not cancel the policy, nor may it change the applicable premium rate schedule at any time during the life of the policy.

    > *Noncancelable and Guaranteed Renewable to Age 65:* This policy is guaranteed renewable upon timely payment of premiums to the first policy anniversary after the insured's 65th birthday and, during that period, can neither be cancelled nor have its terms or premiums changed by the Company.

    This premium guarantee is essentially nonexistent in policies subject to (unscheduled) inflationary pressure, such as major medical policies. If there were a medical policy with this renewability provision, the comments regarding HIPAA which follow would apply to it as well.

    o *Guaranteed Renewable (GR)*. This provision guarantees the insured's right of renewal, by paying the applicable premium. The insurer has the right, however, to change premium rates, subject to any regulatory oversight. This right to change rates is generally interpreted (either explicitly or implicitly) to be limited in that rates will change only on a rating class basis, without consideration of the experience or health status of the individual. (This principle has been tested from time to time by some major medical carriers who have applied some limited rate adjustments to individuals based on their experience.)

    The validity of new state laws requiring changes to the provisions of in force guaranteed renewable policies was tested in the 1970s in New York. It was ultimately found that once the policy is in effect, subsequent state laws cannot be used to force changes in GR policy provisions.[4]

---

[4] New York Court of Appeals, May 1978, citation 376 N.E.2d 1280

When HIPAA arrived in 1996, it brought with it a new meaning to the term "guaranteed renewable" for major medical type policies, making it a bit less stringent than the NAIC's and the industry's previous use of the term. Under HIPAA, individual major medical type policies must be renewable at the option of the insured, unless the insurer, under conditions specified in the law, either (1) offers conversion to any other individual policy it offers, or (2) cancels all such policies in the state. There are also conditions under which policies can be modified under HIPAA. Practitioners often refer to this type of renewability provision as "HIPAA guaranteed renewable." (As an interesting note, this is one of those instances where the federal government, when beginning to regulate in a new area, takes existing jargon and changes its use, leading to some confusion. By force of law, this generally forces the industry to adopt the new meaning. In this case, however, the jargon came from existing state insurance law, so there are now two meanings to the term in each state.)

The ACA also requires guaranteed renewability of coverage in the individual and group markets. Subsequent regulations have largely followed existing HIPAA requirements, although there are some new rules too (for example, the government has defined in much more detail exactly how much a plan may be "uniformly modified" before it is no longer the same plan).

o *Conditionally Renewable.* Under this type of renewal provision, the company agrees that it will not cancel an individual's coverage because of his or her health, but reserves the right to refuse to renew all insureds of the same class. (In this context, a "class" is typically defined as all insureds with the same policy form issued in the same state. This may not be well defined, however.) This type of renewability (and the two that follow) have largely been eliminated from major medical policies due to HIPAA's requirements.

o *Nonrenewable for Stated Reasons Only.* In this renewability provision, the company lists the possible reasons for which it reserves the right to cancel the policy. In most uses, this is almost identical to conditional renewability.

o *Optionally Renewable.* This provision, hardly ever used any more, allows the company to selectively non-renew individual policyholders.

- *Notice of 10 Day Right to Examine Policy*: This is sometimes called the "10 day free look" provision. A longer period (up to 30 days) is sometimes required by law or regulation. This allows the purchaser the right, until the limit has expired, to negate the contract from the beginning, voiding all premium and claim payments.
- *Execution Provision*: This is the part of the contract that actually says that the company agrees to the contract. Reproduced signatures of two high level officers (such as the company president and secretary) are generally included, attesting to the company's agreement to the contract.
- *Form Number*: Each policy form, as well as any portion of the policy form that can appear separately or is optional, is provided a policy form number by the insurer, and is printed in the lower left-hand corner of the first page (and often every page) of the policy. The policy form identifies the version of the contract used. This is separate from the *policy number*, which is assigned by the insurer to identify the specific policy issued to an individual.
- *Reliance Statement*: This is typically a paragraph in which the insurer states that, in issuing the policy, it has relied on the information provided by the applicant, such as:

  > *This policy was issued based on the information you gave us on your application. Omissions or misstatements in the enrollment form can cause claims to be denied or coverage to be rescinded. Please read the enclosed copy of your application. If any information shown is incorrect, incomplete, or if anything is missing, write to us within 10 days.*

  The ability to rescind or reform a contract was historically a very important aspect of individual health insurance. Companies relied on these actions to protect themselves against incorrect information on the applications, and typically had rigorous policies and procedures in place to pursue it. The ACA, however, specifically prohibited rescission of individual major medical health insurance policies except in cases of fraud or intentional misrepresentation of a material fact – in the months leading up to passage of the law, rescission became a lightning rod for critics of the industry. Rescission is discussed further in Chapter 4, "Managing Antiselection."

  If it could be shown that the bad information was provided with the intention to mislead the company, this could be pursued as fraud. Intent to defraud is difficult to prove. Before the ACA, the reliance statement provision often would not require intent, only the fact that the information was false.

If the insurer did not rely on health disclosures in the application (such as for a short term medical contract, or an accident only policy), this provision, of course, would not apply.

If the insurer is using a master group trust to provide benefits, rather than individual contracts, then the language in the document provided to individuals will be modified to refer to the master group policy, and what we here call the policy will then be called a certificate.

TABLE OF CONTENTS

Most policies have a table of contents on the second page (the back side of the face page, typically), which directs the reader to the major sections of the policy.

SCHEDULE PAGE

This section contains all the information that might be unique about this particular policy. It is sometimes called the "specifications page" or "data page." This includes:

- *Information about the owner of the policy and the insured persons:* This would include the name, address, and demographic information of the primary insured or policy owner, the name and demographic information of any other insureds that might be covered under the policy, and the name of the beneficiary (if any) under the policy.

- *Identifying information about the policy:* This includes the *policy number* (the unique identifier for this particular contract with this policyholder – not the *policy form number* which applies to every policy with the same basic contract), the date of issue, the term of initial coverage, the date of first premium renewal, sometimes the state of issue, and (if applicable) the expiration date of the contract.

- *Benefit and Premium information:* Premium information includes a statement of the initial premium due under the policy, information about its periodicity, and sometimes some information about what portion of the premium applies to the base policy or benefits vs. additional benefits or riders. In addition, if there is an increasing premium schedule (typically attained age based), and the coverage is not inflation-driven (such as disability income), the initial premium schedule will be included.

Any attached riders or endorsements will be listed here as well.

Benefit information typically includes information that specifies how certain elements of coverage which are otherwise variable (such as a chosen deductible level, for medical expense coverage) will be determined.

For medical expense coverage, the benefit information might specify deductible levels; maximum coverage limits; co-pay levels for physician visits, ancillary charges, prescription drugs, hospital days, or others; surgical schedule maximums, or other variables. The policyholder often chooses a "plan" from a limited number of plans, which represents a specific combination of these otherwise staggering number of benefit combinations. As described in Chapter 2, the ACA imposes new constraints that will limit the allowable plan designs significantly going forward.

Disability income coverages also have a large number of variables which can define the coverage: the weekly or monthly benefit amount for basic disability coverage, elimination period, benefit period, cost of living increase percentages, partial and/or residual benefits chosen, and any ancillary benefits (typically provided by rider.)

Long term care coverage typically has variables related to the benefit amount, the elimination period, whether there is home health or adult day care coverage (and if so, what benefit), whether there is assisted living coverage (and if so, what benefit), and the maximum benefit payable (or maximum period of payment). Benefits in LTC policies are still evolving, but some of the optional benefits available today include inflation-indexed benefits and nonforfeiture benefits.

For limited benefit plans (such as hospital indemnity, accidental death and dismemberment, specified illness), benefit structures are typically much simpler, and often can be fully described with one or two variables, such as "$$X$ for Y days."

DEFINITIONS

The next section of the typical policy contains definitions for use in the policy. Each type of coverage will feature different defined terms, although some terms (such as "You") tend to be used throughout. Table 3.1 does not distinguish between these, but is meant only to be a sampling across all types of coverages.

Table 3.1

Sample, Partial List of Policy Defined Terms		
Medical Coverages	**Disability Coverages**	**Long Term Care Coverage**
Accidental Death	Beginning Date (of disablement)	Activities of Daily Living (ADL):
Copayment	Consumer Price Index	Dressing
Covered Charges	Full Benefit	Eating
Covered Dependent	Elimination Period	Transferring
Deductible	Insured	Toileting
Emergency Treatment	Licensed Physician	Bathing
Hospital	Maximum Benefit Period	Continence
Illness	Owner	Assisted Care Living Facility
Injury	Partial Disability	Care Coordinator
Insured	Residual Disability	Nursing Care
Inpatient	Regular (Own) Occupation	Nursing Care Facility
Medical Necessity	Social Insurance Supplement	Personal Care Services
Mental Illness	Total Disability	Plan of Care
Outpatient		Severe Cognitive Impairment
Prescription Drug		
We, Us, Our		
You, Your		

PREMIUMS AND REINSTATEMENT

There is typically a section of the policy that describes the terms and conditions under which coverage starts and ends. This includes defining the effective date.

For medical coverages, the terms under which newly covered dependents can be added is described. Newborns or newly adopted children are typically covered for up to 60 days initially, since many states have adopted this requirement. Most companies require notification of the newly covered person within a certain period such as 60 days, in order for the person to be covered. Other dependents will typically be medically underwritten before being added to the policy (although this is not allowed for major medical starting in 2014).

The conditions under which the policy terminates are included in this section. These include non-payment of premium, or notice of termination by the insured. This is where the conditions would be listed if the policy were conditionally renewable, such as the insured no longer being in the sponsoring association. This is also where the HIPAA guaranteed renewable condition would be listed, and how termination would occur if all policies are non-renewed that were issued in that state.

If there are conversion privileges, where a covered dependent might have the right to obtain his own policy when he or she is no longer eligible under family coverage, this is where the terms of those privileges are specified. This provision generally allows for the portability of coverage for individuals. If, for example, a couple becomes divorced, a company will generally issue a second policy to cover the spouse that is no longer covered under the original policy.

In addition, the **reinstatement clause** is an important part of this section. Under the NAIC's restatement of the **Uniform Individual Accident and Sickness Policy Provision Law (UPPL)**, there are two required provisions that read:

> **Grace Period**: *This policy has a 31 day grace period. This means that if a renewal premium is not paid on or before the date it is due, it may be paid during the following 31 days. During the grace period the policy will stay in force.*
>
> **Reinstatement**: *If the renewal premium is not paid before the grace period ends, the policy will lapse. Later acceptance of the premium by the Company (or by an agent authorized to accept payment) without requiring an application for reinstatement will reinstate this policy.*
>
> *If the Company or its agent requires an application, the Insured will be given a conditional receipt for the premium. If the application is approved, the policy will be reinstated as of the approval date. Lacking such approval, the policy will be reinstated on the 45th day after the date of the conditional receipt unless the Company has previously written the Insured of its disapproval.*

> *The reinstated policy will cover only loss that results from an injury sustained after the date of reinstatement or sickness that starts more than 10 days after such date. In all other respects the rights of the Insured and the Company will remain the same, subject to any provisions noted on or attached to the reinstated policy.*

The grace period varies (7, 10, and 31 days), depending on premium mode (weekly, monthly, and other premium modes, respectively). These are periods during which a late premium will be accepted by the insurer, and the contract renewed. The ACA establishes new requirements regarding grace periods for medical policies sold on and off exchanges, including a three month grace period for lower income individuals and families who are receiving federal premium subsidies.

This section is also where mention can be made of any extension of benefits during total disability. Alternatively, and more typically, such a benefit is called a *waiver of premium* benefit, and is listed in the benefit section of the policy.

BENEFIT PROVISIONS

There are one or more sections of the policy devoted to defining the benefits. The benefits provided under various policies are described in Chapter 2, "The Products."

EXCLUSIONS AND LIMITATIONS

This section of the policy form lists the exclusions and limitations to coverage. Allowable exclusions vary by coverage, and are specified by state law. (Early law and regulation focused on this subject, to address the public perception of such exclusions being the "fine print" by which insurers sometimes were perceived to avoid paying claims.)

Some of the most common exclusions in medical insurance policies have historically been:

- Illness or injury covered under Worker's Compensation laws. Worker's Compensation laws are state laws covering medical expenses resulting from occupational causes. This exclusion is sometimes waived for an additional premium, for situations in which the insured might own his own business and need that coverage;

- Care or treatment covered by government plans, including Medicare;
- Care or treatment covered by automobile or liability insurance;
- Routine hearing, vision, and foot care;
- Cosmetic services, including those designed to relieve or prevent emotional distress;
- Non-covered services and their complications;
- Custodial care;
- Dental care unrelated to injury;
- Care caused or contributed to by war or act of war; active duty in the armed forces; commission of a felony, crime, or illegal act; participation in a riot; an adult under the influence of illegal drugs; attempted suicide or self-inflicted injury;
- Maternity coverage, unless there is a maternity benefit purchased;
- Infertility;
- Educational or vocational testing or training;
- Genetic testing and other services;
- Sex change treatments;
- "Lifestyle" treatments (including Viagra);
- Mental illness or substance abuse (except where mandated, as it is in a number of states).

The ACA classifies several of these services (including maternity, pediatric dental and vision, mental illness, and substance abuse) as essential health benefits for major medical plans. Those services can no longer be excluded for non-grandfathered, non-transitional plans (see Chapter 4 for definitions of these). The exact list of benefits that must be covered varies from state to state based on a benchmark plan.

Some of the most common disability income exclusions are:

- Pre-existing conditions. In this case, the period measuring such conditions is typically much longer (five years) than that allowed for medical coverage;
- War or act of war;
- Conditions explicitly excluded from coverage through modification of the policy.

The final bullet of the prior list is a bit different than other exclusions, and should be noted. This provision allows insurers to use an underwriting action sometimes called issuing a "waiver" or "exclusion rider." Such riders are typically offered where an applicant has a (typically) uninsurable condition, but is looking for coverage despite this. The insurer may make an offer to the applicant which excludes coverage due to the condition or bodily system involved in the pre-existing condition. This allows for coverage to be issued (for all but the existing conditions) where the insurer might otherwise have to decline coverage.

For long term care policies, the most common exclusions are:

- Services provided by a member of the insured's immediate family, with exceptions, and unless noted as a benefit in the policy (which sometimes happens in LTC contracts);
- Care and treatment provided outside the U.S.;
- Expenses caused by attempted suicide within the first two years of the policy;
- Expenses caused by war;
- Expenses payable by a governmental plan;
- Care or treatment resulting from alcoholism or drug addiction; and
- Mental and nervous conditions, other than those as a result of organic disease (such as Alzheimer's).

OTHER PROVISIONS

There are other provisions that must find a home in the policy, and this is a common place for them to reside. Most of them have minimum wording specified by applicable laws. They include:

- *Conformity with State Statutes*: This standard provision says that, in the event the policy form is not found to be in compliance with state law, it is to be considered automatically amended to be in compliance.
- *Entire Contract; Changes*: This provision is a statement that the policy constitutes the entire contract between the insured and the company, and that no one other than a company officer can modify the contract, and then only in writing by amending the policy.
- *Enforcement of Plan Provisions*: This is a provision used to assert that failure by the insurer to enforce any part of the contract does not waive

their right to enforce it in the future. (The courts can, of course, sometimes have different interpretations than that desired by the insurer, particularly in this area of waiver and estoppel).

- *Notice of Claim*: This provision requires the insured to submit claims within 60 or 90 days of the start of the loss, for the claim to be valid. This provision typically describes the required process for submitting claims, and the promises made by the insurer, such as to provide claim forms in a timely way.
- *Time of Payment of Claims*: For policies paying benefits periodically, such as DI and LTC benefits, this provision states how often payments will be made.
- *Medical or Physical Examinations*: This provision says that the insurer has the right to require a medical examination of the insured in order for benefits to be paid.
- *Recovery; Subrogation and Right of Reimbursement*: For benefits that reimburse due to specific expenses (like medical expense policies), this provision allows the insurer an opportunity to recover money which becomes payable due to other liability, such as for a judgment in an automobile liability suit.
- *Change of Plan*: This provision states the circumstances under which the policy provisions may be changed. Typically, guaranteed renewable and Non-can policies cannot be changed without mutual agreement by the insured and the company. Less strong renewal guarantees provide greater power by the insurer in changing policy provisions, including benefits.
- *Proof of Loss*: For DI and LTC coverages, the policies may require ongoing proof of a continuing loss. This provision spells out the requirements.
- *Misstatements on the Application*: This provision says that, in the event of a misstatement of facts on the application which impact the premium rate (typically age, plus possibly others), the benefits payable are those that would have been purchased with the premium actually paid, and with the corrected premium rate. This provision works better when the premium is stated in terms of units of coverage, rather than indemnity policies such as major medical.
- *Dividends*: In the case that a policy is participating, there will be a provision stating how any dividends will be paid or credited. When this does happen, it is typically in DI or LTC coverage, not medical

coverage. And when it happens, there may be a provision stating that dividends are not anticipated to be paid.

- *Legal Actions*: This provision limits the period in which legal action can be taken by the insured to recover under the policy. The NAIC model limits this period to between 60 days and three years.
- *Time Limit on Certain Defenses*: After three years from issue, the policy cannot be rescinded for misstatements by the insured, unless the misstatements were fraudulent. (For major medical insurance, rescisions are now only allowed in cases of fraud.)
- *Payment of Claims*: This provision specifies that payments made for loss of life (such as supplemental life coverage, or accidental death coverage) will be made to the designated beneficiary (according to other policy provisions), or to the estate of the insured. All other payments are made to the insured, unless payments are assigned by the insured to health care providers.
- *Change of Beneficiary*: The insured can change beneficiaries unless he or she has made an irrevocable designation of beneficiary.

3.3 NAIC POLICY FORM MODELS[5]

In the U.S., the content of individual health contracts is typically governed by the laws of the state where the contract is "delivered or issued for delivery". Most states have policy provisions which were originally (and typically still are) based on model laws developed by the National Association of Insurance Commissioners (NAIC). The model laws applicable to policy forms for this type of insurance include:

- *Uniform Individual Accident and Sickness Policy Provision Law (UPPL)*. This is the original model law, adopted in most states, which has governed policy forms for many years. When readability of policy forms became required in most states, the UPPL was redrafted to be in simplified language, and called "Restatement of UPPL in Simplified Language."

---

[5] For the complete text, see *Model Laws, Regulations, and Guidelines*, published by the National Association of Insurance Commissioners, www.naic.org

- *Model Regulation to Implement Rules Regarding Contracts and Services of Health Maintenance Organizations.*
- *Long-Term Care Insurance Model Act and Model Regulation.*
- *Medicare Supplement Insurance Minimum Standards Model Act, and the related Model Regulation to Implement the NAIC Medicare Supplement Insurance Minimum Standards Model Act.*
- *Noncancelable and Guaranteed Renewable Terminology Defined.*

Most or all state insurance departments have policy form examiners who approve specific policy forms in their jurisdiction. Although a state may have originally adopted an NAIC Model Law with standard policy provisions, decades of legislative activity (and insurance department interpretation) have typically resulted in a collection of state-specific provisions and modifications. It is common, therefore, for a national filing in the U.S. to require substantial modifications by state, as well as numerous rounds of correspondence.

Detailed discussion of the model acts is beyond the scope of this text. For pedagogical purposes, however, it is worthwhile to discuss the major elements of the most important of these, the UPPL. At the time of this writing, the NAIC is discussing significant changes that may be needed to the UPPL – and other model laws – in light of the changes made under the ACA.

THE UNIFORM INDIVIDUAL ACCIDENT AND SICKNESS POLICY PROVISION LAW (UPPL)

The UPPL was originally adopted by the NAIC in 1950, and has been subsequently amended, most recently in 2001, when a change to language that had prohibited coverage of injuries sustained while an insured was intoxicated was adopted.[6] The UPPL is available from the NAIC.

The UPPL defines minimum standards for carriers' policies. When the UPPL is adopted by a state, it is intended that carriers are free to adopt provisions that are more favorable to the policyholder.

---

[6] The new language requires "medical expense" policies to cover these injuries. Over time, it became clear that the original model law language was having unintended consequences (for example, healthcare providers were reluctant to test trauma patients for intoxicants in fear of jeopardizing their insurance coverage).

The most notable provisions of the UPPL model law include the following (the numbers correspond to the section numbers in the model law):

(1) **Definition of Accident and Sickness Insurance Policy**
In defining the applicability of the law, reference is made to the state's statutory coverage definitions.

(2) **Form of Policy**
Various constraints are made on the policy form, including whom it may insure, printing styles, and a requirement that all exceptions or reductions to coverage must be explicit and placed appropriately in the policy form. Each policy form is required to have a unique identifier (called the "policy form number"), in the lower left-hand corner.

(3) **Accident and Sickness Policy Provisions**
This section has two subsections. The first lists the provisions required in all contracts. The second is a list of provisions that are intended to serve as minimum standards regarding the matters they each address. Many of these were described earlier. In NAIC parlance, "Accident and Sickness" insurance references DI coverage and not others. Some state laws use the term to apply to other coverages as well. Those provisions not already described previously are:

(a) *Change of Occupation.* If an insured changes occupation to one which is more hazardous than the original classification, any benefits ("indemnities") payable are reduced to be those which the paid premium would have purchased under the more hazardous occupation. On the other hand, if notice is received of a change in occupation to one less hazardous, any excess premiums beyond those required for the given benefit amounts are to be refunded.

(b) *Overinsurance.* There are different ways of handling overinsurance, depending on the type of coverage involved and the renewal guarantee.

(c) *Unpaid Premium:* The insurer is permitted to deduct unpaid premium from claim payments.

(d) *Illegal Occupation:* If a contributing cause to the loss was an attempt or commission of a felony, or as a result of an illegal occupation, the insurer is not liable for the loss.

(e) *Intoxicants and Narcotics:* The insurer is not liable for losses in consequence of the insured being intoxicated or under the influence of a non-prescribed narcotic. (This provision is not allowed in medical expense policies.)

(4) Conforming to Statute
If a policy is delivered or issued for delivery in the state, but is in violation of this law, the policy will be construed according to this law. (This was mentioned previously, as a common provision in individual contracts.)

(5) Application
An insured is not bound by statements in the application unless a copy is attached to the policy. Other rules about the application are listed.

(6) Age Limit
If an insurer accepts premium beyond a limiting age (such as accepting an annual premium from someone who turns 65 during the year), insurance will continue for the period paid for by the premium.

There are also some provisions in the model law relating to how the provisions are implemented. In drafting policy forms, care must be taken to address all parts of the applicable state law. For our purpose, though, the two major remaining elements in the model law related to policy provisions are:

(f) *Inapplicable or Inconsistent Provisions:* This allows the Commissioner to modify the requirements of this law to the extent they are inconsistent with or inapplicable to the coverage provided.

(g) *Requirements of other Jurisdictions:* This provision allows for provisions that are "not less favorable" than those described in the model law, when issued by foreign or alien insurers. When issued by domestic[7] insurers for delivery outside the state, the insurer is allowed to use policy provisions that comply with the other state's laws, instead of the ones in their state.

---

[7] A *domestic* insurer is one that is formed under the laws of the state, while a *foreign* insurer is one formed under the laws of a different U.S. state. An *alien* insurer is one formed under the laws of any location other than a U.S. state.

3.4 HIPAA'S CONTINUATION REQUIREMENTS

States were incented by HIPAA to comply (through a threat of taking over jurisdiction) with standards designed to make coverage portable from the group market to the individual market. One way HIPAA's requirements could be met was by requiring insurers to offer policies to eligible individuals. The offerings were up to the insurer, and an insurer would have three choices of what to offer: (a) all of its individual market plans, (b) only its two most popular plans, or (c) two representative plans (with a mechanism for subsidy). This is called the "federal fallback" method of complying with HIPAA. About ten states have adopted this method.

The other method allowed by HIPAA is to have an "alternative mechanism." The most popular of these is to have a state high risk pool to provide coverage to eligible individuals. Roughly 30 states have chosen this route. The remaining states have adopted other solutions, typically because they had other existing state laws in effect to achieve similar purposes. Those solutions often feature a requirement of guaranteed issue of individual coverage to HIPAA eligible insureds, either by all individual insurers in the state or by some major carrier(s) like Blue Cross/Blue Shield.

Under HIPAA, different states chose different ways to have their insurance markets provide guaranteed continuation of group coverage into the individual market. According to CMS's website,[8] the HIPAA guarantee to eligible people can be described as:

If you are a HIPAA eligible individual, and you apply for individual health coverage within 63 days after losing group health plan coverage, HIPAA:

- Guarantees that you will have a choice of at least two coverage options;
- Guarantees that you will be eligible, regardless of any medical conditions you may have, to purchase some type of individual coverage, whether from a health insurance issuer, high-risk pool, or other source designated by your State; and
- Guarantees that you will not be subject to any pre-existing condition exclusions.

---

[8] www.cms.hhs.gov

A "HIPAA eligible individual" is one who meets all the following criteria:

- The individual has at least 18 months of creditable coverage without a significant break in coverage, defined as a period of 63 or more days during all of which there was no coverage. If the individual applies for coverage by midnight of the 63rd day, there was not a "significant break";
- The most recent coverage must have been through a group health plan (through an employer or union, either as primary insured or as dependent);
- The individual is not eligible for coverage under any other group health plan;
- The individual is not eligible for Medicare or Medicaid;
- The individual does not have other health insurance;
- The individual did not lose the insurance for not paying the premiums or for committing fraud; and
- The individual accepted and used up any COBRA continuation coverage or similar State coverage if it was offered.

It is notable that HIPAA precludes a policy from terminating due to the insured reaching a specified age (such as 65).

Starting in 2014, all individual medical insurance plans must be offered on a guaranteed issue basis, which essentially means all states can comply with HIPAA by using the federal fallback method. Accordingly, state high risk pools (and other alternative mechanisms) have either terminated or begun winding down starting in 2014. In some cases, modifications to state law were required to accomplish this.

CHAPTER 4

MANAGING ANTISELECTION

The secret to managing antiselection lies, in these authors' judgment, in having an antiselection model that is at least moderately accurate at predicting the impact of antiselection on blocks of policies.

A good model produces forecasts which can be used by management to successfully scenario test (do "what if's"), and thereby choose an optimal management strategy. Often that strategy comes down to implementing rate increases to minimize losses (or, sometimes, generate profits).

This chapter provides a basis for understanding and modeling antiselection, and thus managing it. Sections 4.1 through 4.4 provide a basic understanding. Section 4.5 describes some theoretical considerations that need to be addressed in order to build an effective antiselection model.

Section 4.6 reviews the mechanisms introduced under the ACA to attempt to control antiselection in and out of the public health insurance exchanges. As we will see, the ACA makes sweeping changes that prohibit many of the traditional tools health insurers have used to manage antiselection. It remains to be seen whether the new mechanisms it introduces in their stead will be sufficient to replace them.

4.1 THE THREE FACES OF ANTISELECTION

An elder actuary once offered something like the following about the nature of antiselection:

Antiselection is that annoying tendency people have of doing what's best for themselves.

When people (insureds) do what is best for themselves, at least in this context, they make choices to maximize the value they receive in return for what they pay. When looked at this way, antiselection seems to reflect human nature. It is annoying to those who work in this industry, however, because it keeps sneaking up to bite us in the nose when we least expect it.

Antiselection can occur in a very specific context, such as the antiselection you would expect when providing an optional rider to cover maternity benefits (only the pregnant need apply). It can also be very general, such as that which occurs because someone perceives himself as unhealthy, and is being provided an opportunity for rich coverage. The specific type of antiselection is relatively easy to manage, and typically fairly obvious (if you provide service A, people who need service A will tend to buy it), so will not be dealt with in detail in this chapter. It is the less specific type that will draw our attention.

In general, we can think of antiselection as happening at one of three times in the course of a policy's life: (1) as the person is first becoming insured, (2) while they are insured, and (3) as they make decisions about whether to end the contract. These three situations can be defined as, respectively, *external* antiselection, *internal* antiselection, and *durational (*including *cumulative*) antiselection.

Imagine yourself to be uninsured. Imagine then that you suddenly develop a health condition which makes it very likely that you will become disabled (or have large medical expenses, or need long term care.) It is human nature for you to seek insurance coverage, hoping that someone else (the insurance company) will pay that (perhaps rather scary) claim, in return for a much smaller and more predictable premium payment. This is, however, also contrary to the basic principles of what makes insurance work – that insured events are relatively random, and outside the control of the insured. This situation is an example of **external antiselection** – antiselection which happens as an impaired risk initially seeks coverage.

Imagine now that there are two insureds with major medical coverage have the same deductible – $250. Insured A has developed a severe recurring illness with high medical costs. Insured B perceives himself as healthy, and has no impending claims. The insurer now notifies both insureds of a 25% rate increase, and reminds them that they can offset a good portion of that increase (say $400 a year) by switching plans to a higher deductible ($1,000.) Both insureds are likely to do the arithmetic, comparing a $750 increase in deductible against a $400 savings in premium. Insured A is more likely to say no to the offer of a higher deductible, because the likelihood of having a claim is near 100%. A's additional self-insured cost of $750 will not be worth the $400 savings. Insured B is more likely to think the exchange is worth it, since the likelihood of having to pay that higher deductible is small. This combination of tendencies (A's and B's) causes lower-cost risks to gravitate to leaner plans, while higher-cost risks will tend to take the richest plan possible. This combination results in higher cost to the insurance company. For purposes of this text, this effect will be termed **internal antiselection**, since it occurs while the insureds are internal to the insurance plan.

Finally, imagine now that there is a block of insureds who have all had their coverage for awhile, who are faced with that same 25% (or higher) increase. Higher cost insureds (like Insured A from the previous example) will tend to keep their coverage in force more often than lower cost insureds, implying they find it of greater value compared to the cost. This form of antiselection is called **cumulative antiselection**. The extent to which this is an emotion-based tendency (fear of losing coverage), or a practical consideration (finding it more difficult to obtain other coverage), isn't clear. What is clear, however, is that this tendency seems to happen more when: (1) there are larger rate increases, and (2) lapse rates are relatively high (major medical, for example, with annual lapse rates typically in the 15-40% range, unlike non-can disability income coverage with ultimate lapse rates in the 5% range.)

4.2 UNDERWRITING THE INDIVIDUAL RISK (EXTERNAL ANTISELECTION)

Potential insureds who know they are likely to have a claim are more likely to seek coverage than potential insureds who do not think they will have a claim. This external antiselection is controlled by insurers through a variety of mechanisms, including:

- Individual (medical) underwriting before issue,
- Policy provisions that exclude or limit coverage due to pre-existing conditions,
- Use of an enrollment mechanism that does not permit or minimizes antiselection (such as minimum participation percentages for associations).

In truth, risk selection (underwriting) begins with the initial selection process used by the agent or sales representative who initially contacts the applicant. This is particularly true for coverages that do not provide for heavy underwriting (accident coverages, for example), and must rely on the sales agent to qualify the prospect. Once initial contact is made, an application can be filled out, which begins the medical underwriting process

The term **medical underwriting** is used by different people in the insurance industry to mean two different things: (1) For those schooled in a life insurance company context, medical underwriting means that the insured is required to have a medical examination by a physician before insurance will be offered. **Paramedical** underwriting means the examination can be done by a paramedic. **Nonmedical** underwriting means that there is no medical examination required, although there are still medical questions on the application; (2) For those schooled in a health insurance environment, particularly group insurance companies, the term "medical underwriting" often means that there are medical questions asked on the individual application. The alternative to medical underwriting in this context is **group underwriting**, which refers to the analysis of the whole group's risk profile, rather than that of the individual. For purposes of this text, the second terminology will be used. When the 'medical examinations' meaning of the term is intended, the text will explicitly say so.

Under the ACA, underwriting and pre-existing condition exclusions are no longer allowed for major medical insurance (group or individual). Instead, insurers are required to issue policies to any individual or small group that wishes to purchase it, at least within specified open enrollment periods (this is called **guaranteed issue** or **guaranteed availability**). What's more, rates cannot vary based on the health status of the applicant (other than a surcharge for tobacco use). Later in this chapter, we will discuss the methods employed by the ACA to attempt to mitigate the antiselection that the prohibition on underwriting would otherwise cause.

While the ACA has prohibited the use of most traditional underwriting tools for major medical coverages, many other coverages still permit these tools, which is why they are still discussed in this chapter. Moreover, until the effects of prior underwriting actions gradually fade away, it is also necessary for practitioners working on major medical coverages to understand the underwriting techniques that were used in the past, in order to understand the makeup of the persisting books of business and produce accurate forecasts of future experience.

The emergence of the internet as a marketing tool has created a distribution portal for insurers which did not exist in prior decades. In such situations, the initial contact is typically made by the applicant, and can be (but isn't necessarily) made directly with the company, bypassing the traditional sales force. Of course, this situation also eliminates the opportunity for the sales force to act as an underwriter for the company. Health insurance exchanges under the ACA take this to another level, with the aim of commoditizing health insurance via a web interface. Consumers on exchanges can readily compare plan designs and prices (and someday, quality metrics) for different insurers' products. They also have access to "navigators" and "assisters" – counselors who can help them make decisions in their financial self-interest.

The insurance application typically includes information about the applicant's health history. Other information, relevant to the coverage being applied for, might also be asked. For disability coverage, for example, this would typically include financial information on the insured. The insurer uses that information, sometimes supplemented by additional information from other sources, to make a decision of whether (and under what conditions) to offer coverage to the individual. There are a variety of tools and data sources available to the underwriter in this process.

UNDERWRITING TOOLS

Some carriers are prohibited by law or regulation from underwriting individuals based on their medical history (as noted earlier, the ACA imposes a blanket prohibition on underwriting for major medical coverage). Others are limited in the underwriting actions they can take on that basis. Most of this chapter's attention assumes that there are no limitations in this regard, as this allows an explanation of the full range of possibilities. At the end of this chapter we will discuss in detail the limitations on underwriting for ACA coverages and what has been done to attempt to mitigate insurers' risks for that business.

It is important to understand, however, the implications of any limitations in underwriting. If, for example, a carrier cannot *rate up* (increase rates on) new policies more than, say, 30% of standard, then presumably any applicants whose risk profile is higher than this would have to be declined. If declinations are prohibited, then the rest of the block must subsidize those high risk insureds, rates must be higher, and there are marketing and other strategic implications.

The Individual Application

Applications typically ask for individual identifying information, financial information (for coverages where such information is relevant, such as DI), and medical history questions. The application often also includes a release by the applicant to allow the insurer to obtain information from third parties related to the insured's medical or financial history.

The number of medical history questions varies widely, depending on the underwriting process to be followed. Asking fewer questions can, but does not necessarily, represent looser underwriting standards. Typically, questions include whether the prospective insured (or his/her family):

- Has ever been diagnosed with a list of particular conditions or groups of conditions,
- Has ever had particular symptoms, or
- Has ever seen a doctor or had medication prescribed for particular conditions.

There are also questions relevant to specific coverages. For disability income coverage, the application will usually include questions related to the insured's income, used to determine how much (and perhaps what type of) coverage will be offered to the applicant.

ACA regulations generally require the use of a standardized application. Insurers are generally not allowed to ask questions about medical conditions any more. This can create difficulties for insurers who wish to identify members who might be candidates for disease management programs early on, or who are working to ensure that all appropriate diagnoses are captured under the ACA risk adjustment program (described in Section 4.6).

APS

Any application which is not entirely "clean" (meaning no conditions or symptoms admitted) requires follow-up by the insurer. There are a variety of mechanisms available for such follow up. If the condition is uninsurable, the coverage may be immediately declined. If the insurer's response depends on details of the condition or procedure which are not included in the application, it is necessary to obtain further information. The most common way to obtain further information is to require an **attending physician statement** (APS) from any or all physicians whose identities are disclosed in the application. In doing so, the insurer (or an administrator hired for this purpose) will mail a request to the physician, along with a check to cover the cost of providing the information, and then follow up as necessary to get a response.

Commercial Databases

Another resource which is becoming more useful is third party databases, used to check on the veracity of the applicant. A surprising number of applicants fail to disclose medical conditions on their applications, whether through oversight or intentional misstatement.

Prescription drug databases can often locate prescriptions for undisclosed conditions, prescribed by doctors similarly undisclosed. There are even some cases where the doctor's statements have changed when confronted by actual prescription histories. An example of such a vendor is Milliman's IntelliScript.[1]

Another commonly used database is the **Medical Information Bureau (MIB)**. MIB is an association of over 500 life insurance companies, which provides data gathered from insurance applications and other sources.

Most commercial databases (including the above two) require that the insurer not base its final underwriting decision on information gained from the service. Rather, the information is to be used as a basis for seeking independent verification that must occur before action is taken.

Internal Data

Internal data from the insurer's own records can be a valuable source of information.

Such information can come from other applications which the individual may have submitted. If the applicant applied for life insurance last month, and disclosed an illness which is not disclosed on the current application, the ability to cross reference can be critically important. This is particularly true in the legal context, where a court might bar a defense by the insurer that the condition was not disclosed, since the information actually was available to the insurer if they had researched their internal data more thoroughly.

---

[1] www.rxhistories.com

Some insurers (particularly those in a concentrated geographic region) have also found some success by accessing their own claim and enrollment databases (particularly in group insurance markets) for information about the applicant.

As in all matters related to private data, care must be taken to abide by the applicable privacy laws and regulations. This can typically be addressed by obtaining a signed authorization from the applicant to seek the data on his behalf, in order to complete the application. Privacy requirements under the Health Insurance Portability and Accountability Act (HIPAA) are discussed in more detail later in this chapter.

Telephone Interviews

Many insurers have found the telephone interview to be a major tool used in underwriting, often replacing the need for an APS or other third party information sources. The interviewer often has a complex decision tree to follow (being led by a series of computer screens) as questions are asked and answered on the phone.

Many insurers have found that prospective insureds are much less willing to mislead an insurer's representative on the phone than they are on a written application. If this characteristic of applicants is appropriately leveraged in the interview process, and if the need for APSs is then obviated, the time taken by the insurer to complete the underwriting process (in the case of an applicant with medical conditions) can be reduced from weeks to only a couple of days.

As sophistication in the telephone interview has grown, the process has often changed from the old, limited uses (checking veracity of application answers) to fairly complete underwriting. Today, this field is often called **teleunderwriting**.

Inspection Reports

Telephone interviews are actually a special case of an underwriting tool called **inspection reports**. Inspection reports contain a class of information that the insurer (or someone they contract with to provide this service) obtains through direct contact with the applicant or others related to the applicant. This can be by telephone, in person, or through other sources. Inspection reports are more common in life and disability coverages than in medical coverages. In person inspections are used relatively infrequently, because of their cost. (They appear more commonly in claim investigations.)

The value of inspection reports is demonstrated repeatedly and often. Most underwriters and claim investigators are amazed at the candor given in interviews, even by people who are trying to deceive the insurance company. People will admit illnesses and doctor visits that clearly contradict information given in the applications.

Inspection reports can be particularly valuable in disability and LTC situations, to evaluate first hand the applicant's mobility and ability to perform certain functions. An applicant who cannot get out of bed in order to meet with the investigator, for example, would likely be a questionable candidate for both DI and LTC coverage.

Lab Testing

Some insurers have found that, for certain portions of their business, blood, saliva, or urine testing can be a useful underwriting tool. Such tests can show the use of tobacco, illegal drugs, and some medical conditions. This is a relatively expensive tool, however, so is typically not used over the universe of all applicants. Instead, it is used with subsets such as those above age 40, those who admit to formerly smoking, or those living in particular geographic areas (because some conditions are more prevalent in certain geographic areas).

Medical Exams

Medical exams are still sometimes required in high risk situations, particularly for high amount disability coverages. Because of their relatively high cost and limited marginal value (when other sources of information are available), they are rarely used for medical coverages.

Tax Returns

Financial information provided through the application can be difficult to evaluate, particularly in small businesses where financial flows can vary dramatically at the choice of the owner. Often the best source of information is the tax return of the individual and the business.

Pre-Existing Condition Provisions

This underwriting tool differs from the others, in that it is not used by medical underwriters in evaluating individual risks. Instead, it is a tool used by insurers to provide blanket protection from antiselection, and replaces part or all of the medical underwriting process.

The **pre-existing condition provision (pre-ex provision)**, a provision of the policy form itself, is the tool. This provision typically says that any condition for which there was treatment or symptoms (the specific language allowed depends on the rules of the state in which the policy will be issued) for up to 6-12 months prior to the application, will not be covered for 12-24 months after issue. Conditions that have been disclosed on the application cannot be used to later deny claims under the pre-ex clause, under the argument that the insurer was aware of the condition before issuing the policy, issued it anyway, and therefore waived its right to enforce the pre-ex clause, and would be estopped from enforcing it.[2]

For certain coverages, such as guaranteed issue hospital indemnity coverage, the pre-ex provision takes the place of more rigorous underwriting. This is also true for certain carriers and in certain jurisdictions for group or short term major medical coverage, where insurers may be prohibited from medical underwriting of individuals.

In other cases, such as individual major medical coverage, the pre-ex clause – now prohibited under the ACA – historically supplemented traditional underwriting. By using it, insurers could deny coverage of expenses from undisclosed pre-existing conditions, without going through the sometimes very expensive process of policy rescission.

There are statutory and regulatory limitations on the ability to define and use pre-ex clauses. These typically limit the period for which a pre-ex clause can apply (such as for 6, 12, or 24 months), or even the look-back period (such as 24 months.)

In the initial rollout of the ACA, the definition of "pre-existing condition" became contentious. The law prohibited pre-existing condition exclusions for children starting in the fall of 2010. The administration interpreted this to require guaranteed issue of policies for children, rather than simply prohibiting pre-ex clauses as described in this section, which is how many insurers had expected the law to be applied.

---

[2] Meyer, William F., *Life & Health Insurance Law, A Summary*, 2nd *Edition.* 1990. pp 567-577.

PRIVACY

HIPAA (the Health Insurance Portability and Accountability Act of 1996) is discussed elsewhere in this book with respect to its portability provisions. HIPAA also contains strict provisions regarding security and privacy of individual health data. This applies not just to claim data, but also underwriting information.

HIPAA's privacy rules apply to "covered entities" that are health plans and other related entities.[3] The Department of Health and Human Services (HHS) was required by Congress to develop a rule to implement the privacy standards, which it did.[4] This rule sets out what information is covered ("personal health information"), who is required to comply ("covered entities" and their "business associates"), and the penalties for non-compliance.

HIPAA's privacy provisions had a significant impact on health plans and their business associates, often requiring the re-vamping of information flows and extensive construction of physical and software protections.[5]

ANALYSIS OF THE INFORMATION

Once all the desired underwriting information has been collected, the underwriter puts it together, perhaps also using tools such as diagnosis-based or prescription-based predictors of relative cost. Examples of predictive tools are medical underwriting manuals, risk adjusters, or a simple credibility formula applied to past claim dollars.

Debit Manuals

Debit points originated in "debit point manuals," which were medical underwriting manuals used by insurers. Most such manuals were historically developed either by reinsurers or by consultants. These books are reference manuals which allow the underwriter to find the number of debit points associated with particular conditions. The following is an example of the entry for a particular condition (Chondritis).[6]

---

[3] For specific details, follow: www.cms.gov
[4] www.hhs.gov
[5] A good resource can be found in the article, "Actuarial and Underwriting Implications of the Final Health Privacy Rule," from the Society of Actuaries' *Health Section News*, April, 2001. Despite the name, however, the "final" rule was re-exposed by the federal government, and changed one more time. Further changes have been made in 2013.
[6] Milliman Health Cost Guidelines – Individual Medical Underwriting.

> **Chondritis**
>
> Inflammation of cartilage. Usually occurs at the cartilaginous border of long bones. Most common sites of occurrence are the ribs and the patella of the knee. Called Tietze's Syndrome if costochondral junctions of ribs involved.
>
> *Development:*
> 1. Site of involvement.
> 2. Any underlying systemic or localized disease?
> 3. Treatment.
>
> *Rating:*
> Chondritis of patella or other bone, including Tietze's syndrome
> Present: 40 debit points
> Resolved: 25 debit points (<2 years)
> Standard (>2 years)

Some conditions can bring with them a wide range of possible financial outcomes, and further information might be needed in order to better predict the future. An example of this is cancer, which might result in no load (for a relatively mild cancer with five years of remission), to uninsurable (for a stage four cancer currently in treatment).

Some conditions are typically not specified in the manual, as they require more analysis than can reasonably be included in a manual, or because they are rare enough that there is not sufficient data for a reliable statistical analysis. In that case, there will typically be a suggestion of "individual consideration" or to "refer to medical director."

In applying such techniques, it is important to remember that some rating mechanisms (notably age rating) include an implicit recognition of higher costs due to specific conditions. To the extent that older insureds have higher costs associated with them, it is because they have a greater prevalence of certain conditions, which (if the underwriting were actually done on those individuals) have associated debit points. When developing age factors for rating purposes, it is therefore important that the development be based on an analysis which somehow excludes claims from those conditions that would have been weeded out by medical underwriting. Otherwise, these conditions might be double counted by applying unadjusted age factors on top of individual medical underwriting.

Many age/sex factors, for example, are developed using large group data, which typically represents an average, non-underwritten population. Those age/sex factors will have a much steeper slope by age than individual age/sex factors developed for use in conjunction with a medical underwriting scheme. As an alternative approach, instead of adjusting the age curve, some insurers account for the age curve when setting underwriting loads for individuals by measuring their morbidity relative to their age group, rather than the population as a whole.

Genetic Testing

Public policy makers periodically examine the issues surrounding the use of genetic testing as an underwriting tool in the individual health market. The Genetic Information Nondiscrimination Act of 2008 (GINA) prohibited the use of genetic test results in health insurance underwriting (in both the group and individual markets) and employment.

Predictive Models

A predictive model is any model that provides a prediction (in this context) of future claims. Today there are a number of such models available, and there is much work being done to measure and improve them. The simplest one is a credibility formula – an individual's expected claims will be modified based on past claim dollars, dampened because some part of the claims might be due to random fluctuation. A modified credibility formula, based on a linear combination of past subsets of claims (perhaps inpatient, outpatient, and other claims) provides substantial improvement over a univariate credibility formula, and rivals the predictive ability of commercially produced, diagnosis-based risk adjusters, which are yet another predictive model. Nonlinear models such as neural nets are becoming more prevalent, although at times extremely complex models can be viewed as a "black box," which can lead to a lack of confidence by key stakeholders.

Debit manuals are early versions of predictive models. Today, large data sets and powerful computing power have allowed the development of other predictive models, some of which are commercially sold today. Early commercial risk adjusters were developed in order to retrospectively measure the relative risk of larger populations, such as all Medicare enrollees of an HMO, for reimbursement. More recently, predictive models have evolved to a point where there can be risk prediction used for underwriting or rating purposes.

The Society of Actuaries has undertaken a periodic study of the predictive ability of various commercial risk adjusters.[7] Their efficacy continues to improve over time.

This area continues to advance rapidly. In particular, risk adjustment is now used in the individual and small group major medical markets under the ACA (described more in Section 4.6), and in Medicare Advantage. In addition, insurers are using risk adjustment models more and more often in payment arrangements with providers, underwriting of groups, and to prioritize medical management casework, to name just a few of many applications.

UNDERWRITING ACTIONS

It is most helpful to translate the collection of information about the applicant (and his or her family, if a family contract) into the additional claim dollars expected because of any existing conditions. Sometimes this information is first translated into debit points, and the insurer's rating system does the further translation of debits into dollars.

Ultimately, a decision is made on whether to offer coverage to the applicant, and if so, under what conditions. At one end of the spectrum, the applicant might be offered full coverage with no restrictions. For major medical insurance, this is generally the only legal option starting in 2014 – none of the other options described as follows are allowed any more. At the other end, the insurer will decline coverage completely. In between, there are a number of alternative responses which the insurer might use:

- *Offer coverage at a higher ("substandard") premium rate.* Many carriers will sometimes offer coverage if the applicant is willing to pay some multiple (perhaps 125%-300%) of the standard premium. The added premium load can be either temporary or permanent, depending on the nature of the condition. Most carriers will consider removing the substandard load at a later date if the insured can demonstrate (through underwriting) a better risk profile at that time.

- *Offer a standard policy, but excluding coverage for that specific condition or affected body system.* This is accomplished by use of a "waiver," "impairment," or "exclusion" rider. These riders are often

---

[7] "A Comparative Analysis of Claims-based Methods of Health Risk Assessment," by Ross Winkelman, FSA and Syed Mehmud, published by the Society of Actuaries, April, 2007. www.soa.org

used for recurrent or chronic illnesses. They are useful if the condition can be well defined and isolated, but are less useful for systemic sorts of medical conditions (like obesity) that might impact multiple body systems. This solution is viewed negatively by some regulators, because it excludes coverage for the condition for which the insured has the greatest need. On the other hand, it might provide an opportunity for insurance that might not otherwise be available at all.

- *Offer a different policy or plan than the one applied for.* Some carriers have separate pools used for substandard risks, and may decline to issue unless the applicant is willing to be part of that pool.[8] This has historically been a solution offered by Blue Cross/Blue Shield plans in certain states. Other carriers have had limited benefit plans (with relatively low inside limits or benefit maximums) which they would offer in lieu of the CMM benefit applied for, particularly where the condition carried a risk of catastrophic claim.

- *Offer a different plan of benefits than the one applied for.* This option is useful when, for example, the applicant might have a chronic condition that is unlikely to become high cost, but will likely continue at a low cost. This is particularly useful in DI or LTC coverage, when existing conditions (asthma, for instance) can be addressed by a longer elimination period or shorter benefit period, while still providing full benefits.

Limitations in Underwriting Actions

Depending on the coverage and the jurisdiction, there are a variety of limitations which might apply to the underwriter's ability to take underwriting action.

For Medicare Supplement coverage, the federal government imposes limitations on the underwriting of the coverage, which began with the Omnibus Budget Reconciliation Act of 1990 (OBRA). Insurers are required to offer a six month open enrollment period for new enrollees of Medicare Part B. If an insured enrolls during this period, the insurer cannot decline coverage, and, in many states, cannot charge a different pre-

---

[8] The ACA requires insurers to use a single risk pool for each market and state, so this approach to pooling would no longer be allowed for individual major medical coverage even if the ACA didn't require insurers to sell the applicant any (non-grandfathered, non-transitional) product they request.

mium based on health status. There are some specific additional situations (less frequent) in which the insurer cannot underwrite. Further, preexisting condition clauses for Medicare Supplement policies are limited to six months from issue and cannot be used in certain circumstances.

For CMM coverage, the federal Health Insurance Portability and Accountability Act (HIPAA) put requirements on states to find ways to ensure the insurability of individuals who would otherwise lose their coverage. CMS (the federal agency responsible for administering the law) said the following in their Transmittal No. 99-02.[9]

> Section 2741 of the PHS Act and the implementing regulations at 45 CFR § 148.120(a)(1) set forth the general rule that issuers that sell health insurance coverage in the individual market must offer all policy forms that they actively sell in that market to "eligible individuals," and may not impose any preexisting condition exclusions on those individuals. There are two exceptions to this rule:
>
> - If a State implements an acceptable alternative mechanism under State law, the rules of the alternative mechanism apply; and
>
> - If a State does not implement an acceptable alternative mechanism under State law, the issuer may choose to offer eligible individuals only two policies, which must meet certain specified criteria and which cannot impose any preexisting condition exclusions.

Starting in 2014, these alternative mechanisms are redundant, given that insurers can no longer medically underwrite or reject applicants based on health status.

Pre-Ex Investigation, Material Misrepresentation, and Rescission

Most carriers who rely on the medical underwriting process for protection against antiselection have a rigorous investigation process to uncover cases where the applicant has not disclosed, or has lied about, conditions which existed at the time of application.

---

[9] www.cms.gov

The first step in such investigations is having an effective set of tools for uncovering new data about a condition. This requires a scanning process applied to claims in order to sort out appropriate claims for further investigation. Too tight a sieve (generating a big list of claims to investigate) might require much unnecessary investigation. Too loose a sieve might allow fraudulent claims through the filter. There are a couple criteria which can be used:

- Timing: The policy provision *Time Limit on Certain Defenses* puts a limit on how long after issue the insurer can rescind a contract because of bad information on the application, unless the insurer can prove the misstatement was fraudulent (a much higher legal hurdle than misstatement – it requires demonstration that the misstatement was intentional and with knowledge.) For most carriers, unless the investigation is part of a fraud detection process, they will not want to investigate claims beyond the time limit, since their ability to remedy the situation has been eliminated.

- Conditions: There are many medical conditions that would be virtually impossible to be pre-existing, and could be excluded from investigation. (Accidents, for example.) Interestingly, the capacity for antiselection is not necessarily proportional to claim size. A relatively low cost chronic asthma patient, for example, is generally well aware of the condition, and can knowingly antiselect when given the opportunity. A heart attack patient, on the other hand, may have had no warning that his or her medical episode was on the horizon.

- Size: Of course, the insurer would not want to spend time investigating a claim if the cost of investigation exceeded the cost of the claim itself. On the other hand, the insurer must be careful not to forego acting on new knowledge that a condition was pre-existing, or they run a risk of legally waiving their right to rescind, and be estopped from later enforcing rescission from the same cause.

- Sentinel conditions or procedures: Some conditions and procedures are related to others that lend themselves to antiselection. Pneumocystis Carinii Pneumonia (PCP), for example, is quite commonly associated with AIDS patients. A PCP claim, even without a secondary diagnosis of HIV or AIDS, might still indicate a person with AIDS. If HIV was not disclosed on the application, this might be cause for investigation.

Once an investigation is complete, and full information is now known, the insurer must determine what action to take. One possibility is **reformation** of the contract – to reissue it retroactively to be under the terms which would have been applied had the insurer been fully aware of the pre-existing condition. The common extreme of this is **rescission** of the policy – to declare the policy void from the beginning, since there was not a full meeting of the minds between the insured and the insurer.

Insurers tend to be very careful about taking an aggressive stance on rescission (although most will claim they take such a stance), due to the explosive public relations and litigation risks associated with it. Indeed, rescissions became a major political issue in the debate that preceded the passage of the ACA. Examples of seriously ill individuals whose policies had been rescinded for relatively minor omissions on their applications became national news, and likely contributed to the passage of the reform law. The ACA prohibits rescissions of health insurance policies unless the insurer can prove fraud or intentional misrepresentation of a material fact.

Material misrepresentation occurs when the claimant provides false information on the application. Under the ACA, the claimant must know that the information is false. Many companies work hard at uncovering such situations, both for their direct effect (to avoid paying for uncovered claims) and for their indirect effect (generating a perception in the market that they cannot be conned.)

Even before the ACA, companies many times found themselves paying claims and not pursuing possible rescissions for misrepresentation because the evidence was not strong enough. Sometimes this happened because, while the applicant might have been aware of a material fact, the insurer could not prove that they intentionally misrepresented it. This situation depended on the state; the need to prove that misrepresentation was intentional often depended on state law. This situation could be helped at least somewhat by existence of a pre-ex clause. That is, while an insurer may not have been able to prove material misrepresentation and rescind the contract, they may at least have avoided paying the claim during the pre-ex period.

One important tool that has emerged for both material misrepresentation and pre-ex investigations is the use of prescription drug data. While someone may "not remember" that they saw a doctor six months earlier, the drug prescribed by that doctor will often show up in a drug history; this will provide an opportunity to obtain a medical history and more information. (Online prescription drug companies also provide information about the physician who prescribed the drug.)

4.3 CHANGES IN PLAN (INTERNAL ANTISELECTION)

When policyholders are provided opportunities to antiselect, they will generally do so. This occurs overtly (as discussed in the section on external antiselection) and subtly. There are sometimes unintentional or unexpected opportunities for this when dealing with in force blocks of business. When antiselection occurs within an in force block of business, it can be called **internal antiselection**, which often tends to be this subtle kind of antiselection.

One common example of this is something which might be called **premium leakage**. This usually occurs at rate increase time, when most insurers will allow policyholders to choose higher deductibles at will, and without underwriting. (After all, they argue, what harm could they be doing by *lowering* the insurer's potential risk on those insureds, and having those insureds self-insure more of the risk?)

At the time of the rate increase, however, higher risk policyholders are much less likely to opt for higher deductible plans than are lower risk policyholders. This is consistent with our understanding of antiselection – higher risk policyholders will generally seek, and even more so *keep*, high coverage levels, while lower risk policyholders are much more flexible in their choices. This seems consistent with human nature.

The predicted average value of a change in benefit plan (say to a higher deductible) is typically based on the average cost of a population with higher and lower risks combined. In reality, however, the average profile of those who *do* change plans is healthier, and the savings from the deductible is therefore worth less. Premium leakage is defined as the difference between the two (the expected pure premium if a random sample of the population migrated to the leaner plan minus the actual pure premium that results from internal antiselection).

EXERCISE 4.1: Assuming the following, calculate the amount of premium leakage:
- A group of policyholders all have a $100 deductible plan with a premium of $100, and are faced with a rate increase of 20%. The insurer has no administrative expenses or profits built into premium.
- The expected savings of an average member moving to a $250 deductible is 5% of premium (without antiselection effects).
- Policyholders are composed of 80% relatively healthy insureds with an expected claim cost of $100 when enrolled in the $100 deductible plan, and 20% relatively unhealthy ones, whose expected claims will be double the healthy policyholders'.
- All the healthy policyholders change deductible, and none of the unhealthy ones do.

The solution to this and all other exercises can be found in the electronic files available for download through the publisher's website. □

THE BUY-DOWN EFFECT

The premium leakage effect described earlier often is part of a larger effect which occurs at the time of rate increase implementation – the **buy-down effect**. This effect is most common with coverages that experience high or frequent rate increases, such as CMM coverage.

Suppose an insurer calculates a needed premium rate increase of X%. If that X% rate increase is implemented by raising rate schedules by X%, the company will often discover that the average premium rate per policy actually goes up *less* than X%. A minor part of this may be due to older policyholders reaching Medicare and dropping their coverage. The major part of this effect, however, is caused by policyholders who, faced with a rate increase, look for a way to reduce their premium, and do so by switching to lower cost (higher deductible or copay) plans.

If there were no antiselection, and if the pricing were done correctly, the premium buy-downs would be matched by proportional and corresponding benefit buy-downs, and the premium level *relative to claims* would still go up by X%. Because of the leakage effect, however, claims generally do not drop as much as the premium does, so there is an antiselective jump in the loss ratio.

EXERCISE 4.2: Calculate the buy-down effect from Exercise 4.1. ☐

MODELING AND MANAGING INTERNAL ANTISELECTION

As with other types of antiselection, the best tool to measure internal antiselection is a partitioning model – separating the population into subsets based on perceived health status. Each subset will tend to behave differently from the others. In this situation, we might typically create two classes of insureds, based on their own perceptions of their claim expectations. Then, each subset will be more or less likely to change its benefit plan, and various assumptions can be tested for this. The result can at least provide some boundaries on the value of antiselection. Further, a useful (if still imprecise) value can often be derived based on judgmental assumptions, providing a much better estimate of antiselection than "zero," which is the result of not modeling it at all.

If the model can be calibrated over time by comparing actual results against predicted results, fairly accurate and precise predictions can be made from such a model.

In the past insurers have generally required members wishing to *increase* their benefits (for example, lower their deductible) to go through an underwriting process, but this will no longer be the case under healthcare reform. That means that individuals who develop a serious medical condition will be able to change to a richer benefit plan at their next open enrollment opportunity. This will likely make internal antiselection an even greater concern for individual health insurers going forward.

4.4 ANTISELECTION UPON LAPSE (CAST/DURATIONAL ANTISELECTION)

It is reasonable to assume that, among potentially lapsing policyholders, some will be high risk and some will be low risk. High risk individuals are (1) less likely to be able to find coverage elsewhere, (2) less likely to be willing to become uninsured, since they know claims are likely on the way, and (3) emotionally less willing to change their current insurance situation (at least without a compelling and obvious financial incentive). For all these reasons, as lapses continue year after year, the proportion of persisting policyholders from an initial group of sales who are higher risk will grow. When an unusually large rate increase takes place, the lapse rate on that business typically jumps following that rate change (and for a short while thereafter). There is a parallel jump in the antiselection as well.

It remains to be seen how this dynamic will change for CMM insurance under the ACA. With the elimination of underwriting and the other changes made by the law, it should be easier for unhealthy individuals to find alternative coverage when faced with an increase, at least if there is sufficient competition in the region where they live. On the other hand, some residual antiselective lapsation effects are likely to persist even in the reformed markets, as points (2) and (3) from the previous paragraph will still apply. The remainder of this section discusses cumulative antiselection as it applied prior to the ACA. The last section of this chapter discusses ACA considerations more thoroughly.

The higher the lapse rate is, the more opportunity there is for antiselective lapsation. Non-cancelable disability income coverages, for example, typically have relatively low (in the 5-7% per year range) ultimate lapse rates, which do not then generate much antiselective lapsation. In fact, DI coverages often experience the opposite – the average risk seems to slightly improve over time. (There are a number of possible explanations for this, including that a higher work ethic might possibly be correlated to longer term policyholders.)

Conversely, individual major medical coverage, which often has ultimate lapse rates of 25% or so, seems to provide ample opportunity for antiselective lapsation, and we generally see such blocks steadily deteriorate in health status over time (provided there is a credible coverage alternative available for healthy policyholders).

This effect – the correlation of antiselective lapsation with the size of the lapse rate – is reflected in a **Cumulative Antiselection Theory (CAST)** model[10] by, first of all, assuming that there is an underlying "involuntary" lapse rate, that doesn't vary between healthy and unhealthy policyholders. This recognizes that certain causes of lapsation (that the coverage becomes superfluous because of Medicare or group coverage, or the accidental death of the insured, for example) are not subject to antiselection. It is only lapsation in excess of this involuntary lapse rate that varies between healthy and unhealthy lives. The Academy's Rate Filing Task Force chose, as a consensus estimate among the individual health insurance experts on

---

[10] Bluhm, William F., "Cumulative Antiselection Theory," *Transactions of the Society of Actuaries*, 1982.

the Task Force, an underlying involuntary lapse rate of 5% per year for major medical.

Additionally, the lapse rate of high risk individuals is generally assumed to be less than that of low risk individuals. If the Academy Task Force's formulae for lapse rates are used over various rate increases, the results appear something like this.[11]

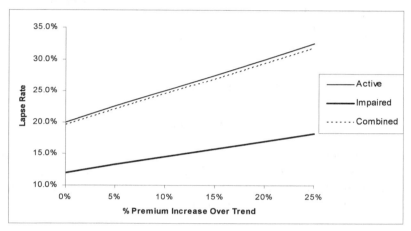

Figure 4.1

When such antiselection occurs year after year, it is referred to as *Cumulative Antiselection*. It is the third type of antiselection – that which occurs as someone is leaving the insured group. It is measured and analyzed by looking at experience over the *durational* dimension, rather than the more typical *calendar* dimension. In other words, to best analyze experience, experience is examined as a function of time since issue of the policy.

In analyzing experience, it is important to understand that the typical CAST model does not attempt to explain the early durational curve caused by the wearoff of initial underwriting. Conceptually, one might think of the typical policy's durational curve as an overlay of the two separate phenomena – wearoff of initial underwriting and cumulative antiselection. The concept is presented in Figure 4.2.

---

[11] This graph is based on durational year 4/5, on the sheet 'Duration,' spreadsheet 'AAA Rate Filing Model – Global Summary," in the electronic files available for download through the publisher's website. In that duration, 5% of the combined population is impaired, and 95% is active.

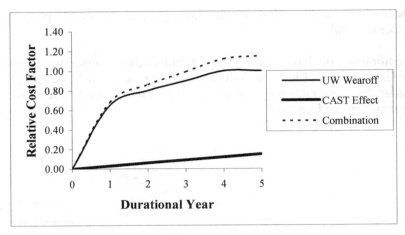

Figure 4.2

There is another phenomenon that occurs over time in this context, which is that insureds who once were healthy can later become chronically ill. Conceptually, we think of this as some portion of the low risk (healthier) group moving to the high risk group each year.

4.5 MODELING ANTISELECTION

THE PARTITION MODEL

By far the most commonly used basis for modeling antiselection is to partition the population in some way, and separately model the resulting subsets. The mathematical and conceptual tools used to process this modeling will vary, depending on the circumstances and the use.

The partitioning of the population can be similar to having the population under study get into a long line, starting with the highest cost person, and having monotonically descending claim levels thereafter, until, at the end of the line, is a group of people who all have zero claims.

One interesting subtlety is the question of whether the line-up is based on: (1) actual claims (which no one can predict), (2) claims expected by the insurer, or (3) claims expected by the insured. For most purposes, the last definition is the one inherent in antiselection models. Individuals cannot perfectly predict their own claim levels, however, so there typically needs to be another function created, which might be called the **antiselection acuity**, representing the insureds' ability to predict their claims. This antiselection acuity will tend to vary by size of claim; high cost claims are on average more predictable than low cost claims.

Once the line-up occurs, we can partition the line-up into relatively unhealthy and healthy insureds. ("Healthy," a handy label for insureds with low expectations of claims, not as a judgment about their healthiness.) We do this by conceptually cutting the line-up into two continuous subsets. The big question in defining the model is: Where to draw the line?

Drawing the Line in a CAST Model

In the prior section the characteristics of a CAST model[12] were described. An approach was suggested whereby the average claims per insured of the unhealthy group are compared with that of the healthy group. The cutoff of the line-up is chosen so that the ratio of the unhealthy to healthy average claim cost is a chosen multiple. If we look at long term CAST projections, it turns out that the ability of the model to make good projections later in the block's lifetime depends on the model still having a sufficient number of members in both the unhealthy and healthy pools. Otherwise, as the projection proceeds, virtually all lives might become "unhealthy," and the model would no longer predict any changes. For this reason, it may be necessary to choose the above multiple relatively high (like 5 to 10), for high lapse coverages such as major medical, so that even after many years there are still sufficient persisting "low" risk insureds in the model to continue to demonstrate antiselection. This model, then, is useful in modeling cumulative antiselection.

Drawing the Line in a MNAM Model

Another situation requires a different condition for creating the partition, and is useful in estimating external antiselection. It was described in the paper "The Minnesota Antiselection Model" (MNAM).[13] That model was developed to find boundary conditions on the antiselection which might occur in a specific situation. The boundary conditions were useful in developing an estimate of the antiselection expected under different scenarios. The situation was one in which uninsureds in a given geographic area were to be provided an offer of guaranteed insurability. In that case, there

---

[12] Op. cit.
[13] "The Minnesota Antiselection Model," William F Bluhm, *Actuarial Research Clearing House*, Jan 01, 1991. www.soa.org

was an "envelope" developed between zero antiselection and maximum antiselection. (Maximum antiselection in this case would occur if every insured were fully prescient about their own future claims, if they acted fully rationally, and if higher cost people were provided the opportunity to buy coverage before lower cost people.) This envelope provided substantial comfort to program designers who wished to measure the risk of antiselection. Reasonable values could be chosen within the envelope, with a degree of comfort about the level of risk in using those values.

Drawing the Line in Internal Antiselection

This type of model is often required when managing existing blocks of individual or small group medical business. A modified CAST model can be used for this purpose, typically with a need to model each of the deductible/plan populations which will be offered the choice of new plans. There are then at least two decrements to those populations – lapsation (as in the CAST model) and plan changes. (It is sometimes helpful to greatly simplify the choices, and assume insureds will only change to a single, most popular alternative plan.) Exercise 4.1 (earlier) is a modeling exercise of internal antiselection.

After the line-up and partition occur, we can choose or derive characteristics of the low risk and high risk subsets. Each subset can be projected separately. Assumptions must be made about relative price elasticity (and lapse rates) of the groups, as well as overall assumptions. Calibration of the model is extremely difficult, because we never know for sure which insureds are in which group (because group membership is based on their self-perceived expectations of claims), so we cannot explicitly measure the results of each group. Instead, we must measure the aggregate results, and deduce assumptions about the underlying pieces. (This can be considered an actuarial equivalent to the Heisenberg Uncertainty Principle. This is the principle in particle physics that says that the more you know about *where* a particle is, the less you know about *what* it is.)

Deterministic vs. Stochastic Models

The typical basic use of an antiselection model (or any actuarial model, for that matter) is to take past history, define it in detail, and project that model into the future, typically (but not always) using deterministic methods based on (mean) expected values. A true picture of the future, including its values and its risks, requires that we work with distributions of potential values, not just the expected values themselves. These distributions are provided by stochastic models. This requires that we distinguish between purely random statistical fluctuations, and the risk of choosing wrong assumptions (including wrong distributions). With the number of variables involved, this type of analysis is not just difficult – it is dauntingly complex – even if we had valid distributions to represent each of the variables. Nonetheless, with the rapid advancement of computing power (including cloud and grid computing resources that can run models in parallel across many machines), there has been renewed interest in stochastic modeling of policyholder behavior.[14]

The partition model is a modeling method which addresses (in a very rudimentary way) the issue of distributions, without moving to a full stochastic model. It does so by saying "rather than characterizing this population in terms of single values, I will create two populations, and let those values vary separately." In doing so, the results are quite substantially more responsive to changing conditions, and reflect the different nature of the subsets and their behavior. Results tend to be much more accurate.

Markov Processes

There is no reason why a population partition need be limited to two subsets. Often, however, once the major internal forces are roughly determined by a two-subset partition model, there seems to not be much additional information to be gained by further partitions. If further partitions are done, however, the multiple subsets can be individually modeled. Typically this modeling uses identical formulas, applied to different assumptions about that subset of the population. In this case, the model lends itself to being treated as a Markov process, where the population at any given point in time can be represented by a $1 \times N$ array, with each element of the array representing the proportion of the population in a given subset (state). The much-recognized *Markov chain* is created by repeatedly applying a linear operator (matrix) to that array, with each subsequent resulting array representing the population in the next time period. (Further, if we had a lot of spare time or were just masochistic, we might develop even more calculationally powerful tools by applying quantum mechanics to the health status vector.)

---

[14] See for instance the following SOA study by Alan Mills:
https://www.soa.org/research/research-projects/health/simulating-health-behavior-a-guide-to-solving.aspx

PROJECTING THE MODEL

Once the subsets are determined and described, the population can be projected forward in time. This process typically requires substantial judgment and understanding of the process and situation being studied. The projection model should require assumptions about how each of the following variables will act on the population over time:

1. Trends in claim costs from policyholder aging, duration (policy aging), secular trend, deductible leveraging, and other causes.
2. Lapsation, separately for each sub-population. This will often vary by size of rate increase, with more antiselective lapsation happening for larger rate increases.
3. Movement between populations, often expressed as a net movement from healthy to unhealthy since the net trend in cumulative antiselection is in this direction.
4. The time value of money (interest).
5. Premium rate increases.

The CAST paper[15] used the following notation:

1. The number of healthy lives (called 'active' in the paper) at age x is $_a\ell_x$, unhealthy (or 'impaired') lives are $_i\ell_x$.
2. The probability of one healthy life becoming unhealthy, issue age x, at duration t, is $q^{(ai)}_{[x]+t}$. (This is assumed net of any flow of unhealthy to healthy lives.)
3. Claim costs for a and i lives, issue age x, at time t, are $_aS^{(d)}_{[x]+t}$ and $_iS^{(d)}_{[x]+t}$.
4. The probabilities of lapsing are $_aq^{(l)}_{[x]+t}$ and $_iq^{(l)}_{[x]+t}$.

Lapses are further defined by:

$$_iq^{(l)}_{[x]+t} = k_1(_aq^{(l)}_{[x]+t} - u) + u, \tag{4.1}$$

---

[15] Bluhm, William, "Cumulative Antiselection Theory," *Transactions of the Society of Actuaries* Volume 34.

where
$$k_1 \in [0,1].$$

The constant u represents an underlying lapse rate that is constant across all risk classes, and which was referred to earlier as the "involuntary" lapse rate. One could think of it as random life circumstances that force a lapse, such as an accidental death, which logically is independent of most pre-existing medical conditions.

Another constant, k_2, is chosen so that

$$_iS^{(d)}_{[x]+t} = k_2 \times {}_aS^{(d)}_{[x]+t}. \tag{4.2}$$

Choosing k_2 implicitly defines the partition between $_a\ell_x$, and $_i\ell_x$, if we know the distribution of claims. This ratio of unhealthy claim cost to healthy claim cost at the same age x was also discussed earlier, when it was mentioned that this ratio is typically chosen in the range of 5-10 for major medical insurance.

Applying the CAST model requires first calibrating the model to past experience (unless and until you are comfortable with choosing the parameters without referencing the block's experience), and then using that calibration to project future results.

The CAST model was a significant step forward in understanding and modeling insureds' antiselective behavior. Since that model was proposed, actuarial observers (largely unpublished) have matured somewhat in outlook regarding that behavior. The CAST model has been found not to be a good fit in certain circumstances: (1) in the first 3-4 durations, when the impact of the wear-off of underwriting overwhelms the CAST effects, (2) in later durations when only a fraction of the original population remains, and (3) at all durations when a rate spiral is severe and volatile.

In early durations, the usual solution is to apply additional underwriting factors. The Academy's Rate Filing Task Force chose the following annual durational adjustment factors for durations 1, 2, 3, and 4+, as representative of a typical fully underwritten CMM situation: 0.65, 0.8, 0.9, 1.0. Without such adjustments, CAST does not adequately explain the dramatic durational change in claim costs from early durations.

The second situation occurs because, over time, the number of healthy lives diminishes dramatically, and the unhealthy lives form a large percentage of the population. Eventually, this causes the model to be inadequately sensitive to the ongoing changes. In essence, the model devolves to a non-CAST model of the unhealthy lives. This problem can be solved by choosing a higher value of k_2, and recalibrating the model. If this is done, we might lose some of the model's sensitivity to early year changes, but gain that sensitivity in the later years. (Ultimately, we might further partition the group into three blocks of policies, but that enormously complicates the calibration process, because there is a much larger number of parameters which must be estimated, with no further guidance than the existing experience. As we gain experience with this calibration problem, and when we feel comfortable at estimating those parameters, we could treat this multi-level CAST model as a Markov process, and use linear algebra to make our projections.) The Academy's group ultimately chose a value of $k_2 = 4.1\overline{6}$, being the ratio of the initial claim cost ${}_i S^{(d)}_{[x]+t}$ (\$375) to ${}_a S^{(d)}_{[x]+t}$ (\$90).

There is some evidence that once the insured population is small, and rates have increased to some level materially higher than market rates (one observer estimates 150-200%), the population can be stabilized.

When a block of policies is in the throes of an antiselection spiral, characterized by large rate increases, high lapse rates, and quickly deteriorating experience, such changes are often too severe to be accurately predictable by a CAST model. A rate spiral can quickly remove most of the healthy lives, making the block mostly unhealthy, and therefore the CAST model less sensitive. This is similar to what happens at later durations even without a severe rate spiral, and so relates to the second situation, described earlier. The projection formulas might, therefore, need stronger terms if they are to be more generalized. There are many curves which can be fit to such data. One example of such a formula was developed by a colleague.[16]

$$Shock\ Lapse = \frac{Rate\ Increase - Trend}{(Rate\ Increase - Trend) + \frac{(1+Trend)}{EF}}, \quad (4.3)$$

where **EF**, the **Elasticity Factor**, is a parameter which measures (not in

---

[16] Stephen T. Custis, FSA, who worked with one of the authors at the time.

the classic economics sense of a linear relationship) price elasticity of the population being modeled. This might be thought of as the ability and willingness of the insured population to take action (finding other insurance or dropping coverage altogether) after a rate increase. In a typical example, the factor for active lives might be 1.3, and for impaired lives 0.8.

A spreadsheet is typically created which describes each of the statistics of interest related to the block of policies. The most recent year's experience is used as a starting point, and each value is built from this, using the formulae described previously combined with normal asset share type calculations. This generally involves separate projections of the $_a\ell_x$ and $_i\ell_x$ lives, based on assumed values and functions for $_aq^{(\ell)}_{[x]+t}$, $_iq^{(\ell)}_{[x]+t}$, and $q^{(ai)}_{[x]+t}$. Each of $_iS^{(d)}_{[x]+t}$ and $_aS^{(d)}_{[x]+t}$ will be projected with the various trends that apply: (1) normal underlying claim cost trend (which itself contains a variety of components), (2) aging of the insureds, and (3) any overlying adjustments (like the early durational adjustments mentioned earlier). The CAST effect is not applied; it's an outcome of the model. The changing mix of $_iS^{(d)}_{[x]+t}$ and $_aS^{(d)}_{[x]+t}$, brought about by the changing values of $_a\ell_x$, and $_i\ell_x$ causes the CAST trend in the overall numbers, even though they are not reflected in the separate sub-populations.

Once the projection of the sub-populations has been made, they can be aggregated. If the projection is being done for calibration purposes, the results can be compared with actual data. One complication with such calibration is that there are many different formulas, such as formula (4.3), which can produce similar results. If, for example, the multiple of high risk to low risk morbidity of insureds were initially chosen to be a lower value, then the partition would yield a larger proportion of high risk insureds. The progression of lapses over the life of the policy would look quite different, yielding a curve which would likely peak much sooner, and flatten out much more in the tail. (In that case, we might need to find a different function to calibrate actual results than we would if we had used a higher value of k_2.)

One additional complication occurs, causing a more level gross premium structure over time. To the extent expenses are materially heavier at issue than renewal (true of many commercial carriers), the total of (claim cost) and (expense cost) can be much more level than considering claim cost alone. If managed knowledgeably, this offsets to some extent the initial steep slope in premiums which would result from consideration of claims alone. This helps alleviate, in turn, some part of the CAST effect.

THE FUTURE

Antiselection models clearly have a significant amount of growth and refinement ahead of them. Even now, however, they are useful tools in predicting a major factor used in managing individual health insurance.

Obviously there is much work that must be done in refining this modeling technique, both through the formulae and through accumulation of data. We might think of the current state of affairs as a "first approximation" toward an ultimate theory. In any event, it is far superior to the prior method often used by actuaries – "let's just assume X% antiselection."

4.6 ANTISELECTION UNDER THE AFFORDABLE CARE ACT

As we have seen throughout this chapter, the ACA prohibited most of the traditional techniques insurers have used to control antiselection in the individual major medical marketplace. In particular, the following were all prohibited starting in 2014:

1. Underwriting, including offering alternative coverage or denying coverage;
2. Health status rating;
3. Pre-existing condition exclusions;
4. Exclusionary riders;
5. Lifetime or annual dollar limits;
6. Limiting benefit coverage or imposing very high cost sharing designed to attract healthier risks;
7. Rescissions, except in cases of fraud or intentional misrepresentation; and
8. Marketing practices that discourage unhealthy risks from signing up.

Given these restrictions, what is to protect insurers going forward from the three faces of antiselection? In the absence of further protections, individuals would simply wait until they need care to purchase insurance (external antiselection), would switch whenever they chose to the plan that provided the best coverage for their conditions (internal antiselection), and would drop coverage as soon as they were well again (cumulative antiselection in its most extreme form). In fact, in the 1990s, several states enacted versions of guaranteed issue or community rating requirements on their individual markets, sometimes without any further protections to limit antiselection.[17] The results were problematic: high premium rate increases and insurers exiting the market. In the case of the state of Washington, the following anecdote reported in the Wall Street Journal[18] gives a sense for how severe antiselection could be in these environments:

> In testimony before a legislative committee, Blue Cross of Washington and Alaska, one of the state's largest health insurers, said its Spokane, Wash., affiliate recently received a letter from an eastern Washington woman who obtained a health-insurance policy under open enrollment. The woman praised the insurer for providing maternity benefits. She added, the insurer said, that she was canceling her policy. But she said she would be sure to come back and get another one if she got pregnant again, Blue Cross says.

Fortunately, the ACA contains a variety of measures aimed at controlling antiselection. These include:

- Coverage mandates (in the form of tax penalties) and premium subsidies to encourage participation;
- Aligning market rules on and off the Exchanges;
- Open enrollment periods;
- Minimum benefit levels; and
- **Premium stabilization** programs (known as **the three R's**).

Each measure is examined in more detail in the next section.

COVERAGE MANDATES AND PREMIUM SUBSIDIES

Perhaps the primary methods employed by the ACA to limit antiselection are two coverage mandates.

---

[17] Wachenheim, Leigh and Leida, Hans, "The Impact of Guaranteed Issue and Community Rating Reforms on Individual Insurance Markets." Prepared for America's Health Insurance Plans. March, 2012. Retrieved April 4, 2014 from http://www.ahipcoverage.com/wp-content/uploads/2012/03/Updated-Milliman-Report.pdf.

[18] Richards, Bill, "Health-Care Reform in State of Washington Riles Nearly Everyone," *The Wall Street Journal*, April 5, 1996.

To limit the risk that employers with relatively less healthy insured lives might cease offering coverage and instead send their employees to the individual market, the ACA requires large employers (with 51 or more employees) to offer affordable insurance coverage meeting a minimum coverage level. Employers that fail to do so may have to pay a significant penalty. This **employer mandate** has been repeatedly postponed – originally scheduled to go into effect in 2014, it is now slated to be phased in over 2015 and 2016.

The second mandate requires all individuals to obtain insurance that provides **minimum essential coverage** or pay a penalty on their tax returns. This is known as the **individual mandate**, and was a focus of the Supreme Court case examining the constitutionality of the ACA (the Court ultimately upheld the mandate – but under Congress' authority to tax, rather than their authority to regulate interstate commerce). Many forms of coverage qualify as minimum essential coverage:

- Medicare;
- Most Medicaid plans, including CHIP;
- Certain other public programs such as TRICARE (military coverage);
- Employer sponsored insurance that meets minimum value;
- Individual major medical insurance; and
- Certain other coverage recognized by CMS.

Requiring all Americans to obtain coverage would have the potential to greatly reduce antiselection in the individual market, but only if (1) individuals believe the penalty is significant in relation to the cost of coverage,[19] (2) the requirement applies to a broad enough population segment of those eligible for individual coverage, and (3) it is enforced.

The individual mandate penalty (formally known as the "individual shared responsibility payment") is scheduled to increase from 2014 through 2016 as follows. For each tax filing household, the penalty is the *greater of* a flat per-person penalty *or* a percentage of all income over the tax filing threshold for the household, as presented in Table 4.1.

---

[19] The following paper investigates this in more detail: Houchens, Paul, "Measuring the strength of the individual mandate," Milliman *Insight*, March, 2012,
http://us.milliman.com/uploadedFiles/insight/health-published/measuring-strength-individual-mandate.pdf.

Table 4.1

Schedule of ACA Individual Mandate Penalties		
Year	Per person (children at 50% of this amount)	% of Income Greater Than Tax Filing Threshold
2014	$95	1.0%
2015	$325	2.0%
2016	$695	2.5%
2017+	Increased by inflation	2.5%

Regardless of household size, the flat amount is limited to a maximum of three times the individual per-person amount. The total penalty for a household cannot exceed the national average premium for a bronze qualified health plan.

There are a variety of exemptions from the individual mandate. In particular, individuals who have incomes below the tax filing threshold are exempt, as are individuals who have suffered a hardship.[20] A number of additional exemptions were granted to individuals affected by the troubled rollout of the insurance exchanges in late 2013 and early 2014.

The mandate also allows individuals to have a gap in coverage of less than three months during a year without having to pay the penalty. This could lead to selection effects when healthy individuals drop coverage for a few months each year and then sign up again in the next open enrollment. (This potential issue may be exacerbated by the three month premium payment grace period[21] afforded to individuals receiving premium subsidies.)

Finally, the premium subsidies available to lower income individuals and families may help reduce antiselection by making coverage more affordable (and hence attractive) to healthier individuals.

---

[20] Examples of hardships include being homeless or recently evicted, the death of a close family member, or being ineligible for Medicaid because your state did not expand the program under the ACA. For a list of hardships that qualify, see
https://www.healthcare.gov/fees-exemptions/exemptions-from-the-fee/#hardshipexemptions

[21] See Kolber, M. and Leida, H. "How Consumers Might Game the 90-day Grace Period and What Can Be Done About It." *Health Affairs Blog*, November 17, 2014.
http://healthaffairs.org/blog/2014/11/17/how-consumers-might-game-the-90-day-grace-period-and-what-can-be-done-about-it/

ALIGNING RULES ON AND OFF EXCHANGES

Besides the overall, market-level selection that we have discussed so far, the ACA creates several distinct blocks of business for insurers – and whenever the population is segmented, it is important to consider the potential for selection.

Other than new start-ups, most insurers will have both **ACA-compliant** and **non-compliant** policies on their books. The ACA-compliant policies may either be **on-exchange** or **off-exchange**. The non-compliant policies may be either **grandfathered** or **transitional**. We will now explore what each of these terms means.

By ACA-compliant plans, we mean those effective January 1, 2014 or later which comply with all the rules that have been presented in this chapter, including guaranteed issue, modified community rating, and the various benefit mandates. These plans may be sold either through a public health insurance exchange (which is the only place premium subsidies are available) or directly by an insurer or its agent as in the past (off-exchange).

In the absence of regulation, it is possible that selection effects would occur between the on- and off-exchange blocks of business. Exchanges assess a fee on each policy (3.5% of premium for 2014 and 2015 in federally facilitated exchanges), and the lower income individuals attracted to the exchanges by the subsidies are likely to differ in health status from the higher income off-exchange population.

To mitigate this selection risk, regulations impose several requirements:

- Insurers must include all ACA-compliant policies, both on- and off-exchange, in a *single risk pool*, meaning that identical plans must have identical rates on and off the exchanges. In particular, if the health status of the exchange pool differs from the off exchange pool, the insurer must average that out across the entire ACA-compliant pool.
- Risk adjustment (as described later) also works to even out risk between insurers, and between the on- and off-exchange portions of the risk pool. Thus, in the event that an insurer only sells plans on or off the exchange, but not both, they still must participate in the overall risk pool through the risk adjustment mechanism.

- Insurers must pay the same commissions to brokers and agents on and off exchanges.
- The exchange fee must be spread across the entire single risk pool, including off-exchange policies.
- Carriers participating in exchanges must offer at least one gold and one silver level plan on the exchange. There is no equivalent requirement off-exchange, however, which could lead to selection issues. States may impose stricter requirements.
- Carriers are prohibited from marketing practices intended to discourage unhealthy individuals from signing up.
- Open enrollment periods are identical on and off the exchange (more on this in the next section).

In general, although on and off exchange rules have been aligned to a great extent, there is still some potential for selection.[22]

The non-compliant policies also come in two flavors: grandfathered and transitional.

Grandfathered policies are those that were in existence when the ACA was signed on March 23, 2010. If benefits or cost sharing are changed too much, these policies lose their grandfathered status. By definition, new grandfathered policies cannot be sold. Grandfathered plans are exempt from most (but not all) of the requirements we have been discussing, and by law they must be rated separately from the ACA-compliant risk pool.

Transitional policies (also sometimes called **grandmothered** plans) are certain policies that were sold after the ACA was passed, but before the major reform changes took effect in 2014. Many of these policies failed to meet one or more of the ACA requirements (such as covering essential health benefits), and hence were going to be canceled. This proved politically awkward given President Obama's promise that "if you like your health care plan, you can keep your health care plan."[23]

Under mounting political pressure, the administration announced in November 2013 that non-compliant plans could be renewed for an additional

---

[22] This NAIC article, while a bit dated, gives a good overview of the considerations. http://www.naic.org/store/free/ASE-OP.pdf

[23] Fact checkers took delight in tracking just how many times the President said this, see for instance http://www.politifact.com/obama-like-health-care-keep.

year – if state regulators chose to allow it, and if insurers chose to do so. While this last minute change created a great deal of consternation on the part of insurers and regulators alike, many insurers did choose to renew non-compliant plans. These plans have come to be called "transitional" because the administration characterized the change as a "transitional policy."

Transitional policies are exempt from many ACA requirements[24] and they are rated separately from compliant plans (that is, they are not part of the ACA single risk pool). They also do not participate in the risk mitigation programs outlined later in this chapter, other than (like grandfathered plans) contributing to the reinsurance program.

In March of 2014, the administration announced that states could allow a further extension of transitional policies for up to two more years (renewals of policies up to October 1, 2016) and that they would consider another one year extension beyond that.

The administration's decision to allow non-compliant transitional policies has raised concerns of potential antiselection against the ACA-compliant individual market. These concerns are heightened because the change was made long after rates were filed and approved for 2014 (and rates cannot be altered). In most cases, the non-compliant plans are likely to cover fewer benefits and have higher cost sharing than compliant plans. Their premium rates may also be lower since they are not subject to guaranteed issue requirements. Thus, healthy policyholders are more likely to keep the non-compliant coverage, while unhealthy policyholders potentially have an incentive to switch to the ACA-compliant pool.

To ameliorate these concerns, the administration made several significant changes to the risk mitigation programs (the three R's), as discussed in the next section.

OPEN ENROLLMENT PERIODS

A proven approach to mitigate antiselection, open enrollment periods have been used for years in the employer group market. This mechanism partially limits the opportunity for antiselection by requiring members to enroll in

---

[24] See Leida, Hans, "Canceled plans, part III: An extension, an expansion, and more changes to 2014 rules," Milliman *Insight*, March 2014,
http://us.milliman.com/insight/2014/ Canceled-plans--part-III-An-extension--an-expansion--and-more-changes-to-2014-rules.

their coverage during a set time period (the open enrollment period) each year. Once a plan has been selected, it generally cannot be changed until the next year's enrollment period – and those that fail to sign up during open enrollment must wait until the next year to obtain coverage, even if they fall ill.

Exceptions to this rule are granted in the case of qualifying life events such as a birth, adoption, or loss of other coverage, each of which would trigger a special enrollment period in which a member has an opportunity to sign up or change plans.

Under ACA regulations, a single annual open enrollment period in the individual market was established each year, and was aligned to be the same on and off of the exchanges. During the initial open enrollment period in late 2013 through early 2014, the government made a number of extensions and exceptions to the open enrollment rules for members who had technical difficulty signing up. Furthermore, the open enrollment period for 2015 was delayed a month in order to give insurers and regulators more time to develop, file, and review premium rates. Even later, a special enrollment period was added (in most states) in the spring of 2015 for individuals and families who discovered that they owed an individual shared responsibility payment when they filed their 2014 tax returns.

MINIMUM BENEFIT LEVELS

As discussed at length in earlier chapters, the ACA places many restrictions on the benefits and cost sharing designs that may be offered to consumers.

In particular, in the individual and small group markets, policies must cover all essential health benefits and must provide at least a bronze actuarial value (catastrophic plans that are slightly less rich than bronze are available to those under 30 or with a financial hardship). Federal rules put a cap on out of pocket spending, and there must be no cost sharing for preventive services.

In the large employer market, plans must meet a *minimum value* of 60% in order for employees to satisfy the individual mandate to purchase insurance (and for large employers to satisfy their mandate to offer insurance). Minimum value is a similar concept to actuarial value, and is measured using a federal tool called the **minimum value calculator** that estimates the percentage of claim costs (not premium costs) covered by the employer plan versus the members. Minimum value differs from actuarial value in that large employers are not required to cover all of the essential health benefits in their plan designs. Preventive services must still be covered with no cost sharing.

In general, these benefit mandates and cost sharing limits set a minimum threshold of coverage that limits antiselection (both external and internal) to a degree, by restricting the ability of healthy individuals to purchase extremely low benefit level plans.

THE THREE R'S

Perhaps the most direct tools used by the ACA to confront potential antiselection are these three premium stabilization programs, which apply to the ACA-compliant individual and small group markets in each state starting in 2014. Two of the programs – **transitional reinsurance** and **risk corridors** – are temporary, phasing out after three years. One – **risk adjustment** – is a permanent feature of the post-ACA marketplace. Together, the programs have come to be known as the three R's. Key parameters and rules related to the programs are released each year in a regulation known as the "Notice of Benefit and Payment Parameters."[25]

Federal Transitional Reinsurance

The federal transitional reinsurance program is a temporary program under the ACA scheduled to run from 2014 through 2016. It reimburses insurers in the ACA-compliant individual market for a portion of high claimants' costs using funds collected primarily from the group major medical market – in other words, it is a temporary, significant subsidy from the group market (including self-funded employer groups) to the individual market. It also serves as a source of revenue for the federal government to recoup monies spent prior to 2014 under the ACA's early retiree reinsurance program. This is worth emphasizing: the federal government is not "reinsuring" the risk in the individual market as in traditional reinsurance (or as in Medicare Part D), as funds ultimately are collected from insurers and employers. This program also does not protect against truly catastrophic claims over $250,000. The government assumes carriers will already have any needed reinsurance for that risk.

---

[25] A good place to find these and other key ACA regulations is the Center for Consumer Information and Insurance Oversight (CCIIO) website, www.cms.gov/cciio/index.html.

Here is how it is supposed to work. In each year, the government imposes a per capita fee on all major medical coverage (individual, small group, and large group, including most self-funded plans). A portion of the fee is used to fund a reinsurance pool, while another portion goes to the Treasury (a relatively small portion is also used to defray costs of administering the program). The statutory collection amounts and per capita fees for each year are given in Table 4.2.

Table 4.2

	Schedule of Transitional Reinsurance Collections			
Year	Total Collection[1]	To Pool[1]	To Treasury[1]	Annual Fee per Capita
2014	$12	$10	$2	$63
2015	$8	$6	$2	$44
2016	$5	$4	$1	$27

[1]In billions. In addition, another $20.3 million in 2014, $25.4 million in 2015, and $32 million in 2016 are to be collected to defray administrative costs of the program.

The reinsurance pool is then used to reimburse insurers for high claims in their ACA-compliant individual line of business. Each year, the government sets an **attachment point**, a **coinsurance rate**, and a **maximum cap** for the program. For each member whose annual claims exceed the attachment point, the insurer is reimbursed the coinsurance rate times the excess, until the member reaches the cap (at which point the coinsurance rate drops to zero). The reinsurance parameters for 2014 through 2016 are listed in Table 4.3.

Table 4.3

Transitional Reinsurance Parameters for 2014 – 2016			
Year	Attachment Point[1]	Coinsurance Rate[2]	Cap
2014 Original	$60,000	80%	$250,000
2014 Revised	$45,000	80%	$250,000
2015 Original	$70,000	50%	$250,000
2015 Revised[1]	$45,000	50%	$250,000
2016 Proposed[1]	$90,000	50%	$250,000

[1]At the time 2015 premium rates had to be set, the government had only stated that it "intends to propose" these revised 2015 parameters, leading to significant uncertainty for health plans. These revisions for 2015 and the 2016 parameters were formally proposed in the Proposed 2016 Notice of Benefit and Payment Parameters, and were then finalized in the final version of that rule.

Under the original 2014 parameters, for example, an individual with incurred claims of $300,000 on an ACA-compliant individual plan in 2014 would result in a reinsurance payment of $152,000 (the $300,000 is capped at $250,000, and then the insurer receives 80% of $250,000 less the $60,000 attachment point).

In Table 4.3, there are two rows for each year. For 2014, the government significantly altered the parameters in response to issuer concerns related to the transitional policy for canceled plans described previously. These changes made the program more generous. For instance, continuing our earlier example, under the revised parameters, the insurer would receive $164,000 (80% of $250,000 less the $45,000 attachment point).

Besides lowering the attachment point, the government has made additional changes to make the program even more generous for 2014:

- If reimbursement requests are lower than available funds, the government will increase the coinsurance rate (up to a maximum of 100%) to use up the excess funds. Under the original rules, the excess funds would have been carried forward to future years.
- Under a new rule, if there is a shortfall in collections, the Treasury will absorb the shortfall first (providing up to a $2 billion cushion in 2014) – under prior rules, the shortfall would have been allocated proportionately to both insurers and the Treasury.

For 2015, the government has stated their intent to propose changes to the reinsurance parameters. At the time rates were set, the parameters had not officially been changed, leading to significant uncertainty among issuers. Another source of uncertainty that actuaries and management must face is the question of whether collections will be more or less than payments calculated under the parameters in each year.

Because the group market is much larger than the individual market, transitional reinsurance has had a material impact on individual market rates in 2014 – perhaps on the order of a 10% reduction relative to where they would have been without the program, although this will vary quite a bit from insurer to insurer and state to state. Of course, as the program is phased out, this reduction will also have to be phased out in order for rates to remain adequate, placing upward pressure on premiums.

The reinsurance program addresses antiselection in at least two ways. First, insurers with a disproportionate share of high claimants will receive higher reimbursement from the program. Second, by lowering the cost of insurance overall, the program may help to encourage more healthy people to purchase coverage.

Given their potentially significant impact on profit margins in the individual market, changes to the reinsurance program will also have a profound impact on the risk corridors program (which shares some gains and losses of insurers in that market with the federal government). This is discussed further later in this section.

Permanent Risk Adjustment

The only permanent "R" of the three, risk adjustment addresses antiselection between carriers by attempting to measure the morbidity difference between them and transfer funds from carriers with low morbidity to those with high morbidity. The program is intended to operate in a revenue neutral manner for the government (funds are transferred between insurers, but there is no net flow of funds to or from the government other than an administrative fee, which was 8¢ per member per month in 2014 and 2015).

States have the option to administer their own risk adjustment program, subject to federal certification. For 2014 and 2015, Massachusetts is the only state that has done so. All other states are subject to the federal methodology. The methodology includes:

- A risk adjustment model;
- The calculation of plan average actuarial risk;
- The calculation of payments and charges (transfers);
- A data collection approach; and
- A schedule.

Risk adjustment applies to all ACA-compliant individual and small group policies in each state. There is a separate risk adjustment pool for the small group and individual markets (unless the state has chosen to merge these markets). Within the individual market, there is also a separate risk adjustment pool for catastrophic plans.

A primary policy goal of the risk adjustment program is to mitigate antiselection due to the elimination of underwriting, the introduction of guaranteed issue, and the potential influx of formerly uninsured risks. If risk adjustment were to work "perfectly," an insurer would in theory be compensated adequately regardless of the demographics and health status of the population they enroll. In that case, insurers would no longer have any incentive to engage in risk selection (although direct risk selection in the form of underwriting or marketing aimed at discouraging unhealthy individuals is prohibited under the ACA, there are still many indirect selection techniques available such as benefit and formulary designs).

In the real world, however, no model is perfect. As of this writing, it remains to be seen how well risk adjustment will operate in practice.

The federal risk adjustment model is known as the **HHS-HCC model**. A risk adjustment model is a predictive model that uses inputs (here, demographics and diagnosis and other codes available on administrative claim data) to create a risk score for an individual measuring his or her relative morbidity. For more on risk adjusters, see Chapter 8.

HHS stands for the **Department of Health and Human Services**, and **HCC** stands for **hierarchical condition category**, which describes the way diagnosis codes are grouped into categories in order to assign each member a risk score. This model was loosely based on the CMS-HCC model that is used by the government to risk adjust Medicare Advantage capitation payments, but with a number of differences:

- The HHS-HCC model is *concurrent* (predicts morbidity in the same year as the diagnosis data) instead of *prospective* (predicts morbidity in the year following the diagnosis data);
- It uses different condition categories and coefficients (pregnancy and neonatal conditions, for example, are much more important for a commercial population than a Medicare population); and
- It transfers money between insurers rather than adjusting capitations paid by the government to insurers.

For much more detail on the development of the HHS-HCC model and the risk transfer formula, the reader may refer to a series of three papers[26] pub-

---

[26] Kautter, J., Pope, G. C., and Keenan, P., "Affordable Care Act Risk Adjustment: Overview, Context, and Challenges." *Medicare & Medicaid Research Review* 2014:Vol. 4, No. 3. Retrieved October 22, 2014 from http://www.cms.gov/mmrr/Downloads/MMRR2014_004_03_a02.pdf

Kautter, J., et al, "The HHS-HCC Risk Adjustment Model for Individual and Small Group Markets under the Affordable Care Act." *Medicare & Medicaid Research Review*

lished by the model developers.

Another unique feature of the HHS-HCC model is that it predicts the relative plan liability net of cost sharing of each member based on the metal level plan they are enrolled in. That is, if an identical member was in a bronze plan instead of a platinum plan, her risk score would be lower to reflect the higher cost sharing she would have to pay.

In addition to the risk scoring model itself, it is vital for insurers to understand the transfer formula used to calculate the dollar transfers between insurers using the risk scores. The formula, which appears as Equation 4.4, depends on many factors in addition to the risk score. Equation 4.4 will be applied separately for each combination of plan and rating area, and then aggregated across all plans and areas to determine the total transfer for the issuer in the state and market. In each application, however, the risk and other factors are measured against the statewide average, so relatively healthy areas will still transfer funds to relatively unhealthy areas.

The formula is:

$$T_i = \left[\frac{PLRS_i \times IDF_i \times GCF_i}{\sum_i (s_i \times PLRS_i \times IDF_i \times GCF_i)} - \frac{AV_i \times ARF_i \times IDF_i \times GCF_i}{\sum_i (s_i \times AV_i \times ARF_i \times IDF_i \times GCF_i)} \right] P_s \quad (4.4)$$

where:
- i is a plan in a rating area;
- $PLRS_i$ is the average[27] plan liability risk score from the HHS-HCC model;
- IDF_i is an induced demand factor that varies based on plan metal level;

2014:Vol. 4, No. 3. Retrieved October 22, 2014 from http://www.cms.gov/mmrr/Downloads/MMRR2014_004_03_a03.pdf

Pope, G. C., et al, "Risk Transfer Formula for Individual and Small Group Markets Under the Affordable Care Act." *Medicare & Medicaid Research Review* 2014:Vol. 4, No. 3. Retrieved October 22, 2014 from http://www.cms.gov/mmrr/Downloads/MMRR2014_004_03_a04.pdf

[27] Average risk scores and other average factors in the transfer formula are generally weighted on member months, though there are some subtleties regarding how "non-billable" children beyond the first three are handled.

- GCF_i is a geographic cost (i.e., area) factor based on average silver plan level premiums in the rating area;
- AV_i is the nominal actuarial value of the plan, (e.g. 60% for a bronze plan);
- ARF_i is the average allowable rating factor (generally the average rating age factor unless the state has imposed tiered or strict community rating);
- s_i is the share of statewide enrollment in plan i; and
- P_s is the statewide average premium in the market.

At a high level, Equation 4.4 can be thought of as follows:

$$T_i = [\text{Premium factor including morbidity} - \text{Allowable rating factor}]P_s$$

Or, put another way, the transfer is roughly based on taking "what you would like to charge" if there were no rating restrictions minus "what you are allowed to charge." In particular, just because an insurer's average risk score is greater than the statewide average, it does not mean that the insurer will receive a transfer under the program. The reason is that the formula takes into account (in the second term) an estimate of the amount of risk that the insurer was able to reflect in rates already, in the form of allowable rating factors such as age.

Another noteworthy feature of the formula is that it is based on statewide average premium rates. This will create leveraging effects for insurers with premium levels significantly higher or lower than the statewide average. The use of premium (rather than claim cost) in the formula also implicitly assumes that administrative costs are proportionate to claim costs, and could create further leveraging effects for insurers with administrative cost loads different than the market average.

The risk adjustment program does not take into account the transitional reinsurance program, so in the first few years insurers could be compensated twice for high risk individuals that trigger reinsurance payments.

There are many other subtleties of the transfer calculations, and this is a rapidly evolving area of regulation. Anyone doing analysis of risk transfers would do well to read the relevant federal regulations[28] and check for any new developments.

Data for the risk adjustment (and reinsurance) programs will be collected in a distributed manner, meaning that:

1. Each insurer will load de-identified member-level data onto a server (called an EDGE server);
2. The government will run software on the EDGE server to calculate risk scores and summarize the data; and
3. The government will receive the summarized data for purposes of calculating risk adjustment transfers and reinsurance payments.

In this way, the government avoids the need to collect member level data to administer the program (although some member level data will need to be collected as part of various audits the government will perform).

EDGE server data for each calendar year must be submitted by April 30 of the following year. The government will notify insurers of their risk adjustment transfers and reinsurance receipts by June 30 of that year, and these amounts must be reflected in insurers' risk corridor and MLR calculations, which must be filed by July 31. Risk adjustment transfers will also eventually be adjusted for error rates measured in risk adjustment data validation (RADV) audits (although there will be a lag: the results of the audits of benefit year 2016 will be used to adjust transfers for benefit year 2017, which will occur in mid-2018).

While risk adjustment is intended to stabilize the markets in the long term, in the short term it has created additional uncertainty for insurers due to the lack of data on what statewide average risk scores are likely to be. Without that information, actuaries must make assumptions to estimate potential transfers for pricing and financial statement purposes. Many insurers may not know whether they made or lost money on their 2014 ACA business until mid-2015 when the three R's are all settled, and after rates for 2016 ACA business have already been filed. As discussed in Chapter 11, forecasting and managing the risk adjustment process will be a key part of managing ACA-compliant health insurance business going forward.

---

[28] Again, a good place to start is the CCIIO website, www.cms.gov/cciio/index.html.

Temporary Risk Corridors

Like the transitional reinsurance program, the risk corridors program is only scheduled to operate for three years, from 2014 through 2016. On its face, the program seems simple: during the transition to new rating rules and given the uncertainty regarding the morbidity of the formerly uninsured (and former state and federal high risk pool members) entering the individual market, insurers will share some gains and losses with the federal government in order to reduce their risk.

In reality, however, looks can be deceiving. The details of the risk corridor program can get quite complex in practice. The program has also become a major political issue, and (perhaps ironically) has become a source of significant uncertainty for issuers in its own right.

The risk corridor program only applies to qualified health plans (QHPs) sold through a public exchange, or substantially similar plans offered by the same issuer off the exchange. The risk corridor protection is, therefore, only available to insurers that choose to participate in the exchanges. The risk corridor calculation depends on the transfer amounts that occur under the risk adjustment and reinsurance programs, so risk corridors must be set after those programs. On the other hand, risk corridors must happen before the calculation of rebates under the minimum loss ratio program, since the risk corridor transfer is an input into that calculation.

The risk corridor formula calculates the ratio of *allowable costs* to a *target amount*. Naively, the allowable costs are the actual claim costs the insurer incurs during a calendar year adjusted for risk adjustment transfers and transitional reinsurance receipts, while the target amount is earned premium less allowable administrative costs. In theory, a ratio less than 100% indicates that the insurer had lower than expected costs, while a ratio greater than 100% indicates that the insurer had higher than expected costs. The value of the ratio then determines what happens next:

- Below 92% of the target, the insurer pays 80% of the "gains" to the government.
- Between 92% and 97% of the target, the insurer pays 50% of the "gains" to the government.
- Between 97% and 103% of the target amount, there is no risk corridor payment or receivable.

- Between 103% and 108% of the target, the government reimburses 50% of the "losses" to the insurer.
- Above 108% of the target, the government reimburses 80% of the "losses" to the insurer.

Due to subtleties in the formulas, "gains" and "losses" here do not necessarily correlate with actual gains and losses for the insurer. In particular, a risk corridor ratio of 100% does not necessarily mean that an insurer broke even – in fact, the insurer could have gained or lost money. Still, a higher ratio does make it more likely that an insurer lost money and vice versa.

A full description of the complexities of the risk corridor calculation is beyond the scope of this book.[29] We will, however, review the risk corridor calculations and a few common pitfalls that can occur. In outline, the calculation is as follows (the parameters given are the original ones for 2014, which were later modified as noted later):

Claim costs = incurred claims + claim reserves
+ any payments/receipts from risk adjustment and transitional reinsurance;

Allowable costs = claim costs + quality expenses
+ health care information technology;

Profits = [premium − allowable costs − non-claim costs], floored at 3% of after-tax premium;

Administrative costs = non-claim costs − taxes/fees;

Allowable administrative costs = taxes/fees +
[administrative costs + profits, capped at 20% of after-tax premium];

Target amount = premium − allowable administrative costs; and

Risk corridor ratio = allowable costs / target amount.

---

[29] For a more thorough primer with examples, see Norris, D., van der Heijde, M. and Leida, H. "Risk Corridors under the Affordable Care Act – A Bridge over Troubled Waters, but the Devil's in the Details." Society of Actuaries *Health Watch,* Issue 73 (October 2013). The reader should be aware that rules are rapidly changing for this program, so some of the information in this article may already be out of date.

The definition of allowable costs parallels that used in the ACA minimum loss ratio program (see Chapter 9 for more on that). Some noteworthy potential pitfalls include the following.

Profits aren't profits. The target amount includes a provision for profit – but it will often not be the profit target the insurer was using when pricing the product. The profit in the risk corridor target is subject to a floor of 3% of *after-tax* premium (many insurers are, of course, used to thinking of profit as a percentage of gross premium, including taxes). In response to the transitional policy for canceled plans, the government made modifications to increase the profit floor in states allowing transitional plans in 2014, and in all states in 2015, among other changes.[30]

Allowable costs are not just claims. Besides the inclusion of risk adjustment, transitional reinsurance, and certain other non-claim expenses such as those related to quality improvement, there are other significant adjustments in determining allowable costs. In particular, there is an adjustment that takes into account the experience on non-risk corridor eligible plans that are still part of the issuer's ACA single risk pool. This further aligns the risk corridor calculation with the MLR calculation – except that the MLR calculation also includes grandfathered and transitional policies that are not part of the ACA single risk pool.

Risk is not shared only with the government. Through the MLR program, insurers with unexpectedly high profits must return some of those profits to policyholders through rebates. To the extent these profits are first shared with the government through the risk corridor program, rebates may be reduced. Thus, the risk corridor formula must strike a balance between the goal of recouping enough money from profitable insurers to offset payments to insurers with losses, and the goal of returning money to policyholders when insurers fail to meet a minimum loss ratio.

Protection is limited. The risk corridor program can dampen gains and losses, but it does not eliminate them. Moreover, for many issuers, only a fraction of their book of business will be eligible for risk corridor protection.

---

[30] See Leida, H. "Canceled plans, part III: An extension, an expansion, and more changes to 2014 rules." Milliman Insight, March 2014. Retrieved October 22, 2014 from http://us.milliman.com/uploadedFiles/insight/2014/canceled-plans-part-III.pdf.

Nothing is set in stone. Finally, there is significant political and legal uncertainty surrounding the program, including whether all payments required under the formula will actually be made.

As noted previously, HHS has changed the parameters and rules of the program significantly after insurers had already set their premium rates and strategies for 2014. The changes generally were intended to make the program more generous to insurers that might have been affected by the administration's decision to allow transitional plans. This will be accomplished by increasing the profit floor and administrative expense cap, which essentially builds more profit into the risk corridor target. For 2014, the adjustment will vary depending on the portion of the market that is in a transitional plan. For 2015, the parameters will be increased by two percentage points (to a 5% profit floor and a 22% administrative cap) in all states.

A central political issue surrounding the program has been whether it can be operated in a budget neutral manner. The risk adjustment program is budget neutral as it just moves money around between insurers, and the reinsurance program is actually designed to be a source of revenue for the U.S. Treasury. The law does not, however, require budget neutrality for the risk corridor program. The government has maintained that they expect collections to equal or exceed payments under the program, at least over the course of the three years that the program exists if not in each year.[31] Other analysts have questioned whether this is likely, however, given that plans with low premiums – which are more likely to lose money – may have greater enrollment than profitable plans with higher premiums.

The other major lever the government has available is the transitional reinsurance program. By making that program more generous for 2014 after premium rates were already set, the government essentially raised the level of profits (or reduced the level of losses) in the entire individual market. Assuming that the collected reinsurance funds are sufficient to pay submitted claims, this higher profit level could help to balance out the risk corridor program for 2014.

Furthermore, as of this writing there is legal uncertainty as to whether HHS will have the necessary authority (i.e., appropriation) to make pay-

---

[31] See https://www.cms.gov/CCIIO/Resources/Fact-Sheets-and-FAQs/Downloads/faq-risk-corridors-04-11-2014.pdf.

ments under the program.³² Given the high profile politics surrounding the issue of budget neutrality, it is possible that new legislation will modify the risk corridors again, even before the first collections and payments occur in 2015 for the 2014 plan year.³³

The Future

In 2017, two of the three premium stabilization programs are scheduled to end. The original idea was that insurers would at that point have sufficient data on the newly enrolled populations and new competitive landscape to support accurate pricing decisions.

Given the delays and challenges that arose in the law's implementation, particularly the decision to allow transitional policies to delay entering the ACA risk pool, it seems likely that pricing actuaries will still face a daunting task after the training wheels come off.³⁴ Valuation actuaries charged with estimating ACA cash flows and settlements for financial statements will face similar challenges, as will the regulators faced with reviewing the premium rates and financial solvency of insurers affected by the ACA. For the next few years at least, uncertainty seems likely to be the norm, rather than the exception.

---

[32] See "Department of Health and Human Services – Risk Corridor Program." U.S. Government Accountability Office, September 30, 2014. Retrieved December 10, 2014 from http://www.gao.gov/assets/670/666299.pdf.

[33] For a more thorough summary, see Perlman, D., Norris, D., and Leida, H.. "Risk corridors episode IV: No new hope." Milliman Insight, December 18, 2014.
http://us.milliman.com/insight/2014/Risk-corridors-episode-IV-No-new-hope/

[34] For an interesting perspective, see Wrobel, K. "The ACA Cost Predictability Question." *The Actuary*, October/November 2014.

CHAPTER 5

SETTING PREMIUM RATES

Before discussing the details of how premium rates are set, it is important to first understand the context and the overall rate setting process. In addition to the information in this chapter, there are valuable guides in the U.S. *Actuarial Standards of Practice*.[1]

5.1 THE RATE SETTING PROCESS

Rate setting generally involves two different approaches, depending on whether rates are being set: (1) based on direct, existing experience (such as the experience of an existing block of policies), sometimes called **rerating**, or (2) based on **fundamental pricing** – rating from other data sources (used as benchmarks), which are adjusted to apply to the current situation. All pricing processes use one or both of these approaches in setting rates. These two methods are discussed in detail later in this chapter.

In all methods of rate setting, the fundamental nature of the process is the same: (1) measuring the past, (2) evaluating and adapting it to the future, and (3) using the results of (1) and (2) to project the future in order to determine needed rate levels. How each of these is accomplished, however, often is challenging in many ways.

Rate setting occurs in multiple contexts, each of which will impact the rate setting process. Some of the major considerations are:

- *The market:* The marketplace itself is a major factor. How the product is priced by competitors sets expectations for consumers, and thereby limits insurers' pricing options. This can apply to rate guarantees, margins, rate structures, and the level and type of prefunding, if any.

---

[1] See www.actuarialstandardsboard.org/asops.asp.

- *Existing products:* If a company is already in the given marketplace, expectations by producers and the market will have an impact. If, for example, a company's strategy is to have a low initial rate for a product, but then apply large rate increases later, this will draw producers and policyholders who prefer that approach. Changing strategies will cause a disruption to the expectation of the groups, and could impact sales. As with all changes in direction, such changes in strategy should be made considering any potential impacts.
- *Distribution system:* The structure, compensation system, and level of control by the company are all relevant to the pricing process, as are expectations and understanding by the producers as to how rates are set and revised. Sudden changes can cause disruption and loss of business.
- *Regulatory situation:* How likely is it that the full needed rate increase will be allowed by the regulatory process? This is an important factor, as are more straightforward concerns, such as explicit limitations on how rates can be set. As an example, the ACA imposed new scrutiny on rate changes in the individual major medical market above certain thresholds (generally 10%).
- *Strategic plan and profit goals:* Pricing is, to borrow a phrase, "where the rubber hits the road" for many individual health (IH) coverages. The ability to price competitively yet profitably is an ongoing (sometimes, seemingly insurmountable) challenge, especially for companies active in the commercial market. Pricing practices and methods should reflect and contribute to achieving the company's strategic goals.

Once the context is understood, it will generally define most aspects of how rates will be structured for a product.

5.2 RATE STRUCTURES USED TODAY

Premium rates could theoretically be set to vary by any factor discovered to have a material correlation to claim costs. In practice, rating variables are generally limited to those that have both a rational causal relationship and such a correlation.[2] Such variables, depending on the coverage, might include: age, gender, occupation, geographic area at time of issue, geographic area at time of renewal, income level, current health status,

---

[2] For a thoughtful discussion of this topic, see the 2011 American Academy of Actuaries monograph "On Risk Classification," available at
http://www.actuary.org/files/publications/RCWG_RiskMonograph_Nov2011.pdf

past claim history, duration of the policy since issue, benefit plan (more on this in a minute), tobacco use status, marital and parental status, presence and nature of other coverage, and sometimes situation-specific factors, such as whether the policyholder converted from another plan of the same insurer.

The term **community rating** is one often used to describe medical insurance rating schemes, and occurs in various forms – "modified community rating," "adjusted community rating," and so forth. The term is a popular one, particularly for public policy purposes, and refers in general to a scheme where many rating variables, which might otherwise be used, are knowingly ignored. Which variables those are will vary from situation to situation, making "community rating" a slippery term to define. Community rates will typically not vary by age, gender, occupation, income level, health status, past claim history, duration, tobacco use status, or the presence or absence of other coverages. It usually allows rates to vary by geographic area (although this variable may often be limited), marital and parental status, and benefit plan. In addition, in various regulatory settings, regulators have redefined the term for their specific use in particular situations. ("Community rating by class" is one such, used by federal regulators in HMO contexts.) The bottom line is: it is important to make sure the term is well defined when using it or relying on it.

For example, the ACA imposed a form of modified community rating for individual and small group major medical coverage starting in 2014 (grandfathered and transitional plans are exempted). The allowable rating variables are:

- Age (carriers must use standard age rating factors which vary by no more than 3:1 from the oldest to the youngest adult ages);
- Tobacco (limited to no more than a 50% surcharge for users);
- Area (rating areas are prescribed by the state, but factors are unlimited unless limited by state law);
- Family tiering/structure (family rates must generally equal the sum of member level rates, with the number of child dependents capped at three); and
- Plan (including benefits, cost sharing, and network).

Health status may not be included in any of the rating factors. States are free to impose more restrictive requirements if they like, and some do.

There is much work being done today on **predictive models**, used to predict future claim costs for individuals and groups based on past claim history, prescription drug use, or other information. These investigations are likely to become an integral part of the underwriting process for most carriers (at least those allowed to underwrite risks), and will likely affect the rate structures.

In the P&C insurance market, there is a controversial issue regarding whether P&C rates should be able to vary based on the insured's credit score. This is an example of consumer data used in underwriting. This is a newly developing area of underwriting in individual and small group health insurance. Its ultimate usefulness has not yet been tested in the market. With the prohibition of underwriting for individual major medical starting in 2014, these tools may instead find their applications in care management or other programs where one needs to stratify the population by health status.

Descriptions of the major rating structure elements follow. In these descriptions, the rating structure variables are related to the corresponding characteristics of the underlying data. In some cases, however, the premium rate relativities chosen may not follow the claim cost relativities for the rating cells, either because of regulatory restrictions or as a business decision by the insurer. To the extent the chosen rate relativities deviate from the underlying claim relativities, subsidies are being created from one rate cell to another. Subsidies can create antiselective situations, and increase the insurer's risk.

AGE

There are three major categories by which rate structures treat the age of policyholders. First, there is **attained age rating**. Under this approach, a policyholder's rate is a function of his age at renewal. Someone age 25 who buys a policy, and pays the age 25 rate, will next year pay the (then current) age 26 rate. If the attained age rates are grouped into rate categories larger than a single age, such as in 5 year (quinquennial) age groupings, this is called **step rating** or **age banding**.

If the rates reflect the age at issue, but not the age at renewal, then the rating scheme is called **entry age** or **issue age rating**. This rating scheme is usually accompanied by a corresponding reserve to offset the increasing costs in future years (called the "active life reserve," "policy reserve," or "contract reserve"). These are described more fully in the chapter on reserves.

In some circumstances, age structures do not recognize age at all, which might be called a **uni-age rating** scheme. Most community rate structures are uni-age. Since age-based rates might vary by a factor as much as 3:1 or 4:1 (for adults under age 65 – if children are included the ratio would be even higher), charging an average rate over all ages creates a significant disparity between the actual cost and the price charged. This leads to a situation ripe for antiselection. (Antiselection, and the art of dealing with it, is discussed further in Chapter 4.) Unless all carriers use similar rate structures in a given market, a company using uni-age rating can experience severe antiselection. One such example occurred with an insurer that determined, while it issued policies from ages 18 to 64 with a common rate, its average policyholder age was 57. (These later ages were the only ones with a premium rate that was competitive with carriers using age-based rating.) Under the ACA, all carriers selling individual major medical must use the same age rating factors in each state. We will discuss this in more detail later.

Medical and Med Supp coverages tend to use attained age rates, or, when regulated to do so, issue age or uni-age rates. These products are most easily characterized as "inflation sensitive" coverages – the claim costs tend to go up each year with increasing health care costs. The impact of claim trend (sometimes 10% to 20% per year, or even more) tends to overshadow the impact of year-to-year age increases (typically 2% to 3% per year), so rate structures intended to level the age increases, such as issue age rate structures, can become fairly ineffective for these types of policies if claim trends remain high.

Non-inflation sensitive coverages, particularly those with relatively fixed benefits, are more prone to use age-leveling premium structures. For this reason, DI, LTC, and HIP coverages all tend to be sold on an issue age basis. In this case, leveling of age increases in the premium structure can be quite effective. In fact, for non-cancelable policies, the premium rates are actually guaranteed not to increase.

Claim costs do vary significantly by age for virtually all coverages. People at older ages tend to generate higher claim costs than people at younger ages for most coverages. (Two counterexamples are maternity coverage and accidental death coverage, but there are not many such examples.)

Underwriting has a particular impact on the age curve. This is because the age curve describes the relative claim costs of *average* insureds at each age. For some products, the average insureds at higher ages have significantly higher expected claim costs than the average younger insured. To the extent underwriting is effective, it has the impact of weeding out those at higher ages with chronic diseases or predictably high claim costs, having a relatively greater impact at the higher ages. This is one reason why the morbidity by age curve for individual insurance has historically tended to be substantially flatter than that of large group insurance, where there was no individual underwriting.

Typical age curves for different coverages are illustrated in Figure 5.1. The relativities have been multiplied by a factor so that the average factor for each coverage, over an assumed typical population, averages to 1.00. (This process is called *normalization* of the factors over that population.) Note that the Accidental Death coverage has factors that *decrease* above the younger ages (and would be even more pronounced if the graph extended to still younger ages); this is one of the few coverages which does so. The slope of most coverages varies by duration; the slope in this graph represents an average slope over all durations.

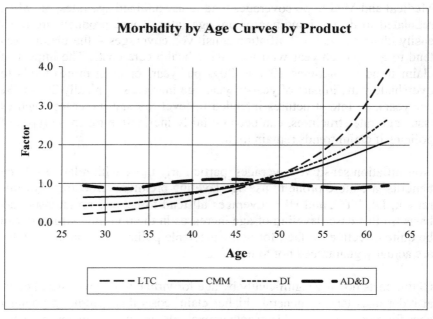

Figure 5.1

As mentioned previously, the ACA requires carriers to use prescribed age factors when setting premium rates in the individual and small group markets starting in 2014. Since all carriers are subject to the same rating rules, there is less chance of antiselection between carriers due to this limitation (but still a chance for antiselection against the market as a whole). While the reason for the overall restriction in the range of the age factors (3:1 for adults) may be political, the reason a standard age curve is required in each market is technical. In order to account for the age rating in the risk adjustment program (discussed in Chapter 4 on antiselection), the government decided to require all carriers in each market to use the same rating factors for age, so that they could be taken into account in the risk adjustment formula. States can propose alternative age curves as long as they vary no more than the 3:1 ratio required by federal law.

DURATION

Rather than "age of the policyholder," duration measures "age of the policy." Many coverages show definite durational trends in claim costs beyond those generated by insured age alone. This typically comes from two sources. The first has to do with initial underwriting, which causes the policyholders at duration zero (time of issue) to be relatively healthy. In major medical coverage, for example, initial underwriting has historically caused first year claims to be roughly 60-65% of average claims over the life of the policy, after adjustment for aging of the insured and trends. Starting in 2014, such underwriting is prohibited in the major medical market.

In DI coverage, the durational claim curve is much more modest; some DI carriers have, in fact, experienced early claim costs higher than in later years. This argues that there is another mechanism at work on the durational costs. LTC durational curves are much steeper than most other coverages, with year one costs sometimes being 20-30% of "ultimate" costs.

Underwriting selection is usually assumed to wear off fully by about duration year four or five for DI coverage, year two for Med Supp, and year 10 for LTC.[3]

---

[3] Early actuarial theory assumed a short-lived selection effect of underwriting on claim costs, perhaps 3 or 4 years, with those costs becoming flat by duration thereafter. This flat period was called the "ultimate" period. This concept only works if durational impacts

The second durational force is known as cumulative antiselection,[4] and is described in detail in Chapter 4.

Some medical carriers build durational deterioration into their rate structure, charging rates which explicitly vary by duration. Others do not do so explicitly, but may close their blocks of business to allow them to sell new policies at lower rates. In the latter case, each year the policies in force in such a closed block will all grow one year older in duration, and this will be reflected (of necessity) in the resulting rate analysis. (If not reflected as explicit durational analysis, it will be implicitly part of the trend analysis.) For major medical, neither of these approaches is allowed beginning in 2014 under the ACA.

Companies that manage their individual business as ongoing, open blocks, will typically not see the same dramatic impact of duration on the results for the block, but such forces are operating nonetheless. (See "the block rating approach," later in this chapter.) Duration can often be found to be the explanation for otherwise puzzling fluctuations in experience.

Durational analysis is vital in evaluating rates and forecasting (projecting) future financial results. Figure 5.2 demonstrates the durational factors that the Academy's Rate Filing Task Force felt were representative of the commercial individual CMM market at the time.

GENDER, MARITAL, AND PARENTAL STATUS

Unless prohibited by law or regulation, most coverages have different rates by gender. (The ACA, for example, prohibits rate structures for major medical coverage that differentiate by gender.) The notable exception to this is in LTC insurance, where market conditions maintained unisex rates for a long time – recently, however, most LTC carriers have moved to introduce gender rating. Sex distinct rates are typical for DI coverage, except in the employer sponsored multi-life market where unisex rates are more common. For most coverages, there is a clear difference in

---

stop at some point, which means it generally doesn't apply to major medical coverage, in the author's judgment, at least through most of its policy life.

[4] Bluhm, William F., "Cumulative Antiselection Theory," *Transactions of the Society of Actuaries*, 1982.

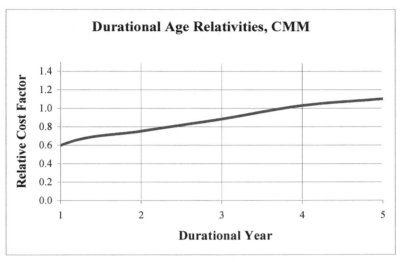

Figure 5.2

experience by gender and by age/gender combinations. Interestingly, experience (even non-maternity experience) can also vary by marital status. In LTC insurance, for example, an important element in determining the likelihood that someone will need care in a nursing home is whether they have a spouse at home – those with spouses have lower claim costs than those without.

Each type of coverage has its own characteristic age/gender curve. A few representative ones are shown in Figures 5.3-5.6. These come from various claim cost tools, based on large and polished databases. Figures 5.3, 5.5, and 5.6 are from proprietary Milliman pricing tools. Figure 5.4 is from SOA study data.[5] Figure 5.7 comes from one analysis of a single carrier's data, so likely is not directly representative of what other carriers should expect.

---

[5] "Report of the Individual Disability Experience Committee Analysis of Experience from 1990 to 1999," Society of Actuaries. This can be found at www.soa.org.

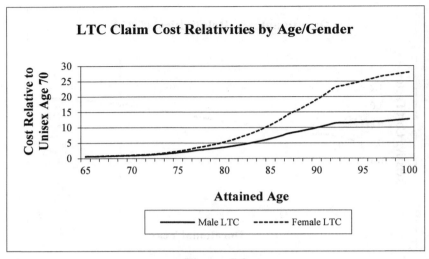

Figure 5.3

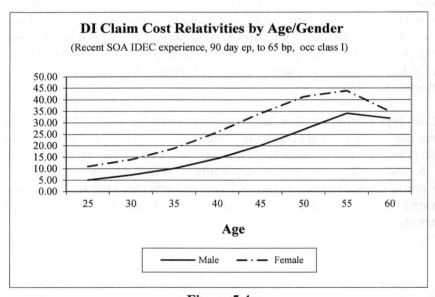

Figure 5.4

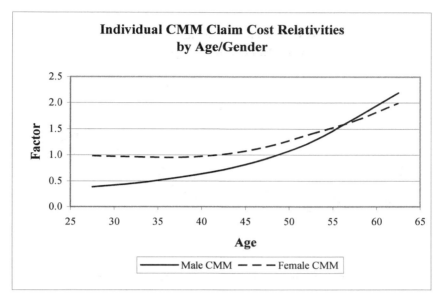

Figure 5.5

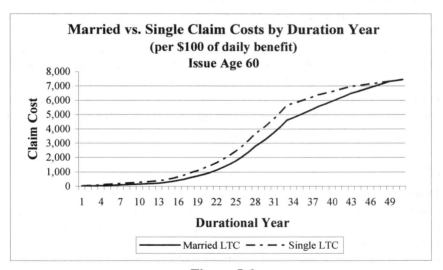

Figure 5.6

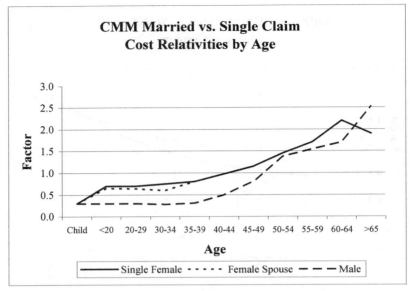

Figure 5.7

Of course, it will cost more to insure a family of four than a single individual, so there is an obvious need to vary premium rates as a function of how many people are insured, and whether they are adults or children. Sometimes, "two person" rates do not differentiate between an adult and child vs. two adults. Some family policies also do not differentiate rates based on how many children there are above some number. (That number might be zero, but typically is higher, so that rates can be competitive for small families. The ACA sets this number at three for major medical coverage in the individual and small group markets.)

OCCUPATION

Disability income insurance is the one area of individual health insurance that relies heavily on occupation, both in underwriting and in rate setting. DI carriers have historically had different sets of rates for different *occupation classes*. In the past, DI companies often had four occupation classes. In recent years, the number of occupation classes has expanded as companies have added multiple occupation classes for medical professionals and separated their top occupation class for non-medical occupations into 2-3 additional classes. This differential is based on historical experience, combined with underwriting judgment.

A variable similar to occupation – income level – was sometimes used to set rates early in the medical insurance market. This was typically done by Blue Shield or Blue Cross plans, in keeping with a perceived social mission by those companies. This was buttressed by a belief (which may have been true at the time, but not any more) that lower income insureds tended to use their benefits less often than higher income insureds, all else being equal.

Today, occupation is generally not used as a rating classification except for DI coverages.

GEOGRAPHIC AREA

There are actually at least *two* geographic locations that are relevant to this discussion: location of *issue* and location of *residence*.

Depending on circumstances, either the state of issue or the state of residence can have jurisdiction over the renewal rates for a policy. This is discussed in the chapters on policy forms and regulation.

Area of residence is an important variable in setting rates for many coverages. Foremost among these is medical coverage, where both utilization and average costs per service might vary from place to place. In particular, there are clear patterns of care which vary geographically. In one area, for example, caesarian sections might be done more frequently than in others. It is sometimes hypothesized that these differences often arise from particular medical schools' teachings. Prevailing charges may be quite different by area as well. In addition, provider contracts may be concentrated in a geographic area, requiring insureds who are treated outside that area to use non-network doctors, which generally results in a higher cost.

Other coverages affected by area include LTC (where one state's much higher availability of nursing homes might cause utilization to be higher), and DI (where varying legal environments by state can cause large differences in claim costs). Granularity of geographic rating areas for medical coverages tends typically to be much finer than for other coverages, often to a level where rates might vary by county or by three digit zip code.

Starting in 2014, rating areas for individual and small group major medical coverage are standardized in each state. States propose the rating areas, which are then subject to federal approval. Carriers are free to set rating factors for each area, provided they can justify them in their rate filings. Again, a likely driver of this regulatory approach was to enable area rating to be taken into account more simply in the ACA risk adjustment program (discussed in Chapter 4).

OTHER FACTORS

Some other factors that might be included in the rate structure are current health status (substandard rates for higher risks), past claim history (sometimes renewal rates can be based on claim experience), tobacco use status (smokers' coverage generally costs more than that of non-smokers), weight (a topic with much recent press coverage and research), presence and nature of other coverage (such as '24-hour' coverage vs. non-coverage of work-related costs, or coordination with OASDI disability benefits), and sometimes situation-specific factors (such as whether the policyholder converted from another plan of the same insurer).

As pointed out previously, under healthcare reform, the only one of the factors in the previous paragraph that is still allowed for individual major medical after 2014 is tobacco use status, with a limit of 1.5:1 on the ratio of smoker to non-smoker rates.

5.3 FUNDAMENTAL PRICING

Fundamental pricing involves using tables or claim costs developed through other sources as the basis for pricing. This is particularly useful when pricing a new benefit, or if the available experience is either inappropriate or insufficient for the current pricing exercise.

Using a company's own experience is generally preferable to using other sources, because it was usually generated by a group of policies that were underwritten in the same way, by the same underwriting department, used the same network of providers, was administered by the same claim department using similar interpretations of provisions, was produced by the same network of producers, and came from a similar pool of prospects. There are a myriad of reasons why, for example, a published table's experience might differ from a company's own experience.

It is the pricing actuary's responsibility to sort through these reasons, and give quantitative estimates of those that are material. It is much easier to start with existing experience, and avoid the higher risk of not seeing or understanding some of the reasons for differences. Of course, even when starting with a company's own experience, there is still no guarantee that the future will resemble the past, and the pricing actuary must still make her best effort to take that into account.

There are three basic methods used in fundamental rate development: (1) tabular, (2) build up and density functions, and (3) simulation.

5.4 FUNDAMENTAL PRICING – TABULAR METHOD

In this method, an existing table, or a modification of it, is used as the morbidity (claim cost) basis for pricing. This method is typically used for long term, non-inflation sensitive products, like DI. (For inflationary policies, where future claims and premiums will both be leveraged upward by unknown and highly unpredictable trend rates, the value of precise calculations, afforded by the tabular method, disappears.)

Today, the most common basis for pricing of disability income is some modification of the 1985 CIDA tables,[6] developed by a Society of Actuaries committee. These modifications reflected companies' own experience. The most recent available public experience[7] shows that the 85CIDA tables overstated claim terminations for the first 18 months of claim, and thus understated claim duration (and claim costs) by a substantial amount. At the same time, frequencies of claim were about on target overall with that predicted by the table, but this varies significantly among certain occupational classes. New industry tables are being developed by the SOA and the AAA to replace the 85CIDA tables. Even after the new tables have been adopted, companies will most likely reflect their own experience to some extent in their pricing of DI products.

---

[6] *TSA XXXVII*, "Report of the Society of Actuaries Committee to Recommend New Disability Tables for Valuation" 1985.

[7] "Report of the Individual Disability Experience Committee Analysis of Experience from 1990 to 1999," op. cit.

The exact method used for the tabular approach depends on the number of "claim states" (and their order) in which a claim can occur. A DI claimant, for example, might be first fully disabled, then partially disabled, then return to fully disabled. Similarly, there tend to be multiple such decrements in LTC insurance as well, such as progression from home health care to assisted living facility to nursing home care.

The modeling technique used for this purpose is typically a deterministic one. (Stochastic models are studied under another pricing method – the simulation method.) A representative policy is followed throughout its potential lifetime, with probabilities of claim at each duration, multiplied by the corresponding cost of that claim. The sum of all such products is then the **claim cost** per unit of coverage (such as 'per $10 of monthly benefit") or **net premium**, which forms the basis (along with expenses and profit) of the gross premium. In symbols, the calculation of the net premium might look like this:

$$NP = \sum_{z=issue\ yr}^{final\ yr} \Pr\{Clm_z\} \times AC_z \times v^z \times \ell_z \qquad (5.1)$$

where

z varies from the year of issue to the final possible year of the contract,

$\Pr\{Clm_z\}$ is the probability of a disability claim occurring ("incidence rate" or "frequency rate") in year z,

AC_z is the average claim (assuming a claim occurs) in year z,

v^z is the present value factor corresponding to year z, $(1+i)^{-z}$, and

ℓ_z is the proportion of originally issued lives still in force in year z, typically calculated by applying decrements for lapsation and death to the starting model population.

In turn, AC_z is calculated as the sum of the product of a number of things. This might be thought of as a conditional calculation – *assuming* a claim occurs in year z, then the average cost of that claim is the sum of the cost calculated in each future period, multiplied by the probability of the claim continuing to the end of that period.

$$AC_z = \sum_{s=1}^{FnlCmPyt} \{Cm\$\}_s \times \Pr\{1-Tn_s\} \times v^s \qquad (5.2)$$

where

s is the claim duration.

(This may not be stated in the same units over its range; in the 85CIDA tables, the units start at days, and end at years);

$Cm\$_s$ is the claim dollars payable at claim duration s;

$\Pr\{1-Tn_s\}$ is the probability of a claimant at claim duration 0 remaining disabled at duration s; and

$FnlCmPyt$ is the claim duration of final possible claim payment.

These calculations are easily done with the aid of today's spreadsheet programs.

EXERCISE 5.1: Using unmodified 85CIDA as the morbidity basis,[8] to a female policyholder age 45, in occupation class 1, with 91 day elimination period, and to-age-65 benefit period, calculate:

(a) the probability of not having a claim in the first policy year, but then having a claim in the second policy year,

(b) the probability of remaining disabled for exactly 6 months, and

(c) the claim cost for a monthly benefit of $5,000 (assuming 5% interest rate). □

For most other coverages, there are no publicly available tables comparable to the CIDA table. As spreadsheet programs have proliferated, there has been greater ability within insurance companies to analyze and create their own claim costs, so the demand for published tables dropped dramatically. Nevertheless, these techniques are still used with a company's home-grown claim cost tables.

Tabular rating calculations can be much more complex than these relatively easy formulae and example. Such complications might be necessary for any or all of the following reasons (or for others, as well):

---

[8] The relevant data and solutions to this and all other exercises are included in the electronic files distributed with this text, which are available through the publisher's website.

- *Modal premiums.* This refers to premiums which might be paid other than annually. Since most tables use annual modes (such as annual claim costs), but most insurance policies are paid more frequently, this needs to be reflected in the calculations.
- *Modal lapse rates.* If premiums are paid more frequently than annually, lapse rates will need to be calculated, and perhaps vary, for matching frequency. This is particularly true at the earliest durations, when lapse rates are still changing sufficiently to make "within the year" variation worth pursuing.
- *Exposure calculations.* Various elements of the premium calculation might be expressed as a function of earned premium, written premium, received premium, incurred claims, paid claims, claim reserves, number of policies, number of premium payments in a year, first year premium, face amount, or others. If they are needed for the calculation, then these exposure values must be calculated.
- *Additional benefits.* DI and LTC policies have a wide array of additional benefits and benefit modifications which complicate these calculations. One add-on benefit might be a DI or LTC benefit that automatically increases claim payments (once the claim occurs) by 3% per year, to address inflation in costs of living. In calculating the claim cost for this modification, then, the pricing actuary must index the stream of benefit payments in Equation 5.2 as follows:

$$CC_z = \sum_{s=1}^{FnlCmPyt} \{Cm\$\}_s \times \{1.03^{s/12}\} \times \Pr\{1 - Tn_s\} \times v^s \qquad (5.3)$$

(The calculation of the index has been simplified for exposition, by assuming the indexing occurs monthly. It would actually most often be a step function, with indexing occurring annually.)

- *Interest.* For many years, interest assumptions for present value calculations were set at a fixed rate over the future life of the policies. In today's environment we often need to view interest in a more complex way. This might be by: (1) varying the interest rate assumed to occur over time in the future, (2) testing alternative interest rate scenarios, or even (3) treating interest as a stochastic variable. For pricing purposes, this is often simplified to a single future rate for each year, or a rate for all years. For coverages under which asset accumulation can be a significant part of the profit equation (such as DI and LTC), care should be taken to adequately assess the interest risk.

- *Multiple decrements.* Most coverages have two "states" that the insured can be in – either on claim or not. Some, however, can have multiple states. LTC coverage, for example, might have care paths which involve no care, home health care, assisted living, and nursing home care. DI coverage might involve full disability, partial disability, and residual disability. Some of these decrements might be conditional on having a prior condition (such as residual disability requiring full disability for a certain period first, or recovery facility care in a medical contract requiring an inpatient stay first.)

There are a variety of actuarial or mathematical techniques available to model such benefits. These include Monte Carlo simulations, in which a specific individual is assigned a path based on random numbers applied to probabilities.[9] Another is Markov processes, which use linear algebra to model the change in claimants' states over time.[10] Yet another is classical multiple, contingent decrement actuarial commutation functions.[11]

Most commonly, though, multiple states are studied using detailed, deterministic models based on computer spreadsheets which successively predict each future year from the prior one, using assumed decrement rates.

5.5 FUNDAMENTAL PRICING – BUILDUP AND DENSITY FUNCTIONS

For inflation-sensitive products, a different approach is more often used than the tabular approach described earlier. There are actually two different approaches, the **buildup** and **density function** approaches, used for this type of pricing. These can be intermingled in the pricing process, depending on the nature of the specific benefits being analyzed.

---

[9] See the December, 1994 report of the American Academy of Actuaries' Task Force on Health Organizations Risk Based Capital, for a classic example.
[10] Jones, Bruce L., "An Analysis of Long-Term Care Data from Hamilton-Wentworth, Ontario," *Actuarial Research Clearing House,* Vol. 1. p. 338-351.
[11] Jordan, Chester Wallace, Jr. *Life Contingencies,* 1967. p. 271-330.

Both methods are based on building a model which describes expected claims in the pricing period. Any changes due to inflationary or other cost trends in the rating period (period in which the rates will be effective) will be taken into account, but not projected into the future.

This discussion will be framed in terms of major medical coverage. Other coverages can generally be considered as simplified versions of the same methodology.

BUILDUPS

The first approach is called a "buildup" or "cost model" method. In this approach, the benefits provided are considered the sum of a number of composing pieces, each of which has its own benefit calculated. This can happen from relatively little detail (such as "hospital" vs. "other") to relatively great detail (perhaps 40-50 categories of claims or more). Each category would have its own claim cost calculation, as the product of claim (service) frequency times the average cost per service. Each of these, in turn, might be calculated from a database kept by the company or purchased, with modifications made to be applicable to the current situation.

This type of calculation lends itself well to "copay" benefits, in which the insured pays a fixed amount for a given service. Because of this, the insurer will pay less to the provider of those services, and this needs to be reflected in the claim cost calculation. The calculation is a simple one, using (frequency of service) × (copay amount) = (reduction in claim cost). This calculation quantifies the primary impact of a copay.

Often there is a secondary calculation which must be made. This is because the change in benefit itself might impact the behavior of insureds. For example, the value of increasing office copays from $10 to $25 will be more than just $15 times the existing frequency of office visits – there will also be some reduction in frequency because of the higher copay.

In some cases there may even be tertiary effects. Increasing a hospital inpatient per diem copay, for example, might have the primary effect of reducing claim costs. It might also have the secondary effect that some inpatient days might be avoided. It might also cause an increase in outpatient frequencies, to the extent patients seek the same treatment on an outpatient basis that they otherwise would have sought on an inpatient basis.

In certain circumstances, such as prescription drug coverage, it is possible for a copay to be more than the cost of some of the associated services (a generic drug copay might, for example, be set at $10 while a particular drug only costs $5). In that circumstance, it is common to cap the actual member liability at the cost of the service. It is important to account for this when valuing the copay. The usual approach is to use a continuance table (e.g., a probability distribution of the cost per generic prescription) to calculate an "effective copay" less than the nominal amount.

Often, the units used in these calculations are "per member per month", or **PMPM**. (Some practitioners loosely (and erroneously) refer to claim costs themselves as PMPMs.) This terminology is primarily used by HMOs and managed care plans, and less frequently in commercial IH insurance.

Such a development of build-up method claim costs might look like that in Table 5.1, using illustrative data.

Table 5.1

	Buildup Method				
Service Category	Annual Utilization per 1,000 (a)	Average Charge (b)	Gross Claim Costs PMPM (c)	Cost Sharing (d)	Net Claim Costs PMPM (e)
Hospital Inpatient					
Medical	130.1	$3,277.00	$35.53		$35.53
Surgical	84.2	$5,369.13	$37.67		$37.67
Psychiatric	25.7	$1,209.23	$2.59		$2.59
Substance Abuse	15.4	$803.91	$1.03	$20	$1.01
Skilled Nursing Care	11.2	$1,008.25	$0.94	$50	$0.89
Hospital Outpatient					
Emergency Room	207	$663.46	$11.44	$5	$11.36
Surgery	122	$3,528.90	$35.88		$35.88
Radiology	190	$728.51	$11.53	$10	$11.38
Laboratory	225	$226.89	$4.25		$4.25
Pharmacy and Blood	160	$219.81	$2.93		$2.93
PT/OT/ST	66	$287.03	$1.58	$15	$1.50
Physician					
...					

In Table 5.1, the less obvious columns were calculated as follows:

$$(c) = (a) \times (b) / (12 \text{ months} \times 1{,}000 \text{ lives}), \quad (5.4)$$

and

$$(e) = (c) - [(a) \times (d) / (12 \text{ months} \times 1{,}000 \text{ lives})]. \quad (5.5)$$

DENSITY FUNCTIONS

The size of a claim can be considered a random variable. In medical insurance, we typically think of this random variable as continuous, or close to it. There is, however, typically no continuous function which adequately describes the claim distribution, so the conceptual continuous function is usually described discretely. Provided the discrete representation is sufficiently granular (detailed), we can interpolate as needed without large errors.

In contrast to the buildup approach, density functions typically (but not always) describe the *total* claims attributable to an individual in a year. The claims result from a given set of benefits, but there are usually no calculations of the cost of component benefits.

Density functions are also sometimes called **continuance** or **continuation** functions. This arose originally in the days before large health care trends. They were often used in fixed indemnity situations, when the size of a claim was simply the number of days or weeks of claim times the amount per day or week. Thus, the curve measured how long the claim *continued*.

Because the density function approach describes a comprehensive benefit, it is very useful when calculating the impact of deductibles, out of pocket limits, and other benefit characteristics which do not depend on the particular service being provided. By itself, however, it cannot reflect the cost sharing elements that might exist at the individual benefit level. Table 5.2 illustrates the density function for a CMM product.

Table 5.2

CMM Product Density Function	
(1) **Annual Frequency**	**(2)** **Total Annual Claim Costs**
0.2427147	$0.00
0.0577467	51.98
0.0777254	134.03
0.0560329	261.61
0.0431136	404.63
0.0346984	557.10
0.0310039	719.65
0.0262755	880.02
0.0454931	1,045.12
0.0529088	1,209.49
⋮	⋮
0.0000161	552,747.44
0.0000203	631,851.06
0.0000129	716,479.28
0.0000128	880,361.43
0.0000049	1,414,459.52
Sum Total 1.0000000	Weighted Average $3,000.00

The distribution function, as you may recall from early statistics classes, is the partial sum of the density function. This table gives us much information. For example:

- The overall claim cost is $3,000.
- 24.3% of insureds will have zero claims. Conversely, 75.7% of them will have claims.[12]

---

[12] When using empirical density tables such as Table 5.2, it is important to understand how members with partial year enrollment were handled. Many plan features like deductibles commonly operate on a per unique individual per year basis, while premiums are often paid monthly. Member turnover must be taken into account when converting from "per unique individual" to "per member month of exposure" values.

EXERCISE 5.2: Calculate the claim cost for a CMM benefit, with a $1,000 deductible, and 80% coinsurance until $2,000 out-of-pocket expenses occur, after which the benefit is 100%. (Table 5.2 is reproduced for use in this exercise in the electronic files distributed with this text. Hint: for each entry in column (2), calculate the benefit corresponding to it using the relevant data in those files.) ☐

The density function approach becomes difficult to deal with when trying to evaluate the impact of changes in portions of the benefits, such as copays. Calculating the impact of a $10 office copay, for example, would be difficult, because we would have to measure what marginal impact that change would have at each level of *total* claim dollars. A claimant with $1,000 in total expenses might have no office visits in that $1,000, he might have the entire $1,000 composed of office visits, or he might have something in-between. To truly evaluate the impact of that $10 copay would require developing a profile of the claims at each level.

A much preferable approach is to modify the underlying claims to reflect what "would have happened if the $10 copay had been in effect," and then develop a density function from that.

This can be approximated, if need be, by calculating the expected value of the copay on the total expected claim cost using the build-up approach, and then allocating that change in value over the whole curve in a way that the resulting new curve has a shape that we believe appropriate. Another approximation might be to interpolate between two known curves – one with office visit benefits, the other without.

COMBINING BUILDUP AND DENSITY IN PPOS AND HYBRID PLANS

Major medical products are often sold as **PPO products**. (PPO stands for "preferred provider organization".) The insurer will have agreements in place with providers, either directly or through a third party who "rents out" the provider network. Benefits differ depending on whether the patient receives services from a participating (**in-network**) or a non-participating (**out-of-network**) provider. This same situation can occur with the out-of-area claims for an HMO's point of service product.

In-network benefits often have copays associated with them. Out-of-network benefits typically have significant deductibles and coinsurance instead. The proportion of claims occurring in each will depend on many things, but most importantly on: (1) the financial incentives between the two sets of benefits, and (2) availability and quality of in-network providers to the insured.

Network provider payments are usually either discounted from otherwise applicable charge levels, or are subject to other payment mechanisms. For this reason, average charge levels are likely to differ significantly between in-network and out-of-network claims. In some cases, carriers have designed tiered network plans with various levels of in-network providers, and further reductions in cost sharing to steer members towards the most preferred tiers.

When calculating claim costs for such PPO programs, the typical approach is to separately calculate in-network claim costs (using the buildup approach) and out-of-network claim costs (using the density approach), and then combine these two claim costs as a weighted average, where the weights are the relative claim dollars expected to occur in and out of network. These weights are typically in the range of 5-15% out-of-network, and 85-95% in-network, but this can and does vary widely.

More recently, fully "hybrid" plan designs which combine copays and a global deductible, coinsurance, and an out of pocket maximum – even on the in-network benefit – have become quite common. There are endless potential variations on this theme (e.g., copays on just the first three office visits, after which the benefit reverts to deductible/coinsurance). Appropriately valuing these benefits requires carefully combining both approaches so that each category of claim cost is allocated to the correct type(s) and levels of cost sharing.

In fact, several ACA mandates led to further complications of hybrid plans in the individual and small group markets. Plans must have a single overall out of pocket maximum for in-network services, not to exceed a statutory level. All cost sharing must accumulate to the maximum, whether copay, coinsurance, or deductible. Thus, if a plan has both a deductible and copays, the actuary must determine an appropriate way to estimate their combined impact on the out of pocket maximum. In another twist, preventive services must have no cost sharing, so it is necessary to carve them out from other services before valuing copays and other cost sharing.

One example of such a calculation that is publicly available is the **actuarial value calculator** published[13] by the federal government. This spreadsheet must be used to estimate the **actuarial value** of each major medical benefit plan offered by an insurer; that is, the ratio of claims net of member cost sharing to the total allowed claim amounts including member cost sharing for a standard population. The actuarial value must fall into certain specified ranges (called metal levels) for the plan to be compliant with the law. If there are plan design features that cannot be valued in the spreadsheet tool, the insurer must obtain a certification from an actuary that the plan meets the requirements.

One new approach that has become possible due to advances in computing power is to take a large claim database in which each member's claim and cost sharing amounts have been broken down into service categories as in the build-up method. Then, in order to price a new benefit, it is possible to do an approximate re-adjudication of the cost sharing in the database to adjust it to the new plan design. This seriatim approach can enable complex interactions between plan elements to be modeled accurately; appropriately adjusting for induced utilization effects can, however, be more challenging (since one would have to estimate how each member might have behaved differently if they had been subjected to different cost sharing requirements).

5.6 FUNDAMENTAL PRICING – SIMULATION

Another pricing approach that builds on the power of seriatim calculations is a stochastic one based on Monte Carlo simulations. (For a refresher on Monte Carlo simulations, see any undergraduate statistics text.)[14] The basis of this method is to use an assumed, existing distribution of expected claims (perhaps the prior year's actual claim costs), and then project each existing policy forward into the rating period, using all known information about the claimants/policyholders.

At an overly simplistic level, the future claim level for a policy can be considered to be a purely random fluctuation from the average (expected) overall claim level. In reality, future claims are fairly highly (at perhaps

---

[13] See http://www.cms.gov/cciio/resources/regulations-and-guidance/index.html
[14] One example is *Applications of Monte Carlo Methods to Finance and Insurance* by Herzog and Lord.

25%) correlated with past claims.[15] This can be built into the projection as a random fluctuation modified by this correlation. As predictive models become more sophisticated, this prediction engine can be further improved by applying correlation values which are dependent on prior claim experience (diagnosis, prescriptions, other claim data). While such methods will probably never be able to predict individual claims with a high degree of confidence, they certainly will provide good estimates for groups of such individuals, which is necessary in setting rates for a whole block.

Such a simulation for an individual's claims can be constructed in various ways. A good method is to first develop an "expected" value based on the whole block's experience. Then the expected value is modified for past experience, claim history, or other medical information about the individual. Finally, it is modified to simulate random statistical fluctuation from this adjusted expected value.

It is important in doing such simulations to differentiate between the statistical fluctuations experienced because the block is not infinite in size (sometimes called "statistical fluctuation"), and the deviations of the block's results because we cannot unerringly predict the block's future average cost, regardless of its size (which ends up being named many things, depending on context, but often called "historical fluctuation"). To construct an accurate model, it is necessary to include both sources of fluctuation in the model, and to calibrate the model to match actual historical experience. This is a concept which the American Academy of Actuaries' Health Organizations Risk Based Capital Task Force adopted and used in developing the original formula used by the NAIC for Risk Based Capital for Health Organizations.

If there are new business policies being sold beyond the experience period, a 'new business module' is probably needed, to generate new issues for the model, and to predict their financial results. This provides for an accurate prediction of total financial results for the whole block in the rating period.

---

[15] Fuhrer, Chuck, "Some Applications of Credibility Theory to Group Insurance," *Transactions of the Society of Actuaries*, Vol. 40 pt. 1. pp 387-404.

The advantage of this stochastic method is that it allows us to examine the projections over the whole distribution of future claim results, over the whole portfolio. To the extent we need to know policyholder behavior (such as the likelihood of lapsing as a result of a rate increase), this method allows behavior to be modeled on a policy-by-policy basis. The other methods all base their calculations on average expected results, rather than the whole distribution of results, and there is a danger that such averages may mislead.

In addition, this method lets us develop extensive and complicated functional relationships between model values. The lapse rate, for example, might depend on the rate increase percentage presented, the prior rate increase, the absolute rate level relative to the marketplace, characteristics of the policyholder, the policyholder's own claim experience, and other factors. Many of these relationships are not linear, so it may be misleading to assume average values for each of them and then calculate average lapse rates. Seriatim calculations let us automatically take those non-linear relationships into account.

5.7 RERATING

If pricing is treated as an adjustment to existing rates (even for a new policy form), the process is a simple one (at least in concept), involving five steps:

- Step 1: Gather Experience.
- Step 2: Restate Experience.
- Step 3: Project Past Results to the Future.
- Step 4: Compare the Projection against Desired Results.
- Step 5: Apply Regulatory and Management Adjustments.

STEP 1: GATHER EXPERIENCE

Start with actual experience on existing business. ("Experience" is a term of art which generally describes the historical premium and claim figures relevant to the block in question.) This is to quantitatively answer the question "What happened?"

There are some clear guidelines which should be used in gathering experience.[16] First, it is usually preferable to deal with *incurred* claims and *earned* premium. By using these, rather than paid claims and premiums received, we are dealing with the financial values actually attributable to the experience period. This removes the vagaries of timing fluctuations in the results. If, for example, we are analyzing experience, we would not want our results to be heavily impacted by whether some sizeable premium payments were received on December 31 versus January 2; we would want the money allocated to the period of time to which it applied. ASOP #8 refers to this as, "The actuary should make adjustments to past experience, as appropriate, in a way that reasonably matches claim experience to exposure."

As with most other situations, there may be circumstances under which data is just not available for earned and incurred calculations. Sometimes this is unavoidable, and an estimate must be made with non-ideal data. In such a situation, actuaries are obliged to address this (due to professional standards of practice)[17] in providing their opinions.

Another important consideration is the generally preferable use of *runout* basis claim experience, rather than *financial* basis experience. Financial basis incurred claims are calculated as (Paid Claims) + (Ending Claim Reserve) - (Beginning Claim Reserve). The last two terms, the change in reserve, can be thought of as being the sum of two things: (1) a reserve estimate for the most recent period, plus (2) corrections to prior reserve estimates based on current knowledge. The latter component can sometimes create distortions in year-to-year measurements, to the extent prior reserve estimates were wrong. An understatement in the prior year's reserves, for example, might cause the second element to be significantly positive, making the current period's incurred claims appear higher than they would if the prior reserving had been accurate. While this is an important calculation for financial reporting purposes, it can be misleading for analytic purposes.

Runout based incurred claims allocate the corrections to prior reserve estimates back to those periods of time (rather than to the time they are recognized), restating the prior reserves (and incurred claims) to the current (and more accurate) estimate of those reserves. Actuarial Standard of

---

[16] ASOP #8: Regulatory Filings for Health Benefits, Accident and Health Insurance, and Entities Providing Health Benefits.
[17] ASOP #23: Data Quality.

Practice #8 says, "The filing actuary should update prior earned premium and incurred claim estimates to reflect premium and claim development experience to date when, in the actuary's professional judgment, the difference is material."

For long term coverages (like DI and LTC), claim reserves are calculated as the present value of future payments. If actual experience equals that expected under the reserve basis, the difference between this year's claim reserve and next year's is the claim payments (as it is for short term coverages) *plus interest earned on the remaining reserve.* This calculation is needed to reconcile financial and runout based claim reserve calculations.

As always, the reliability, applicability, and statistical credibility of the data should be assessed before using it.[18] In addition, it is desirable to have data with sufficient detail that it can be 'sliced and diced' across important variables. Performing *actual-to-expected* (A:E) analysis across such variables is the classical method for adjusting rate slopes and subsidies. Another method, which sometimes yields insights missed by the former method, is to apply rigorous statistical techniques to the data, such as multivariate logistic regression, in order to derive information about the nature of the data.

STEP 2: RESTATE EXPERIENCE

In doing a rerate analysis, if we were to use the experience from Step 1 "as is," we would typically be working with premium that was earned under multiple rate schedules. Judgments we made about the appropriate level of those rates would be with respect to the *average* rate level in effect during the experience period. (This works fine when we are simply looking at past experience, such as an inception-to-date loss ratio calculation. For rate analysis, however, we almost always need to do a projection into the future, either for lifetime loss ratio projections or for future loss ratio projections.) In truth, we want to make judgments about the *current* rate level, because we need to determine the rate change that will apply to the current rate schedules.

To address this issue, we can either: (1) do the analysis with respect to the average rate level, and then adjust for the relationship between average

---

[18] Ibid.

rates in the experience period and the current rate level, or (2) adjust past experience to be on a current rate level, and do the analysis with respect to current rates. The latter approach seems easier to conceptualize, but they are algebraically equivalent. In essence, past experience is adjusted to answer the question, "What would have happened if we had been charging today's rates during the experience period?"

This adjustment process requires careful attention to detail, and typically a computer model. The earned premium in the experience period must be subdivided across any variable relevant to the adjustment. One such variable is the effective dates of rate changes during the experience period. This depends on whether past rate increases were applied on policy anniversaries (as required by some state insurance departments), on policy renewal dates, or on a common date for all policies in a block.

Some policyholders may be under rate guarantees which limited the impact of the rate increase. This can be tricky, since neither the rate at the beginning of the experience period nor the rate at the end might be the current rate; there might well be an additional adjustment built into the premium stream because the impact of the rate guarantee ran out.

Policy Reserve Considerations
Almost all medical rerating is done in the absence of policy reserves. For those few policies that have them, policy reserves are a relatively minor pre-funding element, and (despite their theoretical origin) don't really serve to level premiums over the lifetime of the policies. Coverages like DI and LTC, however, do often carry quite substantial policy reserves.

It may be helpful for the reader to read Chapter 6, "Reserves," in conjunction with this section, to put the theoretical basis for this section's discussion in context.

It is important that policy reserves be appropriately reflected in experience analysis. Experience analysis is typically an A:E comparison in concept, where actual experience (usually meaning loss ratios) are compared against expected loss ratios. It is important that these two experience measures are calculated on a consistent basis. It would be inappropriate, for example, to compare an actual loss ratio without policy reserves against an expected lifetime loss ratio, which would implicitly be on a "with policy reserves" basis.

In a well known paper,[19] Joe Pharr demonstrates that if actual experience exactly matches expected experience (which is also the basis on which policy reserves are, at least theoretically, calculated), it is necessary to make an interest adjustment in the loss ratio calculation, and include the change in policy reserves in the numerator of the calculation as though it equalled incurred claims, in order to achieve an *actual* loss ratio "with policy reserve" exactly equal to the *expected* loss ratio each year. The formula from Pharr's paper is essentially:

$$P_x = \frac{(\text{Policy reserve change plus incurred claims})}{1+i}$$
$$- \left(\frac{i}{1+i}\right) \cdot (\text{Beginning reserve} - 50\% \text{ of incurred claims}).$$

This shows that the net level premium P_x exactly equals the incurred claims, when they are adjusted as shown on the right side of the equation. The net level premium is constant over the life of the policy, and is equal to the gross level premium times the anticipated lifetime loss ratio (if the loss ratio is calculated using the same assumptions as P_x). The adjusted incurred claims will thus be level over the life of the policy. Further, the ratio of incurred claims to P_x will be constant over the life of the policy, and will equal the original lifetime anticipated loss ratio.

In doing A:E analysis, one can thus do it either with or without policy reserves. If done with them, it is important that the loss ratios be interest-adjusted. It is the authors' belief that this basis is preferable, if only for the conceptual understanding of management and regulators. Either, however, will serve if used correctly.

If there is a premium adjustment made to a policy that includes policy reserves, this likely implies that the reserve factors must be revised as well, to reflect the new projections of expected claim costs. The generally accepted methodology for accumulating additional reserves is explained in a classic paper by E. Paul Barnhart.[20] Conceptually, the additional morbidity (claim cost), which is recognized at the time of the rate increase, can be treated as though it were a completely separate benefit which begins at the time of the rate increase. A separate stream of

---

[19] Pharr, Joe B.. "Individual Accident and Health Loss Ratio Dilemma," *Transactions of the Society of Actuaries*, Vol. 31. p. 373-387.
[20] Barnhart, E. Paul, "Adjustment of Premiums under Guaranteed Renewal Policies," *Transactions of the Society of Actuaries*, 1960, p. 472-498

policy reserve factors can be calculated for this additional benefit, and simply added to the reserve factors already calculated.

Because the reserves do not typically accumulate at the same interest rate used to discount values in the rate calculation, it is important to project and model the future impact of such differences, in order to understand the true impact of the rate changes.

STEP 3: PROJECT PAST RESULTS TO THE FUTURE

This step uses the results of Step 2, together with a set of adjustments, to answer the question, "What do we think will happen if we don't change the rates?" The answer is found by taking into account every material element we can identify that might cause future experience to differ from past experience. The following are the changes that most often occur.

Changes in the Covered Population

The experience used in the projection was derived from a population with certain characteristics. If the population in the (projected) rating period will be different than that of the experience period, the resulting changes must be reflected.

Interestingly, if the population changes are for characteristics that are included in the rating variables, then we need not make an adjustment, provided we believe our rate relativities are correct. Suppose, for example, the population in an experience period had an average age factor of 1.10. Suppose further that, based on a separate analysis, we predict the age distribution to be different in the rating period, and have an average age factor of 1.15. This means that the actual rates being charged will have an average factor of 1.15 already built into them, increasing the average rates automatically from 1.10. In a sense, if we believe the rate relativities, we can consider the rates to be immunized to changes in those demographics included in rating.

It is the factors that *are not* included in the rating structure – or those that have been limited by regulation – that have the potential to cause problems. (Ironically, those carriers whose rate structure is simplest, like the community rates of some BCBS plans, are the carriers most at risk. Those simpler rate structures are not robust with respect to some important demographic characteristics.)

The advent of guaranteed issue under the ACA for individual major medical coverage in 2014 created the potential for significant population shifts over the next few years. Accordingly, changes in the covered population became a major driver of some rate actions by insurers.

Changes in Duration

Time and time again, companies have been faced with seemingly inexplicable fluctuations in their experience, causing them to adjust rates – only to find such adjustments to ultimately be the wrong ones. Consider the following example.

Suppose Company A sells individual medical insurance. Since their actuaries do not analyze their experience durationally, they do not know that the relative morbidity of the first and second years' business is 0.65 and 0.85, respectively, nor do they track how much business is in each duration. Company A operates in a competitive marketplace that allows underwriting, with some carriers entering and leaving the market each year. New business volume fluctuates significantly with only minor changes in rates relative to the competition.

Suppose now that Company A has predicted a relatively good year in $201X$, and has a new business premium that, for the year, is relatively low compared to the competition. They sell tons of new business – enough so that, instead of the normal 25% of premium from first year policies, they have 40%.

Before the end of year $201X$, they realize that they underestimated claims for $201X$, and must substantially raise rates in $201X+1$ relative to the competition. When the $201X$ experience is measured early in $201X+1$, however, they are amazed to discover the experience is better than expected. (This is understandable, because on the unusual extra 15% of premium, or $40\% - 25\%$, they had a first year loss ratio 65% of normal. This lowers their overall loss ratio by $0.15 \times (1 - 0.65) = 5\%$ of the loss ratio, giving an A:E ratio of 0.95.) Instead of a 70% targeted loss ratio in $201X$, and instead of the *higher* loss ratio they expected because $201X$ was underpriced, they achieved a 66.3% loss ratio. (If they had done a durational analysis, they would know that this is what they should have expected, not 70%.) So, in $201X+1$, they apply the extra 0.95 A:E factor – just as those first year people from $201X$ move to year 2, and raise experience by $0.85/0.65 - 1$, or 31% on their 40% of the business, and just as the higher rates in $201X+1$ cause a drop-off in new sales to their old levels. So, instead of seeing the 5% better experience they expect, experience worsens by 5%.

This is a whipsaw effect. Just as Company A raised rates in $201X+1$, experience got better. When they then lowered them, it got worse. Yet a durational analysis would have explained all of those changes, and the company could have anticipated the process in advance.

Changes in Benefits

To the extent the benefits under the policy have changed between the experience period and the benefit period, this should be reflected. These changes can either be explicit (such as a change in copays or deductibles), or implicit. Implicit changes can originate within the company (such as a change in how a policy provision is interpreted), or externally (such as when a Medicare Supplement policy changes benefits due to Medicare changes, or because of a new state mandate of additional coverage).

Changes in Claim Costs

These can be examined in a variety of ways, but probably the most helpful is to first look at frequency of claim versus average claim size.

Claim frequency can, and often does, change over time. For medical coverages, claim costs are typically broken down into relatively small component pieces (maybe 10-30 or more), and utilization/claim frequency is examined for each one. Assumed changes in utilization should reflect changes happening in the marketplace being studied. They typically reflect the evolution of medical care toward more cost-effective delivery of care. Over the past few decades, for example, inpatient hospital days have generally continued to decrease in frequency. At the same time, outpatient treatments have increased as those patients who used to get inpatient treatment are now treated on an outpatient basis.

DI coverage has seen decades-long cycles of claim frequency. It is difficult to measure this, however, as DI products have changed over those cycles, and we are not measuring comparable things; a disability in 1975 was subject to a very different level of scrutiny and criteria than a claimant with the same condition today.

LTC coverage is subject to the same measurement issues as DI (only more intensely, because of product changes that have occurred since first introduced). As an example, during the past decade, there has been a shift toward using assisted living facilities in place of nursing homes as these sites of care have become more prevalent.

The other element of claim costs that changes over time is the average claim size. For medical coverage, this includes the impact of a wide array of inflationary forces, market basket changes, and intensity.

One interesting apparent paradox is how the evolution of care management moves treatments to more cost-effective sites. This causes, for example, relatively low cost inpatient stays to be done on an outpatient basis. This raises the average cost of inpatient stays, while it lowers the frequency. At the same time, the procedures that used to be done inpatient tend to be higher cost than the average outpatient procedure, so the shift to outpatient of previous inpatient procedures will similarly raise the average cost of outpatient procedures while also increasing the frequency. In combination, overall costs should be lowered, yet the average cost of services in each part is going up. These changes in average cost can be termed "intensity" changes.

Leveraging
As trends change the average cost of claim over time, the impact of fixed benefit characteristics, such as deductibles, copays, and out of pocket limits, causes a leveraging effect which generally results in claim costs increasing at a higher rate than the underlying costs. Let's look at an example, taking the distribution of major medical expenses shown earlier. Assume this is an enormous and static sample, so that in the absence of other changes, the experience would be repeated each year.

EXERCISE 5.3: Using the same information from Exercise 5.2, calculate:

(1) the claim cost if there is 10% inflation going to the next year, and

(2) the leveraged inflation rate. □

Conceptually, this leveraging comes from two sources. The first source is the mechanics of the arithmetic. For medical expense level X, and deductible Y (with $X > Y$), the benefit calculation is $0.8(X-Y) = 0.8X - 0.8Y$, assuming an 80% benefit above Y. If inflation is 10%, it acts on the X portion of this calculation, but not the Y portion. The benefit calculation then becomes: $0.8 \times (1.1X - Y) = 0.88X - 0.8Y$. However, a pure 10% increase in the benefit calculation would have yielded 110% of the whole benefit, or $1.1 \times 0.8(X-Y) = 0.88X - 0.88Y$. Comparing the two outcomes shows a difference of $0.08Y$. Thus, the actual claim increased by 10% *plus* $0.08Y$.

The second source of leveraging comes from the fact that there are expenses in year X that do not hit the deductible, but with inflation, they do hit it in year $X+1$. A $1000 medical expense this year will be $1100 next year with 10% inflation. With a $1000 deductible, the corresponding claim expense goes from zero to 80% of $100. This is a 10% increase in medical trend, but an infinite increase in claims (admittedly a bit extreme, but it makes the point).

Healthcare Reform Items
When rating individual major medical coverage compliant with the ACA, it is crucial to take into account the effects of the three risk mitigation programs (risk adjustment, transitional reinsurance, and transitional risk corridors). Each of these can create a material cash flow related to the business, which must be estimated and appropriately incorporated into rates. These programs are described more fully in Chapter 4.

Each of the three programs presents unique challenges for the pricing actuary:

- To estimate risk adjustment transfers, one must estimate market-wide risk scores as well as the insurer's own risk score.
- It is not certain that monies collected by the government to fund the transitional reinsurance program will be adequate to fund claims under the program. It is also possible that excess funds will be distributed to insurers if more money is collected than intended.
- The risk corridor program depends on the result of the risk adjustment and reinsurance programs, compounding these uncertainties.
- The government has repeatedly made material changes to the parameters of each of the three programs, often after rates had already been set.

Healthcare reform has other costs that must be included in pricing, including new taxes and fees and also the cost of the administrative work required to comply with all the new rules.

Other Changes
Anything else that will have changed between the experience period and the projection/rating period, and which is relevant to the level of claim costs, needs to be reflected. This includes any changes in how risks are selected or renewed, including:

- Whether the company's renewal business might have been "cannibalized" by re-underwriting existing policyholders into new policies (this is a concentrated form of cumulative antiselection),
- Changes in underwriting, and
- Sudden increases in lapse rates, possibly indicating higher-than-market rates on healthy lives. (Lower than expected lapse rates can also cause problems for certain coverages, such as LTC).

Any changes in policy provisions, business operations, premium and benefit levels, utilization and cost of services, administrative procedures, and the health care delivery system must also be reflected.

A typical projection of claims for a major medical policy might include the following, where s represents the experience period and t represents the projection period:

$$\begin{aligned}
\text{(Projected Claims)}_t = & \ \{(\text{Claim Cost } PMPM)_s\} \\
& \times \{(\text{Number of Members})_t\} \\
& \times \{(1 + \text{leveraged claim cost trend})^{(t-s)}\} \\
& \times \left\{\left(\frac{(\text{Avg Durational Factor})_t}{(\text{Avg Durational Factor})_s}\right)\right\} \\
& \times \{1 + (\text{Antiselection factor due to Lapses})_{t-s}\} \\
& \times \{1 + (\text{Adjustment factor for other changes})_{t-s}\}
\end{aligned}$$

The corresponding premium projection might be:

$$(\text{Projected Premium})_t = (\text{Premium } PMPM \text{ under current rates})_s$$
$$\times (\text{Number of Members})_t$$

There is an interesting effect which historically happened to blocks of individual medical policies over time. There was typically an internal migration within the block toward lower cost plans, which most insurers allowed without underwriting. Because of this, the average premium per policy or per member tended to drop each year from what might otherwise have been expected. If there were no antiselection, and if the various plans were priced appropriately relative to each other, there would have been a drop in the average claims proportionate to the premium drop. In reality, this process was antiselective in nature, and the drop in claims generally did not match that of premium (see the discussion of *premium leakage* and associated exercises in Chapter 4 for more on this). This dynamic will likely change under the ACA, since policyholders will be free to both increase and decrease benefits from year to year in the absence of underwriting.

STEP 4: COMPARE THE PROJECTION AGAINST DESIRED RESULTS

Once the projections have been made, a picture emerges of "this is what will happen if we don't do anything about the rates." This needs to be compared to what we would *like* to have happen. Rate changes (perhaps in combination with other solutions) are then calculated to make the predicted results match the desired results.

Conceptually, we would like to be able to say something like the following. Suppose the predicted loss ratio is 90% in the projection period, and the desired loss ratio is 75%. Then the *needed* rate change (remembering the loss ratio is the ratio of claims over premiums) is the increase in premium rates (call it "x," the percentage increase over current rates) which would reduce the 90% to 75% in the prediction. Or, find x so that:

$$75\% = 90\% \div (1+x), \text{ or } x = 20\%.$$

Interestingly, the calculation of needed rate changes is not as simple as this. It happens that the act of increasing rates (even by 20%) impacts some of the assumptions used to derive the projection in the first place. Unless you are willing to develop a formulaic relationship between the assumptions, the projections, and the resulting rate increase (which would be difficult to do), this becomes a recursive process, requiring successive approximations. Fortunately, unless this is in an extreme situation, the estimates quickly converge. The result of the 20% increase might cause a second order increase of an additional 5%. This convergence becomes less strong as the size of the rate increase goes up; large rate increases require hands-on analysis of the changes in assumptions.

What should be the desired loss ratio? There are many considerations which enter into this decision. The biggest elements are typically the level of expenses attributed to the block, and the company's desired profit level.

Expenses

The expenses reflected in the target loss ratio are those that the company attributes to that line of business. Such an allocation of expenses is inevitably based on at least some level of modeling, because it is not always clear what expenses should be attributed to a particular segment of business. Such expenses are typically expressed as a formula, involving one or more of the following elements:

$$Expenses = \begin{cases} x_1 \times (\$ \text{ of premium}) + \\ x_2 \times (\text{Number of policies, by definition} = 1) + \\ x_3 \times (\$ \text{ of claims}) + \\ x_4 \times (1 \text{ if first } N \text{ years of duration, 0 otherwise}) + \\ x_5 \times (\text{Number of premium payments in a year}) + \\ x_6 \times (\text{Number of members/persons in a contract}) \end{cases}$$

where x_1 and x_3 are typically expressed as percentages (percent of premium, percent of claims), and the other values (per policy, per policy for first N years, per premium payment, and per member) are expressed in dollars. There are many other possibilities; these are the ones most commonly used by companies today.

Individual health businesses that have evolved from a life insurer context (including most DI carriers, many LTC companies, and some CMM companies) tend to use expense formulas that have many elements to them, reflecting fairly sophisticated expense allocation studies and a diverse product mix. Others, such as many Blue Cross plans and HMOs, use just a percent of premium methodology, reflecting the relatively uniform nature of the different products they offer.

To the extent such an expense model represents an approximation of expenses, it is important to understand the limitations inherent in this process. The expenses allocated to that line of business are not the *real* expenses, except for those that are directly related to the business itself. To the extent the model does not reflect reality, there is a risk that it will lead to either inadequate or excessive revenues to cover those expenses. If this happens over a large enough part of the company's business, it can threaten the results of the entire company.

Profit
Not all companies build profit into their formula, but they do all have an element that corresponds to profit. Sometimes it is called "contributions to free reserves," or "contributions to surplus." Sometimes the value used may be zero for a while, such as when a BCBS plan may be limited by statute as to the amount of "free reserves" (meaning surplus) it accumulates.

Generally, however, the owners of the business (whether they be stockholders, policyholders, or the public) are providing a service, taking a risk, and providing capital. They require financial compensation in return, and that is the profit element in the rates.

Similar to expenses, profit can be expressed in a variety of ways, although unlike expenses the profit target is usually expressed as a single unit. In recent years, with the advent of Risk Based Capital formulas, the calculation of target surplus levels (and the profit needed to attain them) has become substantially more sophisticated.

Profit is typically expressed as either a percent of premium (most common with CMM coverages) or a percentage return on equity (ROE, most common with DI and LTC coverages), or a return on investment (ROI). When desired, profit is expressed as ROE, for rerating purposes this typically is translated into a percentage of premium, so that a target loss ratio can be calculated more easily.

Each of the major pricing methods has profit target methods that are consistent with it. Each will be discussed in the next section, as each of those pricing methods is presented.

STEP 5: APPLY REGULATORY AND MANAGEMENT ADJUSTMENTS

After the calculation of needed premium levels is completed, there are often constraints put on those rate changes by management or by regulators, for a variety of reasons.

Management reasons typically might include competitiveness of the premiums for new business, company profitability in other lines, relations with the public or the producer force, or public or social policy. Another management consideration is the desire to manage the block optimally from a long-term perspective. While a large rate increase might be justifiable, modeling might show that this would result in substantial antiselective shock lapses (cumulative antiselection), which would result in unavoidable future losses. It might be better to moderate the current increase in order to keep more healthy lives in the block, to subsidize future experience.

Regulatory interventions typically happen when regulators try to hold down the rising cost of health insurance for the public. This motivation is expressed in at least two different ways. The first is the application of minimum loss ratio standards (or sometimes additional standards), which typically requires that the block of policies meet the minimum loss ratio simultaneously over the *future* lifetime at the time of the rate increase and over the *entire* lifetime (past and future). The other typical regulatory constraint is the requirement in many states that rates be approved by the Insurance Department before being used – this regulatory scrutiny has been amplified under the ACA.

The ACA also sets a minimum loss ratio of 80% for individual major medical business, calculated in a prescribed manner. In the event that the actual loss ratio is less than that, the insurer may have to pay premium rebates to policyholders. This puts insurers in a difficult position, as their upside gain is limited each year, while their downside losses remain unlimited.

These considerations are described more fully in Chapter 9.

5.8 TURNING CLAIM COSTS INTO GROSS PREMIUMS

The methods used to turn claim costs into gross premiums depend on the time horizon being implicitly used in the company's rating philosophy. That choice of rating philosophy has often been determined historically by the type of company. Under the ACA, for major medical rating, companies have had to make fundamental changes in their rating philosophies.

Many Blue Cross plans and HMOs manage their individual blocks of business as open blocks, with new insureds being continually added. They then typically manage the business as a renewal block each year, even when a new policy is introduced. (When a new product is introduced, all policyholders are often "rolled into" the new block – their existing policies are cancelled and immediately replaced by the new one. Typical benefit differences in the new plan are minor, and can be reflected as minor modifications to a renewal rating exercise.) This is a short term profit horizon, with an associated rating approach sometimes called **block rating**.

DI, LTC, and other non-inflationary benefit coverages typically involve long term projections, for a number of reasons: (1) the future claims are predictable, relative to medical coverages, (2) the claim costs increase over time, and (3) the premium structure tends to be issue age based. When pricing these benefits, insurers typically use something called an **asset share model**. This involves a long term (perhaps 40 to 50 years or even more) projection of future claim costs, premiums, associated financial values, and supporting values like exposures, related to a block of policies all issued at the same time, without future policy issues considered (a **closed** block).

Commercial medical insurers, who historically tended to close off existing blocks of business in order to start new ones, tended to price their products using asset shares, but used assumptions that were not realistic over the long term. That is, durational deterioration was recognized and levelized in the pricing, but only to the extent the initial premiums did not become non-competitive. The method thus built in some partial recognition of future reality, but not complete recognition.

Healthcare reform requires the use of a block rating approach for all ACA-compliant major medical plans going forward. That is, insurers are no longer allowed to close off existing blocks of business and rate them separately from new business, but must instead rate all policies as part of a single risk pool in each state. The only exceptions to this are grandfathered and transitional policies that are not required to comply with the ACA.

The single risk pool requirement applies to an insurer's major medical products whether or not they are sold on or off the public Exchanges established under the ACA. The main mechanism for enforcing the single risk pool is the **Uniform Rate Review Template (URRT)** and its associated instructions, which are promulgated by the federal government each year. This form generally must be submitted with all non-grandfathered, non-transitional individual major medical rate filings. Along with an accompanying actuarial memorandum and several other templates, the URRT is used to demonstrate that rates only vary based on the variables allowable under the ACA, as well as to document some of the main drivers of changes in premium rate levels. For more on these filing requirements, refer to Chapter 9 of this text.

BLOCK RATING (SHORT TIME HORIZON) APPROACH

In this approach, representative annual claim costs for the rating period (typically a year) are calculated for the benefits and the population being projected. Gross premiums (the actual premiums charged to policyholders) are calculated in a straightforward way by adding expenses and desired profit to the claim costs.

If the claim cost calculation was performed on an average, block-wide basis, it is necessary to calculate what demographic profile is represented by that average, and adjust for any changes in it when calculating rates. If, for example, a projected average annual claim cost were calculated to be $1,500, this might be based on a population that contains a mix of policyholders at each age. When the age relativities (age/gender factors) for those policyholders are averaged over the existing population, the average age factor might be 1.06.

It is often helpful to translate claim costs into those corresponding to an age/gender neutral basis. This helps put the figures into understandable context, particularly for anyone not personally familiar with what the unadjusted figures mean. It is also helpful for purposes of maintaining an understandable manual rate book. In the above example, the age-neutral claim cost would be $1,500/1.06 = $1,415. This same calculation would need to be done over each rating variable. (In this case, "neutral" means it was adjusted to be the claim cost attributable to a risk with a factor of 1.00. There is nothing special about this value, other than that it standardizes the discussion.)

This process is called "normalization" – we are normalizing the claim cost to be demographically neutral, relative to the rating factors used, over the given population. Once the average claim cost is demographically neutral, the final modeled claim costs (which vary over all the rating factors chosen to be used) can be calculated by applying the demographic rate relativities corresponding to the chosen rating factors. The $1,415 claim cost calculated earlier might, for example, be applied as follows:

Table 5.3

Age Factors			
Age Range	Age Distribution	Age Factor	Modeled Cost
25-29	12.5%	0.596	$843
30-34	14.3%	0.675	$955
35-39	15.5%	0.785	$1,111
40-44	16.4%	0.921	$1,303
45-49	15.4%	1.141	$1,615
50-54	13.3%	1.485	$2,101
55-59	7.6%	1.795	$2,540
60-64	5.0%	2.134	$3,020
Average	100.0%	1.060	$1,500

Thus, $843 = \$1,415 \times 0.596$.

It is important to note that, if we were to graph age factors for underwritten individual insurance against age (at least for most normal coverages), the curve is typically flatter by age than those used for group insurance. This is because individual medical underwriting typically has a bigger impact at higher ages, and is able to screen a greater proportion of claim costs at those ages than at younger ages. (Group insurance, particularly for large groups, is typically sold in a way that both selection and antiselection are minimized, resulting in a collection of "average" risks.) The curve would also change with duration, since underwriting has the most impact in year one, and wears off as duration increases.

Profit targets used in the block approach are usually quite simply expressed as a percentage of the premium in the projection period. If net premium (claim cost) is N, let us assume it is first loaded by those expenses that are a percentage of net, E^N, and fixed expenses, E^F. Then, if the loading for profit and for any remaining expenses that are expressed as percentages of gross premium is E^G, gross premium G can be expressed as:

$$G = \frac{N \cdot (1+E^N) + E^F}{1-E^G}$$

E^G, then, is composed at least in part of profit. Carriers typically target and monitor their experience by looking at loss ratios. It is not misleading for most purposes to express all expenses and profit as a percentage of gross premium, even further simplifying this equation.

Do not be misled by this simplified method of monitoring and targeting experience – the analysis that led to the expense target can be quite sophisticated, reflecting many factors including capital costs (discussed further later).

ASSET SHARE APPROACH

This calculation is generally done for each of a variety of representative rating cells. For a major medical plan, for example, it might be for quinquennial (every five year) ages, for each gender, for each of five plans. A simplified approach would be to do one projection for an average policyholder only. A typical DI asset share model might have one for each quinquennial age, for each of four elimination periods, for each of four benefit periods, for each of five occupation classes. DI riders can typically provide substantial benefits in addition to those in the base policy, so there are usually separate asset share calculations done for those riders, although often with a more limited number of cells. This is also true of asset share models for keyperson and business expense DI policies.

LTC policies will most often have asset share calculations done for representative ages (generally quinquennial), for each elimination period, for each benefit period, for each home care benefit level, and for each inflation protection option. Enough cells should be modeled to capture the different possible relationships between claim costs and premium slopes. As computer power has progressed, it has become more common to simply compute all cells.

Asset share calculations can be done either on a policy year basis or a calendar year basis. Both methods can ultimately be equivalent. The advantage of the policy year basis is the relative simplicity of the cell by cell calculations – no messy partial year calculations are necessary. The downside is that in order to translate the asset share calculation into calendar year financial forecasts for the company, partial year calculations must be made in the aggregate. For this reason, the calendar year approach may be preferred, as it has the added advantage of forcing greater rigor into the pricing actuary's thinking regarding premium modes, the frequency of policy issue over time, and other things, as they relate to the individual policy cells. This ability to distinguish often disappears in the policy year model.

A typical asset share's elements (columns) might be categorized as follows:

1. Exposure Values
These are values needed to calculate other values, which themselves have been expressed in terms of those exposure values. An expense element for "first year per policy expenses", for example, might come from work done elsewhere, and require an exposure figure of "number of policies issued." Such figures can be the number of policies sold or in force, number of claims incurred or claim payments made, number of premium collections, and number of units (such as number of $100 benefit per month, for DI) sold or inforce. Values that depend on dollars of premium or claims will be able to use those values from the revenue and claim sections.

Complexity can arise when it is necessary to differentiate between portions of policy years, in order to model calendar years. If, for example, we are modeling the first calendar year of issue, z, under the form, we might want to look at a policy issued on July 1, z. If the policyholder paid an annual premium, then the premium received on July 1 is one year's premium. We will need a value to prorate that premium into the two calendar years in which it is earned.

Some complexity happens because of the non-symmetric nature of policy issuance. Examine what happens when a company starts issuing its new policies on January 1, and sells them at a constant rate throughout the year. While the average issue date for policies issued that year is July 1, the weighted average date of earned premium is actually later in the year.

(For each policy issued, its average exposure in the year is halfway to the end of the year, assuming it doesn't lapse. Think $\int_{t=0}^{1} \frac{(t+1)}{2} dt = \frac{3}{4}$. Incurred claims also start off year one at negligible levels, and have a fairly steep durational slope within that year. The weighted average incurred claim date is, therefore, even later.

EXERCISE 5.4: Assume a company will start issuing a policy on January 1, and sell policies uniformly throughout the year, with annual premiums received on the date of issue. For this hypothetical exercise, assume all months have the same length. Further, assume claims increase linearly by month within the year, and that claims are paid exactly two months after incurral. Calculate the weighted average date of: (1) premium received, (2) premium earned, (3) claims incurred, and (4) claims paid. □

EXERCISE 5.5: Repeat exercise 5.4, assuming a monthly premium mode. □

2. Revenue Values

Revenue elements are the premium, investment income, and any other revenue items such as explicit subsidies. Premium might be expressed on a: (1) *received* basis (straightforward cash received), (2) *written and renewed* basis (cash received, plus any increase in premium paid in advance, minus any increase in premium due and unpaid), or (3) *earned* basis (written and renewed, minus any increase in unearned premium). For asset share purposes, it is unusual (but not unheard of) to model premiums paid in advance or due and unpaid. These are fairly small items which do not have much impact on the ultimate profitability of the business, but do influence the timing of revenue recognition.

One important consideration in modeling premium (and everything else, for that matter) is the anticipation of possible uses of the asset share model other than the initial pricing. The asset share values are often used as input into the company's forecasting or budgeting process. Elements of the model are also frequently used to form the "expected" part of actual-to-expected experience monitoring.

3. Claim Values

Claim values are typically shown both on a "paid" basis and an "incurred" basis.

There are two definitions of "incurred" in common use; one is the financial definition, the other is the runout definition, as described in Section 5.7. For asset share purposes, for short term coverages which do not involve interest calculations in their claim reserves, they are generally indistinguishable. One exception to this would be if we were doing a stochastic projection of financial results which included a measure of how likely various *mis*estimates of claim liability would be over time. For longer term coverages that involve interest in the claim reserve calculation, as previously described, an interest adjustment is needed to reconcile these two values.

Also important to the projection are various elements of claim reserves and liabilities, and related items. (Development of these items is described in the chapter on reserves and liabilities.) For asset share purposes, there is usually no need to distinguish between reserves (held for payments not yet accrued) and liabilities (held for payments which are accrued), and a single value is calculated. That value might be tabular (such as for DI or LTC), or it might be from a triangulation/development method (such as for major medical).

Another element related to claims is the **Claim Adjustment Expense** or **Claim Administration Expense (CAE)**. (This is sometimes called **Loss Adjustment Expense**, or **LAE**.) This is money needed to cover the cost of administering the claims represented in the claim reserve and liability figures, and so is an additional reserve item.

The final key element is the **policy reserve**. This item is also variously called a contract reserve, additional reserve, or active life reserve. This is money set aside out of early premium revenue, using an assumption of future claim growth, to pay for part of the cost of later claims. In so doing, the premium each year is not purely based on that year's claims, but includes an element of prefunding or leveling over time. It is not conceptually obvious that this item should be considered a claim reserve rather than a premium reserve, but there are compelling reasons for treating it this way.[21] For many years, it was actually treated as a premium reserve or in its own category. Following the publication of the referenced paper, and its acceptance by the actuarial community, the NAIC adopted a change in annual statements in the 1980s which ceased treating policy reserves as a premium reserve, and instead created a separate category.

---

[21] Op. cit., *The Individual Accident and Health Loss Ratio Dilemma.* pp 373-387.

4. Capital Values

Unless the business being studied will be immaterial to the operations of the company, it is important to understand the need for capital created by the line of business, and to model the cost of that capital relative to total return. Elements of this part of the asset share model will depend on how the company looks at the uses and cost of capital. There are sometimes artificial values used for this purpose. The calculations can be very simple, or sometimes very complex, and there are a number of ways to model it. The following exposition is just one of those.

Every company must operate with a positive level of capital, surplus, or free reserves, or they are insolvent. (For this purpose, we will refer to such values generically as 'capital.') The desired level of that capital is set by company management in response to regulation (such as Risk Based Capital Standards), to rating agencies (such as Standard and Poors), or to other factors such as management's own perception of risk and safety. This is discussed further in Chapter 11, "Managing the Business."

Whatever the rationale – when a policy is sold, it explicitly creates a need for additional capital by the company beyond what would otherwise be needed. (This may go beyond the marginal extra capital, since if every policy just had marginal capital allocated to it, the total allocation would not equal the total capital needed.) Presumably that capital belongs to the owners of the company. Because it must be put into the assets of the insurer, it is not available to be used for other purposes, and there is a resulting opportunity cost. The capital itself does earn some return as an invested asset of the insurer, but typically much less than the capital could be earning elsewhere. This opportunity cost is called the **cost of capital** in the asset share model. It is important to note that in this conceptual model the accumulation of the capital itself is not charged against profits in the model – only the cost of that capital.

Another interesting element of this calculation is that the sum of changes in capital over the life of the block is zero – the capital starts and ends at zero. The required capital typically increases monotonically over the beginning of the projection period, then decreases monotonically until the end. The present value of such changes, however, is not zero. In fact, if investment income is accounted for separately elsewhere in the model, the sum of present values of the changes in capital is the time value of those changes, and it can also be considered the opportunity cost of the capital. That is, it is the cost of borrowing that capital until it is repaid.

Some earnings models require the block of business itself to accumulate and pay for the capital being used to support it. In this case, the model becomes an ROE model, where the profit is measured as the return on investment, but the investment includes required capital as equity. Interestingly, if the earnings rate on the capital matches the discount rate (and the model requires it), the two earnings models are identical. This method is discussed further in the next section.

5. Expense and Profit Targets

As mentioned earlier, coverages requiring long term time horizons, such as DI and LTC, can involve quite detailed multivariate expense loadings. The cost of capital can also be treated as an expense for this purpose.

The profit that emerges each future year in the asset share model is discounted with interest back to the point of issue. The profit is calculated in one of three ways. The first method is to calculate the **present value (PV) of future profits**, using a specified interest rate, and compare that to the PV of future premium. The target will be a number or range, such as "the PV of profit is 7-9% of the PV of premium."

The second method is called **return on investment (ROI)**. In this method, there is a presumed investment by the company to issue the policy. This is a negative profit at time of issue. Future positive profits are presumably great enough to offset this initial negative profit, plus provide additional return on that investment. At some interest rate, the PV of those future profits will exactly equal the initial investment. This rate of return is how profit is then measured. It represents the return the company can expect on the investment needed to issue the policy.

If the cost of capital has not been included in the asset share as an expense, it can be included in the profit target measurement. If the initial investment in the ROI calculation is supplemented by the capital that is set aside to cover that business (perhaps a multiple of RBC), then greater profits are needed to cover that expense. (Note that, at an interest rate of zero, the PV of capital set aside at issue is zero, since it is all ultimately released. At non-zero interest rates, future payments must be larger to offset the initial required capital.) This calculation is called **return on equity (ROE)**. A sample target for this might be "profits sufficient to achieve 15% ROE."

CHAPTER 6

RESERVES AND LIABILITIES

6.1 TYPES AND USES OF RESERVES AND LIABILITIES

At any given point in time, there are a number of situations in a typical insurance block where either: (1) a cash flow has occurred but the event to which it applies has not, or (2) vice versa. Reserves and liabilities are used to adjust for these timing differences, so that financial reports can accurately measure various aspects of that operation. Without these adjustments, the financials are on a **cash** basis. With them, they are on an **accrued** (in accounting jargon), or **earned/incurred** (in insurance jargon) basis.

As a simplified illustrative example, suppose a company had one, totally average, policy in force, issued in December. Suppose further that the policyholder paid the whole year's premium at the time of issue. Without a reserve, when calculating results as of the end of the calendar year, the insurer would take in the full year's premium as revenue in the year of issue, with only one month's exposure for claims – a very good year. The following year, the company would have 11 months' exposure, and no premium to offset it, so they would have a very *bad* year. Yet, in total, the results for the policy year might be exactly on target, and exactly represent what was expected.

With a reserve, the same company would not be able to take the full year's premium into profit in the first year, but would set aside or **reserve** 11 months' worth, to be released the following year.

This example illustrates one of the basic principles involved in financial reporting, and a major reason for reserves: the matching of revenues to costs over time. This is the basis for many reserves and liabilities. While this seems a fairly innocuous description, its implications are quite powerful. The holding of such reserves is critical to the measurement and maintenance of company solvency – without reserves, the company would have future obligations that are already owed and unavoidable (even if not yet payable) unstated on its financial statements. This would mean, at the least, the company's financial reports would be misleading. At worst, a company could be insolvent and not know it.

Holding inaccurate reserves yields comparable risks to holding none at all. One might even consider this risk more insidious – inaccurate reserves provide a false sense of security!

In all cases, reserves are held so that the insurer does not take credit in its profit and loss calculation for money which will be needed later to cover expenses which in some way are connected with that money. Those expenses can be related to the coverage itself in an upcoming period (premium reserves), future increases in benefits which are being currently funded (policy reserves), or claims which have already been incurred but which have (for whatever reason) not yet been paid (claim reserves). Or they can be gross premium reserves (or so-called 'deficiency' reserves), where the reserve is an amount which, when combined with future revenue and interest, will be sufficient for the company to meet its obligations over the future lifetime of the policies in force. Reserves can also be held for administrative expense (expense reserves), rather than benefits.

RESERVE VS. LIABILITY

The term "liability," in a generic accounting sense, refers to all the financial obligations of a company that appear on its balance sheet. For insurers and other contingent risk-takers, this includes (among many other things) actuarial reserves and liabilities. For purposes of this book, the term "liability" generally means "actuarial liability."

The distinction between the terms "reserves" and "liabilities," when used in an actuarial sense, comes from NAIC statutory accounting standards and practices. Both concepts are used to set money aside on the valuation date to cover future obligations of the insurer. The term **liabilities** refers to obligations that are already **incurred** and **accrued**. Let's look at an example under DI coverage. Suppose a claim has occurred, and monthly payments are made under the contract on the 15th of each month. On a valuation date at the end of the month, the claim has been incurred, and the benefit has accrued, but it is not yet due for payment. This makes it a liability.

Reserves are for obligations which have not yet been incurred or are not yet accrued. We will spend most of our intellectual effort in this chapter on reserves.

Having made the formal distinction between the actuarial reserves and liabilities, the difference will not be particularly important in practice, except for allocating obligations to the correct exhibits in financial statements. Some people use the terms interchangeably. For most actuarial purposes, including the setting of total reserves and liabilities, there is no distinction made between the two. In fact, most reserve calculations focus almost all effort on calculating the *combined* value of the two, so that the company's total obligations are correctly stated. The allocation between reserves and liabilities is typically based just on a relatively simplistic allocation of the total number between the two. This text will generally refer to the combination of reserves and liabilities as "reserves," in keeping with common practice.

TYPES OF RESERVES

Reserves can be categorized in a number of ways. One major way is by the function they serve in the financial statement.

Functions

Most practitioners divide total reserves into four major categories: (1) premium reserves, (2) claim reserves, (3) policy reserves, and (4) gross premium reserves. Each of these serves a separate and distinct purpose. Each of them has its own calculational techniques and typical assumptions.

Premium and claim reserves are the elements of accounting that convert cash accounting figures into accrual accounting figures. Policy reserves are used to account for any long term differences between the slope of the revenue stream and the benefit (and sometimes expense) stream. Gross premium reserves come into play when the valuation actuary concludes that future revenue streams plus current reserves and liabilities for a given block are not sufficient to cover future costs, and therefore the company needs to set aside money to cover the shortfall.

Contexts for Reserves

Another categorization of reserves depends on the use to which they are being put, each of which is governed by a different authority that sets standards to meet its own goals. Companies today might need to produce financial statements on three or even four bases.

The first type of statement developed, which all licensed insurers produce, is the **statutory statement**. Standards for the development of this statement are set by each state, to be applied to all companies licensed in the state. Since most companies operate in more than one state, without some standardization a collection of varied standards could quickly become a nightmare. Fortunately, all states (except California, with respect to HMOs and Blue Cross/Blue Shield plans) use the statement blanks, instructions, and accounting pronouncements developed by the **National Association of Insurance Commissioners (NAIC)** as the basis for statutory statements, with relatively minor variations required by only a few states. These statements and requirements are contained in *Statutory Statements of Accounting Principles (SSAPs), Model Regulations*, and *Actuarial Guidelines*. Statutory accounting principles are focused on ensuring solvency of the insurer, so tend to be more conservative than other statement bases.

The second type of statement is called a **GAAP (Generally Accepted Accounting Principles) statement**. This is a statement developed under the standards set out by the **Financial Accounting Standards Board (FASB)**. Although FASB is not a governmental body and operates independently, it has for decades been accepted by the Securities and Exchange Commission as the authority for financial accounting standards for publicly traded companies.

GAAP statements focus on a matching of profit streams with revenue streams. Solvency is a secondary concern. GAAP statements are not as conservative as statutory statements, but do have some conservatism explicitly included in both assumptions and process. That conservatism is called "provision for adverse deviation." It is expressed as conservatism in assumptions, which are released over time in a natural way.[1]

A third type of statement is a **tax statement**. In the U.S., the Internal Revenue Service requires that financial statements follow a set of standards designed to make sure that profits beyond a set level (generally based on the least conservative assumptions that still meet state requirements) are recognized immediately, and therefore are taxed immediately.

---

[1] Horn, Richard G. "Life Insurance Earnings and the Release from Risk Policy Reserve System," *Transactions of Society of Actuaries*, 1971.

For companies who operate internationally, or are owned by alien holding companies, another basis of financial statements is sometimes needed, called **embedded value based statements**. Accounting standards are set by the **International Accounting Standards Board (IASB)**, and codified in the **International Financial Reporting Standards (IFRS)**.

6.2 PREMIUM RESERVES

Premium reserves are amounts set aside in financial statements to reflect premiums that have either (1) been received by the valuation date, but provide for insurance coverage after the valuation date, or (2) not yet been received on the valuation date, but which relate to coverage that was provided prior to the valuation date. (The latter amount is actually held as an asset, with the insurer taking credit for anticipated revenue.)

UNEARNED PREMIUMS

This is a reserve that sets aside that part of premium that has been received for coverage which has not yet occurred as of the valuation date. In most cases the calculation of such a reserve is just the pro-rata portion of the actual gross premium received. In this situation, the reserve is said to be a **gross unearned premium reserve (gross UPR)**.

A gross UPR is sometimes approximated by insurers as taking ½ of all modal premiums in force on the valuation date. (e.g., of all annual premiums received and still in force on December 31, it is assumed that half of them are earned, and half unearned.) This is equivalent to an assumption that renewal dates for each modal premium type are uniformly distributed throughout the modal period. This is often an inaccurate assumption – many companies find a disproportionate number of issues on the first of the month, or sometimes the first and the fifteenth. If this is the case, accuracy would require the "½ of all modal premiums" assumption be modified to suitably reflect the difference. (The error, though, is typically conservative, in that more reserve is held than is otherwise needed, so this inaccuracy may be intentionally overlooked. The reader is encouraged to make up an example to verify this assertion)

When a company holds policy reserves for a block of business, the gross UPR reserve is replaced by a *net UPR reserve* for statutory purposes, meaning it is based on the net premium which was used in the calculation of benefit reserve factors. (Net premium generally refers to premium excluding non-claim costs and is described in the following section on policy reserves.) These methods are typically used by life insurers, so often find use in DI and LTC coverages, particularly because these coverages often involve policy reserves. In all cases, however, the gross UPR is typically required as a minimum amount to be held for active life (unearned and policy) reserves, regardless of the active life reserve methods used.

As we will see later, there are several methods used for setting policy reserves. Two of these are known as **mean** and **mid-terminal** reserves. When *mean* reserves are chosen as the method for policy reserves, the reserve is based on a factor that is calculated assuming all premiums payments are annual.[2] To the extent this is not true, this reserve is then overstated, so is offset by a **deferred premium asset**, representing the net premiums which are unpaid for the year, not yet due, but which had been included in the mean reserve.

NAIC REQUIREMENTS FOR UPR

The NAIC's model regulation[3] states that

"unearned premium reserves are required for all contracts with respect to the period of coverage for which premiums, other than premiums paid in advance, have been paid beyond the date of valuation."

Single premium credit insurance is exempted from the requirement of unearned premium reserve, although there are other comparable requirements to hold a liability for refunds.

---

[2] The mean reserve is the average of the reserve on the first and last days of the year, assuming all the premiums are paid on the first day. The mid-terminal reserve is the average of the terminal reserve at the end of the current year and the preceding year. There are other variations on these methods as well. See the section on policy reserves in this chapter for more on this.

[3] *Health Insurance Reserves Model Regulation*, National Association of Insurance Commissioners, NAIC 10-1.

If an insurer carries

> "premiums due and unpaid...as an asset, the premiums must be treated as premiums in force, subject to unearned premium reserve determination. The value of unpaid commissions, premium taxes and the cost of collection associated with due and unpaid premiums shall be carried as an offsetting liability."

The NAIC specifies that the minimum UPR for a given policy is the portion of the modal premium applicable to the period beyond the valuation date. If there is a contract reserve (which necessitates the calculation of a valuation net premium), then the net premium is the minimum; otherwise it is the gross premium. If the basis is net premiums plus contract reserves, then the reserve must still, in the aggregate, at least equal the gross UPR.

PREMIUM PAID IN ADVANCE

Sometimes a policyholder will pay more premium than is strictly required for the current renewal period on the valuation date, such as having paid two monthly premiums on December 15th for a monthly renewal. When this occurs, the insurer must set up a reserve for such premiums until the period occurs for which they apply.

PREMIUM DUE AND UNPAID

Sometimes premium payments are made late. When that occurs, some or all of that premium is expected to be received, and some credit is taken on the statement (as an asset) for such premium due and unpaid (D&U). There is a limit put on this. In statutory accounting this is limited to the smaller of 90 days past due or one modal premium. In any event, such an asset is not taken beyond what might reasonably be expected to be collected. Many companies conduct regular studies to determine the percentage of premium that is typically collectible.

6.3 POLICY RESERVES

Policy reserves are amounts of money set aside to account for current funding of costs over the future lifetime of the policies. This time horizon is different than premium reserves, which typically are concerned mostly with the year following the valuation date. (Policy reserves are also, at times, referred to as "contract reserves," and "additional reserves." The term "active life reserves" is sometimes used for this item, but a more strict use of that term applies to the combination of policy reserves and unearned premium reserves.)

THE THEORY

A valuable way to look at the theoretical basis for these reserves is (in the context of a benefit reserve) to think of the future stream of claim payments, and to replace them with a future stream of net premium payments. (*Net premiums* in this context are those which are sufficient to exactly cover the cost of claims, with no allowance for expenses or profit.) If the premium stream exactly matches the claim stream over time, there is exact matching of income and outflow of dollars, and there is no need for policy reserves. To the extent the premium stream *differs* from the claim stream, however, there is a temporal reallocation of funds.

In many coverages, the claim stream tends to increase over time, and it may be desirable to have a premium stream that does not increase as much or at all. One example of this is when rates are fixed based on the *issue* age rather than changing with *attained* age.

The case in which the net premium is set so that it does not rise at all over the policy lifetime is known as **net level premium** rating or **issue age** rating. In this case, the premium would have to be set higher than the initial claim cost, and end up lower than the final one. (Remember the **Mean Value Theorem**? This implies that, at some point over the policy lifetime, the net premium must equal the cost – at least if we ignore the fact that these are not continuous variables.) The excess money collected in earlier durations is set aside into a reserve account called the policy reserve.

Graphically, the claim cost and net level premium might emerge as displayed in Figure 6.1.

The "wedge" below the dashed net premium line and above the solid claim cost line on the left represents the accumulation of the policy reserve; the reversed wedge on the right represents the natural release of this reserve.

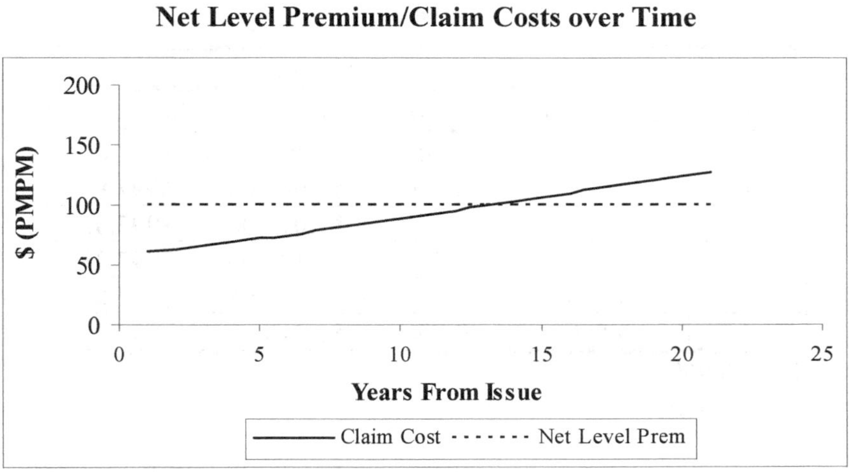

Net Level Premium/Claim Costs over Time

Figure 6.1

We will now work through a simple, sample example as a warm-up, before reviewing the mathematical formulas (for those who want to refer to them, they appear right after this example).

EXAMPLE 6-1

Make the following assumptions:
- An insurance policy is issued to a person aged x;
- Claims are $1,000 in year one, and increase at 7% annually thereafter;
- There is a 90% chance that x will persist each year for years two through five, and a 0% chance that x will persist to year six;
- Interest is 2.0% annually;
- The policy charges a net level premium (with no non-claim expenses); and
- Premiums occur at the beginning of each year, lapses occur at the midpoint of each year, and claims occur at the end of each year.

Table 6.1 shows the persistency at the beginning of each year, discount factors to the beginning of year one, and cash flows.

Table 6.1

| \multicolumn{5}{|c|}{Net Level Premium Example} |

Time (t)	Persistency[1]	Discount[2]	Claims	Net Prem.
0	1.000	1.000	$0.00	$997.85
1	0.900	0.980	$1,000.00	$997.85
2	0.810	0.961	$1,070.00	$997.85
3	0.729	0.942	$1,144.90	$997.85
4	0.656	0.924	$1,225.04	$997.85
5	0.590	0.906	$1,310.80	$0.00

[1] = 0.90^t
[2] = $(1+2\%)^{-t}$

How was the net level premium determined in Table 6.1? By definition, the actuarial present value of the net level premium must be equal to the actuarial present value of the claims. To solve for the premium, we take the present value of claims (sum of the product of the claims column with the persistency and discount columns) and then divide by the sum product of the persistency and discount factors for $t = 0$ through 4 (we are solving equation 6.4 if you want to see the symbols). The reader is invited to check that this results in the net premium of $997.85 in Table 6.1, and to check that the present value of this premium stream does indeed equal the present value of the claim stream.

We will now calculate the policy reserve needed at the end of year three (at $t = 3$, just after claim payments are made for year three and before premium payments are made for year four). We can do this two ways. First, we can look at the reserve accumulated by the past cash flows, taking into account both interest and persistency:

$$
\begin{aligned}
\text{Reserve}_{(t=3)} = &\ \$997.85 \times (1+2\%)^3 \times 0.90^0 \\
+ &\ (\$997.85 - \$1,000.00) \times (1+2\%)^2 \times 0.90^1 \\
+ &\ (\$997.85 - \$1,070.00) \times (1+2\%) \times 0.90^2 \\
- &\ \$1,144.90 \times (1+2\%)^0 \times 0.90^3 \\
= &\ \$162.66
\end{aligned}
$$

This is a *retrospective* calculation. Alternatively, we can calculate the reserve *prospectively*, by taking the present value of future claims less the present value of future premiums, again taking into account interest and persistency:

$$\begin{aligned}\text{Reserve}_{(t=3)} = \ & -\$997.85 \times (1+2\%)^0 \times 0.90^0 \\ + \ & (\$1{,}225.04 - \$997.85) \times (1+2\%)^{-1} \times 0.90^1 \\ + \ & \$1{,}310.80 \times (1+2\%)^{-2} \times 0.90^2 \\ = \ & \mathbf{\$223.13}\end{aligned}$$

But wait – this answer differs from our earlier one. What happened? If you look closely, you will see that the first calculation is *per original policy issued in year one,* while the second calculation gives the reserve in year three *per policy still in force in year three*. In technical terms, the persistency assumption is adjusted in the "per in-force policy" formula to be conditional on policies that remain in force in year three. Since there are 0.730 ($=0.90^3$) policies at the end of year three for each policy in year one, we divide cumulative persistency since inception in each year by 0.730. As a check, if we multiply our second answer by 0.730 we should get the first – and we do, up to rounding. Both of these reserve bases can be useful.

In reality, these simple calculations will be complicated by the introduction of various modifications, which are discussed later in this section. Without modifications, the basic prospective formula (using standard actuarial notation) for the policy reserve on a per original policy basis at time t, for a policy issued at age x, looks like Formula 6.1. (Note that the term "PV" is a common acronym for "present value"):

$$\begin{aligned}{}_t^z V_x &= PV\{\text{Future Claims}\} - PV\{\text{Future Net Premiums}\} \\ &= \sum_{i=t+1}^{\omega} \{{}_i p_x \times v^{i-t} \times {}_i^z C_x\} - \sum_{i=t}^{\omega} \{{}_i p_x \times v^{i-t} \times {}_i^z P_x\},\end{aligned} \qquad (6.1)$$

where

$_i p_x$ = probability of survival to i of policy issued at age x,
v^t = $(1 + \text{annual interest rate})^{-t}$
 = present value factor,
$_i^z C_x$ = claim cost for someone age x at duration i, issued in year z,
$_i^z P_x$ = net premium for someone age x at duration i, issued in year z, and
ω = the latest year where $_i p_x$ is nonzero.

Note in formula 6.1 the addition of z, the calendar year of issue. This is a departure from the annotation of most actuarial texts, but is a necessary distinction for policies like major medical, subject to calendar-based claim trends. Such trends cause the year i claim cost, for a given issue age x, to vary from year to year. This is generally not needed for coverages where claims do not vary significantly because of calendar year.

This and other formulae have assumed that premiums occur at the beginning of the year, and claims occur at the end of the year. They give the reserve at time t (where $t = 0$ is the beginning of year 1, $t = 1$ is the end of year 1 and the beginning of year 2, and so on). By tradition for these sorts of examples, the reserve calculation is assumed to occur in the magic moment between the end of one year (after claim payments are made) and the beginning of the next year (before premium payments are collected). This rigorous development requires the actuary to adjust the summation to appropriately account for the timing of claims and premiums. For example, claims at time t (end of year t) are included in the retrospective calculation, while premiums at time t (beginning of year $t + 1$) are not. Similarly, claims at time t are not included in the prospective formula, while premiums at time t are included.

Formula 6.1 calculates a reserve at time t *per original issued policy*. This is the reserve calculation one might use for asset share purposes, or to project future aggregate reserves. If one wanted to calculate a reserve *per remaining policy in force* or *per surviving* policy, (which we will call $_t^z V_x^s$) then the formula would be

$$_t^z V_x^s = \sum_{i=t+1}^{\omega} \left\{ _{i-t} p_{x+t} \times v^{i-t} \times _i^z C_x \right\} - \sum_{i=t}^{\omega} \left\{ _{i-t} p_{x+t} \times v^{i-t} \times _i^z P_x \right\} \qquad (6.1a)$$

Formula 6.1a might be used to calculate reserve *factors*, which are applied to surviving policies each future year, to calculate statutory reserves. These methods are most useful in non-inflationary coverages such as DI and LTC.

The formulae are further complicated if *p*, *C*, or *P* are on a durational basis, as will happen, for example, if either mortality or lapse rates vary by policy duration.

When $t = 0$, Formula 6.1 is

$$_0^z V_x = \sum_{i=1}^{\omega} \left\{ _i p_x \times v^i \times {_i^z C_x} \right\} - \sum_{i=0}^{\omega} \left\{ _i p_x \times v^i \times {_i^z P_x} \right\} \tag{6.2}$$

But, by definition, $_0^z V_x = 0$ (reserves start at zero), so

$$\sum_{i=1}^{\omega} \left\{ _i p_x \times v^i \times {_i^z C_x} \right\} = \sum_{i=0}^{\omega} \left\{ _i p_x \times v^i \times {_i^z P_x} \right\} \tag{6.3}$$

which happens to be the defining condition of any net premium $_0^z P_x$: that its present value equals the present value of claims at time zero.

Formula 6.1 is the prospective formula for net level policy reserves, where the net premiums are assumed to be a constant percentage of the gross premiums. (This is the usual assumption in such calculations.)

From basic actuarial mathematics, we know there are equivalent prospective formulae (like Formula 6.1) and retrospective formulae. The retrospective formula per original policy corresponding to 6.1 is:

$$\begin{aligned} _t^z V_x &= PV\{\text{Past Net Premiums}\} - PV\{\text{Past Claims}\} \\ &= \sum_{i=0}^{t-1} \left\{ _i p_x \times v^{i-t} \times {_i^z P_x} \right\} - \sum_{i=1}^{t} \left\{ _i p_x \times v^{i-t} \times {_i^z C_x} \right\}, \end{aligned} \tag{6.4}$$

And the retrospective formula corresponding to 6.1a (per surviving policy) is:

$$_{t}^{z}V_{x}^{s} = \sum_{i=0}^{t-1}\left\{\frac{1}{_{t-i}p_{x} \times v^{t-i}} \times {_{i}^{z}P_{x}}\right\} - \sum_{i=1}^{t}\left\{\frac{1}{_{t-i}p_{x} \times v^{t-i}} \times {_{i}^{z}C_{x}}\right\} \qquad (6.4a)$$

Retrospective formulas can be helpful for valuation actuaries and auditors, in calculating and checking reserve factors.[4] They are not often used for other purposes.

The *per surviving policy* formulae shown so far ignore the impact of durational variations in persistency. That is, they assume that the probability that a policyholder aged $x+i$ persists t years is the same regardless of whether that policyholder was issued at age x or some other age. In practice, it is common for persistency to vary by policy duration, especially in early durations. Individual health coverages, for example, tend to have higher lapses in the first year, since some individuals use it as temporary coverage during a transition between other sources of coverage (such as while they are between jobs). The persistency notation in the formulae can be modified to account for this by placing a bracket around the issue age variable (in this case [x]) to indicate that the persistency stream varies by duration.

EXERCISE 6.1: Using the formulae in this chapter, the claim cost stream included in *File 12 - Chapter 6 Data for Exercises.xls* worksheet, tab "6.1 Data" of the electronic files distributed with this text, and the discount rates included in the same spreadsheet, construct the reserve stream shown in that spreadsheet. For the purpose of this exercise, treat claims as occurring at the end of the year and premiums at the beginning of the year. ☐

COMPLICATIONS AND VARIATIONS TO THE RESERVE FORMULA

The basic formula can be complicated in a number of ways. The major complication, however, is how expenses are reflected in reserve calculations. Since early expenses (mostly at issue) are typically higher than later expenses, the double whammy of having to pay those expenses plus start holding policy reserves can put a large strain on the company's bottom line that year. Statutory and GAAP accounting handle this in different ways.

---

[4] Jordan, Chester Wallace Jr.. *Life Contingencies*. pp 115-116.

In statutory accounting, there is no explicit recognition of expenses in policy reserves. By allowing the use of modified reserve methods, however, there is an implicit recognition. The NAIC's model law[5] setting reserve bases allows for **two year full preliminary term (2YFPT)** reserves for coverages other than LTC and return of premium (ROP), and 1YFPT for LTC (except for certain very old policies) and ROP. The NAIC model defines the **Preliminary term reserve method** as follows:

> Under this method of valuation the valuation net premium for each year falling within the preliminary term period is exactly sufficient to cover the expected incurred claims for that year, so the terminal reserves will be zero at the end of the year. As of the end of the preliminary term period, a new constant valuation net premium (or stream of changing valuation premiums) becomes applicable such that the present value of all such premiums is equal to the present value of all claims expected to be incurred following the end of the preliminary term period.

As described in the model law, the modification for preliminary term valuation involves setting an alternative net premium stream for valuation purposes (of course, the actual gross premiums charged by the insurer will differ from this net stream). The reserves are then calculated using the same formulae as for a regular reserve (i.e., 6.1, 6.1a, 6.4, or 6.4a). Because of the way the premiums are chosen, the result is that there are no policy reserves for the first one or two years of the policy, depending on the length of the preliminary term.

The net premiums for a 2YFPT valuation, for example, would be:

$$_t^z P_x^{2PT} = p_{x+t} \times v \times {}_{t+1}^z C_x \text{ for } t = 0 \text{ or } 1, \text{ and}$$

$$= \frac{\sum_{i=3}^{\omega} {}_i p_x \times v^i \times {}_i^z C_x}{\sum_{i=2}^{\omega-1} {}_i p_x \times v^i} \quad \text{for } t \geq 2 \qquad (6.5)$$

Here, the indices on the summation in the denominator differ from those in the numerator because we are again assuming that premium payments happen at the beginning of each year (with the last payment occurring at

---

[5] op. cit., Health Insurance Reserves Model Regulation.

time ω-1), while claim payments happen at the end of each year (with the final claim payment at time ω).

As described previously, brackets could be placed around x in the formulae to indicate that the policyholder was selected (underwritten and issued a policy) at age x.

The 1YFPT reserve has a similar conceptual basis.

EXERCISE 6.2: Construct the two year preliminary term reserve stream corresponding to the net level reserves of Exercise 6.1. □

Many times in practice, especially for medical coverages, calculations are done directly on electronic spreadsheets, without reference to commutation functions or published tables. DI and LTC reserves, on the other hand, are often based on published or collected data sources, and may rely on formulae in their development.

In GAAP accounting, expenses are explicitly reflected. The policy reserve is calculated using net premiums as previously described. If the gross premium structure has future rate changes built into it, net premiums are assumed to change proportionately to gross premiums, and a factor reflecting this change would be included in the stream of ${}_i^z P_x$. (This does not mean that future claim trends are assumed beyond the current rating period – they are usually not. The growth in gross premiums is generally that which occurs without recognition of future increases in the rate schedule itself. It might actually be a better theoretical treatment of this to make reasonable assumptions of future claim growth and premium growth, however this need is now being met through gross premium reserve calculations, discussed later.) This reserve is then referred to as the *benefit reserve,* and notation for the variables related to it are typically endowed with a post-superscripted "B," such as ${}_t^z V_x^B$.

To recognize certain deferrable expenses, a parallel calculation is done using these expenses rather than benefits. This expense "reserve" is actually an asset, but is conceptually equivalent to a *negative* reserve, in that it performs the opposite function of benefit reserves. Benefit reserves cause a company to set aside funds which would otherwise become profit, so that those funds will (appropriately) be used later in the policy lifetime to subsidize later costs. Expense reserves allow a company to postpone recognition of certain expenses, and thus allow funds to flow through to profits earlier than they would if all expenses were fully reflected at the time they are incurred. The equivalent of the reserve in expense terms is called the **deferred acquisition cost**, or **DAC** asset.

The DAC is composed of **deferrable expenses**, which are those incurred to acquire the business. It typically includes the cost of selling, underwriting, and issuing the policy. (There is sometimes also an expense reserve for maintenance expenses, which might increase over time, so are similar in nature to the benefit reserves. When recognized, they are often included as a loading on the benefit reserves.) If we denote the deferrable expenses at time t, from a policy in year z to a policyholder aged x as $_t^z E_x$, then the DAC reserve at time t can be described as in Formula 6.6. Note that "AV" is a term used to represent the accumulated value of past values, in this case with interest and terminations. It is the retrospective equivalent of the prospective case's PV, on a *per surviving policy* basis (in order to calculate factors).

$$_t^z DAC_x^s = AV\{\text{Deferrable Expense}\} - AV\{\text{Net Expense Premiums}\}$$
$$= \sum_{i=0}^{t-1} \left\{ \frac{1}{_{t-i}p_{x+i} \times v^{t-i}} \times {}_i^z E_x \right\} - \sum_{i=0}^{t-1} \left\{ \frac{1}{_{t-i}p_{x+i} \times v^{t-i}} \times {}_i^z P_x^E \right\} \quad (6.6)$$

This is the expense analogue of Formula 6.1a's policy reserve, except that here we have assumed that expenses and net expense premiums occur at the same time (at the beginning of each year). Formulas 6.1 and 6.4 also have analogous expense reserve formulae.

In working with reserves, it is helpful to understand how one year flows into the next. To start this, it is important to keep in mind the difference between the year-end reserve for a year t and the beginning reserve for year $t+1$. The end of year reserve is called a *terminal reserve*. It is fairly standard, in doing financial statement valuations, to aggregate policies of a given issue age and duration, and assume a uniform distribution of issues throughout the year. This results in the average reserve (typically in the form of a *reserve factor* to be multiplied by the appropriate exposure value) being the arithmetic mean of the two terminal reserves. This is called a *mid-terminal reserve* methodology. It is also common to employ weighted average approaches to get a more accurate estimate.

In that magical moment between the end of one year and the beginning of the next, our methods assume the net premium has been paid, and the reserve jumps by the value of that net premium. Then, during year $t+1$, the reserve accumulates with interest (raising the value of the reserve), and claims all occur at the end of the year (lowering the value of the reserve). The reserve that results from these calculations will match the reserve recalculated through the present value formulae, because they are algebraically equivalent.

EXERCISE 6.3: Show how formula 6.1 at time t, when adjusted by the accumulation described in the prior paragraph, is equivalent to formula 6.1 at time $t+1$. □

EXERCISE 6.4: Using the expense and other data from the corresponding worksheet in the electronic files distributed with this text, calculate the stream of DAC shown in the results tab of the spreadsheet. □

PURCHASE GAAP

When a company is acquired, the GAAP effect with respect to an existing block of policies is that the DAC asset, which represents the amortized value of the selling company's original costs, is released. (This makes sense, because the DAC is used to align the timing of acquisition expenses with future premium or profit. When the business is sold, future profit is capitalized into the sales price, so the DAC is as well.) In its place, the acquiring company creates a VOBA (**value of business acquired**). The VOBA is the pre-tax value of the acquired business. (To the extent there are deferrable expenses incurred after the acquisition, such as second year commissions higher than those in years 3+, there will be a DAC asset generated by this, independently of the selling company's DAC.)

VOBAs are usually calculated as the present value of cash profits over the future lifetime of the business assumed, discounted at a risk rate of return. (This is often based on the models used in the appraisal work done to determine purchase price for the business.) The VOBA is then amortized over the future lifetime of the business on a schedule specific to the transaction.

PRE-FUNDING TRENDS

Another complication to the basic policy reserve calculation is caused by the various sources of increasing claim costs. In medical insurance there are at least three sources for increasing claim costs over time: inflationary and similar secular trends, aging of the insured, and durational trends.

The inflationary and related secular trends can be thought of as "environmental" trends – those which would cause increases in costs from year to year with an identical and unchanging insured risk from year to year.

In today's market and with ongoing sizeable claim trends for the foreseeable future, it is not feasible to completely pre-fund the three sources of claim cost increases. Thus, those insurers who pre-fund have funded only some part of that increase. Most typically, they pre-fund aging of the insured and a few years of durational deterioration, but no claim trend. Future rate increases are thus assumed to be sufficient to cover the increased cost due to claim trend, further durational deterioration, and the multiplier/cross product leveraging of those elements of cost increases.

In its work, an American Academy of Actuaries task force indicated that it would be unrealistic to assume carriers' pricing methods implicitly use more than the first five years of durational deterioration. (Some members believed the actual number to be less than five, for most carriers.)

Most major medical premiums do not pre-fund trends, but instead use premiums calculated to exactly match that year's claims. Most DI and LTC products are priced on a level premium basis, recognizing aging and durational effects.

A couple decades or so ago, in a paper proposing a new regulatory reserve standard,[6] a new modified reserve methodology was suggested, which created a modified net premium stream. That net premium stream could be considered as replacing a realistically projected future stream of claim costs with a net premium stream that increases with secular trend plus $x\%$. With $x = 0\%$, the method fully prefunds aging, duration, and the multiplicative compounding element of the combination of the three sources of increasing costs. Premiums are assumed to grow each year proportionately to secular trend. As x increases in value, the level of pre-funding goes down, and more of the growth in costs is borne by future premium increases. The reserves for such a formula would be calculated similarly to Formula 6.1, but perhaps with both the future claims and premium growing annually by some constant value j:

---

[6] Bluhm, William F. "Duration Based Policy Reserves," *Transactions of the Society of Actuaries*, 1993, pp 11-31

$$_t^z V_x = \sum_{i=t+1}^{\omega} \left\{ _i p_x \times v^{i-t} \times {}_i^z C_x \times (1+j)^i \right\} - \sum_{i=t}^{\omega} \left\{ _i p_x \times v^{i-t} \times {}_i^z P_x \times (1+j)^i \right\} \quad (6.7)$$

Formula 6.7 is, once again, a calculation of reserves per issued policy, rather than a reserve per surviving policy, which would be

$$_t^z V_x^s = \sum_{i=t+1}^{\omega} \left\{ _{i-t} p_{x+t} \times v^{i-t} \times {}_i^z C_x \times (1+j)^i \right\}$$
$$- \sum_{i=t}^{\omega} \left\{ _{i-t} p_{x+t} \times v^{i-t} \times {}_i^z P_x \times (1+j)^i \right\} \quad (6.7a)$$

A further assumption in that paper was that assumed lapses be recognized in $_i p_x$. When actual lapses are in excess of that amount, the policy reserves per remaining policy could be increased to recognize the implicit antiselection in that added lapsation.

This is only one of many such schemes which might be constructed for such pre-funding, each based on a differing pattern for the premium stream. Another scheme was proposed by Bob Cumming and Leigh Wachenheim in their article, "A Simplified Method for Calculating Contract Reserves."[7]

TO HOLD OR NOT TO HOLD

That is the question. Whether 'tis nobler in the mind to suffer the slings and arrows of outrageous trends, or to hold reserves against that sea of troubles, and by opposing, end them. (Apologies to The Bard.)

For some coverages, such as DI and LTC, holding policy reserves is obvious. Regulators, in fact, require it. Yet for inflation sensitive coverages (medical), it is not only not required, but regulators often oppose its use in measuring past experience. This may be because of the difficulty in correctly adjusting such experience to make meaningful actual-to-expected comparisons.

In the past, some regulators have also opposed companies holding such reserves, although today there seems to be widespread acceptance by regulatory actuaries. The acceptance reflects an understanding that prefunding

---

[7] Society of Actuaries, *Health Section News*, Issue No. 35, June, 1998.

can be a useful tool in managing in force blocks of business. The inability to use the change in such reserves in demonstrating compliance with minimum loss ratios, however, may impede the use of such reserves.

It is difficult to figure out what "prefunding" (another term for policy reserves) means in today's environment, with multiple trends (durational, aging, and secular) impacting claim costs. If, for example, claim costs are projected to be twice as high as today in six years, and if durational effects are expected to be double, and if aging causes costs to increase by 10% in that time, just how much of that sixth year's costs should be prefunded? The 10% for aging (which is the portion that would typically be prefunded in other coverages) will actually be worth 40% of year one costs when the doubling of secular trend and the doubling of durational trend are also reflected.

Further, any prefunding at all will increase the initial rates, which will hurt competitiveness in this heavily premium-driven marketplace. So, unless prefunding is mandated, it is unlikely to occur to any great degree, unless a particular carrier has another competitive premium advantage that they are willing to sacrifice in order to pre-fund. This whole concept gets even murkier when the medical policy is an attained age policy. In this case, the classical prefunding of age deterioration becomes meaningless (unless age rating is limited, as under the ACA, in which case it is merely dampened). In the authors' opinion, this does not negate the need to prefund at least some part of temporal trends. It is likely that the historical reason age (and not duration or claim trend) was the basis for classical policy reserves was because policyholder aging was the major factor contributing to temporal trends at the time. Further, prefunding of age alone matched the existing life insurance methodology. There is nothing magical about age rather than policy duration or secular trend. If we revert to the fundamental questions of why we would prefund, we arrive at the same answers as the life insurance industry did so long ago – prefunding helps eliminate extreme CAST effects (known also as antiselection spirals.) The only difference today is our relative inability to accurately predict those future trends.

On the other hand, to the extent that durational trends are dampened or eliminated by the prohibition of underwriting under the ACA, it may reduce the level of prefunding needed for ACA-compliant coverage.

Rate Increases

A company will typically calculate reserve values or factors at the time a product is developed. If the product is not inflation sensitive, these reserve factors might well apply every year until the last policyholder lapses. On the other hand, if the product is inflation sensitive, and the premiums are expected to increase over time, the reserve factors might need to change every year as premiums are changed. (The only reason this would not happen would be if the rate increase were already predicted in the premium stream used to calculate the factors, such as with the Duration Based Policy Reserve[8] method.)

Theoretically, the easiest way to calculate changes in policy reserves due to rate increases would be to follow the conceptual basis proposed by E. Paul Barnhart[9] in a classic paper. Conceptually, this method leaves the existing stream of reserve factors alone. Those factors were calculated to recognize a certain stream of net premiums and claim costs. The rate increase could be considered to be a recognition of *increments* to that stream. This allows us to calculate a reserve based solely on the increases in net premium and claim costs. This will likely involve a different pattern of aging and durational factors than the original calculation.

A number of companies have used this methodology. In practice, a stream of reserve factors is stored for each policyholder. Increments to those reserve streams are calculated at the time of rate increases (typically annually), and added to the existing reserve stream. This way, there is no need to regenerate prior calculations, but rather to only build on them.

Reserve Bases

Policy reserves for individual health policies are usually based on those set to meet the NAIC's statutory basis reserve. In the NAIC's model regulation, the current reserve requirements are as follows (policy reserves are called "contract reserves" in the model):

---

[8] "Duration-Based Policy Reserves," op. cit.

[9] Barnhart, E. Paul. "Adjustment of Premiums under Guaranteed Renewal Policies," *Transactions of the Society of Actuaries*, 1960, pp 472-498.

4. Contract Reserves
  A. General
   (1) Contract reserves are required, unless otherwise specified...for:
   (a) All individual...contracts with which level premiums are used; or
   (b) All individual...contracts with respect to which, due to the gross premium pricing structure at issue, the value of the future benefits at any time exceeds the value of any appropriate future valuation net premiums at that time. This evaluation may be applied on a rating block basis if the total premiums for the block were developed to support the total risk assumed and expected expenses for the block each year, and a qualified actuary certifies the premium development...

Subsection B specifies the required basis. It refers to the model's Appendix A for minimum assumption specifications. It requires that net premiums used for contract reserves be "consistent" with the gross premium structure. In practice, "consistent" seems to translate to having net premiums be a constant proportion of gross premiums.

For many years, statutory standards required that there be zero policy lapses assumed in the termination rates for policy/contract reserve valuation; they could recognize mortality only. The current requirement allows for non-zero lapse rates in certain circumstances. A paraphrased version of the model follows. (The original is included in Appendix D.)

  B. (1) Termination Rates. Termination rates used...shall be on the basis of a mortality table as specified in Appendix A except as noted in the following items:
   (i) Under contracts for which premium rates are not guaranteed, and where the effects of insurer underwriting are specifically used by policy duration in the valuation morbidity standard or for return of premium or other deferred cash benefits, total termination rates may be used at ages and durations where these exceed specified mortality table rates, but not in excess of the lesser of:

(I) 80% of the total termination rate used in the calculation of the gross premiums, or

(II) 8%;

(ii) For...(LTC policies issued after 1/1/97 but before 1/1/05)... the contract reserve may be established on a basis of separate:

(I) Mortality (as specified in its Appendix A); and

(II) Terminations other than mortality, where the terminations are not to exceed:

- For policy years 1-4, the lesser of 80% of the voluntary lapse rate used in the calculation of gross premiums and 8%;
- For policy years five and later, the lesser of 100% of the voluntary lapse rate used in the calculation of gross premiums and 4%.

(iii) For...(LTC policies issued after 1/1/05)...the contract reserve may be established on a basis of separate:

(I) Mortality (as specified in its Appendix A); and

(II) Terminations other than mortality, where the terminations are not to exceed:

- For policy year 1 only, the lesser of 80% of the voluntary lapse rate used in the calculation of gross premiums and 6%;
- For policy years 2-4 only, the lesser of 80% of the voluntary lapse rate used in the calculation of gross premiums and 4%;
- For policy years five and later, the lesser of 100% of the voluntary lapse rate used in the calculation of gross premiums and 2%.

Except for LTC and return of premium or other deferred cash benefits, the minimum reserve method is two-year full preliminary term (2YFPT) – terminal reserves are zero at durations 0, 1, and 2. For LTC, the minimum is a function of when the policy was issued. For policies issued before 12/31/91, the minimum is 2YFPT; thereafter it is the 1YFPT. Return of premium and other deferred cash benefits minimum reserve methods depend on the length of the deferral period – 1YFPT for benefits that are provided within 20 years of issue, otherwise 2YFPT.

It is important to keep in mind that the NAIC itself does not have legal authority to effectuate minimum standards in any jurisdiction. It is up to each jurisdiction to adopt the appropriate standards, and this happens on different dates. So, when looking for applicable minimum standards, it is crucial to look to the governing jurisdiction(s) for its (their) minimum standards. (A discussion of which jurisdiction governs is in Chapter 9.)

POLICY RESERVES AND EXPERIENCE MONITORING

One interesting complication of the calculation of policy reserves lies in their use for experience monitoring purposes. This was first described in a paper by Joe Pharr.[10]

If we were to assume a pattern of future claims under a contract, and then create a level gross premium rate scheme, the resulting net premium rate scheme would likewise be level, and be a constant percentage of the gross premium. The ratio of net to gross would be the lifetime anticipated loss ratio under the policy.

If actual experience unfolded to exactly match the pricing assumptions, we would expect to see the actual reported loss ratio equal the lifetime anticipated loss ratio. It turns out that, algebraically, this will only happen if we do two things which are not otherwise intuitively obvious:
  (1) Increases (decreases) in policy reserves each year must be added to (subtracted from) the incurred claims that year, and
  (2) An interest adjustment must be made to claims, to account for that year's interest earnings on reserves assumed in the reserving process.

This is discussed further in Chapter 5, "Setting Premium Rates."

Before publication of that paper, changes in policy reserves had often been treated as equivalent to a premium reserve rather than a claim reserve, which had led to misleading experience reporting.

Unfortunately, statutory accounting does not allow for a clean application of this concept. The use of the preliminary term reserve method (or *any* modified reserve method, for that matter), and the limitations of statutory claim costs for this purpose, both create disruption that make a simple ap-

---

[10] Pharr, Joe B. "The Individual Accident and Health Loss Ratio Dilemma," *Transactions of the Society of Actuaries*, 1979, pp 373-387.

plication of Pharr's rule difficult. With some intellectual sweat invested, however, a modified version can be made to apply.

6.4 CLAIM RESERVES

Claim reserves and liabilities are amounts set aside to cover future payments for claims which have been incurred under the contract, but which have not yet been paid. This sounds like a straightforward statement, but the difficulty of determining exactly when a claim is incurred makes it more complex.

The simplest (but unfortunately not final) test of whether a claim payment has been incurred as of a given date is whether the company would be legally obliged to pay the claim even if the contract ended at the moment following that date. If so, the answer is clear that the subject payment should be included in claim reserves. Otherwise, it is not yet clear.

One question is whether the future payment is subject to future contingencies, such as the continuation of the policy, or the continuation of disablement by the insured. Claim reserves are generally held regardless of the answers to these questions.

Whereas premium and policy reserves are intended to reallocate the timing of premiums to match claims, claim reserves are more commonly thought of as the mechanism to actually quantify the claims attributable to a period of time but paid later.

There are basically seven methods commonly used in calculating claim reserves. Each will be described in detail. Some new methods have been proposed recently, and the Society of Actuaries released a useful study[11] in 2009 that compares various methods.

---

[11] The study aims to compare the effectiveness of various methods in different circumstances, and includes helpful descriptions and further references. It also comes with an Excel model illustrating many of the methods:
Cabe Chadick, Wes Campbell, and Finn Knox-Seith. Comparison of Incurred but not Reported Methods, October 2009. Retrieved October 16, 2014 from
https://www.soa.org/research/research-projects/health/research-ibnr-report.aspx.

1. TRIANGULATION METHOD

This method of calculating claim reserves uses past claim runout history (how payments occurred over time for past incurral dates) as a predictor for future runout. For that reason, this is sometimes called the **runout** method, or **development** method. (We study how the claims for a given time period "develop" over time.)

The most common time frame for the triangulation method is the month. Past claim data are accumulated into a two dimensional array, with "month of incurral" along one axis and "month of payment" along another. For example, a single claim incurred in June of year z, with payments of $1,000 each in June through September, would be included as follows:

Table 6.2

Paid Claim Runout						
Month of Payment	...	Month of Incurral				
		May, z	June, z	July, z	Aug, z	...
...	—	—	—	—	—	—
May, z	...	0	—	—	—	—
June, z	...	0	1,000	—	—	—
July, z	...	0	1,000	0	—	—
Aug, z	...	0	1,000	0	0	...
Sep, z	...	0	1,000	0	0	...
Oct, z	...	0	0	0	0	...
...	...	...	...	...	...	...

Notice that, since payments do not happen in advance of the claim being incurred, there are entries only in the lower left triangular half of the array. Hence the name "triangulation method." Note also that there is nothing magic about the orientation of the entries (top down, left to right) or the axes (paid date vertically, incurred date horizontally); in practice this triangle comes in all permutations.

Once claims have been entered into the triangle, the analysis begins. The concepts used in this analysis are universal, although the details of the analysis differ. There are published variations which are useful to read.[12][13] We will describe the basic process here; the footnoted references provide many additional details which are helpful. Note that the process as described has been simplified in a number of ways versus the methods commonly used in practice. The reader is encouraged to explore the footnoted references throughout this chapter for more details on the many variations of the triangulation method.

The next step in the analysis is to take partial sums (accumulations) of the claim development. Another matrix is created, of identical size to the paid claim matrix, but each entry consists of paid claims *through* that paid month of the claims incurred in that column's month. The sample single claim shown in Table 6.2 would contribute the following to the cumulative paid claim matrix:

Table 6.3

Month of Payment	Cumulative Paid Claims					
		Month of Incurral				
	...	May, z	June, z	July, z	Aug, z	...
...	-	-	-	-	-	-
May, z	...	0	-	-	-	-
June, z	...	0	1,000	-	-	-
July, z	...	0	2,000	0	-	-
Aug, z	...	0	3,000	0	0	...
Sep, z	...	0	4,000	0	0	...
Oct, z	...	0	4,000	0	0	...
...	...	...	...	...	...	...
Ultimate	0	0	4,000	0	0	

We can see that, once a claim is complete, its ultimate value will continue on down the table unchanged. In fact, this characteristic is typically used as a test for whether the data goes back far enough in time to represent fully completed claims. If observation shows consistent figures (within a column) in the bottom left corner of the array, then we can feel comfortable (assuming there is no separate reason to believe otherwise) making an assumption that those claims are fully complete, and can be

---

[12] Litow, Mark. "A Modified Development Method for Deriving Health Claim Reserves," *Transactions of the Society of Actuaries*, 1989, pp 89-126.

[13] Bluhm, William F. *Group Insurance, Sixth Edition,* ACTEX Publications, pp 699-715.

used to represent the entire payout pattern. (If there is not sufficient data to have a complete runout pattern, we must find another means to estimate how much more payout there is for the leftmost columns in our table, and build that into our estimates.)

The next step is to build an arithmetic model of the claim payout pattern. This is typically done by comparing each element of the cumulative paid claim table to the element below it in the table. We will call those the "completion ratios". (The terms "completion factors" and "completion ratios" are not well defined in general usage, and are commonly used to mean various things. It is important to define these terms, when encountered.)

For those incurred months which are not yet complete (in our simplified example, all columns other than the first one in the table), we can use the months to the left of them as a pattern for completion. Suppose, for example, claims are deemed complete at 24 months. When we look at the first incurred month (call it month x) from the left which is not fully complete, it will have 23 months of payments. We can use the ratio of (incurred month $x-1$'s ultimate payout at 24 months) to ($x-1$'s payments through 23 months), as an estimate of how much month x's payments must be increased to be completed. We present Example 6-2 to demonstrate.

Suppose cumulative paid claims look like this:

EXAMPLE 6-2

Table 6.4

Ex. 6-2 Cumulative Paid Claims						
Month of Payment		Month of Incurral				
	...	May, z	June, z	July, z	Aug, z	...
...		—	—	—	—	—
May, z	...	600	—	—	—	—
June, z	...	800	1,000	—	—	—
July, z	...	900	2,000	800	—	—
Aug, z	...	950	3,000	1,200	700	...
Sep, z	...	980	4,000	1,300	1,100	...
Oct, z	...	1,000	4,000	1,700	1,100	...

Suppose further that, upon examining the experience, we are convinced that all claims are substantively complete by the sixth month of runout. Also, we are doing this analysis with paid data through October of z. This means that incurred month May, z, is the most recent fully complete month in our data.

Table 6.5

Month of Payment	Ex. 6-2 Completion Ratios					
		Month of Incurral				
	...	May, z	June, z	July, z	Aug, z	...
...		–	–	–	–	–
May, z	...	0.750	–	–	–	–
June, z	...	0.889	0.500	–	–	–
July, z	...	0.947	0.667	0.667	–	–
Aug, z	...	0.969	0.750	0.923	0.636	...
Sep, z	...	0.980	1.000	0.765	1.000	...
Oct, z	...	1.000*	n/a	n/a	n/a	...

*This value is assumed, since May is deemed complete.

These completion ratios can then be used to develop **completion factors**, which represent, for a given payment month and incurral month, the ratio of that month's cumulative payments to the ultimate total of payments for that incurral month. They are calculated by taking the cumulative product of the completion ratios from the bottom of the column upward. (Alternatively, they could be calculated directly from cumulative paid claims, as the ratio of an incurral month's cumulative paid claims to the ultimate paid claims for that incurral month.)

Here is an important point, though: Months of June, z, and later are not complete, so we do not yet know the ultimate runout of those claims. We therefore cannot find the completion factors for those months until we make an assumption about that missing piece – how they will become complete in the future. So, step 1 is to calculate completion factors for the months that are complete. Table 6.6 shows this for May, z.

Table 6.6

Ex. 6-2 Completion Factors - Step 1						
Month of Payment		Month of Incurral:				
	...	May, z	June, z	July, z	Aug, z	...
...		–	–	–	–	–
May, z	...	0.600	–	–	–	–
June, z	...	0.800	–	–	–	–
July, z	...	0.900	–	–	–	–
Aug, z	...	0.950	(3)	–	–	...
Sep, z	...	0.980	(2)	–	–	...
Oct, z	...	1.000	(1)	–	–	...

The next step is to complete June, z, using the payout pattern of May, z. Since June is only five months complete, if it follows May's runout pattern this will be 98% of the ultimate, and we will put the figure 0.980 in (1). This was taken from the completion factor for May's fifth payment month (Sep). Once we have (1), (2) can be calculated from the corresponding June number in Table 6.5, which happens to be 1.000. (This is just a coincidence, whereas the 1.000 in the most recent payment month for May, z was the result of assuming that month was complete.) So, (2) equals $0.980 \times 1.000 = 0.980$. Similarly, (3) is then (2) times the corresponding Table 6.5 figure of 0.750. Then $(3) = 0.980 \times 0.750 = 0.735$. Once June's payout pattern is completed, July's can be calculated similarly, using incurral month June's fourth payout month completion factor (Sep, again) to complete July's four months of experience. The table can be completed this way, and is shown in Table 6.7.

Table 6.7

Ex. 6-2 Completion Factors – Final						
Month of Payment		Month of Incurral				
	...	May, z	June, z	July, z	Aug, z	...
...		–	–	–	–	–
May, z	...	0.600	–	–	–	–
June, z	...	0.800	0.245	–	–	–
July, z	...	0.900	0.490	0.462	–	–
Aug, z	...	0.950	0.735	0.692	0.477	...
Sep, z	...	0.980	0.980	0.750	0.750	...
Oct, z	...	1.000	0.980	0.980	0.750	...

In general, the completion factor F_i^p, for given incurral month i and payment month p, is determined using completion ratios R_i^p, as follows. When i is the earliest incurral month and $p = \omega$, the latest payment month, then $F_i^\omega = R_i^\omega = 1.000$. Otherwise,

$$F_i^p = R_{i-1}^{p-1}, \text{ for } p = \omega, \text{ and}$$
$$= R_i^p \times F_i^{p+1}, \quad \text{for } i \leq p < \omega. \tag{6.9}$$

If we set $R_i^\omega = R_{i-1}^{\omega-1}$ for incurral months i after the first (earliest) one, then this latter equation is the iterative representation of:

$$F_i^p = \prod_{t=\omega}^{p} R_i^t, \quad \text{for } i \leq p < \omega \tag{6.10}$$

where we have run the index backwards on the product to follow the order of the prior calculation.

Now, finally, we are ready to declare what we think the ultimate claim payouts will be for each incurral month – they are the cumulative paid claims as of Oct, z, for each incurral month (Table 6.4), divided by each corresponding completion factor in Table 6.7. These values are often displayed as part of the "cumulative paid claims" table, as shown here by modifying Table 6.4:

Table 6.8

Ex. 6-2 Cumulative & Ultimate Paid Claims					
Month of Payment		Month of Incurral			
	...	May, z	June, z	July, z	Aug, z	...
...		–	–	–	–	–
May, z	...	600	–	–	–	–
June, z	...	800	1,000	–	–	–
July, z	...	900	2,000	800	–	–
Aug, z	...	950	3,000	1,200	700	...
Sep, z	...	980	4,000	1,300	1,100	...
Oct, z	...	1,000	4,000	1,700	1,100	...
Ultimate	...	1,000	4,081	1,735	1,467	...

If we were to accept this calculation as the source of our final incurred claim estimate, then the reserve would be the sum of the entries in the "ultimate' row, minus the sum of the entries in the row immediately above it, which represents all payments to date.

In practice, these calculations are typically done using a variety of adjustments, and the results of these alternative calculations are all compared and weighed. Some of the adjustments include:

- Averaging the completion ratios attributable to a given month of payout (perhaps using a variety of different averaging methods).
- Averaging the completion factors used to calculate ultimate claims (ditto).
- Developing and using "seasonality" factors, which use month (or season) based completion factors.
- Taking rolling sums of multiple months of incurrals, to smooth the results.

One major assumption in this whole development is that *the past claim runout pattern is representative of the future one.* If there is any reason to believe otherwise, this analysis must be modified to address that issue. Examples of such reasons are: (1) the company's payment mechanism changed to or from electronic submission of claims, (2) a change in claim administration IT systems with a concomitant change in work flow, (3) slow-downs or speed-ups in the claim administration department – including unusual holidays and vacations, (4) changes in benefits, (5) changes in the level of claim backlog during the historical period, or (6) many others. Each of these requires special consideration and adjustment.

In addition, there are quite often unexplained fluctuations in the claim payouts. The practitioner is inevitably presented with a difficult question: How much do I want to believe (and thus reflect in my calculations) this fluctuation? In addition, where does this fluctuation occur in the calculations? It might be inappropriately skewing most or all other reserve estimates. The answers to these questions must be translated into the triangulation process, which requires thinking through the logic of how to make corresponding adjustments.

There is, however, a major shortcoming of this method of claim estimation. As we work with months closer to the current time, where there is less and less actual data on which to base our estimates, the most complete months may only have a fraction of total claims paid at the time of the analysis. The most severe case would be a month with only one month of paid claims. That one month of paid claims can fluctuate significantly, because it is a relatively small sampling of the month's ultimate total payout. However, the completion method treats that single month of paid claims as fully indicative of future payouts for that month.

If, for example, the first month's paid claims correspond to a completion factor of 10%, then the paid claims for that month are multiplied by a factor of 10 to get incurral estimates. Suppose there was a relatively minor fluctuation from 10% to 15% of ultimate payout (for reasonableness, look at the first diagonal in Table 6.7, and notice the ratio varying from 0.245 to 0.600.), which might be the result of perhaps one large claim being paid on the 31st of the month, rather than the 1st of the following month. Then that added claim is also multiplied by the factor of 10, and the incurred claim estimate for that month increases by 50%. A sizeable jump in reserves can thus emerge from a minor fluctuation.

For this reason, actuaries have developed various methods to replace the estimates in those recent months. Most commonly, either the claim cost method or a regression method is used to replace triangulation in recent periods.

2. CLAIM COST METHOD

This method is sometimes called the **loss ratio** or the **pure premium** method. All are logically equivalent, if used correctly. The method is used in two different ways, depending on whether the policy form or plan is a new one (with no data) or an existing one.

For new policy forms or plans, where there is not completion data from which to estimate ultimate claims, claim costs are typically based on pricing costs, then gradually replaced by actual claim data.

For existing policy forms, the method involves developing an estimate of claim cost (being the incurred claims in a month divided by the exposure, such as number of members) for older months, and using it to estimate the claim cost for the recent months. When this is combined with the triangulation method, the claim cost method is used for recent months, and the triangulation method for older months.

Trend is typically taken into account in this process, and the choice of trend can be very important. Normally, the trend implicit in the fully complete months (and perhaps some of the not fully complete ones, as well) is taken into account, as well as environmental trends and any other knowledge brought to the process.

When the recent months' claim costs have been estimated (whether by history or by rating assumptions), they can provide an estimate for incurred claims by simply multiplying them by exposures for the months in question.

It is important to examine how to combine the claim cost method with the triangulation method. Substitution of claim cost method figures for triangulation-produced figures can be considered a credibility question — we are substituting because we do not believe the recent months' calculations are credible. One way to do this is to choose a completion value as a 'cliff.' That is, months where the completion factor is at least this large (typically set in the range of 50-75%) are considered fully credible, and months where the completion factor is not met are considered fully non-credible, and the claim cost estimates fully replace the triangulation results.

Perhaps a bit more sophisticated would be a method shown in a classic paper by Bornheutter and Ferguson,[14] wherein they proposed the better result to be a weighted average of the triangulation method and its replacement. The weights to be used are the completion factors themselves. That way, a month only 10% complete would only rely on 10% of its calculated value, and substitute 90% with the claim cost estimates. (This proportional relationship between completion factors and weights is not altogether theoretically derived, as can be seen by noticing that credibility would reasonably be expected to increase with the square root of the sample size. Completion factors will resemble a square root function only by accident. Our actuarial world is filled with practical solutions which are not strict to the theory, and this is one of them. Even if imperfect, it certainly does a better job than the cliff method, which is still in wide use.)

---

[14] Bornhuetter, Ronald L. and Ferguson, Ronald E., "The Actuary and IBNR," *Proceedings,* Casualty Actuarial Society, 1972, pp 181-195

3. TABULAR METHODS

Some coverages are characterized by a relatively low number of high cost claims. They may also have claim payouts that extend over a long period of time. The notable coverages subject to this are disability income and long term care. Most carriers will not have a sufficiently large claim base, under these coverages, to develop a reliable triangulation process. Even the largest carriers will have difficulty in measuring the probability of claims continuing at very long durations. For that reason, there have been industry-wide efforts to accumulate and evaluate claim data, in order to provide a basis for claim reserves that can be relied on by regulators and carriers.

The tabular method produces a separate claim reserve figure for each claim which exists on the valuation date. The company's total reserves are the sum of these separate reserves.

Most early tabular claim reserve methods were explicitly stated as tables of actual reserve factors. The 1964 Commissioners Disability Table, or 64CDT, for example, was the standard in the 1970s and early 1980s. These reserve factors are typically expressed on a per unit basis, perhaps per $100 of face amount of claim. Terminal claim reserve factors are found in a table (or a book of tables), and usually depend on one or more of: age at incurral of claim, duration of the claim, benefit parameters, gender, and other characteristics.

The current standard for disability income reserves is the **1985 Commissioners' Individual Disability-C**, or **85CIDC** table. The 85CIDC table was adopted by the NAIC to replace the 85CIDA in the late 1990s. The claim termination rates of the 85CIDC table are equal to the 85CIDA claim termination rates multiplied by scalar factors during the first five claim years. The DI valuation table is based on a new kind of table. Rather than articulating the reserve values themselves (which would be an enormous volume of data), the table is defined in terms of factors which can be used by each user to construct each reserve factor.

The 85CIDA table was based on a much more rigorous statistical analysis than had ever been used before for such tables.[15] This included the analysis of a much larger number of variables than ever before, and em-

---

[15] Kidwell, W. Duane and Taylor, William J. "New Disability Tables for Valuation," *Transactions of the Society of Actuaries*, Vol. 37. pp 181-195.

ployment of a SAS model called the "log linear" model. (This model employs a neat algebraic fact – that the log of products is the sum of the logs. By doing a log transformation on data points, performing linear regression, and then doing an exponential transformation, data for multiplicative variables can be processed using linear regression.) Unfortunately, this also caused the resulting number of possible reserve values to increase exponentially as each new variable was added. This was complicated by the expanding number of interest rate bases needed in those calculations, because of changing valuation and tax laws. The new valuation tables being developed presently to replace the 85CIDA tables have even more variables than the 85CIDA tables.

The solution was to express the table in terms of factors used to develop tabular values, rather than the values themselves. This made the result more manageable and publishable. This approach also allowed for a differing number of variables used to determine claim termination rates, depending on duration of the claim. In addition, the factors do not follow equal time intervals – termination rates are stated weekly for early claim durations, then monthly, then yearly, and then by attained age only. A claim with a 30 day elimination period, for example, would have a weekly termination rate for the first week that depends on age at disablement, gender, cause (accident or sickness), and occupation class. Six months into the claim, the termination rate would be monthly, and depend only on age, gender, and cause. In year five of claim, an annual termination rate applies, depending only on age and gender. Claims over 10 years in duration become "ultimate," and have annual termination rates that depend only on attained age and gender.[16]

> **EXERCISE 6.5:** Suppose we were constructing the claim reserve for a policy with the following characteristics: Male, age 35 at disablement, occupation class 1, 7 day elimination period, accident claim, currently in week 12 of the claim.

---

[16] Ibid, Exhibit 1.

Table 6.9
Multiplicative Factors for Calculation of Termination Rates

	Week 12				Week 13			
Duration Rate	0.094				0.082			
Age 35:	1.049				1.027			
EP-0,7,14,30	0.985	1.049	1.008	.955	0.971	1.038	0.989	0.992
Class-1,2,3,4	0.974	0.994	1.009	1.002	0.962	0.993	1.012	1.032
Sex- M,F	0.959	1.039			0.967	1.026		
Cause- A,S	0.950	1.040			0.984	1.006		

Month 4

Duration Rate	0.224	
<90 day ep	1.172	
Male:	0.989	
Age 35 A, S	1.039	1.103

Using the Table 6.9 factors for calculation of termination rates, from the 85 CIDA Table,

    a. construct the remaining weekly termination rates for weeks 12 and 13, and the monthly termination rate for month 4, then

    b. assuming 100,000 such claimants entering week 12 of claim, calculate the number remaining after week 12, week 13, and month 4.[17]   ☐

The Society of Actuaries sells a program, developed by the committee that developed the CIDA table, which calculates reserves and net premiums based on CIDA. It is available through the SOA's website.[18] There is a committee of the Society of Actuaries that, at the time of this writing, is developing a table which is expected to replace the 85CIDA table. That committee's report on recent DI experience is also available on the Society's website.[19]

For LTC insurance, there is, unfortunately, no standardized table for this purpose. Nonetheless, tabular methods are useful, in order to smooth and

---

[17] Op. cit., DTS committee, exhibits 3a and 3b
[18] www.soa.org
[19] 1990-1999 Individual Disability Experience Committee Report accessed at: www.soa.org

extrapolate long term claims. A single table poses several challenges, due to: (1) the wide variation of policy provisions which lead to differing definitions of a claim, and (2) the enormous number of different claim states which can occur. For this purpose, it may be useful to develop a stochastic approach, where a Monte Carlo simulation can be used to measure the volatility of claim reserve projections.

4. REGRESSION METHODS

When rigorous new work is done in the area of claim reserves, it seems to generally involve regression methods. There have been a variety of ways in which regression has been applied. In various papers and talks, actuaries have applied such methods to the reserving process. Peter Reilly,[20] for example, shows an application of regression to the determination of reserves for backlog claims. Another example was presented at a Valuation Actuary Symposium,[21] where Rob Lynch described a regression method to predict actual claim payments by lag month (rather than completion factors), and Doug Fearrington described a time series model which uses a time series polynomial to predict reserves.

5. AVERAGE SIZE CLAIM METHOD

This is a simple method of applying an average expected claim size against a count of known claims. (Thus, the method is not usable for unreported claims.) This is most useful for estimating the value of reported but unprocessed claims (backlog claims), where there is a count of claims but no other information.

6. FORMULA METHOD

This refers to a methodology where the past relationship of the reserve to other statistics (such as number of policies in force, premium in force, paid or incurred claim counts, or number of pending claims) is calculated, and is then applied to those statistics on the valuation date. The validity of this method depends on the predictive ability of these relationships. In using them, it is important to be aware of any potential variations (particularly one-time events) in the statistics which are not reasonably related to reserves.

---

[20] Reilly, Peter K. "A Practical Method for Incorporating Pended Claims in Medical IBNR Estimates", *Health Section News,* Issue # 45

[21] Fearrington, Doug and Lynch, Robert, "New Approaches to Determining Unpaid Claim Liabilities: Old and New," Valuation Actuary Symposium. 2004

7. Seriatim Case Reserves

Case reserves are reserves set based on judgment applied to each individual claim (case). There are multiple situations in which this method might be appropriate. Reserves for claims that are being contested in judicial proceedings, for example, might be held based on the company's attorneys' opinions. (Sometimes companies avoid this method, however, because the amounts so held might be discoverable by the opposition, and used in court in an attempt to sway the decision.) Another situation is when there are catastrophic medical claims, and knowledge of the details of the claim by claim examiners can yield much more accurate predictions of ongoing claim payments than an application of other (more mechanical) methods.

When case reserves are used, it is important to keep in mind that, even though such values might be demonstrably more accurate than other methods, the reserves must still meet minimum standards. This is a particularly meaningful limitation for coverages with tabular reserve methodologies, like DI. While a claim examiner may know that a claimant is only temporarily injured (such as due to a broken leg), the statutory minimum claim reserve must still be held.

Other Considerations

The Actuarial Standards Board has promulgated ASOP #5, which was most recently revised in 2000.[22] That standard refers to many additional things that the insurer and its valuation actuary need to keep in mind in setting claim reserves. A list of other important governing documents is included at the end of this chapter.

6.5 Deficiency and Other Reserves

Another statutory reserve requirement was established relatively recently (compared to the other reserves discussed earlier) as part of the NAIC's recodification of its model laws and regulations. The new requirement is for health insurers to hold **deficiency reserves**. (This term may be confusing to those who are familiar with the life insurance reserves of the same name. Those reserves are set up to fund the shortfall when gross

---

[22] www.actuarialstandardsboard.org

premiums are less than valuation net premiums. That is not the meaning of the term in the current context.)

Deficiency reserves are a slightly specialized form of gross premium reserve. The specialization occurs because the reserves are developed specifically for the statutory blank, and therefore there are boundaries set by regulators on how such reserves can be calculated. These reserves are commonly intended to be only for: (1) a specific block of policies (rather than the insurer's entire business, as might be used for gross premium reserves) grouping blocks of business only with methods acceptable to regulators, and (2) the limited period of time for which the current rates are expected to be valid. (Implicitly, the latter requirement is equivalent to an assumption that future rates can be raised to a self-sufficient level.)[23]

A gross premium reserve is basically the present value on the valuation date of the difference between (future benefit and expense costs) and (current reserves plus future revenue). If this difference is a positive number, then in simple terms, there will not be enough money available in the future to pay the bills. So, the insurer must set aside more money now to cover that shortfall.

A gross premium reserve will typically occur when future premium levels cannot be raised enough to cover the future expense (including both benefit and non-benefit expenses). Some reasons might be: (1) the policy is non-cancelable, and premium rates cannot be raised, (2) regulators are unlikely to allow the premium rates to rise to self-sufficient levels, or (3) even without regulatory restrictions, the size of increases needed to avoid losses might trigger an antiselection spiral that makes it impossible to ever break even.

It is a relatively recent development (within the past couple decades) that deficiency and gross premium reserves have been given the respect they deserve, and that there are explicit requirements for actuaries to perform such calculations when needed. The NAIC-defined deficiency reserve

---

[23] Some regulatory guidance on how to calculate deficiency reserves can be found in the NAIC's "Health Reserves Guidance Manual." In addition, the following paper by Michael Weilant provides helpful discussion and references to several other sources of guidance: "Premium deficiency reserve requirements for accident and health insurance," retrieved October 16, 2014 from http://publications.milliman.com/research/health-rr/pdfs/premium-deficiency-reserve-requirements.pdf.

and the more generic gross premium reserve do have some differences, not all of which are clear.[24]

One important issue has arisen regarding the appropriate level of grouping of business, for purposes of calculating the deficiency reserves. Unfortunately, the NAIC's SSSAP 54 (the defining document for this purpose) is not entirely clear on this issue. There is much disagreement, and many companies are in unique circumstances that seem to justify unique treatment. If, for example, a company is knowingly subsidizing one block of business with another, should they be prohibited, allowed, or required to group those blocks together for deficiency reserves? The papers noted in the footnotes are useful sources for trying to sort this out. Even so, to the extent practicable it is prudent to get auditors' and examiners' buy-in ahead of time on the methods used.

The GAAP equivalent to a gross premium projection is **recoverability testing**. In recoverability testing, a projection of future results is made to determine whether there is sufficient margin in the future rates to cover future costs. If not, the DAC is written off, as necessary to correct this imbalance. If the DAC is not sufficient, the original GAAP assumptions in the (policy, not claim) reserves, which until then have been "locked in," are released under a process known as **loss recognition**. In these circumstances, a new set of assumptions is made about future experience, including a new provision for adverse deviation. These new assumptions then become locked in, unless and until another loss recognition is needed. This process causes a one-time increase in reserves due to the assumption change, aside from the natural year-to-year progression of the calculated reserves.

OTHER RESERVES

Any insurer subject to the Standard Valuation Law, which includes many (but not all) issuers of individual health policies, must file an actuarial opinion under the NAIC's **Actuarial Opinion and Memorandum Regulation (AOMR)**. This law requires an insurer to have an **appointed actuary**. The appointed actuary must annually file an opinion which includes an **asset adequacy analysis**, which determines the likelihood that

---

[24]American Academy of Actuaries, "Report of the American Academy of Actuaries Health Practice Financial Reporting Committee Presented to the National Association of Insurance Commissioners Accident and Health Working Group," January 2002, www.actuary.org

current assets plus future revenue will be able to cover future liabilities. This analysis includes **cash flow testing**.

Most medical coverages tend to be relatively short term, for a number of reasons. First, lapse rates tend to be high relative to (for example) life or DI coverages. For this reason, there tends to be substantially lower asset accumulation over time. Most coverages also do not have cash values or nonforfeiture benefits. (LTC is the large notable exception.)

There have been six risks identified by the NAIC as being important (in general) to cash flow testing: morbidity, mortality, lapse, asset credit quality, reinvestment, and disintermediation.[25] For individual medical coverage, the morbidity risk overpowers the others. In truth, there is another risk not officially recognized in that list – the risk that insurers will not be able to raise rates to a level adequate to offset losses, whether due to regulatory limitation or being in a CAST-induced assessment spiral – that is a major one for individual medical coverages. These two risks, morbidity and premium increase limits, tend to drive the cash flow projections for carriers in the individual medical market.

The medical cash flow testing in this case becomes more of a classical gross premium or deficiency reserve calculation, which essentially tests whether future premiums will be adequate to cover the future losses. Assets are most often limited to those backing claim reserves, which are on the order of ¼ of a year's claims. A major downturn in the value of the invested assets (10%, for example), would result in a shortfall of about 2% of premium, which can most likely be easily built into the next premium increase.

Certain individual coverages, such as DI and LTC, develop substantial reserves relative to premium, and typically will require more conventional cash flow testing. In this case, a longer term projection is made (typically at least 20 years, and often longer) of the expected cash flows under the block. The assets supporting those future needs are modeled stochastically, and the appointed actuary must become comfortable that the assets will be sufficient.

---

[25] "Health Practice Note 1995-1," American Academy of Actuaries, www.actuary.org

TIME PERIODS

Most of the literature, including the earlier discussion, is focused on the annual calculation of policy reserves. Historically, most insurers have used simplified methods between year-end calculations to generate quarterly results. There has been increasing focus on obtaining accurate quarterly statements, however, particularly for publicly held companies.

In this context, there is a question of whether it is appropriate to hold reserves for purposes of reallocating revenue within a given year to properly express seasonality. High deductible, calendar year plans have become quite prevalent, and are subject to more severe seasonality than low deductible plans. Claims under Medicare Part D benefits, on the other hand, are more heavily concentrated earlier in the year, but have the same fundamental issue – claims are predictably non-uniform throughout the year.

A company generally needs to determine intra-year reserves in relation to two contexts: (1) for purposes of management monitoring of experience, and (2) for financial reporting purposes. Certainly it is important that management understand the impact of seasonality in monitoring its actual-vs.-expected financial results. Otherwise, there will be an annual cycle of missed predictions. For financial reporting, the insurer must consider both what the regulatory imperatives are as well as the expectations of the stock market.

MISCELLANEOUS RESERVES

There are a number of reserves that might appear in a company's balance sheet in addition to the major ones already defined. These generally are related to government plans (refund reserves for Medicare Supplement, risk-sharing reserves for Medicare Part D, or special reserves needed for state Medicaid programs), ACA-compliant plans (which may need to reserve for risk adjustment, reinsurance, risk corridors, MLR rebates, or reconciliations of various government subsidies), or for contracts with providers (such as for withholds, bonuses, or other risk-sharing mechanisms). There will generally be a reserve needed any time there are obligations payable after the valuation date that arise from the period prior, or where there is a leveling of experience desired.

Such reserves must typically be addressed on a case-by-case basis, reflecting the terms of the contracts, laws, or regulations involved. These must generally be handled by relying on basic principles, rather than on nonexistent prevailing practice.

Actuaries responsible for setting up reserves for potential future cash flows under the ACA's premium stabilization programs (risk adjustment, transitional reinsurance, and risk corridors) have faced particular challenges as the government has repeatedly changed the rules for those programs. Furthermore, the outcomes under the programs may depend on market level results that cannot be known at the time that financial statements must be prepared.

6.6 RESERVE BASES

Statutory minimum reserve bases are set by each state in which an insurer operates. For multistate carriers, this can become a burden, as the standard effectively becomes the most conservative basis of all the states in which it operates. Many states adopt the NAIC's model standards without change. The current NAIC model is included in Appendix D.

For GAAP accounting, there is not as well-defined a standard. Assumptions equal or comparable to statutory assumptions are typically used, without statutory modifications like preliminary term methods, and with the necessary GAAP modifications (including provision for adverse deviation and calculation of the DAC asset).

Tax reserves are set based on Statutory Accounting Principles, but with limitations that require reserves be recalculated (if not already on this basis) to minimums specified in the IRS Code. For many coverages, one of the main distinctions between the two is the interest rate used for discounting purposes.

These bases are discussed further in Chapter 7, "Financial Reporting and Solvency."

6.7 Governing Documents

Each of the ruling bodies has its own official documents that govern the setting of reserves and liabilities. In the U.S., insurers have financial statements defined by (1) state governments (and the NAIC, to the extent NAIC models are used) for statutory statements, (2) the Financial Accounting Standards Board for GAAP statements, and (3) the IRS Code and Treasury regulations for tax statements. In Canada, statutory standards are set by both provincial and federal authorities, although federal authorities (Office of the Superintendent of Financial Institutions, or OSFI) supervise the vast majority of health insurance business in Canada.

Actuaries who set reserves are subject to professional standards of practice. In the U.S. these standards are set by the Actuarial Standards Board; in Canada by the Canadian Institute of Actuaries.

U.S. Statutory Governing Documents

In the U.S., the NAIC is responsible for most governing documents used by state governments, although there are some states that deviate from the NAIC models in some ways. (NAIC models have no force of law themselves; they must be adopted by states in order to have effect.) The most applicable documents are.[26]

> *NAIC Accounting Practices and Procedures Manual (APPM)*, including *Statements of Statutory Accounting Principles (SSAPs)*. This manual contains the official policies adopted by the NAIC, and is updated annually.
>
> *NAIC* model *Standard Valuation Law (SVL)*. This law has formed the basis of most reserve setting and asset/liability matching for many years. Many issuers of individual health insurance (such as HMOs and many BCBS plans) are not subject to the SVL.
>
> *NAIC* model *Actuarial Opinion and Memorandum Regulation (AOMR)*. This model provides guidance on what should be contained within actuarial statements of opinion which are attached to statutory financial statements of companies subject to the SVL.

---

[26] The product listing can be found at www.naic.org

NAIC model *Health Insurance Reserves Model Regulation.* This was described earlier in this chapter. This model technically applies only to companies subject to the SVL. All of its provisions, however, have been adopted within the NAIC APPM (as Appendix A-010), effectively extending the guidance in the regulation to all companies subject to statutory accounting requirements.

NAIC Health Reserve Guidance Manual. This manual contains detailed guidance useful to actuaries, explaining how the NAIC's Life and Health Actuarial Task Force interprets the application of model laws and regulations.

CANADIAN GOVERNING DOCUMENTS

Canadian insurers are not permitted to publish financial statements on multiple bases (such as statutory versus GAAP) as is required in the U.S. for publicly held companies. For fiscal years starting on or after January 1, 2011, Canadian regulators require that International Financial Reporting Standards (IFRS) be used in preparing insurers' annual statements (formerly, Canadian GAAP was generally used). GAAP principles are published by the *Chartered Professional Accountants of Canada* (CPA Canada, formerly the *Canadian Institute of Chartered Accountants* (CICA)), in the *CPA Canada Handbook.*

The *Canadian Income Tax Act* governs the tax basis for insurers.

U.S. GAAP GOVERNING DOCUMENTS

The governing documents for U.S. GAAP purposes include the following:

Financial Accounting Standards Board (FASB) Statements and Interpretations. FASB is the official promulgator of GAAP accounting standards.

Accounting Principles Board (APB) opinions, statements, and interpretations. The APB was the precursor of FASB. Their original pronouncements are published in FASB's *Accounting Standards: Original Pronouncements* and the AICPA's *Opinions of the Accounting Principles Board.*

There are additional documents that provide guidance as well, including:

American Institute of Certified Public Accountants (AICPA) Statements of Opinion.

FASB Technical Bulletins, and

AICPA Industry Audit and Accounting Guides.

TAX GOVERNING DOCUMENTS

There is only one in the U.S.: the IRS code, and related documents (regulations, opinions, tax court decisions, legislative committee reports, and IRS private letter rulings). In Canada, there are no separate financial statements for tax purposes, although there are some required adjustments made to statutory numbers for tax purposes.

ACTUARIAL GOVERNING DOCUMENTS

Actuaries providing an actuarial opinion for financial statements are subject to a number of specific professional documents:

Actuarial Standards Board (ASB) Actuarial Standards of Practice (ASOPs). These are professional standards developed to apply to specific situations in the U.S. The most relevant ones for this purpose are:

ASOP #5:	Incurred health and disability claims.
ASOP #7:	Analysis of Life, Health, or Property/Casualty Insurer Cash Flows.
ASOP #10:	Methods and Assumptions for Use in Life Insurance Company Financial Statements Prepared in Accordance with GAAP.
ASOP #11:	Financial Statement Treatment of Reinsurance Transactions Involving Life or Health Insurance.
ASOP #12:	Risk Classification.
ASOP #18:	Long-Term Care Insurance.
ASOP #21:	Responding to or Assisting Auditors or Examiners in Connection with Financial Statements for All Practice Areas.

ASOP #22:   Statements of Opinion Based on Asset Adequacy Analysis by Actuaries for Life or Health Insurers.

ASOP #23:   Data Quality.

ASOP #28:   Statements of Actuarial Opinion Regarding Health Insurance Liabilities and Assets.

ASOP #41:   Actuarial Communications.

ASOP #42:   Determining Health and Disability Liabilities Other than Liabilities for Incurred Claims.

Aside from the official pronouncements of the ASB, there is helpful literature which describes common practices, including the American Academy of Actuaries' series of Practice Notes.

Chapter 7

Financial Reporting and Solvency

This chapter discusses the major elements of financial reporting and solvency as they relate to individual health insurance. It assumes the reader already has a basic understanding of accounting principles.

7.1 Financial Reporting

"Financial reporting" is a term usually used to describe the process by which a business organization periodically reports its financial results to its owners and regulators. In doing so, insurers will prepare such reports using a set of accounting principles and practices which are specific to the purpose of the reports. In the U.S., there are two major sets of such principles and practices, sometimes called accounting bases, named *statutory* and *GAAP*. (There is a third, a *tax* basis, which restates financials in ways required by the IRS for federal income tax purposes. This is ubiquitous, but not useful for financial reporting in a traditional sense.)

Statutory reporting is a set of accounting principles and practices prescribed by the regulators who supervise insurers; this is almost always the state of domicile. There is much effort expended by the National Association of Insurance Commissioners (NAIC) to standardize this reporting, and all states (except for California, with respect to certain HMOs and BCBS plans) rely on the principles, bases, and reporting blanks of the NAIC, although some states do require unique supplements for specific purposes.

In Canada, statutory accounting authorities historically required statements to be prepared using Canadian GAAP (Generally Accepted Accounting Principles), specified by the Canadian Institute of Chartered Accountants (CICA) in a handbook. For statements for fiscal years starting on or after January 1, 2011, however, the Canadian Accounting Standards Board requires publicly accountable enterprises (including insurance companies) to use International Financial Reporting Standards (IFRS) in the preparation of financial statements. In another change, CICA joined with other Canadian accounting professional organizations in 2013 and 2014 to form a national organization called CPA Canada.

In the U.S., there are different statement blanks for use by life companies, health insurers (combining what was previously a number of different blanks), and property-casualty companies. (A **statement blank** is the form, provided by the NAIC, that an insurer must fill out and file. It provides a strict format for reporting financial results. The different blanks are often identified by the unique color of their covers: a life blank is blue, health is orange, and P&C is yellow.) Copies of selected portions of the life and health blanks are included in the electronic files distributed with this text with permission from the NAIC. The NAIC provides tests to determine which type of statement blank an organization must file, based mostly on what type of business it writes, rather than just how it is licensed. This brings an important level of consistency between carriers. In the past, reporting requirements and solvency standards were quite different, depending on whether a company was licensed as an HMO, health service company, life and health insurer, or property-casualty insurer.

Some carriers must now test the business they had in force for the year, to determine what kind of annual statement blank they must complete and file. The two major ones for individual health insurance are the Orange (Health) and Blue (Life) blanks.

There are annual statement blanks and quarterly statement blanks. The annual statement blank is the most important one, for a number of reasons. First, the annual statement reporting is more complete and detailed than quarterly versions. (In 2013, the quarterly health blank had 39 pages, while the annual blank had 87 – not including the many supplements.) The work done by insurers to obtain values for quarterly statements is sometimes based on extrapolations of annual statement values, and a "back to basics" recalculation might only occur once a year for the annual statement. In addition, most financial statistics about insurers, used for a variety of purposes, are based on annual statement numbers. Finally, the much discussed "Actuarial Statement of Opinion," in its various formats for different blanks, is required only for the annual statement, not for quarterly filings.

GAAP (Generally Accepted Accounting Principles) reporting in the U.S. is based on a different set of accounting principles and practices, determined by the Financial Accounting Standards Board (FASB).[1] For actuarial liabilities of insurance companies, the primary relevant portion of FASB guidance is in its **Statement of Financial Accounting Standards (SFAS) No.60: Accounting and Reporting by Insurance Enterprises**. Companies whose stock is publicly traded are required by the federal Securities and Exchange Commission to prepare financial reports on this GAAP basis. For the past decade or so, mutual companies have been required by the American Institute of Certified Public Accountants (AICPA) to produce GAAP statements, or have their audit opinions be qualified.

Each country has its own reporting standards for insurers. The International Accounting Standards Board (IASB) is attempting to codify international rules that will be adopted in many countries, and possibly be harmonized with U.S. GAAP. IASB rules (known as IFRS) are already relevant to U.S. subsidiaries of European companies. As another example, Canada recently adopted IFRS to replace its prior reporting standards (which were known as Canadian GAAP). Canadian GAAP differed in major ways from U.S. GAAP. In this book, references to "GAAP" will refer to the U.S. version, unless otherwise specified.

While statutory accounting tends to focus most heavily on solvency protection for the public, and is therefore relatively conservative, GAAP reporting focuses more on accurate reporting of revenue and earnings, and has only limited and explicit conservatism.

GAAP financials and statutory financials are very close to each other in many ways. Most companies will maintain their general ledger on one basis or the other, and make adjustments to get to the other basis when needed for filing. In moving from statutory to GAAP, the major aspects of such modifications are:

- Capitalization of deferred acquisition costs (**DAC**). DAC reallocates the higher initial expense of acquiring business, which would otherwise be charged at the time it is incurred, proportionately to the future earnings attributable to that business, with a modest amount of conservatism, called, in GAAP parlance, **provision for adverse deviation**. Statutory accounting does not allow a DAC asset.

---

[1] www.fasb.org

- Replacement of statutory conservatism in policy reserves with the provision for adverse deviation, a less conservative basis. This includes allowing lapse assumptions in such calculations, as opposed to the strict limitations on lapse rates found in statutory accounting (described in Chapter 6, "Reserves and Liabilities."
- Some differences in recognition of deferred taxes, all receivables and allowances (not just the statutorily defined ones called **admitted assets**), and the market value of most assets.
- Reporting of reserves is net-of-reinsurance in statutory reporting. In GAAP reporting, reserve credits for cessions to reinsurance are shown as assets, and the liability item for reserves is shown prior to reinsurance ceded.

One other important difference between statutory and GAAP reporting is that statutory reporting tends to provide both asset and liability values on a basis which would demonstrate solvency if the insurer closed its doors on the date of the valuation. GAAP reporting, on the other hand, is on a **going concern basis**, meaning that values in the statement assume that the enterprise will continue into the future. One might assume, for example, that there will be a level of future sales sufficient to create normal economies of scale in expense projections. Future sales, however, are not included directly.

Further discussion of the statutory and GAAP bases, and how their presence guides reserve calculations, is included in Chapter 6, "Reserves & Liabilities."

Tax Basis reserves, a third basis of reporting, is required by the U.S. tax law. The Tax Reform Act of 1984 put into place the current tax law for insurance companies. The Tax Reform Act of 1986 extended taxation to some individual health insurers that were previously tax exempt, mostly BCBS type plans. Some HMOs remain exempt from federal taxation to this day. The 1984 act prescribes a tax basis for reserves that includes specified reserve methods, interest assumptions, and morbidity assumptions. The purpose of this basis "is to limit the amount of tax deductible life insurance reserves to the minimum level under the prevailing valuation standards of the States."[2] Various limitations are placed on different types of reserves, depending on whether the policies are "noncancelable" (the

---

[2]*Internal Revenue Manual*, U.S. Internal Revenue Service. www.irs.gov

IRS definition, which, in more common parlance, would include policies with either non-cancellable or guaranteed renewable renewability provisions), disability income coverage vs. long-term care coverage vs. other coverages, and claim vs. other (which they call "active life" for this purpose) reserves.

As with GAAP accounting, tax reserve calculations are generally a modification of the statutory calculations.

With both GAAP and tax accounting, the year of issue of the policy, and the year of incurral of a long term claim, will define the assumptions to be used in calculating the reserves. These assumptions will change over time, and as they do, there may accumulate a large number of assumptions applicable to a company's business. In the past this has, on occasion, created computer programming nightmares – forcing programmers to choose between carrying forward sets of pre-calculated reserve factors and the computation-heavy alternative of calculating reserve values from scratch at each valuation date. In today's era of very powerful computing power, and large available memory, this is less of a problem.

One interesting set of IRS code requirements, for a reserve to be allowed as a **life insurance reserve** (i.e., be deductible), is in the following excerpt from the code:

- The reserves must be computed or estimated on the basis of recognized mortality and/or morbidity tables, and assumed rates of interest;
- They must be set aside to mature or liquidate, by payment or reinsurance, future unaccrued claims. Such future claims must:

  o arise under....noncancelable A & H insurance contracts.

  o involve at the time the particular reserves are computed... accident, or health contingencies (i.e.,...morbidity risks); and
- The reserves must be required by law (i.e., by state law, rules or regulations), except for two special cases cited in IRC section 816(b).[3]

Health insurers can be taxed either as life insurers or as non-life insurers. The IRS uses a test that says an insurance company will be taxed as a life

---

[3] A useful website containing the IRS Code, maintained by Cornell Law School, is www.law.cornell.edu

insurance company if its life insurance reserves, plus unearned premiums, and unpaid losses, on "noncancelable life, health, or accident policies", comprise more than 50 percent of its total reserves. Being taxed as a life insurer can greatly increase a company's tax liability, so some companies work hard at maintaining their non-life insurance company status.

NOTABLE PORTIONS OF THE ORANGE ANNUAL STATEMENT BLANK

Most elements of the annual statement will be applicable in some way to individual health insurance. The exhibits that display assets and their related investment income, for example, include assets that are typically being held to support all the company's business, including the individual health line. For purposes of this chapter, though, we will concentrate on the portions of the statement of greatest interest to the actuary.

The orange blank is the one probably being filled out by (medical) health insurers in the U.S., including Blue Cross/Blue Shield plans, HMOs, and many other commercial (mutual or stock) companies who specialize in health insurance. Because of this, all parts of the blank (except the Life and P&C supplements) are relevant to health business. There are a few pages, exhibits, and supplements of particular note to those in the IH business.

Liabilities, Capital, and Surplus

This is the second part of the balance sheet (the page labeled *Assets* being the first.) The following lines of the statement are of greatest interest:

- Line 1: Claims unpaid (less $..... reinsurance ceded).

    This is the amount for claims incurred but not reported (IBNR), claims in course of settlement, percentage withholds of provider payments, and anticipated coordination of benefits and subrogation recoveries. In other words, claims incurred but not *paid* (IBNP);
- Line 2: Accrued medical incentive pool and bonus amounts;
- Line 3: Unpaid claims adjustment expenses;
- Line 4: Aggregate health policy reserves, including the liability of $..... for medical loss ratio rebate per the Public Health Service Act (from Part 2D of the underwriting and investment exhibit);

- Line 7:   Aggregate health claim reserves.

    This is from the same source as line 4, and represents the present value of amounts not yet due, reserves for future contingent benefits, and any write-in claim reserves; and

- Line 8:   Premiums received in advance.

All these items are aggregate amounts; they summarize the liabilities for which there is greater detail later in the annual statement.

This page also splits the aggregate total amounts between **covered** and **uncovered** amounts. Generally, covered liabilities and claims are those associated with services provided within the carrier's provider network. Uncovered claims and liabilities are for care provided by nonparticipating or out-of-network providers. These terms are carried over from the predecessor HMO statutory reporting blank.

Analysis of Operations by Line of Business (Gain and Loss Exhibit)

This exhibit provides an overview of the net underwriting gain (or loss), and the major elements which generated it, in total and split by 9 lines of business. The gain or loss (with line numbers in square parentheses,[ ]) is calculated as follows. Note that this calculation uses a 'stepping stone' approach, common in the annual statement, of calculating intermediate subtotal values.

Gain[24] = Total Revenues [7] – Total Underwriting Deductions [23]

In turn,

Total Revenues [7]
 = Net premium income [1]
  + Change in UPR and reserve for rate credit [2]
  + Fee-for-service (net of $...medical expenses) [3]
  + Risk revenue [4]
  + Aggregate write-ins for other health care related revenues [5]
  + Aggregate write-ins for other non-health care related revenues [6]

"Deductions" from revenue are the expenses associated with doing the business. This includes the direct costs (such as medical claims) plus the increase in reserves associated with them. The increase in reserve can, in turn, be thought of as two pieces (although not expressed as such, at least here.) The first piece is the current estimate of the most recent year's outstanding IBNP. The second piece is a correction of last year's reserve.

Total Underwriting Deductions [23]
= Total hospital and medical [17]
+ Non-health claims (net) [18]
+ Claims adjustment expenses including
$.... cost containment expenses [19]
+ General administrative expenses [20]
+ Increase in reserves for accident and health contracts [21]
+ Increase in reserves for life contracts [22]

Total hospital and medical is further broken down by certain categories: hospital/medical, other professional, outside referrals, emergency room and out-of-area claims, prescription drugs, and a couple others.

In order to evaluate the financial results by line of business (LOB), the LOBs reported in the analysis of operations exhibit (and which constitute its column headings, along with "Total") are:

(1) Comprehensive (Hospital & Medical),
(2) Medicare Supplement,
(3) Dental Only,
(4) Vision Only,
(5) Federal Employees Health Benefit Plan,
(6) Title XVIII Medicare,
(7) Title XIX Medicaid,
(8) Other Health, and
(9) Other Non-Health.

Underwriting and Investment Exhibit

This is a multi-part exhibit in the blank. The first part (called "Part 1 - Premiums") shows the premiums earned by line of business. The lines of business are almost the same ones as listed for the Gain and Loss Exhibit, except that the "Other Non-Health" item is broken down into two categories: Life and Property/Casualty. The other 8 categories are also presented as a "Health subtotal." The premiums that are shown in this part include: (1) Direct Business, (2) Reinsurance Assumed, (3) Reinsurance Ceded, and (4) Net Premium Income (1+2-3). This breakdown allows the reader to see the financial results on both a direct basis (to evaluate the company's business), and net of reinsurance (to evaluate the ultimate risk it is taking, net of the reinsurance protections it has put in place to absorb fluctuations.)

The next part is "Part 2 - Claims Incurred During the Year." It shows the development (for each of the Gain and Loss Exhibit categories) of the Incurred Benefits for the year, and separately, incurred medical incentive pools and bonuses. The calculation is again based on payments made plus the increase in reserves and liabilities.

Part 2B- Analysis of Claims Unpaid – Prior year net of reinsurance

This is an exhibit that *restates* the prior year's claim reserve, and substitutes what we know now for what we knew then, and compares it to our estimate then. This is useful in evaluating the sufficiency of the reserve basis and method being used.

This analysis is done by breaking down the two elements of Incurred Claims (Claims paid during this valuation year, and Claim reserve and Claim liability as of the valuation date) into two categories – those dollars related to claims incurred during the valuation year and those related to claims incurred prior. Then:

"Claims Incurred in Prior Years"
= (Claims Paid this year on prior year's incurrals)

+ (The portion of this year's ending reserve applicable to prior years' incurrals).

This is then compared against the estimated claim reserve and liability from the prior year.

Part 2C- Development of Paid and Incurred Health Claims

This exhibit contains three sections. The first is a matrix showing the cumulative paid health claims for incurrals in the valuation year, each of the prior four years, and for all years prior to that combined. The payments are shown for the most recent five years.

The second section is identical to the first, except that the claim liability and reserve from each year-end is added to the entries in the matrix. This represents, then, the incurred health claims, as estimated over a five year period.

The third section has various ratios of paid claims and unpaid claims, with and without their associated claim adjustment expenses, to earned premium.

Part 2D- Aggregate Reserve for Accident and Health Contracts Only

This part develops the detail of the totals which are brought forward to lines 4 and 7 of the liability page (mentioned earlier.) This part accumulates all the major reserves and liabilities for the business. The calculations are as follows:

Health policy reserves (named "Totals (Net)" in the exhibit) [8]
 = Unearned premium reserves [1]
  + Additional policy reserves (with a footnote of the portion arising from premium deficiency reserves) [2]
  + Reserve for future contingent benefits [3]
  + Reserve for rate credits or experience rating refunds (including $...) for investment income [4]
  + Aggregate write-ins for other policy reserves [5]
  − Reinsurance ceded [7]

Health claim reserves (similarly named) [14]
= Present value of amounts not yet due on claims [9]
+ Reserve for future contingent benefits [10]
+ Aggregate write-ins for other claim reserves [11]
− Reinsurance ceded [13]

In this calculation, "claim reserves" is using the strict definition, and excludes claim liabilities. These therefore represent amounts held to support claims which have been incurred but not yet accrued, such as future DI claim payments to an existing claimant. They do not include accrued but unpaid benefits, such as claims in course of settlement.

Lines [3] and [10] are entries for 'future contingent benefits.' The NAIC explains[4] that these entries are for "the extension of benefits after termination of the policy or of any insurance hereunder. Such benefits, that actually accrue and are payable at some future date, are predicated on a condition or actual disability that exists at the termination of the insurance and that is usually not known to the insurance company. An example…is the coverage for hospital confinement after the termination of (coverage)" where the policy had a provision which provides such an extension of benefits.

Line [4], the reserve for rate credits or experience rating refunds, doesn't normally apply to individual coverage.

Part 3 – Analysis of Expenses

This exhibit breaks total expenses into dozens of categories. Further, each of these must be broken down into Claim Adjustment Expenses (CAE), General Administrative Expenses, and Investment Expenses. Further, the CAE is broken down between Cost Containment Expenses and Other CAE. In some situations, cost containment expenses are treated differently from other CAE, for policy reasons.

Medicare Supplement Insurance Experience Exhibit

This is a supplementary exhibit which was originally developed in response to the federal law Omnibus Budget Reconciliation Act of 1990 (OBRA 1990). That law required substantial reform in the Medicare Supplement market, including expanded reporting.

---

[4] *2005 Health Quarterly and Annual Statement Instructions*, National Association of Insurance Commissioners.

Medicare Part D Coverage Supplement

This supplementary exhibit provides a detailed breakdown of financial items pertaining to prescription drug policies sold to the Medicare-eligible population, split into individual and group coverage. The Medicare Part D prescription drug program has several features that complicate financial reporting, including risk adjustment, federal reinsurance, and risk corridors. (If these features sound familiar, it may be because they were used as a model for similar programs under the ACA for the commercial market.)

Accident and Health Policy Experience Exhibit for Year

This is a very useful supplementary exhibit that provides basic information by line of business, separately for individual and group coverage. The information includes earned premiums, incurred claims, changes in contract reserves, and exposure values (number of policies, lives, and member months).

Supplemental Health Care Exhibit

This supplementary exhibit was introduced for 2010 financial statements and provides a wealth of information by state and line of business, including information needed to calculate preliminary medical loss ratios for testing against the minimums required under the ACA (these preliminary ratios are still subject to additional claim runout and various other adjustments before the final ratio for rebate purposes is calculated several months later).

This information (together with information insurers must report separately due to MLR reporting required by the ACA) has made it possible to study financial results for the individual, small group, and large group markets separately, whereas previously it was difficult to get a full picture by line of business. One recent study[5] by Paul Houchens, Jason Clarkson, and Colin Gray has done this. They found that, in 2013, direct individual insurance averaged a 3.9% underwriting loss across the 10.9 million covered lives, as compared to average gains of 2.8% in the small group market and 2.0% in the large group market.

---

[5] Houchens, Paul, Clarkson, Jason, and Gray, Colin. 2013 Commercial health insurance: Overview of financial results. Milliman Insight, November 2014. Retrieved 1/14/2015 from http://us.milliman.com/insight/2014/2013-Commercial-health-insurance-Overview-of-financial-results

Long-Term Care (LTC)
Experience Reporting Forms 1, 2, 3, 4, and 5

These supplemental forms report the experience of the company in its LTC products. These forms were new in 2009, replacing prior forms A, B, and C.

Form 1 focuses on current and recent morbidity and persistency experience, and loss ratios. (The prior forms required substantially more detail in loss ratio reporting.) It does so comparing actual to expected values, and puts LTC policies into three categories: comprehensive, institutional only, and non-institutional only. There are separate exhibits for individual and group coverage.

Form 2 details the major elements of current and recent experience, by policy form.

Form 3 focuses on a runout of claim reserves, with interest adjusted restatements of reserves for incurral year and eight years after. This is to evaluate the adequacy of the reserve basis.

Form 4 relates to LTC accelerated benefits attached to certain life and annuity products, while Form 5 includes basic information on LTC business for each state.

NOTABLE PORTIONS OF THE BLUE ANNUAL STATEMENT BLANK

The Blue Blank is used for Life and Accident and Health (A&H) Companies. Until relatively recently, the applicable valuation laws called for different actuarial opinions ("Section 7 opinions," and "Section 8 opinions"), depending on the size of the company. Smaller companies could avoid the more rigorous Section 8 requirements and have Section 7 opinions. Section 7 opinions were not required to contain asset adequacy opinions, while Section 8 opinions did.

The NAIC has adopted a revised version of the Actuarial Opinion and Memorandum Model Regulation, which now requires all insurers filing the blue blank to have asset adequacy testing, thus eliminating the Section 7 option. This change only becomes applicable state by state, as each state adopts the new models. As of the end of 2013, however, 48 states, the District of Columbia, and Puerto Rico have all adopted some version of the revised model regulation.

Actuarial opinions are required to be from qualified Members of the American Academy of Actuaries, who must attest to the reasonableness of the liabilities being held by the company. Asset adequacy opinions also include opinions regarding the assets being held to cover the liabilities. If the asset risks are material, developing this opinion may require rigorous, complex, and time consuming modeling of future assets, liabilities, and their interaction.

With most medical coverages, the asset risk is largely negligible, because the amount of assets is relatively small. Cash flow testing is used to demonstrate asset adequacy, but without that requirement, gross premium reserve calculations or even just policy reserve calculations (without asset testing) are often done. Some actuaries build investment income into their gross premium and deficiency reserve calculations, and consider that sufficient asset adequacy testing for this purpose. A good source for considerations regarding this process is the American Academy of Actuaries' Health Practice Note.[6] Notably, such asset adequacy testing is not required for companies that are not life insurers.

For coverages other than LTC and DI, asset adequacy testing has largely been replaced by premium deficiency reserve testing. This testing focuses on the long term adequacy of current reserves and future premiums to fund future benefits and future expenses, and is discussed further in Chapter 6, "Reserves and Liabilities."

LTC and DI coverages often generate substantial assets which are needed to fund claim payments many years in the future. For this reason, asset adequacy testing is generally considered very important to the solvency monitoring of insurers that issue them.

The notable elements of the blue blank relating to individual health insurance are as follows.

Liabilities, Surplus and Other Funds

As in the orange blank, there are certain lines of particular interest:

- Line 2: Aggregate reserve for accident and health contracts. This is the Exhibit 6 total reserve amount, net of reinsurance.

---

[6] www.actuary.org

- Line 4.2: Accident and health contract claims. This is the amount from Exhibit 8 due to A&H insurance.
- Line 8: Premiums...for...A&H contracts received in advance.

As before, these are amounts that are generally brought forward from other parts of the statement where greater detail is provided.

Summary of Operations

This exhibit shows the amounts flowing in and out of the company's accounts, which have generated the changes in the balance sheet. The most relevant items to our discussion are:

- Line 1: Premiums...for...A&H contracts.
- Line 13: Disability benefits and benefits under A&H contracts.
- Line 16: Group conversions.
- Line 19: Increase in aggregate reserves for life and A&H contracts.

Analysis of Operations by Line of Business (Gain and Loss Exhibit)

This exhibit is very similar to the one contained in the orange blank. The line numbers are different, and there is more detail in matters related to life insurance, and less in those related to health insurance. Of the 11 lines of business (in columns), seven are related to life and annuity business, 3 to A&H, and one "Aggregate of All Other Lines of Business." Of the 3 A&H columns, there are only two related to individual health coverage:

- Column 10: Credit (Group and Individual), a specialty line of business relating to coverage (usually disability) designed to pay loan payments in event of disablement.
- Column 11: Other, which would contain all other individual A&H business.

The lack of detail in this exhibit is echoed in many other exhibits and schedules, because the blue blank has a major focus on life insurance.

It is worthwhile noting that some life insurance contracts have relatively minor amounts of disability coverage attached to them. In this case, the financial aspects of such DI coverage are generally reported as part of the life coverage. For example, the exhibit entitled **Analysis of Increase in Reserves During the Year** refers to reserves "Involving Life or Disability Contingencies." However, the instructions to the blank clarify that this exhibit "applies to items reported in Exhibit 5," which does not actually include A&H policies, just life policies.

There are a few more places of particular interest to us in the blue blank.

Exhibit 6- Aggregate Reserves for Accident and Health Contracts

This exhibit shows, for each of nine columns, a development of total active life reserve (ALR), total claim reserve (CR), and tabular fund interest. In both reserve amounts, the exhibit shows results both before (gross of) and after (net of) reinsurance.

Total ALR (Gross) [7] = Unearned premium reserves [1]
+ Additional contract reserves [2]
+ Additional actuarial reserves
− Asset/Liability analysis [3]
+ Reserve for future contingent benefits [4]
+ Reserve for rate credits [5]
+ Aggregate write-ins for reserves [6]

With respect to line [2], the blank requires that the insurer disclose the valuation standard used, including the basis, interest rates and methods.

Line [3] includes any premium deficiency reserve amounts which must be held.

Total CR (Gross) [14]
= Present Value of Amount Not Yet Due on Claims [10]
+ Additional actuarial reserves − Asset/Liability analysis [11]
+ Reserve for future contingent benefits [12]
+ Aggregate write-ins for reserves [13]

Each of these line items is calculated for each of the categories of policies specified in the blank, and listed as column headings in Exhibit 6. Aside from the "total" column, they are: Group Accident and Health, Credit Accident and Health (Group and Individual), Collectively Renewable, and Other Individual Contracts (which has five subheadings, based on the renewability provisions of the contracts. This is discussed in the Chapter 3, "Policy Forms.")

Exhibit 8- Claims for Life and Accident and Health Contracts

This exhibit shows breakdowns of the liabilities and incurred claims for the year. It has two parts. Part 1 shows four categories of claim liabilities (both gross and net of reinsurance) as of the statement date. The four categories of liability are *Due and Unpaid, In course of settlement (resisted), In course of settlement (other),* and *Incurred but unreported.*

Part 2 of Exhibit 8 displays the incurred claims for the year, again gross and net of reinsurance, for *Settlements* (paid claims) *during the year; Liability December 31, current year from Part 1; Amounts recoverable from reinsurers December 31, current year* (this one and its prior year counterpart do not have the further reinsurance breakdown, for obvious reasons); *Liability December 31, prior year;* and *Amounts recoverable from reinsurers December 31, prior year.*

Exhibit 6 contains the reserve items related to non-accrued payments for claims (a rigorous definition of 'reserve'), while Exhibit 8 contains the accrued portions ('liabilities'). A discussion of the calculation of these reserves is in Chapter 6, "Reserves and Liabilities."

Schedule H – Accident and Health Exhibit is THE major schedule of A&H experience in the blue blank. It has five parts.

Schedule H, Part 1 – is the *Analysis of Underwriting Operations.* For the familiar nine categories of business, this schedule shows the development of gain or loss from underwriting. (It is interesting to note that the definition of 'gain' in this use does not include investment income.) The formula is worth noting, because of the important terms it defines, as follows:

Gain from underwriting before dividends or refunds [12]
= Premiums earned [2]
- Incurred claims [3]
- Cost containment expenses [4]
- Increase in contract reserves [6]
- Total other expenses incurred [10]
- Aggregate write-ins for deductions [11],

where

Premiums earned [2] = Premiums written [1]
- (The increase in reserves from Part 2, A, [6])

Schedule H, Part 2 – details the breakdown of the three reserve categories. It also develops the increase in these reserves over the year. *Reserves and Liabilities* provides detail on the reserve calculations for each line of business (column). There are three sections, one each for premium reserves, contract reserves, and claim reserves and liabilities. The first section, A, breaks down the total premium reserves for the year into some component pieces; *unearned premium reserves, advance premium*, and *reserve for rate credits*.

Similarly, Section B, for contract reserves, shows two elements – *Additional reserves*, and *Reserve for future contingent benefits*. The additional reserves include any premium deficiency reserve which might be needed, as well as the more classical contract reserves.

Section C is for claim reserves and liabilities. Since these are largely detailed in Exhibits 6 and 8, there is no breakout of these.

Schedule H, Part 3 – Test of Prior Year's Claim Reserves and Liabilities calculates a one year restatement of the prior year's reserve estimates. It compares the sum of: (1) the current year's estimate of reserves on claim incurred prior to the current year, and (2) the current year's payments on those same claims, against last year's estimate. In essence, it answers the question, "What is your current best estimate of what you should have held as reserves last year, compared to what you actually held?"

Schedule H, Part 4 – Reinsurance is a simple exhibit showing, for each column, for (A) reinsurance assumed, and (B) reinsurance ceded, the premiums written, premiums earned, incurred claims, and commissions.

Schedule H, Part 5 – Health Claims shows the development/relationship between incurred claims and paid claims, and the starting and ending reserves, for direct (gross of reinsurance) business, assumed reinsurance, ceded reinsurance, and net (of reinsurance). The last section of this part makes the same calculation, on a net of reinsurance basis, for incurred claims and cost containment expenses. The columns for this schedule are simpler than the other parts of Schedule H; Medical, Dental, Other, and Total.

Schedule S is often mentioned as an important schedule, which details the reinsurance values that are used elsewhere in the statement.

The blue blank includes several other important supplements similar to those described earlier for the orange blank:

- the *Medicare Supplement Insurance Experience Exhibit*,
- the *Medicare Part D Coverage Supplement*,
- the *Long-Term Care Experience Reporting Forms*,
- the *Accident and Health Policy Experience Exhibit for Year*,
- the *Supplemental Health Care Exhibit.*

7.2 SOLVENCY TESTING

The primary purpose of statutory financial reporting is to expose the company's financial results to the light of day, to ensure that the company is, and is likely to remain, solvent. Because insurance obligations are long term, and people's financial and even physical well being often depend on the company meeting those obligations, it is seen as an important public policy goal to provide a high degree of security that health companies will remain solvent.

The bulk of today's statutory annual statement blank was originally devised in the 1920s, following some scandals that rocked the industry, particularly for mutual insurers. At that point, much of the modern annual statement approach was developed. It was not until relatively late in the century that the next quantum step was taken in solvency regulation – a turn toward risk-based analysis. The first step in this regard was the development of risk-based capital standards for insurers. This allowed regulators to maintain consistent capital requirements between diverse insurers, with diverse risk profiles. Risk-based analysis is still evolving, through the advent of **enterprise risk management**. It will be interesting to watch this evolution continue.

The major tool currently used by regulators in monitoring and evaluating capital adequacy is **the risk-based capital (RBC)** formula. There are separate formulas for life companies, health companies, and P&C companies. Chapter 11, "Managing the Business," includes discussion of many RBC issues from a strategic management point of view. Here, we will have a more detailed discussion of the actual mechanics of the health formula calculations.

Risk Based Capital monitoring is conceptually quite simple:

- First, company data is put into the RBC formula to calculate the benchmark **Authorized Control Level (ACL)** RBC value.
- Second, the company's capital and surplus is taken, with some adjustments specifically for this purpose, to find **Adjusted Capital**.
- Third, the ratio of the Adjusted Capital to the ACL level is calculated. If the value of that ratio falls under 200%, corrective action is specified by the RBC law. The severity of that action depends on how far under the 200% trigger it falls.

The **Risk-Based Capital for Health Organizations Model Act (HORBC)** was adopted in 1998, about five years after the Life and P&C equivalent was adopted. In 2009, a trend test was added to the model law that generates a company action level event in certain circumstances where RBC is declining over time.

As with any NAIC model, implementation requires adoption by individual states. As of this writing, the majority of states have adopted a version of this model law.

The complexity of RBC monitoring mostly lies in the first of the above steps, calculating the ACL value for the company. In order to understand the formula, it is helpful to first have some context.

THE THEORY

Risk Based Capital formulae, and in particular the HORBC formula, are designed to be a set of *relativities* that reflect the widely varying risk profiles that different kinds of coverage and insurers experience.

Suppose, for example, there are two carriers that are identical in all ways except the coverage they issue. Carrier A issues a coverage that is predictable and produces results year after year within a narrow range around expected values. (Hospital indemnity coverage, for example.) Carrier B, however, issues a highly volatile coverage that fluctuates significantly from expected levels – a very high deductible major medical coverage, perhaps. If these two carriers are of comparable size and otherwise similar, it makes perfect sense that Carrier B should hold a higher level of capital than Carrier A, in order to achieve the same level of risk of insolvency as Carrier A.

The HORBC formula was developed based on the presumption that risk is embodied as unexpected negative fluctuations in financial results. (Conversely, if something can be accurately predicted, assuming that there is an available response to it and that management reacts rationally to that knowledge, it is not a risk.) These unexpected fluctuations can be measured by looking at fluctuations in actual historical results.[7]

Fluctuations were assumed to be composed of two elements: (1) *statistical fluctuations*, which were purely random fluctuations based on the probability distributions of individuals in the group and the size of the portfolio, and (2) *historical* (or residual) *fluctuations*, which were the remaining fluctuations, assumed to be based on everything else, but which did not vary by size of the portfolio.

This combination of risks is what led to the tiered, size-based factors the NAIC ultimately adopted. The historical data was subdivided and examined according to every relevant risk factor that the working group found. Among others, these factors included: type of reimbursement method, speed of growth of the block of insurance, and type of coverage. (A further risk factor, degree of regulation, was demonstrated to have a very high degree of correlation to risk. The regulators rejected this factor, however,

---

[7] This work was done by a task force of the American Academy of Actuaries, the Health Organizations Risk Based Capital Task Force, www.actuary.org

because of its implication that heavier rate regulation would result in higher risk of insolvency.)

The theoretical formula was developed using a Monte Carlo simulator that was designed specifically for that purpose, combined with a ruin model that simulated ongoing capital levels of a block of business. A multitude of cells were simulated. For each cell, historical variance, related to that cell's non-size characteristics, was combined with statistical variance, based on the block's size and intrinsic variance of the individual risk, along with a formula that provided for management response to each fluctuation and relevant prior ones. The simulation modeled seven years of results for each cell, but the results from the first two years were not used. (This was to better model five years of risk to ongoing business.) Over 10,000 simulations for the cell, given a starting level of capital, measured how often that block of business became insolvent; that provided a relative risk measure.

The resulting theoretical formula was modified for simplicity and accessibility (i.e., so that the formula could be completed using only annual statement values), and was adopted after being vetted in the NAIC's public exposure process.

USING THE FORMULA

Each year, the NAIC publishes a document and diskette entitled "(Year X) Forecasting". This tool is a useful one for insurers in predicting and modeling their RBC levels, but cannot be used for an official filing of the RBC calculation.

The overall HORBC formula (repeated in Chapter 11, "Managing the Business") is:

$$ACL = 0.5 \times (H0 + \sqrt{H1^2 + H2^2 + H3^2 + H4^2}) \qquad (7.1)$$

Each of these H factors represents a category of risk defined by the NAIC. The ACL value, as mentioned earlier, is the specific RBC benchmark of the authorized control level of capital for this insurer. If a carrier's adjusted capital is less than this value, regulators are authorized to take control of the company. This is the basic RBC calculation, with other benchmarks keyed from the ACL value.

It is interesting to note the reason for the (essentially) root-mean-square nature of the calculation. It is intended to reflect a belief that the categories of risk under the radical are relatively independent of each other. Thus, for example, the H1 risk of invested assets losing value is considered independent of H2, the risk of underpricing products. If they were fully correlated, the capital needed for their combined risk would be the sum of the two. The root-mean-square method calculates a value less than the sum, to reflect their independence.

The most important item in this list for most health insurers is H2, the **Underwriting Risk**. This is the risk due to the possibility that the business will incur underwriting losses – that the claims and expenses will exceed the revenue, and put the company's capital at risk.

The H2 value is calculated separately for Medical and other coverage, DI, LTC, and certain Limited Benefit Plans.

H2 for Medical Coverages

This is calculated as the larger of the calculated RBC capital value and an alternate risk charge, and separately for five lines of business: Comprehensive Medical, Medicare Supplement, Dental & Vision, Stand-Alone Medicare Part D Coverage, and Other. The main RBC value is calculated using the following nested logic:

$$\text{RBC after Managed Care Discount} = (\text{Base Underwriting Risk RBC}) \times (\text{Managed Care Discount Factor})$$

$$\text{Base Underwriting Risk RBC} = (\text{Underwriting Risk Revenue}) \times (\text{Underwriting Risk Claim Ratio}) \times (\text{Underwriting Risk Factor})$$

$$\text{Underwriting Risk Claim Ratio} = \frac{(\text{Underwriting Risk Incurred Claims})}{(\text{Underwriting Risk Revenue})}$$

(You might notice that when the loss ratio (their "Claims Ratio") is multiplied by the Underwriting Risk Revenue, the revenue figures cancel out, and the Base Underwriting Risk RBC becomes simply Incurred Claims times the Risk Factor.)

Underwriting Risk Factor is defined in this table:

Table 7.1

Coverage	Underwriting Risk Revenue (millions)		
	$0-3	$3-25	$25+
Comprehensive Medical	0.150	0.150	0.090
Medicare Supplement	0.105	0.067	0.067
Dental & Vision	0.120	0.076	0.076
Stand-Alone Medicare Part D	0.251	0.251	0.151
Other	0.130	0.130	0.130

The Alternate Risk Charge is the largest of the applicable following values:

Table 7.2

Coverage	For each coverage, the lesser of:	
Comprehensive Medical	$1,500,000	2 times the Maximum Individual Risk (6 times for Medicare Part D)
Medicare Supplement	$50,000	
Dental & Vision	$50,000	
Stand-Alone Medicare Part D	$150,000	
Other	$50,000	

Managed Care Discount Factor

This factor deserves some special discussion, because of both its theoretical basis and its application.

Managed care provider payments occur in a variety of ways, with a wide range of impacts on underwriting risk. For each of these, the paid claims in each category is weighted by a corresponding discount factor, and merged to a single factor.

At the minimalist end of the spectrum is the (not very helpfully named) *Category 0 - Arrangements not included in Other Categories.* This category includes fee for service arrangements, discounted fee for service, usual and customary arrangements, stop loss payments (including retrospective settlements) to providers having capitated arrangements[8] or withholds[9] or bonus arrangements. Payments under this category receive zero credit.

The next level is *Category 1 - Payments Made According to Contractual Arrangements*. This includes payments under hospital per diems, case rates (including DRGs – diagnosis related groupings), non-adjustable professional case and global rates, provider fee schedules, ambulatory payment classifications (APCs), and relative value schedules (RVSs) where the payment base and factor are fixed by contract for more than a year. The discount factor for this category is 15%.

Category 2 is for payments subject to withhold or bonus arrangements, and has two sub-categories. Both categories have a credit calculated the same way, using a formula applied to the *prior* (year before the year being reported) year's values. (Category 2b has a minimum factor of 15%, Category 2a has no minimum. Both have a maximum of 25%.) This credit is based on a realization that withholds and bonuses can act as buffers for needed capital, but only if they are set at levels that are likely to realistically be at risk.

$$\text{Discount Factor} = (\text{average withhold rate}) \times (\text{MCC multiplier}),$$

where

$$\text{Average withhold rate} = \frac{(\text{withholds \& bonuses available})}{(\text{Claims subject to them})},$$

and

$$\text{MCC Multiplier} = \frac{(\text{withhold \& bonus payments})}{(\text{withholds \& bonuses available})}.$$

Category 2a is for *Payments Made Subject to Withholds or Bonuses with No Other Managed Care*. This is for payments made for arrangements subject to withhold or bonus arrangements, but where, in the absence of those withholds or bonuses, the payments would have fallen into category 0. *Category 2b* is for *Payments Made Subject to Withholds or Bonuses that Are Otherwise Managed Care Category 1*.

---

[8]A **capitation** is a contractual, fixed payment, typically paid monthly, made by an insurer to a health care provider on behalf of a plan member. The provider, in turn, provides whatever services may be required with respect to that member, within the realm of the contract between provider and insurer.

[9]A **withhold** is a portion of a provider payment that is held back by an insurer, and is only paid if the provider's performance meets targeted standards.

The next category is *Category 3*, which includes capitated payment arrangements (caps). There are three subcategories in this one. *Category 3a* is for caps directly with providers, and is shown split between medical groups and all others. *Category 3b* is for payments to regulated intermediaries which in turn pay providers. *Regulated* in this case refers to entities who are subject to their own RBC requirements under the insurance law, and which are regulated by the state. *Category 3c* is for payments to non-regulated intermediaries which in turn pay providers. Each of these Category 3 subcategories has a 60% credit factor. Category 3c, however, has a limit of 5% of its claims in this category which are paid to providers or other corporations with no contractual relationship with the intermediary. Amounts in excess of 5% must be reported as Category 0 claims.

The final category is *Category 4 - Medical & Hospital Expense Paid as Salary to Providers*. This includes "non-contingent salaries" to those providing care, payments to affiliates who pay such salaries, facility expenses of owned and operated facilities, and aggregate cost payments. The discount factor for this category is 75%.

Stand-Alone Medicare Part D plan experience has its own categories and factors depending on whether or not it is subject to federal reinsurance and risk corridor protections.

Each of the managed care discount factors represents the relative lessening of risk (defined in terms of the likelihood of a theoretical financial ruin) caused by that reimbursement method. Withholds and bonuses were perceived to act somewhat as a financial buffer, for example – that these monies could be permanently withheld if the financial results were negative.

The factors for withholds and bonuses were developed at a time when such arrangements were usually based directly on financial results or on utilization. An interesting question arises as to whether the quality-based withholds and bonuses in use today are an equal financial buffer as the originally contemplated utilization- or financial-based versions. Arguably, unless the quality-based withhold uses measures that are highly correlated to the company's financial results, they are less effective as a financial buffer.

H2 for DI

Disability income coverage has tiered factors similar to, but much less complicated than, medical coverage. There are only two categories of this coverage for individual insurance: Noncancelable and Other. The factors are applied against earned premium (EP), as follows:

Table 7.3

Coverage	Amount Multiplied	Factor
Non-Can	First $50 million EP	0.35
	Over $50 million EP	0.15
Other Individual	First $50 million EP	0.25
	Over $50 million EP	0.07

There are a variety of other DI coverages with similar tiered factors (such as for credit or group DI coverage).

One of the major criteria used in deriving the RBC formula was the ability of carriers to quickly and effectively respond (via rate actions) to unanticipated losses. Non-can policies have guaranteed premiums, and therefore the company can never adjust rates on existing policies. This limits their ability to respond, and therefore creates higher risk. Hence the higher factor.

H2 for LTC

For LTC, there are factors that apply to earned premium, incurred claims, and claim reserves. Further, there are different factors depending on whether the coverage is non-can. The factors are:

Table 7.4

Coverage	Amount Multiplied	Factor
Non-Can	Same as Other Individual +	
	Earned Premium	0.10
Other Individual	First $50 million EP +	0.10
	Excess over $50 million +	0.03
	First $35 million incurred claims +	0.37
	Excess over $35 million +	0.12
	Claim Reserves	0.05

For both DI and LTC, each of the lines of business need only meet the first tier once. That is, the amount to which the first "other individual factor" applies is the total earned premium minus the amount already counted in the non-can first tier. If, for example, a company had exactly $50 million each in non-can and other DI premium, the first tier factor of

0.35 from Table 7.3 would apply to the Non-can premium, but the 0.07 factor from that table would apply to the Other premium.

H2 for Limited Benefit Plans

There are three categories of such plans included in the HORBC calculation.

If a company has *Hospital Indemnity* and/or *Specified Disease* plans, the factor is 0.035 times premium, plus $50,000.

For *Accidental Death and Dismemberment* (AD&D), the calculation starts with a tiered one, similar to that for other coverages. The amount of premium for the tier, however, is much higher: $10 million, with a factor of 0.055 applying to the first tier (up to the $10 million), and 0.015 above it. To this is added the lesser of $300,000 or 3 times the maximum retained risk for any single claim. This formula reflects the much lower frequency and higher variance of AD&D coverage, which then requires much higher premium levels to achieve the same level of risk.

The final category, *Other Accident*, has a flat factor of 0.05 applied to premium.

There is an offset in the formula that gives partial credit for any premium stabilization reserves associated with the business.

Excessive Growth: This is one additional element of the RBC calculation which should be discussed. This element was originally suggested to the NAIC due to a belief by some practitioners that one highly correlated predictor of significant losses within a short period of time is rapid growth in the size of the block of business. This is because: (1) a common error for the uninitiated in this business is to underprice initial rates, and (2) this business is highly premium driven. In combination, this underpricing leads to large product sales, with the losses only becoming obvious after a couple of years.

This element of RBC is in *H4 – Business Risk*. The NAIC chose to change this factor to represent risk due to growth of the H2 RBC amount by more than 10% over the growth in revenue. The resulting formula is:

Excessive growth risk
$$= 0.5 \times (\text{Excess of H2 RBC growth above safe harbor}),$$

where

Safe Harbor = (Last Year's H2 RBC)
　　　　　　× (Growth in H2 revenue figures this year/last year + 10%)

It has been pointed out that this formula does not achieve the intended effect. Rather than penalizing a company for excessive growth (an indicator in many markets that they might be underpriced and heading for a difficult time), it penalizes companies whose *factor* grows excessively. The Academy Task Force did not examine the impact of changes in average H2 factors over time, but did discuss excessive changes in total H2 growth.

Calculation of Total Adjusted Capital

Once the ACL level of RBC has been calculated, and related benchmarks determined (see Chapter 11, "Managing the Business"), the insurer must then compare its own level of capital against those benchmarks. In doing so, there are a few (usually minor) adjustments made to the statutory capital and surplus figures from the company's balance sheet, generating a value known as the **Total Adjusted Capital (TAC)**.

The calculation of TAC involves making a couple specific adjustments for values from Life and P&C subsidiaries.

After the initial calculation, a sensitivity test is done by adjusting capital to check what the TAC would be without deferred tax assets and liabilities.

7.3 Results of the Calculation

Once the values of H0 through H4 are calculated, the RBC benchmarks can be calculated. Formula 7.1 shows the calculation of ACL. The ACL value is the level at which, if TAC falls below this number, regulators are authorized to take control of the company. There are actually four such levels, each representing successively more dire situations, with successively more severe corrective actions:

- Company Action Level, 200% of the ACL. If adjusted capital falls below this level, the company is required to submit a plan of action to the regulators, to address the capital shortfall. Under the most recent model law, this can also be triggered by failing a **trend test**.

- Regulatory Action Level, 150% of ACL. If adjusted capital falls below this level, regulators can specify the corrective action to be taken by the company.
- ACL, described previously.
- Mandatory Control Level, 70% of ACL. If adjusted capital falls below this level, regulators are *required* to take over management of the company.

If TAC falls below any of these values, or even threatens to do so, it indicates a serious situation requiring management attention.

It is worth mentioning some of the theoretical framework of this RBC benchmarking process. There is some level of conservatism included in virtually all statutory and GAAP reserve calculations. That conservatism provides for a probability greater than 50% (or a *one tailed confidence interval*) that the reserves will be adequate. If they are not, then the company's capital is available to buffer any excess losses. The presence of that capital provides yet another (higher) confidence interval. If, for example, the reserves are 80% likely to be adequate to cover losses in a given year, then the reserves plus available capital might be 99.5% likely to be adequate.

This confidence interval rationale lies behind the development of the health risk-based capital formula. Ultimately, the decisions made to choose a specific level of capital were not measured relative to the original ruin theory model, so the actual modeled confidence interval cannot be measured.

It is worthwhile noting, however, that to produce the same level of statistical confidence, there are a variety of combinations of reserve conservatism and capital levels that would achieve the same result. Unfortunately, much of reserve conservatism is implicit in the calculations, and therefore cannot be measured. Some observers are hopeful that eventually all such margins will be made explicit, allowing a more intentionally chosen confidence interval, via the level of surplus and capital.

Chapter 8

Forecasting and Modeling

This chapter discusses the modeling techniques used to forecast financial results of blocks of individual health insurance business, in a business setting.

8.1 Purpose and Uses of Models

In this context, a **financial model** means a mathematical representation of financial flows connected with an insurance business. Models of large organizations are typically comprised of component blocks of business, sometimes in a nested way. An insurer may, for example, have a model of all its individual health businesses, consolidated from models for each type of policy, perhaps in turn comprised of models of individual policy forms, which, in turn, might be made of models of different issue ages and/or plans within that block of policies. At the bottom level, the groups of models are typically called the **model cells**.

There are a number of purposes for which financial models are created in individual accident and health business. These include:

(1) Pricing. Financial and sales models are typically used to determine the premium rates necessary to achieve goals;

(2) Reserve calculations and reserve basis evaluation. Some reserves (such as gross premium reserves and deficiency reserves) are actually the result of a forecasting model;

(3) Monitoring of results. This can be done to test the validity of assumptions (possibly for future use in a subsequent product), to warn of deviations from expected values, for resource planning, or for other reasons;

(4) Solvency testing. Gross premium reserves are the ultimate test of the need for additional financial reserves to fund future experience. Within

this category we might also consider models used to measure and analyze risk, including those used for enterprise risk management (ERM);

(5) Financial forecasting. For many reasons, corporations need to be able to forecast financial results, and a model is needed to do so; and

(6) Appraisals. Actuarial appraisals are studies of the value of a block (or blocks) of business, typically used when transferring ownership of the block. The actuarial value is usually equal to the present value of future profits or distributable earnings. The future profits come from financial projections of the business.

For all of these reasons, models are a critical part of an insurer's (and their consultant's) toolkit. The strength of decision making is only as strong as the information used in making those decisions, and the information in this case is usually the output of a model.

DETERMINISTIC VS. STOCHASTIC

There are two basic approaches to modeling – **deterministic** and **stochastic**. Deterministic models show the interrelationships of variables, but each piece of output is a single value – the expected value of that variable under the assumptions chosen. In a pricing model, for example, the cost of claims in a given year is often calculated as the number of policies expected to be in force at that time (calculated in a stepwise fashion from the originally issued radix of policies by applying successive lapse and possibly mortality rates) times the expected claim cost for the cohort being modeled. (A **cohort** is the group of insureds being represented by a particular cell and year of issue.)

Stochastic models treat one or more variables stochastically, meaning that, rather than representing the variable's value at a point in time by a single point estimate, the variable's whole distribution of possible results is used. Sometimes this representation is **parametric**, meaning that the distribution is assumed to match a particular known distribution (with parameters suitably chosen), such as an F-distribution, or a normal (Gaussian) distribution. By making this assumption, and using a parametric representation of the variable, powerful tools can be applied, since the characteristics of such distributions have been studied for many years. In health insurance, unfortunately, there just have not been good parametric representations found for many variables, and particularly for claim costs.[1] (There are exceptions to this, most notably accidental death coverages, whose distributions can be easily matched.)

Without parametric representations, we are usually forced to use a brute force technique – **Monte Carlo Simulations**.[2] This is a technique used to develop stochastic results when we do not know the underlying parametric distribution (possibly because it does not exist). Monte Carlo simulations were long considered too onerous to often be useful, since the model would have to be recalculated tens of thousands of times in order to have sufficient data points to understand the true distribution. With the enormous advances in personal computing power, simulations that used to take hours of mainframe time can now be done in minutes on a personal computer – or even faster using a grid or cloud computing resources.

So why do we care whether the model is deterministic or stochastic? Stochastic models give us information about the *distribution* of results, not just their average or expected value. This is particularly important when the impact of such results is not linear.

One example of such a non-linear function involves stop-loss reinsurance. Suppose an insurer were able to purchase 110% aggregate stop-loss reinsurance for its block of business. (This means that the insurer has contracted with a reinsurer to provide insurance that, if the insurer's aggregate claim experience exceeds 110% of expected, and a claim occurs, the reinsurer must reimburse the insurer for the portion in excess of 110%.) If f_x is the density function for the universe of possible aggregate claims by the insurer (treating this as a continuous function for ease of understanding; in reality this would be the discrete analogue), and if C represents the dollar amount of 110% of expected claims, then the numerically calculated value of this coverage to the insurance company would be:

$$\int_C^\infty (x-C) f_x dx \qquad (8.1)$$

---

[1] One promising candidate that might be worth another look is the Tweedie family of distributions, which allow for a point mass at zero.
[2] There are other techniques available, such as Markov chains and other multi-state models. See *Actuarial Models for Disability Insurance*, by Haberman and Pitacco. These are growing in prevalence, but have not yet found widespread use by practitioners.

Clearly, to calculate such a value we need to have more than just the expected value of claims.

Another example of such a case is a **ruin theory** model. This type of model evaluates the potential of future losses being sufficient to completely absorb a company's surplus, and thus cause financial 'ruin.' An excellent example of this is the American Academy of Actuaries' model, developed to provide a risk based capital formula for health insurers, at the request of the National Association of Insurance Commissioners. This model (known as the HORBC model) was a Monte Carlo simulator which measured, for a given level of starting surplus, how likely it was that an insurer with particular characteristics would exhaust that surplus over a given number of years.

Deterministic models can still be helpful. When we want to test the impact of specific alternative situations (**scenario testing**), they can be quite useful. If, for example, we had built a financial forecasting model of an insurer's block of business, we might want to be able to answer the question, "What would be the impact if lapses were 20% higher than expected?" or other, similar questions. This process of testing alternative sets of assumptions is called **sensitivity testing**, since it measures the sensitivity of model results to those alternatives. In the above example of the HORBC model, a deterministic model was actually discussed and discarded by the task force, as it would have only provided sensitivity testing (answering the question, "What would the most likely outcome be of a single trial, if reality varied from assumptions by x?"), not variance information ("How often would companies fail if reality varied from assumptions by x?").

Before computing capacity and understanding allowed the actuarial profession to stochastically test economic scenarios in its asset/liability matching, deterministic models were often used. In some cases, regulators actually specified the economic scenarios to be tested. Such models require good fundamental thinking about the variance inherent in our assumptions, since, in order to test alternative assumptions, we have to have some idea about how likely such alternatives are.

8.2 Characteristics of a Good Model

The list of desirable characteristics of a model could be a long one. The environment and intended use of the model will determine some of these. There are also characteristics of a model that are driven by the coverage being modeled. There are, however, a relatively small number of general characteristics that are essential. They are as follows:

- *Reliable Accuracy.* A model isn't worth much if it does not do a good job of predicting the future. How accurate should it be? Not meaning to be flippant, the answer is, "As accurate as needed." The real issue, which is discussed further later, is determining not only the accuracy needed, but how to go about achieving it.

  Another aspect of this is the need for **robustness**. A model is robust (either in total or with respect to a given element of the environment) if it continues to be a good model, and does not fail in some way as the input situations being modeled are varied over the range of possible values.

- *Suitability for use.* The model should produce the results it is designed for, including all appropriate aspects of design and detail, without adding unnecessary complications.

  A major element of model definition is the level of **granularity** of the component model cells. (Granularity is a term used to describe the level of precision defined by models. A model with 100 cells, for example, is more granular than a similar one with 10 cells.) For some purposes, a **windshield** model, which uses very little granularity, might be sufficient. For other purposes, the same block might require many cells (perhaps in the hundreds) to be modeled, in order to achieve the sensitivity and robustness needed.

- *Appropriate Precision.* How many decimal places should be kept, used, and displayed in the values?

- *Sensibility.* The underlying basis of the model should reflect a logical, theoretical construction of what is being modeled. Any counterintuitive aspects should be investigated and rationalized (or fixed).

  Another aspect of this element is that the model should be theoretically sound. After all, it does no good to accurately portray a bad theory.

  In the past, many models for individual major medical business were constructed using data from the group market. Predictably, this created results that varied significantly from reality. This is one example where failing to ensure the data used to build the model are appropriate for the intended purpose (or have been appropriately adjusted) sometimes resulted in an unsound model.

- *Effectively Communicated.* The results of the model are useless unless they can be effectively communicated to the users or clients. The communication should include everything necessary to understand and use the model's results.

8.3 Building a Model

The process of building and using a model involves seven major steps.

Step 1: Choosing the Basic Structure of the Model

There are as many types of models as there are uses for them. Actuaries and individual health insurers generally run into only a few basic models.

Modeling Tools

Spreadsheets are, by far, the most common tool for building and managing models. These are straightforward, easily modified, and relatively easily de-bugged. They are the most suitable solution for one-time analyses and modeling. There are, however, circumstances where other tools are preferred. In a post Sarbanes-Oxley world where many financial matters are undergoing increased scrutiny, spreadsheet models may be more vulnerable. One real drawback of spreadsheet models is that they blur the lines between *data* and the *algorithms* acting on that data. It is also easy for assumptions to be hidden (as, for example, a "magic number" embedded in a formula).

Database models are useful (and sometimes even necessary) when large amounts of data must be manipulated. Some database languages have powerful statistical functions built into them – functions that cannot easily be performed in other languages.

Sequential programs are written in computer languages, where the programs are invoked. (These are equivalent to 'macros' in spreadsheet or database programs.) These can be most appropriate when a user-friendly interface is important, such as building a model that will be accessed by many users, when there may be multiple or ongoing iterations of the model, when there are vast amounts of data to be processed, or when the model needs to use advanced statistical or other mathematical techniques available in existing code libraries.

Asset Share Type Models

This is the most common model type. It is usually created using spreadsheet programs. Each sheet will typically represent a given model cell, with each column representing an element of needed input, intermediate results, and output values. Each row typically represents a given point or period in time, although on occasion the axes are reversed. (Some variables, such as "premium earned" will only be meaningful with respect to a period of time, such as "premium earned in policy year one." Others, such as "number of policies in force" will have meaning only with respect to a given point in time, such as the beginning, mid-point, or end of that year.) More detail on such column definitions is included in Chapter 5, "Setting Premium Rates."

When used for pricing, asset share models are typically done on a "per policy" or "per unit of coverage" basis. Asset share models can also be used in projecting future earnings for appraisal work. When used for this latter purpose, the component model cell pieces must be scaled to represent their actual proportion of the business, before being included in the total.

Reserve Development Models

These models come in a number of flavors: claim lag (development) models, tabular reserve models, and active life reserve models. Each is discussed in more detail in Chapter 6, "Reserves and Liabilities." In the individual health (IH) marketplace, it is relatively unusual to use parametric models (à la property and casualty actuaries) to model reserves, since such methods are more useful with longer tailed coverages. In IH, the longer tailed coverages are DI and LTC, which tend to use tabular (or at least factor-based) methods.

Agent-Based Models

These models (also known as **micro-simulation models**) are used to try to predict the behavior of various **agents** (which might include policyholders, insurers, regulators, and other decision makers) under various scenarios or strategies. There has been significant interest and work in developing such models in order to forecast the potential movement of individuals between various sources of coverage due to the ACA.[3]

---

[3] See for instance the following SOA study by Alan Mills: https://www.soa.org/research/research-projects/health/simulating-health-behavior-a-guide-to-solving.aspx

These models are generally stochastic and often require significant computing resources. A major advantage to such models is their ability to reveal potentially unexpected and nonlinear relationships between variables. They also have the ability to test various theories about policyholder behavior (including research from behavioral economics about common ways humans fail to act rationally). Besides the computational effort required, another disadvantage to these models is the difficulty in selecting assumptions for all the agents' behaviors. There are often multiple solutions when calibrating such a model to base data, and it can be difficult to find ways to uniquely specify the model.

Deterministic vs. Stochastic

A stochastic model requires significantly more effort to build, use, and interpret than deterministic models. For that reason, stochastic models are reserved for situations that require their unique output, and deterministic ones are used otherwise. It is relatively unusual to use stochastic models, although becoming less so.

Cell Definition

How many cells will be needed to build an accurate picture of the business being modeled, and how will they be defined? It is important to think through how each potential cell might behave, and whether it behaves differently from other cells in the projection, to determine whether it is a valuable addition to the cell definition library.

If, for example, we were building a detailed model of a large block of disability income insurance policies for appraisal purposes, we might want hundreds of cells in the model. This is because of the wide variation in financial values (and their relationship to each other) that is generated by the disparate policies included in the block.

At the other extreme, if we were projecting a block of comprehensive major medical (CMM) policies for a Blue Cross plan, for financial forecasting purposes, and we knew the block to be stable in all important policy characteristics (benefit plan, duration of policies, demographics of insureds), we might have only one cell, which projects all policies in one group.

Durational Characteristics

As you have learned, measuring and managing durational effects on claim costs is critical to success in the medical insurance market. In other financial models and for other coverages, however, it is also important to address durational effects.

Policies for most coverages will have modeled characteristics (claim costs, accumulated policy and claim reserves, persistency, etc.) that vary substantially over the policy life cycle. An average DI block, for example, may have accumulated claim reserves of two or three times annual premium in its later years, but have practically none in the early years.

In building detailed projection models that require an accurate picture of these various financial elements, it is common to have cells that reflect the same policy characteristics, but which vary by duration.

In the DI appraisal example described earlier, there might be a cell defined by a coverage/demographic combination of:

- Benefit period: to age 65.
- Elimination period: 90 days.
- Occupation class: IV.
- Issue age: 45.
- Gender: Male.

An underlying model might first be built to describe the life cycle of this average policy. If we think of this (perhaps asset share) spreadsheet model as a matrix S, we can represent an element of that matrix as $S_{t,c}$, where t is the time element (row of the matrix) and c is the particular data element being modeled. This model might generate values for a single policy form, or for $100 of face amount. In using this underlying model to perform an appraisal, we might want to use it to create three cells, represented by policies that, in the first year of the model, are in policy years 1, 4, and 10. So, S must be scaled (say using scaling factors $f_1, f_2,$ and f_3) so that the model matches the number of policies actually in force in these durations. The total contribution to the master projection matrix M from the cells based on S would then be:

$$M_{t,c} = (f_1 \times S_{t,c}) + (f_2 \times S_{t+3,c}) + (f_3 \times S_{t+9,c})$$

Not all elements of S are scalable and combinable in this way. For this reason, each element must be considered individually when combining cells.

STEP 2: CHOOSING THE INFORMATION TO BE CARRIED

We need to carefully choose the information that will be carried forward in the model. The information needed will depend, of course, on the purpose of the model. Going back to the list of purposes at the beginning of this chapter:

Pricing Models

Pricing models typically project model offices, spreadsheet representations of an expected mix of policies. For each cell modeled, an asset share calculation is made, which is a comprehensive projection of all relevant financial values. If modeling a disability income policy, for example, one representative policy being modeled might be a total disability basic policy benefit only, issue age 35, elimination period 90 days, 'to age 65' benefit period, male, occupation class I. If 10,000 policies are being modeled in total, this cell might have 500 policies in its asset share calculation. This cell's model would need to have appropriate data elements, for each year being modeled, of all the major financial elements: exposure (numbers of policies in force at appropriate points in the year), premium, claims, reserves, expenses, profit, and required capital. Some of these values will necessitate carrying other values which are not needed in and of themselves.

A detailed asset share model might carry a number of exposure values, such as the number of policies at the start of the year, the number of policies in force at the end of the year, and an average number in force for the year. If the level of detail calls for calculations based on modal premiums, there may be additional exposure items required, representing exposures for modal premiums within the year. In addition, if the asset share is calendar year-based, rather than policy year, there will need to be appropriate exposure factors so that the impact of two policy years within a calendar year can be calculated. (In the second calendar year of a calendar year projection model, for example, there would normally be exposures from both policy years one and two. Different commission scales might apply to the two policy years, so we must carry both pieces of information to calculate commissions in that year.) Premium values that might be carried in the calculation include premium received, premium written and renewed, earned premium, and average premium per policy. If modal premiums or calendar year projections enter the picture, additional values will need to be included.

Claim values that might be carried include paid claims, incurred claims (financial basis), and incurred claims (runoff basis). If there are different types of claim payments (which will depend on the coverage), these may need to be projected separately. For disability coverage, for example, residual or partial disability payments might be tracked separately from total disability. For medical coverages, we might want to track claims by type of provider, by type of service, by network, or many other breakdowns. For LTC, we might want to track home health care, assisted living payments, or other service categories separately from nursing home payments. Calendar year-based claim projections are a complication, as with other values.

Reserve values carried might include premium reserves (unearned premiums, premiums paid in advance, premiums due and unpaid), policy reserves, claim reserves (rarely broken down into component pieces for modeling purposes), and gross premium reserves (including deficiency reserves.)

Expense values carried will vary widely, depending on the company's particular circumstances. DI carriers, for example, who might also sell life insurance, are likely to have many different expense items tracked, consistent with their internal expense allocation formulae, and reflecting often complex commission and agency support schemes. An HMO or BCBS plan, on the other hand, may have a very simplistic expense allocation scheme, reflecting the relative uniformity of its products. For GAAP purposes, where certain items are amortized over time, amortization schedules or factors must be carried as well.

For coverages subject to the ACA, there are a number of new values that may need to be estimated and carried through models. These include the net impact of the "3R" risk mitigation programs (transitional reinsurance, risk adjustment, and risk corridors), minimum loss ratio rebates, new taxes and fees, and subsidy amounts receivable from the government (including advance premium tax credits and cost sharing reduction payments). Many of these will be extraordinarily difficult to estimate in the early years of ACA implementation.

Profit is calculated on either a statutory or GAAP basis (depending on the purpose of the projection), as a dependent variable. This might be calculated both pre-tax and post-tax, which then necessitates tracking the financial items required for tax calculations, including (most likely) reserves calculated under an alternative (tax) reserve basis. Profit that is not paid out is retained in capital and surplus (or free reserves).

For many purposes, it is important to know how much capital is required to support the block of business over time, given the company's chosen capital and surplus targets. There is a cost associated with this capital, because the assets must be used for this purpose instead of being invested in other, perhaps riskier but more profitable, opportunities. This is the **opportunity cost** of holding this capital, and can be treated as an expense when evaluating the true value of the block of business.

Reserve Models

Reserve models for developing short term claim reserves (claim triangles) are usually based on paid claims and exposure. They are generally created and used at the time they are needed, to actually calculate the reserves.

Reserves for tabular claims are usually either taken directly from a table or based on promulgated factors. Under some circumstances, modified tabular reserves are held. Models for tabular claim reserves are often created in order to compare actual claim termination rates or payout rates against the existing tabular reserve basis. Thus, they involve claim data in their calculation.

Reserve models for policy reserves involve exposures and claims, and may involve premium.

Those for gross premium reserves involve all the major financial elements, and are essentially asset share calculations of in-force business.

Recoverability Tests

Recoverability tests for GAAP purposes are similar to gross premium reserve calculations. They test whether, under updated assumptions, current premium levels are sufficient to cover benefits, deferred acquisition costs (DAC, which a company is amortizing over the future lifetime of the business), and maintenance costs. The DAC calculation requires a projection using the original DAC schedule, applied to projected exposures under current conditions.

Monitoring

Monitoring of financial (or other) results is generally a comparison of recent actual results against expected results, and is typically part of an information system used to manage the business. This is discussed further in Chapter 11, "Managing the Business." The data elements to be kept for this purpose are highly variable, and entirely dependent on the study being conducted. One such study might monitor policy lapse rates, while another monitors the effectiveness of a disease management program.

Solvency Testing and Risk Analysis

Risk analysis, in the insurance company context, is generally modeled as financial risk. This is an analysis of the likelihood of various unexpected, negative financial results. A related analysis is the likelihood that existing capital and surplus (or free reserves) will not be sufficient to fund those results, a ruin model. These projections most often use asset share models, so carry the information elements described earlier.

Ruin models require information about the distribution of results which occur over time (perhaps even the distribution itself), and so are stochastic in nature. While it is helpful to evaluate what the financial impact is of specific alternative outcomes (sensitivity testing), this is not ultimately the information needed to evaluate the risk, which requires confidence interval information (that is, how often this alternative outcome might happen.) This requires a different approach (parametric or simulation) to modeling than the typical spreadsheet (deterministic) approach.

Financial Forecasting

Financial forecasting can be used for many purposes. The most common approach is an asset share calculation, used for short term budgeting for the corporation. (Some people use the term 'asset share' to only apply to such projections made of policies that are not yet in force. It can be used, as well, for in-force projections, as it is here.)

Corporate models typically include projection of needed capital, including risk-based capital requirements. They are not solely concerned with rate adequacy, capital adequacy, or value of the business. They are used for a number of other purposes, including cash flow projections and corporate resource assessments. The variables carried for these projections will depend on their intended uses.

Appraisals

Actuarial *appraisals* are long term financial projections, used to set a value on a block of business. The appraisal value is usually calculated as the present value of projected future profits or distributable earnings, typically based on an asset share calculation, with the usual required data elements. The earlier comment on the opportunity cost of capital is particularly important here. (**Distributable earnings** are often defined as the present value of future profits, plus the present value of changes in required capital, plus investment returns on that required capital.)

STEP 3: CHOOSING ASSUMPTIONS AND BUILDING A PROTOTYPE PROJECTION

Asset Share Models

An asset share projection is typically created as a two dimensional matrix. Each column represents a data or information element. Each row represents a time period (or vice versa.) The most common time period in such calculations is the year; particularly for long term projections. Some short term projections (such as financial forecasting for budgeting or experience analysis purposes) may use quarterly (or perhaps even monthly) time periods, in order to provide enough sensitivity to short term changes, such as changes in rate or payment levels or seasonality.

Some of the informational data elements of an asset share model are explicitly assumed. An example of this is the exposure value for the number of policies (or coverage units) starting at time $t=0$. Sometimes this value is meaningful, such as the forecasting of an expected production number. More often, the value is set at an arbitrary radix, such as 10,000. The number of policies at time $t \geq 1$ is usually successively calculated from the time $t=0$ value, with assumptions as to lapse and sometimes other decrements applied. If, for example, $\ell_0 = 10,000$, and the lapse rate is $p_0^{lapse} = 0.25$ (in this case, including mortality), then $\ell_1 = 10,000 \times (1 - p_0^{lapse}) = 7,500$.

Other elements of the asset share model are derived. The above calculations for $\ell_{t \geq 1}$ are an example of this. All data elements must either be assumed or derived; sometimes (as in the ℓ_t case) both. The next section discusses assumptions in more detail, by coverage.

For new business asset share calculations, the year $t = 0$ values are theoretical, and represent initial assumed or derived values. Sometimes, especially for in-force asset share calculations, the $t = 0$ calculation represents a picture of recent, actual experience. On occasion, especially for validation purposes (see Step 5), more than one year of actual experience is used.

For either new business or for in-force projections, once the values for year $t = 0$ are input, year $t = 1$ is built for the first prototype cell. These calculations are usually based on a combination of year $t = 0$ values and other basic assumptions. The calculations for the second year of the projection ($t = 1$) are very similar to (if not identical to) the calculations to be made for subsequent ($t \geq 2$) years. As with all such work, it is important to fully identify the extent to which such calculations must be modified as they are extended.

One characteristic that is an important choice of assumption is the number of years of projection to be made. For non-inflationary coverages, it is common to make pricing projections for many years in the future. For inflationary coverages, the gross variability of future claim and premium trends tend to make long term projections much less relevant (except for LTC coverage, where inflation must be planned for, and typically prefunded. Even then, the rates of inflation are far less than typical medical expense trends.)

An interesting anomaly occurs when this logic is extended to appraisal work. Many users of actuarial appraisals of health insurance blocks will tend to use only the first 5-10 years of such projections, and then replace the remainder of the projection with their own rules of thumb for value. For that reason, some actuaries have shortened their projections in anticipation of such a treatment. (One interesting exception to this is the annual Medicare Board of Trustees Report prepared by the Office of the Actuary at CMS. This report – available at www.cms.gov – projects the entire Medicare program many years into the future under several scenarios.)

While actuaries may not have a crystal ball that provides a high confidence level to long term projections, they are still better equipped than anyone else to make a best estimate of that value. Failure to make a long term projection is, in essence, a projection itself – setting the value at zero. Even a bad projection is likely to be better than such an assumption. Replacing actuarial judgment about long term assumptions with those that underlay investment bankers' rules of thumb does not make much sense. (Of course, it is the bankers who must be the arbiter of this decision, so the authors' opinion is of limited relevance.)

The real challenge in using such long term assumptions lies in adequately communicating the level of uncertainty that goes with it, as that uncertainty increases over time. It is far better to have an actuarial rule of thumb for years 6+, based on realistic (albeit volatile) assumptions, than one based on historical precedent (which might actually come from a very different industry and a very different analysis.)

Development Reserve Models

For reserving models using the development method, an insurer's business is typically separated into a number of cells. The number of cells used varies quite dramatically from insurer to insurer. Some insurers may have upwards of a hundred cells. There are rarely more than a couple dozen. Because this is (usually) a retrospective analysis rather than a prospective projection, each of these cells is most often addressed individually. Thus, there is no prototype cell, but rather a collection of cells, each of which is subjected to a customized (at least to some extent) analysis.

The development reserve process is described in more detail in Chapter 6, "Reserves and Liabilities." The most significant assumptions or choices needing to be made include:

(1) Number of months' experience to use and method of averaging;

(2) Whether to account for seasonality;

(3) The method to use for recent, less than fully credible, months of experience;

(4) The denominator to use for trending purposes (claims per policy, per member, per dollar of premium, etc.); and

(5) The trend rate to use to determine the recent period.

Other Models

Most other models, including experience monitoring and risk analysis models, tend to be specialized, designed and built in a way that is dependent on the coverages being modeled. They may or may not have a prototype cell, depending on the homogeneity of the cells being modeled.

STEP 4: EXTENDING THE PROTOTYPE

For a prototype model, once the major step of building the prototype cell (proto-cell) is finished, then comes the task of extending the prototype. The proto-cell has been chosen to represent a given subset of the business being modeled.

The proto-cell will be composed of policies that, for purposes of this modeling, are identical to it. In reality, the cell is one that is chosen to represent all the policies which will be mapped to it. In doing so, there are two things that might happen in that cell: (1) we might use average values for the cell, such as average policy reserve values, or (2) we might give the cell values for a specific, representative policy that is chosen to represent the policies being mapped to that cell.

An example of a cell for which average policies might be used would be in a financial forecast for a block of medical policies, where the proto-cell might represent a $1,000 deductible, all ages, all areas, all everything else. On the other hand, if we were doing an appraisal of a disability income block of policies, and needed to validate policy values over time (like policy reserves), we might map all policies issued to ages 20-29 into a representative cell of age 25, for a given combination of policy parameters (elimination period, benefit period, occupation class, etc.).

The choice of whether to use average or specific representative values is an interesting one. The decision typically depends on the coverage being modeled, the use to which it is being put, and the expectations of the users. Non-inflation sensitive coverages (like DI and LTC) tend to use specific representative cells, and inflation sensitive coverages (like medical) tend to use averages. Given computational advances, it is also becoming somewhat more common to perform seriatim (i.e., policy by policy or member by member) projections to retain maximum granularity in the model.

STEP 5: VALIDATING THE MODEL

Let us suppose we are building an asset share model of an insurer, perhaps for purposes of an appraisal. We took company data to find representative cells. We built a proto-cell for each major line of business and then extended each to a set of cells which we hope will represent those lines of business. After we have done this, how do we know how well the model represents the business? We answer this question using **model validation**.

There are four general ways in which models are validated. Each of these methods has its strengths and weaknesses, and they are typically used in different situations. They are:

(1) The values of the model in the starting year are compared directly to the actual values for that year. (The starting year of the model is generally the year with the latest available information, so that it can be used for just this purpose.) This is a measure of how well the model represents the book of business at the start date. Typical measures include earned premium, number of policies, incurred claims, loss ratios, policy reserves, claim reserves, and others. If there are any cash values or nonforfeiture benefits associated with the policies, those can be tested as well.

(2) The year-to-year changes produced in the model are compared to actual past historical results. This might involve having the model work backward from the first model year $(t=0)$, to one or more years in the past. More typically, the model might actually start, say, in year $t=-1$. Rather than calibrate the model to year $t=-1$, however, the calibration might still be to year $t=0$, but the resulting values for year $t=-1$ can be compared to statement values. This is an important test for long term asset shares, particularly when it is important to be sure the year-to-year operators are working in a way that reproduces reality.

In some cases, such as in retrospective modeling, it is necessary to calibrate the model extensively to longer term historical values. One major application of this methodology is in calculating the profit shares attributable to classes of policies for demutualization purposes.

(3) The results of the model can be (and virtually always are) subjected to reasonableness checks by people familiar with the business. This is a normal part of any model development.

(4) Another way models can be validated is by "stress testing" them. That is, see how the modeled results behave when some of the underlying assumptions are changed. There are two ways to do this. First, the changes can be relatively small. In this case, the resulting studies are typically called "sensitivity tests." The results of such tests are then reviewed for reasonableness.

The second method is to make much more major changes in underlying assumptions. This process is typically used to check for

robustness, or the ability of the model to stand up to (i.e., still be valid under) varying conditions. Again, the results are checked for reasonableness. This approach can be very useful to flush out simple errors – for instance, if mortality, lapse, and future sales are all set to zero, the number of policies had better remain constant.

STEP 6: DOCUMENTING THE MODEL

Documenting a model is tedious, difficult, and impeding. It is also very important, both for business reasons and professional ones. There is nothing particularly unique about individual health insurance in this regard; it is true of all actuarial models. In fact, the Actuarial Standards Board, in ASOP #8, Regulatory Filings for Health Plan Entities,[4] sets out specific documentation requirements that actuaries must adhere to in setting health plan rates. ASOP #41, Actuarial Communications, also requires appropriate documentation.

Why is documentation important? First, there is the professional reason. A professional should be able to adequately describe the work he or she has done, and stand ready to defend it. Without documentation, the work is not presented in a way that can be evaluated by other professionals.

There are multiple business reasons why documentation is important. The first is that the employer or client may want to duplicate the underlying work, modify it, discuss it, or otherwise refer to it. The only time this can be done is when the underlying work is adequately described, and the description can thus be readily referenced. In addition, even those with the best of memory cannot rely on remembering details of the model over time – even if all the work was performed personally. Many models must also be modified over time, and will evolve. Without documentation, this process is fraught with error and inefficiency.

STEP 7: DESIGNING OUTPUT AND COMMUNICATING RESULTS

The humorous science fiction series of books called *The Hitchhiker's Guide to the Galaxy*, by Douglas Adams, included a scene in which the most powerful computer ever devised was given the task of finding the ultimate solution. After enormous time and energy was spent, and with much fanfare, the computer finally gave the answer: 42. The problem was that no one had thought to find out what the question was.

---

[4] www.actuarialstandardsboard.org

So it is with actuarial models. Unless we design the output in a way that puts it into the context of the question being asked, it can be useless. Teaching how to write effective reports is beyond the scope of this text. There are, however, some important things that are worth mentioning.

First, if the author of the report is an actuary, it is important to remember that the report is subject to the actuarial Code of Professional Conduct. The author should only provide results if he or she is qualified to do so. If the report includes matters that are beyond the individual's actuarial expertise, it is important to be clear where this is the case. It may be worthwhile to identify (sometimes in the documentation, not the report itself) the ASOPs which apply.

An effective report states its intent early and clearly. The issues to be addressed and the approach used to do so are necessary elements. Limits and caveats to the study should be identified clearly as well.

Some analyses present the calculation of future values without regard to any expected values. An example of this would be an appraisal, which is typically done without reference to earlier such calculations. (An exception to this appraisal situation would be when an update is being done to an earlier appraisal, so that there might be a comparison made of the new values to the prior ones.)

Most analyses, however, are projections of values that the user of the information intends to compare against some standard. That standard might be:

- Original pricing targets (to evaluate original pricing relativities and levels);
- Current pricing targets (to evaluate current re-rating processes);
- Corporate performance (including prior projection) targets (for a multitude of reasons, including profitability, evaluation of the projection process itself, underwriting effectiveness, identifying antiselection issues, measuring medical management, etc.); and
- Management basis targets (for similar reasons).

It is usually worthwhile exploring the expectations of the report's users, to ascertain exactly to what purpose the report will be put, and what metric will be used to measure the results.

Another important aspect of such reporting, often overlooked, is the reporting of *variance* information, along with expected values. It is, for example, much less helpful to know there are 125% of expected catastrophic claims in this year's experience than it would be to also know that this fluctuation is only expected to happen once every 10 years. That added information about confidence levels can help management understand the significance of deviations.

8.4 CHOICE OF ASSUMPTIONS

There are some standard assumptions which must be made for all coverages. Some of these are lapse, mortality, claim cost, expense, profit, and model office assumptions. Other assumptions are coverage-specific.

For major medical coverage governed by the ACA, the rules and parameters of the government programs involved have been rapidly evolving as the law is implemented. It is thus often just as important to understand and validate the legal and regulatory assumptions made by a model of such coverage as well as more traditional economic and actuarial assumptions.

LAPSE ASSUMPTIONS

Lapse rates vary widely by product, by duration, and by company. For this reason, there are no available intercompany studies (except for LTC), as we can sometimes find with respect to claim costs. Lapses are generally highest in year one, and decrease thereafter. It is common to assume they level out at some future time (such as year 5) to an ultimate level. They will also vary by age, occupation, and sometimes benefit plan. In fact, lapse rates can probably be measured and used as a function of any rating variable, if desired. There will generally be a great deal of simplification in choosing lapse rates, limiting the number of total variables used.

It is commonly observed that rate increases (at least those that are material in size) cause a higher lapse rate in the period following the increase, often called a **shock lapse**. The shock lapse often does not occur more than marginally at the time of the first, higher premium billing, but rather at the next one. (This makes sense, if the insured uses that time period to seek out alternative coverage before dropping his existing coverage.)

In cumulative antiselection models, where healthy and unhealthy lives are being modeled separately, healthy lives are assumed to have a higher lapse rate (that is, they drop their coverage more often) than unhealthy lives. Unhealthy lives are also perceived (and modeled) to exhibit much lower shock lapse impact from rate increases than healthy lives. This is logical, since the unhealthy lives: (1) are less insurable, so probably less able to find replacement coverage, and (2) tend to hang on to their coverage more than healthy lives, regardless of rate increases. (There have even been cases where blocks of largely unhealthy lives are unwilling to accept a change in deductible of $\$X$, even if the resulting premium savings are materially greater than $\$X$.)

For major medical coverage, many of the prospects seeking such coverage are actually in short term situations, looking only for interim coverage in anticipation of starting a new job, or school, or some other situation where other (usually group) coverage will apply. This historically caused first year lapse rates to be quite high, sometimes over 50%. Many companies then developed short term products, which are sold in this market space. These products are not underwritten rigorously, relying instead on pre-existing condition exclusions to counter antiselection. When these products are actively marketed alongside the longer term major medical products, the first year lapse rates in the major medical product are much lower.

It remains to be seen how lapse rates for major medical coverage will change in the wake of exchanges and the guaranteed issue requirements of the ACA. Since federal premium subsidies are tied to the second lowest cost silver plan in each market, it is possible that many lower income enrollees will churn from insurer to insurer in order to stay in the lowest priced plan after subsidy. Less healthy insureds will no longer have an underwriting barrier preventing them from switching plans.

For LTC coverage, lapse rates tend to be lower than most other coverages. This is consistent with the way LTC is purchased – to guard against financial loss due to a risk that is far in the future. Because of this, a relatively large portion of policyholders keep their policies for long durations. Lapse assumptions, which drive this leveraging, are therefore an unusually important assumption.

MORTALITY

Some models treat mortality as a separate decrement, applying appropriate, usually age-based, mortality rates. These are usually tabular, from a published table. Most often, however, lapse rates and mortality rates are actually combined to a single decrement, which might be called **termination rates**. Even when mortality is included separately, health actuaries will often refer to 'lapse rates' when they mean 'termination rates,' because: (1) lapse rates are so much larger than mortality rates that they essentially overpower them, (2) there is typically nothing in the policy provisions that depends on the manner of termination, and (3) it is very difficult to determine the cause of termination – often the only thing the company knows is that premiums stopped being paid.

One exception to this typical treatment of mortality occurs in Long Term Care insurance. Based on recent surveys, LTC products are typically purchased by older insureds (in the range of 50 to 70 years old) when mortality starts having a more significant impact. At the same time, lapse rates are low relative to other coverages. In combination, this makes mortality a much more relevant variable, and it is almost always included as a separate contingency in the calculations. This is also true of Medicare Supplement, which similarly targets an elderly population.

CLAIM COSTS

Claim costs are the element of ratemaking that typically gets (for good reason) the most attention. These are the assumptions as to what the benefits are actually going to cost the insurer, and these costs generally are much bigger than all other costs.

In virtually all cases and for all coverages, if the company has good, credible, relevant experience under similar contracts, it is better to use that experience than a theoretical one. Where such experience is not as large as desired, we need to rely on other sources, at least in part. When actual experience is used, the actuarial challenge lies in quantifying the differences to be expected between the experience period and the modeled projection period.

For medical coverages, claim cost assumptions will reflect all things that impact the benefit – benefit design, characteristics of the claim payment process (including networks and their related payment arrangements, if applicable), characteristics of the insured population, and regulatory impacts. If the company's own data is not available, databases can be purchased.[5] It is common to separately choose the claim cost *level* (representing an average assuming a certain fixed population) from the claim cost *relativities*. Relativities might be based on studies from the same data set, but are not typically revised nearly as frequently as the overall claim cost level. Further discussion of this topic is included in Chapter 5, "Setting Premium Rates."

For disability coverages, a tabular approach is generally taken. Simple modifications to an existing table (today, usually the 85 CIDA table)[6] are used, such as X% of incidence rates, and Y% of termination rates, perhaps varying over one or two variables. Termination rate adjustments often vary by duration of claim, since actual experience seems to diverge at differing levels for claims in shorter and longer durations.

LTC coverage often uses a tabular approach, but without the benefit of having a standardized table. Original assumptions for this coverage were based on population statistics. Today, they are based on the accumulated experience and knowledge of the company or the consultant involved.

For forecast models, an important consideration is projecting how claim costs (and all other assumptions, for that matter) will change over time. This amounts to making assumptions about future claim trends. For medical coverages, assumptions often start at current trend levels and grade to a long term trend that is likely to be sustainable in the economy. For all coverages, it is important to reflect any major shifts or cycles likely to apply to the claims.

EXPENSE ASSUMPTIONS

Expenses are an interesting, and often problematic, part of modeling. Very rarely are we lucky enough to know exactly what expenses are attributable to the model we are building. More often, we are modeling only one segment of a company's business, which requires that many of the company's expenses be allocated to the block in a meaningful way. For example, the president of the company has an expense associated with her, which is not attributable to any single line of business, but yet is attributable to all.

---

[5] One example is the *Milliman Health Cost Guidelines*™. Other firms have similar products.
[6] *TSA XXXVII*, "Report of the Society of Actuaries Committee to Recommend New Disability Tables for Valuation." 1985.

Those material expenses that *can* be directly attributed to the block are modeled that way. These include commissions, underwriting costs, premium taxes, and similar expenses. Other expenses are attributed based on an allocation formula.

One interesting expense, which has become more important over time, is the cost of capital for the block of business. As companies have become more aware and sophisticated in their outlooks toward capital over the past few decades, their modeling has begun to include capital and its cost. Most approaches are equivalent to each other, once we understand them, but they vary widely in their conceptual complexity. A popular approach is to model the company's capital level (target capital if doing future projections, actual capital if modeling the past) associated with the block. Then the expense of holding this capital is the cost of capital, which is typically assumed to be the difference in earnings rate between what the capital actually earned (as the company's invested assets) relative to what it *could* have earned if used elsewhere. (This latter value, the amount it *could* have earned, is typically the desired rate of return of the investor. It is also, therefore, typically the discount rate used in calculating present values of profit in an appraisal. This is sometimes called the **hurdle rate**.) This capital was essentially borrowed from the owners of the insurance company (whether it be stockholders for stock companies, policyholders for mutual companies, or the public for not-for-profit companies), and in so doing, the purchasers of that business should reasonably pay a premium for the use of that capital.

It is useful to differentiate between the concepts of a **profits released** and a **profits retained** model. A profits released model projects future profits according to the model's assumptions, and those profits no longer impact values within the projection because they are assumed to be paid out to the company's owners.

A profits retained model might generate the same profit in that year, but that profit then accumulates over time and generates additional investment income on it. If the rate of growth of the accumulated profits (the investment earnings rate) is different from the discount rate later used to bring profits back to time zero, anomalous results can emerge. (Suppose, for example, our model showed a $100 profit in year 1, and we accumulated that profit for ten years at an investment earnings rate of 8%, and discounted it back over those same ten years at 15%. We then end up with the present value of that profit being $53. How can $100 be worth $53 at the same time?)

All expenses are usually expressed in a "per unit" basis. The most common such expense units are per policy, percentage of premium, percentage of claim, and per premium collection. Some larger companies (typically in a life insurance environment) may have even more sophisticated formulae, including expenses that are expressed relative to other expenses. (Agency expenses can be expressed as separate percentages of first year and renewal commissions, for example.) Often the expenses will vary between first year and renewal, and sometimes for more durations than that. (Commissions are a prime example; they may have a high first year value, lower values in some subsequent years, and finally leveling off in some future year to an ultimate level.)

There is an important subtlety to keep in mind with respect to "percent of premium" expenses. There is a clear conceptual difference between percent of *net* premium (net premium being the claim cost, perhaps levelized to a specific premium pattern) and percent of *gross* premium. When building gross premium using expenses that are a percentage of net premium, we can express gross premium as:

$$\text{Gross Premium} = (1+e) \times (\text{Net Premium}),$$

where e is the loading percentage. This is conceptually straightforward. On the other hand, when building gross premium using expenses that are a percentage of that same gross premium, the calculation is sometimes confusing. In this case, we want the loading to be a percentage of *the premium we will get after it is loaded.* The formula for this is then:

$$\text{Gross Premium} = \frac{(\text{Net Premium})}{(1-e)}.$$

PROFIT ASSUMPTIONS

All insurers put margin in their rates. Not-for-profit companies do not literally have capital, but they have the equivalent, typically called **free reserves**. The real difference comes in the long-term management of those reserves. For-profit companies manage their business in order to generate profit for their owners. Not-for-profit companies must limit how much profit they generate, in order to maintain their not-for-profit mission.

In doing retrospective models, profit is actually a dependent variable – it is the difference between revenue items (premium, interest) and expense items (claims, expenses, cost of capital).

For prospective models, there are two approaches. The modeling situation will determine which is used. In the first, a target profit is chosen, and the needed premium level for each cell is calculated. If the premium levels must then be modified to fit market pressures, the model must revert to the second approach, which is to set the premium levels based on other sources (competitive analyses, prior rate levels, etc.), and solve for the profit.

Profit can be measured or targeted using a number of methods. The simplest, and historically most common, method is to express profit as a percentage of annual premium. In doing asset share calculations, where profit may vary from year to year as a percentage of premium, this is sometimes calculated as the present value of profit as a percentage of the present value of premium. This can be done on either a pre-tax or a post-tax basis.

Another profit measure is the Return on Investment (ROI). Under this method, the stream of year by year profit is calculated, and an interest rate is determined such that the present value of the profit flows is equal to zero. This is, in essence, a problem of finding the root of a fairly complicated equation. If there is not at least one year when an investment is made into the block (i.e., negative profit), then there is not a real root to the equation, just complex ones, which are not useful as profit measures.

A related measure of profit is the Return on Equity (ROE). This is the same as the ROI method, except that an additional component is added to the calculation of profit: the investment of capital. Under this method, early investment is much more likely. (Capital needs are often on the order of 25-30% of premium. Since the aggregate premium for a block is typically largest in the first year, before lapses start impacting the size of the block, this results in the biggest investment in year one. There is a gradual release of that capital over time, as the aggregate premium decreases.) The calculated discount rate for the resulting profit stream is profit expressed as a return on equity.

It is interesting that ROI and ROE are not well defined, and have many different definitions.[7] One other version views ROI and ROE both as being calculated post-tax and after cost of capital, but differentiating between them by ROE being on a GAAP basis and ROI being on a statutory basis.

MODEL OFFICE ASSUMPTIONS

These are the assumptions that provide the proportion of business in the block being contributed by each model cell. If a model office is a theoretical one, modeling policies that have not yet been issued, then the assumptions are typically based on sales projections, informed by past performance.

If the model is designed to model existing business, then the assumptions are taken from actual data about the block. To do so, if the modeled cells do not exactly match all the business, there will need to be a mapping, so that each actual policy is mapped to its representative model cell. (Hence the need for model validation – to show that the mapping is appropriate.)

The simplest way to develop model office assumptions is to assume the variables are independent. An asset share model office might, for example, be done for a disability income policy with 320 cells; for each of 4 issue ages (25, 35, 45, and 55), there might be 4 elimination periods (30, 90, 180, and 365 days), 4 benefit periods (2-year, 5-year, to age 65, and lifetime accident), and 5 occupation classes. Independence between variables allows for assumptions that are one-dimensional. The proportion of business to be issued at ages 25, 35, 45, and 55 might be 10%, 20%, 30%, and 40%, respectively, regardless of the combination of elimination period, benefit period, and occupation class. If the assumptions were not independent, then, for example, the 10%, 20%, 30%, and 40% proportions might be used for the longer benefit periods, but the shorter benefit periods might use 25%, 25%, 25%, and 25%.

---

[7] A helpful article in this regard is: Robert W. Beal, "Bridging The Gap Between ROE and IRR," *North American Actuarial Journal*, October 2000.

8.5 AUTO-CORRELATIVE MODELS

In recent years, much attention has been paid to the subject of how past experience for an individual (and the groups to which they belong) can be used to predict his or her future experience. Early treatments of this subject were discussed elsewhere in this text, under the heading of "credibility." Underwriters (more specifically, medical or individual underwriters) are responsible for assessing individual risks. They do so by using all available medical and claim information, and providing a risk relativity or **risk score** for the individual, which is a prediction of the expected claim results for that individual. Even after the prohibition of medical underwriting for major medical coverages in 2014, there is still great interest in predicting individual risks. Insurers or clinicians may, for example, want to make such predictions in order to focus care management efforts where they are likely to do the most good.

Since the risk involves an individual, the prediction does not have a high degree of statistical confidence about it, unless combined with the scores of many other, similar individuals. Conceptually, this high expected variance level has often (or even usually) been confused with a lack of accuracy, and little work was historically done to measure outcomes relative to predictions, or to improve the predictive models being used.

Credibility theory, as it has been used classically, was mostly based on models that presumed independence of individual claims between the experience and projection period. More recently, models have been used that recognize the dependence (or **auto-correlative**) nature of these claims. Conceptually, this is fairly obvious, even without consideration of specific diagnoses. If, for example, someone has a major claim in one year, they are more likely (than someone who has not) to have a sizeable claim in the next year. When specific diagnoses are considered, the correlation is even stronger. Someone with severe diabetes, for example, has a chronic illness that carries with it substantially higher expectation of claim than the average person would have.

More recently, as an outgrowth of interest by the federal government in classes of predictive models called **risk adjusters**, and with the help of some ongoing research sponsored by the Society of Actuaries,[8][9][10] there

---

[8] "A Comparative Analysis of Methods of Health Risk Assessment," by D.L. Dunn, A. Rosenblatt, D.A. Taira, E. Latimer, J. Bertko, T. Stoiber, P. Braun and S. Busch, published by the Society of Actuaries, SOA Monograph M-HB96-1.

has been explosive growth in the development and use of computerized models to predict future claims for individuals and groups. These risk adjusters[11] tend to be based on demographics and either diagnoses or drug history (or both). Recent research has started exploring other data sources, such as electronic medical records or lab data, as well as "lifestyle" data available from consumer marketing databases.

There is some evidence that a predictive model based on a small number of categories of claims can produce a reasonably good prediction, with results comparable to some commercial risk adjusters.[12]

This area promises exciting growth and advancement in understanding over the next few years. These models are substantial improvements over past models and practices.

Another interesting auto-regressive model application is in the area of analysis of claim trends. Some practitioners use **Box-Jenkins ARIMA**[13] models (auto-regressive integrated moving average), which are econometric models that create linear combinations of leading indicators (with derived lags and weights) to predict claim trends.

Finally, as mentioned earlier, agent-based models and other ideas from complexity science are making inroads into actuarial practice. Sophisticated machine learning algorithms are also starting to be used, such as gradient boosting[14] techniques. These algorithms go far beyond the simple linear regressions used by many early risk adjusters.

---

[9] "A Comparative Analysis of Claims-based Methods of Health Risk Assessment for Commercial Populations," by Robert B. Cumming, FSA, MAAA, David Knutson, Brian A. Cameron, FSA, MAAA, and Brian Derrick, published by the Society of Actuaries, May, 2002, www.soa.org

[10] "A Comparative Analysis of Claims-Based Tools for Health Risk Assessment," by Ross Winkelman, FSA, MAAA and Syed Mehmud, published by the Society of Actuaries, April 2007, www.soa.org

[11] See also the useful textbook *Healthcare Risk Adjustment and Predictive Modeling*, Ian Duncan, FSA, FIA, FCIA, MAAA, published by Actex Publications, Inc., 2011.

[12] "Optimal Small Group Renewal Methods," by Ross Winkelman, Society of Actuaries, *Health Section News*, August 2005.

[13] http://en.wikipedia.org/wiki/ARIMA

[14] http://en.wikipedia.org/wiki/Gradient_boosting

CHAPTER 9

REGULATION

This chapter discusses various ways in which individual health insurance is regulated. Emphasis is given to rate regulation (including both traditional regulation at the state level and also regulation at the federal level under the ACA), federal back door regulation, and market conduct, including advertising and sales. Financial reporting and solvency regulation are discussed in Chapter 7. Many regulatory requirements and other programs under the ACA are discussed further throughout the rest of this text.

In 1944, insurance was deemed by the United States Supreme Court to be interstate commerce when transactions cross state lines.[1] Congress responded by passing the **McCarran-Ferguson Act**, preserving the states' roles as the pre-eminent regulators of insurers.[2]

> "The business of insurance, and every person engaged therein, shall be subject to the laws of the several States which relate to the regulation and taxation of such business... No Act of Congress shall be construed to invalidate, impair, or supersede any law enacted by any State for the purpose of regulating the business of insurance..."

This law held for many years without modification. In recent years, however, the federal government has begun taking back federal authority for regulation of insurance. This is usually done by coercing states to comply with federally mandated standards, the coercion being the threat of federal regulation if the states do not comply. The Baucus Amendment and HIPAA (discussed later) both are examples of this. In addition, the creation of federally qualified HMOs (via the HMO Act of 1973) had a substantial impact on the development of the managed care insurance marketplace, and ultimately on all health insurance.

The ACA greatly expands the role of the federal government in the regulation of health insurance generally and individual health insurance in particular. At the same time, the law and its regulations do attempt to preserve

---

[1] U.S. v South-Eastern Underwriters Ass'n.
[2] 15 U.S.C.A. 1012(a) and (b).

the traditional role of the states in regulating insurance where possible. Title I of the ACA states.[3]

> "No Interference With State Regulatory Authority – Nothing in this title shall be construed to preempt any State law that does not prevent the application of the provisions of this title."

On the other hand, this does mean that the ACA preempts any state laws that provide less stringent consumer protections. The National Association of Insurance Commissioners (NAIC) has promulgated a model act[4] implementing many of the ACA market rules. Some states have enacted new laws and regulations at the state level to harmonize their rules with the ACA – and in some cases, to set requirements beyond the baseline now required at the federal level. As a result, insurers must exercise caution to ensure they are complying with these rapidly evolving requirements in all the jurisdictions in which they operate.

9.1 RATE REGULATION IN GENERAL

AUTHORITY

Some state laws explicitly require that individual health insurance rates be *approved* by the Insurance Commissioner. (The Commissioner does not personally approve the rates; it is done by employees in the Insurance Department that the Commissioner leads.) The majority of the time this is *prior approval*, which is a term used to describe a situation in which Commissioner must approve rates before they are used. Sometimes, though, the right of approval is retrospective, in that an insurer can use the rates before they are approved, but if they are subsequently disapproved in favor of lower rates, the difference must be refunded. The right of prior approval of rates is not always explicit in the law. The New York State Insurance Department, for example, believes its right to prior approval of rates is based on its right to prior approval of policy forms, and that for individual insurance the rates are actually part of the policy form (and therefore subject to their approval, since the right to approve policy forms is explicitly given in the law).

Other states require that the rates be *filed* with the Commissioner. Some Commissioners accept all such filings, and treat their duty as administra-

---

[3] §1321(d).
[4] MDL-36

tive. (These are considered **file and use** states.) Others believe they have the right to refuse to accept filings, if the filings do not meet their standards. In the latter case, there is no practical difference between "filing" of rates and a requirement of "approval"; as insurers generally feel that they must obtain an affirmative response from the Commissioner's office before being able to use the rates.

Some state laws were written to have **deemer** provisions. Those laws state that when a rate filing is made with a department, the department has a limited time period in which to object to the filing. If they do not object within that time period, the rates will be "deemed" approved, and the department can no longer object.

The determination of where certain states lie in the spectrum of rate regulation can be difficult. There are comprehensive lists from many different sources, each purporting to list the approval/filing situation in each of the states. While there are many states for which the situation is clear, for many other states those lists disagree with each other to a surprising degree. This lack of clarity argues the importance of having good legal advice, particularly in those states where the situation is not crystal clear.

In addition, even when a state's interpretation or position on a matter is determined, that position can change quite dramatically over time, especially when new commissioners are appointed. (At one NAIC meeting, someone commented that the average tenure of the sitting commissioners was under two years.)

While the ACA requires rate review of *potentially unreasonable* rate increases (generally defined in regulation[5] as those exceeding 10%), it did not give the federal government authority to approve or deny rates. Instead, the federal government has required insurers to file rate increases with them as well as with state authorities. In states deemed to have an *effective rate review program*, the federal government will generally rely on state review of rates and rate increases, although there is still federal review of certain outliers. As of this writing, the great majority of states have been deemed to have effective rate review programs.

In other states, the federal government will review increases and publicly disclose its determination as to whether they are reasonable or not. Insurers are still free to implement rate increases, however, even if they are deemed

---

[5] 45 C.F.R. §154

unreasonable by the federal government, unless the state has the power to deny such increases and chooses to exercise it.

JURISDICTION

The authority to regulate the rates under a particular policy generally follows the jurisdiction of the policy itself. Classically this was the state where the policy was delivered or issued for delivery.

More recently, some policy forms (when allowed by the state of issue) now contain language that gives jurisdiction to where the policy form is "issued and renewed." This gives some weight to an argument that the state of renewal would have jurisdiction. Some have argued in the past that, even without the "issued and renewed" language in the policy form, the right to approve new rates should be in the state of current residence of the policyholder, rather than the state of original issue, at least for policies which are not guaranteed renewable. Under this argument, each renewal of the contract constitutes a new contract, subject to the laws of the state where the new contract was executed.

There are complications implied by either interpretation. If the "state of issue" jurisdiction applies, then each state's Commissioner must approve rates to be applied to policyholders residing in many other states or countries. In essence, each state (at least where approval is required) must approve a nationwide set of rates to be applied to all policies originally issued in that state – a very complex rate structure. This might also lead to very different rates being paid by essentially equivalent risks living next door to each other.

Suppose, for example, that two Minnesota residents live in the same neighborhood, with comparable policies, from the same company, issued at the same time, but where one of the residents had lived in Wisconsin at the time the policy was delivered. Under the 'state of issue' legal construction, the Wisconsin Insurance Department then has jurisdiction over the set of rates for one person, and the Minnesota Insurance Department has jurisdiction over the other set. Those departments might approve very different rates for the two policies, even though the policies may provide identical benefits for identical risks.

On the other hand, if the "state of residence" standard applies, then each Commissioner must approve rates that will apply to all residents of the state, even if they hold policy forms that were never approved (and might not be approvable) under that state's laws.

Qualified health plans sold through an ACA exchange generally have a service area restricted to a single state, and individuals that move outside the service area will have to purchase a different plan when their current plan year ends.

The determination of jurisdiction is a specialized legal area, so it is worthwhile seeking legal advice before relying on a particular position.

HEARINGS

Some carriers who are geographically concentrated, (most often Blue Cross plans and HMOs), are sometimes required to participate in public hearings regarding any rate increases. Sometimes such hearings happen automatically; sometimes they must be requested, either by the public or by another public official (like the state Attorney General).

Hearings are an administrative proceeding, so are subject to the administrative code of the state in which they are held. Often, public disclosure is mandated in the law or in the administrative code, and public testimony may be heard, in addition to the insurer's testimony.

Sometimes such proceedings are adversarial, with experts (like the insurer's in-house or consulting actuary) being examined and cross examined. Sometimes they are not, and prepared statements are supplemented by questions from the hearing officer(s).

Historically, public hearings were typically only held for not-for-profit companies, and not for commercial companies. One reason for this different treatment was the difference in basic ownership interest between the types of carriers (the public's perceived ownership interest in a not-for-profit, policyholders owning a mutual company, and stockholders owning a stock company).

Given the large amount of political and media attention focused on health insurance rate increases in the wake of the ACA, rate hearings have become more prevalent even for commercial companies. This leads to practical difficulties for companies that are not geographically concentrated. Commercial companies are often licensed and do business in multiple states, without major concentration in any one state.

Even for companies not subject to required rate hearings, under state administrative codes insurers can bring administrative actions against insurance departments if the two parties cannot agree on appropriate rate actions. Subsequently, court actions may be needed to resolve the matters.

The ACA has also led to more required rate filing documents (discussed in more detail later in this chapter), and many of these documents are now available to consumers and other interested stakeholders through the internet.

9.2 REASONABLENESS STANDARDS

LOSS RATIOS AS A METRIC

It is helpful to know a bit of the history behind loss ratios.

When regulators first began to look into the regulation of premium rates, they struggled with determining what constituted a "reasonable" rate. For some years they were unable to define the term, in some part because insurers were afraid of being locked into a possibly inappropriate standard. The first mention of such a measure by regulators is in a speech made by New York's then Insurance Superintendent Alfred J. Bohlinger, following a study by the department[6] (italics added):

> "Our law provides that the *benefits must not be unreasonable in relation to the premium charge* for accident and health coverage...Upon considering that point, we invariably come down to a question of: 'What constitutes a reasonable loss ratio?' It has been suggested by our Department – not as a rigid rule but rather as, shall I call it, a benchmark – that in our individual accident and health coverages, the loss ratio anticipated to be produced or to result under a given form should, in the case of accident and health coverages, be in the neighborhood of 50%, and as to straight accident coverage, in the neighborhood of 45%."

This standard was proposed in 1952 to the NAIC by the New York Insurance Department. In 1953, the NAIC adopted a standard based on the New

---

[6] Address at the 54th Anniversary Dinner of the New York Insurance Brokers Association, as reported by the *Insurance Advocate*, Nov. 29, 1952, p.11.

York proposal.[7] This adoption of **minimum anticipated loss ratio (MALR)** standards initially treated the standard as a safe harbor – if insurers demonstrated compliance with the MALR standard, their rates would then be presumed to be reasonable. This still allowed insurers the opportunity to demonstrate that the rates they proposed for a policy form were reasonable by some other standard, provided the regulator would agree to it.

Most state laws, for similar historical reasons, require that the *benefits* be reasonable in relation to *premium*, rather than the other way around. This relationship can be assumed to be commutative, so will be discussed as the rates being reasonable in relation to benefits.

As we will see, minimum loss ratio (MLR) requirements for major medical insurance and Medicare Advantage plans were introduced as part of the ACA. These new federal requirements are having far-reaching consequences for the U.S. health insurance market. Before discussing the details of this new requirement, it is helpful to review other historical definitions of loss ratios (indeed, in many cases, ACA policies are also subject to state loss ratio rules in addition to the federal MLR rules).

Defining Loss Ratios

A loss ratio, in simplest terms, is a ratio of claim expense to premium revenue. This seems simple enough, but has a surprising number of definitional nuances. These nuances can be categorized in different ways.

An important differentiator is whether the loss ratio is retrospective (in which case it is composed of actual, historical numbers) or prospective (in which case it is composed of projected, future numbers).

Retrospective loss ratios can be characterized by whether the claim and premium figures in them are composed of paid claims and paid premiums, or of incurred claims and earned premiums. The former is typically referred to as a **paid loss ratio**, the latter an **earned/incurred loss ratio**, or something similar. Even though historical loss ratios are based on past actual experience, if they are at all recent (as most analyses require), some

---

[7] Max J. Schwartz, "Accident and Health Insurance Rates, Rating Plans, and Commissions," from *Examination of Insurance Companies*, prepared under the direction of Deputy Superintendent Adelbert G. Straub, Jr. (New York City: New York State Insurance Department, 1955), Vol VI, Chapter 11.

portion of the claim experience will still be based on estimates. This is to account for the claims that were incurred in the experience period (the period being analyzed), but which have not yet been paid at the time of the data collection. For some coverages, like DI and LTC, these unpaid portions of claim can be quite a sizeable portion of the incurred claim figure, since much of the claim payment for a given claim occurs quite some time after incurral. In most actuarial analyses, earned/incurred loss ratios are used, so as to allocate the financial flows back to the appropriate point in time from which they arose. When paid loss ratios are used, there can be unknown biases created in the analysis by uneven cash flows.

In certain contexts, particularly HMOs, retrospective loss ratios for the plan are called **medical loss ratios**. Sometimes the unmodified term *loss ratio* is also intended to include all expenses associated with the block of business in question, although more commonly that situation is described with the property & casualty term **combined ratio**.

Prospective loss ratios are projections, and virtually always on an earned/incurred basis. Often such a loss ratio is called an **anticipated loss ratio (ALR)**, meaning it is the loss ratio anticipated to occur over the policy lifetime. Such a loss ratio is usually calculated as the present value of future claims divided by the present value of future premium. This calculation can be made either before issue (during the product development process) or during the policy lifetime. Sometimes the prospective ALR is combined with the accumulated historical loss ratio to develop a **lifetime loss ratio** for the business from the time the first policy was issued until the (projected) time the last policy lapses.

The impact of using paid/paid vs. earned/incurred values will vary by type of coverage. This is because the difference between these bases represents timing differences – determining when in the projection period the claim payments represented by contributions to (or release of) reserves are recognized. Reserves are simply the early recognition of those amounts before they are actually paid. The significance of these timing differences will depend on the amounts involved and the length of time involved, both of which will vary by coverage and by circumstances.

We will now take a look at how this difference occurs, using a hypothetical projection of a cohort of three-year-term policies, that all: (1) are issued simultaneously at time $t = 0$, (2) experience lapses over three years, and (3) terminate immediately following the end of the third duration.

First, the earned/incurred calculation:

Table 9.1

Time	Number of Policies	Present Value Factor	Premium Rate	Earned Prem (000)	Claim Cost/Pol	Incurred Clms (000)	Earned /Inc LR
t	N	$(1+i)^{-t}$	P	$EP = P \times \frac{N}{1000}$	C	$IC = C \times \frac{N}{1000}$	IC/EP
0	1,000	1.0000	$1,000	$1,000	$600	$600	60.0%
1	750	0.9524	$1,150	$863	$720	$540	62.6%
2	640	0.9070	$1,300	$832	$864	$553	66.5%
3	550	0.8638	$1,500	$825	$1,037	$570	69.1%
PV				$3,289		$2,108	64.1%

The present value at time 0 of incurred claims ($3,289), divided by the present value of earned premium ($2,108), is 64.1%. This is the original lifetime ALR. Note that this differs somewhat from the loss ratio you would get if there was no discounting of the claim and premium values.

Now let us look at the calculation of loss ratios using paid claims rather than incurred claims. The following table shows the development of the paid claims, and thus the paid/earned loss ratio.

Table 9.2

Time	Claim Res (000)	Paid Claims	P/E Loss Ratio
t	V_t	$PC = IC - (V_t - V_{t-1})$	PC/EP
0	150	$450	45.0%
1	135	$555	64.3%
2	138	$550	66.1%
3	143	$565	68.6%
3+	0	$143	
PV[1]		$2,083	63.3%

[1] In taking the present value we have assumed that claim payments in years 3+ actually all occur in year 4, and have used a discount factor of 0.8227 for that year.

A similar analysis could be done converting earned premium to paid premium. The effect would be similar to Table 9.2, although somewhat smaller because premium reserves tend to be a much smaller portion of premiums than claim reserves are of claims.

The paid loss ratio for this same period is 63.3%. This is sometimes a difficult fact to intuitively accept on its face. After all, the lifetime loss ratio is calculating the same total claim payments and the same total premium over the policy lifetime. Why isn't the loss ratio the same?

The difference is timing, and the impact of taking the present value of payments. In the incurred calculation, all payments are assumed to occur at the moment the claim is incurred, and they are discounted from that point in time. (Even though payments might occur after the point of incurral, they are recognized at that point by means of the reserves which are set up for that purpose.)

On the other hand, in the paid calculation, the portion of claims and premium that is paid after the incurral date is discounted from the point in time that these amounts are paid. Because that is later than the incurral date, they are more discounted, and therefore contribute less to the numerator of the loss ratio calculation. Hence, this loss ratio is smaller than the earned/incurred one.

Claim costs and claim reserve factors for DI insurance and LTC insurance generally use a claim cost methodology that somewhat corrects for this timing issue. For these coverages, insurers typically use a tabular approach for claim reserves, which includes the application of present value factors to future claim payments. That is, the present value (PV) of claim costs is the sum of a series of claim costs (one for each duration), just as it is with other coverages. Each of those durational-specific claim costs, however, is itself a present value calculation of the expected payouts of such a claim over time.

We could actually correct for the same claim payment timing difference in our example calculations by including present value discounts in the reserve calculation. This is rarely done for coverages other than DI and LTC, however, because: (1) the impact is relatively minor most of the time, (2) it is conservative (produces higher reserves) for solvency purposes, and (3) when compared to normal claim reserve fluctuations, the discounting is typically inconsequential.

CREDIBILITY

Many insurance department examiners would prefer data specifically from their state, from which to draw their conclusions regarding the reasonableness of rate levels. Unfortunately, multi-state carriers often do not have sufficiently sized blocks of business to support that analysis. Compounding this issue is the lack of uniform treatment of the problem by regulators.

The concept of credibility can be viewed as a confidence interval issue. If an actuary can identify the level of confidence they wish to have in an estimate (e.g., "95% probability that the estimate is within +-5% of the estimate"), then it is a relatively simple exercise (assuming a claim distribution is available) to perform a Monte Carlo simulation to determine the number of insureds or claims needed to obtain that level of credibility.

One aspect of this issue, often discussed by industry and actuarial representatives with regulators, is the desire to have a credibility system that is a zero sum process –the post-credibility (pooling) process results in the same needed premium level overall as the pre-credibility one, at least across the insurer's entire block of business that is included in the rating exercise.

As will be discussed later in this chapter, the minimum loss ratio requirement under the ACA makes explicit adjustments for credibility as part of the measurement process.

MINIMUM ANTICIPATED LOSS RATIOS

The standard most often used to determine whether rates are reasonable in relation to benefits is the **minimum anticipated loss ratio (MALR)**. The projected loss ratio for a given block of policies is compared against this MALR, to determine or prove reasonableness.

Setting minimum loss ratios is sometimes viewed as a way to ensure that a certain proportion of premium dollars is returned to the policyholders as benefits. One problem with this view is that it ignores those expenses (such as expenses for disease management programs) that benefit policyholders and help limit unnecessary claims, but that increase expenses. These expenses thus lower the loss ratio (and this makes it more difficult to meet a loss ratio minimum), despite being of benefit to everyone and in keeping with public policy goals. For this reason, many observers had suggested that the NAIC (and states that adopt versions of the NAIC models) allow certain cost containment expenses such as these to be considered part of the loss ratio. This is the approach taken in the ACA MLR requirement, which includes certain quality improvement and healthcare information technology costs with claims in the numerator.

The application of the MALR standard is different for rate revisions of existing policies than it is for new policy forms. Often these standards do not apply to HMOs or Hospital Service Corporations (Blue Cross plans), because those carriers' loss ratios are often much higher than the minimum (in excess of 80%) anyway, and the rating process (as described earlier) is different.

Such MALR standards vary by state. Often the standard applicable to a given policy will depend on the type of coverage, the renewability provision of the policy, and the average premium under the policy. The NAIC has adopted a model[8] which includes MALR standards, and is similar to those adopted in a number of states. Any such state requirements are in addition to the federal MLR requirements for major medical plans under the ACA. It is important to distinguish between minimum *anticipated* loss ratios (which are projections commonly used to evaluate reasonableness of premium rates) from the ACA's minimum *historical* loss ratio requirements which are used to determine rebates due to policyholders after the fact.

The MALR standard adopted by the NAIC for new policy forms includes the following standards. Items in italics are the author's clarifying language. Standards for LTC and Medicare Supplement polices will be discussed separately.

(1) With respect to a new form under which the average annual premium *(defined in the model)* is expected to be *within a defined range*, benefits shall be deemed reasonable in relation to premiums provided the anticipated loss ratio is at least as great as shown in the following table:

Table 9.3

Type of Coverage	Renewal Clause			
	OR	CR	GR	NC
Medical Expense	60%	55%	55%	50%
Loss of Income and Other	60%	55%	50%	45%

---

[8] Model law 134 Guidelines for Filing of Rates for Individual Health Insurance Forms, http://www.naic.org/store/free/MDL-134.pdf.

(2) Definitions of Renewal Clause

> OR - Optionally Renewable: renewal is at the option of the insurance company.
>
> CR - Conditionally Renewable: renewal can be declined by class, by geographic area or for stated reasons other than deterioration of health.
>
> GR - Guaranteed Renewable: renewal cannot be declined by the insurance company for any reason, but the insurance company can revise rates on a class basis.
>
> NC - Non-Cancelable: renewal cannot be declined nor can rates be revised by the insurance company.

The premium range referenced in (1) is defined in terms of a maximum and a minimum, each of which is indexed so that it will increase over time. The index used for this purpose is the CPI-U, and the formula's starting point is framed in terms of the CPI-U for 1982.[9] For policies with average premiums falling outside the range, the MALR is adjusted formulaically.

According to the NAIC, as of April 2014 there are 25 jurisdictions that have either never adopted or adopted and then repealed this model law, 9 that have adopted the model or a similar law, and 22 that have adopted something related to the model, but not close enough to be called "similar." (These figures are intended only as general information, as they appear to be based on broadly different judgments as to the meaning of the words "similar" and "related." There are, for example, at least two states in the "no action taken" list that appear to have adopted some related standards.)

It is noteworthy that the NAIC MALR values in Table 9.3 are quite a bit lower than the minimum loss ratio requirement for individual insurance under the ACA, which is 80%. As we will see, adjusting to this more stringent requirement was a major undertaking for insurers.

DISCOUNT RATES

In calculating the present value of future or past experience for loss ratios, a discount (interest) rate must be assumed. For most underwritten coverages, early premiums are relatively higher as compared to claims and later

---

[9] www.bls.gov

claims are higher relative to premiums, so higher discount rates result in lower ALRs. Lower ALRs may result in the need to lower premiums to achieve a minimum ALR. When meeting the minimum is at risk, therefore, companies would tend to want to use a lower discount rate. (Some even go so far as to assume no discounting, equivalent to a discount rate of 0%.) Regulators tend to want to limit the interest rate used, and may require a minimum discount rate, perhaps related to the minimum interest rate used in the state's valuation law.

POLICY RESERVES

Policy reserves are conceptually designed to pre-fund future increases in claim costs, expected to occur later in the policy lifetime. Those future claim costs come from claims that have not yet occurred, and will not occur until those future years. This is conceptually different from claim reserves, which are held to fund future payouts of already existing claims. It is also different from premium reserves, which are held so that premium payments will be attributed to the correct contractual period.

In pre-funding future claim increases, policy reserves make incurred claims (and therefore incurred loss ratios) more level over time. Since they are calculated by comparing the average claims over the policy's lifetime against each year's own projected claims, we might even expect that, if actual experience matches that assumed in the reserve basis, such reserves would completely levelize loss ratios over time. As discussed in Chapter 6, "Reserves and Liabilities," it turns out that, in order to make this happen, we have to make a couple very specific adjustments to this calculation. The earned/incurred loss ratios are, in fact, level only when: (1) changes to policy reserves are included in the numerator, and (2) an appropriate adjustment is made for interest on the policy reserve.[10]

Thus, if: (1) the actual experience matches expected experience, (2) contributions to policy reserves are included in the numerator, and (3) the appropriate adjustments are made, the actual loss ratio will emerge as identically equal to the original anticipated lifetime loss ratio. To the extent experience varies from expected, they will not be equal. The comparison of adjusted historical loss ratios against the original anticipated lifetime loss ratio can be very useful, particularly in discussions with non-actuaries who might be looking to the original ALR as an important measure of reasonableness.

---

[10] Pharr, Joe B. "The Individual Accident and Health Loss Ratio Dilemma," *Transactions of the Society of Actuaries*, 1979, pp 373-387.

Regulators have been known to apply their minimum loss ratio standard by comparing actual year-to-year loss ratios *without* reserve adjustments against original anticipated lifetime loss ratios (in contravention of the theory, described earlier). This led to disapproval of rate increases for the carriers until cumulative actual loss ratios (without reserves) equaled the lifetime ALRs. By that point, it was too late to take effective corrective action, and the block was forced into an antiselection spiral. At times, this has been a major problem for some insurers.

In reality, a comparison of actual loss ratios against expected ones (an "actual to expected" or "A:E" analysis) can be done on virtually any basis, including on a paid basis, *provided that the actual and expected values have been calculated consistently.* The example discussed in the last paragraph is one where this comparison was not made correctly. When choosing the basis of comparison for a particular situation, there are, of course, many practical and theoretical considerations that should be taken into account. This includes the likelihood of successfully communicating appropriate expectations to the user.

For a variety of reasons, claim experience with and claim experience without policy reserve adjustments are not directly comparable with one another. In fact, it can be (and often is, for medical coverages) that the historical unadjusted loss ratios for a block of policies, a few years after initial issue, are running significantly higher than planned, indicating that corrective rate action is needed. At the same time, those actual yearly loss ratios (and the cumulative loss ratio to date) may still be significantly lower than the original anticipated lifetime loss ratio.

Suppose, for example, we are analyzing a medical policy a few years after issue. The original anticipated lifetime loss ratio under a policy might be 60%. The unadjusted cumulative actual historical loss ratio might be 56%. At first glance, it is tempting to conclude that this is a fortunate deviation. If the experience was modified, however, according to the Pharr adjustments (changes in reserves and interest adjustments in the numerator of the loss ratio), the adjusted loss ratios in that period could well be 66%, indicating the experience is significantly worse than expected – 110% of expected, in fact.

In this situation, it is important that either (1) the unadjusted actual loss ratios be compared against the unadjusted expected loss ratios, or (2) the adjusted actual loss ratios be compared against the lifetime ALR (which is the level expected loss ratio). The first method seems less prone to misinterpretation. In the example from the last paragraph, an adjusted actual loss ratio of 66%, compared to an anticipated loss ratio of 60%, might cause one to (erroneously) conclude that the actual experience is 10% higher than expected. In truth, the 66% is composed of two pieces: (1) the actual claim experience, and (2) an accumulation of policy reserves and interest (adjustments to claim experience described earlier, based on the *original expected experience*, not *actual* experience). Therefore, in order to measure the actual A:E ratio of experience, we must account for the leveraging caused by the change in policy reserves and the interest adjustment. If the expected claims were understated, then the claim adjustments (based on those expected claims) were similarly understated. In this case, the actual A:E is more nearly 112%, rather than 110%.

When looking at unadjusted claim experience, for A:E analysis, it is helpful to think of the unadjusted expected loss ratios as "durationally adjusted" loss ratios. This can be understood by realizing that, at any given point in time, the experience thus far under a block of policies represents a mix of experience by duration. The experience in each of those durations has an expected loss ratio connected with it. The true expected loss ratio for that mix of durations is the weighted average of those duration-specific loss ratios.

One very common application of this durational A:E analysis is when regulators test actual experience against MALRs. Actual year-by-year experience is accumulated (using the same interest rate as used for the original ALR calculation), but cannot be compared directly against the minimum ALR. The minimum should be adjusted to account for the durational mix, typically by multiplying it by the ratio of [the weighted average expected loss ratio by duration] to [the ALR].

STATE LEVEL LOSS RATIO GUARANTEES

In a few states, there are "loss ratio guarantee" laws in effect. Those laws permit insurers to change rates under their policies at will, provided the insurer guarantees to pay out a given minimum percentage of their premiums in the form of claims, or otherwise refund money to policyholders. As a typical example of how this works, Kentucky has a **deemer**-type law. Under this law, a company can voluntarily use the loss ratio guarantee, and obtain rate increases without stringent rate regulation.

If a company chooses not to avail itself of the loss ratio guarantee, they can **file and use** the rates, and there is a 60 day deemer provision in the law. If the filing is disapproved, however, the commissioner can order a retroactive rate reduction.[11]

If a company *does* choose to use the loss ratio guarantee alternative to approval, rate filings are "file and use," being deemed approved immediately. The company's loss ratio guarantee is stated at the time the policy form is originally approved, and the insurer must later make whatever adjustments are necessary to fulfill that guarantee, if claims should happen to be less than expected. The law provides for a list of the information that must be included in the filing. It is useful to see how such requirements are worded.[12]

1. An actuarial memorandum specifying the expected loss ratio that complies with the standards as set forth in this subsection;
2. A statement certifying that all rates, fees, dues, and other charges are not excessive, inadequate, or unfairly discriminatory;
3. Detailed experience information concerning the policy forms;
4. A step-by-step description of the process used to develop the experience loss ratio, including demonstration with supporting data;
5. A guarantee of a specific lifetime minimum loss ratio, that shall be greater than or equal to the following, taking into consideration adjustments for duration as set forth in administrative regulations promulgated by the commissioner:
    a. Sixty-five percent (65%) for policies issued to individuals or for certificates issued to members of an association that does not offer coverage to small employers;...
6. A guarantee that the actual Kentucky loss ratio for the calendar year in which the new rates take effect, and for each year thereafter until new rates are filed, will meet or exceed the minimum loss ratio standards referred to in subparagraph 5. of this paragraph, adjusted for duration;
7. A guarantee that the actual Kentucky lifetime loss ratio shall meet or exceed the minimum loss ratio standards referred to in subparagraph 5. of this paragraph; and

---

[11] KRS 304.17A-095.
[12] Ibid.

8. If the annual earned premium volume in Kentucky under the particular policy form is less than two million five hundred thousand dollars ($2,500,000), the minimum loss ratio guarantee shall be based partially on the Kentucky earned premium and other credibility factors as specified by the commissioner.

When actual loss ratios do not meet the guarantee, this mechanism causes a refund of premiums to occur, sufficient in size to bring the actual loss ratio up to the minimum. In return for this, the insurer need not go through the sometimes arduous task of obtaining approval from regulators before implementing a rate increase.

As described in a separate subsequent section, a loss ratio guarantee now applies at the federal level for all issuers of individual major medical insurance (and in fact, similar requirements also apply to small and large employer coverage, as well as Medicare Advantage plans). There are, however, a number of key differences in how this federal MLR operates.

MINIMUM LOSS RATIOS AT RENEWAL

One very important aspect of MALR regulation is how it is applied in the calculation of renewal rates for individual health insurance. This is of occasional importance to DI and LTC coverages, which have less frequent rate increase filings compared to medical insurance coverages. It is of critical importance to medical insurance coverages, which have very frequent (usually annual) rate increases.

The underlying concept of the NAIC's approach, which is repeated in virtually all states that have implemented similar regulations, is the requirement that a rate increase be calculated to meet two standards at renewal:

1. The policy form (or rating block) must meet the MALR over its future lifetime, as of the point in time the new increase becomes effective, and

2. The policy form must meet the MALR over its *entire* (past and future) lifetime, as of the same point in time.

The combination of these two requirements has an interesting impact on rate calculations. To see this, we need to understand the various pieces of this situation.

If we call the original projection of loss ratios "expected", we first should recognize that these do not necessarily equate to a lifetime ALR equaling the MALR. For many reasons, an insurer might choose rates that result in a loss ratio higher than the minimum. When applying the above MALR standard some years after introduction of the policy form, we should realize that the regulation compares the actual stream of loss ratios (actually the sum of the present values of that stream) against a stream of loss ratios that is consistent with the MALR, *not* against the true expected loss ratio stream.

To illustrate this situation, examine the following example. Let us assume the numbers here represent the company's *expected* results, which were used in pricing:

Table 9.4

Time	Number of Pols	Present Value Fctr	Premium Rate	Earned Prem (000)	Claim Cost/Pol	Incurred Claims (000)	Earned/ Inc LR
t	N	v	P	$EP = P \times \frac{N}{1000}$	C	$IC = C \times \frac{N}{1000}$	IC/EP
0	1,000	1.0000	$1,000	$1,000	$483.50	$484	48.4%
1	750	0.9524	$1,200	$900	$714.10	$536	59.5%
2	563	0.9070	$1,440	$810	$964.00	$542	66.9%
3	422	0.8638	$1,728	$729	$1,221.10	$515	70.7%
4	316	0.8227	$2,074	$656	$1,546.70	$489	74.6%
PV				$3,761		$2,333	62.0%
MALR							60.0%

The ALR is calculated as follows:

$$ALR = \frac{\sum_t IC_t \times v^t}{\sum_t EP_t \times v^t} \tag{9.1}$$

and equals 62.0%. The company has intentionally chosen an ALR of 62%, by setting its premium rates at a level that generates it. This ALR is greater than the MALR of 60%, as it must be in order to comply with the regulation.

We will now assume that the policy has been introduced, and that in the middle of the second year (time = 1 in Table 9.4), we have measured the first year's results, compared this actual against expected, calculated the earned/incurred loss ratios, and found that the experience is 110% of expected:

Table 9.5

Time	Expected Loss Ratio	Actual Loss Ratio	A:E
0	48.4%	53.2%	110%

In order to determine the appropriate rate increase, we will certainly need a prospective projection for management. We will also need to take the past history (shown in this table) into account, to meet the regulatory dual MALR (future lifetime and total lifetime) requirement.

To do this, assume that future experience will stay at 110% of the originally expected level. Further, for this illustration assume that exactly one year will pass between the $t = 1$ experience period for the analysis, calculation, approval, and 100% implementation of the rate change, at time $t = 2$.

Without a rate increase, our projection of the lifetime of experience looks like this:

Table 9.6

Time t	Number of Pols N	Present Value Fctr v	Premium Rate P	Earned Prem (000) $EP = P \times \frac{N}{1000}$	Claim Cost/Pol C	Incurred Clms (000) $IC = C \times \frac{N}{1000}$	Earned/ Inc LR IC/EP
0	1,000	1.1025	$1,000	$1,000	$531.90	$532	53.2%
1	750	1.0500	$1,200	$900	$785.50	$589	65.5%
2	563	1.0000	$1,440	$810	$1,060.40	$596	73.6%
3	422	0.9524	$1,728	$729	$1,343.20	$567	77.7%
4	316	0.9070	$2,074	$656	$1,701.40	$538	82.1%
Total				$4,095		$2,822	

If we calculate the year 2-4 loss ratio (the future ALR at the time of the rate increase), using a present value calculation similar to the one shown earlier, we get an ALR for years 2-4 of 77.4%. This is 110% of the expected value of 70.3% for the same years. Calculating the total lifetime loss ratio in the same way yields 68.2%.

To achieve a future ALR of 60%, the future premium rates would need to increase by (77.4 – 60.0) / 60.0 = 29% The rate increase needed to achieve the original lifetime ALR (62%) is 25%. The rate increase needed to achieve the original year 4 results of 74.6% is 10% (since the A:E is 110%.)

(It is interesting to note that at least one state insurance department–Florida–has implemented a rule that rate increases can only be made to bring ALRs in line with the originally intended loss ratios for those durations, in this case 70.3%.)

If the 29% rate increase took place, and we ignore the real world antiselective shock lapse that would take place as a result, the revised projection would look like this:

Table 9.7

Time	Number of Pols	Present Value Fctr	Premium Rate	Earned Prem (000)	Claim Cost/Pol	Incurred Clms (000)	Earned/ Inc LR
t	N	v	P	$EP = P \times \frac{N}{1000}$	C	$IC = C \times \frac{N}{1000}$	IC/EP
0	1,000	1.1025	$1,000	$1,000	$531.90	$532	53.2%
1	750	1.0500	$1,200	$900	$785.50	$589	65.5%
2	563	1.0000	$1,857	$1,045	$1,060.40	$596	57.1%
3	422	0.9524	$2,228	$940	$1,343.20	$567	60.3%
4	316	0.9070	$2,674	$846	$1,701.40	$538	63.6%
PV				$4,755		$2,829	59.5%

The resulting year 2-4 ALR is 60.0% and the total lifetime ALR is 59.5%. We have calculated a rate increase so that the future loss ratio will meet the MALR standard. In this case, however, we have run afoul of the other rule – the lifetime loss ratio is 59.5%, which is lower than the MALR. Because of this, we must recalculate the rate increase to a lower number in order to meet the minimum. It is a relatively simple algebraic calculation to find the needed rate increase of 27.1% (as opposed to 29.0% before the lifetime restriction was applied). The following projection shows the result expected after the 27.1% rate increase:

Table 9.8

Time t	Number of Pols N	Present Value Fctr v	Premium Rate P	Earned Prem (000) $EP = P \times \frac{N}{1000}$	Claim Cost/Pol C	Incurred Clms (000) $IC = C \times \frac{N}{1000}$	Earned/ Inc LR IC/EP
0	1,000	1.1025	$1,000	$1,000	$531.90	$532	53.2%
1	750	1.0500	$1,200	$900	$785.50	$589	65.5%
2	563	1.0000	$1,830	$1,029	$1,060.40	$596	57.9%
3	422	0.9524	$2,196	$927	$1,343.20	$567	61.2%
4	316	0.9070	$2,635	$834	$1,701.40	$538	64.6%
PV				$4,716		$2,829	60.0%

Now the year 2-4 ALR is 60.9%, and the total lifetime ALR is 60.0%. In this example, the lifetime MALR standard had a relatively minor impact on the resulting rate increase. In contrast, however, for some policy forms that have been in force for many years, past experience may overwhelm future experience in the rate calculation. Earlier experience that was less than the MALR might be virtually impossible to offset with future high loss ratios, even if those future loss ratios are *very* high. In this instance, it probably makes sense for the insurer to hold gross premium reserves or deficiency reserves for these policies, since the insurer is unlikely to be able to charge self-supporting premium rates. (This is the purpose of such reserves.)

The dual lifetime and future loss ratio tests have sometimes been considered a prohibition against an insurer "recovering past losses." This is a rating requirement that allows the insurer to raise rates as needed in order to achieve a lifetime ALR, but only provided that the future loss ratio does not fall below the minimum to offset higher past loss ratios (i.e., "past losses").

It is important to keep in mind that, for most coverages (and particularly those that are underwritten), loss ratios increase with policy duration. It is therefore inappropriate to compare either past or future experience against a single "expected" number (like the MALR or original ALR), unless that expected number has been calculated using durational adjustments.

FEDERAL MINIMUM LOSS RATIO REQUIREMENTS UNDER THE ACA

The MALR standards examined previously set limits on *anticipated* loss ratios over the lifetime or future lifetime of a block of policies. The *federal minimum medical loss ratio* – commonly referred to as MLR – requirements under the ACA, however, limit the *actual* loss ratios that insurers can achieve, requiring them to pay rebates if the actual loss ratio is lower than the minimum. This fundamentally changes the risk that insurers are taking on, making it asymmetrical – years with large gains can no longer be used to offset years with large losses, since the extra gains in the profitable years may need to be paid out as rebates.

As we will see next, the actual calculation of the MLR rebate for an insurer includes certain adjustments aimed at smoothing experience out over multiple years and dampening the impact for non-credible blocks of business. These may help to address the asymmetry in risk, but only partially. It also includes adjustments to credit insurers for certain quality improvement expenses and to take into account taxes and fees insurers must pay.

ACA MLR requirements took effect for commercial insurers beginning in 2011, with rebates payable in 2012. The NAIC was heavily involved in developing certain aspects of the requirements, and has published a model law[13] on the subject.

MLR is applied separately in each state for three market segments: individual, small group, and large group. The minimum loss ratio for individual and small employer group health insurance is generally 80%, while the standard for the large employer group market is 85%, although some states[14] obtained waivers to phase in these requirements over time in the individual market. The MLR requirement applies to all fully insured coverage in these markets (including grandfathered business); self-insured coverage is not, however, subject to MLR. Insurers must provide MLR reports to the Department of Health and Human Services (HHS) by July 31 in the year following each calendar year.

Starting in 2014, MLR standards also apply to Medicare Advantage and Part D plans. These requirements will not be covered in detail in this text. Like large employer business, the MLR standard for Medicare Advantage and Part D plans is 85%. Unlike in the commercial market, plans that drop

---

[13] MDL-190
[14] See http://www.cms.gov/CCIIO/Programs-and-Initiatives/Health-Insurance-Market-Reforms/state_mlr_adj_requests.html.

below the minimum pay a rebate to the federal government, rather than to policyholders. Medicare Advantage or Part D plans that fail to meet the MLR for multiple years will face sanctions, and will eventually have their contracts with the federal government terminated.

Medicare supplement plans are not subject to ACA MLR requirements. These plans were already subject to their own MLR requirements prior to the passage of the ACA, as described elsewhere in this chapter. Long term care, dental, vision, or most other limited benefit plans also are not subject to ACA MLR, though there are special rules for expatriate and mini-med plans.

For the first three years of the program (2011 through 2013), HHS estimates that individual and employer plan enrollees received approximately $1.9 billion in MLR rebates.[15]

A recent analysis[16] of insurer financial statements found the following experience in the individual market over the past few years:

Table 9.9: Commercial Individual Market Financial Results

Year	Covered Lives (Millions)	Earned Premium PMPM	Claim Expenses PMPM	Preliminary MLR	MLR Rebates*†	Under-writing Margin*	Admin Expense Ratio*
2013	10.9	$247.41	$209.62	86.7%	0.4%	(3.9%)	17.4%
2012	10.7	$240.10	$199.47	86.0%	0.6%	(2.0%)	16.0%
2011	10.7	$234.17	$188.47	83.5%	1.3%	(1.1%)	16.4%
2010	10.1	$214.11	$166.14	80.8%	0.1%	(0.3%)	19.1%

*Expressed as a percentage of earned premium.
†MLR rebates reported in 2010 likely reflect either state minimum loss ratio requirements that predate the ACA or reporting errors.

Over recent years, the preliminary MLR in the individual market has risen and the portion of premiums rebated back to policyholders has fallen – as have insurer's average profit margins on this business, from a slight loss of

---

[15] Department of Health and Human Services, "Consumers Benefitted From 80/20 Rule in 2013," retrieved 1/14/2015 from http://www.cms.gov/CCIIO/Resources/Forms-Reports-and-Other-Resources/Downloads/Final-MLR-Report_07-22-2014.pdf .
[16] Houchens, Paul, Clarkson, Jason, and Gray, Colin. 2013 Commercial health insurance: Overview of financial results. *Milliman Insight*, November 2014. Retrieved 1/14/2015 from http://us.milliman.com/insight/2014/2013-Commercial-health-insurance-Overview-of-financial-results

0.3% in 2010 to a loss of nearly 4% in 2013. This may indicate insurers adjusting pricing to meet the MLR requirement. Many other important drivers of insurer financial results were also changing over this same time period, making it difficult to draw conclusions. More stringent rate increase review requirements, for example, also went into effect over this same time period in many jurisdictions.

The MLR formula has already changed somewhat over its short lifetime. Starting in 2014, the formula was modified to account for the impact of the ACA premium stabilization programs: transitional reinsurance, risk adjustment, and risk corridors. These programs are discussed in Chapter 4.

For reporting year 2014, the main MLR formula[17] is as follows:

$$\text{MLR} = \left[\frac{\text{Incurred Claims} + \text{Quality Improvment Expenses}}{\text{Earned Premiums - Taxes and Fees}}\right]$$
$$+ \text{Credibility Adjustment} \qquad (9.2)$$
$$= \frac{i+q-s+n-r}{(p+s-n+r)-t-f-(s-n+r)} + c$$

where

i = incurred claims,
q = expenditures on quality improving activities,
p = earned premiums,
t = Federal and State taxes and assessments,
f = licensing and regulatory fees, including trans. reinsurance contributions,
s = issuer's transitional reinsurance receipts,
n = issuer's risk corridors and risk adjustment related payments,
r = issuer's risk corridors and risk adjustment related receipts, and
c = credibility adjustment, if any.

Note that, in the denominator, the adjustments to premium for reinsurance, risk adjustment, and risk corridors are made and then reversed. This is due to legal technicalities – the law required that these amounts be treated as premium adjustments, but it was later determined that for MLR purposes it

---

[17] Department of Health and Human Services. 2014 Notice of Benefit and Payment Parameters. Federal Register, March 11, 2013 p. 15505.

would be better to treat them as adjustments to claims (which is why they are in the numerator).

To reduce volatility of results, the MLR formula is generally based on three year aggregate values. The credibility adjustment in the formula is intended to further protect small blocks of business from having to pay a rebate simply due to statistical fluctuations in claim levels. It is determined based on a published table, and there is a further adjustment to take into account the portion of business in high deductible plans (which can have more volatile experience). There is also a special rule for carriers with newer blocks of business that allow them to defer MLR reporting in certain circumstances.

Once the MLR is calculated, if it is less than the minimum, the rebate for a given block of business (state and market) is.[18]

$$\text{Rebate} = (m-a)[(p+s-n+r)-t-f-(s-n+r)], \qquad (9.3)$$

where m is the applicable minimum MLR standard for the state and market, a is the insurer's MLR, and the other variables are as in equation 9.2. Thus, the insurer must rebate a portion of after-tax premiums sufficient to bring the MLR back to the applicable minimum.

There are many subtleties in exactly how the items in the MLR formula are defined, so actual reporting calculations require careful study of the applicable regulations[19] and guidance. Commercial reinsurance arrangements, for example, and the treatment of policy reserves may require special consideration, and there are various adjustments that only apply to certain reporting years or situations. As further examples of the latter, for the 2014 reporting year, insurers that provided transitional coverage in a state are allowed to multiply their claims and quality improvement expenses by a factor of 1.0001, and insurers that participated in ACA exchanges can multiply the same values by a factor of 1.0004.

The dependency of the MLR on the three premium stabilization programs will create challenges for insurers, because those premium stabilization program payments and receipts are subject to significant uncertainty (see Chapter 4 for more on this). This may make it difficult for insurers to forecast whether they will owe a rebate or not, at least until more data is avail-

---

[18] Ibid.
[19] 45 C.F.R. Part 158.

able on the post-reform marketplace. Managing MLR is likely to be an ongoing area of concern for insurers (see Chapter 11 for more on this).

OTHER REASONABLENESS MEASURES

The MALR test is by far the most common one used by both the industry and regulators to determine the reasonableness of rates. Nonetheless, there are some circumstances in which other measures can and have been used for this purpose.

One measure that is sometimes used with rate filings is called a "me too" filing. In such a filing, the insurer does not build a new rate structure and actuarial memorandum. Instead, it relies on the previously approved rates used by their competitors. The logic that an insurer uses is something like this: "We are providing the same (or similar) benefits as our competitor. We will be charging the same (or similar) rates. The product will be sold in the same market, to similar insureds. You (the insurance department) have already approved the competitor's rates as being reasonable in this situation, so we argue that ours must be reasonable as well." This type of filing is generally acceptable to regulators, although they may still require affirmative demonstration that other standards, which may vary by insurer, are being met, such as how the rates relate to other, similar products the company may have.

Another test that is sometimes applied by regulators can be called the **reasonable expectations** test. This situation occurs when an insurer may have neglected to analyze or implement rate increases in the past on an inflation sensitive policy (such as major medical). As a result, an unusually large increase might be needed to achieve the company's desired loss ratio targets. Even though such an increase might meet the regulators' MALR standards, they might argue that the policyholders have a right to expect the percentage increase they face in any year be reasonably related to the increase for other, similar policies. A typical manifestation of this argument would allow an insurer to increase rates to achieve the current year's correction, plus recover some portion of the prior years' foregone corrections. It might take a few years to achieve all of the needed recovery.

Unfortunately for insurers, some regulators have interpreted the reasonable expectations rule in seemingly unfair ways. In one such instance, a regulator has maintained that when an insurer fails to correct its rate levels in a given year, they are *forever* prohibited from correcting the rates for that rate increase, so the rates will forever be inadequate in that block. In other instances, insurers have been prevented from implementing increases they felt were needed because regulators overruled the assumptions or methods chosen by the company. When the company projections proved correct, and the approved increases proved inadequate, the companies are then prohibited from immediately recovering the difference because of the rule.

Insurers have generally been reluctant to challenge the reasonable expectations rule and its unusual regulatory implementations previously described. This is not unusual, for two important reasons: (1) Most insurers are reluctant to "take on" insurance departments in this regard, as they are afraid of hurting their relationships with the departments, which might result in even further future problems. (2) Administrative and judicial proceedings typically take a long time and are expensive. By the time an insurer's position might be found legitimate, the ability to apply the resulting increase in a meaningful way might have already passed years earlier.

MEDICARE SUPPLEMENT RATE REGULATION

Medicare Supplement contracts are generally not included in such MALR regulation. Because of perceived federal concerns over abuses in the elderly market, Medicare Supplement loss ratios have been separately regulated since the Baucus Amendment was passed in 1980.[20] States have been required to pass legislation at least as restrictive as that laid out by the NAIC in its Medicare Supplement Insurance Minimum Standards Model Act and the complementary Model Regulation,[21] or risk federal intervention.

The Baucus Amendment initially established a lifetime loss ratio standard of 60% for individual Medicare Supplement policies, and 70% for group coverage. The Omnibus Reconciliation Act of 1990 (OBRA-90) increased these standards to 65% and 75%, effective November 15, 1991. The OBRA-90 regulation also required that the benefits of the policies be standardized. The loss ratios of existing, pre-standardized policies were held to their original loss ratio standards until OBRA Technical Corrections were passed in the mid-'90s. After that, the future loss ratios of pre-standardized policies ("future" meaning from the date of the Technical Corrections on) were also subjected to the 65/75% standards.

Policies issued as a result of mass media advertising are deemed to be individual policies under OBRA-90, although some states have subjected

---

[20] Public Law 96-265
[21] MDL-650 and MDL-651, freely available at the NAIC website.

these policies to the 75% group standard.

One additional loss ratio requirement that was added with the OBRA legislation was that the third year loss ratio must be greater than or equal to the required minimum. This can present some difficulty for companies with issue age premiums, which have significant pre-funding.

Loss ratios for Medicare Supplement are specifically defined to exclude expense loadings and active life reserves, and modal loadings (extra premiums charged when premiums are paid in modes more frequently than annually) must be included. Subsidies by rating class are allowed, meaning that the test is applied overall, rather than rating cell by rating cell. If a company files an expected lifetime loss ratio that exceeds the statutory minimum, it is held to the higher filed loss ratio.

The OBRA-90 legislation introduced a new regulatory requirement – an annual Rate Refund Calculation – aimed at ensuring that policyholders do not pay excessive rates. A prescribed refund form, calculated separately for every plan type in every state, must be filed by May 31 of each calendar year. If a company's actual loss ratios have fallen below specified benchmarks, a rate refund or premium credit is required, subject to credibility tolerance thresholds.

Medicare Supplement rates are generally increased annually, to keep pace with increases in Medicare deductibles and with inflation. The Model Regulation requires that an annual filing, justifying rate levels and providing past actual and projected future experience, be submitted to states, whether an increase is being requested or not. The NAIC created a Compliance Manual for states, providing specific guidance on the types of items and justifications that should be included in these annual filings.

The Medicare Supplement model regulation was updated in 2008[22] to implement requirements under the Genetic Information Nondiscrimination Act (GINA) and the Medicare Improvements for Patients and Providers Act (MIPPA). GINA generally prohibits insurers from using genetic information in underwriting decisions for Medicare Supplement products, and generally prohibits insurers from requiring individuals to undergo a genetic test except in certain limited circumstances. As discussed in Chapter 2, MIPPA made changes to certain of the standardized plan designs.

---

[22] Further technical revisions were made in 2014.

LONG-TERM CARE INSURANCE MODEL REGULATION

The version of the LTC model regulation, adopted in August of 2000, made significant changes to the required actuarial certification made at the time of rate filings. The intent of that model was to focus attention away from minimum loss ratios (a major focus of regulation of most other coverages) and toward premium rate stability. An amendment to the model regulation was adopted by the NAIC effective September 2014, furthering the rate stability concept while putting in place additional consumer protection provisions.

Older LTC policies issued prior to the adoption of the 2000 model regulation required the actuary to certify that a minimum 60% loss ratio would be met over the life of the policy. The 2000 model regulation and 2014 model amendment are designed to minimize the need for future rate increases. The actuary must include:

- Certification that the initial premium rate schedule is sufficient to cover anticipated costs under moderately adverse experience;
- A statement that policy design and coverage have been reviewed and taken into consideration;
- A statement that the underwriting and claim adjudication processes have been reviewed and taken into consideration;
- A statement that the premium rate schedule is not less than that of existing, similar policy forms except for reasonable differences attributable to benefits;
- A comparison of the premium schedules for similar policy forms currently sold by the insurer, with an explanation of the differences; and
- A complete description of the basis for contract reserves that are anticipated to be held under the form, including sufficient detail or sample calculations, a statement that the assumptions used for reserves contain reasonable margins for adverse experience, a statement that the valuation net premium is not assumed to increase over time, and a statement that the difference between the gross and valuation net premium for renewal years is sufficient to cover expected renewal expenses.

In addition to this certification, the commissioner may request an actuarial demonstration that benefits are reasonable in relation to premiums.

As of this writing, 44 states (including the District of Columbia) have adopted the 2000 model regulation or one substantially similar to it. Because similar rates between states is usually a goal for LTC insurance, the pricing actuary is in the difficult situation of having to certify to a 60% minimum loss ratio in some states, and for others certify that the rates are sufficient under moderately adverse experience.

The 2014 model amendment aims to advance rate stability by requiring the actuary to make a statement that the premiums contain at least the minimum margin for moderately adverse experience which, in most cases, is 10% or more of lifetime claims. The model also requires an annual rate certification to be submitted to the states adopting the regulation, stating that the premium rate schedule is sufficient to cover anticipated costs under moderately adverse experience and that the premium rate schedule is reasonably expected to be sustainable over the life of the form with no future premium increases anticipated. If the actuary cannot make this statement, a plan of action to re-establish the margin for moderately adverse experience must be submitted to the state.

The requirement for an annual rate certification encourages companies to file for needed rate increases sooner, which may allow for smaller, more frequent rate increases. The 2014 model amendment also allows for companies to disclose the rate increase needed to certify to rate stability, but request a lower rate increase if it is in the opinion of the commissioner to be in the best interest of policyholders.

Minimum Loss Ratios

Under the new model, it is required that premium rate schedule *increases* meet a minimum test: the accumulated value of past incurred claims, plus the present value of future incurred claims, without the inclusion of changes in policy reserves, must not be less than the sum of:

1. The accumulated value of initial earned premium times fifty-eight percent,
2. Eighty-five percent of the accumulated value for prior premium rate schedule increases on an earned basis,
3. The present value of future projected initial earned premiums times fifty-eight percent, and

4. Eighty-five percent of the present value of future projected premiums not included in (3), on an earned basis.

In essence, this requirement uses a 58% MALR applied to the original rate schedule, and an 85% MALR applied to increases in premium. A more liberal 70%, rather than 85%, is used if the increase is considered "exceptional." Exceptional increases are those required due to changes in laws or regulations applicable to LTC coverage, or due to increased and unexpected utilization that affects the majority of insurers of similar products. Accumulations and present values are calculated using valuation interest rates specified in the Health Reserves Model Regulation.

Included in the 2014 model amendment is a new standard for the acceptance by states of premium rate schedule increases. For policies issued prior to the adoption of the 2014 model amendment, the minimum loss ratio as described previously continues to apply. For those policies issued after the adoption of the 2014 model amendment, the greater of a 58% MALR and the original pricing loss ratio is used in place of the prior 58% MALR requirement (items 1. and 3. above).

GROUP HEALTH INSURANCE MANDATORY CONVERSION PRIVILEGE MODEL ACT

For decades, there have been laws in some states, and an NAIC Model Act, that requires group medical contracts to contain **conversion** provisions. Conversion provisions allow an eligible person (typically covered three months or longer under the group policy) to purchase a particular type of individual health insurance contract, a **conversion contract**, which has minimum benefits defined under the law, whenever their group coverage ceases (unless the termination was due to failure to pay premiums or the coverage was replaced by similar coverage within a short period). Quite often, the minimum benefits required under state law for conversion policies are quite limited relative to the comprehensive benefits of the prior group coverage.

Most terminations of group coverage historically happened when an individual leaves the employ of the sponsoring employer. Of those that chose conversion coverage, a disproportionate number of them had higher than expected costs. Such experience often had antiselection sufficient to generate experience at a level three times that of comparable underwritten individual business.

In many states, and in the NAIC model, the premium rates for conversion policies were severely limited. The most recent version of the NAIC's Model, the **Group Health Insurance Mandatory Conversion Privilege Model Act**, was adopted in 2005 (the original version was adopted in 1976). The rate limitations in that model are designed to require a minimum loss ratio of 120%, which is twice the typical loss ratio of a corresponding individual major medical policy (60%). If, however, experience itself runs at three times the typical rate (which is a commonly observed morbidity level), this implies the rates allowed for the coverage are at roughly 150% of those charged by individual insurers $\left(60\% \times \frac{3}{120\%}\right)$.

The limited rate level, combined with antiselection, results in significant losses by carriers. Most carriers built subsidies into this line of business from the group line, since the guarantees which generated the losses were arising from group insurance.

The cost of conversion could be quite a drain on a group's financials. This was one of the contributing factors to the adoption of the Employee Retirement Income Security Act (ERISA) in 1974, which exempted self-insured plans from state laws, including conversion laws.

The lack of guaranteed conversion laws for self-insured plans was a major factor in the adoption of COBRA (the Consolidated Omnibus Budget Reconciliation Act) in 1985. In that act, employees and their dependents, whose coverage might otherwise terminate for various reasons, were guaranteed the right to continue their coverage for at least 18 months. (Under some circumstances, the continuation lasts longer.) In return they could be required to pay up to 102% of the average employee rate. This coverage is typically better than group conversion coverage, and the rates are significantly lower. As a result, most employees who need or want a continuation of coverage do so by continuing their group coverage under COBRA. By the time the 18 month period ends, there are far fewer eligible persons who still want to exercise their conversion privilege (although the conversion mandate would still apply, since the person is leaving their group coverage), and therefore there are far fewer convertees in the block of conversion policies. This has greatly reduced the cost of subsidies to conversion policies. At the same time, the comparable benefits, combined with the limitation on the cost to policyholders of COBRA continuation, has led to greater participation of COBRA benefit extensions by terminating employees than the previous conversions, when conversion premium may have been significantly higher. This has helped dampen the antiselection that used to be rampant in conversion blocks.

In 1996, another federal law, HIPAA, was passed which again impacted this market segment. That law required each state to provide a solution to meet federal policy goals in the small group and individual market. That policy goal was to require that, through whatever mechanism was adopted by the state, an employee who had been covered under a group contract, and who had exhausted his COBRA extension, would be guaranteed to be eligible for insurance under at least two individual plans by each carrier. It turns out that such experience, like other conversion experience, is much worse than that of a comparable individual policy form.

Because of these alternative solutions for providing guaranteed continuation of individual medical coverage, the importance of conversion policies to insurer and group financials has dwindled in recent years. Under the ACA, this trend is likely to continue, since individuals leaving group coverage are now able to purchase individual market coverage on a guaranteed-issue basis during open and special enrollment periods, and may also qualify for premium subsidies through public exchanges.

9.3 OTHER REGULATORY RESTRICTIONS

A number of states have implemented (usually through statute) restrictions on insurer's standard set of individual health management tools. The major categories of these include rate restrictions and underwriting restrictions. The ACA applied many of these restrictions to major medical coverage sold nationwide starting in 2014, as we have discussed already in Chapters 2, 4, and 5 of this text.

OTHER RATING RESTRICTIONS

There are various rating restrictions that states have put into effect, usually limiting the rating variables over which rates are permitted to vary. The earliest such restriction was four or five decades ago, when "race" was eliminated as a rating variable. At one time, there were demonstrable claim cost differences by race in many coverages. There were arguments made, however, that: (1) such differences might be a result of other social injustices, rather than inherently different risks; i.e., while there was correlation, there might not be causation, and (2) this variable would be eliminated regardless, as a matter of public policy.

In the 1970s, there was a movement toward a similar social policy, only with reference to gender-based rating. Ultimately, a few states adopted rules requiring unisex rating for medical insurance. Disability income carriers were able to successfully argue against such a rule for DI insurance in all but one state, at least in part because of a major study done by the New York State Insurance Department which demonstrated a significant gender-based difference in cost that was independent of occupation.[23] In 2014, the ACA required unisex rating nationwide for major medical coverage, among other rating restrictions.

One rating concept that has been around for many years, and is generally used only in medical insurance, is the concept of **community rating**. While not well defined, this term generally means a rating structure that does not vary rates based on age, gender, health status, claim experience, occupation, or (sometimes) by area. The rates usually do vary by rate tier (single/family, or single/two person/family, etc.), and by product. This rate structure was historically often required of not-for-profit companies, such as some Blue Cross plans and HMOs, in return for certain advantages they were given in the marketplace (such as exemption from premium tax, or in some cases, statutory discounts in payment levels). A **modified community** *rating* approach is one where some variation is still allowed based on age or some other variables, but only to a limited degree. Under the ACA, for example, age rating is permitted, but only using prescribed factors that vary by no more than 3:1 from the oldest to the youngest adult age. See Chapter 5 for more detail on ACA rating restrictions.

A few states have adopted strict community rating for all individual medical carriers. New York is one example. In New York, this requirement was coincident with the implementation of guaranteed issue coverage. Ultimately, all commercial carriers withdrew from the state, and only HMOs, BCBS plans, and similar plans remained in that market.[24]

---

[23] "Differences in Disability Claim Costs by Sex," Publications Unit, New York State Insurance Department.
[24] Wachenheim, Leigh and Leida, Hans, "The Impact of Guaranteed Issue and Community Rating Reforms on Individual Insurance Markets." Prepared for America's Health Insurance Plans. March, 2012. Retrieved April 4, 2014 from
http://www.ahipcoverage.com/wp-content/uploads/2012/03/Updated-Milliman-Report.pdf.

In any market, if there are restrictions on rating variables that are otherwise demonstrably correlated to varying claim costs, the result will be antiselection. As long as individuals have knowledge about their own claim expectations (which they often do, due to chronic conditions), they can and will make rational decisions. If expecting high claims, they will migrate toward rich benefits. If expecting low claims, they will migrate toward low premiums. If rating restrictions apply equally to all insurers in the market, the selection will tend to be against the market as a whole. If, however, different rules apply to different insurers, selection will often occur between insurers rather than – or in addition to – at the market level.

A particular BCBS plan, for example, was historically required to offer guaranteed issue, community rated coverage. Commercial carriers in the same market were allowed to underwrite, and could charge age-based rates. As might be expected, the financial experience of the BCBS plan in this market was terrible, with an average age in the upper 50s. This was a clear result of the effect that, for those who could pass underwriting, the commercial carrier's coverage was much cheaper except at those higher ages.

The strength of the antiselection which results from such rate restrictions is a function of many variables, including the stringency of the restrictions and the availability of alternative coverages. This antiselective behavior is discussed further in Chapter 4, "Managing Antiselection," which also contains a section detailing further the restrictions imposed under the ACA and the provisions of the ACA aimed at mitigating the associated antiselection effects.

UNDERWRITING RESTRICTIONS

There are a number of restrictions on underwriting, imposed by both federal and state laws and regulations.

As discussed previously, the ACA requires insurers to accept all applicants for individual medical coverage during the specified open enrollment periods, regardless of the presence of any pre-existing medical conditions.

Medicare Supplement policies are required to be guaranteed issue for the first six months following the day the person is both: (1) 65+ years old, and (2) eligible for Medicare Part B. This is called the "open enrollment" period. If an applicant applies during this time period, and has had a "continuous period of creditable coverage of at least six months," the insurer cannot apply a pre-existing condition exclusion. Other qualifying individuals can obtain coverage through the "guaranteed issue" provisions. Individuals become "qualified" by meeting one of the criteria listed in the model, most of which relate to having prior coverage that terminated.[25]

In 2006, a new Medicare program, Medicare Part D, began providing prescription drug coverage to Medicare recipients. The coverage was either included in the individual's Medicare Advantage coverage, or was offered as a free standing policy by participating Part D carriers. Individuals could enroll any time up to May 15, 2006. Just as in the case of Medicare Part B, which permanently increases premiums for late entrants (10% for each 12 month period of lateness), Part D premiums will increase 1% per month as a late enrollment penalty.

Some states have restricted various underwriting tools which would otherwise be available. Such restrictions include requiring guaranteed issue, limitations on pre-existing conditions, and prohibition of exclusionary riders. When designing or evaluating individual A&H programs, it is best to investigate each applicable state's requirements (in addition to federal requirements under the ACA), since they can and do vary quite widely by state and by coverage.

MEDICARE ADVANTAGE AND PART D BIDS

One interesting variation on normal rate filings is with respect to Medicare Advantage and Part D prescription drug plans. Those who offer these plans act as a contractor with the U.S. government, providing health care to Medicare beneficiaries. The controlling government agency is the **Centers for Medicare and Medicaid Services (CMS)**, part of the **Department of Health and Human Services (HHS)**.

Medicare Advantage and Medicare Part D rate filings – generally known as "bids" – are simultaneously a proposal to a contracting agency and a regulatory filing, and CMS is filling those dual roles. The rate filings follow detailed instructions by CMS each year, with simultaneous nationwide due dates.

---

[25] NAIC 651-1, *Model Regulation to Implement the NAIC Medicare Supplement Insurance Minimum Standards Model Act,* Section 12, Guaranteed Issue for Eligible Persons.

In this text, "rate filings" will generally not refer to Medicare Advantage or Part D rate filings, unless this is specified. See the section in Chapter 2 for more about the Medicare Advantage and Part D program.

9.4 Required Information in Rate Filings

One major ingredient of all state rate regulations is the list of information that an insurer must provide to the Commissioner's office to demonstrate that its rate filing meets the requirements of that state. The list of information required in a particular state will vary, depending on: (1) the type of carrier, (2) the type of coverage, (3) whether the rate filing is for a new policy form or is a rate revision to an existing block of policies, and (4) the specific requirements of that state.

In addition to state requirements, insurers must also submit a significant amount of documentation required by the federal government under the ACA for major medical coverages. These are described separately after the following outline of state requirements.

Not-for-Profits

Some states have different statutes and/or regulations applicable to different types of carriers. Not-for-profit medical insurance companies (like some Blues plans) and HMOs are usually regulated under somewhat different statutes and regulations than commercial carriers. Because not-for-profits and HMOs tend not to close off blocks of business, but rather roll all existing policyholders into new policy forms, there are different rating methods used, and different information required by regulators. Often in those cases, the insurer's filing includes financial projections of the entire line of business, or even of the entire company. Because the existing policyholders will form the starting book of business under the new form, the rating exercise is essentially a renewal rating, with modification for policy differences. In addition, because there are typically a limited number of such plans in a state, the state's requirements (including required exhibits, formats, data, etc.) may not all be codified into published rules and regulations, and therefore require substantially more state-specific knowledge and/or interaction with the state before filing.

As an example, here is an excerpt from the regulation describing the information required by New York, when rate revisions are being made for such plans.[26]

Section 52.40. Procedures and requirements for filing of rates…

(3) With respect to applications for revisions of previously approved rates of article 43[27] corporations and health maintenance organizations:

    (i) information with respect to claim or utilization frequencies, claim costs and expenses shown for all contracts and riders, or for each coverage separately if more than one coverage is provided by a contract or rider, for a period of at least two years prior to the calendar year in which the new rates are effective, even though rates for some contracts, riders or coverages are not being changed;

    (ii) the information required in subparagraph (i) of this paragraph projected for a period not more than two years beyond the effective date of the new rates;

    (iii) a summary of projected changes in claim or utilization frequency, average claim costs and expenses;

    (iv) the current financial condition of the corporation and the financial condition projected to the effective date of the new rates and to the end of the period during which the new rates will be in effect;

    (v) the projected operating results for the period during which the new rates will be in effect, showing premiums, claims and expenses;

    (vi) such additional information as may be needed in order to assist the superintendent in determining whether the application shall become effective as filed, shall become effective as modified, or shall be disapproved;

    (vii) as respects rate adjustment applications where such adjustment is only requested to reflect anticipated payments to or from the demographic or specified medical condition

---

[26] 11 NYCRR 52, Regulation 62.
[27] This is a reference to the portion of the New York Insurance Law that authorizes hospital, medical, and dental insurers (HMDI). The most typical example of these are Blue Cross, Blue Shield, and Delta Dental plans.

pooling funds, such applications shall contain such information as may be needed in order to assist the superintendent in determining the amount of the adjustment which is necessary in order to recognize such payments. Such information shall be in lieu of the material requested in subparagraphs (i), (ii), (iii) and (vi) of this paragraph; and

(viii) a jurat (*a legal term; a certification on an affidavit declaring when, where, and before whom it was sworn*) subscribed to by the corporation's president or chief executive officer, treasurer or chief financial officer, and chief actuary...

COMMERCIAL CARRIERS

As a management tool, commercial carriers selling individual medical coverages historically tended to close off blocks of business, without rolling existing insureds to the new policy form. Business under the new form will be mostly or all newly underwritten policyholders, so there is no explicit experience available based on their own claims. In this situation, the rating process for a new policy form is not a projection of an existing block, but is a development of new rates for a new policy.

This practice is no longer allowed for major medical coverage since the ACA requires carriers to rate all such business (with a few exceptions) in a single risk pool. However, it still may apply to other coverages not subject to the ACA.

When available, insurers usually calculate rates for a new policy form using past experience of a similar policy form. When the rates are not based on related company experience, then other sources must be used. Sometimes the rate development might use a combination of sources of information. Specified required information in the rate filing must be flexible enough to account for all these situations.

A typical set of information required for new policy forms for commercial carriers is contained in the NAIC's model regulation.[28]

I. Policy Form, application, and endorsements...

---

[28] Excerpt from *Guidelines for Filing of Rates for Individual Health Insurance Forms*.

II. Rate Sheet *(the rates being proposed)*
III. Actuarial Memorandum
   A. Brief description of the type of policy, benefits, renewability, general marketing method, and issue age limits.
   B. Brief description of how rates were determined, including the general description and source of each assumption used. For expenses, include percent of premium, dollars per policy or dollars per unit of benefit, or both.
   C. Estimated average annual premium per policy.
   D. Anticipated loss ratio, including a brief description of how it was calculated.
   E. Anticipated loss ratio presumed reasonable according to the guidelines.
   F. If Subsection D is less than Subsection E, supporting documentation for the use of the proposed premium rates.
   G. Certification by a qualified actuary that, to the best of the actuary's knowledge and judgment, the rate submission is in compliance with the applicable laws and regulations of the state and the benefits are reasonable in relation to the premiums.
IV. A statement as to the status of this rate filing in the company's home state. *(if applicable and required by this state)*

Renewal rating for commercial carriers, like not-for-profits, is typically based on a projection of existing experience. Unlike not-for-profits, however, the projection is limited to the block in question, and there is no explicit reference to financial results from other parts of the company.

The NAIC's list of information for rate renewals is this.[29]

I. New Rate Sheet
II. Actuarial Memorandum
   A. Brief description of the type of policy, benefits, renewability, general marketing method and issue age limits.

---

[29] Ibid.

B. Scope and reason for rate revision including a statement of whether the revision applies only to new business, only to in force business, or to both, and outline of all past rate increases on this form.

C. Estimated average annual premium per policy, before and after rate increase. Descriptive relationship of proposed rate scale to current rate scale.

D. Past experience, as specified in Section 2D of the guidelines, and any other available data the insurer may wish to provide.

E. Brief description of how revised rates were determined, including the general description and source of each assumption used. For expenses, include percent of premium, dollars per policy, or dollars per unit of benefit, or both.

F. The anticipated future loss ratio and description of how it was calculated.

G. The anticipated loss ratio that combines cumulative and future experience, and description of how it was calculated.

H. Anticipated loss ratio presumed reasonable according to the guidelines.

I. If Subsection F or G is less than Subsection H, supporting documentation for the use of such premium rates.

J. Certification by a qualified actuary that, to the best of the actuary's knowledge and judgment, the rate submission is in compliance with the applicable laws and regulations of the state and the benefits are reasonable in relation to the premiums.

RATE FILING REQUIREMENTS UNDER THE ACA

A significant component of federal healthcare reform is the additional review it requires of insurers implementing premium rate increases. While the federal government does not have the authority to deny rate increases, it does have the ability to publicly declare an increase to be unreasonable, and in some cases may be able to bar an insurer with a pattern of unreasonable increases from participating in public health insurance exchanges.

As of this writing, the specific requirements for rate filings under the ACA have undergone multiple revisions, and this is a rapidly evolving area of practice. Accordingly, practitioners would be well advised to review the latest published regulatory guidance.[30]

As noted earlier in this chapter, most states have been deemed to have an "effective rate review process" for purposes of the ACA, which means that the federal government will generally defer review of rate filings to the state. Filing documents must still be submitted to the federal government as well as with state regulators, however.

Only rate increases exceeding a threshold (initially set at 10%, though states were able to submit proposals for different thresholds) were originally subject to additional reporting and review as "potentially unreasonable." More recently, the reporting threshold has been lowered to 0%, meaning that most of the additional documentation has come to be required to be filed every year for all products contained in the ACA single risk pool,[31] both on and off of the exchanges. The threshold triggering additional review remains at 10% unless a state has received approval for an alternative threshold.

The ACA filing documents are known as the **rate filing justification** and include Parts I, II, and III. The American Academy of Actuaries has published a series of helpful practice notes on this subject. The current draft practice note[32] includes the following description of Parts I, II, and III:

- Part I is the Unified Rate Review Template (URRT). The URRT is an Excel spreadsheet that includes experience period and projected data and information for all products and plans from an issuer in a market (i.e., individual, small group, or combined), which is essentially the single risk pool of products and plans.

  There are two worksheets in Part I – Worksheet 1 includes aggregate information across the entire risk pool and Worksheet 2 includes information by product and plan within a product.

---

[30] A good place to start is the web page of the Center for Consumer Information and Insurance Oversight (CCIIO), http://www.cms.gov/cciio/index.html.

[31] Grandfathered plans are not subject to ACA rate review requirements or documentation (unless a state requires it, and even then they are filed separately). Transitional plans are subject to ACA rate review, but use the old process in place prior to 2014.

[32] As of this writing, the most recent is still in draft form, though a final version is expected to be released soon. See *Actuarial Practices Related to Preparing, Reviewing, and Commenting on Rate Filings Prepared in Accordance with the Affordable Care Act for 2015 and Beyond,* September 2014. Retrieved January 16, 2015 from http://www.actuary.org/files/RRPN_exposure_draft_092614.pdf.

- Part II includes a summary description of the rate changes and is filed whenever a rate increase is greater than the threshold for rate review.
- Part III is the actuarial memorandum and certification that describes and supports the development of the information provided in Part I. Part III includes additional required documentation to show the development of rates from the index rate.

These documents fulfill several different purposes. First, they allow independent reviewers (typically actuaries) to assess the reasonableness of the requested rate increase. Second, they aim to promote transparency with consumers and other stakeholders – this information is generally posted publicly by the government, although insurers can argue that certain portions constitute trade secrets. The narrative justification in Part II is intended to be a plain-language description of the drivers of the rate changes understandable by the general public. Finally, the filing documents are intended to demonstrate compliance with ACA rating restrictions, such as the single risk pool and limitations on allowable rating variables.

Detailed instructions are available for each part of the rate filing justification. In particular, the Part III memorandum has specific required elements that must be included (more on this in the section on actuarial memoranda which follows).

Besides Parts I, II, and III, there are a host of other required components when insurers wish to file qualified health plans (QHPs) on an ACA exchange. Many of these are known as "templates," and take the form of Excel workbooks that the issuer must fill in. Examples of such templates are listed in Table 9.10.

Creating and filling out these required documents and forms is a challenging and time consuming exercise, compounded by the fact that updated instructions and forms for each year are typically not available until relatively close to filing deadlines each spring. In many ways, this exercise is not dissimilar from the bid process familiar to Medicare Advantage and Part D plans.

Important pieces of regulatory guidance are released by the government each year in addition to the updated filing templates and instructions, including draft and final versions of the annual Notice of Benefit and Payment Parameters and the Letter to Issuers in the Federally-facilitated Marketplaces.

Table 9.10: Overview of QHP Templates

Template Name	Brief Description*
Administrative Template	Collects general company and contact information.
ECP Template	Collects identifying information for Essential Community Providers.
Plan/Benefit Template	Collects plan and benefit data for medical and dental.
Prescription Drug Template	Collects formulary data for plans.
Network Template	Information identifying a provider's network.
Service Area Template	Information identifying a plan's geographic service area.
Rate Data Template	Rating Tables.
Business Rule Template	Supporting business rules.
Accreditation Templates	Collects information related to an issuer's NCQA and/or URAC accreditation status.
Unified Rate Review Template	This is a federal data collection template designated to capture information at the market level, consistent with the requirement to set premium rates using a single risk pool.
Network Adequacy Template	Collects information on provider networks.
Plan ID Crosswalk Template	The Plan ID Crosswalk template will be used by issuers to map 2014 Qualified Health Plan (QHP) or Stand Alone Dental Plan (SADP) Plan ID and service area combinations (e.g., Plan ID and County combinations) to a 2015 Plan ID.

* Taken from http://www.serff.com/plan_management_data_templates_2015.htm.

Table 9.11: Part III Actuarial Memo Contents

Required Element	Required Element, cont'd.
General Information	Market Adjusted Index Rate
Proposed Rate Increase(s)	Plan Adjusted Index Rates
Experience Period Premium and Claims	Calibration
Benefit Categories	Consumer Adjusted Premium Rate Development
Projection Factors	AV Metal Values
Credibility Manual Rate Development	AV Pricing Values
Credibility of Experience	Membership Projections
Paid to Allowed Ratio	Terminated Products
Risk Adjustment and Reinsurance	Plan Type
Non-Benefit Expenses, Profit, & Risk	Warning Alerts
Projected Loss Ratio	Effective Rate Review Information
Single Risk Pool	Reliance
Index Rate	Actuarial Certification

ACTUARIAL MEMORANDA

Virtually all policy form filings and rate change filings require an actuarial memorandum to be included in support of them. While the NAIC's model does contain a good generic list of requirements, many states have unique requirements for the memorandum, and may have differing interpretations of the NAIC's list.

As mentioned previously, many different states have adopted rate regulations that specify what material must be filed, and what the filings should demonstrate. In addition, the federal government has promulgated a detailed list of requirements for actuarial memoranda satisfying Part III of an ACA rate filing justification, which are summarized in Table 9.11. Depending on what a state requires and allows, actuaries may choose to include all required elements in a single document or submit two separate memoranda to satisfy state and federal requirements. What's more, while there is major overlap in these requirements from state to state, there is still wide variation in the list of required information and in its interpretation. This poses a logistical challenge for insurers operating in many different states.

From a practical standpoint, an efficient approach to such memoranda is to create a *generic* memorandum first, which either (1) demonstrates compliance with the NAIC's model by following the same format as the model regulation, referring to each requirement by item number, or (2) demonstrates compliance with the federal Part III memorandum, if applicable. The generic memorandum is then supplemented with state-specific memoranda. Those memoranda refer specifically to the state's requirements. It is helpful to have the supplements refer back to the generic memorandum, in answering some required information.

This approach is useful both to regulators (who have to read many such filings and seem to appreciate the direct, ordered approach) and to the actuaries preparing it (since it provides a recipe approach to the organization).

There are a number of Actuarial Standards of Practice (ASOPs) that might impact such rate filings. The Academy's guide[33] lists 15 as applying to this situation (1, 3, 5, 6, 7, 8, 11, 12, 18, 23, 25, 26, 41, 42, 45), but ASOP #8, *Regulatory Filings for Health Benefits, Accident and Health Insurance, and Entities Providing Health Benefits* applies directly, and is most relevant to this discussion. A prior version of ASOP #8 defined an important purpose of its existence:

> Proper actuarial practice in this area involves the use of reasonable and appropriate assumptions and procedures. Given the regulatory nature of these filings, it is possible that techniques may be employed and assumptions may be chosen so as merely to meet the regulatory requirements, without consideration of sound actuarial principles and practices. A purpose of this standard is to guide the actuary in avoiding such a practice.

Even though this language has been removed from the current version of ASOP #8 (which has also been revised in response to the ACA's changes), the authors believe it is still sage advice. This ASOP also contains a nicely compact and general list of the things that a rate filing actuary should con-

---

[33] www.actuary.org

sider in developing assumptions for an actuarial memorandum. This is discussed further in Chapter 5, "Setting Premium Rates."

MARKET REFORM: PAST, PRESENT, AND FUTURE

As should be clear by now, regulatory reform in the individual health insurance market has taken a long and winding road over the years, culminating in the recent major changes under the ACA.

Early efforts were aimed at renewability, portability, and rating restrictions. Renewability and portability were largely addressed by the federal law called HIPAA, as described earlier in this book, although the ACA significantly amplified consumer protections with regard to guaranteed issue and renewability.

Rate regulation, however, has remained a sore point for regulators and carriers alike, for many years. The historical dynamics of the underwritten commercial individual medical marketplace often caused individual medical premium rates to rise much faster than the underlying cost trends, as described in Chapter 11, "Managing the Business." Regulators' responses have been varied, but usually default to finding ways to limit the size of those increases. In return, this has historically led to losses by carriers as they strive to keep their rates where the marketplace and their experience dictate they must be.

Long before healthcare reform was finally passed into law in 2010, there were many different proposals made to reform rating practices in the individual market. In the early 2000s, a task force appointed by the American Academy of Actuaries examined these proposals, in response to a request by the NAIC. The Rate Filing Task Force (RFTF) produced a final report, model, and documentation that is included with the electronic files distributed as a supplement to this text[34] (See also Appendix B). That model includes a baseline scenario that represents the Task Force's view of a typical, generic, commercial individual health insurer (prior to the advent of the ACA). The reader is cautioned that this model is very complex, and the assumptions used in it are interrelated.

Although it is perhaps growing a bit dated, this material is being included because this study represents an excellent and rigorously tested and docu-

---

[34] With permission of the American Academy of Actuaries.

mented model, which illustrates many of the concepts described in this text. Its inclusion should not be taken to endorse any particular policy position, or even technical conclusion, about the subject matter or the results. It shows how modeling can be done to test such hypotheses. While the model and its results represent the collected wisdom of the task force that produced it, it should be recognized that this work was done in order to respond to a specific request by the NAIC. If the work had been done by or for others, we can presume that different defining parameters would have been specified, perhaps other closed block solutions presented, and different results would have emerged. The model was not intended for any use other than its stated one.

One other proposal that has been regularly discussed is a federal proposal that would allow consumers in one state to purchase policies offered in other states. One major supporting argument for this is the concept of making individual health insurance available nationwide the same way as other financial services products (like mutual funds).

This proposal exemplifies an idea that has been common in many health care reform schemes that have been proposed in the past – to wit, it attempts to cut through the frustrating issues of regulation of individual health insurance that might be stifling accessibility of coverage for people in a given state. Unfortunately, such initiatives sometimes do not take into account the complexities and nuances of health insurance. One such complexity is the fundamentally local nature of provider contracting.

The latest iteration of this approach is perhaps embodied in the concept of a **multi-state plan** under the ACA. These plans are regulated by the Office of Personnel Management (OPM), the same agency that administers the health plan for federal employees. They allow an insurer or group of insurers to offer a plan on multiple state exchanges with a partially streamlined regulatory arrangement (plans certified by OPM will not have to obtain separate certification from each state's exchange). In 2015, there will be a multi-state plan available in 35 states. It remains to be seen whether the program will be able to be expanded to meet the statutory requirement of offering coverage in all 50 states and the District of Colombia.

Multi-state plans are just one of a bewildering array of experiments unfolding in the wake of the ACA. As of this writing, there are still significant court cases pending, and a real possibility of further changes after the 2016 elections. Regardless of one's politics, it is a historic time for the health insurance industry in the U.S., and there is plenty of work to be done.

CHAPTER 10

OTHER INSURER FUNCTIONS

This chapter describes a number of the professional functions that an insurer must perform in order to successfully sell and administer its individual health business. The chapter begins by describing the many ways in which individual health insurance is marketed. It then describes the underwriting, claim administration, and policy administration and service functions.

Perhaps one way to think of the functions performed at an insurer is to examine the roles played by various insurer personnel over the life of a policy. Initial contact is made through the sales function. Then the underwriting area comes into play, determining whether and on what terms coverage will be offered. (Underwriting is discussed in Chapter 4, Managing Antiselection.) If the policy is offered and accepted, policyholder services enter the picture, to issue and maintain the policy. Later, claim administration will become involved if and when there is a claim.

10.1 SALES AND MARKETING

As you have probably noticed throughout this text, in many ways the individual health insurance market is not a single market, but rather a collection of small market segments, varying by product and type of insurer. Sales and marketing is no different, and the characteristics of the market will depend on the market segment being studied.

At the same time, there are a limited number of production conduits available. Products are sold via personal sales by agents, by telephone (telemarketing), or by mass marketing methods. Mass marketing can occur through various media (including television, radio, the internet, billboard advertising, or flyers), or brochures provided through and with other media (such as a credit card bill or a paycheck). Sometimes leads produced through mass marketing methods are handed off to agents or telemarketers for follow-up.

In the commercial major medical, disability income, and long term care markets, most products are sold by independent brokers, although there are a small number of insurers with captive agency forces of their own, usually managed through a general agency system. Most brokers who are active in these markets specialize in the coverage being sold, as success demands specialized knowledge about the current conditions in these quickly-changing marketplaces. Brokers will sometimes "spreadsheet" rates – comparing the rates of a variety of insurers, in order to obtain the lowest rate for a particular prospect.

Captive agents are usually not as specialized as brokers, and instead are focused on providing a spectrum of products from the same company to their customers. In some schemes, with general agencies of sufficient size, and products that require specialized knowledge (such as DI or LTC), a general agency might have a product specialist who supports the non-specialized agents in the agency.

Blue Cross and Blue Shield plans are no longer homogeneous in their approach to sales. Some rely on their own employees to produce sales, either directly or through telemarketing, some rely on the broker community, and some do both.

Insurers are constantly re-evaluating their products. In the major medical market, this is most notable with respect to premium rates. Seemingly minor changes in rate relativities between areas can cause significant shifts in production volume. Often the difference between selling a high volume of business and selling a little can revolve on a rate difference as little as 5%. The DI and LTC markets are often more driven by product design, although premium levels are never absent from the list of important issues.

Except for telemarketing or mass marketing, selling in these markets usually occurs through personal contact between an agent (whether employed directly by the insurer, a general agent, or a broker) and the prospect. The agent often helps the prospect fill out the application, and creates a personal connection with him or her. (For some coverages, agents are sometimes asked by the company to also perform some field underwriting, by doing a limited amount of simplified underwriting while interfacing with the client.) Some products, particularly those covering basic needs, require more sales effort to sell than does a lower cost supplemental policy.

General agents (GAs) are typically (but not always) appointed by an insurer to be responsible for all business provided in a given geographic area. They will hire sub agents, on behalf of the insurer, to be the actual business producers, and will manage those agents. A **brokerage** is an entity formed of a group of agents, not affiliated with any particular insurer, although they may form exclusive working arrangements with them from time to time.

Within every product type, some products are designed to cover basic needs, while others are more supplemental. Most typically, it is supplemental products that are more easily sold using mass marketing methods, while basic coverages are less often sold that way. There are several reasons for this, but it seems mostly driven by the cost of underwriting. Basic coverages typically have much larger claims, and therefore constitute a much bigger risk to the insurer. Antiselection under supplemental coverages can more often be controlled by other means, such as contract language and product design.

The market for basic medical coverage (major medical) is most often self-employed persons, and individuals who are not covered (for whatever reason) by a group contract. Sometimes that lack of coverage arises because an employee is temporarily between jobs, or is a college graduate looking for a first post-graduate job. This short term need is usually met with a short term medical contract.

Another common situation (not met by short term coverage) is when individuals are employed by a small business without group health insurance. This situation is becoming more frequent, as small employers are less able to afford the cost of health insurance as an employee benefit.

A somewhat less comprehensive medical coverage, addressing hospitalization only, is sometimes used to provide a lower cost alternative to major medical coverage, while still protecting against major illnesses or injuries. Such limited coverage will generally not satisfy the requirement to purchase health insurance mandated by the ACA.

There are similar comparisons that can be made between basic and supplemental DI coverages. Because U.S. Social Security provides a significant disability benefit, DI products tend to be built around this. When looking at the market in total, companies will tend to disproportionately focus on higher income individuals, because those are the prospects who have the most meaningful need (if defined as the portion of earnings being replaced) for coverage above Social Security.

As discussed in Chapter 1 and throughout this text, the ACA introduced a new distribution channel for individual major medical coverage starting in 2014: the public insurance exchange. While brokers and agents can still assist individuals in obtaining coverage, there are also new options for those seeking assistance in purchasing coverage: navigators, in-person assisters, and certified application counselors.

Participating in exchanges can involve significant administrative hurdles for an insurer. For instance, the insurer must interact with the exchange to verify eligibility and coverage, and must also complete the complex certification process for qualified health plans outlined in Chapter 9. Brokers generally have to be registered with the exchange to be compensated for exchange policies. Some carriers may question whether they need brokers involved at all, or whether they should instead focus on signing up consumers directly through the exchange. The impact of the exchanges on existing distribution channels will likely take some years to play out, and will be interesting to watch.

Even outside of the exchanges, internet sales are becoming more and more common. These occur both directly through the insurer's own website, and also through web brokers that offer multiple insurers' products.

COMPENSATION

Sales personnel are typically compensated by means of commissions payable on business they sell and have in force. Many times, a company with a captive agency force will provide a stipend in the first year or two of agents' careers (typically grading down over time, often to zero), in order to provide them with income while they learn their trade and build their portfolios of customers.

Commission rates are usually expressed as percentages of premium, and can vary by product, by duration (most commonly first year vs. renewal), by persistency of the agent's business, by volume of business placed, or by other factors. Schedules with higher first year (and possibly for a few subsequent years) commissions are said to be *heaped,* or *graded,* although "graded" sometimes refers to differences by other variables such as volume. Heaped commissions occur in both broker-driven markets and captive agencies, although more frequently in the broker market. They also are more often used by companies that have a life insurance focus, and are less prevalent among P&C companies, because the comparable scales for those other coverages are more heaped (life) or less heaped (P&C). One school of thought is that heaped commissions tend to attract brokers that are more likely to replace the business elsewhere (and thereby earn yet another first year commission), which argues that insurers' best interests lie with flat commission scales. Another consideration is that levelized commissions tend to generate better returns on investment (or equity) in pricing models. Prevailing practice in the marketplace will generally dictate whether a heaped commission scale is needed.

For coverages that are not inflation-sensitive, such as DI, non-scheduled increases in coverage are often treated as though they are first year premium for commission purposes, under the rationale that such an upgrade in coverage required selling comparable to a new policy of that premium size, and avoids the cost of issuing a new policy.

Sometimes a company will change its commission schedule in order to achieve a sales or tactical goal, such as a year-end push for new policies, or intentionally converting an existing policy to a new one.

It is important to understand that the more independent a producer is (i.e, they can go to competitors' products at will), the more competitive the compensation scheme needs to be. While we would like to think that an agent will always put their customer's needs first, the value of the commission to the agent will always have an impact on the success of the product.

For coverages that are inflation sensitive, it has long been a practice not to consider regular rate increases as first year premium. In recent years, there has also been a movement among some carriers to not consider the premium from rate increases even as renewal premium for commission purposes. This is particularly true for major medical and Medicare supplement coverages, where premium increases can consistently outpace actual cost trends by a sizeable margin. Some argue that salesmanship is needed to keep policies in force in the light of such increases. A middle ground between these arguments is to allow the increases to be commissioned, but at a lower rate. Over the past decade or so, there has been a growing movement toward paying flat commissions per policy or per member, rather than commissions based on a percentage of premium.

Sometimes service fees are paid to agents, to compensate for services provided through the renewal process. Renewal commissions might be composed partly of an element intended to compensate for ongoing service (service fees) and partly a payment of commission in renewal years for the original sale.

Another element of commission scales is the vesting schedule. Commissions generally become **vested** at the point when commissions become due to an agent regardless of whether the agent continues to be employed by the agency or the insurer.

General agents and brokerages are sometimes paid a commission override. This is an additional commission payable to the GA or broker, typically significantly smaller than the commission itself. Sometimes the combined commission and override is paid to the GA or broker, who then distributes the commission out of the total.

Group conversion policies generally exist in order to comply with the law, rather than as a source of profits. They are usually marketed through the employer, or directly with the insurer. Even when there are agents involved, there may not be any commissions payable.

The ACA requires insurers to pay the same commissions for major medical products sold in and out of the public exchanges. At the same time, minimum medical loss ratio requirements are putting significant pressure on administrative costs, of which commissions make up a large part. It is unclear how these changes will affect the traditional roles of brokers and agents in the individual health market in the long term.

Since OBRA 1990 became law, first year commissions on Medicare Supplement policies have been limited to two times renewal (defined as years 2-6) commission rates, presumably to help limit potential **churning** (intentional, unnecessary replacement of coverage by another carrier). This 2:1 limitation can be applied either on a dollar basis or a percentage basis.

Marketing's literal meaning is defined as "the act or process of buying and selling in a market.[1]" In an insurance company context, marketing typically involves developing all the sales material, (including research), addressing

---

[1] *The American Heritage Dictionary of the English Language,* Fourth Edition, Houghton Mifflin Co., 2000.

the product. Product design and development, market research, sales brochures, and market strategies are typically all functions of the marketing department. In a **direct marketing company**, the marketing department also designs the interactions with customers and manages the sales process.

Some individual coverage is sold to associations of various types. An important aspect of marketing to these collections of individuals is the understanding and management of the **affinity level** of this target audience. A group with a high affinity level is one whose individuals have a strong sense of identification with the group (such as a medical association, bar association, or actuarial association). At the other end of the spectrum are groups that are essentially formed only to provide a vehicle for insurance. Other things being equal, high affinity groups tend to have better response rates to marketing programs, and have resulting better experience results.

An important function of the marketing area is to develop market strategies. It is important to segment the marketplace, defining sub-segments which differ in important ways. The differences most often are defined because either: (1) the competitive situation is different in one market segment than another, or (2) the population being served is heterogeneous, and can be better targeted as multiple sub-populations. One of the critical success factors of most companies is adequately defining these market segments. A major medical carrier will typically have its biggest division be geographic, for reasons described earlier. DI carriers will more typically segment their market by occupation class, or even by subdivisions of those occupation classes.

A major part of the last remaining pool of uninsured has been the young, healthy people who do not purchase coverage. At least a few insurers have tried to penetrate this market segment with new products designed to appeal to this segment. The ACA's individual mandate intends to induce all such "young invincibles" to sign up for coverage. In most cases, however, the penalty for flaunting the mandate is much lower than the cost of coverage, even after premium subsidies are taken into account.

Another important marketing function is the management of the renewal process. Particularly in inflation sensitive products, it is crucial that the block be managed in a way that avoids an antiselection spiral. This renewal management can take the form of alternatives to rate increases, where an insurer might offer the policyholder an X% rate increase or a Y% rate increase if they accept a higher deductible. It might also take the form of intentionally lowering needed rate increases, trading short term losses for the ability to retain better risks and the long term impact of those better risks' premiums. It might also extend to programs whereby agents are provided with information about pending lapses, so they can make personal calls to retain the business.

10.2 Policy Administration and Services

Once the insurer receives a completed application, the underwriting area will determine whether, and on what basis, to make an offer to the prospective policyholder (subject to any regulatory restrictions, such as guaranteed issue under the ACA for major medical). If the policyholder accepts, then a policy is issued, and the company enters the new policy on its books. The area of the company that issues the policy is typically called *policy administration*. Sometimes this area is split between policy issue and policy service functions.

This area might also be responsible for any home office interactions with the policyholder. This might include responding to questions or complaints, or providing the status of any pending policy changes or claims. There are sometimes legal ramifications to these interactions, so the policy services area will often involve the company's legal counsel in crafting appropriate responses to inquiries.

Policyholder services typically include all the interactions a company has with its customers. For this reason, most of a company's self-measurement (and most of others', including regulators', measurements) are focused on the speed and efficiency of how such interactions are handled. Examples of important measures of a company's service include:

- Statistics (such as mean, median, 90th percentile, maximum) that measure the time a caller must spend on hold before speaking with a representative,
- Number of mailed claims received but not yet processed,
- Number of claims pending (in process of being administered), and
- Statistics on the processing time of claims.

One interesting question for management to answer is, "What is the right target for such service measures?" Some companies feel it is worthwhile pushing for the best possible scores. Others believe that the performance targets in these areas should be chosen after weighing the public's perception of various performance levels against the marginal cost of achieving those various levels of performance. It seems valid, for example, to question whether it is worth reducing the average telephone response delay from 10 seconds to 5 seconds, if it requires adding enough staff to raise the costs of that area by 20%. The answer depends, in part, on the impact of that 5 second gain on the attitudes of customers, and the company's strategic and tactical goals.

10.3 CLAIM ADMINISTRATION

Claim administration refers to the process that a company uses to process claims under its policies. The claim administration (often shortened to *claim admin*) process has four steps, which will be discussed next. Company management must monitor this process to maintain appropriate performance, as the repercussions of bad claim management can be disastrous for the company.

Aside from the desire most companies have to provide good service, there is also an NAIC model law which many states have adopted, called the **Unfair Claims Settlement Practices Act**, which provides some minimum standards in this area. This model law (when adopted by a state) requires that an insurer abide by certain broad performance standards in responding to requests for claim forms and in processing claims. This law has been in effect for decades. More recently, many states have enacted **prompt pay** laws, which require medical insurers to pay providers within a specified period, such as 30 or 45 days. Failure to act in a timely way can induce both regulatory and customer problems, both of which can hurt the company's ability to sell its products.

RECEIPT OF THE CLAIM

An insurer must obviously be notified of a claim's existence before it can start the process of paying it. This notification generally happens in one of two ways: (1) by paper claim, whereby the claimant asks for the company's claim form, fills it out, and returns it to the company, or (2) by electronic claim, when the company is automatically notified of the claim by the service provider. In the paper claim case the claim form may be accompanied by receipts if the claim is for reimbursement of expenses.

Electronic claims generally only exist in the medical insurance arena. In the past, they were usually employed only by large, geographically concentrated insurers, or by Medicare intermediaries. This was because electronic claim filing was only worth the trouble and expense if a particular provider had a sufficiently large number of such claims to make it worthwhile. Now, electronic clearinghouses are common, and the vast majority of claims are electronic.

When a paper claim form is received by the company, an employee of the company logs the claim into the claim system and gives it a claim number, so that it can be tracked and monitored by the company's systems. These records can be used to measure the company's backlogs at various points in the claim admin process, and help management alleviate any bottlenecks in processing. Statistics on such backlogs are also used in the reserve setting process, as a way to estimate the value of unpaid claims.

The policy form itself usually contains provisions that place restrictions on the length of time a person has to file a claim (perhaps 60 days), and the length of time required to provide proof of loss. This limit is typically waived if the person is unable to file the claim within the specified time period because of illness or disability.

VERIFYING COVERAGE AND PROOF OF LOSS

An insurer is obliged to verify that the person on whom a claim is submitted actually had coverage at the time the claim was incurred. Putting a date to the claim, or **incurral dating**, is therefore sometimes a critical matter in claim administration. For medical coverages, claims are typically dated on the date a service is provided, or on the first date of a multi-day claim such as an inpatient stay. For disability policies, it is typically the date the person first becomes disabled, even though they have not yet fulfilled the elimination period. In LTC, it is either the date the disability begins or the date the first paid service is provided, depending on contract language. In reality, the claim is incurred on the date it becomes a legal obligation under the contract.

Incurral dating should conceptually be differentiated from claim *accrual*, which is a term often used to describe the point at which dollars of expense, periods of disablement, or services are provided, and in which dollars of claim start occurring. The day a DI claimant becomes disabled, for example, is the date a claim is incurred, even though there are no accrued benefits under the claim until the elimination period has passed.

A claimant is required to provide **proof of loss** to the insurer. For an expense reimbursement policy, this is usually accomplished by including copies of receipts for services. If the service provider is **participating (par)**, meaning it is a contracted provider in the insurer's network, the claim may be made on behalf of the insured, who need only show his insurance card to the provider. If the provider is **non-participating (non-par)**, it might still file the claim on behalf of the insured. In this case, the provider will ask the insured to sign an **assignment of benefits**, which allows the insurer to pay the provider directly. The provider will then bill the claimant for any remaining balance due. Many insurers' provider contracts require the provider to accept the insurer's fee schedule as full payment for services. This is an added benefit to the insured, as his remaining liability to the provider is reduced by any discounts. Suppose, for example, a claimant sees a physician for an office visit, and that the undiscounted charge for that service is $150. The insurer might have $100 as its discounted payment for that service, and the claimant's liability might be a $10 copay. Then the provider will receive $10 from the claimant and $90 from the insurer ($100 covered expense minus $10 copay), and waive the $50 discount.

In medical insurance, aside from the consumer directed and health savings account products described in Chapter 2, "The Products," some carriers (particularly those geographically concentrated) are developing or renting alternative (sometimes tiered) networks, so the insured can choose the level of payment he wants and the providers he would use. This can happen in two ways; (1) The insured may be required to 'declare' the network he wants to use for services at the time the policy is issued. There might be significant premium differences by network (sometimes increased further by benefit differences); and (2) in a "point of service" plan, the insured picks the network (or out-of-network services) implicitly by choosing a provider at the time of the service. In this case, the benefits usually differ between networks, to provide incentives for insureds to patronize network providers.

Narrow network plans have become a hot topic, as they are one of the few remaining levers insurers have to differentiate products and lower price points under ACA restrictions. Geographically focused plans with extremely narrow networks (sometimes comprised of a single provider system) are becoming more and more common. It remains to be seen whether consumers will be willing to embrace such products.

For DI and LTC policies, and sometimes for medical coverages, there is more to providing proof of loss than simply filling out the claim form. Proof is required under the policy that the insured event has occurred. For a DI policy, for example, the insured might need to demonstrate: (1) that they are under the regular care of a licensed physician, (2) the amount of lost income and other financial information, and (3) that, not only their personal physician, but another one appointed by the insurer agrees that the insured is disabled.

LTC coverage, even more than DI, can consist of a number of separate causes of loss which require various proofs that are specific to that cause (proof of a clinical diagnosis of Alzheimer's disease, for example, in relation to an Alzheimer's benefit). A written certification by a health care practitioner may be needed for most benefits, along with a care plan approved by the insurer.

Both DI and LTC coverage might require ongoing proofs of loss over time, to demonstrate that the insured event is still, in fact, occurring.

In any event, it is this part of the claim administration process in which the important facts related to the case are gathered, for subsequent evaluation by the **claim examiner** or **claim administrator**. The fact-gathering portion of claim admin is often delegated to less skilled clerical staff, since it is somewhat formulaic and requires less skill and experience than the later parts of claim administration.

EVALUATING THE CLAIM AGAINST POLICY PROVISIONS

Once the initial data is received, the claim moves on to the evaluation stage. This part of claim administration is what is often perceived as the most important (or at least the most visible) part. The claim examiner (or administrator) must take the data provided by the claimant and his or her appointees, and evaluate whether the claim meets the conditions of the contract, and if so, what claim is payable.

For medical coverages, this claim administrative function may be largely mechanized, and the claim may not be viewed by a human claim examiner at all. This is particularly true if the claim is submitted electronically by the provider. Even when mechanized, however, the electronic review process will usually have some algorithmic logic that separates out claims that need human viewing. Reasons for such a viewing might include:

- *Potential for pre-existing condition investigation.* If the claim occurred during the period of time when a pre-existing condition provision would have applied, the insurer might need to examine the claim against the original application and underwriting file, or seek other data sources for additional information. (The ACA has eliminated pre-existing condition exclusions in the individual major medical market, however.)

- *Potential fraud.* There are a variety of ways in which either an insured or a provider might intentionally mislead the insurer into paying a claim that should not be paid. These might include, among many others:

  o Payment for services that have not actually been provided.

  o A provider submitting claims for services that were not actually rendered.

  o Failure to disclose earnings while supposedly disabled.

- *Unusual claim characteristics.* Sometimes claimants ask for coverage which is not otherwise included under the policy, but which makes sense in lieu of other claim payments. Coverage of rental of a medical device (such as a hospital bed), for example, which will allow a claimant to go home early from the hospital is likely an efficient use of claim dollars, even if the rental is not otherwise covered. If the rental were not covered, the insured probably has a financial incentive to stay in the hospital, costing the insurer much more than the rental.

  Another example occurs when a DI insurer might allow a claimant to try a part-time job for a short while to test out recovery, without putting the existing total disability claim at risk, even though there is no explicit policy provision in place. Without the company's willingness to do this, the claimant might view such a return to work as too financially risky to try.

- *Claim negotiation.* Sometimes an insurer or the insured may initiate a negotiation, either with the service provider (in medical coverage) or the claimant (in DI) to propose different terms of payment.

  In the case of medical coverage, there are sometimes significant hospital claims that occur out of network where no negotiated discounts exist. In these cases the hospital often bills the claimant at full (undiscounted) charge levels. An insurer's claim admin department can often negotiate a reasonable discount from billed charges on these claims, even though there is not a pre-existing contractual relationship.

  Another common circumstance arises when benefits must be coordinated among several sources of coverage (members who have duplicative health insurance coverage through their own and their spouse's employer, for example) or when an insurer must pursue reimbursement for a claim through **subrogation** (e.g., if a health insurer paid for accident claims that end up being covered by auto insurance or worker's comp).

  In DI coverage, an insured may sometimes prefer a lump sum payout of the claim, rather than continuing to receive periodic payments. This might be used, for example, to set the claimant up in a new business, when he cannot continue in his old occupation. Capitalization of such a claim is in the best interests of the insured, and normally will be at a somewhat discounted present value of future payments, reflecting the change in the financial risks.

The claim examiner (whether human or electronic) will need to determine whether expenses are covered by the policy, and if so, the covered charge amount. Policy limitations and exclusions must be applied, and are not always obvious. If the claim examiner suspects the possibility that some aspect of the claim does not measure up to the requirements of the policy, he can further investigate the claim.

DI AND LTC

For DI and LTC policies, the claim administration process, typically much more through human claim examiners than through electronic processing, will pursue similar issues. There are two additional functions for these coverages, however, that the claim examiner needs to fill. The first is the evaluation of the claimant, to determine whether his physical condition meets the terms required under the policy for a claim to occur, specifically if the physical condition prevents the insured from performing the material and substantial duties of his or her occupation. Because such claims occur over time (as opposed to a medical claim which has a shorter time horizon for accrual of benefits), periodic revalidation of the claimant's condition is often required. The tools available for this include:

- *Examination by Company Physicians:* Most policies contain language that allows the insurer to require that a physician of its choice examine the claimant, to validate (or not) the claimant's physician's opinions. Discussions and negotiation may occur, in the event of differing opinions.

- *Telephone Validations.* A common practice for claim departments is to simply call the claimant and discuss the claim. The level of candor that a claimant or their family will provide to a telephone investigator can be surprising. In one case, the claimant could not come to the phone because "they are at their job" (in a case where they claimed to be unable to work in any occupation).

- *Field Examinations.* One of the more amusing types of stories one hears in insurance work is about field exams that uncover the claimant performing functions that he claims to be unable to perform. In one case, a field investigator took pictures of a claimant putting a new roof on his house, carrying heavy loads of tiles up a ladder, while claiming he was disabled and barely able to move because of a back injury.

The amusing stories from claim administration are exceptions, rather than the rule. Most claimants receive appropriate benefits for valid claims, and the insurance serves the valuable purpose for which it was intended. The occasional problem case, however, is what necessitates the cautionary practices of insurers.

The second unique characteristic of DI and LTC claim adjudication is that the claim examiner may need to determine the amount of benefit that is due under the policy. Unlike a medical policy, a DI or LTC policy may (and usually does) have language that specifies different amounts payable, depending on the circumstances of the claim.

Under DI policies, the coverage may be based on lost income, which may require that a determination be made of the size of that lost income. Or the policy might pay a lesser amount for partial or residual disability than for total disability, and the examiner must determine which situation applies.

Under LTC policies, payments may be limited by a maximum daily amount, with separate maximums payable for various elements of the coverage, such as nursing facility care, home health care, adult day care, informal caregiver training, respite care, or others.

Under either coverage, the benefits may be indexed, either before or after claim occurs, which requires calculations to be applied to the benefit amounts.

MEDICARE SUPPLEMENT

There is a different approach usually used in the administration of Medicare Supplement policies. They pay portions of the insured's costs which remain after Medicare pays its portion of those claims. In this regard, the Med Supp carrier must wait until a claim is administered by Medicare, in order to determine what benefits are payable under the Med Supp claim. This can cause some delay in claim payment.

Medicare chooses private administrators (typically insurance companies) to be their intermediaries (administrator) for a particular geographic area. This administrator then deals directly with providers throughout the region, and sets up electronic communication channels for claim processing. This helps Med Supp carriers by unifying the sources of reliable claim data, at least somewhat offsetting the delay caused by having two carriers involved.

THE END OF THE PROCESS

When the evaluation of a claim is finished, the result is one of four possibilities:

1. The claim (or a part of it) is approved, and an amount of claim is calculated.
2. The claim (or a part of it) is disapproved.
3. The claim examiner requires more information in order to make a determination.
4. The contract is rescinded, because of misrepresentation.

If the claim is disapproved, the company will generally notify the claimant with an explanation. The provider may also be notified, if the provider had made the initial submission for the claim. The insurer establishes a process for appeal of the claim so that, if the insured chooses to do so, the claim can be reexamined in light of additional information, and probably moved to a senior level examiner to evaluate. If a claimant exhausts the company's appeals process, he can then appeal to the state's Insurance Department, and ultimately, to the courts. Most insurers have court cases every year in which a claimant believes himself unfairly treated, and the insurer believes it justly denied the claim.

The fourth possible outcome of the claim, rescission, occurs when the insurer discovers intentional misinformation (misrepresentation) on the application, and, when allowed by policy provisions, rescinds the contract. (The legal argument is that, because of the misrepresentation, the insurer and the applicant never had a true meeting of the minds, so a contract never existed.) This action carries some risk with it that the insured will litigate the action. Some insurers feel that rescission is necessary, however, to demonstrate to the marketplace their willingness to stand up to such misrepresentations. Without that demonstration, a company might be victimized by those actively looking to misrepresent. As mentioned in previous chapters, the ACA prohibits rescissions of major medical policies except in cases of fraud or intentional misrepresentation of a material fact, a much higher hurdle for the insurer to prove in court.

If the claim is approved, payment occurs. Payment can occur electronically through bank transfers, or by check. Transfers are often used for recurring reimbursements to large providers or to group policyholders, but can also be used for direct deposit into individuals' accounts for DI or LTC plans. Checks are used otherwise. In the case of medical coverage, an **explanation of benefits** or **EOB** is usually provided to the policyholder regardless of how payment occurs. The EOB explains how the benefit was calculated.

CHAPTER 11

MANAGING THE BUSINESS

This chapter discusses the critical elements of successfully managing a block of individual health insurance policies. Each type of coverage carries a unique blend of risks, and requires a similarly unique blend of expertise to successfully manage it. Of course, the elements discussed in this chapter represent the authors' opinions, in an area that tends to be subjective. The reader is encouraged to seek alternative views.

The first section discusses the strategic context of an individual health insurance business.

It is important to understand that there are many expertises needed to successfully manage individual health insurance. Most of these can be monitored quantitatively through appropriate design and use of management information systems. The chapter on "Other Insurer Functions" discusses some of these. Analysis of data to extract underlying information is critical. This is often the most effective way in which challenges to profitability can be identified. The second section of this chapter discusses the needed management information systems and analyses.

The next two sections discuss capital management, specifically how this interrelates to risk based capital and the individual major medical product cycle, which is a major challenge to the successful management of IH portfolios.

Finally, a discussion of the product development and product management processes is given.

This chapter is somewhat different than other chapters in this text. Managing individual health insurance business involves important technical and planning expertise, much of which is described in other chapters. Putting all the pieces together, however, involves a little subjective magic.

11.1 Strategic Context

Any successful business organization must operate with a fundamental understanding of what it is meant to accomplish. This is sometimes called the organization's 'mission.' A conceptual picture of what success looks like is typically called the organization's 'vision.' The plan to get from here to there is the strategic plan. These are all big picture, long time period concepts.

The importance of a valid strategic plan to the success of a health insurance enterprise cannot be overemphasized. Such a plan takes into account the organization's mission, its competitive situation, and the organization's own strengths and weaknesses. It has been said that, "The only good thing about not having a strategic plan is that failure comes as a complete surprise."

11.2 Management Information

One critical prerequisite for the successful management of individual health insurance is the ability to effectively extract a wide variety of information from company data. This requires the establishment of a well designed data warehouse for use by those whose job it is to monitor and study the company's book of business.

There are a large number of processes that all must be performed correctly in order to manage this business. Each type of product requires some core functions plus some functions unique to (or uniquely important to) that coverage. Most of those "things that must be done right" can be explicitly measured, or at least have quantitative measures that can tell the insurer whether they point in the right direction.

Those processes include (but are not limited to):

- New business underwriting. This is measured in various ways, including:
  - Durational claim curves, and
  - Benchmarked measures of underwriting ratios, such as the percentage of policies ultimately rescinded or reformed.

- Network contracting. The attractiveness and coverage of the network to insureds is measurable (at least somewhat) by the policyholders' use of network providers versus non-network providers. Another measure is the relative efficiency (perhaps measured by severity-adjusted number of hospital days) of the network in managing patients. Recently, much effort has been expended on studying efficiency and quality of care in order to identify narrower networks of providers that can achieve quality care at low cost. This also requires analysis of referral patterns and the geographic distributions of providers and policyholders.
- Claim administration. Performance measures include days of inventory, or dollars of payments versus dollars submitted or allowed. For DI and LTC, performance might also be measured by the claim frequency and termination rates.
- Pricing. Measured by actual-to-expected ratios, with the 'expected' numbers based on the pricing structure.
- Investment performance. Perhaps measured by portfolio rates of return versus those assumed in pricing.
- Quality producers. One analysis might compare producer-specific loss ratios or financial results, but this is usually not a large enough sample to be usable. It certainly can be useful, however, with data grouped in appropriate ways (by broader distribution channels, for example).
- Managing by geographic area or regulatory jurisdiction. This might require geographic-specific analysis of loss ratios.

There are many such reports that can be produced; these are just a sampling. In order to effectively manage this information flow, the carrier's analytic area (usually the actuarial department or a consultant) must have access to ongoing data from the company's main files (perhaps supplemented by external data and other internal databases.) This is typically done via a data extract to an actuarial database, which contains the data needed by that department to do this monitoring.

11.3 BASELINE ANALYSIS

At the heart of every successful individual health insurer, particularly for medical coverage insurers, lies a complex and robust analytic model that compares actual results against expected results.

First, it is absolutely essential that any of the measurements we are discussing be put in the proper context when communicated. At a very basic level, this means communicating how the results compare to expectations. It also means clarity about what inferences can and cannot be drawn from the analysis.

In measuring the loss ratio occurring in the first year of a new medical product, for example, suppose the measured incurred/earned loss ratio is 45%, and this is communicated to management without context. Since management might well remember choosing a 60% lifetime loss ratio for this product, they might conclude that 45% is an excellent result for the first year, and might actually put pressure on the actuaries to avoid a rate increase.

In truth, the 45% might be 125% of an expected first year loss ratio of 36%. If the results are shown in context, management might be justifiably worried about how to correct such a problem. Further, they might want clarity on the cause of this deviation. Was it just a misestimation of the underlying claim costs by the actuaries, without other causes? (If so, the 125% is likely to continue in subsequent years' experience.) Does it mean the underwriting was poor (or the estimate of its impact was incorrect)? (In that case, the 125% might not continue, but could regress to a 100% level even without corrective action.) Were the promised network savings illusory? (In which case, other solutions must be sought, such as finding a new network.)

Ideally, a monitoring system and metric would be developed for every quantifiable risk faced with respect to a block of business. This might mean monthly or quarterly monitoring of actual results, measured against expected (benchmark) results, examined in ways that will highlight those risky areas. Such areas might include (but not be limited to):

- Overall results for the block.
- Results by state or other geographic area.
- Results by benefit plan.
- Results by producer network, or even producer. This might also involve looking at exchange business separately from off-exchange business for major medical policies. Off-exchange may be further bro-

ken down into ACA compliant, transitional, and grandfathered policies.
- Results by healthcare provider network.
- Results by calendar period of issue.
- Results by duration.
- Historical results by calendar period.
- Results by underwriting method, segment, era, or even underwriter.
- Results by rating variable or class.

Besides measuring claims, revenue, and enrollment, it is essential to ensure that other key assumptions such as sales, lapse rates, and (for longer term coverages) investment earnings are also monitored closely.

In order to measure results in these and other dimensions, these characteristics must be gathered and maintained in the database. All of these analyses can be useful in pinpointing flaws in the company's ratings or operations which may be leading to worse than expected results. If overall results are at least as good as expected, there is likely to be much less emphasis on this analysis.

Aside from the eternal need to monitor the number of claims occurring, success for coverages like DI and LTC, which have long term claims, require ongoing analysis of existing claims. This is typically done by measuring the "claim termination rate" A:E. Because the frequency of such claims is relatively low, and because there are few claims terminating in each claim duration being measured (even for the largest carriers), aggregating and smoothing methods must be used. Typically, overall A:E claim termination rates are calculated, and compared to a standard (usually a published table or a pricing table based on external data, but occasionally for the largest companies, a pricing table based on its own data.) One such result might be, "Claim terminations are running at 98% of 85CIDA levels, for claims over one year in duration."

11.4 "EXPECTED" RESULTS

What is the "expected" to which actual results are compared in an "A:E" analysis? This is an interesting question, to which each person in the company may have a different answer. There are only a few definitions which seem to have the most universal relevance. Other bases can also be important, in specific circumstances.

ORIGINAL PRICING

The original assumptions used to develop premiums are relevant for two reasons. The first reason is that it is likely that many of the stakeholders, including senior management, looked closely at the assumptions and the related expectations set out in the original product development for that product. They likely have a mental picture of (and perhaps emotional attachment to) that basis. For that reason, it can be most meaningful to those people to put current results in those terms. They might be looking for an A:E analysis to say something like, "The first year's incurred claims are at 98% of the level we anticipated when doing the pricing work. Plan A is at 102%, and Plan B is at 96%."

The second reason is that, quite often, prior product development is used as a basis for the next product's development. Putting actual results in terms of those original assumptions provides an easy and automatic experience update to those assumptions in time for the next product development. For this reason, even when it is not the basis provided to management, it can be helpful to have this analysis for future rating purposes.

This basis for expected results is most useful for non-inflation sensitive[1] coverages like DI or LTC. In those cases, the monitoring results simultaneously serve as much of the analysis for the next generation of product's pricing basis.

For many coverages (mainly the inflation sensitive ones like major medical), the original pricing basis becomes meaningless over time, as original assumptions must be abandoned because reality has differed greatly from them. In this case, the second basis is useful.

---

[1] Although we have generally referred to these coverages as "non-inflation sensitive" in comparison to inflationary coverages like major medical, it is of course important to recognize the potential for inflationary effects even in these less sensitive coverages as well– for instance, if benefits are expressed as a percentage of salaries, which also go up over time.

Profit Targets

This basis replaces the original full set of product development assumptions with a limited set – the original *profit* targets, and whatever current assumptions there are which would be consistent with that. Since this is typically the bottom line in which most senior management is interested, and since quoting a myriad of actual-to-expected ratios may lead to a glazed look in your boss' eyes, it can be very helpful to focus on this metric.

If the original pricing assumptions are not important to maintain, this method allows you to update the expected basis to keep pace with the changing situation, but doing so in a way that will still maintain the original pricing targets. As mentioned previously, this is most useful for inflation-sensitive policies, and particularly so over time, since inflation targets are not very reliable beyond a year or so. A result of this A:E analysis might be expressed as, "This year's claim experience is at 103% of the level needed to achieve profits consistent with the original profit targets."

One common version of this basis is the following one ('current pricing'), particularly for organizations that manage their business with year-to-year rate changes, such as HMOs.

Current Pricing

This may be the most useful measure for inflation sensitive products. Rather than relying on a static view of the original pricing assumptions for an "expected" basis, this method treats the pricing basis as constantly evolving. Provided the users of the information understand the current assumption basis, then it seems meaningful to compare actual results against this benchmark.

Tabular

As described earlier, for DI coverage a published table is often used for comparison. (LTC coverage does not enjoy the same advantage of having a commonly accepted public table, so one must rely on other measures.) It is also possible for companies to develop their own internal table, based on their historical experience, and use that as a tabular basis. For DI and LTC, this would require a very large block of experience, far beyond the capabilities of most carriers.

Most commercial individual carriers specialize in their market segments, and have developed unique sets of reports that they use to monitor their experience. They will typically use one of these bases for comparison. Such reports are most typically produced automatically each month, and interpreted each time they are generated. There may also be: (1) periodic reports that are generated less frequently, perhaps on a rotating basis with other reports, and (2) ad hoc studies. An example of such a report might be one that analyzes the company's experience by deductible or elimination period.

Regardless of the basis for comparison, interpretation of the results requires an understanding of whether a particular deviation is material, and whether it is statistically reliable. Unfortunately, this information is often missing from management reports. When it does appear, it most often is provided subjectively, based on the analysts' gut feel of what constitutes a "credible" amount of business.

11.5 CONFIDENCE INTERVALS

Some reports are built in a context whereby the size of the business is relatively predictable, and they need not have measures that test varying sizes for statistical reliability. An example of such an environment is in dental coverage, in which there tends to be a large number of relatively small claims, which therefore tend to be statistically reliable at exposures much smaller than that for medical coverages. This practice is fraught with peril, however, as it can lead to a presumption that all numbers in the reports are valid and reliable measures. This might be proven wrong at just the wrong time.

It is, therefore, important to provide some quantified measure of 'credibility' or 'reliability' to deviations from expected values, even if rudimentary. One method of doing this is to use the A:E ratio, along with an assumed or constructed distribution of expected claims, and compare the ratio to values which are 1σ (one standard deviation), 2σ, or 3σ from expected. From our basic statistics classes, we know that if we are looking at a two-tailed test (in this case, we are testing whether the A:E ratio is either unusually high or unusually low), the probability of exceeding a deviation of 1σ even though we have the right underlying assumptions is about 32% if the underlying distribution is approximately normally distributed. Similarly, for 2σ and 3σ, it is 5% and 3/10%. The level (or levels) used in a monitoring system should be discussed and understood by management for this exercise to have meaning.

At times (depending on the purpose), A:E values can be suppressed from a report if they appear to signal a deviation, but because of small exposure they did not exceed the chosen significance level (perhaps 1σ, for this purpose), for fear that management might draw inappropriate conclusions. In order to accomplish this, though, it is important to get a clear understanding of the level of deviation that management considers to be significant.

One of the easiest ways to provide this "significance of the deviation" information is to determine whether the *number of claims* meets a specific criterion. In that case, if you have a measure for the expected frequency of such claims (and therefore, by multiplying by the exposure, the expected number of claims), this distribution can be developed by considering this a binomial distribution – i.e., each sample (member) either meets the condition (with likelihood p) or does not (with likelihood $1-p$.) The standard deviation is given by $\sqrt{np(1-p)}$.

This can sometimes be approximated by the Poisson distribution. The Poisson expected value is the same as the binomial, np. The Poisson standard deviation is $\sqrt{np}$. The approximation error in the standard deviation is therefore $\sqrt{1-p}$, which is close to 1 when p is close to zero. This approximation therefore works best when p is close to zero (or 1, since defining p also defines $(1-p)$, so the analysis is symmetric).

When p is not close to 0 or 1, a better approximation is the Normal approximation. Once the sample exceeds 20 or so in size (usually exceeded in our context by a multiple of 10,000 or so), the Normal curve closely approximates the Binomial. (In fact, it is the limiting distribution of the Binomial as $n \to \infty$.)

If the sample is quite small (say 10-20 or so), then Student's T distribution is useful[2].

---

[2] According to www-stat.stanford.edu, "the T distributions were discovered by William S. Gosset in 1908. Gosset was a statistician employed by the Guinness brewing company which had stipulated that he not publish under his own name. He therefore wrote under the pen name 'Student'." I couldn't help offer this as a footnote, just in case anyone else

Exercise 11.1: Suppose you are a consultant whose client has asked you whether the number of large claims (defined as claims in excess of $100,000) in a company's major medical block was significantly larger than the expected number of such claims. Further questioning of the client yields the following information:

- It is appropriate to use Table 5.2 (the full version is included with the electronic materials provided with the book) as the expected distribution of claims per member for this population and benefit set.
- The company has 100,000 members.

Calculate the expected number of large claims, and the endpoints of the two-tailed confidence intervals corresponding to 1σ, 2σ, and 3σ deviations. ☐

For a more rigorous application of this, I use a Monte Carlo simulation of the individual claim distribution (either the company's own distribution or a sample one we have developed over the years as representative of an average population), on a population size matching the size of the exposure in each of the cells being measured.

11.6 MANAGING CAPITAL

Management's job is to run a business to generate reliable profits which match or exceed the organization's target profit level. Profits are reliable either when (1) management is lucky (which only works for a time), or (2) management successfully manages (not necessarily eliminating) the risks associated with the business, without unduly hampering the generation of profit.

The overall capital level of a company is an important aspect of company management. In order to manage this, most senior management teams develop a target relative to a benchmark. Because of its ubiquity (particularly among regulators, rating agencies and stock analysts), a version of the NAIC's Risk Based Capital (RBC) is usually used as the

---

had wondered about that, as I have, since first encountering the name in 1972. And particularly because it's a beer reference.

benchmark. In doing this, the company's target is typically expressed as a multiple of either its "Company Action Level" or its "Authorized Control Level" RBC benchmark.

There are two fundamental goals of capital management: (1) hold appropriate levels of capital, and (2) have regulators, rating agencies, and stock analysts judge the capital levels to be appropriate.

In order to manage the level of capital relative to RBC (the **RBC ratio**), management can change either the numerator (the level of capital held), or the denominator (the RBC benchmark). Changing the denominator is typically accomplished by focusing on those product lines, provider payment methods, etc., which will result in a lower benchmark value. Changing the numerator requires finding more capital – either through profits or other investors.

To understand the benchmark, it is useful to look at the conceptual work done to support development of the NAIC's Risk Based Capital Formula. In this work, the actuarial profession first categorized the risks associated with the entire field of health and life insurance into four categories, called C-1 through C-4 risks. There was similar work done for Property & Casualty companies. The NAIC later chose to recategorize these risks into the following categories for health companies:

- *H0*, "Asset Risk - Affiliates," the risk of asset default for certain affiliated investments.
- *H1*, "Asset Risk - Other," the risk of asset default or fluctuation in market value.
- *H2*, "Underwriting Risk," the risk of inadequately measuring liabilities, or of inadequately pricing business.
- *H3*, "Credit Risk," the risk of not recovering amounts due from debtors.
- *H4*, "Business Risk," the general risks of doing business.

As discussed in Chapter 7, "Financial Reporting and Solvency," a value is calculated for each of these risks, and combined to a final RBC value for the authorized control level (ACL) using the following formula:

$$ACL = 0.5 \times \left(H0 + \sqrt{H1^2 + H2^2 + H3^2 + H4^2} \right) \quad (11.1)$$

Early work on risk based capital was done for life insurers, which resulted in a relatively heavy focus on investment risks and a somewhat lighter focus on business risks. For most health insurance (the possible exceptions being LTD and LTC coverage, which rely heavily on asset accumulation to fund future benefit payments), the opposite is true – investment risk is relatively minor, and underwriting risk is the key element. This is illustrated by looking at formula (11.1). By squaring the elements under the radical, differences in relative size become much more pronounced, and somewhat smaller H# values can become insignificant. This can be easily illustrated using a simplified, artificial calculation such as this:

$$\text{Let:} \quad H0 = 0$$
$$H1 = 10$$
$$H2 = 100$$
$$H3 = 10$$
$$H4 = 20$$

$$ACL = 0.5 \times (0 + \sqrt{10^2 + 100^2 + 10^2 + 20^2}) = 0.5 \times 103 = 51.5$$

While these numbers and relativities are obviously artificial, they do illustrate the point – the RBC values for $H1$, $H3$, and $H4$, while in total being 40% of the $H2$ value of 100, only add 3% (100→103) marginally to $H2$'s RBC contribution.

During development of the health RBC formula, some members of the task force voluntarily applied the formula to their portfolios. Interestingly, where health was a separate line of business to a life insurer, the $H2$ risks became relatively minor (on the order of the post-square root marginal value of about 15% of the pre-square root value). This was due to the heavy asset-related elements in those insurers' calculations.

In a panel discussion[3] in 2002, Rowen Bell recounted the marginal impact on final Health RBC for all Blue Cross/Blue Shield plans. If each of the factors $H1$ through $H4$ separately had a $100 increase in their value, the result on final RBC would be as follows:

---

[3] *Record*, the Society of Actuaries, Vol. 28, No. 2, June, 2002.

$H1$ $32
$H2$ $93
$H3$ $8
$H4$ $15

This demonstrates clearly the enormous importance of $H2$, relative to the other risks.

Since most health insurers have substantially more $H2$ risk than any other, the management of RBC for most health insurers is largely a challenge of effectively managing their own capital levels (the numerator) and the $H2$ component of ACL (the denominator). Following introduction of the RBC formulas, most companies spent a few years restructuring their capital, in order to achieve their desired ratio of capital to ACL. This target ratio is typically a higher multiple of ACL than we have been discussing – perhaps even 500-600% (or 2.5 to 3 times the Company Action Level.)

11.7 THE LIFE CYCLE OF COMMERCIAL MAJOR MEDICAL INSURANCE

Individual major medical insurance, when issued by commercial insurers, has tended to have a recognizable and predictable life cycle, driven by the unique characteristics of this business. The historical cycle is discussed in this section, together with some thoughts on how this may change going forward under the ACA.

THE CHARACTERISTICS

Regulatory Setting

Setting the stage for this life cycle is a common regulatory approach (at least for most commercial insurers and some not-for-profits), where the experience and resulting rate action for a policy form are considered independently of any other experiences that a carrier may be having on other policy forms. This causes the insurer to manage this collection (typically called a "block") of policies independently of other blocks.

As we will discuss at length later in this chapter, the ACA completely changes this regulatory environment by prohibiting underwriting and requiring insurers to rate all policies as a single risk pool (other than grandfathered and transitional policies). Still, understanding the cycle is important for insurers managing blocks of pre-ACA policies, as well as for coverages in which underwriting and block rating are still permitted.

Durational Effects

Before a new policy is issued, it is underwritten. This is a protection against antiselection, which, without underwriting, would result in claim experience far in excess of average. (In Chapter 4, "Managing Antiselection," this is called 'external antiselection.') As a result of underwriting, however, initial claim experience is generally much lower than average. The experience quickly deteriorates as the effects of initial underwriting wear off. This wear-off of underwriting causes a highly steep durational effect on claim experience for these policies. This underwriting effect, by policy year, might look like this (with the year one value arbitrarily set at 1.00):

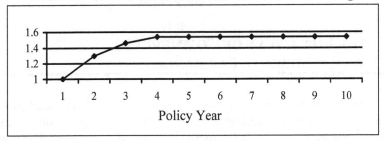

Figure 11.1

There is a second durational effect which causes higher claim experience over time. Once policies have been issued, there is a natural tendency for healthier policyholders (who can successfully pass underwriting at another carrier) to lapse their policies at a higher rate than unhealthier policyholders. Over time this effect accumulates to a significant degree. It intensifies when there are larger rate increases and higher rate levels. This effect has been termed "Cumulative Antiselection"[4] or CAST. (In extreme cases, this effect, when combined with resulting rate increases, is called a "death spiral" or "antiselection spiral.")

The combination of these durational effects has a significant impact on experience. When the two are combined, a typical durational curve for a

---

[4] "Cumulative Antiselection Theory," by William F. Bluhm, *Transactions of the Society of Actuaries*, 1982.

rigorously underwritten individual policy might look like this: (Note the scale of the Y axis has changed to accommodate the larger values.)

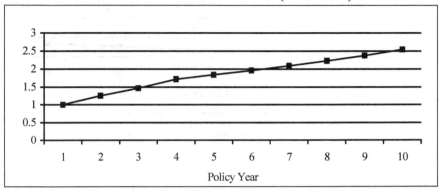

Figure 11.2

This graph shows that, in this illustrative case without particularly strong CAST effects, the claim cost per policy will be 50% higher in year three than in year one, simply because of the durational effects.[5]

Other Temporal Effects

Claim costs increase over time due to underlying trends in claim costs (higher cost of services, changing mix of services, deductible leveraging, changes in utilization rates of services, changing technology), plus changes due to aging of the policyholder. Claim trends can vary widely, but it is not unusual to see actual underlying claim trends well in excess of 10% per year. Aging trend typically averages 2.5-3% per year[6].

Putting together all the time-related changes in cost, and using 15% as a representative cost trend, total claim trends by policy cohort would typically look something like the following. A pure 15% trend is included as well, for reference.

---

[5] Similar effects were reported in the research report, "Variation by Duration in Individual Health Medical Insurance Claims," by Leigh M. Wachenheim, FSA, MAAA, published October 3, 2006, by the Society of Actuaries. www.soa.org

[6] These values are intended to be illustrative, and shouldn't be relied upon for any other purpose without being validated.

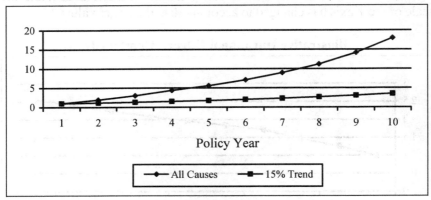

Figure 11.3

There are times when this is a realistic picture of what experience for a given cohort can look like over a ten year period. Some might feel this is extreme. Even so, it demonstrates the profound impact that compounding of temporal effects has on experience over time. Note that the cost per policy has *doubled in two years from issue*. While the environmental trend is 15%, the (geometric) average annual trend experienced by these policies, including durational effects over the ten years, is 31%.

THE MARKET IMPLICATIONS

The individual major medical market is extremely price-sensitive, meaning that purchasers tend to make decisions based mostly on cost differences. Product, company, or other product differentiations, such as having a premier reputation in the industry, can only protect against a 5-10% difference in premium level.

This means that a company that can find a way to sell its product at a lower price will have significantly better sales. This fact, combined with the underlying characteristics of this product, have led to pressure on issuers to charge premiums for new issues that reflect as much as possible the low claim levels expected from new policies.

Prudent product management, in the absence of other forces (like the need for competitive premiums), would seem to argue that some level of pre-funding would make sense – charge a bit more in the beginning, so that the policies can be subsidized later, and you will not need rate increases to be as large. Lower rate increases would lead to lower CAST (durational antiselection) effects, and ultimately to even lower premiums and more healthy lives staying with the block.

Once a single company charges lower rates for new issues, however, others must follow suit or risk being priced out of the market. Hence, the prefunding scenario fails if even one company fails to follow it, and premiums tend to fall to a level near the lowest rate level in the market just from market pressure. Or, if the other carriers believe the low-priced carrier to be temporarily pricing inappropriately, they might wait for a year or so, until the carrier discovers its error.

It is also worth mentioning that the 'sky is falling' implications of CAST on claim costs can be mitigated to a great extent by consideration of the durational incidence of expenses that some carriers have for individual health insurance. Those expenses are typically heavily weighted toward early durations, at least somewhat offsetting the durational slope of claims in calculating durational costs.

COHORT GROUPING

The graphs shown earlier are those for a single cohort of policyholders. Imagine, if you will, a steady stream of new issues being generated by a company, starting on January 1 of a given calendar year, z. In z, all policies (that were issued uniformly throughout the first year) are in durational year 1. Policies issued at each moment could be represented by the single cohort graph.

If we turn to calendar year $z+1$, we note that those policies that were issued on January 1, z, enter their durational year 2 on January 1, $z+1$, and immediately begin contributing 48% higher claims. Those year z issues all turn 2 years old in $z+1$ (uniformly throughout the year), and similarly contribute higher claims. The combined impact of those year z issues in year $z+1$ is that the claims move from first durational year levels on January 1 to second durational year levels by December 31.

At the same time in year $z+1$, there are new issues still coming along, whose experience is still in their first duration. Their volume (and thus their contribution to the aggregate results) is growing throughout the year. For these reasons, the premiums in the second year need not be increased by the full 48% suggested by the earlier graph.

This situation is great news for the issues from year z, whose experience in $z+1$ is being combined with the lower experience of the new $z+1$ cohort. Because of that, the $z+1$ cohort's premiums must be high enough to cover not only their own duration year 1 experience, but also some part of the duration year 2 experience of the z cohort. Thus, premiums for the $z+1$ cohort contain a subsidy for the z cohort.

The same thing happens yet again in $z+2$, but with three cohorts this time. The impact of the duration 1 issues (the $z+2$ cohort) on aggregate experience will be significantly less than in $z+1$, because there are now two cohorts at higher cost, including the z cohort whose claims are now at duration 3 levels – even higher.

By the time the block has moved to the third year from first issue, it is typically becoming difficult to make the experience both self supporting and competitive.

Many companies who are active in this market feel that if they were to sell the same policy form for a fourth year, and not differentiate by duration in the rate schedule, self-supporting rates could become uncompetitive in the market, and new sales would drop dramatically. Rather than face this situation, carriers tend to either: (1) introduce a new product sometime before or at the beginning of the fourth year of issue, or (2) build durational rating elements into their rate structure.

If the company introduces a new product, it allows the "new low premium" cycle to begin again with a new block of policies. The existing block of policies is then "closed" to new issues (this practice is also prohibited under the ACA). The old and new blocks are then managed separately with respect to rate increases.

Durational Rating

Another common solution to the product cycle problem is the use of durational rating. In this approach, rates are increased automatically (as part of the rate schedule) by duration of the policy. This allows a company to charge higher rates to their longer-standing policyholders to reflect the durational deterioration of the experience. In this way, they can avoid tying the durational management of the block to the introduction of new policy forms.

The major shortcoming of this approach is that the company is tied into rate actions for the entire portfolio. If it becomes strategically desirable to partition the business for experience grouping, it is more difficult, because it becomes a change in methodology that is likely to be scrutinized more heavily by regulators. This practice is also prohibited for ACA-compliant individual major medical policies, since duration is not among the permitted rating variations.

WHAT HAPPENS TO A CLOSED BLOCK?

If a block is closed, as soon as the flow of new issues stops or substantially slows (either due to explicitly closing the block or raising the premiums substantially above the market rate), there are no more low cost policies entering the block to help buffer the otherwise substantial claim increases which almost inevitably occur at later durations.

After being closed, the block's experience typically shows a significant acceleration of claim cost per policy. Depending on the level of shock lapse experienced, and the resulting CAST effects, trends may gradually slow, as all policies in the block reach later durations.

A critical element in managing such a closed block is the correct anticipation of the CAST effects which will occur, and taking appropriate rate action *in anticipation* of their occurrence. This can involve some judgment, since a similar rate increase might have very different impacts on two comparable populations. It is important to understand the relative health characteristics of the remaining policyholders. If, for example, a block has been subject to substantial rate increases in the past, and the rates are well above current market rates for new business, it is likely that the remaining policyholders have a relatively high expectation of claims, and a relatively high tolerance for future increases. In such a case, additional antiselective lapsation might be more limited than it would for a similarly sized increase applied for the first time, to a relatively healthy group of policyholders.

Without a strategy which models future experience and needed rate increases, it is impossible to test the impact of alternative strategies on a company's portfolio. Sometimes, for example, there are blocks of business for which, once they are in a given loss situation, it is impossible to financially rehabilitate them to a return to profitability. The best that can be achieved in that regard may be to minimize future losses.

A good approach to understand, anticipate, and manage such blocks of business is to create CAST models, calibrate them, and get to know the block. It is also important to understand and take account of how expenses are distributed by duration, to help temper the need for durational increases.

OTHER IMPLICATIONS

Anticipation of the CAST effects in projections and planning does not necessarily mean that those anticipated costs must be borne by the remaining policyholders. To fully allocate those costs to the remaining group is to flirt with an antiselection spiral – the risk that, merely by anticipating the deterioration, even higher antiselective lapsation occurs, that causes even worse CAST effects, that results in even higher premiums, etc.

To the extent such deterioration can be either pre-funded or subsidized by better risks, the block will be that much easier to manage without antiselective lapsation. It turns out (mostly because of the high lapse rates in such business at early durations) that a relatively minor investment from earlier durations (either through prefunding or subsidy) is heavily leveraged, and can have a major impact on the rate levels of later durations.

There are a number of schemes possible for subsidization. These include explicit prefunding (such as using Duration Based Policy Reserves, referenced earlier in this text), durational rating, and limitations on the variation of rates allowed between blocks. Each has its advantages and disadvantages, as might be expected. Ultimately, the last of these alternatives is what was implemented under the ACA.

MANAGING THE PRODUCT CYCLE

As described earlier, the highly sloped temporal claim cost curve (driven in early years mainly by durational effects but also materially by environmental trends), in combination with the fact that the major medical market is very price sensitive, creates a strong incentive for carriers to charge less initially, and follow this by large rate increases. This can either be done explicitly, through higher rate increases on a block, or implicitly, through durational rating.

Some carriers have one or more characteristics that allow them to avoid (either partially or in total) succumbing to the pressure to durationally rate their individual medical business. Those characteristics can include low cost local networks (reducing competitive pressure in the claim cost element), major market presence (reducing competitive pressure in the premium element), or others.

There are some states that have implemented policies that limit the ability of carriers to differentiate their rate levels (either by durational rating or by segmenting policy forms) by duration or policy era. Such limitations are usually (but not always) applied to all carriers in the market. (The exception might be where a particular dominant carrier, such as a Blue Cross plan, is perceived as having a unique social obligation because of their position, so a state legislature or regulators might impose different standards for that carrier.)

In order to effectively market in a commercial marketplace where durational rating is not allowed or feasible, carriers generally feel they must develop and introduce new products every two to four years, closing off the existing block of policies, so that their deteriorating experience does not force the new business rates to rise above competitive levels.

The rate increases that result in the closed blocks can be quite substantial, year after year, and appear to have resulted in regulatory pressure to reduce those rate increases, sometimes regardless of their actuarial justification. To the extent that regulatory pressure is successful, those blocks of business become less profitable or more unprofitable. This has led many companies that previously were active in this market to leave it.

Other regulatory solutions have been implemented, with varying success. Experiments with mandated community rates seem to have resulted in a major reduction in the number of companies competing, and a shrinking of the market.[7] Less draconian measures, such as a California law[8] that requires the pooling (or, alternatively, a version of open enrollment) seems to have been successful at limiting the closed block problem.

The Academy's Rate Filing Task Force[9], referenced previously in this book, began its work by discussing all potential solutions identified by its 40+ members, and ended up (with some input from the NAIC as to what was politically feasible) categorizing those potential solutions into four categories, represented by four illustrative regulatory plans. The Task Force then modeled those solutions, and compared the results to a baseline

---

[7] Wachenheim, Leigh and Leida, Hans. "The Impact of Guaranteed Issue and Community Rating Reforms on States' Individual Health Insurance Markets," prepared for America's Health Insurance Plans, March 2012. Retrieved October 20, 2014 from http://www.ahipcoverage.com/wp-content/uploads/2012/03/Updated-Milliman-Report.pdf.
[8] Health & Safety Code §1367.15
[9] See Appendix B

model of the "current market." Durational effects, and models of them, are discussed in more detail in Chapter 4, "Managing Antiselection."

CHANGES UNDER THE AFFORDABLE CARE ACT

Starting in 2014, the ACA changed many key elements of the regulatory setting underlying the life cycle presented previously, and it is already having profound impacts on the way insurers manage their individual major medical portfolios. In fact, the changes in the major medical market are also having ripple effects on other markets, such as the markets for short term medical, hospital indemnity, and other limited benefit products.

For ACA-compliant individual major medical insurance in 2014 and beyond, insurers must (among many other requirements):
- Issue and renew policies at modified community rates without regard to health status or pre-existing conditions;
- Allow individuals to purchase any non-grandfathered, non-transitional plan "approved for sale" in a state (so blocks can no longer be closed, although an insurer is not obliged to market all plans);
- Rate each individual market pool for each legal entity in a state as a **single risk pool**;
- Rate all policies on a calendar year basis, and set rates in the spring of the preceding year (after which they cannot be changed until the following year);
- Participate in the transitional reinsurance, risk adjustment, and risk corridor programs (as discussed in Chapter 4, risk corridors only apply to carriers participating in the public exchanges).

The advent of the public insurance exchanges created by the ACA presents individual market carriers with a new key strategic decision: should they participate in the exchanges or not? If so, in how many states? Exchange participation provides access to a potentially large market of consumers seeking subsidized insurance plans, but it also requires a significant amount of administrative effort to complete the QHP application process and interface with the exchange.

Instead of a "product cycle" of introducing new products every few years, carriers now face a "bid cycle" similar to that familiar to Medicare Advantage carriers – whether they are participating in exchanges or not. Each spring (or, often, starting in the preceding winter), analysis must be performed in a tight timeframe to adapt to any new regulatory guidance and to analyze the most recent data available in order to set rates for the following year's open enrollment period, which occurs in the fall. The requirement to file and lock in rates longer in advance materially increases the risk that carriers take on.

The risk adjustment program aims to force carriers to price to the market average morbidity (and hence remove the incentive to compete based on risk selection). It is still unclear how well the risk adjustment process will work in practice. Until actual data is available, estimating risk adjustment transfers will be a large source of uncertainty for many carriers (those who have dominant market shares have, of course, a good idea what the market average risk score will be).

As they are managing their new ACA blocks of business, carriers will also have to be mindful of market dynamics affecting any transitional or grandfathered business they (or their competitors) may have. No new members can enter these plans, but to the extent leaner benefit plans with lower rates are available in the non-ACA market, it is possible that these closed blocks could experience favorable selection whereby the less healthy members leave to purchase ACA-compliant plans with richer benefits.

Finally, the minimum 80% loss ratio (MLR) requirement for individual business (including transitional and grandfathered policies) will pose an ongoing challenge. The MLR essentially caps the amount of profit an insurer can make in a given year for a given claim cost and administrative expense level. Unless the insurer can reduce administrative expenses as a percentage of premium, there will be a maximum upside profit margin they can achieve in good years. The downside risk, however, (while temporarily dampened somewhat by risk corridors for some insurers) is still ultimately unlimited in bad years.

The MLR formula includes credibility and multi-year averaging provisions that aim to somewhat help smooth out volatility. Carriers may also find however, that they need to pursue new contractual arrangements with providers to try to manage their MLR due to this asymmetry. One approach is through vertical integration, in which the insurer is the healthcare provider (e.g. a traditional HMO). In another approach the insurer uses risk sharing contracts with the provider to smooth out claim costs from year to year.

In the near term, of course, estimating the MLR position of a block is difficult, since the MLR depends on the risk adjustment, reinsurance, and risk corridor results for the block, all of which will be difficult to estimate for the first few years when data is limited.

11.8 RISK PREDICTION AND RISK ADJUSTMENT

A major element of success in individual health insurance lies in the ability to predict an individual's future claims. A subset of this is the detection and prevention of antiselection. Carriers would also like to be able to have lower than average claims and administrative costs, in order to be able to offer lower premiums to those risks.

For many years, the main tool used by most companies in evaluating and predicting the individual new business risk has been the underwriter. While underwriting has been prohibited for individual major medical coverage subject to the ACA, it remains important for many other individual health coverages. The medical underwriter ("medical" referring to the process the underwriter follows – using medical history and status in the risk evaluation) has tools available for this process, including (typically) a **debit manual**. This is described in detail in Chapter 4, "Managing Antiselection." Debit manuals have gradually evolved, from a purely judgment-based set of relativities, to one based primarily on rigorous analysis of data, with steadily decreasing amounts of judgment used to set relativities.

Debit manuals are actually versions of predictive models – medical profiles, as disclosed on the application and through any ancillary sources, are used to develop a best estimate of the coming year's (or years', depending on the coverage and the conditions) claims. Another such model is experience rating – using an individual's past claim history as a predictor for future claims. (There is a surprising amount of credibility to this measure, contrary to the classical beliefs of some actuaries.)

Over time, many other predictive models have been developed, which are advancing carriers' ability to create an accurate automatic (non-human underwriter) process. Such models often come in three types: (1) diagnosis based risk adjusters, which provide an estimate of the coming year's claims based on the diagnoses coded in the person's recent claim history; (2) prescription based risk adjusters, which provide a similar estimate based on the individual's prescription history; and (3) modified experience rating, where predictions might be made based on a more complex algorithm than simply a factor times the dollars of past claims. There might be, for example, a linear combination of the hospital claim dollars, medical claim dollars, and prescription claim dollars, which provides a higher degree of predictive accuracy than another method.

A number of commercially available risk adjusters have been periodically evaluated in studies funded by the Society of Actuaries.[10] More recently, there has been growing interest in predictive models that use alternative data sources (such as electronic medical records or consumer marketing databases) and more advanced statistical and machine learning techniques (such as gradient boosting techniques). For more on this, see Chapter 8.

Two of the best known risk adjusters are the CMS-HCC model used to risk adjust capitation payments from the federal government to Medicare Advantage plans and the HHS-HCC model used to transfer funds between insurers in the ACA markets (both on and off exchange). The HHS-HCC model is described further in Chapter 4. Risk adjusters are also commonly used in a variety of other capitation or pay for performance arrangements (such as managed Medicaid programs or accountable care contracts between insurers and provider systems).

As a result, risk score management (the operational and analytical work needed to ensure that risk scores are accurate and reflect all appropriate diagnoses or other indicators) is now a crucial part of managing many lines of business. Carriers or healthcare providers that do not "keep up with the pack" in terms of the accuracy of their submitted risk adjustment data will tend to be undercompensated for the true risk of their population, with potentially significant financial consequences. At its simplest, this analysis might involve using prescription drug or other data sources to identify members with potentially missing diagnosis codes who are then flagged for medical record review. Much more complex algorithms are also being used.

Insurers are still working to find optimal predictive models, and link them to their underwriting (where permitted), rating, and (for group insurance)

---

[10] The most recent as of this writing is the following, although the SOA also just released a request for proposals to perform an updated study in 2015. "A Comparative Analysis of Claims-Based Tools for Health Risk Assessment," by Ross Winkelman, FSA, MAAA and Syed Mehmud, published by the Society of Actuaries, April, 2007, www.soa.org

rerating algorithms. A part of this challenge will be to optimally integrate these predictive models with existing underwriting methods.

One other common use of such predictive models is in identifying candidates who would benefit from disease management programs. Such programs can be most useful in preventing certain chronic illnesses (such as diabetes and asthma) from worsening, by the use of good disease management. Predictive models are ideal for this purpose.

Finally, predictive modeling is commonly used as one part of analyzing the relative efficiency of different healthcare providers (in order to adjust for the differing morbidity loads of their panels of patients). This can be a crucial part of designing a narrower network product with an attractive price point, even if the provider is not taking on financial risk.

Predictive modeling is still a rapidly advancing field of practice, and will likely transform many aspects of insurance as it matures. Insurers are well advised to stay abreast of changes in this area, or risk being significantly outpaced by their competitors.

11.9 THE PRODUCT DEVELOPMENT AND MANAGEMENT PROCESSES

A product development process generally begins with a core idea for the product. The product development process, if done correctly, takes this core idea and turns it into a fully developed product concept.

A company will involve a collection of internal, and possibly external, experts, to address all important aspects of the development. This expertise will include all operational areas of the company. Most often, the marketing area is responsible for managing the product development process. Ideas are generated over time and accumulated within the company, and typically gathered up for discussion at the time the new product is being conceptualized. Sometimes regulatory changes drive or require new product development, such as insurers' rapid development of new ACA-compliant products to be sold on and off the public insurance exchanges in 2014.

If the product involves a major change in direction for the company, they may choose to use outside advisors to help develop the first version of the policy, even if they later plan on developing revisions in-house. If the product is only the latest revision in an ongoing series of policies, the company most likely has sufficient expertise in-house to keep the product up to date.

All aspects of selling, administering, and maintaining the policy come into play in the product development process. Benefits and other policy provisions can only be finalized when the corresponding price tag is known. This process is typically an iterative one. ("Oh, the price goes up too much with that new benefit package, so let's try this other one, instead.")

There are actually two price tags to consider. The first is the premium rate to be charged for the coverage. The second is the cost to the insurer to implement and administer the new policy. Both have their impact on the new product.

A new product is typically only one product out of an array that the company offers. The product design must then fit well into the overall strategic marketing plan.

The product development process is where a critical element of effective management comes to play – the feedback loop. In particular, appropriate and detailed monitoring of prior product experience is a crucial input to the successful design of new products.

11.10 IN SUMMARY

There are specific expertises that have historically been shown to be necessary for the successful management of individual health insurance. Many of those expertises are different than the ones needed for group health insurance management. There are also additional skills and knowledge currently being added to the mix, which will challenge carriers in all lines of business.

Each coverage requires its own knowledge base and expertise for success. Medical coverages require dealing with the impact of duration and inflationary trends, as well as the unfolding changes and many challenges related to healthcare reform. DI and LTC require dealing with long-term claim management and measurement.

Writing and managing these coverages involves working with many factors, and is higher risk than many other coverages. Much can (and does) go wrong, so it is critical to identify these sources of risk, monitor them, and correct for them when necessary.

As the implementation of the Affordable Care Act continues, we are entering an unprecedented era of both risk and opportunity for individual health insurers. Actuaries have a key role to play in helping insurers navigate these uncharted and sometimes stormy waters, and helping to ensure the financial stability of the market as a whole.

INDEX

1985 Commissioners' Individual Disability-C (85CIDC) table 248
85CIDA table 248

Accidental Death and Dismemberment 96, 290
Accountable care organizations 14
Accrued 213
Active purchaser model 17
Activities of daily living (ADL) 4, 70-75
Actual to expected (A:E) 190, 208, 232, 337
Actuarial Control Cycle 88
Actuarial Opinion and Memorandum (AOMR) 254, 258, 275
Actuarial Standards Board 252, 258, 260
Actuarial Standards of Practice 161, 260, 369
Actuarial value 41, 147, 186, 294
Actuarial value calculator 41, 186
Adjusted capital 282, 284, 291-292
Administration
  claims 381-389
  policy 380-381
Admitted assets 266
Advance notice 60
Affinity level 379
Affordable Care Act (ACA) 7, 61
  antiselection 140-160
  compliant, non-compliant 144
  major medical lifecycle 412-413
  multi-state plan 371
  rate filing justification 365
  rate review 364
Age banding 164
Agents
  captive 25, 384
  general 374
  managing general 15
Allowed charges 31
Alternate Plan of Care (APC) 75
American Institute of Certified Public Accountants (AICPA) 259-260, 265
America's Health Insurance Plans (AHIP) 10
Announcement 60
Anticipated loss ratio (ALR) 330
Antiselection
  ACA 140-160
  acuity 133
  cumulative 23, 111, 129-140
  durational 129-132
  external 82, 110, 111-127
  internal 111, 127-129, 134
  models 132-140
  upon lapse 129-132
Appointed actuary 254
Appraisals 294, 306
Asset adequacy analysis 254
Asset share 206-211
Asset share model 203, 299, 306
Assignment of benefits 383
Assisted living facility (ALF) 74-75
Associations 16-20
Attachment point 149
Attained age 220
Attained age rating 164

419

Attending physician's statement (APS) 114
Authorized Control Level (ACL) 282, 401
Auto-correlative 321
Average Size Claim Method 251

Balance billing 31
Balanced Budget Act of 1997 52, 56
Baucus Amendment 21, 51, 323, 350
Benchmark plan 40
Benefit limit 5, 76
Benefit period (BP) 64
Benefit triggers 71
Billed charges 31
Block rating 203-204
Blue Cross/Blue Shield (BCBS) 5, 12-14
Bona Fide Associations 19-20
Bonus payments 59
Box-Jenkins ARIMA 322
Broker 16
Brokerage 375
Build-up 179-180
Business overhead expense 69, 70
Business protection coverage 69-70
Buy-down effect 128

Canada 22, 258, 263-265
Captive agents 374
Care management services 75
Case reserves 252
Cash basis 213
Cash benefit plan 74
Cash flow testing 255
Catastrophic Medical 36
Cause 49
Center for Medicare and Medicaid Services (CMS) 56-62, 152, 359
Churning 378
Claim Adjustment Expense or Claim Administration Expense (CAE) 209
Claim administrator 384
Claim Cost Method 246-247

Claim costs 195-196, 202-204, 315-316
Claim examiner 384
Claim reserves 238-252, 272-273
Claim reserve methods
  average size claim 251
  claim cost 246-247
  formula 251
  regression 251
  seriatim case reserves 252
  tabular 248-251
  triangulation 239-246
Clearinghouse model 17
Closed block 203
COBRA 50
Cognitive impairment 72
Coinsurance 31
Coinsurance rate 149
Combined ratio 330
Commercial carriers 362
Commissions 376
Community rating 163, 357
Company action level 291
Completion factors 242
Comprehensive Major Medical (CMM) 6, 13, 29-30, 35, 168-174
Conditionally renewable 63, 93
Confidence intervals 398-400
Consolidated Omnibus Budget Reconciliation Act of 1986 (COBRA) 50, 355-356
Consumer directed plans 38
Continuance, Continuation functions *See* Density functions
Contract of adhesion 87
Conversion 354
Conversion contract 354
CO-OP 14
Copays 34
Cost of capital 210
Cost of living adjustments 67
Cost sharing 30
Cost sharing limit 41
Covered expenses 29
Covered services 29, 74-75

Credibility 332
Critical illness 3, 48-49
Cumulative Antiselection (CAST)
 23, 111, 129-140, 403-410

Debit manuals 119-120, 414
Deductibles 30
Deemer 325, 338
Deferrable expenses 229
Deferred Acquisition Cost (DAC)
 229, 265
Deferred premium asset 218
Deficiency reserves 252-253
Defined standard plan 57
Density functions 179-180, 182
Dental coverage 80-83
Department of Health and Human
 Services (HHS) 152, 359
Desk review 60
Deterministic models 134, 294, 300
Development method 239
Direct marketing 16
Direct marketing company 379
Direct subsidy 59
Disability 63
 partial 65
 recurring 66
 residual 66
 total 64-65, 70
Disability buyout 69-70
Disability income (DI) 1, 62-69, 248
Disability model - LTC 74
Disablement 63
Discount rates 335-336
Discretionary Group Trusts 20
Distributable earnings 306
Distribution Channels 15-16
Dread Disease 48-49
Durational antiselection 129-132
Durational deterioration limitation
 period 168, 231, 408, B-15

Earned/incurred loss ratio 213, 329
Earned premium 156, 189, 289
Elasticity factor (EF) 138

Elimination period (EP) 47, 63-64, 73
Elimination period effect 64
Embedded value based statements 217
Employer mandate 142
End stage renal disease (ESRD) 57
Enhanced benefit plans 57
Enterprise risk management 282
Entry age rating 164
Essential health benefits (EHBs) 40
Exchanges 7
Exclusions 99
Expenses 200, 211, 316
Experience rating 414
Explanation of benefits (EOB) 389
Extension of Benefits (EOB) 80
External antiselection 82, 110-127, 140

Federally facilitated exchange (FFE) 17
File and use 325, 338
Financial Accounting Standards Board
 (FASB) 216
Financial model 293
Five-star quality rating 59
Formula Method 251
Formulary 34
Free reserves 318
Fundamental pricing 161, 174-188

GAAP reserves 216, 230, 257
General agent (GA) 374-375
Generally Accepted Accounting
 Principles (GAAP) 216, 226, 230, 258
Genetic Information
 Nondiscrimination Act of 2008 52
Genetic testing 121
Geographic area 173
Going concern basis 266
Grace period 98
Grandfathered policies 14, 144
Grandmothered plans 145
Granularity 297
Gross premium 202-211
Gross unearned premium reserve
 (gross UPR) 217
Group conversion 49-50, 277

Group Health Insurance Mandatory
 Conversion Privilege Model Act 355
Group wraparound 68
Guaranteed availability 112
Guaranteed issue 112
Guaranteed insurability 67
Guaranteed Renewable (GR) 62-63,
 92-93

Habilitative 41
Health Insurance Portability and
 Accountability Act (HIPAA) 7, 71,
 92-93, 107, 116, 119, 124, 356, 370
Health Maintenance Organization
 (HMO) 34, 38, 104, 323, 361
Health Policy 22-27
Health Savings Account (HSA) 7, 26,
 39, 383
HHS-HCC model 152
Hierarchical condition category
 (HCC) 152
High Deductible Health Plan
 (HDHP) 39
High Risk Pool 12, 37, 107-108
Home and community-based care
 74-76
Hospice care 75
Hospital Indemnity plans 47
Hurdle rate 317

Incurral dating 382
Incurred claims 188, 213, 214, 245-
 247, 271
Indemnity 47, 63, 74
Independent Marketing Organization
 (IMO) 16
Individual Accident and Health Rate
 Filing Guidelines 21
Individual Health (IH) 1
Individual Health Rate Filing Task
 Force (RFTF) 23-25, 370, Appendix
 B, Appendix C
Individual mandate 142
Individual medical pool 25
Inflation protection 76

Inside limits 5
Inspection reports 116
Insurer of last resort 12
Intensive Care Unit 47
Interblock subsidy
 durational pooling 25
 rate compression 25
Internal Antiselection 110-111, 127-
 129, 134
Internal limits 33
International Accounting Standards
 Board (IASB) 217
International Financial Reporting
 Standards (IFRS) 217
Issue age 220
Issue age rating *See* entry age rating

Jurisdiction 326

Kaiser Family Foundation 9
Keyperson insurance 69

Leveraging 196-197
Liability 214
Life insurance reserve 267
Lifetime loss ratio 330
Limitations 99
Limited Benefit Medical Coverages
 46-49
Limits
 benefit 76
 internal 33
 maximum 32
 out of pocket 32
Long Term Care (LTC) 4, 70-80, 96-
 97, 104, 110, 248, 260, 275, 315, 352,
 374
Loss Adjustment Expense (LAE) 209
Loss Ratio 246
 anticipated 330
 combined 330
 earned 331, 394
 guarantees 338-340
 minimum anticipated 329, 333

minimum at renewal 340
paid 329
Loss recognition 254

Major Medical *See* Comprehensive Major Medical
Managed Care Plans 14, 56, 181
Managing General Agents (MGA) 15
Mandatory control level 292
Market reform 370-371
Marketing 378
Marketplaces 17
Markov processes 135-136
Material misrepresentation 124, 126
Maximum cap 149
Maximum Limits 32
McCarran-Ferguson Act 323
Mean Value Theorem 220
Meaningful difference 42
Medical
  catastrophic 36
  comprehensive major (CMM) 6, 13, 29-30, 35, 168-174
  limited benefit 46-49
  savings accounts 38-39
  short term 36
  underwriting 112
Medical Information Bureau (MIB) 115
Medical loss ratios 330
Medical Savings Accounts 38
Medicare Advantage 8, 55-62, 329, 359, 412
  bid process 60
Medicare Advantage Organization (MAO) 56
Medicare Benefits 51-56
Medicare Cost plans 56
Medicare Improvements for Patients and Providers Act (MIPPA) 52
Medicare Modernization Act (MMA) 51, 56
Medicare Part D 51, 56, 256, 274
Medicare Part D Plan Sponsors 56

Medicare Supplement 6, 13, 15, 51-55, 104, 123-124, 273, 350, 388
Medigap 51
MedSupp 51, 55
Mental Health Parity and Addiction Equity Act of 2008 (MHPAEA) 33
Metal level 11, 42
Micro-simulation models 299
Minimum anticipated loss ratio (MALR) 329
Minimum essential coverage 142
Minimum medical loss ratio, federal 345
Minimum value 41
Minimum value calculator 147
Minnesota Antiselection Model (MNAM) 133
Model cells 293
Modeling tools 234
Models
  agent-based 299
  antiselection 132-140
  asset share 203, 206, 299, 306
  auto-correlative 321-322
  Cumulative Antiselection (CAST) 23-24, 111, 129-140
  deterministic 294, 296, 300
  disability 74
  financial 293
  Minnesota antiselection 133
  parametric 294
  partition 132
  predictive 121, 152, 164, 414-416
  pricing 302
  reserve 299, 304, 308
  robustness 297, 311
  service indemnity 74
  service reimbursement 73
  stochastic 134-135, 294, 300
  validation 309
  windshield 297
Modified community rating 357
Monitoring 305
Monte Carlo simulations 186, 295

NAIC Medicare Supplement Insurance Minimum Standards Model Act 52
National Association of Insurance Commissioners (NAIC) 17, 52, 92, 103-106, 216, 218, 227, 263, 296, Appendix D, Appendix E
Net level premium 220
Networks 30-31, 33
Networks for hire 43
New York Regulation 62 21, 30, Appendix A
Non-Bona Fide Associations 20
Non-Cancelable (non-can) 3, 62, 79
Nonforfeiture benefits 77
Non-participating (non-par) 383
Non-renewable for stated reasons only 63
Normalization 166, 205
Not-for-profits 360-362
Nursing home care 74

OASDI *See* Social Security
Occupation 64-65, 172
Off-exchange 144
Omnibus Budget Reconciliation Act (OBRA) 51, 123, 273, 350, 355, 378
On-exchange 144
Open Enrollment 57-58
Opportunity cost 304
Optionally renewable 63, 93, 335
Out of pocket limits 32
Overinsurance 1, 68, 105
Override 15, 378

Paid loss ratio 329
Partial disability 65
Participating (par) 383
Partition model 132-135
Patient Protection and Affordable Care Act (ACA) 7
Per member per month (PMPM) 181
Personal spending account 38
Pharmacy benefits manager (PBM) 35, 88

Policy form 85
Policy reserves 209, 219-238, 237, 336-338, 353
Preauthorization 82
Predictive models 121, 152, 164, 414-416
Pre-existing conditions 37, 47, 57, 82, 100, 107, 111, 118, 126, 140, 385, 412
Pre-Existing Condition Insurance Plan (PCIP) 37-38
Preferred Provider Organizations (PPO) 43, 184
PPO product 6, 43, 184
   in-network 184
   out-of-network 184
Prefunding 25
Preliminary term reserve method 227
Premium leakage 127
Premium reserves 217-219
Premiums
   gross 202-211
   net 221-222
   waiver of 68
Premium stabilization 141, 148
Prescription drug plan (PDP) 56
Present value (PV) of future profits 211
Pricing methods
   simulation 186-187, 251, 284, 295, 299
   tabular 175-179, 248-252, 304, 397
Privacy 119
Profit 201, 211, 318, 397
Profits released 317
Profits retained 317
Prompt pay 381
Proof of loss 383
Provider network 42
Providers 45
Provision for adverse deviation 265
Public insurance exchanges 17
Pure premium method 246

Qualification period 65
Qualified health plans (QHPs) 17

Rate Filing Task Force *See* Individual Health Rate Filing Task Force
Rate setting process 161
Rating
  block 203-204
  community 22, 163, 357
  entry age 164
  issue age 164, 220
  step 164
  uni-age 165
RBC ratio 401
Reasonable expectations 349
Reasonableness standards 328-356
Rebate 58
Rebate reallocation 61
Recoverability testing 254
Recurring disability 66
Reformation 126
Regression methods 251
Regulatory action level 292
Regulation 18-22, 30, 323-371
Reinstatement 97-99
Reinstatement clause 98
Reinsurance, federal transitional 148
Renewability 62-63
Replacement benefit 69
Replacement ratio 68
Rerating 161, 188-202
Rescission 124, 126
Reserves 213-261
  mean 218
  mid-terminal 218
Reserve bases 234, 257
Reserve types
  claim 238-252, 272-273
  deficiency 252-253
  GAAP 216, 230, 257
  policy 209, 219-238, 237, 336-338, 353
  premium 217-219
  seriatim 252
  statutory 225, 252
  tax 257, 267
  unearned premium 217-218
Residual benefits 65

Residual disability 66
Respite care 75
Return on Equity (ROE) 211
Return on Investment (ROI) 211
Risk adjusters 321
Risk adjustment 148
  ACA, 151
Risk analysis 305
Risk-Based Capital (RBC) 282, 400
Risk-Based Capital for Health Organizations Model Act (HORBC) 282, 290
Risk corridors 148, 156
Risk score 321
Ruin theory 296
Runout 239

Sales and marketing 373-380
Savings 58
Scenario testing 296
Sensitivity testing 296
Seriatim 186
Seriatim case reserves 252
Service fees 378
Service indemnity 74
Service reimbursement 73-74
Shock lapse 313
Short term medical 36-37
Simulation 186-188
Single risk pool, 144, 412
Social insurance supplements 68
Social Security 68
Solvency testing 281-291, 293, 305
Specified illness policy 2-3
State-based exchange (SBE) 17
State Children's Health Insurance Program (SCHIP or CHIP) 7
State partnership exchange (SPE) 17
Statement blank 264
Statement of Financial Accounting Standards (SFAS) 265
Statutory
  blanks, 268-281
  reporting 263

reserves 225, 252
statement 216
Step rating 164
Stochastic models 134-135, 294, 300
Stop loss 32
Subrogation 386

Tabular method 175-179, 248
Tax reserves 257, 267
Tax statement 116
Teleunderwriting 116
Terminal reserve 229
Termination rates 315
Testing
  recoverability 254
  scenario 296
  sensitivity 296
  solvency 281-291, 293, 305
Three R's, the 141, 148
  risk adjustment 148
  risk corridors 148
  transitional reinsurance 148
Tiered 34
Transfer formula 153
Transitional policies 14, 144
Transitional reinsurance 148
Trend test 292
Triangulation method 239-246
Two year full preliminary term (2YFPT) 227

Underwriting
  group 112
  medical 112
  nonmedical 112
  paramedical 112
Underwriting restrictions 358
Underwriting Risk 285
Underwriting tools 113
Unearned premium reserves 217-218
Unfair Claims Settlement Practices Act 381
Uni-age rating 165
Uniform Individual Accident and Sickness Policy Provision Law (UPPL) 98, 104
Uniform Rate Review Template (URRT) 204

Value of Business Acquired (VOBA) 230
Variable deductible 30
Vested 378
Vesting 378
Voluntary insurance 16

Waiting period *See* elimination period
Waiver of premium 68, 99, D-23
Workplace insurance 16
Wraparound 5, 68

APPENDIX A

SECTION 52.7 OF NEW YORK'S REGULATION 62

SECTION 52.7 MAJOR MEDICAL INSURANCE

Major medical insurance is an insurance policy which provides coverage for each covered person, to a maximum of not less than $100,000; copayment by the covered person not to exceed 25 percent; a deductible stated on a per-person, per-family, per-illness, per-benefit period, or per-year basis, or a combination of such bases, not to exceed five percent of the lowest overall maximum limit under the policy, unless the policy is written to complement underlying hospital and medical insurance, in which case such deductible may be increased by the amount of the benefits provided by such underlying insurance, for at least:

(a) daily room and board, as defined in section 52.5(a) of this Part;

(b) miscellaneous hospital services, as defined in section 52.5(b) of this Part; provided, however, that the maximum amount limitation shall not apply;

(c) surgical services, as defined in section 52.6(a) of this Part;

(d) anesthetic services, as defined in section 52.6(b) of this Part;

(e) in-hospital medical services, as defined in section 52.6(c) of this Part;

(f) mental health care consisting of coverage for diagnosis and treatment of mental illness for at least:

    (1) 30 days per year of inpatient care in a hospital as defined by subdivision ten of section 1.03 of the Mental Hygiene Law;

(2) 30 outpatient visits per year at no less than $30 per visit and a yearly maximum of no less than $1,500 with reimbursement for early visits greater than or at least equal to reimbursement for subsequent visits in a facility issued an operating certificate by the Commissioner of Mental Health pursuant to the provisions of article 31 of the Mental Hygiene Law, or in a facility operated by the Office of Mental Health, or by a psychiatrist or psychologist licensed to practice in this State, or a professional corporation thereof; and

(3) outpatient crisis intervention services consisting of at least three psychiatric emergency visits per year. Upon certification, by a licensed mental health care provider whose services are covered under the policy, that a visit was the result of a psychiatric emergency (one where the person appears to have a mental illness for which immediate observation, care and treatment is appropriate and which is likely to result in serious harm to himself or others), benefits for such a visit shall be no less than $60 per visit. However, benefits provided under this paragraph may be used to reduce benefits otherwise payable under paragraph (1) or (2) of this subdivision;

(g) out-of-hospital care, consisting of physicians' services rendered on an ambulatory basis, where coverage is not provided elsewhere in the policy, for diagnosis and treatment of sickness or injury, including the cost of drugs and medications available only on the prescription of a physician, and diagnostic X-ray, laboratory services, radiation therapy, chemotherapy and hemodialysis ordered by a physician; and

(h) prosthetic appliances, meaning artificial limbs or other prosthetic appliances (including replacements thereof which are functionally necessary), and rental or purchase (at insurer's option) of durable medical equipment required for therapeutic use, including repairs and necessary maintenance of purchased equipment, not otherwise provided for under a manufacturer's warranty or purchase agreement.

APPENDIX B

REPORT TO THE NAIC'S A&H WORKING GROUP OF THE LIFE AND HEALTH ACTUARIAL TASK FORCE

Reprinted with permission from American Academy of Actuaries

American Academy of Actuaries

May 13, 2004

To: Julia Philips, Chairperson, NAIC's Accident and Health Working Group and Leslie Jones, Chairperson, NAIC's Life and Health Actuarial Task Force

From: Bill Bluhm, Chairman, American Academy of Actuaries' Rate Filing Task Force

Dear Julia,

I am pleased to send you the enclosed report from our Task Force. After five years and thousands of hours of volunteer work, the American Academy of Actuaries' Rate Filing Task Force is pleased (and relieved) to submit the enclosed, computer model, and documentation, in response to your request.

The Task Force report describes the current situation in the individual health market, and outlines four alternative regulatory solutions to the closed block problem, called Prefunding, Inter-Block Subsidy–Durational Pooling, Inter-Block Subsidy–Rate Compression, and Individual Market Pools. The computer model being presented analyzes the result of each of those closed block solutions.

Several members of the Rate Filing Task Force, including myself, will be present at your meeting in San Francisco on June 11 to present this report in more detail and to answer any questions you may have about it. We thank you for your consideration, and look forward to discussing our findings with you.

This work is intended to be an interim step in re-writing the NAIC's Individual Health Rate Filing Guidelines. It is our expectation that the NAIC will choose a single closed block solution for inclusion in its Rate Filing Guidelines. When that choice has been made, we would be pleased to assist your groups with the drafting of model guidelines or regulations to implement your choice.

Sincerely,

W. F. Bluhm

William F. Bluhm
Chairperson, Rate Filing Task Force American Academy of Actuaries

Cc: Dennis Hare, Mark Peavy

Report to the NAIC's A&H Working Group of the Life and Health Actuarial Task Force

May 12, 2004

By the American Academy of Actuaries' Rate Filing Task Force

Table of Contents

Volume I
Report

Section I. Executive Summary B-7
Section II. Background B-9
Section III. Overview and Global Assumptions B-12
Section IV. Current Market Model B-17
Section V. Discussion of the Sub-Issues B-19
Section VI. New Business Rates and Competition B-21
Section VII. Potential Closed Block Solutions B-22
Individual Medical Pool (IMP) B-24
Prefunding B-26
Inter-block Subsidy – Durational Pooling B-28
Inter-block Subsidy – Rate Compression B-29
Section VIII. Findings and Analysis of Solutions B-31
Section IX. Sensitivity Testing B-51

Appendices
Appendix A: Relevant portions of LHATF's Dec., 2000, meeting minutes: B-53
Appendix B: The Drivers of Rate Increases B-57
Appendix C: Competitive Markets B-59
Appendix D: The Current Marketplace B-62
Individual Major Medical Marketplace Attractiveness Scale B-63
Summary of Current State Individual Major Medical Market Environment B-63
Appendix E: Claim Trend Scenarios B-64
Appendix F: Survey of State Regulatory Environment of Premium
Rates for Individual Major Medical Insurance Policies B-65
Tabulation of Responses From the State Regulatory Environment
Survey of Premium Rates for Individual Major Medical Insurance B-66

Volume II
Model Documentation

Volume III
Detailed Modeling Results

Section I. Executive Summary

In late 1999, the NAIC's Accident and Health Working Group (a subcommittee of its Life and Health Actuarial Task Force, or LHATF), under the leadership of Julia Philips, FSA, MAAA, asked the American Academy of Actuaries for assistance in developing rate filing regulatory methodologies for health insurance products. The Academy subsequently appointed a Task Force, under the leadership of William Bluhm, FSA, MAAA, FCA, to help the NAIC. That task force is called the Health Rate Filing Task Force (RFTF). Its mission is to help redraft the NAIC's *Guidelines for Filing of Rates for Individual Health Insurance Forms*.

The RFTF met a number of times throughout 2000 and 2001 to define the scope of the project and to begin work. As discussion progressed, it became clear that the issues needing to be addressed in the RFTF's work were much larger than a simple rewrite of the NAIC's guidelines. Aside from being simply an update of recommended rate filing techniques and practices, it included two major issues: (1) a proposed solution to the "closed block problem," which we will discuss in greater detail later in this report, and (2) inclusion of elements which would make the individual health market more attractive to insurers.

The RFTF spent much time discussing various potential solutions to the closed block problem. It also sought and received input from LHATF as to the policy goals they viewed as being paramount in any solution. Ultimately, the RFTF concluded that there are four major categories of potential closed block solutions, each of which would require a very different regulation to be drafted in order to implement it.

Therefore, this report to the NAIC is a document presenting two major results to LHATF, with a request for decision:

- It presents four major alternatives intended to help solve the closed block problem, along with a discussion of the advantages and disadvantages of each. If the NAIC decides which solution it prefers, the RFTF can continue its work in drafting a proposed regulatory guideline; and
- It presents the RFTF's thinking on a number of other issues related to rewriting the guidelines. We ask that the NAIC review the proposals contained herein, and, if necessary, provide specific guidance on how they might need to be changed. In this way, we can redirect our work before we commit further resources to a proposal that would be unacceptable.

It is important to note that our work product was designed to respond to a specific charge from LHATF. LHATF members attended our meetings and provided input along the way. The boundaries of our discussion were often determined by those regulators who provided input as to what the acceptable answers might be to various questions the group put to them. For that reason, it should not be assumed that any particular decision regarding the shape of this report are necessarily based on the preferences of either LHATF or RFTF, but represent a merging of the two.

May 12, 2004

Membership of the Task Force

The Task Force was composed of various volunteer members of the American Academy of Actuaries. The meetings also were attended by interested parties. Members of the Task Force were asked to act and speak in an unbiased manner, to provide advice to the NAIC regarding the impact of policy decisions, without advocating any. Each member agreed to do so. Those who decided to pursue a given public policy goal or goals declared themselves as part of the "interested party" group, along with others who decided not to be official Task Force members. In practice, interested parties contributed to our final work product alongside members.

As with any other project, individual members of the Task Force might be viewed as having a potential conflict between the Academy's goal of an unbiased work product and their employers' or other goals. We believe that by making such potential clear through membership status, by being alert to the potential for such conflicts on specific subjects, by having broad representation from competing market segments and geographies, and by fully disclosing and discussing all parts of our work with all members and interested parties (including regulators), we have successfully produced an unbiased work product.

Participants are listed below, along with their status as members, interested parties, or staff:

Members
William F. Bluhm, FSA, MAAA, FCA, Chair
James E. Oatman, FSA, MAAA, FCIA, Vice Chair

Michael S. Abroe, FSA, MAAA
Rowen B. Bell, FSA, MAAA
Karen Bender, ASA, MAAA, FCA
Damian A. Birnstihl, FSA, MAAA
Cecil D. Bykerk, FSA, MAAA
Kenneth L. Clark, FSA, MAAA
Steven M. Dziedzic, FSA, MAAA
Paul R. Fleischacker, FSA, MAAA
James M. Gabriel, ASA, MAAA
John A. Hartnedy, FSA, MAAA
Richard H. Hauboldt, FSA, MAAA
Peter G. Hendee, FSA, MAAA
Steven Kessler, MAAA
Mark E. Litow, FSA, MAAA
Julia T. Philips, FSA, MAAA
Richard J. Ruppel, ASA, MAAA
Daryl M. Schrader, FSA, MAAA
Martha M. Spenny, ASA, MAAA
Roderick E. Turner, FSA, MAAA
Thomas F. Wildsmith, FSA, MAAA
Jerome Winkelstein, FSA, MAAA

Interested Parties
Timothy I. Martin, FSA, MAAA
Bernard Rabinowitz, FSA, MAAA, FCIA, FIA
Randi Reichel
Diane R. Seaman, FSA, MAAA
David A. Shea, Jr., FSA, MAAA
Thomas J. Stoiber, FSA, MAAA
Ronora E. Stryker, ASA, MAAA
John F. Troy, JD

Staff
Joanna Ossinger, MPP, HIA

Particular Thanks

The chairman would like to particularly thank Messrs. Wildsmith, Hauboldt, Birnstihl, and Turner, for their extraordinary personal commitment to this project, which was evidenced by their enormous time commitment.

May 12, 2004

Section II. Background

The NAIC's current rate filing guideline ("Guidelines for Filing of Rates for Individual Health Insurance Forms") was adopted in 1980, with amendments in 1983.

As health care rate reform has attempted to address consumer-oriented concerns such as portability, the individual major medical marketplace has, in general, been subject to much less reform than the small group market. One of the major issues in this market is the relatively large size of rate increases relative to trend. Often the cause of this is attributed to what has become commonly labeled as the "closed block problem." No completely satisfactory solution has yet been found for this problem, although recently individual states have used various regulatory techniques in an attempt to address the issue.

Another underlying cause of large rate increases may be the differential between medical trend and wage growth. This difference affects consumer affordability and can result in high lapses causing adverse selection and consequently higher rate increases. The models in this report do not address this overall issue of affordability. The drivers of rate increases are discussed in Appendix B.

In presenting the analysis, the task force is not advocating for any particular approach among the four described, nor does the task force believe that any approach is preferable from the standpoint of any individual company. The task force is not advocating, directly or indirectly, for any approach that would unreasonably limit companies' ability to make competitive market decisions or to compete effectively in the marketplace.

The Closed Block Problem

It is a commonly observed practice of the current individual health insurance market that an insurer will periodically "close" a block of business (meaning they will no longer issue new business in that pool of policies). There can be many reasons for closing a block of business. Regardless of why a block of business is closed, that block will typically experience claim costs rising more rapidly than would a block that was still open. If the insurer raises premiums at an equally rapid rate, policyholders may find it difficult to keep their policies in force due to the increased cost, which is a particular problem for those who have developed serious health conditions and are unable to find new policies. If the insurer does not continue to raise rates, then claims will eventually exceed premiums, and the resulting losses must be funded from some other source (such as premiums on other blocks of business, reserves established in earlier years, or company surplus).

Whether a block is open or closed, each year a substantial number of existing policyholders typically reconsider whether they should keep their existing policies in force. This process tends to be biased against the block, because standard insureds are more likely than impaired insureds to find less expensive coverage elsewhere, or to decide that the benefits they are likely to receive no longer justify the cost of coverage. As a result, lapse rates for standard insureds tend to be significantly higher than those for individuals who have become impaired. This is described as antiselection at lapse, and the cumulative impact of this over time is known as Cumulative Antiselection (CAST). This happens when a portion of standard policyholders (who can easily pass underwriting under another company's standards for new business) leave the closed block, resulting in a greater portion of impaired policyholders (who have greater trouble finding coverage) maintaining their coverage in the closed block.

Because there are no new entrants to a closed block, experience in the closed block often worsens over time, leading to relatively large rate increases. This typically happens in cases where rate increases are based on the experience of that closed block only, rather than on multiple blocks, including currently sold business. Larger rate increases, in turn, raise the level of antiselection at lapse by further increasing the financial incentive for standard individuals to shop for more attractive prices or drop coverage. This increased antiselection leads to even higher rate increases. This process is known variously as a "premium rate spiral," "death spiral," or "antiselection spiral." In some cases, a point of equilibrium may be reached, where most of the policyholders who are inclined to change coverage have already done so, and experience and premium levels may stabilize, albeit at levels higher than would be typical for an open block of policies. In other cases, the process may continue indefinitely, leading to a situation where only the sickest policyholders remain covered, paying very high premiums, with no standard policyholders in the block to subsidize costs.

The claim costs experienced in individual insurance tend to initially be relatively low, then rise dramatically over time. This is due to the effect of initial underwriting, including possibly an initial pre-existing condition period as well as due to the CAST effect described above.

This market is very price sensitive. Insurers can charge the lowest prices by charging premium rates which mirror the increasing nature of claim costs over time. This results in relatively low initial rates followed by sizeable rate increases. To the extent insurers follow this philosophy, the CAST effect is magnified, increasing the likelihood of an antiselection spiral.

The RFTF feels that this evolution of the marketplace, combined with the current regulatory approach, have encouraged the closed block problem. In many cases, it is very difficult for insurers to keep rates at a level adequate to cover the losses caused by this rating spiral.

For purposes of this report, this dilemma in the current marketplace is what we refer to as the 'closed block problem.'

LHATF's Goal:

During its discussions, the RFTF determined that, in order for the Task Force to be able to help the NAIC in its redrafting goal, the NAIC needed to prioritize its public policy goals behind the request. We asked for and received guidance from LHATF, in the form of their top three policy goals, in order of priority: (1) rate stability over time, (2) consumer choice, and (3) disclosure. Further descriptive material is included as Appendix A of this report, which includes the relevant portions of the A&H Working Group's minutes from the applicable meeting.

LHATF also asked the RFTF to identify and propose changes in the rate filing guidelines that might make the individual major medical marketplace more attractive to insurers, without compromising the public policy goals. This report addresses one such change (Section V). We intend to address this more fully in our subsequent work.

May 12, 2004

Other Considerations

Many other public policy considerations were discussed by the Task Force as it developed these alternative solutions to the closed block problem. In many cases, results associated with these solutions will not create ideal solutions to the regulators' goals described above. As is often the case, the regulators' dilemma will be to balance these solutions optimally.

Our work included measurement of a variety of statistics which might be used by regulators in evaluating the efficacy of various closed block solutions.

Representative Market

The work of the task force was focused on modeling the relative impact of alternative regulatory approaches– not on measuring the impact that any particular state, or even the average state, would experience if a particular approach were adopted. The diversity and complexity of state specific market and rating rules (see Appendices D and F) precluded any effort to model state-specific results, or even results for an "average" state. While a baseline "current market" model was developed as a point of comparison for the various alternatives, it is a representative approximation of the current rating environment in states that have not enacted comprehensive individual market reforms. This current market baseline illustrates some of the important dynamics seen in today's markets – particularly those relevant to the closed block problem - but ignores other important factors, such as the federal Health Insurance Portability and Accountability Act of 1996 (HIPAA), guaranteed issue rules, and the prevalence of state high-risk pools. The presence of these, and any state reform efforts such as guaranteed issue, community rating, or rate band rules, must be taken into account in interpreting these results and evaluating their relevance for any particular state.

Scope

Our work is designed to study and apply to individual major medical policies. By this, we mean insurance contracts made directly between the carrier and the individual. It is not intended to apply to plans other than major medical plans, such as those for Medicare Supplement, Limited Benefit, Hospital Indemnity, Critical Illness, Long Term Care, Dental, or Vision plans. In some cases, major medical plans sold to individuals take the legal form of group master policies in which certificates of insurance are issued to individuals instead of policies. Our work could be applied to these types of plans, as well as to true individual policies.

In our modeling, we have assumed that all legal entities in a state (insurance companies, HMOs, Blues plans, and others) would follow the same set of rules in each state under each of these methods. Other situations would create different environments, requiring a different analysis.

We warn strongly that these results were modeled to take into consideration only policies issued after enactment of these solutions. We have not modeled the effect of in force policies on the results. These transition impacts will need to be addressed to fully understand how these solutions would work, including, possibly, additional modeling.

Section III. Overview and Global Assumptions

In order to evaluate alternative solutions to the closed block problem, a financial model was developed. The model is not intended to be a pricing model for a given policy form. The intent of the model is to provide a means to compare the financial implications of the alternative solutions to current market behavior. In addition, and most importantly, the model results should be viewed as a relative basis for comparing one method to another.

The Current Market Model provides an overview of the average behavior of the carriers in the market and is not intended to model the experience of any particular carrier. In fact individual carriers will have experience varying from the average based upon each carrier's underwriting, marketing, pricing, network arrangements, managed care activities and claim adjudication practices. The RFTF believes that these individual variances in experience and practice do not distort the validity of the Current Market Model's representation of the market as a whole.

The following points summarize the key components, assumptions, and structure of the model:

- It is a prospective view from the effective date of implementation of a particular closed block solution through the 30th year after the original effective date;
- A policy form or group of policy forms is assumed to be open for new sales for a three year period (an 'era'), and then it is subsequently replaced by another policy form or group of policy forms;
- Five such policy eras were modeled. New policies are thus issued for the first 15 years of the 30 year model;
- The insured population was divided between 'standard' and 'impaired' segments. They were modeled separately, and then were combined to show the total experience;
- As new business rates change over time, both in absolute dollars and relative to other insurers in the market, sales levels are assumed to change inversely;
- Covered claim costs increase each year based on trend and deductible leveraging. (Deductible leveraging is an acknowledged phenomenon where observed claim trend is higher than the underlying cost trend due to having a fixed deductible applied to trended costs.) Claim costs do not include cost containment expenses as defined by the NAIC;
- Lapse rates are adjusted based upon the level of the rate increase implemented, as well as the absolute level of the resulting premium. Larger than expected rate increases and larger premiums can increase lapse rates, and lower rate increases can reduce lapse rates; and
- Effective rate increases (the increases actually experienced by the block) will be lower than requested rate increases (those calculated as needed), due to regulatory limits and constraints. This effect is assumed to be more pronounced on larger rate increases.

The baseline for comparisons is called the Current Market Model. This is a projection of premium, claims, expenses, enrollment, and other key variables based on a set of global assumptions and a premium rate calculation that we believe to be common. The Current Market Model was constructed to represent what is currently happening in the individual market in general (but, again, is not intended to represent any particular state).

Each of the potential solutions to the closed block problem has its own model. For consistency in comparing the output of these models and the Current Market Model, the same set of global assumptions is used for each. These assumptions are not necessarily reflective of conditions at any particular company, nor are they intended to suggest any particular set of conditions to which insurers should conform their operations. Rather, these assumptions are used for illustrative purposes only, recognizing that individual insurers' circumstances can and will differ, perhaps significantly, from the assumptions the task force selected. In addition, each closed block solution's model may contain some specific assumptions that are unique to it, some of which modify portions of the global assumptions.

Global Assumptions

These assumptions recognize the following list of key global forces and parameters common to all spreadsheets. Rigorous definitions for all variables are contained in Volume II of this report, entitled "Documentation." For some of the major assumptions, a separate discussion is provided in this section of the report immediately following the discussion of the Current Market Model.

At a conceptual level, it is important to understand that the models first mimic the original rate calculation done by an insurer in setting rates. These assumptions produce an initial premium rate which is a starting value for the projection. The assumptions used in developing the starting premium rate do not necessarily match the assumptions used in the projection, which is intended to model emerging experience that will naturally vary from original assumptions.

- Claim Trend – Premium Rates

    This assumption reflects the claim trend used in the initial premium rate development of each block of business. Claim trend assumptions reflect the underlying base trend, deductible leveraging trend, and the impact of benefit reductions or "buy-downs".

    The initial premium rates for each block of business are based on a level claim trend rate assumption of 12%. No fluctuations in the claim trend rate are anticipated when a new product is being priced. This 12% trend assumption assumes the actuaries pricing the product have gone through an analysis of trend which matches the analysis described elsewhere in this report.

- Premium Rate Increases

    Premium rate increases are applied to both new business premiums and renewal premiums for a given era's block of policies. The first rate increase is based on the expected claim trend in the first renewal year, since sufficient experience is not available in time to influence it. After the first rate increase for a policy form, future premium rate increases are based on actual claims experience and reflect the most recent actual claim trend pattern.

- Claim Trend - Actual Claims

    This assumption allows us to test various scenarios of how actual trend might unfold over the projection period of the model. As described above, these claim trends are different than the trend assumed in the initial rate computation. Claim trend assumptions reflect the underlying base trend, deductible leveraging trend, and the impact of commonly observed voluntary benefit reductions or "buy-downs".

- Interest Rate

    This assumption is used as the discount rate to calculate an initial premium rate in each spreadsheet.

- Target Lifetime Loss Ratio

    A target lifetime loss ratio is chosen for purposes of initial premium rate development in all but the Prefunding model (described later in this report). In that model, a target is not used directly, but intended to be met via other means of calculating premium that is intended to be equivalent.

- Maximum Allowable Loss Ratio

    A maximum allowable experience loss ratio for any one year, used for purposes of renewal rate increases.

- Initial Claim Cost Level – Standard Lives and Impaired Lives

    Distinct claim cost level assumptions for the first year of each block for standard and impaired lives.

- Base Lapse Rates – Standard Lives

    This assumption reflects the underlying annual lapse rates for standard lives before the impact of rate increases in excess of claim trend and aging, as well as other adjustments described below.

- Base Lapse Rates – Impaired Lives

    This assumption reflects the underlying annual lapse rates for impaired lives before the impact of rate increases in excess of claim trend and aging as well as other adjustments described below.

- Adjustments to Base Lapse Rates Adjustments to base rates are made in the following situations:

    – premium rates change at a different rate than the actual claim trend;
    – the ratio of the company's renewal premium rate to the market new business premium is other than 1.0 (this applies only to standard lives' base lapse rates);
    – the ratio of the company's initial premium rate to the reference premium rate is other than 1.0 (this applies only to standard lives' base lapse rates).

    However; the composite adjustments from all sources are limited such that no annual lapse rate shall be less than 15% or greater than 80% for standard lives, or less than 5% or greater than 50% for impaired lives.

- Reference Premium

    Defines the aggregate level of premium that exists in today's market. Over time, market rates may move away from the reference premium rate as the model causes them to separate. For example, if a new model law causes an abrupt change in the average market rate, a portion of the difference from the reference premium rate is used to adjust lapse rates as noted above in the adjustments to base lapse rates.

- Rate of Impairment

    This assumption reflects the net migration from standard to impaired status from one year to the next.

- Durational Deterioration Limitation Period (DDLP)

    This durational period is used in the initial pricing calculation, to reflect the period of time within which the insurers' pricing model portrays deterioration of overall claim costs by duration. This reflects the limited way in which durational deterioration is recognized in today's rate practices. It also determines the time period after which the pricing recognizes no variation in persistency between standard and impaired lives.

    The term "durational deterioration limitation period" was coined for this report; it is not standard actuarial nomenclature. The DDLP is an important parameter in our model. It represents a common aspect of individual medical pricing that is not always explicitly recognized by the pricing actuary.

- Aging

    This assumption models the increase in claim costs and premium rates due to annual increases in attained age of the insured block.

- Durational Rate Increases

    This assumption reflects a pricing practice which has automatic increases in premium rates due to duration, in addition to annual attained age and claim trend rate increases. The model generates additional lapses due to such increases.

- Production Assumptions

    Production reflects underlying uniform sales volumes adjusted for market and carrier price sensitivity.

- Expenses and commissions

    The assumptions reflect commissions paid on initial policy premium, but not on rate increases.

- RBC levels and the cost of capital

    The models estimate the amount of capital which will be held by insurers, as a flat 24% of premium. A separate assumption is made for the opportunity cost of capital (the difference between what that money *could* be earning vs. what it earns as conservatively invested assets in an insurers general fund). The opportunity cost is currently set at five percent. These are both global assumptions common to all of the models. (This should not be confused with the separate, global interest rate assumption, which is only used to calculate net present values for summarizing the results of each model.)

    To calculate the opportunity cost of capital, each of the models calculates target capital and surplus held each year, and the net opportunity cost of that capital. The Prefunding model also reflects a portion of the Prefunding reserve when modeling the cost of capital. The reserve margin is currently set at 10 percent. Because "natural" reserves (reserves calculated with no margin or modifications) are assumed to be funded out of premiums, and ultimately go to pay claims, they are not treated as capital. The margin on the reserves, however, is treated as an additional capital requirement for the block, and is added to the RBC when calculating the opportunity cost of capital. Considered over the lifetime of a policy, reserve margins are not funded out of premiums, but are in the nature of a loan; the margin set up in early years (reducing earnings in those years) is released back into the profit stream at later durations.

- Regulatory dampening of rate increases and maximum rate increase levels

  Rate increases actually approved and implemented are assumed to be less than those filed, due to restrictions placed on rate increase levels in the current regulatory environment.

Sensitivity testing of the model, described in detail later in this report, involves varying the global assumptions to determine what effect they have on the results. With respect to the actual future claim trend assumption, we tested multiple alternative trend scenarios, both in terms of level and pattern. See Section IX for additional details.

Section IV. Current Market Model

This spreadsheet contains the financial model describing today's market. The assumptions in the model were chosen by task force members to reflect realistic levels based on historical information and observations within the individual health insurance industry. Individual insurers' circumstances will undoubtedly differ from those modeled in the spreadsheet.

Initial premium rates are set to achieve a target lifetime loss ratio (assuming an illustrative target loss ratio). After the first renewal (when rates are set on expected trend), rates are assumed to be recalculated based on an actual-to-expected analysis. Expected loss ratios are based on the durational loss ratio patterns which formed the basis of initial pricing, and are not adjusted to reflect past deviations from expected levels.

The first era of policies is assumed to be issued evenly over three years. Subsequent eras of policies are modeled in a similar manner, with initial premium rates based on the market new business premium rate level, which is based on actual emerging claim trend levels. A key characteristic of the Current Market Model is that the rates for each era are modeled independently, without regard to the experience of the other eras.

Appendix E lists the various trend scenarios used to "stress test" each of the models. Our baseline trend scenario was the one called "Medium", which is a constant claim trend over time. The results of the tests are described in Section IX, Sensitivity Testing.

Detailed Discussion of Major Assumptions

- Overall Average Claim Trend Assumptions

    The starting point in developing the overall average claim trend assumption was the historical mean change in the Medical CPI for the period 1970 to 2000. This change averaged 7% per year. To reflect typical health insurance experience, the Medical CPI must be adjusted for a number of factors including: different medical services included in the Medical CPI versus those typically included in a health insurance product; changes in claim utilization patterns; cost shifting; medical technology; leveraging of medical costs due to deductibles, co-payments and maximum out-of-pocket limits; and benefit plan changes over time. These were estimated to be an additional 5% above the overall Medical CPI average claim trend of 7%, for a total claim trend of about 12%. The overall average claim trend of 12% does not include the impacts of aging and the wear-off of underwriting selection over time.

- Claim Trends-Actual Claims

    As mentioned above, the baseline projection assumes a constant claim trend. This is shown in Appendix E, Claim Trend Scenarios, and labeled Medium, a level 12% annual trend rate per year. Cyclical claim trend patterns, such as those described as Cyclic A and Cyclic B, are representative of typical cycles of trends seen historically. Running the model with Cyclic A and Cyclic B demonstrate the effects of implementing these closed block solutions at different points in the cycle.

May 12, 2004

- Standard vs. Impaired Claim Cost Assumption

  A certain portion of insured lives is assumed to become impaired after issue. Impaired lives are assumed to have an average morbidity cost about four times that of standard risk lives. The proportion of standard versus impaired lives changes over time based on lapse rates that vary for standard and impaired lives. Standard lives have higher lapse rates than impaired lives. Also, in each year there is a net transfer of policies from a standard to an impaired status. Initially, no impaired lives are assumed. This assumption would not be true in states that impose HIPAA guarantee issue requirements on the individual market.

- Persistency Assumption

  The Current Market Model, which we sometimes refer to as the baseline scenario, assumes an annual lapse rate that varies by the policy year since issue (duration), by standard and impaired lives, and the following three relationships:

  - The difference in the premium rate change versus the actual claim trend;
  - The ratio of renewal premium rate to market new business rate (this applies only to base lapse rates for standard lives);
  - The ratio of initial premium rate to reference premium rate (this applies only to base lapse rates for standard lives).

  However; the composite adjustments due to these relationships are limited such that no annual lapse rate shall be less than 15% or greater than 80% for standard lives, or less than 5% or greater than 50% on impaired lives.

  The functional relationship of lapse rate to these three variables was based upon the combined expertise of the authors of this report.

- Other Assumptions

  Other assumptions typically made for pricing of individual policies were made in a simplified manner for modeling purposes, but did not vary by model. These are based on typical assumptions readily verifiable by information often available in actuarial memoranda filed with DOIs.

Section V. Discussion of the Sub-Issues

Early in our discussion of how to address the major issues of the 'closed block' problem, we realized how important it would be to at least recognize the series of underlying issues that may cause us difficulty in arriving at a clear-cut solution. Any model legislation or regulation that may ultimately result from the work here of the RFTF may also have to address these underlying, but important issues. Consequently, we discuss them here.

We group our discussion of the sub-issues into three major categories: actuarial, industry, and consumer issues.

Actuarial Issues

- Should the numerator be net of changes in policy reserve in the reported loss ratio? Current guidelines indicate that the numerator of the loss ratio calculation be stated before adjustment for contract reserves (including durational reserves). While such an approach does avoid the risk of potential manipulation (not seen as a significant long term risk by the RFTF), it may be counter to the NAIC's primary goal of rate stability. This is because the use of unadjusted claims figures tends to cause an increasing durational loss ratio.
- Should the reported loss ratio include certain cost containment expenses? LHATF has already addressed this issue, and agreed conceptually to the inclusion of such expenses within the numerator of the loss ratio.
- Can past losses be recovered, up to the lifetime loss ratio (which reflects past and anticipated future experience), or must the future loss ratio match the originally anticipated loss ratio over the same period? This would seem to be a public policy question, as each of the options implies a separate public policy standard.
- What are parameters for assessing credibility of a block's experience? How can theoretically sound credibility rules be structured so that there is consistency among states?

Industry Issues

- If a closed block solution requires insurers to establish additional contract reserves, such reserves should be deductible for federal income tax purposes. Lack of tax deductibility would create substantial incentive for insurers to minimize these reserves, making the prefunding method problematic.
- The framework for any proposed solution must include prompt review of filings on the part of regulatory authorities. Regulatory responses and actions must be fact-based and rational, not arbitrary.
- Proposed solutions must provide for consistent rules and application, both among states and within a state.
- Solutions should create an environment of consistent regulation among all insurers participating in the individual market.

May 12, 2004

Consumer Issues

- From the consumer perspective, the main problem with the current market situation is large percentage rate increases relative to perceived inflationary trends. Consumers generally do not understand the drivers of premium rate increases.

- Potential solutions will greatly impact availability and affordability of individual medical insurance. Reducing the cost of coverage for some consumers requires increasing premiums for others. Since the primary direction given to this task force is to reduce premium increases on policies in later durations to make them easier to keep in force, all solutions studied ultimately end up increasing premiums at the earlier durations – often including new business premiums. Since the cost of coverage is one of the primary reasons so many individuals are uninsured, in evaluating the results of this study it will be important to consider the impact each potential solution would have on the new business premiums.

- Consumers probably need assurance that any solution will entail rate structures that produce reasonable equity between similarly situated risks.

- Disclosure of rating methodologies at the time of purchase is essential to consumer understanding of expected future rating actions.

May 12, 2004

Section VI. New Business Rates and Competition

It became clear in both the RFTF and the LHATF discussions that the level of premium rates for people buying new individual major medical policies is not a major concern of regulators for purposes of this work, so long as the subsequent rate increases are within an acceptable range. If a particular market could be demonstrated to be competitive, the RFTF feels that those competitive pressures are more than sufficient to ensure the rates are no higher than needed to achieve target profit. However, each solution studied will have differing impacts on the level of these initial premiums. Regulators will need to decide if any methods affect initial premiums in such a way as to put them outside of an acceptable range.

It cannot be assumed that higher initial premium rates will guarantee lower renewal rate increases or even, if set high enough, renewal rate increases equal to trend. There is also a behavioral effect that needs to be taken into consideration; as initial premium rates increase, the underlying morbidity level of the insureds that purchase coverage also increases. Taking this to the extreme, if the initial premium rates are set too high, the only purchases who will buy coverage are those who will expect to have claims greater than the premium; this will require the carrier to increase rates, and will lead to an insured pool with even higher morbidity levels, etc; thus, if initial premium rates are too high, an assessment spiral could be created.

For any given solution, if a company's new business rate is higher than needed to achieve target profit, any such overpricing will be corrected in future years because of the minimum lifetime loss ratio requirement. In such a case, the result would be smaller rate increases after issue than would have occurred with a lower initial rate.

The RFTF has investigated standards for a competitive marketplace. As a result of that research, we propose the following rule for LHATF decision:

New business rates are not subject to prior approval where there is a competitive market in that geographic area. The definition of such a competitive market is one where the Herfindahl Index (HI) is .4 or less across a state, or .7 or less for a smaller geographic area. The Herfindahl Index is defined as: $HI = \sum (MSn)^2$, where MSn is the market share of competitor n.

The assumption here is that competition will motivate insurers to develop rates consistent with state regulation that attract and keep the most customers. See Appendix C for a more detailed discussion of competitiveness within the Individual Medical Marketplace.

May 12, 2004

Section VII. Potential Closed Block Solutions

The Task Force discussed many different potential solutions for the closed block problem. In our early deliberations, we asked for all potential solutions to be put on the table by all stakeholders, and we then worked at categorizing the solutions.

The Task Force developed four generic categories of solutions to the closed block problem:

1. Individual Medical Pooling (IMP)
   The IMP method assumes that all carriers in the individual medical market will share the cost of financing individual policies by providing an industry wide safety-net for policies that may be rated high in relation to the market. This method does not solve the closed block problem, but provides a safety net for those who might be in a rate spiral.

2. Prefunding
   Prefunding operates on the premise that each issue year cohort of policies must be financed with premiums and claims from that cohort. Reserves are set aside at early durations when loss ratios are low to fund claims at later durations when loss ratios are higher. The advantage of this method is that the carrier may discontinue sales at any time and the in-force business will be self-supporting and future rate increases after that point should parallel new business rate increases in the market. The disadvantage of this method is that the size of the reserves depends upon the slope of expected loss ratios by duration which may vary widely by carrier and by block of business. Another disadvantage is that this method does not provide for any direct recognition of high policy acquisition costs which results in a combined ratio that varies less over time than the medical loss ratio. This method also has the intention of preventing a rate spiral, but does not guarantee the avoidance of a rate spiral, since no relationship is specified between new business premiums and renewal premiums and no relationship is specified between renewal premiums and market premiums.

   This method also has the disadvantage of establishing large reserves which will increase prices for all policyholders and those reserves may not be deductible by the carrier for federal income tax purposes.

3. Interblock Subsidy – Durational Pooling
   Interblock Subsidy – Durational Pooling (referred to as Durational Pooling) is a method that combines the experience of all policy forms of a duration greater than N for all blocks of business with similar characteristics in a given business segment of one insurer for experience rating purposes. This results in policyholders on some forms subsidizing policyholders on other forms. It does not limit the maximum rate increase for the blocks, but it does reduce the rate increases needed by the blocks with the worst experience as they will be subsidized by the blocks with better experience.

4. Interblock Subsidy – Rate Compression
   Interblock Subsidy – Rate Compression (referred to as Rate Compression) is a method that limits the rate differential for similar (after adjustment for benefits, area, demographics, etc.) policies in different blocks of business, within a given business segment of one insurer, to a maximum amount. Rate increases will still be requested separately by block, but the method will generate subsidies between blocks. This occurs when the rate increases for the blocks with the highest rates are restricted by the maximum differential, and the lowest rated blocks are increased to subsidize these other blocks.

In addition a fifth (experience rating, or reclassifying individuals' rate class at renewal based on their health status) was later raised, given initial consideration, and ultimately excluded at the direction of the NAIC.

These four approaches have been modeled in order to determine not only the extent to which the objectives can be achieved, but also to evaluate the implications these approaches may have on the individual major medical insurance industry. This section describes each of those four approaches. Following is a brief key word summary of each of the approaches, followed by a separate section for each. Each section attempts to describe in a more thorough manner several aspects of the approach in narrative form, including its principles, specific objective, and mechanics. A later section describes the implication of each, such as a risk of capital, reserves, and existing model laws and regulations.

Before discussing each approach individually, it is useful to describe a few terms:

- **Policy**

    A "policy" is the unit of individual medical insurance coverage that controls the premium payment, typically covering the policyholder and possibly his or her family. Many individuals purchase and are covered by a policy that, as far as that person is concerned, behaves very similarly to an individual policy, but, in fact, the individual enrolls, usually showing evidence of insurability, as a "subscriber" to a master policy which may be a trust or association plan. In such case, the individual is provided a "certificate" certifying his or her coverage as a member covered under a master policy. For the purpose of this section, both these "certificates" and "policies" are referred to as "policies." The approaches are intended to cover both situations in identical manners.

- **Duration**

    "Duration" is the ordinal number measuring the time since the policy became effective, usually expressed in years. For example, if a policy was effective 9 months ago, it is said to be in its first policy duration, or Duration 1.

- **Form**

    In an individual insurance policy situation, a "form" is the collection of the legal document pages that together form the unique set of policy benefits and terms to which the respective state insurance department approves, These forms provide for a limited number of variable items which usually depend upon the selections made by the policyholder (deductible, coinsurance, riders for maternity, drugs, etc.). As described in the definition of policy, for this section, form also refers to the set of benefits and terms to which the certificate applies if individual coverage is provided through associations or group trusts.

- **Block**

    A "block" is an aggregation of policies of one or more forms having similar claim cost characteristics over time, which an actuary has grouped together for the purposes of determining appropriate premium rates.

May 12, 2004

- **Incurred claims**

    "Incurred claims" are claims that are ultimately to be paid by the terms of the policy, that were incurred during a specified period of time. The period of time usually is a calendar year or duration. A claim is incurred, for the purpose of this definition; in the period a claim becomes a liability as determined by the policy (usually, the period in which a hospital admission occurs or a medical service is rendered). It does not include any change in contract reserves, or any similar reserves that might come about due to the approaches described in this study. The amount of claims that ultimately will be paid is often estimated to be the paid claims plus the change in claim reserves from the beginning to the end of the period, or the cumulative incurred and paid claims with an estimate of the remaining payments to be made. Incurred claims can include cost containment expenses that are defined by the NAIC, but these expenses are included with claim expenses in our model.

- **Segment or Era**

    A "segment" or "era" is a logical grouping of all blocks of business that for reasons other than benefit differences have similar expectations for developing experience. The following are some possible, but not the only, reasons for which a carrier may establish multiple segments:
    - Blocks closed to new sales,
    - Blocks open to new sales,
    - Blocks of obsolete forms,
    - Blocks whose business originates from different distribution sources,
    - Blocks whose business originates from distinctly different underwriting practices (such as guaranteed issue during an open enrollment period vs. medically underwriting each and every application), and
    - Blocks with different claim management practices, including network differences.

Individual Medical Pool (IMP)

This approach allows an insured who is covered by an individual policy, and whose rates have increased beyond a trigger level, to move to a separate state-authorized program (the IMP) that offers policies with premiums that are limited to a fixed percentage above current market rates, and whose rate increases are limited to the average increase in the entire individual market. As we have envisioned the program, the insured is eligible if they purchased their current coverage after the effective date of the IMP, they have been continuously insured for a specified number of years, and their current premium rate exceeds the pool rate. The IMP would be comprised solely of such individuals who are eligible under these criteria and who choose to move to it. The premium rate would be restricted to an actuarial equivalent of a fixed percentage, such as 150%, of standard premium rates. Due to this formula method of determining the IMP rates, the IMP's annual rate increases will mirror the average increase in rates of the individual market each year. The rate increases will not be based on the experience of the IMP. The losses of the IMP program would be funded solely by the individual major medical insurers in that state.

Elements of Implementation

Eligible insureds (under individual major medical products) would be notified of their potential eligibility to move to the IMP with their rate increase notices. The RFTF believes that the number of years of coverage needed before eligibility would likely be in the area of five years. In addition, the price of their current product must exceed the benefit-adjusted price of the IMP product before they are eligible to move to the IMP. The IMP would be open to state residents only.

IMP plan benefits would be similar to products purchased in the state's individual major medical market. Multiple deductibles would need to be offered, so that insureds could obtain comparable coverage under the IMP. Since the purpose of this program is to control rates, not provide additional coverage, any exclusionary waivers attached to an insured's existing policy would be attached to the IMP policy.

Premiums for the IMP would include variations by age, gender, geography, etc. in the same manner as allowed for the other individual plans in the state. We believe that anti-selection would be a problem for the pool without these variations.

The IMP products would be administered by one entity, and governed by a board of directors who are elected by the insurers selling individual insurance in the state. The board would be responsible for selecting the administrator, and all other administrative aspects of the program

Losses from this program would be distributed back to the individual major medical insurers in the state. We believe it is important that this assessment on individual companies be allocated based on two factors: first, the number of insureds in the IMP from each company, and second, the number of lives that company has in force in the individual major medical market.

Discussion

The objective of this approach is to limit the ultimate spread between premium rates at later durations and those charged to new business. This is achieved through a mechanism that gives customers choice, without hampering an individual carrier's ability to charge appropriate rates based on experience. The assessment mechanism is designed to discourage companies from using a rate increase strategy that would generate significant movement of policyholders into the IMP. (It does this through higher assessments charged to insurers with more people in the IMP.)

Certain insurers try to minimize lapses by moderating the size of rate increases at early durations. The IMP method would allow insurers to continue this practice. The IMP approach will not altogether stop the need for large rate increase filings at later durations, but it gives policyholders another option once their rate levels exceed the IMP rates.

Other Comments

A new NAIC model regulation will be needed to define the operating parameters of the Individual Medical Pool, including specific carrier reporting and/or filing requirements and assessment authority. Consideration must be given for the benefit structure and range of options available in the pool, including the extent to which optional coverages are to be made available, if at all. Specifics regarding the details of the two-part assessment formula will berequired. Procedures are also needed for

May 12, 2004

the selection process and responsibilities of the board of directors and overall IMP governance.

Prefunding

This approach requires insurers to fund in advance some of the expected future claims at later policy durations. The claims arising from antiselection at lapse and the "wear-off" of underwriting are the claims that are prefunded.

As modeled, within any one block, the same level of rate increases must be applied uniformly to new business rates and to all existing policies. Policies within a block are pooled for determining these rate increases. The more significant "pooling" or subsidy, however, occurs between durations within a block, as explained above.

Mechanically, premiums collected during early durations are significantly higher than necessary to cover current year claims and expenses. The excess of the premiums over these claims and expenses are used to establish reserves that are later drawn down to reduce premium increases from levels dictated by their experience.

Elements of Implementation

This approach requires the creation of reserve factors by duration that will be applied to the incurred claims per policy, or possibly to the earned premium, to build up a new type of contract reserve. This new reserve is used to offset future needed premium rate increases of the block. This new reserve must also be recognized on carrier financial statements.

This approach establishes required prefunding reserves, based on reserve factors which are a function of duration, claim experience, and lapse experience. The methodology follows that outlined in the paper "Duration-Based Policy Reserves", published in the Transactions of the Society of Actuaries, volume 45, 1993.

Only the claim costs that are reasonably expected to increase as a function of duration and antiselection at lapse are prefunded into a reserve. For ease of reference, this document refers to these increases as "durationally induced" increases. Increases in coverage costs that are unrelated to the duration of the policy or the age of the block of policies are not pre-funded. Claim costs that increase due to chronological aging of individuals, secular trend (net of buy-downs), benefit changes, rating characteristic changes, and deductible leveraging are specifically excluded from funding through the prefunding reserve mechanism.

Nonforfeiture values do not accrue, so lapses will not release any part of the prefunding reserve directly to the individual in any form. The release of these reserves to the funding of the block is critical to the success of this approach.

The prefunded reserve is used to offset premium rate increases that would otherwise be needed to offset increases in claim cost antiselection at lapse, and durationally-induced claim increases.

Prefunding does not preclude rate increases for losses in excess of anticipated levels arising from other forms of adverse experience, such as medical trend that is greater than anticipated.

May 12, 2004

Because of the substantial reserves involved, the Prefunding model incorporates three additional financial assumptions: (1) a reserve discount rate, (2) an assumed level of investment earnings on reserves, and (3) a required reserve margin. The reserve discount rate is currently set at 3.5 percent. This discount rate is used in calculating the reserve factors used to establish the required reserve levels. The assumed rate of investment earnings on reserves is currently set at five percent, and is applied to the Prefunding reserves held each year to determine the investment earnings on those reserves. Because the assumed earnings rate exceeds the discount rate, there is an interest spread on Prefunding reserves that is an additional source of profit.

Discussion

Premium increases at renewal may be attributed to the following six broad causes:

1. aging of the policyholder,
2. rising medical care costs,
3. changes in the regulatory environment,
4. changes in utilization of health care services,
5. wear-off of underwriting, and
6. self-selection at renewal (Cumulative anti-selection, or CAST).

The first four are not part of the "closed block" problem, and this model assumes that premiums would still rise for those reasons. Appendix B provides more detail on this subject. Numbers five and six above are at the heart of the "closed block" problem, and eliminating "planned" or expected rate increases due to those effects would, if all the pricing assumptions hold, place a closed block policyholder in the same position as an open block policyholder. This model pre-funds for the expected cost increases from numbers five and six, while assuming premium increases are needed to fund numbers one through four.

The model develops a series of reserve factors by duration. In calculating these factors, claims are assumed to increase with age, trend, and duration. Differing lapse rates are assumed for standard and impaired lives. Premiums are assumed to increase with age, trend, and a flat chosen percentage each year. Net annual premiums are calculated under these assumptions. Reserve factors are calculated as a percentage of claims. The model estimated annual claim levels, but did not distinguish between paid and incurred claims. One important implementation issue would be deciding whether reserve factors should be applied to paid claims or incurred claims. Gross premiums are generated by adding in expenses and profit charges, and expected gross premium loss ratios are calculated.

In projecting the financial results of a block of business, reserves are calculated by year and by cohort. In developing these reserves, the reserve factors developed in the initial pricing process are adjusted using CAST factors as described in Bill Bluhm's paper "Cumulative Antiselection Theory", published in the TSA, Volume 34, 1982, and also in the Society of Actuaries' 50th Anniversary Monograph. In addition, the CAST factors increase the required reserve level as lapse rates increase in order to adjust for an assumed increase in lapse-related antiselection.

If actual experience is the same as the pricing assumptions, premiums will increase with age, trend, and the assumed flat chosen percentage. If lapse rates are higher than expected, a reserve adjustment is made, and premiums increase as the loss ratio deteriorates. The reserve adjustment means that the loss taken by the company in the year the adjustment is made is larger than it would be in the absence of prefunding, and, as these reserves are released in later years, future rate increases are correspondingly smaller than they would be in the absence of prefunding. The model calculates the year-end reserve by applying a reserve factor to premiums. The reserve change is the difference between the current year's reserve and the prior year's reserve. If claims increase by more than the expected amount, the reserve charge will need to be correspondingly larger.

In situations where the claim cost experience on a *block* is not realized due to lapses exceeding that assumed, the carrier will be required to use the release in *prefunding* reserves to offset the otherwise justified increase in premium rates.

How a company is required to set the prefunding reserves will affect the pricing assumptions and methods used by the company. Guidelines would be needed to determine how these reserves are to be set. Companies would use these guidelines for their pricing, and regulators would use them for their reviews.

As discussed previously, prefunding will not fund changes in the economic environment or adverse claims experience that varies from that priced for. When these events occur, reserve adjustments will be needed to cover the change in expected future claims

Guidelines for regulating this methodology must consider the extent that the prefunding must balance between the smoothing of the premium for the customer, and the reserve adjustment and solvency issues resulting from adverse claims experience of the company.

Other Comments

The current NAIC model law calls for a minimum contract reserve method of two-year preliminary term (2YPT). The prefunding approach would be severely undermined if no additional reserve were required during the first two years as 2YPT calls for, or if a similar method were applied.

The current model uses a one-year preliminary term reserve. Given the high lapse rates in the first two years after issue and the front-loading of expenses into the first year, moving to two-year preliminary term reserves may not be practical.

Inter-block Subsidy – Durational Pooling

Durational pooling is a method in which the computation of renewal business rates requires a carrier to pool the experience of its policies after they reach a chosen duration, across all *blocks* within the applicable business segment. This means that premium rate increases will be the same percentage increase for all policies in the pool. The effect of this is to cause some policy premiums to be lower than they otherwise would have been, and others to be higher.

Elements of Implementation

Prior to duration N, renewal business rate increases are calculated as in the Current Market Model, where each block is rated on its own experience. For each issue year within a block of policies upon reaching duration N, the experience must be pooled with that from all other forms and blocks defined to be included in the pool for duration N or greater. For the first 2 years of the pool, if there is no experience base yet, anticipated trend can be used for pooled rate increases. Our modeling uses this approach for simplicity. Thereafter, the experience of the pool, relative to expected loss ratios reflecting the durational mix for the pool, is used to adjust rate increases.

May 12, 2004

Definitions would have to be developed for what forms and blocks within segments would have to be pooled. The pooling should only occur among forms and blocks with broad yet somewhat homogenous risk characteristics such as comprehensive major medical policies.

It may be necessary to file anticipated loss ratios by duration for each block that will be in the pools so that regulators have some means of verifying the variation of the pool's actual loss ratios versus expected loss ratios.

Discussion

Adoption of this approach in some states but not in others, or adoption with significant modification, can undermine the effectiveness of this potential closed block solution, even in the state in which the model was adopted intact. Uniformity across states is important, so that any subsidy between blocks can also take place across state lines. The larger the pool of business over which the subsidy can be spread the more likely rate stability can be achieved.

The effectiveness of pooling of forms across blocks, particularly in the form of a limitation on rate increases in some fashion, is risky because the forms have different benefit designs. This is because each benefit design may have differing trend experience potential. For example, forms with rich prescription drug benefits will expect to experience different cost increases for trend. The same is true for forms with a mix of deductibles.

Pooling of durations still in the select underwriting period can limit the effectiveness of underwriting, and minimize the effect of any new underwriting standards a carrier would like to implement. Thus, if possible, N should be set to be a duration beyond the select underwriting period.

Other Comments

The current NAIC model law allows for combining forms for purposes of improving credibility of experience. This component of the model may need to be modified in order to accommodate blocks of business, as well as subsets of forms, such as only those policies within a form that exceed duration N.

Inter-block Subsidy – Rate Compression

Rate compression is a method in which premium rates for individuals with comparable demographics, geographic location and benefits must be within a specified high-to-low range. The comparison is made for all policy forms within a specified segment of forms to which the rate compression requirement applies.

The effect of this is to cause rate increases on some policy forms to be artificially adjusted from their true experience levels so that the resulting rates stay within the specified high-to-low range. The result is that some policy premiums can be lower than they otherwise would have been without the compression, and others can be higher.

Elements of Implementation

Renewal business rate increases (after the first renewal) would initially be calculated based upon actual experience. After that, premium rates for persons of like demographics, area and benefits would be compared between forms within that segment. Adjustments would then be applied as needed to bring the form rates within the high-to-low range. The result would be that some forms would need to have their rates raised, and others lowered. It is anticipated that these adjustments would be made in such a manner that, to the extent possible, a carrier would maintain its calendar year profit objective that existed prior to the impact of rate compression.

Definitions would have to be developed to determine which forms and blocks within a market segment would be subject to rate compression. The compression should only occur among forms and blocks with broad yet somewhat homogeneous risk characteristics.

Rate compression is performed so that rates are within the required range, exclusive of benefit differences and predefined allowable characteristics. These would most likely follow the state allowable rating characteristics, such as age, gender, and area.

An annual filing of a certificate of compliance may be required, similar to what is done under many group insurance laws. This would allow the regulators to have a signed statement of compliance for their records. The company should have a methodology statement available for the regulators to show its process for compliance.

Discussion

The high-to-low range chosen can have an effect that varies from negligible to dramatic, as illustrated in the following table:

Effect of Range Width on the Impact of Rate Compression

Relatively Narrow Range	Relatively Wide Range
Similar rates for all policyholders	Rates similar to current rates; potentially wide variations among policyholders
Higher new business rates	Small impact on new business rates
Smaller durational rate increases	Little or no limitation on durational rate increases
Could discourage people from purchasing	Not likely to discourage purchases

If this method is applied to products that are priced using durational rating, it will minimize the effectiveness of the durational rating due to the ultimate compression of rates.

Other Comments

A new NAIC model regulation would be necessary to define what types of forms are to be combined for purposes of rate compression, and to discuss what types of rating factors could be excluded from the compression tests.

May 12, 2004

Section VIII. Findings and Analysis of Solutions

This section discusses the results of our modeling efforts. We attempted to "even the playing field" between the models, by having standardized assumptions and scenarios for testing. Even so, each of these closed block solution models should be considered a specific example of a spectrum of such solutions. Each of them can be made more or less extreme than what is illustrated, by changing the parameters used in defining the method. This might include choosing:

- The degree of prefunding, in the prefunding method;
- The width of the rate corridor allowed, in the rate compression method;
- The duration in which pooling occurs, for durational pooling and the individual medical pool method; and
- The rate level trigger for pooling, for the individual medical pool method.

For this reason, care should be taken in evaluating the relative size of observed effects; qualitative comparisons are much more helpful than quantitative ones.

The RFTF developed a sizeable number of metrics for possible use by the NAIC in evaluating the results of the modeling. The stated primary goal of the LHATF was "rate stability", which was defined as having "rate increases... within a corridor of trend that reduces the probability of spirals." For this reason, our models report a number of statistics aimed at measuring this.

This section first discusses results from each of the four solutions (models); this is followed by a comparison between the four.

The Individual Medical Pool (IMP):

Under the IMP solution, people in the individual major medical market are guaranteed the availability of a product whose rate cannot exceed a fixed percentage of the average rate available in the current individual major medical market, and whose rate increases will be limited to the average increase for the individual market. Once eligible for the IMP, the choice to move to it or keep their current product is up to them.

The IMP has no initial effect on the current marketplace since people cannot move into the pool until their rate exceeds the IMP premium and they have kept their product for N years. This means that market premiums would not be affected initially when the method was introduced. As people move into the pool, the program will begin to generate losses. Assessments to pay for the losses are charged to all the companies in the individual marketplace. The assessments will, in turn, be included in the rates the companies charge to their customers. Like all solutions in this report, the model is based on prospective application of this reform to people who buy a new individual major medical policy after the requirement is in effect. Transition issues for previously inforce policies would require other modeling.

As the IMP grows, so will the losses from it, and the resulting assessments.

In discussions of potential market situations, we decided to test a scenario where companies are using aggressive rating practices in the individual major medical market. This was done to emulate situations that may currently exist in some markets. Aggressive pricing would include a larger amount of durational rating, and a shorter pricing horizon than we used in the Current Marketplace scenario. In testing

May 12, 2004

this scenario we see a greater number of people moving to the IMP, and at earlier durations. As a result of this, the ultimate assessment level would be more than double the assessment otherwise, based upon our modeling. This would increase premiums for the individual major medical market correspondingly, with a corresponding decrease in participants in the future.

One result of increased premiums in the future would be a slight reduction in policies purchased. We measured this effect by measuring the number of covered lives in the market.

Our model proposes that assessments should be in two parts; one part would be based on participation in the marketplace, the other based on how many former policyholders are in the IMP. Companies with higher assessments would have to build a larger amount into their premiums than their competitors.

The IMP does not directly control the level of rate increases that non-IMP products will need at any duration. It does give the policyholder, once they are eligible, an option to choose a product whose rates are limited to a fixed percentage of the average individual major medical market rates, and whose rates will increase at the same rate as the average individual major medical market rates.

In testing the various trend scenarios, it was discovered that varying the trend scenario had little effect on the ultimate level of the assessment.

Due to the gradually increasing rate and the ultimate level of the amount of the assessments, we do not feel that this method would create an unpredictable pricing situation for the companies in the individual major medical market. A prospective assessment method, compared to a retrospective method, would improve predictability even more. A prospective method does, however, require the ability of the IMP to do special assessments on insurers if the program runs short of funds. Insurers must be allowed to pass these special assessments directly to non-IMP policyholders in the form of extra premiums. This situation currently exists with assessments made for some state high risk pools.

Prefunding:

If cost increases attributable to the wear off of underwriting and adverse selection at lapse are fully prefunded, consumers buying individual health insurance can expect renewal premiums that increase at approximately the same rate as new business premiums. In other words, their rate increases would equal the increase in costs due to age plus medical trend. New business premiums would, however, be substantially higher. As with entry-age Medicare Supplement policies, the higher initial cost would provide more stable premiums over time. Consumers expecting to remain in the individual market for an extended period of time would likely benefit from stable rate increases and lower ultimate rates, relative to the other solutions. Consumers needing transitional coverage who expect to remain in the individual market for a shorter period would likely find other solutions more attractive.

As with the other approaches, there are ways to moderate the effect of prefunding. The current projections are based on prefunding part – but not all – of expected durational cost increases. Specifically, premiums and reserves were developed to produce expected premium increases equal to medical trend, plus the normal increase in costs due to age, plus two percent. Allowing this additional two percent in expected renewal rate increases cut the required increase in new business premiums roughly in half. It is important to note that we are not modeling a rate band; rather, this is a change in the *target* level of future rate increases, which is used to develop expected loss ratios for renewal rating purposes and reserve factors. Implementing a hard rate cap would have different results when experience deviated from expected, and was not modeled.

Prefunding would significantly change the market. Higher initial premiums would reduce new business sales. Lower renewal rate increases would reduce lapse rates, and increase the number of long-duration policies. Total enrollment did not, during the 15 years in which new business was being sold, reach the levels produced by the current market model. The improved persistency did, however, result in total enrollment climbing to within three to five percent of current market levels.

Reduced renewal rate increases mean that the higher cost of a prefunded policy is gradually reduced over time. Our modeling suggests that the renewal premium for a prefunded policy would fall below that for the current market around year 13. Rate increases are also more stable – the minimum, maximum and average rate increases for an insurer's entire book of business are grouped more tightly together than under the other models (although a rate compression approach, through the size of the rate band selected, directly controls this relationship).

Prefunding also changes the pattern of gains and losses for an insurer. The combination of higher initial premiums and a one-year preliminary term reserving method serves to offset the high expenses associated with selling new business. After the first year, early duration profits are reduced relative to the other rating approaches. However, as reserves are released to offset high claim levels at later durations, profitability is preserved on older policies.

The presence of substantial prefunding reserves does serve to moderate rate increases and reduce market turnover. However, they also make results more sensitive to changes in trend rates and assumptions. When experience deviates from what was expected when a policy was initially priced, reserve adjustments are necessary in addition to changes in premiums.

Durational Pooling:

Durational pooling is a method in which the computation of renewal business rates requires a carrier to pool the experience of its policies after they reach duration N across all *blocks* within a limited number of segments of its business. Company new business rates are affected indirectly by the pooling.

The following general observations of results under durational pooling are relative to the Current Market Model.

- In general, fewer lives are covered than under the Current Market Model.
- Lapses vary by block/cohort with older blocks having fewer lapses, more covered lives than under the current model because of subsidized rate increases.
- Newer blocks/cohorts show fewer covered lives and increased lapse compared to the Current Market Model because they are subsidizing older blocks/cohorts and rate increases are higher.

- Durational pooling can affect company new business rates because the model new business rates for a block are increased each year after the initial year of issue by the effective rate increase applied for the block. This method of determining new business rates can cause the company new business rate to be higher or lower than under the current market resulting in opposite changes in new sales volume. At later years when rate increases become larger for newer blocks because they are subsidizing older blocks, new sales levels drop.
- Profitability to the insurer is slightly better across all blocks but varies dramatically by block or cohort. Older blocks, because of subsidies from newer blocks, could have significant losses and newer blocks could have substantial profits.
- Average rate increases in general tend to be minimally more than in the current market, but there is significant variation by block and cohort because of the subsidization of rate increases across blocks.

There is more variation in the number of lives, rate increases and profitability when looking at cohorts than can be seen in averages across all blocks.

The interblock subsidy durational pooling baseline model starts pooling in duration 1. We tested pooling starting at durations through 31. Based on the economic gain, number of covered lives and magnitude of rate increases, durational pooling starting at duration 7 appears optimal. The economic gain is maximized with durational pooling starting at duration 7, almost 15% higher than the current market. In aggregate, the number of covered lives does not vary significantly with the starting duration, however, there can be substantial variation by issue year and duration. Rate increases were reviewed for durational pooling starting at durations 1, 4, 7, 10 and 15. For cohorts 5 through 15 the minimum rate increases are about 2% to 5% higher than the current market with durational pooling starting before duration 7. For pooling starting after duration 7, the most notable impact is that the block 1 maximum rate increase is significantly higher by 13% to 16%. By starting pooling in late durations, the initial pool entrants have quite poor experience. There is significant variation of rate increases by issue year and duration as compared to the current market.

If durational pooling starts during the DDLP, company underwriting changes in more recently issued blocks may not be as effective since generally newer blocks subsidize older blocks in durational pooling. In addition, the shorter the period from issue to the duration when pooling starts, the less time a company has to fix any initial pricing inaccuracies before pooling dilutes any remedial action.

If pooling starts after duration 7, in general our tests indicate the solution's effect is minimized because the high lapse rates indicative of the individual market result in pooling applied to only a small portion of the initial exposure since issue.

We performed some sensitivity tests for claim level experience deviations under durational pooling. If poor experience deviations were modeled, the impact before durational pooling starts would be the same as in the Current Market Model since each block would still be rated independently of the others. Rate increase corrective actions on/or after durational pooling starts would be dampened, in most cases, due to the cross-subsidies. Thus older business would not benefit fully from the corrective action while new business would see higher rate increases and more lapses due to the subsidy inherent in durational pooling. If experience deviations develop in more recently issued blocks, durational pooling will still show dampened rate increases for that block because all other blocks subsidize the needed increase for the experience deviation. However, the average rate increases for more recently issued blocks would increase relative to that in the current market and the minimum rate increases would be even higher since there are fewer policies in older issued blocks to add to the subsidy. Aggregate lives and the economic gain in dollars would drop from that in the current market. If there were issues modeled after year 15, this result would not be as pronounced.

This solution requires a definition of what "blocks" get pooled: similar benefits, deductible levels, level of network restrictions, etc. The model does not show premium rate differences by age/gender, area, industry, benefits and health status (claim costs by impaired vs. standard are in the model, however).

There also needs to be a definition of duration: examples include true duration, year of issue, year that block was closed, or other. The model uses year of issue but with true policy year. This definition will impact both the carrier and the regulatory agency. The definition needs to allow some carrier flexibility while still allowing for appropriate regulatory controls. The definition that facilitates one carrier's rating system may be very difficult to implement for another carrier.

Rate Compression:

Rate compression is a method in which premium rates for blocks with comparable demographics, networks, geographic location and benefits must be within a specified high-to-low range.

The baseline rate compression (2:1) model results as compared to the Current Market show no change in sales because compression is not necessary until later years since there is little variation between the five blocks in the Current Market Model.

The following general observations of results under rate compression are relative to the Current Market Model.

- Total lives covered in the market are slightly down but almost the same as compared to the Current Market Model.
- Rate increases are almost the same as Current Market.
- Profitability is almost the same as in the Current Market, just slightly higher.

However, these results vary by block because, as with the durational pooling model, rate compression results in newer blocks subsidizing older blocks.

Rate compression at 3:1 or 4:1 shows little or no impact primarily due to little or no variation between blocks. Using assumptions of more heterogeneous blocks of business may result in more rate compression. However, the higher this rate compression ratio is, the closer results will be to those of the Current Market Model.

The rate compression models attempts to restore lost profits due to compression by increasing rate increases in aggregate up to 2% of premium each year. Block 1 loses considerably more money because rate compression limits its rate increases and all blocks attempt to maintain the original annual profit objective by increasing all rates slightly. Significant rate increases to maintain profitability likely would not be allowed due to the regulatory review. A macro in the spreadsheet performs the profit restoration process. It is imperative that the macro be run every time any change is made to the assumptions that would affect the rate compression model.

To create some variation between blocks, we increased claim level experience on the two oldest blocks by 40% and 20%, respectively. When the claim level adjustment is also made to the current market, the current market economic gain and covered lives drop substantially. Comparison of the rate compression and current market models with this adjustment shows the economic gain under rate compression is now about 1% less than the current market and the covered lives in total are about 500 less. Rate increases under rate compression, however, are about 8% lower in block 1 around years 13 and 14 as compared to the current market but in later years the increases stay in the 20% to 24% range. Whereas, in the current market with the claim experience adjustment, the rate increases at these later years typically range from 16% to 24%.

The 2:1 rate compression scenario is the minimum ratio tested in our model and is in our baseline scenario since the small group market uses +/- 25% to +/-35% in most states and that has shown to be difficult for survival of some insurers and the viability of small group markets. We believe that any rate compression used in the individual market should have a wider range than that in the small group market such as 2.5:1 or greater.

It will be necessary to define what "blocks" are subject to rate compression. Note that all models in our analysis do not show rate differences by age/gender, area, benefits, industry and health status.

Operationally, insurers need to standardize rates among blocks for differences in allowable rating characteristics such as age/gender, area, industry, benefits or health status. This will add complexity to a company's rating procedure since first they have to standardize rates to a common basis and determine if they then meet the rate compression range. If not, then they need to adjust rates, rebalance rates and likely try to build in a margin to restore lost profits due to compression. A company may not be able to recoup lost profits due to compression if the compression impact is too large.

The model assumes that a carrier will decrease their older rates to conform to the necessary rate compression range. This assumption was made because it was assumed that it would be preferable that new business rates, which are typically the lowest rates, would usually be unadjusted or be impacted the least. Other methodologies could be used, but were not modeled.

New Business rates could be affected by rate compression, except that compression in our modeling usually starts after new business has stopped, unless significant variation among blocks is assumed. Rate compression could cause new business rates to increase and in that case rate compression limits the premium effect of any change in underwriting criteria.

The following is a discussion of model results in terms of the impact of each potential solution on the indicated components.

A. Market and Company New Business Premium Rates

In general, only the Prefunding solution has a material impact on new business rate levels, estimated to be approximately 32% above that of the Current Market. The characteristics of the other solutions do not call for remedial action until future years. In fact under the baseline scenario, the initial company new business rates for the IMP and Rate Compression solutions do not vary from the Current Market. Company rates under the Durational Pooling solution actually decrease slightly in years 4 through 10, then increase to minimal levels relative to the Current Market.

The IMP Model is the only model that uses issues beyond year 15; this was necessary for the pool to reach an ultimate state. The IMP model spreads the cost of the market pool over all in-force premiums. If new business sales are discontinued during the projection period, pool assessments will begin to spiral rapidly upwards. To produce stable pool assessments we modeled new business sales for the entire thirty year projection period. However, to place the results of the IMP model on a comparable basis with those of the other models, the exhibits only include experience from the first 15 years of issues. This provides full run-out for those blocks, with assessment levels consistent with an active, ongoing market.

May 12, 2004

B. New Business Sales

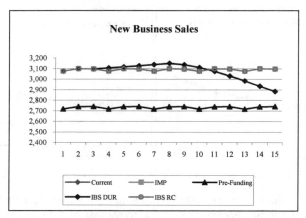

Results are consistent with the company new business premium results. The Prefunding solution results in much lower sales, while Durational Pooling sales increase slightly in years 4 through 10, then decreases relative to the Current Market.

C. Total Enrollment

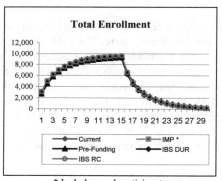

* Includes pool participants

Total enrollment is dependent on new business sales as well as persistency. It must be noted that the significant drop in total enrollment after fifteen (15) years is due to the lack of new business sales in our model after that time.

For Prefunding, enrollment is lower than the Current Market as well as the other solutions for the first 16 years. Enrollment is also lower than the other models in total. Although, for years 16-30, the year-by-year enrollment is slightly higher for prefunding than the Current Market and other solutions.

None of the potential solutions, other than Rate Compression, reach an enrollment level as high as the Current Market in terms of total life years under the 30 years modeled. Durational Pooling reaches levels slightly above Current Market in years

7-10. Prefunding reaches levels above Current Market by year 15 and increases relative to the Current Market thereafter. Among the potential solutions, Rate Compression and IMP come closest to matching the Current Market. The Durational Pooling pattern relative to the Current Market tends to mirror the pattern of new business sales.

D. Impaired Lives as a Percentage of Total Enrollment

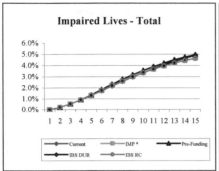 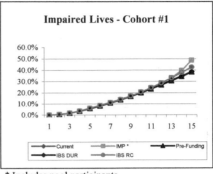

*Includes pool participant   * Includes pool participants

It must be noted that the impaired lives percentage increases dramatically after fifteen (15) years. This is due to the fact that new business, assumed to be 100% standard lives, is not modeled after fifteen (15) years.

None of the proposed solutions show significant differences in impaired percentages relative to the Current Market.

For IMP, the impaired percentage roughly matches the Current Market through year 18, and then decreases steadily thereafter. As the impaired lives move to the pool, the rate increases for the remaining standard lives are lower than they would be otherwise, resulting in lower lapse rates for the standard lives. In order to compare the IMP results on an equivalent basis, the pool enrollment was extended beyond the 15 year time horizon for new policy issues.

For Prefunding, the impaired percentage actually increases relative to the Current Market and then declines to levels below the Current Market starting in year 18 and decreases steadily thereafter.

For durational pooling, the impaired percentage follows the Current Market through year 10, increasing thereafter.

Rate Compression matches the Current Market in all but a few years.

May 12, 2004

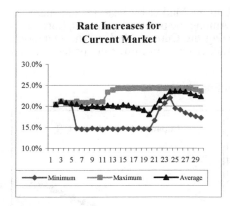
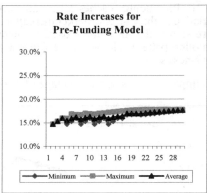
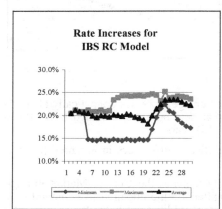
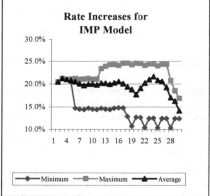
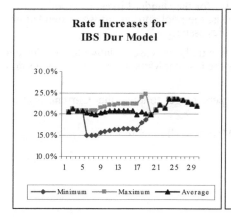
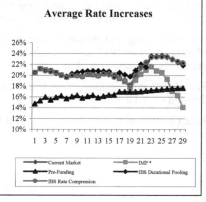

May 12, 2004

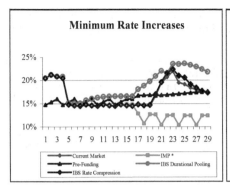 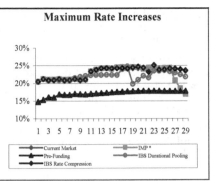

Rate increase results are presented in terms of the minimum, maximum, and average of the fifteen issue year cohorts modeled.

The Prefunding solution has the greatest impact on rate increase variation and level due to the limitation on rate increases of trend plus 2%.

Both the IMP and Durational Pooling solutions show the same level of rate increase variability as the Current Market until later years. For Durational Pooling, uniformity takes over in year 20 at levels relatively close to those of the Current Market. For IMP, rate increase variability continues, although the average rate increases ultimately decrease steadily to levels below the Current Market as well as all other potential solutions.

Rate Compression is not significantly different than the Current Market.

F. Premium Rates by Cohort

Results are presented for issue year cohorts 1, 5, 10, and 15.

It must by noted that the in later years in which significant rate impact takes place, a minimal number of insureds remain in force. Durational Pooling, however, results in significant subsidization for later issues in relatively early policy years.

Cohort #1

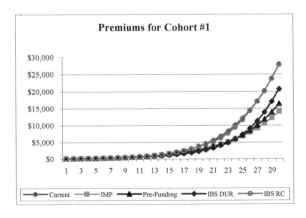

The IMP solution follows the Current Market through year 14, and then begins to steadily decrease relative to the Current Market to a level of roughly 50% of the Current Market by year 30.

The Prefunding solution naturally begins with a rate level approximately 32% above the Current Market decreasing steadily relative to the Current Market due to rate increase limitations. It takes 13 years for the rate level to reach a level below the rate level of the Current Market and ultimately reaches a level of approximately 59% of the Current Market.

The Durational Pooling solution generally follows the Current Market through year 5, and then begins to steadily decrease relative to the Current Market to a level of roughly 74% of the Current Market by year 30.

Rate Compression generally follows the Current Market.

Cohort #5

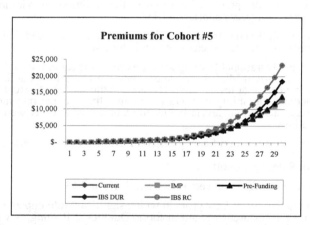

Cohort #5 results generally show the same pattern as Cohort #1 relative to the Current Market.

The IMP solution generally follows the Current Market through year 18 (policy year 14), then begins to steadily decrease relative to the Current Market to a level of roughly 54% of the Current Market by year 30 (policy year 26).

The Prefunding solution naturally begins with a rate level approximately 32% above the Current Market, decreasing steadily toward the Current Market. It takes 12 policy years (year 16) for the rate level to reach a level below that of the Current Market. The ultimate level is approximately 59% of the Current Market.

The Durational Pooling solution is fairly close to the Current Market through year 13 (policy year 9), then begins to steadily decrease relative to the Current Market to a level of roughly 79% of the Current Market by year 30 (policy year 26). It is apparent that Durational Pooling has a greater impact on the older cohorts, as one would expect.

Rate Compression generally follows the Current Market.

May 12, 2004

Cohort #10

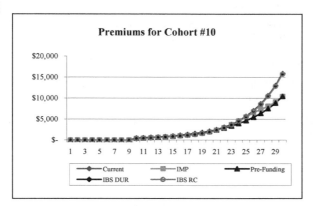

A review of Cohort #10 appears to reveal a general pattern emerging. For IMP and Prefunding, while the impact is slightly less than for older cohorts, the pattern is generally the same. For Durational Pooling, differences from the older Cohorts is much more pronounced and later issue years are clearly subsidizing earlier issue years to the extent that rate levels are in excess of Current Market levels. Rate Compression has no impact.

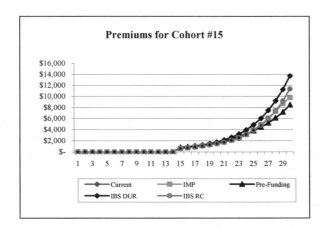

For IMP and Prefunding, the impact is actually greater than for Cohort #10. Premium rates for the IMP will begin having subsidies in them after about year 14. For Durational Pooling, subsidization is even more pronounced in later years. Rate Compression has no impact.

May 12, 2004

G. Rate Increases by Cohort

These results are consistent with the new business rates, overall rate increases, and rate levels by Cohort already presented.

Results are presented for issue year cohorts 1, 5, 10, and 15.

It must by noted that in later years in which significant rate impact takes place, a minimal number of insureds remain in force.

Durational Pooling, however, results in significant subsidization for later issues in relatively early policy years.

Cohort #1

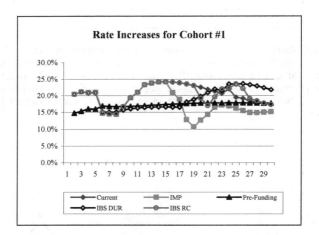

The IMP solution follows the Current Market through year 14, then reaches a steady rate increase level consistently lower than the current market for people in the IMP. People choosing to keep their current policy will have increases similar to the Current Market.

The Prefunding solution is characterized by rate increase limits of trend plus 2%, which is generally, but not always, lower than the Current Market.

The impact of Durational Pooling results in rate increases lower than the Current Market starting in year 9, but gradually increasing (due to the lack of new business) and exceeding the rate increases of the Current Market at year 22.

Rate Compression follows the Current Market through year 19, then decreases relative to the Current Market for three (3) years as rates become compressed, and thereafter increases relative to the Current Market. This is caused by no new business after year 15.

Cohort #5

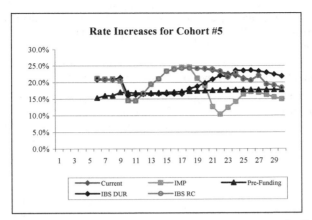

The IMP solution follows the Current Market through year 18 (policy year 14), then reaches a steady rate increase level consistently lower than the Current Market for people in the IMP. People choosing to keep their current policy will have increases similar to the Current Market.

The Prefunding solution is characterized by rate increase limits of trend plus 2%, which is generally, but not always lower than the Current Market.

The impact of Durational Pooling results in rate increases that alternate at levels lower than the Current Market through year 8 (policy year 4), then higher than the Current Market through year 11 (policy year 7) then lower than the Current Market starting in year 12 (policy year 8), but gradually increasing (due to the lack of new business) and exceeding the rate increases of the Current Market at year 24 (policy 20).

Rate Compression follows the Current Market through year 19 (policy year 15), and then varies slightly year to year from the Current Market.

Cohort #10

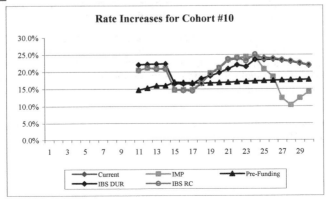

May 12, 2004

The IMP solution follows the Current Market through year 24 (policy year 15), then reaches a steady rate increase level consistently lower than the Current Market for people in the IMP. People choosing to keep their current policy will have increases similar to the Current Market.

The Prefunding solution is characterized by rate increase limits of trend plus 2%, which is generally, but not always lower than the Current Market.

The impact of Durational Pooling results in rate increases greater that the Current Market through year 18 (policy year 9), thereafter reaching levels lower than the Current Market despite gradually increasing due to the lack of new business. Rate Compression follows the Current Market through year 19 (policy year 10), then varies slightly year to year from the Current Market.

Cohort #15

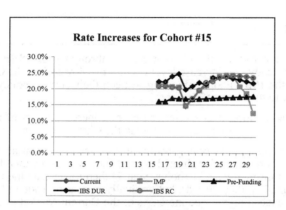

The IMP solution exhibits rate increases greater than the relatively low increases of the Current Market through year 27 (policy year 13) thereafter decreasing to levels consistently lower than the Current Market for people in the IMP. People choosing to keep their current policy will have increases similar to the Current Market.

The Prefunding solution is characterized by rate increase limits of trend plus 2%, which is generally, but not always lower than the Current Market.

The impact of Durational Pooling results in rate increases greater that the Current Market through year 24 (policy year 10), thereafter reaching levels slightly lower than the Current Market. Unlike earlier issue years, these rate increases are relatively level through the modeling period due to the fact that subsidization of the older blocks does not allow for significantly lower rate increases relative to the Current Market.

Rate Compression follows the Current Market through year 19 (policy year 5), and then varies slightly year to year from the Current Market.

May 12, 2004

H. Annual Premium

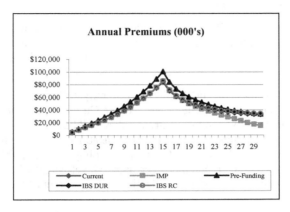

Annual Premiums are dependent on the rate level and enrollment, presented above. It must be noted that the significant drop in total premium after fifteen (15) years is due to lack of new business sales in our model.

On a present value basis, Prefunding generates the greatest volume of premium, while Durational Pooling is slightly lower than the Current Market and Rate Compression. IMP generates the lowest premium, although it should be noted that pool premium is not included with these results.

With respect to the premium pattern, the IMP solution follows the Current Market through year 13 then drops steadily relative to the Current Market for people in the IMP. People choosing to keep their current policy will have increases similar to the Current Market. Prefunding is consistently well above the Current Market until many years later. Durational Pooling generally follows the Current Market through year 13, and then decreases to levels slightly below the Current Market. Rate Compression is virtually identical to the Current Model.

I. Annual Claims

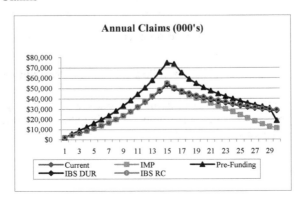

May 12, 2004

It must be noted that the significant drop after fifteen (15) years is due to lack of new business sales in our model.

On a present value basis, Prefunding generates the greatest volume of claims (including reserves), while Durational Pooling is slightly lower than the Current Market and Rate Compression. IMP generates the lowest claims, although it should be noted that pooled claims are not included with these results.

With respect to pattern, the IMP solution generally follows the Current Market through year 15 then drops steadily relative to the Current Market for people in the IMP. People choosing to keep their current policy will have increases similar to the Current Market. Prefunding is consistently well above the Current Market with exception of the first and last year. Durational Pooling generally follows the Current Market through year 11, and then decreases to levels slightly below the Current Market. Rate Compression is virtually identical to the Current Model.

J. Annual Expenses

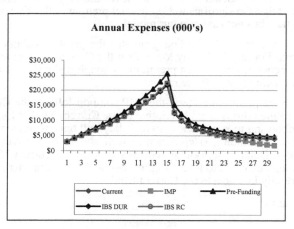

It must be noted that the significant drop after fifteen (15) years is due to lack of new business sales in our model.

Expense levels and patterns generally follow the Annual Premium results. Profitability
Profitability results are presented in terms of pre-tax underwriting profit (Annual Gain/Loss) before and after the opportunity cost of capital (Economic Gain/Loss), both in dollars and percent of premium.

May 12, 2004

Annual Gain/Loss

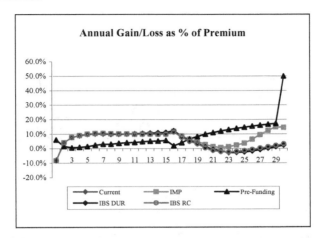

On a present value basis, IMP is the most profitable, both in terms of dollars and percent of premium. Durational Pooling generates slightly higher profits than the Current Market, both in terms of dollars and percent of premium. Prefunding generates higher profit dollars than all but the IMP, but the lowest profits as a percent of premium. Rate Compression is virtually identical to the Current Market.

With respect to pattern, surplus strain impacts all but the Prefunding solution in the first year. With the exception of Prefunding, profit margins increase steadily in future years then begin to erode beginning in year 17, reaching minimum levels at about year 22, and increasing thereafter. The IMP model in particular increases to significant levels in future years.

The Prefunding solution has a much different pattern than the other models. As mentioned, the high initial rate levels eliminate surplus strain in year one. Thereafter, moderate to low profit margins are achieved (although much lower than the other models) through year 17, then increases steadily to levels significantly higher than the other models, no doubt generated by reserve releases. This slow emergence of profits will be a concern to a number of carriers in the market and may be a barrier to new carriers entering into the market.

May 12, 2004

Economic Gain/Loss

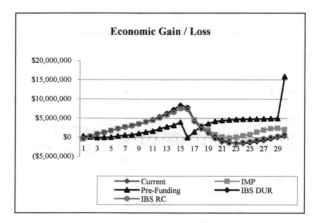

Economic Gain/Loss generates generally the same pattern as Annual Gain/Loss with the following exceptions.

On a present value basis, Prefunding generates the lowest profits, both in terms of dollars and percent of premium. This appears to be caused by higher cost of capital due to reserves.

When comparing the results of these models to each other, it is assumed that all external forces stay consistent. This would include such things as rating characteristics, state mandates and rating rules, taxation, and other factors affecting the rating of individual health policies.

Another factor affecting comparison of these methods is the relative provider payment levels that competing companies pay. There may be situations where some companies, who may pay lower claim costs per person, perhaps due to negotiated discounts being significantly larger than their competitors, may already be using a different form of rating methodology than some of their competitors. If this is the case, then the resulting comparisons from one method to another may be appropriate for each company, but may not be appropriate for the market in general in that state.

For example, assume a state has a carrier that uses some form of a prefunding type rating method and has competitive premiums because of their superior provider discounts. If the state were to move to a prefunding rating approach the effect on this company could be minimal. Also, assume that the other competitors in the state are using rating methodologies closer to what we have modeled as the current marketplace in order to be competitive with the previous carrier. If they were to move to the new prefunding approach, their rates might then become non-competitive due to their lack of the same level of negotiated discounts. In the most extreme situation this could result in a significant competitive advantage for the carrier with the low rates.

May 12, 2004

Section IX. Sensitivity Testing

We tested the sensitivity of changes in the following global modeling assumptions on the output of the model for each of the four potential solutions:

1. Reducing the Market Price Sensitivity and Carrier Price Sensitivity by 50% (these Sensitivities essentially adjust new business sales due to the relationship between the Market premium versus the Reference premium and the Carrier Premium versus the Market Premium, respectively)
2. Increasing the Reference Premium (essentially the overall needed premium) by $10/month
3. Decreasing the Reference Premium by $10/month
4. Discounting the initial Premium by 20%
5. Loading the initial Premium by 20%
6. Increasing the Standard lives Lapse Rate by 50%
7. Reducing the Impaired Lives Lapse Rate from 12% to 5%
8. Each of the alternative trend scenarios listed in Appendix E.

The results of these Sensitivity Tests on the outputs from the model are as follows:

Test #1: Total enrollment was 2% less under all modeling assumptions, except for Prefunding where it was 5% higher. Similarly, the Net Economic Gain to the carrier was virtually unaffected under all modeling assumptions, except for Prefunding where it was 5% higher.

Test #2: Total enrollment was 2% higher under all modeling assumptions, except for Prefunding where it was 4% higher. However, the Net Economic Gain to the carrier was 2% lower under all modeling assumptions, except for Prefunding where it was 6% higher.

Test #3: Total enrollment was 2.0% lower under all modeling assumptions, except for Prefunding where it was 5% lower. Again, the Net Economic Gain to the carrier was 2% higher under all modeling assumptions, except for Prefunding where it was 7% lower.

Test #4: Total enrollment was 12% higher for Individual Medical Pool and for Inter-block Subsidy – Rate Compression; was 3% higher for Inter-block Subsidy – Durational Pooling; and was 15% higher for Prefunding. The Net Economic Gain to the carrier was 41% - 49% lower for Individual Medical Pool and for Inter-block Subsidy – Rate Compression; was 9% lower for Inter-block Subsidy – Durational Pooling; and was 60% lower for Prefunding.

Test #5: Total enrollment was 17% lower for Individual Medical Pool and for Inter-block Subsidy – Rate Compression; was 4% lower for Inter-block Subsidy – Durational Pooling; and was 19% lower for Prefunding. The Net Economic Gain to the carrier was 13% - 17% higher for Individual Medical Pool and for Inter-block Subsidy – Rate Compression; was 5% higher for Inter-block Subsidy – Durational Pooling; and was 19% higher for Prefunding.

Test #6: Total enrollment was 37% lower for Individual Medical Pool and for Inter-block Subsidy – Rate Compression; was 39% lower for Inter-block Subsidy – Durational Pooling; and was 37% lower for Prefunding. The Net Economic Gain to the carrier was 59% lower for Individual Medical Pool and for Inter-block Subsidy

– Rate Compression; was 57% lower for Inter-block Subsidy – Durational Pooling; and was 63% lower for Prefunding.

Test #7: Total enrollment was 1% - 3% higher under all modeling assumptions, except for Inter-block Subsidy – Durational Pooling where it was 1% lower. The Net Economic Gain to the carrier was 15% lower for Individual Medical Pool; was 26% lower for Inter-block Subsidy – Rate Compression; was 30% lower for Inter-block Subsidy – Durational Pooling; and changed enormously from a $31 million gain to a $36 million loss for Prefunding.

Test #8: Projected trends were replaced by each of the alternatives in Appendix E. Under each of the ten claim trend scenarios, the current market and the four solutions maintained the same relative positions with respect to each other, by duration, with respect to:

- Market New Business Premiums, - Total Enrollment,

- Average Rate Increases,

- Maximum Rate Increases, and - Annual Claims.

Economic gain maintained a consistent relationship by duration for each solution except for the Prefunding solution, which was somewhat more volatile. Prefunding premium levels were generally more stable than the others.

Conclusions
1. None of the models are sensitive to changes in Market Price Sensitivity, Carrier Price Sensitivity, or Reference Premium.
2. All the models are very sensitive, and equally sensitive, to a change in the Standard lives Lapse Rate
3. All the models are sensitive to loading the initial premium. The Prefunding model is the most sensitive and the Inter-block Subsidy – Durational Pooling model seems to "self-adjust" and be the least sensitive.
4. All the models are very sensitive to discounting the initial premium. The Prefunding model is the most sensitive and the Inter-block Subsidy – Durational Pooling model seems to "self-adjust" and be the least sensitive.
5. The Net Economic Gain produced by the models is very sensitive to the Impaired Lives Lapse Rate. In particular, the Prefunding models swings from a sizable gain to a sizable loss. The other models still show gains, but with reductions of 15% - 30%.

In summary, the economic results produced by the Inter-block Subsidy – Durational Pooling model appear to be the least sensitive to changes in the underlying assumptions, while the results produced by the Prefunding model are the most sensitive.

Appendix A: Relevant portions of LHATF's Dec., 2000, meeting minutes:

Rate Adequacy – Medical

The working group sent a letter to the AAA (Attachment L of the Dec. 3, 1999, minutes of the Accident and Health Working Group) requesting assistance concerning possible replacements for the Accident and Health Individual Rate Filing Guidelines. The working group held an additional half-day meeting on Dec. 1 to give feedback to the American Academy of Actuaries' committee that is studying revised approaches to rate regulation of medical expense insurance.

Ms. Philips opened the discussions by reviewing desirable criteria underlying rate regulation that were identified during an interim meeting of the Accident and Health Working Group on Aug. 6-7, 1997 (see Attachment B of the Sept. 19, 1997, minutes of the Accident and Health Working Group). The working group then reviewed the prior criteria in the current environment and agreed that the desirable criteria underlying rate regulation for medical products, in order of priority, are as follows:

a) Rate Stability
b) Consumer Choice c) Disclosure

The working group noted that historically regulations addressing medical rating have been based on "premiums being reasonable in relation to benefits" (reasonableness test). Some of the working group members felt that the reasonableness test was equally applicable regardless of whether rates were excessive or inadequate; however, it was noted that historically, the reasonableness test had been used to address primarily excessive rates.

Mr. Batte stated that most states have two basic versions of rate regulations. One version is primarily applicable to property and casualty business and requires that premiums not be unfair, inadequate, or discriminatory. A second version is primarily applicable to life and health business and requires that premiums be reasonable in relation to benefits. The working group agreed that the property and casualty approach would not be appropriate for medical rate regulations because property and casualty business is sufficiently different in the following ways:

a) Property and casualty products are primarily one-year term products, whereas medical business may be inforce for a lifetime
b) Trend is smaller for property and casualty business
c) Property and casualty business is a totally different environment

The working group agreed that the current belief is that competition will control excessive rates. Ms. Philips also noted that if people have choices then reasonableness is not as much of an issue. However, the issue of consumer choice also has sub-issues of suitability and availability.

William Bluhm (Milliman & Robertson, Inc. representing the American Academy of Actuaries) requested that the working group define the terms "rate stability," "consumer choice," and "disclosure."

May 12, 2004

The working group agreed that rate stability exists when rate increases are within a corridor of trend that reduces the probability of spirals. Rate stability also has the following characteristics:

a) Carrier should not become insolvent
b) Reduce the probability of rate spirals

c) Long term rate increases should not be greater than the trend in the underlying healthcare costs

Ms. Philips stated that rate stability implies an annual limit on rate increases (such as trend). Mr. Diamond added that even if annual increases are minimal, it is possible for rates to not be stable if the cumulative effect of the annual increases is sufficiently large.

The working group agreed that the following characteristics were associated with consumer choice:

a) Availability
b) Affordability
c) Suitability
d) Portability within carrier

The working group also discussed portability across insurers and determined that portability across insurers is outside the scope of this charge. Mr. Sky also noted that rate stability and consumer choice are conflicting goals.

Mr. Dino suggested that disclosure could encompass rate history disclosure. He further stated that he discovered that, historically, some insurers selling attained-age policies had not always disclosed the entire rate schedule applicable to a particular insured.

The working group agreed that rate regulations should be constrained by the following:

a) Do not unfairly discriminate
b) Do not be arbitrary
c) Do not take away power to purchaser
d) Minimize amount of bureaucratic paperwork
e) Do not impose burdens on companies or states
f) Do not disadvantage existing insurers in the market

The working group next focused on the Oct. 30, 2000, memorandum from Mr. Bluhm. The working group agreed to the following concerning methods of dealing with closed blocks:

#	Method	Comments
a)	A high risk pool	There was no consensus of the working group as to whether this was a viable option or not. A key point was whether individuals may enter a risk pool if they have existing coverage. Some states permit this where other states do not.
b)	A reinsurance mechanism (one that is transparent to the policy-holder)	The working group thought this option could be worthwhile to explore.
c)	Pool of all business or a subset of all business	The working group thought that this option would be acceptable.
d)	Limit rate increase (i.e., equal to new business rates, fixed percent-age or based on some index such as the CPI)	The working group thought that this option was probably not feasible.
e)	Use rating bands similar to the small group model	Mr. Rink expressed concerns with rating bands causing rates for younger insureds to increase and force them out of the market. Mr. Dino suggested that rating bands could impose limitations on underwriting loads or discounts rather than across age bands.
f)	Rate guarantees	The working group thought that this option was probably not feasible.
g)	Prefunding	The working group believes that this option is consistent with the desired goals. How-ever, the working group did acknowledge that the biggest obstacle to this option is affordability.
h)	Disclose prior rate increases or anticipated premiums	The working group thought this option could be worthwhile to explore.
i)	Require a higher loss ratio on the portion of any premium that is in excess of the initial premium	The working group thought that this option would be acceptable.
j)	Adjust deductibles/co-pays with trend	The working group thought they would be willing to consider this option.
k)	Full guaranteed issue or guaran-teed portability to another carrier	During the discussions concerning con-sumer choice (see above), the working group determined that this option is not within the scope of the charge.

May 12, 2004

Additionally, Mr. Dino proposed that one more option be added for consideration. The new option would be to limit the extent that insurers could include catastrophic claims in a single policy form. Catastrophic claims above a certain level would be pooled across all policies.

Next, the working group addressed loss ratios. In particular, Ms. Philips raised the question of whether insurers should be permitted to recoup past losses. Ms. Philips drew a chart where the projected slope of loss ratios was flatter after a proposed rate increase than what

was originally anticipated in the original pricing assumptions. There was no consensus among the working group members as to whether the flatter loss ratio slope should be permitted.

Mr. Foley emphasized that options other than fixed loss ratios might be more effective.

Mr. Sky stated that the numerator and denominator should be on a consistent basis, such as incurred claims and earned premium.

The working group discussed what should be included in the numerator of the loss ratio. In particular, the issue of whether a subsidy should be included in the numerator. Mr. Diamond stated it should. Mr. Weller inquired as to whether the numerator would include the cost of a managed care network. Ms. Philips noted that the Codification Subteam of the Accident and Health Working Group is addressing whether claim adjustment expenses should be included with losses. Mr. Rink noted that the work of the Codification Subteam is limited to statutory reporting and was not being recommended for rate increase determination at this time.

The working group next discussed on what basis is a lifetime period determined – an average policy, a policy form, or block of business. Mr. Diamond stated that the lifetime should be based on the policy form. Ms. Philips and Mr. Sky agreed that the lifetime should be based on an average policy.

With regard to Mr. Bluhm's question regarding the standard of review, Mr. Diamond stated that the review should be less initially.

The working group agreed to defer discussions concerning competitive markets until some other issues have been addressed.

Additionally, the working group agreed that it would be difficult to not require loss ratio minimums until it is known what could replace them. The working group requested that the Academy task force provide feedback on the existence of any viable alternatives to loss ratios, that would do a better job of ensuring that premiums are reasonable.

May 12, 2004

Appendix B: The Drivers of Rate Increases

Not including changes that might be necessary due to increased distribution costs, administrative costs, taxation, or cost of capital, there are three classes of drivers that impact the size of a needed rate increase.

1. Overview of Drivers
  a) External Cost Drivers
       i) These are factors driving up medical costs in the economy that are independent of the individual marketplace and independent of any specific insurer's pricing, marketing, underwriting, and product management practices.
  b) Internal Cost Drivers
       i) These are factors relating to the selection dynamics in the individual marketplace.
  c) Correction of Prior Actuarial Estimates
       i) These factors are due to an unanticipated change in an external or internal cost driver; or a data analysis error.
       ii) The impact of these factors on rate increases is directly related to the time delay in the detection of the change or error and in implementing the corrective action.

2. Expanded Analysis of Drivers
  a) External Cost Drivers
       i) Medical CPI represents the cost change for a defined market basket of medical services.
       ii) Change in utilization represents the change in the frequency of services provided for similar insureds with similar medical conditions. Intensity represents the change in the level of services provided (i.e. comprehensive office visit vs. brief office visit) for similar insureds with similar medical conditions.
       iii) Change in intensity represents the change in the level of services provided (e.g. comprehensive office visit vs. brief office visit) for similar insureds with similar medical conditions.
       iv) New technology represents the cost change of new innovations, including new equipment, new procedures and new medications.
       v) Deductible leveraging represents the impact of calendar year deductibles on plan costs. This reflects the fact that due to cost increases a greater percentage of costs will exceed a fixed deductible. The impact of deductible leveraging depends on the insurer's mix of business by plan type and deductible.
       vi) Cost shifting is caused by payments to providers for Medicare, Medicaid, and indigent care that are often paid at a level that doesn't cover fully allocated costs. To compensate for this, providers typically increase their revenue demands from insurers and other payors.
       vii) Increases in disease prevalence over time. AIDS was a disease unknown prior to the 1980's. Cancer rates for many classes of tumors are on the rise. This may be due to increased environmental risks, poorer health maintenance or other causes. Obesity is on the increase and is a known cause of increased disease prevalence.

May 12, 2004

viii) State benefit mandates add additional costs to benefit plans that insurers and their customers had previously decided to exclude from coverage.
ix) Federal benefit mandates are a relatively new driver. Since the mid-1990's the federal government has become active in adding benefit entitlements to health plans, and some of these impact individual plans.
x) Other Legislative/Regulatory activity also drives increased costs. HIPAA portability in many states requires additional costs for portability rights to be assigned to individual policies. Government extensions of drug patents and refusal to move drugs to over the counter status increase costs. Legislative requirements often increase administrative expenses, as well.
xi) Increases in the supply of providers, including increases in hospital beds, physicians and other health care providers drive supply-based cost increases.
xii) Aging of the population increases the prevalence of disease throughout the adult lifetime of covered individuals.
xiii) Consolidation in the provider community can lead to greater leverage for providers and correspondingly less leverage for insurers in reimbursement rate negotiations.

b) Internal Cost Drivers
i) As the market price of individual insurance increases, more of the healthier individuals become, or stay, self-insured. The remaining purchasers are relatively more costly and are higher utilizers of health care services. This drives up new business costs.
ii) New buyers of insurance who expect to use fewer health care services purchase lower cost and/or higher deductible products. The effect of this is to reduce the overall income to the block of business from people who would normally have few or no claims. This can increase the overall loss ratio of the block.
iii) Standard insureds drop coverage instead of renewing it.
iv) Standard insureds switch insurers instead of renewing with the same company.
v) Standard insureds reduce coverage at renewal, thereby reducing the premium coming into the block of business.
vi) Wear off of new business underwriting and pre-existing condition clauses
vii) Inflation erodes the deterrent effect of co-pays and deductibles, and more insureds reach their out-of-pocket maximums.
viii) Inability to predict the timing and amount of rate increases when actually approved by the states

c) Inaccuracies of Prior Actuarial Estimations
i) Failure to appropriately predict claims by duration.
ii) Failure to use appropriate seasonality adjustments.
iii) Failure to estimate appropriate claim reserves.
iv) Failure to estimate future claims level due to not adjusting for anticipated future changes in claim levels that could reasonably have been foreseen. For example, the announcement of a new high cost treatment for a relatively common condition that is currently treated at lower cost.
v) Lack of timeliness or unavailability of data.

Appendix C: Competitive Markets

Characteristics of a Competitive Marketplace
- Number of Sellers and Concentration of Market Share Among Sellers Concentration Ratios
  - This measure is the market share of the top five competitors, individually and
    in aggregate.
  - One possible definition of a competitive market is that the largest competitor has no more than 60% market share and the top five competitors together have more than 80% of the market.

Herfindahl Index.
  - This measure of market concentration is defined as:

    $HI = \sum (MSn)^2$, where HI is the Herfindahl Index, and MSn is the market share of competitor n
  - Normally an index of less than 0.2 indicates that the attributes of a competitive market exist.
  - An index above 0.7 indicates the market is operating as a monopoly.
- Level of Margins and Return on Capital

  In order to have many players in a market there must be the expectation of consistent returns in excess of the cost of capital. Extremely low or extremely high returns are evidence that there may not be a competitive marketplace.

  Individual medical insurance is a very capital intensive business often requiring capital in the range of 15% to 25% of earned premium. The risks imposed by an uncertain regulatory environment combined with the volatility of underwriting cycles result in a need for higher returns in order to attract capital from increasingly competitive capital markets.

  Consistent profit margins in excess of 10% of premium or return on equity consistently above 40% for the market as a whole may indicate a lack of competitiveness. Consistent margins of less than 3% or returns on equity for the market as a whole of less than 15% may indicate the market is over-regulated or has some structural deficiency making the market unattractive to new entrants.

- Low Barriers to Market Entry by Sellers

  In order for a market to be competitive it must be relatively easy for new competitors to enter the market.

  For individual medical this usually means that the initial capital requirements should not be excessively high, the regulations should not be unduly harsh or complex, and access to health care provider contracts at competitive rates must be available.

When new competitors enter a market, it is likely a sign of a healthy competitive market.

- Access to Product by Purchasers and Ability of Purchasers to Switch Insurers

In order for markets to be competitive the prices must be low enough to attract purchasers, and there must be relative ease for the majority of purchasers to switch insurers.

However, this access must not restrict or hinder the market. For example:

Guaranteed issue provisions often result in prices so high that purchasers exit the market. This shrinks the market, since only those with a very high utility for health care will be purchasers. This typically will continue to spiral, as impaired members of the large pool of uninsured enter the market, driving prices even higher.

In a marketplace that allows underwriting and has a risk pool the market can operate more efficiently, since prices will be lower and impaired non-purchasers can access coverage via the risk pool. Also current purchasers who are impaired have an option to switch to the risk pool.

- Ability of Purchaser to Evaluate Fairly and Choose Among Products

In order for a competitive market to operate efficiently, consumers must be able to compare and contrast the economic value of various benefit options. They must also make assessments not only about issue prices but also about anticipated future renewal increases.

Educated insurance advisors and disclosure can enable consumers to make good economic decisions based on the best available information.

Disclosure of historical rate increases over several years, disclosure of rating methodologies, and anticipated loss ratios may assist the consumer in making informed choices.

- Price of the Product and the Level of Quality and Innovation

Important attributes of a competitive market are a wide variety of product choices and the ability for insurers to innovate and improve the quality of their product offering.

A large number of insurers with a large number of product options would be indicative of a relatively competitive market.

- Access of Sellers to Competitive Supply of Health Care Services

It is important that no one or two insurers monopsonize the purchase of health care services. In a small markets one vertically integrated supplier of health coverage and health care services may monopsonize the market for health care services and monopolize the market for individual health insurance. This could prevent entry of more competitors into this market by placing them at a significant cost disadvantage.

- Fair and Consistent Set of Rules for All Insurers

  Most policymakers feel there should be a level playing field for all insurers. Examples of violations of this characteristic are application of unique rate review requirements, differing mandated benefits, or varying premium tax rates by types of insurers.

Examples of Market Attributes That Hinder Competition

- Mandated Guaranteed Issue of All Products

  This will cause prices to spiral upward preventing access.

- Mandated Exclusive Offering of Standardized State Plans Fixed product designs preclude innovation and quality improvements.

- Rate Controls that Preclude a Fair Return on Capital or Impose Excessively Burdensome Administrative Costs

  The inability to attract capital will result in fewer competitors and less competition.

- Dominance of the Purchasing of Healthcare by a Few Insurers Precluding Other Insurers Access to Health Care Purchasing at Comparable Rates

  This situation, with one carrier having greater purchasing power will lead to a reduction in insurers, less choice and higher premiums for insurers trying to compete.

- Rate Corridors, Rate Caps, High Minimum Loss Ratios, Modified Community Rating, and/or Limits on Rating Variables

  These pricing controls increase the variance between anticipated claim costs and price, causing the price to increase beyond the purchasing utility of many buyers, since the price is higher than the perceived benefit. These controls may also cause insurers to exit the market due to inadequate return on investment.

- Mandated Coverages

  These mandates force buyers to purchase coverage options for which they may have no utility at all. Buyers may choose instead to exit the market as the mandates drive up premiums.

May 12, 2004

Appendix D: The Current Marketplace

In order to evaluate the alternatives presented in this paper, it is important that there be agreement as to the characteristics of the current market, including the regulatory environment. It may be that what is presented here becomes controversial; it is not meant to be. It is meant to be a recitation of facts relevant to the problem at hand.

The Individual Major Medical Marketplace

Within the individual marketplace, it is common practice to close off periodically a policy form to new business and introduce a replacement form. This closes off the inflow of newly underwritten entrants into the closed form. As a result, average claim cost levels will tend to rise above those experienced under forms that are open to new business, and pricing of the closed form will tend to reflect the higher costs. Standard policyholders will be more likely than impaired to terminate their policies, either because they can qualify for a more favorable new business premium with another carrier, or because they feel more confident about their prospects for going without insurance. This again increases average claim costs, which tends to increase further premiums on the closed form beyond the premium levels on open forms, and the cycle continues. This is the "closed block" problem.

Some contributors to the problem include pricing structures that link higher morbidity associated to underwriting wear-off and renewal antiselection to rate increases, and greater ability of standard lives than impaired to move within the market or to exit the market.

Rate increases in individual major medical insurance are influenced by a large number of potential drivers as described in Appendix B.

The current marketplace consists of a multitude of individual insuring entities, each with unique procedures and philosophies regarding marketing and insured selection and underwriting. At the time of initial premium rate development, each entity is faced with a decision, whether explicit or implicit, in terms of the extent to which the durational change in future claim costs are reflected in new business rates. The decision involves a trade-off between future renewal rate increases and the new business rate level. In a competitive marketplace, these decisions cannot be made in a vacuum. Rather, consideration must be given to competition within a target market and an understanding of the market viewpoint regarding the relative desirability and/or merits of initial rate level versus future rate action. Whether or not this understanding is reality or perception, the current marketplace appears to be generally characterized by a strong emphasis on initial rate level.

Attractiveness of the Marketplace

Other attributes that affect the attractiveness of a market are: speed to market, regulatory responsiveness, regulatory flexibility, allowable rating frequency, market adaptability, the litigation environment, and the size of the potential market. Each of these will be considered before a carrier decides to operate in a state.

The following exhibits show how specific factors affect the attractiveness of states for companies marketing individual major medical policies. Exhibit 1 shows individual factors and how they range from attractive to unattractive. Exhibit 2 gives a summary of the current environment and shows the number of states in each category, according to our subcommittee which looked at this.

May 12, 2004

Exhibit 1

Individual Major Medical Marketplace Attractiveness Scale
(Insurer Perspective)

Regulatory Environment:
◄ Highly Attractive Markets   Unattractive Markets ►

Price Controls	No Filing	Info Only Filing		File and Use Rates	File and Approve Rates
Expected Minimum Lifetime Loss Ratio	None, or < 60%	65% and Adj. For MHC, Prem Tax, and Assessments		65%	> 65%
Rate Corridor	No Rate Corridor Limitation	Rate by class/ Block based on experience	± 35%	± 25%	± 0%
Underwriting Limitations	Rate, Rider and Decline	Rate w/limits, Rider w/limits, Decline	Rate w/ limits, no riders, decline	Accept Decline Only	Guaranteed Issue Only
HIPAA Portability	Risk Pool	Two Representative Plans, no limits on substandard	Two Most Popular Plans, 300% rate-up limit	All Plans, 100% rate-up limit	Full Guaranteed Issue
Mandates	None	Mandated Benefits	Mandated Benefits and Beneficiaries	Mandated Benefits, Beneficiaries, Providers	Mandated Benefit Options (Choice), Beneficiaries, Providers

Exhibit 2

Summary of Current State Individual Major Medical Market Environment

◄ Highly Attractive Markets   Unattractive Markets ►

A	B	C	D	F
18 States	13 states	7 states	7 states	6 states

May 12, 2004

Appendix E: Claim Trend Scenarios

			\multicolumn{8}{c}{Scenario}		
From Year		To Yr	Medium	High	Low	Jump	Drop	Peak	Valley	Baseline Cyclic A	Cyclic B	Medical CPI+5% History
1	-	2	12.0%	18.0%	6.0%	12.0%	12.0%	12.0%	12.0%	12.0%	12.0%	9.6%
2	to	3	12.0%	18.0%	6.0%	12.0%	12.0%	13.0%	11.0%	15.0%	9.0%	8.3%
3	to	4	12.0%	18.0%	6.0%	12.0%	12.0%	14.0%	10.0%	18.0%	6.0%	10.3%
4	to	5	12.0%	18.0%	6.0%	12.0%	12.0%	15.0%	9.0%	15.0%	9.0%	17.6%
5	to	6	12.0%	18.0%	6.0%	12.0%	12.0%	16.0%	8.0%	12.0%	12.0%	14.8%
6	to	7	12.0%	18.0%	6.0%	18.0%	6.0%	17.0%	7.0%	9.0%	15.0%	15.0%
7	to	8	12.0%	18.0%	6.0%	18.0%	6.0%	18.0%	6.0%	12.0%	12.0%	13.9%
8	to	9	12.0%	18.0%	6.0%	18.0%	6.0%	19.0%	5.0%	15.0%	9.0%	13.8%
9	to	10	12.0%	18.0%	6.0%	18.0%	6.0%	20.0%	4.0%	18.0%	6.0%	15.1%
10	to	11	12.0%	18.0%	6.0%	18.0%	6.0%	19.0%	5.0%	15.0%	9.0%	14.9%
11	to	12	12.0%	18.0%	6.0%	18.0%	6.0%	18.0%	6.0%	12.0%	12.0%	17.5%
12	to	13	12.0%	18.0%	6.0%	18.0%	6.0%	17.0%	7.0%	9.0%	15.0%	16.0%
13	to	14	12.0%	18.0%	6.0%	18.0%	6.0%	16.0%	8.0%	12.0%	12.0%	11.4%
14	to	15	12.0%	18.0%	6.0%	18.0%	6.0%	15.0%	9.0%	15.0%	9.0%	11.1%
15	to	16	12.0%	18.0%	6.0%	18.0%	6.0%	14.0%	10.0%	18.0%	6.0%	11.8%
16	to	17	12.0%	18.0%	6.0%	18.0%	6.0%	13.0%	11.0%	15.0%	9.0%	12.7%
17	to	18	12.0%	18.0%	6.0%	18.0%	6.0%	12.0%	12.0%	12.0%	12.0%	10.8%
18	to	19	12.0%	18.0%	6.0%	18.0%	6.0%	12.0%	12.0%	9.0%	15.0%	11.9%
19	to	20	12.0%	18.0%	6.0%	18.0%	6.0%	12.0%	12.0%	12.0%	12.0%	13.5%
20	to	21	12.0%	18.0%	6.0%	18.0%	6.0%	12.0%	12.0%	15.0%	9.0%	14.6%
21	to	22	12.0%	18.0%	6.0%	18.0%	6.0%	12.0%	12.0%	18.0%	6.0%	12.9%
22	to	23	12.0%	18.0%	6.0%	18.0%	6.0%	12.0%	12.0%	15.0%	9.0%	11.6%
23	to	24	12.0%	18.0%	6.0%	18.0%	6.0%	12.0%	12.0%	12.0%	12.0%	10.4%
24	to	25	12.0%	18.0%	6.0%	18.0%	6.0%	12.0%	12.0%	9.0%	15.0%	9.9%
25	to	26	12.0%	18.0%	6.0%	18.0%	6.0%	12.0%	12.0%	12.0%	12.0%	8.9%
26	to	27	12.0%	18.0%	6.0%	18.0%	6.0%	12.0%	12.0%	15.0%	9.0%	8.0%
27	to	28	12.0%	18.0%	6.0%	18.0%	6.0%	12.0%	12.0%	18.0%	6.0%	7.8%
28	to	29	12.0%	18.0%	6.0%	18.0%	6.0%	12.0%	12.0%	15.0%	9.0%	8.4%
29	to	30	12.0%	18.0%	6.0%	18.0%	6.0%	12.0%	12.0%	12.0%	12.0%	8.7%
30	to	31	12.0%	18.0%	6.0%	18.0%	6.0%	12.0%	12.0%	9.0%	15.0%	9.2%

May 12, 2004

Appendix F: Survey of State Regulatory Environment of Premium Rates for Individual Major Medical Insurance Policies

The RFTF determined that there was value to the readers of the report, as well as a need to develop a common starting point for RFTF members, to be familiar with key elements of the current regulatory environment that affect premium rates in today's market. Since regulation of insurance companies still remains primarily with state government, and there is no central location from which to capture how each state handles this regulation, the RFTF sought to compile this information by going to the State regulatory body in each of the 50 states. Rather than researching thousands of pages of states' laws, regulations and bulletins, and recognizing that provisions in some states give regulators the right to form interpretations, we conducted the research in the form of asking the key regulator on premium rates in each state to complete a survey. The RFTF constructed the questions of the survey to capture the most important elements of this study.

The survey was sent out in March 2003. Responses were tabulated for the 23 states that returned them.

Each state was asked to complete a separate survey for HMO type policies and another for indemnity and preferred provider policies, if the laws or regulations within a state regulated them differently. A similar request was made for distinctions in regulations for Blue Cross type policies. None of the 23 states responding reported any separate laws or regulations for Blue Cross type policies. Only two states reported regulating HMOs differently for premium rates than for the other types of policies. For these two states, the variances were minimal. Due to the low response and the nominal differences, the RFTF chose not to compile the HMO surveys for this report. We called the non-HMO responses "commercial" for the purposes of this report.

The industry uses a mix of legal contracts to insure individuals in this market, including individual, group association, and group discretionary trust policies. When the group master policy is issued outside of the state in which the individual resides, the regulation may differ from that applicable to policies issued inside the state. Some states have no regulation on premium rates if the individual is covered by an out-of-state group association or trust policy. Other states have separate regulations for these types of polices, and other states regulate them the same, even if they have no specific regulatory language to do so. Recognizing this industry movement, the RFTF felt it important to make the distinction in compiling the results of the survey. The responses indicated that almost half of the states responding have no regulatory authority on premium rates for individuals residing in their state if they are covered by an out-of-state master group policy. More specifically, ten responded they have no jurisdiction, eleven responded they do have jurisdiction, and two did not respond.

The RFTF concluded from the survey responses that regulation of individual health insurance policies is far from consistent, ranging from no specific requirements in a few states (i.e., no filing requirement or reference exists in the state's regulations) to very extensive regulation (e.g., requiring filing and approval, demonstration that experience and assumptions be proven, limitations on premium rate size by duration since a policy is issued, etc.). The survey questions, along with the responses, are shown in the following table:

May 12, 2004

Tabulation of Responses from the State Regulatory Environment Survey of Premium Rates for Individual Major Medical Insurance

States that responded for commercial or all types of legal entities:

AL, AR, AZ, CT, FL, ID, IN, KY, LA, MA, MS, MN, NC, ND, NH, NJ, NV, OK, OR, SD, VT, WA, WY

Does my state have any rate jurisdiction for out-of-state master policies?

YES	NO	NO RESPONSE
11	10	2

Comments on above question

- #6: "only on groups formed for purposes of issuing insurance"
- #17: "Answers below apply to trusts and associations"
- #20: "Statutes apply extraterritorially to group health plans covering residents of our state, regardless of where group contract is issued or delivered."
- #11: "Yes, but only for certificates issued in the state."

	Item	Yes	No	Sometimes (please comment)	Amt. or Percent	Comments &/or Citation
1.	New Form Rate approval required?	14	9			#6: out of state discretionary group, informational
2.	New Form Rate approval is not required if a loss ratio is guaranteed?	4	17			
3.	New Form Rate must be filed only?	9	13			#6: out of state discretionary group, informational
4.	New Form Rate filing is unnecessary?	2	19			#6: out of state discretionary group, informational
5.	Rate change approval required?	14	9			
6.	Rate change approval is not required if a loss ratio is guaranteed?	6	15			#2: "must file changes" #6: "out of state not required"
7.	Rate changes must be filed only?	5	16			#2: "must explain impact" #6: "out of state not required"

May 12, 2004

8.	Rate change filing is unnecessary?	3	18		
9.	Are periodic Rate filings or experience filings required even if no changes in rates? (If yes, please comment on the frequency)	6	18		#1: "annually" #6: "requires an annual filing that the rates are adequate"
10.	Are there any restrictions on filing/applying rate changes more frequently than annually? If yes, please specify.	8	14		#10: "Department guidelines: no more frequently than every 12 months" #1: "unreasonable to file on change more than annually" #12: "12 month rate guarantee required"
11.	Do you require new business rate filings to indicate the anticipated loss ratio minimums? If yes, indicate the minimum allowed %.	15	9	50%: #5, #18 55%: #19 65%: #6, #9 60,68 or 72%: #1 70%: #23, #8 75%: #3, #11	#1: "depends on market size" #12: "varies per NAIC model"
12.	Do you allow rate change filings to change the anticipated loss ratio, as long as it is still above the minimum?	18	3		#6: "subject to justification & prior approval"
13.	Do you have any other restrictions, other than items 11 & 12, on the magnitude of rates, or their change? If "yes", please respond to a-f below	11	11	#8: 20%	
a.	On range by age? If yes, specify amt. (example: 5:1)	8	8	#3: 1:1 #15: 75% #23: 5:1 #9: 4:1 #7: 1.5:1 #1: 3:1	#23: "also includes geography, gender and industry" #9: also "includes geography in combination"
b.	On range by area? If yes, specify amt. (example: 1:1, 2:1, etc.)	5	9	#23: 5:1 #9: 1.5:1 #1: 0.8:1 #18: 1:1 #3: 1:1	#2: "only 6 areas," responded "sometimes" #23: also "includes age, gender and industry"

May 12, 2004

c.	On health status, including smoker status? If yes, specify amt. (example: +/- 35% of index rate)	8	7		#2: 15% #23: +or-35% #9: 0 #1: 1.67:1 #18: 1.5:1 #7: +or-30% #22: +75%	#18: AAA Task Force comment – additional 1.5:1 for smokers #2 & #9: "but no smoker status restrictions"
d.	Do any of the above restrictions apply across more than the filed form? (example: rates must be within 20% of an index rate between blocks of business, which may be forms or groupings of forms.)	6	9	1	#23: 10% #2: 50% between blocks #7: +or-30% of index	#23: "for different classes of business" #2: "one class of business" #9: "sometimes" response; "if small closed blocks" #1: "across entire individual block"
e.	On the magnitude of the rate increase? If possible, specify amt. (example: 15% plus trend)	5	10	1	#23: trend + 20% #2: 39% age; 28.5% trend 15% health #8: 20%	#2: "trend & 15% plus age change – geo change" #11: "Department guidelines of reasonableness" #1: "Cannot be much larger than trend" #10: "No more than 25% from all sources in any one policy year.'
f.	Other? Please comment.	4	4		#3: 1:1	#1: "health status at issue is prohibited"
14.	Is reunderwriting prohibited, i.e., may an individual be changed from the health status rating class assigned at issue any time while he/she is covered?	14	8			#2: "must be at next rating period" #23: responded "no", "but health status cannot be considered at issue or at renewal" #20: "is proposing legislation this year" #4: "since individual is guaranteed renewable, it goes against concept to reunderwriting" #8: "reunderwriting and health status is prohibited"
15.	Are there any restrictions on premium rates by duration?, i.e., are there any prohibitions for premium rates to vary by the length of time since coverage was issued? If yes, please comment.	12	10		#2: part of 15% of question no. 13.e. 0%: #9, #1, #18, #3, #22, #17	#2: "risk characteristics – health, claims experience, duration" #23: 12 month rate guarantee #20: responded "no"; "is proposing legislation this year" #9: "no variation by duration" #1: "no variation by duration" #12: "do not approve year of issue nor duration as rating categories"

May 12, 2004

		<5	5-10	11-20	>20	Comments &/or Citation
16.	Please check the box that most closely indicates the approximate number of carriers that…					
a.	Are PPO or indemnity carriers, currently sell policies to individuals	5	10	2	3	#9: "only 1"
b.	Are PPO or indemnity carriers, currently sell out-of-state based master policy coverage to individuals	8	2	1	3	#9: "none legally" #1: "none, prohibited"
c.	Are PPO or indemnity carriers, no longer sell, but insure individuals via policies	7	3	2	6	#12: indicates 28
d.	Are PPO or indemnity carriers, no longer sell, but insure individuals via out-of-state master policy coverage	7	1	2	2	#2: "none"
e.	Are HMO carriers, no longer sell, but insure individuals via policies	13	2	2		#12: "by law conversions only; no HMO direct sold"
f.	Are HMO carriers, currently selling policies to individuals	15	2			#9: required by law #12: "all full service HMOs are required to offer individual conversion policy, but none offer any other individual business."

What problems in general would you like to share with the NAIC regarding rate increase, and other premium rate filings?

#2: "Despite implementing NAIC Model Act and Regs, no one interpretation is available; the process of applying rating requirements, specifically reference to 'sum of'" is particularly difficult as 'actuaries' are not willing to take a position."

If your state regulates insurance companies differently by the construction of the legal entity (commercial insurance carrier, health maintenance organization, Hospital, Medical, Dental, Indemnity service type organizations, HMDIs, such as a Blues Plan, etc.), please make copies of the above form, and submit a separate form for each, indicating what the entity is.

May 12, 2004

Table of Contents
Volume III
Tables and Graphs

American Academy of Actuaries
Rate Filing Task Force

Page	
Market New Business Premiums	71
Company New Business Premiums	72
New Business Sales	73
Total Enrollment	74
Percentage of Cohort 1 Enrollees who are Impaired	75
Percentage of All Enrollees who are Impaired	76
Summary of Rate Increases (tables)	77
Summary of Rate Increases (graphs by model)	78
Summary of Rate Increases (graphs by minimum, maximum & average)	79
Premiums for Cohort #1	80
Rate Increases for Cohort #1	81
Premiums for Cohort #5	82
Rate Increases for Cohort #5	83
Premiums for Cohort #10	84
Rate Increases for Cohort #10	85
Premiums for Cohort #15	86
Rate Increases for Cohort #15	87
All Blocks Combined Annual Premiums (in $1,000s)	88
All Blocks Combined Annual Claims (in $1,000s)	89
All Blocks Combined Annual Expenses (in $1,000s)	90
All Blocks Combined Annual Gain (Loss)	91
All Blocks Combined Annual Gain (Loss) as Percentage of Premium	92
All Blocks Combined Annual Economic Gain (Loss) – Includes Cost of Capital	93
All Blocks Combined Annual Economic Gain (Loss) as Percentage of Premium	94

May 12, 2004

AAA Rate Filing Task Force Model — Summary Values
Trend Scenario: 1
Market Results

Market New Business Premiums

Year	Current	IMP	Pre-Funding	IBS DUR	IBS RC	Current	IMP	Pre-Funding	IBS 'DUR	IBS 'RC
1	$127	$127	$167	$127	$127	100.0%	100.0%	131.9%	100.0%	100.0%
2	$142	$142	$187	$142	$142	100.0%	100.0%	131.9%	100.0%	100.0%
3	$159	$159	$209	$159	$159	100.0%	100.0%	131.9%	100.0%	100.0%
4	$178	$178	$234	$178	$178	100.0%	100.0%	131.9%	100.0%	100.0%
5	$199	$199	$263	$199	$199	100.0%	100.0%	131.9%	100.0%	100.0%
6	$223	$223	$294	$223	$223	100.0%	100.0%	131.9%	100.0%	100.0%
7	$250	$250	$329	$250	$250	100.0%	100.0%	131.9%	100.0%	100.0%
8	$280	$280	$369	$280	$280	100.0%	100.0%	131.9%	100.0%	100.0%
9	$313	$313	$413	$313	$313	100.0%	100.0%	131.9%	100.0%	100.0%
10	$351	$351	$463	$351	$351	100.0%	100.0%	131.9%	100.0%	100.0%
11	$393	$393	$518	$393	$393	100.0%	100.0%	131.9%	100.0%	100.0%
12	$440	$440	$580	$440	$440	100.0%	100.0%	131.9%	100.0%	100.0%
13	$493	$493	$650	$493	$493	100.0%	100.0%	131.9%	100.0%	100.0%
14	$552	$552	$728	$552	$552	100.0%	100.0%	131.9%	100.0%	100.0%
15	$618	$619	$815	$618	$618	100.0%	100.2%	131.9%	100.0%	100.0%
16	$692	$695	$913	$692	$692	100.0%	100.4%	131.9%	100.0%	100.0%
17	$775	$780	$1,023	$775	$775	100.0%	100.6%	131.9%	100.0%	100.0%
18	$868	$876	$1,146	$868	$868	100.0%	100.9%	131.9%	100.0%	100.0%
19	$973	$983	$1,283	$973	$973	100.0%	101.1%	131.9%	100.0%	100.0%
20	$1,089	$1,102	$1,437	$1,089	$1,089	100.0%	101.2%	131.9%	100.0%	100.0%
21	$1,220	$1,236	$1,609	$1,220	$1,220	100.0%	101.3%	131.9%	100.0%	100.0%
22	$1,366	$1,386	$1,802	$1,366	$1,366	100.0%	101.5%	131.9%	100.0%	100.0%
23	$1,530	$1,553	$2,019	$1,530	$1,530	100.0%	101.5%	131.9%	100.0%	100.0%
24	$1,714	$1,742	$2,261	$1,714	$1,714	100.0%	101.6%	131.9%	100.0%	100.0%
25	$1,919	$1,952	$2,532	$1,919	$1,919	100.0%	101.7%	131.9%	100.0%	100.0%
26	$2,150	$2,187	$2,836	$2,150	$2,150	100.0%	101.7%	131.9%	100.0%	100.0%
27	$2,408	$2,451	$3,176	$2,408	$2,408	100.0%	101.8%	131.9%	100.0%	100.0%
28	$2,696	$2,746	$3,557	$2,696	$2,696	100.0%	101.8%	131.9%	100.0%	100.0%
29	$3,020	$3,075	$3,984	$3,020	$3,020	100.0%	101.8%	131.9%	100.0%	100.0%
30	$3,382	$3,446	$4,462	$3,382	$3,382	100.0%	101.9%	131.9%	100.0%	100.0%

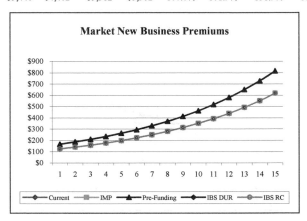

Market New Business Premiums

AAA Rate Filing Model – Exhhibits.xls
Global Summary

Trend Scenario: 1

Company New Business Premiums

Year	Current	IMP	Pre-Funding	IBS DUR	IBS RC	Current	IMP	Pre-Funding	IBS DUR	IBS RC
1	$127	$127	$167	$127	127	100.0%	100.0%	131.9%	100.0%	100.0%
2	$141	$141	$186	$141	141	100.0%	100.0%	131.9%	100.0%	100.0%
3	$158	$158	$208	$158	158	100.0%	100.0%	131.8%	100.0%	100.0%
4	$178	$178	$234	$177	178	100.0%	100.0%	131.9%	99.3%	100.0%
5	$198	$198	$261	$197	198	100.0%	100.0%	131.9%	99.6%	100.0%
6	$222	$222	$292	$220	222	100.0%	100.0%	131.8%	99.3%	100.0%
7	$250	$250	$329	$246	250	100.0%	100.0%	131.9%	98.6%	100.0%
8	$278	$278	$367	$275	278	100.0%	100.0%	131.9%	98.9%	100.0%
9	$312	$312	$411	$309	312	100.0%	100.0%	131.8%	99.1%	100.0%
10	$351	$351	$463	$348	351	100.0%	100.0%	131.9%	99.2%	100.0%
11	$391	$391	$516	$393	391	100.0%	100.0%	131.9%	100.6%	100.0%
12	$438	$438	$577	$444	438	100.0%	100.0%	131.8%	101.4%	100.0%
13	$493	$493	$650	$503	493	100.0%	100.0%	131.9%	102.0%	100.0%
14	$549	$549	$724	$569	549	100.0%	100.0%	131.9%	103.6%	100.0%
15	$615	$615	$811	$644	615	100.0%	100.0%	131.8%	104.6%	100.0%
16	$0	$694	$0	$0	–	0.0%	0.0%	0.0%	0.0%	0.0%
17	$0	$773	$0	$0	–	0.0%	0.0%	0.0%	0.0%	0.0%
18	$0	$876	$0	$0	–	0.0%	0.0%	0.0%	0.0%	0.0%
19	$0	$981	$0	$0	–	0.0%	0.0%	0.0%	0.0%	0.0%
20	$0	$1,093	$0	$0	–	0.0%	0.0%	0.0%	0.0%	0.0%
21	$0	$1,247	$0	$0	–	0.0%	0.0%	0.0%	0.0%	0.0%
22	$0	$1,385	$0	$0	–	0.0%	0.0%	0.0%	0.0%	0.0%
23	$0	$1,543	$0	$0	–	0.0%	0.0%	0.0%	0.0%	0.0%
24	$0	$1,766	$0	$0	–	0.0%	0.0%	0.0%	0.0%	0.0%
25	$0	$1,951	$0	$0	–	0.0%	0.0%	0.0%	0.0%	0.0%
26	$0	$2,173	$0	$0	–	0.0%	0.0%	0.0%	0.0%	0.0%
27	$0	$2,493	$0	$0	–	0.0%	0.0%	0.0%	0.0%	0.0%
28	$0	$2,745	$0	$0	–	0.0%	0.0%	0.0%	0.0%	0.0%
29	$0	$3,058	$0	$0	–	0.0%	0.0%	0.0%	0.0%	0.0%
30	$0	$3,512	$0	$0	–	0.0%	0.0%	0.0%	0.0%	0.0%

* Includes impaired lives in the pool

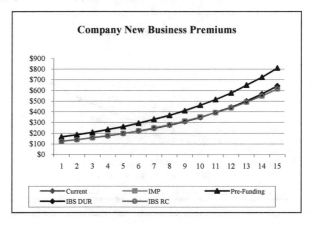

Company New Business Premiums

Trend Scenario: 1

New Business Sales

Year	Current	IMP	Pre-Funding	IBS DUR	IBS RC	Current	IMP	Pre-Funding	IBS DUR	IBS RC
1	3,075	3,075	2,716	3,075	3,075	100.0%	100.0%	88.3%	100.0%	100.0%
2	3,100	3,100	2,738	3,100	3,100	100.0%	100.0%	88.3%	100.0%	100.0%
3	3,097	3,097	2,740	3,097	3,097	100.0%	100.0%	88.5%	100.0%	100.0%
4	3,075	3,075	2,716	3,107	3,075	100.0%	100.0%	88.3%	101.0%	100.0%
5	3,100	3,100	2,738	3,116	3,100	100.0%	100.0%	88.3%	100.5%	100.0%
6	3,097	3,097	2,740	3,127	3,097	100.0%	100.0%	88.5%	101.0%	100.0%
7	3,075	3,075	2,716	3,138	3,075	100.0%	100.0%	88.3%	102.1%	100.0%
8	3,100	3,100	2,738	3,150	3,100	100.0%	100.0%	88.3%	101.6%	100.0%
9	3,097	3,097	2,740	3,138	3,097	100.0%	100.0%	88.5%	101.3%	100.0%
10	3,075	3,075	2,716	3,111	3,075	100.0%	100.0%	88.3%	101.2%	100.0%
11	3,100	3,100	2,738	3,074	3,100	100.0%	100.0%	88.3%	99.2%	100.0%
12	3,097	3,097	2,740	3,031	3,097	100.0%	100.0%	88.5%	97.9%	100.0%
13	3,075	3,075	2,716	2,984	3,075	100.0%	100.0%	88.3%	97.0%	100.0%
14	3,100	3,100	2,738	2,934	3,100	100.0%	100.0%	88.3%	94.7%	100.0%
15	3,097	3,097	2,740	2,884	3,097	100.0%	100.0%	88.5%	93.1%	100.0%
16	–	–	–	–	–	0.0%	0.0%	0.0%	0.0%	0.0%
17	–	–	–	–	–	0.0%	0.0%	0.0%	0.0%	0.0%
18	–	–	–	–	–	0.0%	0.0%	0.0%	0.0%	0.0%
19	–	–	–	–	–	0.0%	0.0%	0.0%	0.0%	0.0%
20	–	–	–	–	–	0.0%	0.0%	0.0%	0.0%	0.0%
21	–	–	–	–	–	0.0%	0.0%	0.0%	0.0%	0.0%
22	–	–	–	–	–	0.0%	0.0%	0.0%	0.0%	0.0%
23	–	–	–	–	–	0.0%	0.0%	0.0%	0.0%	0.0%
24	–	–	–	–	–	0.0%	0.0%	0.0%	0.0%	0.0%
25	–	–	–	–	–	0.0%	0.0%	0.0%	0.0%	0.0%
26	–	–	–	–	–	0.0%	0.0%	0.0%	0.0%	0.0%
27	–	–	–	–	–	0.0%	0.0%	0.0%	0.0%	0.0%
28	–	–	–	–	–	0.0%	0.0%	0.0%	0.0%	0.0%
29	–	–	–	–	–	0.0%	0.0%	0.0%	0.0%	0.0%
30	–	–	–	–	–	0.0%	0.0%	0.0%	0.0%	0.0%

* Includes impaired lives in the pool

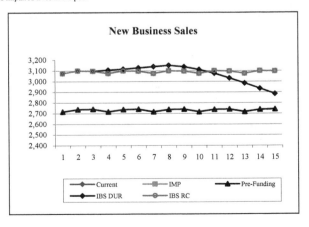

Trend Scenario: 1

Total Enrollment

Year	Current	IMP*	Pre-Funding	IBS DUR	IBS SRC	Current	IMP	Pre-Funding	IBS UR	IBS RC
1	3,075	3,075	2,716	3,075	3,075	100.0%	100.0%	88.3%	100.0%	100.0%
2	4,957	4,957	4,514	4,957	4,957	100.0%	100.0%	91.1%	100.0%	100.0%
3	6,147	6,147	5,750	6,147	6,147	100.0%	100.0%	93.6%	100.0%	100.0%
4	6,960	6,955	6,626	6,992	6,960	100.0%	99.9%	95.2%	100.5%	100.0%
5	7,588	7,581	7,286	7,616	7,588	100.0%	99.9%	96.0%	100.4%	100.0%
6	8,066	8,062	7,765	8,117	8,066	100.0%	99.9%	96.3%	100.6%	100.0%
7	8,434	8,427	8,093	8,524	8,434	100.0%	99.9%	96.0%	101.1%	100.0%
8	8,761	8,752	8,400	8,855	8,761	100.0%	99.9%	95.9%	101.1%	100.0%
9	8,990	8,984	8,629	9,073	8,990	100.0%	99.9%	96.0%	100.9%	100.0%
10	9,151	9,143	8,776	9,206	9,151	100.0%	99.9%	95.9%	100.6%	100.0%
11	9,313	9,304	8,941	9,272	9,313	100.0%	99.9%	96.0%	99.6%	100.0%
12	9,411	9,405	9,059	9,288	9,411	100.0%	99.9%	96.3%	98.7%	100.0%
13	9,472	9,464	9,120	9,268	9,472	100.0%	99.9%	96.3%	97.8%	100.0%
14	9,560	9,551	9,217	9,219	9,560	100.0%	99.9%	96.4%	96.4%	100.0%
15	9,601	9,596	9,280	9,151	9,601	100.0%	100.0%	96.7%	95.3%	100.0%
16	6,544	6,522	6,582	6,235	6,544	100.0%	99.7%	100.6%	95.3%	100.0%
17	4,718	4,687	4,892	4,502	4,718	100.0%	99.4%	103.7%	95.4%	100.0%
18	3,544	3,519	3,751	3,361	3,544	100.0%	99.3%	105.8%	94.8%	100.0%
19	2,731	2,710	2,933	2,571	2,731	100.0%	99.2%	107.4%	94.2%	100.0%
20	2,143	2,127	2,321	1,996	2,142	100.0%	99.2%	108.3%	93.1%	99.9%
21	1,671	1,659	1,843	1,545	1,667	100.0%	99.3%	110.3%	92.5%	99.8%
22	1,295	1,287	1,468	1,192	1,291	100.0%	99.4%	113.4%	92.1%	99.7%
23	1,002	997	1,173	927	998	100.0%	99.5%	117.1%	92.6%	99.6%
24	773	770	941	716	771	100.0%	99.6%	121.8%	92.6%	99.7%
25	600	598	758	556	599	100.0%	99.8%	126.4%	92.8%	99.8%
26	468	466	613	434	467	100.0%	99.7%	131.1%	92.9%	99.9%
27	367	366	497	342	367	100.0%	99.6%	135.5%	93.1%	100.0%
28	291	290	405	271	291	100.0%	99.7%	139.4%	93.4%	100.0%
29	232	230	331	217	232	100.0%	98.8%	142.8%	93.7%	100.0%
30	187	183	272	176	187	100.0%	97.9%	145.7%	94.1%	100.0%
	146,050	145,815	142,954	143,803	146,033	100.0%	99.8%	97.9%	98.5%	100.0%

* Includes impaired lives in the pool

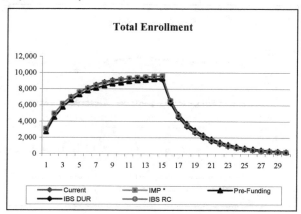

May 12, 2004

Trend Scenario: 1

Percentage of Cohort 1 Enrollees who are Impaired

Year	Current	IMP*	Pre-Funding	IBS DUR	IBS RC	Current	IMP	Pre-Funding	IBS DUR	IBS RC
1	0.0%	0.0%	0.0%	0.0%	0.0%	0.0%	0.0%	0.0%	0.0%	0.0%
2	0.6%	0.6%	0.5%	0.6%	0.6%	100.0%	100.0%	93.9%	100.0%	100.0%
3	1.8%	1.8%	1.7%	1.8%	1.8%	100.0%	100.0%	91.8%	100.0%	100.0%
4	3.7%	3.7%	3.4%	3.7%	3.7%	100.0%	100.1%	90.5%	100.0%	100.0%
5	6.2%	6.2%	5.6%	6.2%	6.2%	100.0%	100.1%	91.5%	100.0%	100.0%
6	8.7%	8.7%	8.1%	8.7%	8.7%	100.0%	100.1%	94.1%	100.1%	100.0%
7	11.3%	11.3%	10.8%	11.3%	11.3%	100.0%	100.0%	95.8%	100.2%	100.0%
8	14.1%	14.1%	13.7%	14.2%	14.1%	100.0%	100.0%	97.0%	100.4%	100.0%
9	17.2%	17.2%	16.8%	17.2%	17.2%	100.0%	100.0%	97.3%	100.0%	100.0%
10	20.7%	20.7%	20.0%	20.5%	20.7%	100.0%	100.0%	96.7%	98.9%	100.0%
11	24.5%	24.5%	23.4%	23.9%	24.5%	100.0%	100.0%	95.7%	97.5%	100.0%
12	28.7%	28.7%	27.0%	27.4%	28.7%	100.0%	100.0%	94.0%	95.6%	100.0%
13	33.2%	33.1%	30.6%	31.1%	33.2%	100.0%	100.0%	92.4%	93.8%	100.0%
14	37.9%	39.7%	34.4%	34.8%	37.9%	100.0%	104.7%	90.9%	92.0%	100.0%
15	42.7%	48.7%	38.3%	38.7%	42.7%	100.0%	114.0%	89.6%	90.5%	100.0%
16	47.7%	59.9%	42.2%	42.5%	47.7%	100.0%	125.8%	88.5%	89.2%	100.0%
17	52.6%	71.4%	46.1%	46.3%	52.6%	100.0%	135.7%	87.7%	88.2%	100.0%
18	57.4%	77.7%	50.0%	50.3%	57.4%	100.0%	135.4%	87.1%	87.7%	100.0%
19	62.0%	80.7%	53.8%	54.3%	62.0%	100.0%	130.2%	86.8%	87.6%	100.0%
20	66.3%	83.5%	57.6%	58.2%	65.8%	100.0%	126.0%	86.8%	87.9%	99.3%
21	70.3%	86.7%	61.2%	62.2%	69.1%	100.0%	123.4%	87.0%	88.5%	98.3%
22	73.9%	91.4%	64.6%	66.1%	72.6%	100.0%	123.6%	87.4%	89.4%	98.2%
23	77.2%	97.1%	67.9%	69.7%	76.1%	100.0%	125.8%	87.9%	90.3%	98.5%
24	80.4%	103.2%	71.0%	73.4%	79.3%	100.0%	128.5%	88.3%	91.3%	98.7%
25	82.9%	109.2%	73.9%	76.7%	82.4%	100.0%	131.7%	89.1%	92.5%	99.4%
26	85.2%	114.6%	76.6%	79.8%	85.0%	100.0%	134.5%	89.9%	93.7%	99.8%
27	87.1%	119.2%	79.0%	82.6%	87.1%	100.0%	136.8%	90.7%	94.8%	99.9%
28	88.8%	123.3%	81.3%	85.0%	88.8%	100.0%	138.8%	91.5%	95.7%	100.0%
29	90.3%	127.2%	83.4%	87.2%	90.3%	100.0%	140.8%	92.3%	96.5%	100.0%
30	91.6%	131.0%	85.3%	89.0%	91.6%	100.0%	143.0%	93.1%	97.2%	100.0%

*Includes impaired lives in the pool.

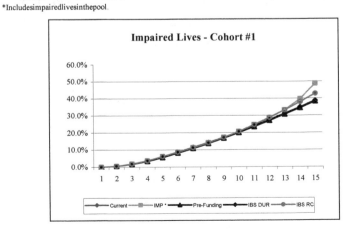

Impaired Lives - Cohort #1

Trend Scenario: 1

Percentage of All Enrollees who are Impaired

Year	Current	IMP *	Pre-funding	IBS DUR	IBS RC	Current	IMP	Pre-Funding	IBS DUR	IBS RC
1	0.0%	0.0%	0.0%	0.0%	0.0%	0.0%	0.0%	0.0%	0.0%	0.0%
2	0.2%	0.2%	0.2%	0.2%	0.2%	100.0%	100.0%	98.6%	100.0%	100.0%
3	0.5%	0.5%	0.5%	0.5%	0.5%	100.0%	100.0%	99.6%	100.0%	100.0%
4	0.9%	0.9%	0.9%	0.9%	0.9%	100.0%	100.0%	101.1%	99.6%	100.0%
5	1.3%	1.3%	1.4%	1.3%	1.3%	100.0%	100.0%	103.1%	99.7%	100.0%
6	1.8%	1.8%	1.8%	1.8%	1.8%	100.0%	99.9%	104.4%	99.5%	100.0%
7	2.2%	2.2%	2.3%	2.2%	2.2%	100.0%	100.0%	105.3%	99.1%	100.0%
8	2.6%	2.6%	2.8%	2.6%	2.6%	100.0%	100.0%	105.5%	99.1%	100.0%
9	3.0%	3.0%	3.2%	3.0%	3.0%	100.0%	99.9%	105.4%	99.4%	100.0%
10	3.4%	3.4%	3.6%	3.4%	3.4%	100.0%	100.0%	105.7%	100.0%	100.0%
11	3.7%	3.7%	3.9%	3.7%	3.7%	100.0%	100.0%	105.8%	101.1%	100.0%
12	4.0%	4.0%	4.2%	4.1%	4.0%	100.0%	99.9%	105.9%	102.2%	100.0%
13	4.2%	4.2%	4.5%	4.4%	4.2%	100.0%	100.0%	106.4%	103.3%	100.0%
14	4.4%	4.5%	4.7%	4.7%	4.4%	100.0%	100.2%	106.7%	104.8%	100.0%
15	4.6%	4.7%	5.0%	4.9%	4.6%	100.0%	100.3%	106.9%	106.0%	100.0%
16	7.1%	7.1%	7.3%	7.5%	7.1%	100.0%	100.5%	103.3%	106.0%	100.0%
17	10.0%	10.0%	10.0%	10.5%	10.0%	100.0%	100.5%	100.9%	105.7%	100.0%
18	13.0%	13.0%	13.0%	13.8%	13.0%	100.0%	100.2%	99.8%	106.1%	100.0%
19	16.2%	16.1%	16.1%	17.3%	16.2%	100.0%	99.6%	99.4%	106.6%	100.0%
20	19.4%	19.2%	19.3%	20.8%	19.4%	100.0%	99.1%	99.6%	107.2%	100.1%
21	22.9%	22.5%	22.7%	24.6%	23.0%	100.0%	98.2%	99.0%	107.5%	100.3%
22	26.8%	26.0%	26.2%	28.8%	26.9%	100.0%	97.2%	97.7%	107.4%	100.3%
23	31.0%	29.8%	29.8%	33.1%	31.1%	100.0%	96.1%	96.2%	106.7%	100.4%
24	35.6%	33.7%	33.6%	37.8%	35.7%	100.0%	94.6%	94.4%	106.2%	100.3%
25	40.4%	37.5%	37.4%	42.6%	40.4%	100.0%	92.8%	92.7%	105.6%	100.1%
26	45.3%	41.2%	41.3%	47.6%	45.3%	100.0%	91.0%	91.3%	105.1%	100.0%
27	50.2%	44.6%	45.2%	52.5%	50.2%	100.0%	88.7%	90.1%	104.5%	100.0%
28	55.1%	47.3%	49.1%	57.3%	55.1%	100.0%	85.8%	89.2%	104.0%	100.0%
29	59.8%	49.5%	53.0%	61.9%	59.8%	100.0%	82.7%	88.5%	103.4%	100.0%
30	64.3%	50.8%	56.7%	66.2%	64.3%	100.0%	79.0%	88.2%	102.8%	100.0%

* Includes impaired lives in the pool.

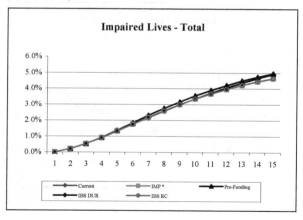

May 12, 2004

Trend Scenario: 1
Premiums

Yr	Current Market			Summary of Rate Increases IMP*			Pre-funding			UBS Durational Pooling			IBS Rate Compression		
	Min	Max	Avg	Min	Max	Avg	Min	Max	Avg	Min	Max	Avg	Min	Max	Avg
1															
2	20.5%	20.5%	20.5%	20.5%	20.5%	20.5%	14.7%	14.7%	14.7%	20.5%	20.5%	20.5%	20.5%	20.5%	20.5%
3	21.2%	21.2%	21.2%	21.2%	21.2%	21.2%	15.3%	15.3%	15.3%	21.2%	21.2%	21.2%	21.2%	21.2%	21.2%
4	20.9%	20.9%	20.9%	21.0%	21.0%	21.0%	16.0%	16.0%	16.0%	20.9%	20.9%	20.9%	20.9%	20.9%	20.9%
5	20.5%	20.9%	20.7%	20.5%	21.1%	20.8%	14.7%	16.0%	15.5%	20.9%	20.9%	20.9%	20.5%	20.9%	20.7%
6	14.8%	21.2%	20.5%	14.7%	21.2%	20.5%	15.3%	16.9%	15.9%	15.1%	20.8%	20.4%	14.8%	21.2%	20.5%
7	14.6%	20.9%	20.0%	14.5%	21.0%	20.1%	16.0%	16.7%	16.2%	15.1%	20.8%	20.0%	14.6%	20.9%	20.0%
8	14.5%	20.9%	19.6%	14.4%	21.1%	19.7%	14.7%	16.7%	15.7%	15.1%	20.8%	19.8%	14.5%	20.9%	19.6%
9	14.8%	21.2%	20.0%	14.7%	21.2%	20.0%	15.3%	17.0%	16.1%	15.7%	21.5%	20.3%	14.8%	21.2%	20.0%
10	14.6%	20.9%	19.9%	14.5%	21.0%	20.0%	16.0%	16.9%	16.3%	16.0%	21.8%	20.5%	14.6%	20.9%	19.9%
11	14.5%	21.0%	19.7%	14.4%	21.1%	19.8%	14.7%	16.9%	15.8%	16.3%	22.1%	20.7%	14.5%	21.0%	19.7%
12	14.8%	23.4%	20.2%	14.7%	23.4%	20.2%	15.3%	17.0%	16.1%	16.4%	22.3%	20.8%	14.8%	23.4%	20.2%
13	14.6%	23.9%	20.1%	14.5%	23.9%	20.2%	16.0%	17.1%	16.3%	16.5%	22.4%	20.8%	14.6%	23.9%	20.1%
14	14.5%	24.3%	19.9%	14.4%	24.3%	19.9%	14.7%	17.2%	15.9%	16.6%	22.4%	20.8%	14.5%	24.3%	19.9%
15	14.8%	24.3%	20.3%	14.7%	24.3%	20.3%	15.3%	17.3%	16.2%	16.6%	22.4%	20.8%	14.8%	24.3%	20.3%
16	14.6%	24.2%	20.2%	14.8%	24.1%	20.5%	16.0%	17.4%	16.4%	16.6%	22.4%	20.7%	14.6%	24.2%	20.2%
17	14.5%	24.3%	19.7%	14.8%	24.6%	20.1%	16.0%	17.5%	16.4%	16.5%	22.3%	19.9%	14.5%	24.3%	19.7%
18	14.8%	24.3%	19.4%	12.9%	24.6%	19.4%	16.7%	17.6%	17.0%	18.1%	24.0%	20.5%	14.8%	24.3%	19.4%
19	14.6%	24.2%	19.0%	10.7%	24.2%	18.8%	16.8%	17.7%	16.9%	18.8%	24.8%	20.1%	14.6%	24.2%	19.0%
20	14.5%	24.3%	18.1%	12.7%	24.6%	17.7%	16.8%	17.7%	17.0%	19.8%	19.8%	19.8%	14.7%	24.5%	18.2%
21	16.6%	24.3%	19.8%	12.6%	24.5%	19.1%	16.7%	17.8%	17.0%	20.9%	20.9%	20.9%	17.0%	24.7%	20.0%
22	19.5%	24.2%	21.4%	10.4%	24.1%	20.2%	16.8%	17.8%	17.0%	22.1%	22.1%	22.1%	19.6%	24.4%	21.5%
23	20.7%	24.2%	22.3%	12.4%	24.4%	21.0%	16.9%	17.8%	17.1%	21.6%	21.6%	21.6%	21.6%	23.2%	22.4%
24	22.0%	24.3%	23.5%	12.5%	24.4%	21.6%	17.0%	17.8%	17.2%	23.6%	23.6%	23.6%	22.4%	25.2%	23.4%
25	19.5%	24.2%	23.6%	10.3%	24.0%	20.8%	17.1%	17.8%	17.3%	23.5%	23.5%	23.5%	21.0%	23.8%	23.4%
26	19.2%	24.3%	23.6%	12.4%	24.3%	20.5%	17.2%	17.8%	17.4%	23.7%	23.7%	23.7%	20.6%	23.9%	23.4%
27	18.4%	24.3%	23.5%	12.4%	24.3%	19.3%	17.3%	17.8%	17.5%	23.4%	23.4%	23.4%	19.1%	24.2%	23.4%
28	18.0%	24.2%	23.0%	10.3%	20.8%	17.1%	17.4%	17.8%	17.6%	23.0%	23.0%	23.0%	18.4%	24.1%	23.0%
29	17.6%	24.0%	22.6%	12.4%	18.5%	16.3%	17.5%	17.8%	17.6%	22.4%	22.4%	22.4%	17.7%	23.9%	22.5%
30	17.3%	23.6%	22.3%	12.4%	16.9%	14.1%	17.6%	17.8%	17.7%	21.9%	21.9%	21.9%	17.3%	23.6%	22.3%

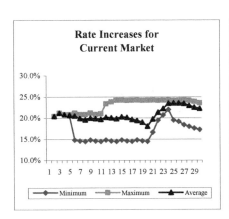

Rate Increases for Current Market

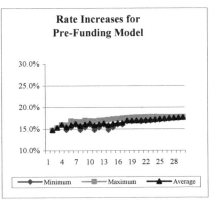

Rate Increases for Pre-Funding Model

AAA Rate Filing Model – Exhhibits.xls
Global Summary

American Academy of Actuaries
Rate Filing Task Force

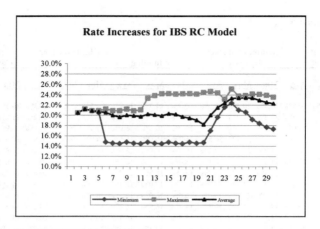

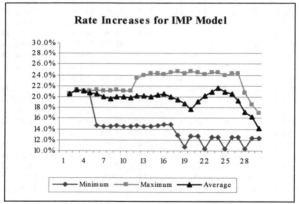

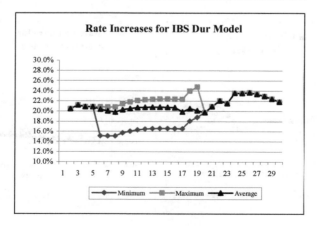

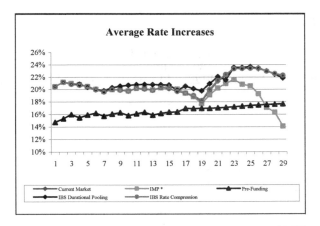

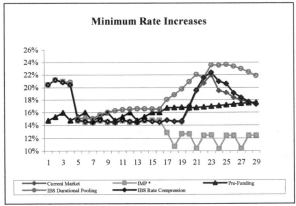

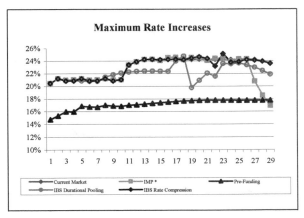

Trend Scenario: 1
Premiums

Premiums for Cohort #1

Year	Current	IMP	Pre-Funding	IBS DUR	IBS RC	Current	IMP	Pre-Funding	IBS DUR	IBS RC
1	$127	$127	$167	$127	$127	100.0%	100.0%	131.9%	100.0%	100.0%
2	$152	$152	$192	$152	$152	100.0%	100.0%	125.6%	100.0%	100.0%
3	$185	$185	$221	$185	$185	100.0%	100.0%	119.5%	100.0%	100.0%
4	$223	$224	$256	$223	$223	100.0%	100.1%	114.7%	100.0%	100.0%
5	$270	$271	$297	$270	$270	100.0%	100.3%	110.0%	100.0%	100.0%
6	$310	$311	$347	$311	$310	100.0%	100.2%	112.0%	100.3%	100.0%
7	$355	$356	$405	$357	$355	100.0%	100.2%	114.1%	100.7%	100.0%
8	$407	$407	$473	$411	$407	100.0%	100.1%	116.3%	101.2%	100.0%
9	$474	$475	$552	$476	$474	100.0%	100.1%	116.4%	100.3%	100.0%
10	$567	$567	$644	$552	$567	100.0%	100.0%	113.7%	97.4%	100.0%
11	$686	$686	$753	$642	$686	100.0%	100.0%	109.8%	93.6%	100.0%
12	$846	$846	$881	$747	$846	100.0%	100.0%	104.1%	88.3%	100.0%
13	$1,048	$1,048	$1,031	$871	$1,048	100.0%	100.0%	98.4%	83.1%	100.0%
14	$1,302	$1,302	$1,208	$1,015	$1,302	100.0%	100.0%	92.8%	78.0%	100.0%
15	$1,619	$1,618	$1,417	$1,184	$1,619	100.0%	100.0%	87.6%	73.1%	100.0%
16	$2,010	$1,957	$1,664	$1,380	$2,010	100.0%	97.4%	82.8%	68.6%	100.0%
17	$2,492	$2,328	$1,956	$1,608	$2,492	100.0%	93.4%	78.5%	64.5%	100.0%
18	$3,080	$2,627	$2,300	$1,898	$3,080	100.0%	85.3%	74.7%	61.6%	100.0%
19	$3,793	$2,909	$2,706	$2,256	$3,793	100.0%	76.7%	71.3%	59.5%	100.0%
20	$4,651	$3,278	$3,186	$2,702	$4,523	100.0%	70.5%	68.5%	58.1%	97.3%
21	$5,674	$3,749	$3,752	$3,267	$5,291	100.0%	66.1%	66.1%	57.6%	93.3%
22	$6,886	$4,367	$4,420	$3,988	$6,329	100.0%	63.4%	64.2%	57.9%	91.9%
23	$8,312	$5,115	$5,207	$4,848	$7,727	100.0%	61.5%	62.6%	58.3%	93.0%
24	$10,148	$5,978	$6,134	$5,992	$9,458	100.0%	58.9%	60.4%	59.0%	93.2%
25	$12,128	$6,948	$7,226	$7,402	$11,692	100.0%	57.3%	59.6%	61.0%	96.4%
26	$14,453	$8,025	$8,512	$9,155	$14,288	100.0%	55.5%	58.9%	63.3%	98.9%
27	$17,112	$9,224	$10,024	$11,294	$17,023	100.0%	53.9%	58.6%	66.0%	99.5%
28	$20,189	$10,598	$11,802	$13,889	$20,157	100.0%	52.5%	58.5%	68.8%	99.8%
29	$23,738	$12,188	$13,892	$17,006	$23,722	100.0%	51.3%	58.5%	71.6%	99.9%
30	$27,838	$14,038	$16,348	$20,724	$27,830	100.0%	50.4%	58.7%	74.4%	100.0%

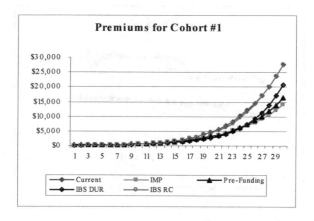

May 12, 2004

Trend Scenario: 1

Rate Increases for Cohort #1

Year	Current	IMP	Pre-Funding	IBS DUR	IBS RC	Current	IMP	Pre-Funding	IBS DUR	IBS RC
1										
2	20.5%	20.5%	14.7%	20.5%	20.5%	100.0%	100.0%	72.0%	100.0%	100.0%
3	21.2%	21.2%	15.3%	21.2%	21.2%	100.0%	100.0%	72.2%	100.0%	100.0%
4	20.9%	21.0%	16.0%	20.9%	20.9%	100.0%	100.7%	76.6%	100.0%	100.0%
5	20.9%	21.1%	16.0%	20.9%	20.9%	100.0%	100.9%	76.5%	100.0%	100.0%
6	14.8%	14.7%	16.9%	15.1%	14.8%	100.0%	99.5%	114.1%	102.0%	100.0%
7	14.6%	14.5%	16.7%	15.1%	14.6%	100.0%	99.5%	114.7%	103.2%	100.0%
8	14.5%	14.4%	16.7%	15.1%	14.5%	100.0%	99.6%	115.3%	104.0%	100.0%
9	16.6%	16.6%	16.7%	15.7%	16.6%	100.0%	99.8%	100.3%	94.2%	100.0%
10	19.5%	19.4%	16.8%	16.0%	19.5%	100.0%	99.5%	86.1%	82.4%	100.0%
11	21.0%	21.0%	16.9%	16.3%	21.0%	100.0%	100.0%	80.1%	77.4%	100.0%
12	23.4%	23.4%	17.0%	16.4%	23.4%	100.0%	99.9%	72.6%	70.3%	100.0%
13	23.9%	23.9%	17.1%	16.5%	23.9%	100.0%	100.0%	71.5%	69.2%	100.0%
14	24.3%	24.3%	17.2%	16.6%	24.3%	100.0%	100.0%	70.9%	68.3%	100.0%
15	24.3%	24.3%	17.3%	16.6%	24.3%	100.0%	100.0%	71.3%	68.2%	100.0%
16	24.2%	20.9%	17.4%	16.6%	24.2%	100.0%	86.6%	72.0%	68.4%	100.0%
17	24.0%	18.9%	17.5%	16.5%	24.0%	100.0%	79.0%	73.1%	69.0%	100.0%
18	23.6%	12.9%	17.6%	18.1%	23.6%	100.0%	54.5%	74.5%	76.6%	100.0%
19	23.1%	10.7%	17.7%	18.8%	23.1%	100.0%	46.3%	76.3%	81.3%	100.0%
20	22.6%	12.7%	17.7%	19.8%	19.2%	100.0%	56.1%	78.4%	87.5%	85.1%
21	22.0%	14.4%	17.8%	20.9%	17.0%	100.0%	65.4%	80.8%	95.1%	77.2%
22	21.4%	16.5%	17.8%	22.1%	19.6%	100.0%	77.1%	83.3%	103.3%	91.8%
23	20.7%	17.1%	17.8%	21.6%	22.1%	100.0%	82.7%	86.0%	104.1%	106.7%
24	22.1%	16.9%	17.8%	23.6%	22.4%	100.0%	76.3%	80.6%	106.8%	101.4%
25	19.5%	16.2%	17.8%	23.5%	23.6%	100.0%	83.2%	91.2%	120.7%	121.0%
26	19.2%	15.5%	17.8%	23.7%	22.2%	100.0%	80.8%	92.8%	123.5%	115.8%
27	18.4%	14.9%	17.8%	23.4%	19.1%	100.0%	81.3%	96.6%	127.0%	104.1%
28	18.0%	14.9%	17.7%	23.0%	18.4%	100.0%	82.8%	98.6%	127.8%	102.4%
29	17.6%	15.0%	17.7%	22.4%	17.7%	100.0%	85.4%	100.7%	127.7%	100.6%
30	17.3%	15.2%	17.7%	21.9%	17.3%	100.0%	87.9%	102.4%	126.6%	100.3%

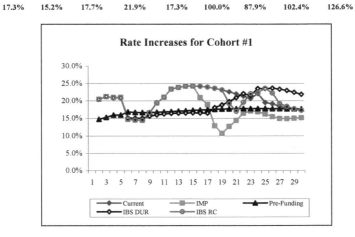

Trend Scenario: 1

Premiums for Cohort #5

Year	Current	IMP	Pre-Funding	IBS DUR	IBS RC	Current	IMP	Pre-Funding	IBS DUR	IBS RC
1	$-	$-	$-	$-	$-	0.0%	0.0%	0.0%	0.0%	0.0%
2	$-	$-	$-	$-	$-	0.0%	0.0%	0.0%	0.0%	0.0%
3	$-	$-	$-	$-	$-	0.0%	0.0%	0.0%	0.0%	0.0%
4	$-	$-	$-	$-	$-	0.0%	0.0%	0.0%	0.0%	0.0%
5	$198	$198	$261	$197	$198	100.0%	100.0%	131.9%	99.6%	100.0%
6	$240	$240	$301	$238	$240	100.0%	100.0%	125.5%	99.3%	100.0%
7	$290	$290	$349	$288	$290	100.0%	100.1%	120.4%	99.3%	100.0%
8	$351	$352	$405	$348	$351	100.0%	100.3%	115.6%	99.3%	100.0%
9	$423	$424	$474	$423	$423	100.0%	100.2%	112.2%	100.0%	100.0%
10	$484	$485	$554	$490	$484	100.0%	100.2%	114.5%	101.3%	100.0%
11	$554	$555	$648	$570	$554	100.0%	100.1%	116.8%	102.9%	100.0%
12	$647	$647	$756	$664	$647	100.0%	100.1%	116.9%	102.7%	100.0%
13	$773	$773	$883	$774	$773	100.0%	100.0%	114.2%	100.2%	100.0%
14	$935	$935	$1,031	$902	$935	100.0%	100.0%	110.3%	96.5%	100.0%
15	$1,154	$1,154	$1,206	$1,052	$1,154	100.0%	100.0%	104.5%	91.1%	100.0%
16	$1,429	$1,432	$1,412	$1,226	$1,429	100.0%	100.2%	98.8%	85.7%	100.0%
17	$1,776	$1,783	$1,655	$1,428	$1,776	100.0%	100.4%	93.2%	80.4%	100.0%
18	$2,208	$2,222	$1,942	$1,687	$2,208	100.0%	100.7%	87.9%	76.4%	100.0%
19	$2,742	$2,693	$2,279	$2,004	$2,742	100.0%	98.2%	83.1%	73.1%	100.0%
20	$3,399	$3,205	$2,678	$2,401	$3,405	100.0%	94.3%	78.8%	70.6%	100.2%
21	$4,201	$3,610	$3,149	$2,903	$4,222	100.0%	85.9%	75.0%	69.1%	100.5%
22	$5,173	$3,985	$3,704	$3,544	$5,207	100.0%	77.0%	71.6%	68.5%	100.7%
23	$6,343	$4,481	$4,360	$4,308	$6,331	100.0%	70.6%	68.7%	67.9%	99.8%
24	$7,739	$5,118	$5,134	$5,324	$7,778	100.0%	66.1%	66.3%	68.8%	100.5%
25	$9,391	$5,958	$6,046	$6,577	$9,410	100.0%	63.4%	64.4%	70.0%	100.2%
26	$11,337	$6,979	$7,121	$8,134	$11,350	100.0%	61.6%	62.8%	71.7%	100.1%
27	$13,841	$8,159	$8,388	$10,034	$13,847	100.0%	59.0%	60.6%	72.5%	100.0%
28	$16,541	$9,488	$9,879	$12,340	$16,546	100.0%	57.4%	59.7%	74.6%	100.0%
29	$19,712	$10,959	$11,633	$15,110	$19,715	100.0%	55.6%	59.0%	76.7%	100.0%
30	$23,339	$12,596	$13,697	$18,413	$23,341	100.0%	54.0%	58.7%	78.9%	100.0%

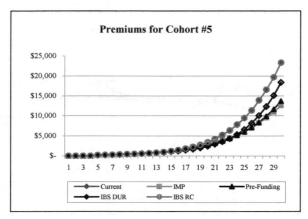

May 12, 2004

Trend Scenario: 1

Rate Increases for Cohort #5

Year	Current	IMP	Pre-Funding	IBS DUR	IBS RC	Current	IMP	Pre-Funding	IBS DUR	IBS RC
1										
2										
3										
4										
5										
6	21.2%	21.2%	15.3%	20.8%	21.2%	100.0%	100.0%	72.2%	98.3%	100.0%
7	20.9%	21.0%	16.0%	20.8%	20.9%	100.0%	100.7%	76.7%	99.8%	100.0%
8	20.9%	21.1%	16.0%	20.8%	20.9%	100.0%	100.9%	76.6%	99.7%	100.0%
9	20.5%	20.5%	17.0%	21.5%	20.5%	100.0%	99.7%	82.9%	104.5%	100.0%
10	14.6%	14.5%	16.9%	16.0%	14.6%	100.0%	99.5%	115.8%	109.9%	100.0%
11	14.5%	14.4%	16.8%	16.3%	14.5%	100.0%	99.6%	116.1%	112.5%	100.0%
12	16.6%	16.6%	16.7%	16.4%	16.6%	100.0%	99.8%	100.4%	98.8%	100.0%
13	19.5%	19.4%	16.8%	16.5%	19.5%	100.0%	99.5%	86.2%	84.9%	100.0%
14	21.0%	21.0%	16.9%	16.6%	21.0%	100.0%	100.0%	80.1%	78.7%	100.0%
15	23.4%	23.4%	17.0%	16.6%	23.4%	100.0%	99.9%	72.6%	70.9%	100.0%
16	23.9%	24.1%	17.1%	16.6%	23.9%	100.0%	100.9%	71.5%	69.3%	100.0%
17	24.3%	24.6%	17.2%	16.5%	24.3%	100.0%	101.2%	70.9%	68.1%	100.0%
18	24.3%	24.6%	17.3%	18.1%	24.3%	100.0%	101.3%	71.2%	74.5%	100.0%
19	24.2%	21.2%	17.4%	18.8%	24.2%	100.0%	87.7%	71.9%	77.8%	100.0%
20	24.0%	19.0%	17.5%	19.8%	24.2%	100.0%	79.3%	73.0%	82.6%	100.9%
21	23.6%	12.6%	17.6%	20.9%	24.0%	100.0%	53.6%	74.5%	88.6%	101.6%
22	23.1%	10.4%	17.6%	22.1%	23.3%	100.0%	44.9%	76.2%	95.3%	100.9%
23	22.6%	12.4%	17.7%	21.6%	21.6%	100.0%	55.0%	78.3%	95.4%	95.5%
24	22.0%	14.2%	17.7%	23.6%	22.9%	100.0%	64.6%	80.6%	107.2%	103.9%
25	21.4%	16.4%	17.8%	23.5%	21.0%	100.0%	76.8%	83.2%	110.2%	98.2%
26	20.7%	17.1%	17.8%	23.7%	20.6%	100.0%	82.8%	85.9%	114.3%	99.5%
27	22.1%	16.9%	17.8%	23.4%	22.0%	100.0%	76.6%	80.5%	105.8%	99.6%
28	19.5%	16.3%	17.8%	23.0%	19.5%	100.0%	83.4%	91.1%	117.8%	99.9%
29	19.2%	15.5%	17.8%	22.4%	19.2%	100.0%	80.9%	92.7%	117.1%	99.9%
30	18.4%	14.9%	17.7%	21.9%	18.4%	100.0%	81.2%	96.4%	118.8%	100.0%

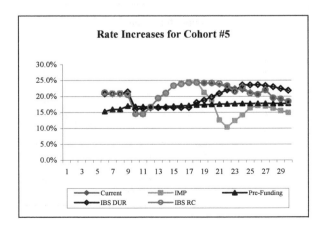

Trend Scenario: 1

Premiums for Cohort #10

Year	Current	IMP	Pre-Funding	IBS DUR	IBS RC	Current	IMP	Pre-Funding	IBS DUR	IBS RC
1	$-	$-	$-	$-	$-	0.0%	0.0%	0.0%	0.0%	0.0%
2	$-	$-	$-	$-	$-	0.0%	0.0%	0.0%	0.0%	0.0%
3	$-	$-	$-	$-	$-	0.0%	0.0%	0.0%	0.0%	0.0%
4	$-	$-	$-	$-	$-	0.0%	0.0%	0.0%	0.0%	0.0%
5	$-	$-	$-	$-	$-	0.0%	0.0%	0.0%	0.0%	0.0%
6	$-	$-	$-	$-	$-	0.0%	0.0%	0.0%	0.0%	0.0%
7	$-	$-	$-	$-	$-	0.0%	0.0%	0.0%	0.0%	0.0%
8	$-	$-	$-	$-	$-	0.0%	0.0%	0.0%	0.0%	0.0%
9	$-	$-	$-	$-	$-	0.0%	0.0%	0.0%	0.0%	0.0%
10	$351	$351	$463	$348	$351	100.0%	100.0%	131.9%	99.2%	100.0%
11	$423	$423	$531	$425	$423	100.0%	100.0%	125.6%	100.6%	100.0%
12	$512	$512	$612	$520	$512	100.0%	100.0%	119.5%	101.4%	100.0%
13	$619	$620	$710	$636	$619	100.0%	100.1%	114.7%	102.7%	100.0%
14	$748	$751	$824	$778	$748	100.0%	100.3%	110.1%	104.0%	100.0%
15	$859	$861	$964	$907	$859	100.0%	100.2%	112.2%	105.6%	100.0%
16	$985	$989	$1,127	$1,057	$985	100.0%	100.4%	114.5%	107.4%	100.0%
17	$1,127	$1,135	$1,316	$1,232	$1,127	100.0%	100.7%	116.8%	109.3%	100.0%
18	$1,315	$1,327	$1,536	$1,455	$1,315	100.0%	100.9%	116.9%	110.7%	100.0%
19	$1,571	$1,588	$1,794	$1,729	$1,571	100.0%	101.1%	114.2%	110.1%	100.0%
20	$1,901	$1,926	$2,097	$2,071	$1,905	100.0%	101.3%	110.3%	108.9%	100.2%
21	$2,346	$2,379	$2,452	$2,504	$2,357	100.0%	101.4%	104.5%	106.8%	100.5%
22	$2,906	$2,953	$2,871	$3,057	$2,924	100.0%	101.6%	98.8%	105.2%	100.6%
23	$3,610	$3,674	$3,365	$3,716	$3,603	100.0%	101.8%	93.2%	102.9%	99.8%
24	$4,487	$4,571	$3,947	$4,592	$4,509	100.0%	101.9%	87.9%	102.3%	100.5%
25	$5,573	$5,524	$4,633	$5,673	$5,583	100.0%	99.1%	83.1%	101.8%	100.2%
26	$6,909	$6,551	$5,444	$7,016	$6,916	100.0%	94.8%	78.8%	101.6%	100.1%
27	$8,539	$7,365	$6,401	$8,656	$8,543	100.0%	86.2%	75.0%	101.4%	100.0%
28	$10,516	$8,126	$7,530	$10,644	$10,518	100.0%	77.3%	71.6%	101.2%	100.0%
29	$12,894	$9,134	$8,863	$13,034	$12,894	100.0%	70.8%	68.7%	101.1%	100.0%
30	$15,730	$10,425	$10,436	$15,883	$15,730	100.0%	66.3%	66.3%	101.0%	100.0%

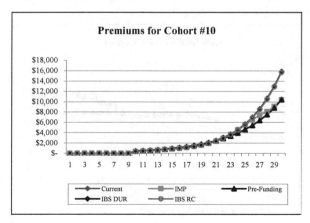

May 12, 2004

Trend Scenario: 1

Rate Increases for Cohort #10

Year	Current	IMP	Pre-Funding	IBS DUR	IBS RC	Current	IMP	Pre-Funding	IBS DUR	IBS RC
1										
2										
3										
4										
5										
6										
7										
8										
9										
10										
11	20.5%	20.5%	14.7%	22.1%	20.5%	100.0%	100.0%	72.0%	107.9%	100.0%
12	21.2%	21.2%	15.3%	22.3%	21.2%	100.0%	100.0%	72.2%	105.0%	100.0%
13	20.9%	21.0%	16.0%	22.4%	20.9%	100.0%	100.7%	76.7%	107.2%	100.0%
14	20.9%	21.1%	16.0%	22.4%	20.9%	100.0%	100.9%	76.6%	107.3%	100.0%
15	14.8%	14.7%	17.0%	16.6%	14.8%	100.0%	99.5%	115.0%	112.0%	100.0%
16	14.6%	14.8%	16.9%	16.6%	14.6%	100.0%	101.5%	115.8%	113.5%	100.0%
17	14.5%	14.8%	16.8%	16.5%	14.5%	100.0%	102.0%	116.1%	114.1%	100.0%
18	16.6%	16.9%	16.7%	18.1%	16.6%	100.0%	101.7%	100.4%	108.7%	100.0%
19	19.5%	19.7%	16.8%	18.8%	19.5%	100.0%	101.3%	86.2%	96.7%	100.0%
20	21.0%	21.3%	16.9%	19.8%	21.3%	100.0%	101.0%	80.1%	94.0%	101.0%
21	23.4%	23.5%	17.0%	20.9%	23.8%	100.0%	100.7%	72.6%	89.5%	101.6%
22	23.9%	24.1%	17.1%	22.1%	24.1%	100.0%	100.9%	71.5%	92.5%	100.8%
23	24.3%	24.4%	17.2%	21.6%	23.2%	100.0%	100.7%	70.9%	88.9%	95.7%
24	24.3%	24.4%	17.3%	23.6%	25.2%	100.0%	100.5%	71.2%	97.1%	103.6%
25	24.2%	20.9%	17.4%	23.5%	23.8%	100.0%	86.2%	71.9%	97.3%	98.4%
26	24.0%	18.6%	17.5%	23.7%	23.9%	100.0%	77.6%	73.0%	98.8%	99.7%
27	23.6%	12.4%	17.6%	23.4%	23.5%	100.0%	52.6%	74.5%	99.0%	99.6%
28	23.1%	10.3%	17.6%	23.0%	23.1%	100.0%	44.7%	76.2%	99.3%	99.9%
29	22.6%	12.4%	17.7%	22.4%	22.6%	100.0%	54.9%	78.3%	99.3%	99.9%
30	22.0%	14.1%	17.7%	21.9%	22.0%	100.0%	64.2%	80.6%	99.4%	100.0%

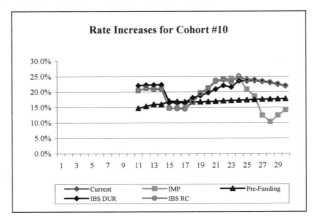

Rate Increases for Cohort #10

Trend Scenario: 1

Premiums for Cohort #15

Year	Current	IMP	Pre-Funding	IBS DUR	IBS RC	Current	IMP	Pre-Funding	IBS DUR	IBS RC
1	$—	$—	$—	$—	$—	0.0%	0.0%	0.0%	0.0%	0.0%
2	$—	$—	$—	$—	$—	0.0%	0.0%	0.0%	0.0%	0.0%
3	$—	$—	$—	$—	$—	0.0%	0.0%	0.0%	0.0%	0.0%
4	$—	$—	$—	$—	$—	0.0%	0.0%	0.0%	0.0%	0.0%
5	$—	$—	$—	$—	$—	0.0%	0.0%	0.0%	0.0%	0.0%
6	$—	$—	$—	$—	$—	0.0%	0.0%	0.0%	0.0%	0.0%
7	$—	$—	$—	$—	$—	0.0%	0.0%	0.0%	0.0%	0.0%
8	$—	$—	$—	$—	$—	0.0%	0.0%	0.0%	0.0%	0.0%
9	$—	$—	$—	$—	$—	0.0%	0.0%	0.0%	0.0%	0.0%
10	$—	$—	$—	$—	$—	0.0%	0.0%	0.0%	0.0%	0.0%
11	$—	$—	$—	$—	$—	0.0%	0.0%	0.0%	0.0%	0.0%
12	$—	$—	$—	$—	$—	0.0%	0.0%	0.0%	0.0%	0.0%
13	$—	$—	$—	$—	$—	0.0%	0.0%	0.0%	0.0%	0.0%
14	$—	$—	$—	$—	$—	0.0%	0.0%	0.0%	0.0%	0.0%
15	$615	$615	$811	$644	$615	100.0%	100.0%	131.8%	104.6%	100.0%
16	$744	$747	$940	$788	$744	100.0%	100.5%	126.5%	105.9%	100.0%
17	$899	$908	$1,091	$964	$899	100.0%	101.1%	121.4%	107.2%	100.0%
18	$1,083	$1,097	$1,277	$1,195	$1,083	100.0%	101.2%	117.8%	110.3%	100.0%
19	$1,304	$1,323	$1,492	$1,491	$1,304	100.0%	101.5%	114.5%	114.4%	100.0%
20	$1,492	$1,517	$1,743	$1,786	$1,495	100.0%	101.7%	116.8%	119.7%	100.2%
21	$1,741	$1,771	$2,034	$2,160	$1,749	100.0%	101.8%	116.9%	124.1%	100.5%
22	$2,080	$2,117	$2,376	$2,637	$2,092	100.0%	101.8%	114.2%	126.8%	100.6%
23	$2,518	$2,564	$2,776	$3,205	$2,554	100.0%	101.8%	110.3%	127.3%	101.5%
24	$3,106	$3,164	$3,247	$3,961	$3,126	100.0%	101.9%	104.5%	127.5%	100.7%
25	$3,848	$3,923	$3,802	$4,894	$3,865	100.0%	101.9%	98.8%	127.2%	100.4%
26	$4,781	$4,877	$4,455	$6,052	$4,787	100.0%	102.0%	93.2%	126.6%	100.1%
27	$5,942	$6,064	$5,226	$7,466	$5,945	100.0%	102.0%	87.9%	125.7%	100.1%
28	$7,380	$7,323	$6,135	$9,182	$7,379	100.0%	99.2%	83.1%	124.4%	100.0%
29	$9,148	$8,681	$7,209	$11,243	$9,145	100.0%	94.9%	78.8%	122.9%	100.0%
30	$11,308	$9,758	$8,476	$13,701	$11,302	100.0%	86.3%	75.0%	121.2%	99.9%

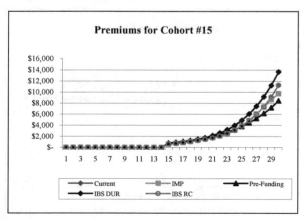

May 12, 2004

Trend Scenario: 1

Rate Increases for Cohort #15

Year	Current	IMP	Pre-Funding	IBS DUR	IBS RC	Current	IMP	Pre-Funding	IBS DUR	IBS RC
1										
2										
3										
4										
5										
6										
7										
8										
9										
10										
11										
12										
13										
14										
15										
16	20.9%	21.4%	16.0%	22.4%	20.9%	100.0%	102.7%	76.7%	107.3%	100.0%
17	20.9%	21.6%	16.0%	22.3%	20.9%	100.0%	103.4%	76.6%	107.1%	100.0%
18	20.5%	20.8%	17.0%	24.0%	20.5%	100.0%	101.2%	82.9%	116.8%	100.0%
19	20.3%	20.6%	16.9%	24.8%	20.3%	100.0%	101.5%	83.1%	121.9%	100.0%
20	14.5%	14.7%	16.8%	19.8%	14.7%	100.0%	101.2%	116.1%	136.6%	101.4%
21	16.6%	16.8%	16.7%	20.9%	17.0%	100.0%	100.7%	100.4%	125.8%	102.1%
22	19.5%	19.5%	16.8%	22.1%	19.6%	100.0%	100.3%	86.2%	113.4%	100.7%
23	21.0%	21.1%	16.9%	21.6%	22.1%	100.0%	100.3%	80.1%	102.4%	104.9%
24	23.4%	23.4%	17.0%	23.6%	22.4%	100.0%	100.1%	72.6%	100.9%	95.8%
25	23.9%	24.0%	17.1%	23.5%	23.6%	100.0%	100.4%	71.5%	98.6%	98.9%
26	24.3%	24.3%	17.2%	23.7%	23.9%	100.0%	100.3%	70.9%	97.6%	98.4%
27	24.3%	24.3%	17.3%	23.4%	24.2%	100.0%	100.2%	71.2%	96.2%	99.6%
28	24.2%	20.8%	17.4%	23.0%	24.1%	100.0%	85.9%	71.9%	95.0%	99.6%
29	24.0%	18.5%	17.5%	22.4%	23.9%	100.0%	77.4%	73.0%	93.7%	99.9%
30	23.6%	12.4%	17.6%	21.9%	23.6%	100.0%	52.6%	74.5%	92.6%	99.9%

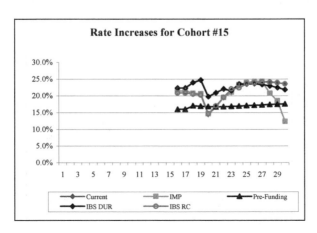

Trend Scenario: 1
Company Financial Results

All Blocks Combined Annual Premiums (in $1,000's)

Year	Current	IMP	Pre-Funding	IBS DUR	IBS RC	Current	IMP	Pre-Funding	IBS UR	IBS RC
1	$4,670	$4,670	$5,441	$4,670	$4,670	100.0%	100.0%	116.5%	100.0%	100.0%
2	$8,640	$8,640	$10,191	$8,640	$8,640	100.0%	100.0%	117.9%	100.0%	100.0%
3	$12,323	$12,323	$14,685	$12,323	$12,323	100.0%	100.0%	119.2%	100.0%	100.0%
4	$16,007	$16,007	$19,237	$16,028	$16,007	100.0%	100.0%	120.2%	100.1%	100.0%
5	$19,897	$19,898	$23,867	$19,922	$19,897	100.0%	100.0%	120.0%	100.1%	100.0%
6	$24,068	$24,068	$28,777	$24,111	$24,068	100.0%	100.0%	119.6%	100.2%	100.0%
7	$28,558	$28,557	$34,007	$28,651	$28,558	100.0%	100.0%	119.1%	100.3%	100.0%
8	$33,483	$33,482	$39,754	$33,602	$33,483	100.0%	100.0%	118.7%	100.4%	100.0%
9	$38,890	$38,888	$46,081	$39,016	$38,890	100.0%	100.0%	118.5%	100.3%	100.0%
10	$44,828	$44,824	$53,009	$44,948	$44,828	100.0%	100.0%	118.3%	100.3%	100.0%
11	$51,432	$51,429	$60,704	$51,463	$51,432	100.0%	100.0%	118.0%	100.1%	100.0%
12	$58,770	$58,764	$69,255	$58,634	$58,770	100.0%	100.0%	117.8%	99.8%	100.0%
13	$66,888	$66,880	$78,693	$66,541	$66,888	100.0%	100.0%	117.6%	99.5%	100.0%
14	$75,976	$75,858	$89,244	$75,272	$75,976	100.0%	99.8%	117.5%	99.1%	100.0%
15	$86,123	$85,782	$101,031	$84,923	$86,123	100.0%	99.6%	117.3%	98.6%	100.0%
16	$71,844	$71,205	$84,324	$70,825	$71,844	100.0%	99.1%	117.4%	98.6%	100.0%
17	$62,775	$61,714	$73,550	$61,789	$62,775	100.0%	98.3%	117.2%	98.4%	100.0%
18	$56,789	$55,205	$66,287	$55,809	$56,789	100.0%	97.2%	116.7%	98.3%	100.0%
19	$52,396	$50,200	$60,813	$51,376	$52,396	100.0%	95.8%	116.1%	98.1%	100.0%
20	$48,835	$45,852	$56,394	$47,862	$48,825	100.0%	93.9%	115.5%	98.0%	100.0%
21	$45,873	$41,993	$52,495	$44,874	$45,843	100.0%	91.5%	114.4%	97.8%	99.9%
22	$43,419	$38,525	$49,070	$42,355	$43,378	100.0%	88.7%	113.0%	97.6%	99.9%
23	$41,356	$35,213	$46,069	$40,138	$41,310	100.0%	85.1%	111.4%	97.1%	99.9%
24	$39,677	$32,121	$43,447	$38,388	$39,637	100.0%	81.0%	109.5%	96.8%	99.9%
25	$38,251	$29,158	$41,163	$36,925	$38,226	100.0%	76.2%	107.6%	96.5%	99.9%
26	$37,070	$26,117	$39,181	$35,744	$37,066	100.0%	70.5%	105.7%	96.4%	100.0%
27	$36,130	$23,101	$37,469	$34,795	$36,127	100.0%	63.9%	103.7%	96.3%	100.0%
28	$35,349	$20,080	$35,996	$34,056	$35,347	100.0%	56.8%	101.8%	96.3%	100.0%
29	$34,736	$17,419	$34,739	$33,492	$34,734	100.0%	50.1%	100.0%	96.4%	100.0%
30	$34,305	$15,241	$33,672	$33,078	$34,301	100.0%	44.4%	98.2%	96.4%	100.0%
LT PV	$594,496	$560,865	$688,788	$587,905	$594,428					

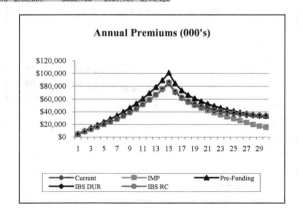

May 12, 2004

Trend Scenario: 1

All Blocks Combined Annual Claims (in $1,000's)

Year	Current	IMP	Pre-Funding	IBS DUR	IBS RC	Current	IMP	Pre-Funding	IBS DUR	IBS RC
1	$2,125	$2,125	$2,020	$2,125	$2,125	100.0%	100.0%	95.0%	100.0%	100.0%
2	$4,262	$4,262	$5,688	$4,262	$4,262	100.0%	100.0%	133.5%	100.0%	100.0%
3	$6,390	$6,390	$9,174	$6,390	$6,390	100.0%	100.0%	143.6%	100.0%	100.0%
4	$8,660	$8,653	$12,644	$8,686	$8,660	100.0%	99.9%	146.0%	100.3%	100.0%
5	$11,087	$11,074	$16,206	$11,114	$11,087	100.0%	99.9%	146.2%	100.2%	100.0%
6	$13,750	$13,740	$19,875	$13,808	$13,750	100.0%	99.9%	144.5%	100.4%	100.0%
7	$16,695	$16,678	$23,859	$16,806	$16,695	100.0%	99.9%	142.9%	100.7%	100.0%
8	$20,012	$19,987	$28,390	$20,146	$20,012	100.0%	99.9%	141.9%	100.7%	100.0%
9	$23,624	$23,604	$33,117	$23,761	$23,624	100.0%	99.9%	140.2%	100.6%	100.0%
10	$27,589	$27,562	$38,416	$27,693	$27,589	100.0%	99.9%	139.2%	100.4%	100.0%
11	$32,066	$32,028	$44,374	$31,979	$32,066	100.0%	99.9%	138.4%	99.7%	100.0%
12	$36,935	$36,904	$50,736	$36,669	$36,935	100.0%	99.9%	137.4%	99.3%	100.0%
13	$42,315	$42,275	$57,919	$41,813	$42,315	100.0%	99.9%	136.9%	98.8%	100.0%
14	$48,430	$48,302	$66,060	$47,467	$48,430	100.0%	99.7%	136.4%	98.0%	100.0%
15	$55,114	$54,853	$74,791	$53,693	$55,114	100.0%	99.5%	135.7%	97.4%	100.0%
16	$50,908	$50,206	$73,645	$49,712	$50,908	100.0%	98.6%	144.7%	97.7%	100.0%
17	$47,683	$46,346	$65,298	$46,760	$47,683	100.0%	97.2%	136.9%	98.1%	100.0%
18	$45,326	$43,355	$59,166	$44,396	$45,326	100.0%	95.7%	130.5%	97.9%	100.0%
19	$43,238	$40,611	$54,944	$42,305	$43,238	100.0%	93.9%	127.1%	97.8%	100.0%
20	$41,775	$38,247	$51,028	$40,706	$41,768	100.0%	91.6%	122.1%	97.4%	100.0%
21	$40,187	$35,709	$47,782	$39,076	$40,161	100.0%	88.9%	118.9%	97.2%	99.9%
22	$38,536	$33,109	$44,829	$37,429	$38,501	100.0%	85.9%	116.3%	97.1%	99.9%
23	$36,947	$30,186	$42,206	$36,046	$36,908	100.0%	81.7%	114.2%	97.6%	99.9%
24	$35,364	$27,228	$39,845	$34,504	$35,329	100.0%	77.0%	112.7%	97.6%	99.9%
25	$33,958	$24,439	$37,712	$33,129	$33,937	100.0%	72.0%	111.1%	97.6%	99.9%
26	$32,704	$21,253	$35,776	$31,875	$32,689	100.0%	65.0%	109.4%	97.5%	100.0%
27	$31,586	$18,151	$34,012	$30,780	$31,577	100.0%	57.5%	107.7%	97.4%	100.0%
28	$30,638	$15,234	$32,400	$29,831	$30,632	100.0%	49.7%	105.7%	97.4%	100.0%
29	$29,824	$12,829	$30,921	$29,023	$29,819	100.0%	43.0%	103.7%	97.3%	100.0%
30	$29,102	$11,292	$18,679	$28,342	$29,098	100.0%	38.8%	64.2%	97.4%	100.0%
LT PV	$413,639	$378,368	$538,027	$407,548	$413,573					

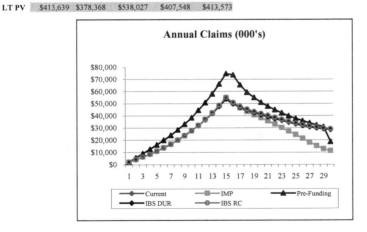

Annual Claims (000's)

Trend Scenario: 1
All Blocks Combined Annual Expenses (in $1,000's)

Year	Current	IMP	Pre-Funding	IBS DUR	IBS RC	Current	IMP	Pre-Funding	IBS DUR	IBS RC
1	$2,933	$2,933	$3,094	$2,933	$2,933	100.0%	100.0%	105.5%	100.0%	100.0%
2	$4,022	$4,022	$4,352	$4,022	$4,022	100.0%	100.0%	108.2%	100.0%	100.0%
3	$4,983	$4,983	$5,504	$4,983	$4,983	100.0%	100.0%	110.5%	100.0%	100.0%
4	$5,913	$5,912	$6,626	$5,935	$5,913	100.0%	100.0%	112.1%	100.4%	100.0%
5	$6,848	$6,845	$7,711	$6,862	$6,848	100.0%	100.0%	112.6%	100.2%	100.0%
6	$7,830	$7,828	$8,842	$7,861	$7,830	100.0%	100.0%	112.9%	100.4%	100.0%
7	$8,882	$8,879	$10,027	$8,946	$8,882	100.0%	100.0%	112.9%	100.7%	100.0%
8	$10,071	$10,067	$11,384	$10,132	$10,071	100.0%	100.0%	113.0%	100.6%	100.0%
9	$11,343	$11,341	$12,854	$11,398	$11,343	100.0%	100.0%	113.3%	100.5%	100.0%
10	$12,728	$12,723	$14,437	$12,765	$12,728	100.0%	100.0%	113.4%	100.3%	100.0%
11	$14,310	$14,303	$16,257	$14,252	$14,310	100.0%	100.0%	113.6%	99.6%	100.0%
12	$16,021	$16,017	$18,247	$15,878	$16,021	100.0%	100.0%	113.9%	99.1%	100.0%
13	$17,901	$17,894	$20,408	$17,664	$17,901	100.0%	100.0%	114.0%	98.7%	100.0%
14	$20,060	$20,031	$22,902	$19,629	$20,060	100.0%	99.9%	114.2%	97.9%	100.0%
15	$22,411	$22,349	$25,643	$21,797	$22,411	100.0%	99.7%	114.4%	97.3%	100.0%
16	$12,751	$12,620	$15,053	$12,427	$12,751	100.0%	99.0%	118.1%	97.5%	100.0%
17	$10,257	$10,049	$12,196	$9,998	$10,257	100.0%	98.0%	118.9%	97.5%	100.0%
18	$8,627	$8,350	$10,248	$8,388	$8,627	100.0%	96.8%	118.8%	97.2%	100.0%
19	$7,446	$7,094	$8,797	$7,231	$7,446	100.0%	95.3%	118.1%	97.1%	100.0%
20	$6,824	$6,367	$8,024	$6,608	$6,822	100.0%	93.3%	117.6%	96.8%	100.0%
21	$6,293	$5,721	$7,380	$6,082	$6,287	100.0%	90.9%	117.3%	96.7%	99.9%
22	$5,840	$5,147	$6,841	$5,638	$5,833	100.0%	88.1%	117.1%	96.5%	99.9%
23	$5,460	$4,606	$6,387	$5,273	$5,452	100.0%	84.4%	117.0%	96.6%	99.8%
24	$5,140	$4,111	$6,005	$4,960	$5,133	100.0%	80.0%	116.8%	96.5%	99.9%
25	$4,874	$3,663	$5,683	$4,703	$4,871	100.0%	75.2%	116.6%	96.5%	99.9%
26	$4,656	$3,207	$5,410	$4,492	$4,655	100.0%	68.9%	116.2%	96.5%	100.0%
27	$4,478	$2,773	$5,180	$4,320	$4,478	100.0%	61.9%	115.7%	96.5%	100.0%
28	$4,333	$2,364	$4,985	$4,182	$4,333	100.0%	54.6%	115.0%	96.5%	100.0%
29	$4,217	$2,017	$4,820	$4,073	$4,216	100.0%	47.8%	114.3%	96.6%	100.0%
30	$4,125	$1,760	$4,681	$3,987	$4,125	100.0%	42.7%	113.5%	96.7%	100.0%
LT PV	$140,225	$135,623	$159,988	$138,597	$140,212					

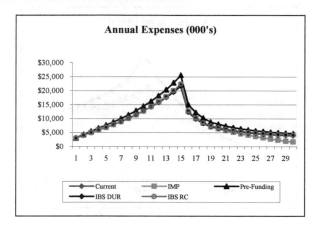

May 12, 2004

Trend Scenario: 1

All Blocks Combined Annual Gain (Loss)

Year	Current	IMP	Pre-Funding	IBS DUR	IBS RC	Current	IMP	Pre-Funding	IBS DUR	IBS RC
1	($388,531)	($388,531)	$326,891	($388,531)	($388,531)	100.0%	100.0%	-84.1%	100.0%	100.0%
2	$356,070	$356,070	$150,589	$356,070	$356,070	100.0%	100.0%	42.3%	100.0%	100.0%
3	$950,286	$950,286	$81,311	$950,286	$950,286	100.0%	100.0%	8.6%	100.0%	100.0%
4	$1,433,189	$1,441,911	$176,385	$1,407,624	$1,433,189	100.0%	100.6%	12.3%	98.2%	100.0%
5	$1,961,953	$1,978,369	$343,262	$1,945,817	$1,961,953	100.0%	100.8%	17.5%	99.2%	100.0%
6	$2,488,053	$2,499,720	$682,975	$2,442,368	$2,488,053	100.0%	100.5%	27.5%	98.2%	100.0%
7	$2,981,081	$3,000,774	$1,015,103	$2,899,315	$2,981,081	100.0%	100.7%	34.1%	97.3%	100.0%
8	$3,400,213	$3,428,338	$1,194,217	$3,323,064	$3,400,213	100.0%	100.8%	35.1%	97.7%	100.0%
9	$3,922,984	$3,943,225	$1,699,344	$3,857,962	$3,922,984	100.0%	100.5%	43.3%	98.3%	100.0%
10	$4,510,863	$4,539,256	$2,168,604	$4,490,747	$4,510,863	100.0%	100.6%	48.1%	99.6%	100.0%
11	$5,057,226	$5,097,239	$2,567,494	$5,232,199	$5,057,226	100.0%	100.8%	50.8%	103.5%	100.0%
12	$5,813,604	$5,842,225	$3,312,219	$6,087,209	$5,813,604	100.0%	100.5%	57.0%	104.7%	100.0%
13	$6,671,208	$6,711,154	$4,009,886	$7,065,054	$6,671,208	100.0%	100.6%	60.1%	105.9%	100.0%
14	$7,486,828	$7,524,929	$4,603,747	$8,176,048	$7,486,828	100.0%	100.5%	61.5%	109.2%	100.0%
15	$8,597,736	$8,580,507	$5,678,956	$9,432,373	$8,597,736	100.0%	99.8%	66.1%	109.7%	100.0%
16	$8,185,188	$8,379,145	$1,544,226	$8,685,610	$8,185,188	100.0%	102.4%	18.9%	106.1%	100.0%
17	$4,835,162	$5,318,311	$2,906,414	$5,031,341	$4,835,162	100.0%	110.0%	60.1%	104.1%	100.0%
18	$2,836,558	$3,500,019	$4,367,367	$3,026,216	$2,836,558	100.0%	123.4%	154.0%	106.7%	100.0%
19	$1,711,990	$2,494,960	$5,001,547	$1,840,753	$1,711,990	100.0%	145.7%	292.1%	107.5%	100.0%
20	$235,123	$1,238,827	$5,585,578	$548,725	$235,762	100.0%	526.9%	2375.6%	233.4%	100.3%
21	($606,054)	$562,968	$5,765,015	($284,085)	($604,545)	100.0%	-92.9%	-951.2%	46.9%	99.8%
22	($957,722)	$269,096	$5,917,944	($711,959)	($955,778)	100.0%	-28.1%	-617.9%	74.3%	99.8%
23	($1,051,063)	$421,426	$5,983,693	($1,181,208)	($1,048,928)	100.0%	-40.1%	-569.3%	112.4%	99.8%
24	($826,735)	$782,454	$6,012,526	($1,076,359)	($824,952)	100.0%	-94.6%	-727.3%	130.2%	99.8%
25	($581,993)	$1,056,308	$6,016,135	($906,880)	($581,103)	100.0%	-181.5%	-1033.7%	155.8%	99.8%
26	($289,754)	$1,657,182	$6,006,427	($622,414)	($277,870)	100.0%	-571.9%	-2072.9%	214.8%	95.9%
27	$65,494	$2,176,574	$5,989,294	($304,667)	$72,873	100.0%	3323.3%	9144.7%	-465.2%	111.3%
28	$377,393	$2,482,661	$5,968,435	$42,417	$382,834	100.0%	657.8%	1581.5%	11.2%	101.4%
29	$695,707	$2,572,757	$5,945,086	$396,753	$698,395	100.0%	369.8%	854.5%	57.0%	100.4%
30	$1,077,766	$2,189,270	$16,801,397	$748,398	$1,078,706	100.0%	203.1%	1558.9%	69.4%	100.1%
LT PV	$40,632,500	$46,874,520	$44,708,508	$41,760,091	$40,643,295					

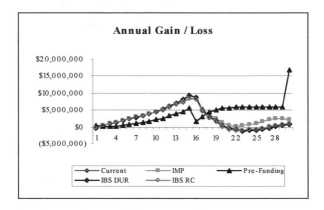

Annual Gain / Loss

Trend Scenario: 1
All Blocks Combined Annual Gain (Loss) as Percentage of Premium

Year	Current	IMP	Pre-Funding	IBS DUR	IBS RC	Current	IMP	Pre-Funding	IBS DUR	IBS RC
1	-8.3%	-8.3%	6.0%	-8.3%	-8.3%	100.0%	100.0%	-72.2%	100.0%	100.0%
2	4.1%	4.1%	1.5%	4.1%	4.1%	100.0%	100.0%	35.9%	100.0%	100.0%
3	7.7%	7.7%	0.6%	7.7%	7.7%	100.0%	100.0%	7.2%	100.0%	100.0%
4	9.0%	9.0%	0.9%	8.8%	9.0%	100.0%	100.6%	10.2%	98.1%	100.0%
5	9.9%	9.9%	1.4%	9.8%	9.9%	100.0%	100.8%	14.6%	99.1%	100.0%
6	10.3%	10.4%	2.4%	10.1%	10.3%	100.0%	100.5%	23.0%	98.0%	100.0%
7	10.4%	10.5%	3.0%	10.1%	10.4%	100.0%	100.7%	28.6%	96.9%	100.0%
8	10.2%	10.2%	3.0%	9.9%	10.2%	100.0%	100.8%	29.6%	97.4%	100.0%
9	10.1%	10.1%	3.7%	9.9%	10.1%	100.0%	100.5%	36.6%	98.0%	100.0%
10	10.1%	10.1%	4.1%	10.0%	10.1%	100.0%	100.6%	40.7%	99.3%	100.0%
11	9.8%	9.9%	4.2%	10.2%	9.8%	100.0%	100.8%	43.0%	103.4%	100.0%
12	9.9%	9.9%	4.8%	10.4%	9.9%	100.0%	100.5%	48.3%	104.9%	100.0%
13	10.0%	10.0%	5.1%	10.6%	10.0%	100.0%	100.6%	51.1%	106.5%	100.0%
14	9.9%	9.9%	5.2%	10.9%	9.9%	100.0%	100.7%	52.3%	110.2%	100.0%
15	10.0%	10.0%	5.6%	11.1%	10.0%	100.0%	100.2%	56.3%	111.3%	100.0%
16	11.4%	11.8%	1.8%	12.3%	11.4%	100.0%	103.3%	16.1%	107.6%	100.0%
17	7.7%	8.6%	4.0%	8.1%	7.7%	100.0%	111.9%	51.3%	105.7%	100.0%
18	5.0%	6.3%	6.6%	5.4%	5.0%	100.0%	126.9%	131.9%	108.6%	100.0%
19	3.3%	5.0%	8.2%	3.6%	3.3%	100.0%	152.1%	251.7%	109.7%	100.0%
20	0.5%	2.7%	9.9%	1.1%	0.5%	100.0%	561.2%	2057.2%	238.1%	100.3%
21	-1.3%	1.3%	11.0%	-0.6%	-1.3%	100.0%	-101.5%	-831.2%	47.9%	99.8%
22	-2.2%	0.7%	12.1%	-1.7%	-2.2%	100.0%	-31.7%	-546.7%	76.2%	99.9%
23	-2.5%	1.2%	13.0%	-2.9%	-2.5%	100.0%	-47.1%	-511.1%	115.8%	99.9%
24	-2.1%	2.4%	13.8%	-2.8%	-2.1%	100.0%	-116.9%	-664.2%	134.6%	99.9%
25	-1.5%	3.6%	14.6%	-2.5%	-1.5%	100.0%	-238.1%	-960.6%	161.4%	99.9%
26	-0.8%	6.3%	15.3%	-1.7%	-0.7%	100.0%	-811.8%	-1961.3%	222.8%	95.9%
27	0.2%	9.4%	16.0%	-0.9%	0.2%	100.0%	5197.8%	8818.0%	-483.0%	111.3%
28	1.1%	12.4%	16.6%	0.1%	1.1%	100.0%	1158.0%	1553.0%	11.7%	101.4%
29	2.0%	14.8%	17.1%	1.2%	2.0%	100.0%	737.5%	854.5%	59.1%	100.4%
30	3.1%	14.4%	49.9%	2.3%	3.1%	100.0%	457.2%	1588.2%	72.0%	100.1%
LT PV	6.8%	8.4%	6.5%	7.1%	6.8%					

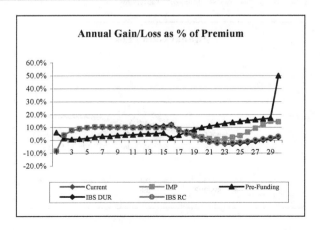

May 12, 2004

Trend Scenario: 1
All Blocks Combined Annual Economic Gain (Loss) - Includes Cost of Capital

Year	Current	IMP	Pre-Funding	IBS DUR	IBS RC	Current	IMP	Pre-Funding	IBS DUR	IBS RC
1	($444,566)	($444,566)	$261,602	($444,566)	($444,566)	100.0%	100.0%	−58.8%	100.0%	100.0%
2	$252,388	$252,388	$21,491	$252,388	$252,388	100.0%	100.0%	8.5%	100.0%	100.0%
3	$802,412	$802,412	($113,976)	$802,412	$802,412	100.0%	100.0%	−14.2%	100.0%	100.0%
4	$1,241,110	$1,249,830	($90,230)	$1,215,283	$1,241,110	100.0%	100.7%	−7.3%	97.9%	100.0%
5	$1,723,187	$1,739,592	$232	$1,706,752	$1,723,187	100.0%	101.0%	0.0%	99.0%	100.0%
6	$2,199,240	$2,210,907	$256,322	$2,153,036	$2,199,240	100.0%	100.5%	11.7%	97.9%	100.0%
7	$2,638,384	$2,658,085	$496,626	$2,555,504	$2,638,384	100.0%	100.7%	18.8%	96.9%	100.0%
8	$2,998,419	$3,026,549	$572,683	$2,919,840	$2,998,419	100.0%	100.9%	19.1%	97.4%	100.0%
9	$3,456,304	$3,476,569	$963,423	$3,389,764	$3,456,304	100.0%	100.6%	27.9%	98.1%	100.0%
10	$3,972,931	$4,001,370	$1,305,719	$3,951,367	$3,972,931	100.0%	100.7%	32.9%	99.5%	100.0%
11	$4,440,037	$4,480,091	$1,562,721	$4,614,642	$4,440,037	100.0%	100.9%	35.2%	103.9%	100.0%
12	$5,108,370	$5,137,056	$2,149,912	$5,383,598	$5,108,370	100.0%	100.6%	42.1%	105.4%	100.0%
13	$5,868,552	$5,908,594	$2,672,655	$6,266,557	$5,868,552	100.0%	100.7%	45.5%	106.8%	100.0%
14	$6,575,111	$6,614,636	$3,070,856	$7,272,782	$6,575,111	100.0%	100.6%	46.7%	110.6%	100.0%
15	$7,564,266	$7,551,120	$3,928,636	$8,413,295	$7,564,266	100.0%	99.8%	51.9%	111.2%	100.0%
16	$7,323,065	$7,524,681	($90,528)	$7,835,714	$7,323,065	100.0%	102.8%	−1.2%	107.0%	100.0%
17	$4,081,861	$4,577,748	$1,342,511	$4,289,871	$4,081,861	100.0%	112.1%	32.9%	105.1%	100.0%
18	$2,155,084	$2,837,563	$2,851,130	$2,356,502	$2,155,084	100.0%	131.7%	132.3%	109.3%	100.0%
19	$1,083,238	$1,892,556	$3,522,333	$1,224,237	$1,083,238	100.0%	174.7%	325.2%	113.0%	100.0%
20	($350,892)	$688,598	$4,142,331	($25,624)	($350,140)	100.0%	−196.2%	−1180.5%	7.3%	99.8%
21	($1,156,533)	$59,054	$4,360,794	($822,574)	($1,154,661)	100.0%	−5.1%	−377.1%	71.1%	99.8%
22	($1,478,744)	($193,206)	$4,555,635	($1,220,222)	($1,476,319)	100.0%	13.1%	−308.1%	82.5%	99.8%
23	($1,547,333)	($1,132)	$4,665,796	($1,662,866)	($1,544,651)	100.0%	0.1%	−301.5%	107.5%	99.8%
24	($1,302,862)	$397,006	$4,741,351	($1,537,015)	($1,300,600)	100.0%	−30.5%	−363.9%	118.0%	99.8%
25	($1,041,001)	$706,409	$4,793,841	($1,349,978)	($1,039,819)	100.0%	−67.9%	−460.5%	129.7%	99.9%
26	($734,600)	$1,343,779	$4,835,075	($1,051,340)	($722,662)	100.0%	−182.9%	−658.2%	143.1%	98.4%
27	($368,067)	$1,899,368	$4,870,868	($722,212)	($360,654)	100.0%	−516.0%	−1323.4%	196.2%	98.0%
28	($46,794)	$2,241,695	$4,904,870	($366,249)	($41,336)	100.0%	−4790.5%	−10481.7%	782.7%	88.3%
29	$278,874	$2,363,731	$4,938,275	($5,154)	$281,593	100.0%	847.6%	1770.8%	−1.8%	101.0%
30	$666,108	$2,006,376	$15,902,667	$351,462	$667,091	100.0%	301.2%	2387.4%	52.8%	100.1%
LT PV	$33,498,544	$40,144,136	$31,177,343	$34,705,229	$33,510,155					

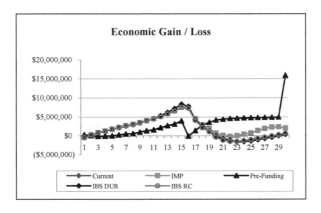

Economic Gain / Loss

Trend Scenario: 1

All Blocks Combined Annual Economic Gain (Loss) as Percentage of Premium

Year	Current	IMP	Pre-Funding	IBS DUR	IBS RC	Current	IMP	Pre-Funding	IBS DUR	IBS RC
1	9.5%	-9.5%	4.8%	-9.5%	-9.5%	100.0%	100.0%	-50.5%	100.0%	100.0%
2	2.9%	2.9%	0.2%	2.9%	2.9%	100.0%	100.0%	7.2%	100.0%	100.0%
3	6.5%	6.5%	-0.8%	6.5%	6.5%	100.0%	100.0%	-11.9%	100.0%	100.0%
4	7.8%	7.8%	-0.5%	7.6%	7.8%	100.0%	100.7%	-6.0%	97.8%	100.0%
5	8.7%	8.7%	0.0%	8.6%	8.7%	100.0%	100.9%	0.0%	98.9%	100.0%
6	9.1%	9.2%	0.9%	8.9%	9.1%	100.0%	100.5%	9.7%	97.7%	100.0%
7	9.2%	9.3%	1.5%	8.9%	9.2%	100.0%	100.7%	15.8%	96.5%	100.0%
8	9.0%	9.0%	1.4%	8.7%	9.0%	100.0%	100.9%	16.1%	97.0%	100.0%
9	8.9%	8.9%	2.1%	8.7%	8.9%	100.0%	100.6%	23.5%	97.8%	100.0%
10	8.9%	8.9%	2.5%	8.8%	8.9%	100.0%	100.7%	27.8%	99.2%	100.0%
11	8.6%	8.7%	2.6%	9.0%	8.6%	100.0%	100.9%	29.8%	103.9%	100.0%
12	8.7%	8.7%	3.1%	9.2%	8.7%	100.0%	100.6%	35.7%	105.6%	100.0%
13	8.8%	8.8%	3.4%	9.4%	8.8%	100.0%	100.7%	38.7%	107.3%	100.0%
14	8.7%	8.7%	3.4%	9.7%	8.7%	100.0%	100.8%	39.8%	111.6%	100.0%
15	8.8%	8.8%	3.9%	9.9%	8.8%	100.0%	100.2%	44.3%	112.8%	100.0%
16	10.2%	10.6%	-0.1%	11.1%	10.2%	100.0%	103.7%	-1.1%	108.5%	100.0%
17	6.5%	7.4%	1.8%	6.9%	6.5%	100.0%	114.1%	28.1%	106.8%	100.0%
18	3.8%	5.1%	4.3%	4.2%	3.8%	100.0%	135.4%	113.3%	111.3%	100.0%
19	2.1%	3.8%	5.8%	2.4%	2.1%	100.0%	182.4%	280.2%	115.3%	100.0%
20	-0.7%	1.5%	7.3%	-0.1%	-0.7%	100.0%	-209.0%	-1022.3%	7.5%	99.8%
21	-2.5%	0.1%	8.3%	-1.8%	-2.5%	100.0%	-5.6%	-329.5%	72.7%	99.9%
22	-3.4%	-0.5%	9.3%	-2.9%	-3.4%	100.0%	14.7%	-272.6%	84.6%	99.9%
23	-3.7%	0.0%	10.1%	-4.1%	-3.7%	100.0%	0.1%	-270.7%	110.7%	99.9%
24	-3.3%	1.2%	10.9%	-4.0%	-3.3%	100.0%	-37.6%	-332.3%	121.9%	99.9%
25	-2.7%	2.4%	11.6%	-3.7%	-2.7%	100.0%	-89.0%	-427.9%	134.3%	99.9%
26	-2.0%	5.1%	12.3%	-2.9%	-1.9%	100.0%	-259.6%	-622.7%	148.4%	98.4%
27	-1.0%	8.2%	13.0%	-2.1%	-1.0%	100.0%	-807.1%	-1276.1%	203.7%	98.0%
28	-0.1%	11.2%	13.6%	-1.1%	-0.1%	100.0%	-8433.1%	-10293.2%	812.4%	88.3%
29	0.8%	13.6%	14.2%	0.0%	0.8%	100.0%	1690.3%	1770.7%	-1.9%	101.0%
30	1.9%	13.2%	47.2%	1.1%	1.9%	100.0%	678.0%	2432.3%	54.7%	100.2%
LT PV	5.6%	7.2%	4.5%	5.9%	5.6%					6

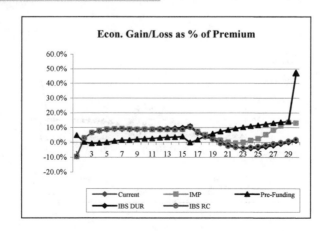

Econ. Gain/Loss as % of Premium

May 12, 2004

APPENDIX C

RATE FILING TASK FORCE MODEL USER HINTS

The following tips will be helpful as you use the task force's models distributed electronically by the publisher.

USER'S GUIDE

Read the Model User's Guide found on pages 5-8 of the Model Documentation PDF. Note there are model specific instructions for each of the Current Market, Pre-Funding, Interblock Subsidy, and Individual Market Pool spreadsheets.

REVIEW INPUT

Always review the input sheet of the AAA Rate Filing Model – Exhibits.xls spreadsheet to ensure that the input is as you intended. In making multiple tests, it is quite easy to forget to undo previous changes in assumptions.

RUN RATE COMPRESSION MACRO

You must run the IBS Rate Compression model's macro to restore profit each time you modify any global or model specific assumptions that affect the IBS Rate Compression model. Depending on the speed of your computer and the type of assumption being tested, the macro can take quite some time to run. The macro button is found in the AAA Rate Filing Model – Interblock Subsidy.xls spreadsheet, Rate Compression Assumptions sheet, cells AO2 through AQ and is labeled as Set Profit Difference % to Zero.

EXPECTED PREMIUM RELATIONSHIP TO COMPANY NEW BUSINESS RATES

The Expected Premium assumption for each model should generally be within $1 of the Company New Business rate. The Expected Premium value should be the same for the Current Market, Individual Market Pool and Interblock Subsidy models. The Pre-Funding model requires a different Expected Premium. This value is entered in the following cells:

AAA Rate Model – Current Market.xls, Current Market Assumptions sheet cell E15

AAA Rate Model – Pre-Funding.xls DBPR Assumptions, cell E10

AAA Rate Model – Individual Market Pool.xls, IMP Assumptions sheet, cell R43

AAA Rate Model – Interblock Subsidy.xls, Current Market Assump 5 blocks sheet, cell M15

The need for an Expected Premium arose when developing the Pre-Funding model. With that model we need to start the pricing process with some idea of what the final premium will be, in order to adjust the lapse rates used in setting the reserve factors. Manually setting an Expected premium allows us to avoid circular formula references. Once we introduced the Expected Premium concept in the Pre-Funding model, we also included it in the other models, which made the pricing more accurate. The Pre-Funding model is a bit more sensitive than the other models to getting the Expected Premium right, because missing it does not just give you the wrong first year premium, it also gives you the wrong reserve factors.

PARTIAL PRE-FUNDING INPUT

You can do partial pre-funding in the Pre-Funding model by setting the "Excess of Premium Trend over Claim Trend" assumption in the DBPR Assumptions sheet, cell F11, to something greater than 0%. "Full Pre-Funding" means that premiums are expected to increase with age and medical trend; all durational effects are pre-funded. "Partial Pre-Funding" means that premiums go up not just with age and trend, but also by a bit more for durational effects. Reserves are set up to reduce the amount of increase due to duration, but do not eliminate durational increases.

REVIEW OUTPUT AT DETAIL LEVEL

The AAA Rate Filing Model – Exhibits.xls spreadsheet summarizes many variables but by necessity does not contain all the detailed results. Some results are shown as averages and the direction or magnitude of an assumption change may not be readily apparent. It is often helpful in these situations to track the effect of an assumption change at a detailed level for an issue year cohort. The models contain up to 15 years of issues and each issue year cohort may react differently to any assumption change.

UNDERSTAND WHAT YOU ARE CHANGING

Review the Documentation to be sure you understand what the values in the Global Assumptions sheet of the AAA Rate Filing Model – Global.xls spreadsheet are intended to do and where they might be used. Note each model, Current Market, Pre-Funding, Interblock Subsidy, and Individual Market Pool, picks up its global assumptions from the AAA Rate Filing Model – Global.xls spreadsheet. There are unique assumptions for each model which are also summarized in the Input sheet of AAA Rate Filing Model - Exhibits.xls spreadsheet.

ONLY OPEN ONE VERSION OF EXHIBITS.XLS SPREADSHEET

Do not open more than one AAA Rate Filing Model – Exhibits.xls spreadsheet at a time. If, for example, you run several tests and save the results as AAA Rate Filing Model - Exhibits1.xls, AAA Rate Filing Model – Exhibits2.xls, AAA Rate Filing Model – Exhibits3.xls, etc., we have observed values in these spreadsheets change when several are open at the same time, even if you did not update links. Even though links are not updated, there seems to be some sort of logic conflict in Excel in that each Exhibits.xls spreadsheet refers to certain assumptions, but those assumptions are not necessarily the same for the different versions of the AAA Rate Filing Model – Exhibits.xls spreadsheets created. We recommend printing the Global Summary and Input sheets for each run you make. Then the printed versions can be compared or you can view one of the AAA Rate Filing Model – Exhibits.xls spreadsheets and compare it to previously printed versions.

APPENDIX D

Model # 10

National Association of Insurance Commissioners

Health Insurance Reserves Model Regulation

© NAIC
Reprinted with permission from NAIC.
Further distribution is strictly prohibited.

© 2006 National Association of Insurance Commissioners
All rights reserved.

National Association of Insurance Commissioners
Insurance Products & Services Division
816-783-8300
Fax 816-460-7593
www.naic.org/insprod
prodserv@naic.org

Printed in the United States of America

No part of this book may be reproduced, stored in a retrieval system, or transmitted in any form or by any means, electronic or mechanical, including photocopying, recording, or any storage or retrieval system, without written permission from the NAIC.

Executive Headquarters	Securities Valuation Office	Government Relations
2301 McGee Street, Suite 800	48 Wall Street, 6th Floor	Hall of States Bldg.
Kansas City, MO 64108-2662	New York, NY 10005-2906	444 North Capitol NW, Suite 701
816-842-3600	212-398-9000	Washington, DC 20001-1509
		202-624-7790

HEALTH INSURANCE RESERVES MODEL REGULATION

TABLE OF CONTENTS

Section 1. Introduction
Section 2. Claim Reserves
Section 3. Premium Reserves
Section 4. Contract Reserves
Section 5. Reinsurance
Section 6. Effective Date
Appendix A. Specific Standards for Morbidity, Interest and Mortality
Appendix B. Glossary of Technical Terms Used
Appendix C. Reserves for Waiver of Premium

Section 1. Introduction

A. Purpose and Scope

The purpose of this regulation is to implement [cite section of law which sets forth the NAIC Standard Valuation Law].

These standards apply to all individual and group health [accident and sickness] insurance coverages including single premium credit disability insurance. All other credit insurance is not subject to this regulation.

When an insurer determines that adequacy of its health insurance reserves requires reserves in excess of the minimum standards specified herein, such increased reserves shall be held and shall be considered the minimum reserves for that insurer.

With respect to any block of contracts, or with respect to an insurer's health business as a whole, a prospective gross premium valuation is the ultimate test of reserve adequacy as of a given valuation date. Such a gross premium valuation will take into account, for contracts in force, in a claims status, or in a continuation of benefits status on the valuation date, the present value as of the valuation date of: all expected benefits unpaid, all expected expenses unpaid, and all unearned or expected premiums, adjusted for future premium increases reasonably expected to be put into effect.

Such a gross premium valuation is to be performed whenever a significant doubt exists as to reserve adequacy with respect to any major block of contracts, or with respect to the insurer's health business as a whole. In the event inadequacy is found to exist, immediate loss recognition shall be made and the reserves restored to adequacy. Adequate reserves (inclusive of claim, premium and contract reserves, if any) shall be held with respect to all contracts, regardless of whether contract reserves are required for such contracts under these standards.

Whenever minimum reserves, as defined in these standards, exceed reserve requirements as determined by a prospective gross premium valuation, such minimum reserves remain the minimum requirement under these standards.

B. Categories of Reserves

The following sections set forth minimum standards for three categories of health insurance reserves:

Section 2. Claim Reserves
Section 3. Premium Reserves
Section 4. Contract Reserves

Adequacy of an insurer's health insurance reserves is to be determined on the basis of all three categories combined. However, these standards emphasize the importance of determining appropriate reserves for each of the three categories separately.

C. Appendices

These standards contain two appendices which are an integral part of the standards, and one additional "supplementary" appendix which is not part of the standards as such, but is included for explanatory and illustrative purposes only.

Appendix A. Specific minimum standards with respect to morbidity, mortality and interest, which apply to claim reserves according to year of incurral and to contract reserves according to year of issue.

Appendix B. Glossary of Technical Terms used.

Appendix C. (Supplementary) Waiver of Premium Reserves.

Section 2. Claim Reserves

A. General

(1) Claim reserves are required for all incurred but unpaid claims on all health insurance policies.

(2) Appropriate claim expense reserves are required with respect to the estimated expense of settlement of all incurred but unpaid claims.

(3) All such reserves for prior valuation years are to be tested for adequacy and reasonableness along the lines of claim runoff schedules in accordance with the statutory financial statement including consideration of any residual unpaid liability.

B. Minimum Standards for Claim Reserves

(1) Disability Income

(a) Interest. The maximum interest rate for claim reserves is specified in Appendix A.

(b) Morbidity. Minimum standards with respect to morbidity are those specified in Appendix A, except that, at the option of the insurer:

(i) For individual disability income claims incurred on or after [January 1, 2005], assumptions regarding claim termination rates for the period less than two (2) years from the date of disablement may be based on the insurer's experience, if such experience is considered credible, or upon other assumptions designed to place a sound value on the liabilities.

(ii) For group disability income claims incurred on or after [January 1, 2005]:

(I) Assumptions regarding claim termination rates for the period less than two (2) years from the date of disablement may be based on the insurer's experience, if the experience is considered credible, or upon other assumptions designed to place a sound value on the liabilities.

(II) Assumptions regarding claim termination rates for the period two (2) or more years but less than five (5) years from the date of disablement may, with the approval of the commissioner, be based on the insurer's experience for which the insurer maintains underwriting and claim administration control. The request for such approval of a plan of modification to the reserve basis must include:

- An analysis of the credibility of the experience;
- A description of how all of the insurer's experience is proposed to be used in setting reserves;
- A description and quantification of the margins to be included;
- A summary of the financial impact that the proposed plan of modification would have had on the insurer's last filed annual statement;
- A copy of the approval of the proposed plan of modification by the commissioner of the state of domicile; and
- Any other information deemed necessary by the commissioner.

(iii) For disability income claims incurred prior to [January 1, 2005] each insurer may elect which of the following to use as the minimum morbidity standard for claim reserves:

(I) The minimum morbidity standard in effect for claim reserves as of the date the claim was incurred, or

(II) The standards as defined in Items (i) and (ii), applied to all open claims. Once an insurer elects to calculate reserves for all open claims on the standard defined in Items (i) and (ii), all future valuations must be on that basis.

Drafting Note: It is recommended that these amended standards apply to claims incurred on or after January 1, 2005, however, the state should insert the date on which these standards will apply to newly incurred claims in its jurisdiction.

Drafting Note: For experience to be considered credible for purposes of Item (ii), the company should be able to provide claim termination patterns over no more than six (6) years reflecting at least 5,000 claims terminations during the third through fifth claims durations on reasonably similar applicable policy forms.

For claim reserves to reflect "sound values" and reasonable margins, reserve tables based on credible experience should be adjusted regularly to maintain reasonable margins. Demonstrations may be required by the commissioner of the state of domicile based on published literature (e.g., Goldman, TSA XLII).

(c) Duration of Disablement. For contracts with an elimination period, the duration of disablement should be measured as dating from the time that benefits would have begun to accrue had there been no elimination period.

(2) All Other Benefits

(a) Interest. The maximum interest rate for claim reserves is specified in Appendix A.

(b) Morbidity or Other Contingency. The reserve should be based on the insurer's experience, if the experience is considered credible, or upon other assumptions designed to place a sound value on the liabilities.

C. Claim Reserve Methods Generally

A generally accepted actuarial reserving method or other reasonable method, if, after a public hearing, the method is approved by the commissioner prior to the statement date, or a combination of methods may be used to estimate all claim liabilities. The methods used for estimating liabilities generally may be aggregate methods, or various reserve items may be separately valued. Approximations based on groupings and averages may also be employed. Adequacy of the claim reserves, however, shall be determined in the aggregate.

Section 3. Premium Reserves

A. General

(1) Except as noted in Paragraph (2), unearned premium reserves are required for all contracts with respect to the period of coverage for which premiums, other than premiums paid in advance, have been paid beyond the date of valuation.

(2) Single premium credit disability insurance, both individual and group, is excluded from unearned premium reserve requirements of this Section 3.

(3) If premiums due and unpaid are carried as an asset, the premiums must be treated as premiums in force, subject to unearned premium reserve determination. The value of unpaid commissions, premium taxes and the cost of collection associated with due and unpaid premiums shall be carried as an offsetting liability.

(4) The gross premiums paid in advance for a period of coverage commencing after the next premium due date which follows the date of valuation may be appropriately discounted to the valuation date and shall be held either as a separate liability or as an addition to the unearned premium reserve which would otherwise be required as a minimum.

B. Minimum Standards for Unearned Premium Reserves

(1) The minimum unearned premium reserve with respect to a contract is the pro rata unearned modal premium that applies to the premium period beyond the valuation date, with the premium determined on the basis of:

(a) The valuation net modal premium on the contract reserve basis applying to the contract; or

(b) The gross modal premium for the contract if no contract reserve applies.

(2) However, in no event may the sum of the unearned premium and contract reserves for all contracts of the insurer subject to contract reserve requirements be less than the gross modal unearned premium reserve on all such contracts, as of the date of valuation. The reserve shall never be less than the expected claims for the period beyond the valuation date represented by the unearned premium reserve, to the extent not provided for elsewhere.

Drafting Note: States should be aware that while single premium credit disability insurance is excluded from unearned premium reserve requirements, there may be requirements elsewhere in statutory accounting to test reserves against the premium refund net liability.

C. Premium Reserve Methods Generally

The insurer may employ suitable approximations and estimates; including, but not limited to groupings, averages and aggregate estimation; in computing premium reserves. Approximations or estimates should be tested periodically to determine their continuing adequacy and reliability.

Section 4. Contract Reserves

A. General

(1) Contract reserves are required, unless otherwise specified in Section 4A(2) for:

(a) All individual and group contracts with which level premiums are used; or

(b) All individual and group contracts with respect to which, due to the gross premium pricing structure at issue, the value of the future benefits at any time exceeds the value of any appropriate future valuation net premiums at that time. This evaluation may be applied on a rating block basis if the total premiums for the block were developed to support the total risk assumed and expected expenses for the block each year, and a qualified actuary certifies the premium development. The actuary should state in the certification that premiums for the rating block were developed such that each year's premium was intended to cover that year's costs without any prefunding. If the premium is also intended to recover costs for any prior years, the actuary should also disclose the reasons for and magnitude of such recovery. The values specified in this subparagraph shall be determined on the basis specified in Subsection B of this section.

Drafting Note: Language permitting a rating block test was added because a concern arose that the existing minimum reserve standards could be interpreted as requiring contract reserves on a per contract basis for products that are community rated or that use other rating methodology based on cross-subsidies among contracts within the block. If rates are determined such that each year's premium is intended to cover that year's cost, the rating block approach results in no contract reserves unless required by Subsection D. If rates are designed to prefund future years' costs, contract reserves will be required.

(2) Contracts not requiring a contract reserve are:

(a) Contracts that cannot be continued after one year from issue; or

(b) Contracts already in force on the effective date of these standards for which no contract reserve was required under the immediately preceding standards.

(3) The contract reserve is in addition to claim reserves and premium reserves.

(4) The methods and procedures for contract reserves shall be consistent with those for claim reserves for a contract, or else appropriate adjustment shall be made when necessary to assure provision for the aggregate liability. The definition of the date of incurral shall be the same in both determinations.

(5) The total contract reserve established shall incorporate provisions for moderately adverse deviations.

B. Minimum Standards for Contract Reserves

(1) Basis

(a) Morbidity or Other Contingency. Minimum standards with respect to morbidity are those set forth in Appendix A. Valuation net premiums used under each contract shall have a structure consistent with the gross premium structure at issue of the contract as this relates to the advancing age of insured, contract duration and period for which gross premiums have been calculated. Contracts for which tabular morbidity standards are not specified in Appendix A shall be valued using tables established for reserve purposes by a qualified actuary and acceptable to the commissioner. The morbidity tables shall contain a pattern of incurred claims cost that reflects the underlying morbidity and shall not be constructed for the primary purpose of minimizing reserves.

Drafting Note: Section 4B(1)(a) only applies to the premium structure applicable to each contract. The relationship among gross premiums for different contracts (e.g., variations by age) has no bearing on the net premium structure. If for a policy form there is no gross premium variation by age, the valuation net premiums will nonetheless vary based on age at issue for each contract since at issue the present value of valuation net premiums for a contract must equal the present value of tabular claim costs.

(i) In determining the morbidity assumptions, the actuary shall use assumptions that represent the best estimate of anticipated future experience, but shall not incorporate any expectation of future morbidity improvement. Morbidity improvement is a change, in the combined effect of claim frequency and the present value of future expected claim payments given that a claim has occurred, from the current morbidity tables or experience that will result in a reduction to reserves. It is not the intent of this provision to restrict the ability of the actuary to reflect the morbidity impact for a specific known event that has occurred and that is able to be evaluated and quantified.

Drafting Note: The last sentence is intended to provide allowances for a known event, such as a new drug release, but at the time of this writing, there are no specific examples that could be pointed to in the recent past that would have met this standard. This is intended to be an extremely rare event.

(ii) Business in force as of the effective date of Section 4B(1)(c)(iii) may be permitted to retain the original reserve basis which may not meet the provisions of Item (i) above, subject to the acceptability to the commissioner.

Drafting Note: The consistency between the gross premium structure and the valuation net premium is required only at issue, because the impact on such consistency after issue of regulatory restrictions on premium rate increases is still under study.

(b) Interest. The maximum interest rate is specified in Appendix A.

(c) Termination Rates. Termination rates used in the computation of reserves shall be on the basis of a mortality table as specified in Appendix A except as noted in the following items:

(i) Under contracts for which premium rates are not guaranteed, and where the effects of insurer underwriting are specifically used by policy duration in the valuation morbidity standard or for return of premium or other deferred cash benefits, total termination rates may be used at ages and durations where these exceed specified mortality table rates, but not in excess of the lesser of:

(I) Eighty percent of the total termination rate used in the calculation of the gross premiums, or

(II) Eight percent;

(ii) For long-term care individual policies or group certificates issued after January 1, [1997], the contract reserve may be established on a basis of separate:

(I) Mortality (as specified in Appendix A); and

(II) Terminations other than mortality, where the terminations are not to exceed:

- For policy years one through four (4), the lesser of eighty percent (80%) of the voluntary lapse rate used in the calculation of gross premiums and eight percent (8%);

- For policy years five (5) and later, the lesser of one hundred percent (100%) of the voluntary lapse rate used in the calculation of gross premiums and four percent (4%).

(iii) For long-term care individual policies or group certificates issued on or after January 1, [2005], the contract reserve shall be established on the basis of:

(I) Mortality (as specified in Appendix A); and

(II) Terminations other than mortality, where the terminations are not to exceed:

- For policy year one, the lesser of eighty percent (80%) of the voluntary lapse rate used in the calculation of gross premiums and six percent (6%);

- For policy years two (2) through four (4), the lesser of eighty percent (80%) of the voluntary lapse rate used in the calculation of gross premiums and four percent (4%); and

- For policy years five (5) and later, the lesser of one hundred percent (100%) of the voluntary lapse rate used in the calculation of gross premiums and two percent (2%), except for group insurance as defined in [insert reference to Section 4E(1) of the NAIC Long-Term Care Insurance Model Act, i.e., employer groups] where the 2% shall be three percent (3%).

(iv) Where a morbidity standard specified in Appendix A is on an aggregate basis, the morbidity standard may be adjusted to reflect the effect of insurer underwriting by policy duration. The adjustments must be appropriate to the underwriting and be acceptable to the commissioner.

(2) Reserve Method.

    (a) For insurance except long-term care and return of premium or other deferred cash benefits, the minimum reserve is the reserve calculated on the two-year full preliminary term method; that is, under which the terminal reserve is zero at the first and also the second contract anniversary.

    (b) For long-term care insurance, the minimum reserve is the reserve calculated as follows:

        (i) For individual policies and group certificates issued on or before December 31, [1991], reserves calculated on the two-year full preliminary term method;

        (ii) For individual policies and group certificates issued on or after January 1, [1992], reserves calculated on the one-year full preliminary term method.

    (c) (i) For return of premium or other deferred cash benefits, the minimum reserve is the reserve calculated as follows:

           (I) On the one year preliminary term method if the benefits are provided at any time before the twentieth anniversary;

           (II) On the two year preliminary term method if the benefits are only provided on or after the twentieth anniversary.

        (ii) The preliminary term method may be applied only in relation to the date of issue of a contract. Reserve adjustments introduced later, as a result of rate increases, revisions in assumptions (e.g., projected inflation rates) or for other reasons, are to be applied immediately as of the effective date of adoption of the adjusted basis.

(3) Negative Reserves. Negative reserves on any benefit may be offset against positive reserves for other benefits in the same contract, but the total contract reserve with respect to all benefits combined may not be less than zero.

(4) Nonforfeiture Benefits for Long-Term Care Insurance. The contract reserve on a policy basis shall not be less than the net single premium for the nonforfeiture benefits at the appropriate policy duration, where the net single premium is computed according to the above specifications.

Drafting Note: While the above consideration for nonforfeiture benefits is specific to long-term care insurance, it should not be interpreted to mean that similar consideration may not be applicable for other lines of business.

  C. Alternative Valuation Methods and Assumptions Generally

    Provided the contract reserve on all contracts to which an alternative method or basis is applied is not less in the aggregate than the amount determined according to the applicable standards specified above; an insurer may use any reasonable assumptions as to interest rates, termination and mortality rates, and rates of morbidity or other contingency. Also, subject to the preceding condition, the insurer may employ methods other than the methods stated above in determining a sound value of its liabilities under such contracts, including, but not limited to the following: the net level premium method; the one-year full preliminary term method; prospective valuation on the basis of actual gross premiums with reasonable allowance for future expenses; the use of approximations such as those involving age groupings, groupings of several years of issue, average amounts of indemnity, grouping of similar contract forms; the computation of the reserve for one contract benefit as a percentage of, or by other relation to, the aggregate contract reserves exclusive of the benefit or benefits so valued; and the use of a composite annual claim cost for all or any combination of the benefits included in the contracts valued.

D. Tests For Adequacy and Reasonableness of Contract Reserves

Annually, an appropriate review shall be made of the insurer's prospective contract liabilities on contracts valued by tabular reserves to determine the continuing adequacy and reasonableness of the tabular reserves giving consideration to future gross premiums. The insurer shall make appropriate increments to such tabular reserves if such tests indicate that the basis of such reserves is no longer adequate; subject, however, to the minimum standards of Section 4B.

In the event a company has a contract or a group of related similar contracts, for which future gross premiums will be restricted by contract, insurance department regulations, or for other reasons, such that the future gross premiums reduced by expenses for administration, commissions, and taxes will be insufficient to cover future claims, the company shall establish contract reserves for such shortfall in the aggregate.

Section 5. Reinsurance

Increases to, or credits against reserves carried, arising because of reinsurance assumed or reinsurance ceded, must be determined in a manner consistent with these minimum reserve standards and with all applicable provisions of the reinsurance contracts which affect the insurer's liabilities.

Section 6. Effective Date

The regulation shall be effective on [insert date].

APPENDIX A. SPECIFIC STANDARDS FOR MORBIDITY, INTEREST AND MORTALITY

I. MORBIDITY

A. Minimum morbidity standards for valuation of specified individual contract health insurance benefits are as follows:

(1) Disability Income Benefits Due to Accident or Sickness.

(a) Contract Reserves:

Contracts issued on or after January 1, 1965 and prior to January 1, [YEAR]:

The 1964 Commissioners Disability Table (64 CDT).

Contracts issued on or after January 1, [YEAR]:

The 1985 Commissioners Individual Disability Tables A (85CIDA); or

The 1985 Commissioners Individual Disability Tables B (85CIDB).

Contracts issued during [YEAR or YEARS]:

Optional use of either the 1964 Table or the 1985 Tables.

Each insurer shall elect, with respect to all individual contracts issued in any one statement year, whether it will use Tables A or Tables B as the minimum standard. The insurer may, however, elect to use the other tables with respect to any subsequent statement year.

(b) Claim Reserves:

(i) For claims incurred on or after [effective date of this amendment]:

The 1985 Commissioners Individual Disability Table A (85CIDA) with claim termination rates multiplied by the following adjustment factors:

Duration	Adjustment Factor	Adjusted Termination Rates*
Week 1	0.366	0.04831
2	0.366	0.04172
3	0.366	0.04063
4	0.366	0.04355
5	0.365	0.04088
6	0.365	0.04271
7	0.365	0.04380
8	0.365	0.04344

(cont.)

Duration	Adjustment Factor	Adjusted Termination Rates*
9	0.370	0.04292
10	0.370	0.04107
11	0.370	0.03848
12	0.370	0.03478
13	0.370	0.03034
Month 4	0.391	0.08758
5	0.371	0.07346
6	0.435	0.07531
7	0.500	0.07245
8	0.564	0.06655
9	0.613	0.05520
10	0.663	0.04705
11	0.712	0.04486
12	0.756	0.04309
13	0.800	0.04080
14	0.844	0.03882
15	0.888	0.03730
16	0.932	0.03448
17	0.976	0.03026
18	1.020	0.02856
19	1.049	0.02518
20	1.078	0.02264
21	1.107	0.02104
22	1.136	0.01932
23	1.165	0.01865
24	1.195	0.01792
Year 3	1.369	0.16839
4	1.204	0.10114
5	1.199	0.07434
6 and later	1.000	**

* The adjusted termination rates derived from the application of the adjustment factors to the DTS Valuation Table termination rates shown in exhibits 3a, 3b, 3c, 4, and 5 (*Transactions of the Society of Actuaries* (TSA) XXXVII, pp. 457-463) is displayed. The adjustment factors for age, elimination period, class, sex, and cause displayed in exhibits 3a, 3b, 3c, and 4 should be applied to the adjusted termination rates shown in this table.

** Applicable DTS Valuation Table duration rate from exhibits 3c and 4 (TSA XXXVII, pp. 462-463).

The 85CIDA table so adjusted for the computation of claim reserves shall be known as 85CIDC (The 1985 Commissioners Individual Disability Table C).

(ii) For claims incurred prior to [effective date of this amendment]:

Each insurer may elect which of the following to use as the minimum standard for claims incurred prior to [effective date of this amendment]:

(I) The minimum morbidity standard in effect for contract reserves on currently issued contracts, as of the date the claim is incurred, or

(II) The standard as defined in Item (i), applied to all open claims. Once an insurer elects to calculate reserves for all open claims on the standard defined in Item (i), all future valuations must be on that basis.

(2) Hospital Benefits, Surgical Benefits and Maternity Benefits (Scheduled benefits or fixed time period benefits only).

(a) Contract Reserves:

Contracts issued on or after January 1, 1955, and before January 1, 1982:

The 1956 Intercompany Hospital-Surgical Tables.

Contracts issued on or after January 1, 1982:

The 1974 Medical Expense Tables, Table A, *Transactions of the Society of Actuaries,* Volume XXX, pg. 63. Refer to the paper (in the same volume, pg. 9) to which this table is appended, including its discussions, for methods of adjustment for benefits not directly valued in Table A: "Development of the 1974 Medical Expense Benefits," Houghton and Wolf.

(b) Claim Reserves: No specific standard. See (6).

(3) Cancer Expense Benefits (Scheduled benefits or fixed time period benefits only).

(a) Contract Reserves:

Contracts issued on or after January 1, 1986:

The 1985 NAIC Cancer Claim Cost Tables.

(b) Claim Reserves:

No specific standard. See (6).

(4) Accidental Death Benefits.

    (a) Contract Reserves:

        Contracts issued on or after January 1, 1965:

        The 1959 Accidental Death Benefits Table.

    (b) Claim Reserves:

        Actual amount incurred.

(5) Single Premium Credit Disability.

    (a) Contract Reserves:

        (i) For contracts issued on or after [effective date of this amendment]:

            (I) For plans having less than a thirty-day elimination period, the 1985 Commissioners Individual Disability Table A (85CIDA) with claim incidence rates increased by twelve percent (12%).

            (II) For plans having a thirty-day and greater elimination period, the 85CIDA for a fourteen-day elimination period with the adjustment in Item (I).

        (ii) For contracts issued prior to [effective date of this amendment], each insurer may elect either Item (I) or (II) to use as the minimum standard. Once an insurer elects to calculate reserves for all contracts on the standard defined in Item (i), all future valuations must be on that basis.

            (I) The minimum morbidity standard in effect for contract reserves on currently issued contracts, as of the date the contract was issued, or

Drafting Note: If the state does not have a minimum morbidity standard in effect for contract reserves on currently issued contracts, the state shall accept the methodology approved by the commissioner in the state of domicile.

            (II) The standard as defined in Item (i), applied to all contracts.

    (b) Claim Reserves:

        Claim reserves are to be determined as provided in Subsection 2C.

(6) Other Individual Contract Benefits.

    (a) Contract Reserves:

        For all other individual contract benefits, morbidity assumptions are to be determined as provided in the reserve standards.

(b) Claim Reserves:

For all benefits other than disability, claim reserves are to be determined as provided in the standards.

B. Minimum morbidity standards for valuation of specified group contract health insurance benefits are as follows:

(1) Disability Income Benefits Due to Accident or Sickness.

(a) Contract Reserves:

Contracts issued prior to January 1, [YEAR]:

The same basis, if any, as that employed by the insurer as of January 1, [SAME YEAR];

Contracts issued on or after January 1, [YEAR]:

The 1987 Commissioners Group Disability Income Table (87CGDT).

(b) Claim Reserves:

For claims incurred on or after January 1, [YEAR]:

The 1987 Commissioners Group Disability Income Table (87CGDT);

For claims incurred prior to January 1, [YEAR]:

Use of the 87CGDT is optional.

(2) Single Premium Credit Disability

(a) Contract Reserves:

(i) For contracts issued on or after [effective date of this amendment]:

(I) For plans having less than a thirty-day elimination period, the 1985 Commissioners Individual Disability Table A (85CIDA) with claim incidence rates increased by twelve percent (12%).

(II) For plans having a thirty-day and greater elimination period, the 85CIDA for a fourteen-day elimination period with the adjustment in item (I).

(ii) For contracts issued prior to [effective date of this amendment], each insurer may elect either Item (I) or (II) to use as the minimum standard. Once an insurer elects to calculate reserves for all contracts on the standard defined in Item (i), all future valuations must be on that basis.

(I) The minimum morbidity standard in effect for contract reserves on currently issued contracts, as of the date the contract was issued, or

(II) The standard as defined in Item (i), applied to all contracts.

(b) Claim Reserves:

Claim reserves are to be determined as provided in Subsection 2C.

(3) Other Group Contract Benefits.

(a) Contract Reserves:

For all other group contract benefits, morbidity assumptions are to be determined as provided in the reserve standards.

(b) Claim Reserves:

For all benefits other than disability, claim reserves are to be determined as provided in the standards.

II. INTEREST

A. For contract reserves the maximum interest rate is the maximum rate permitted by law in the valuation of whole life insurance issued on the same date as the health insurance contract.

B. For claim reserves on policies that require contract reserves, the maximum interest rate is the maximum rate permitted by law in the valuation of whole life insurance issued on the same date as the claim incurral date.

C. For claim reserves on policies not requiring contract reserves, the maximum interest rate is the maximum rate permitted by law in the valuation of single premium immediate annuities issued on the same date as the claim incurral date, reduced by one hundred basis points.

III. MORTALITY

A. Unless Subsection B or C applies, the mortality basis used for all policies except long-term care individual policies and group certificates and for long-term care individual policies or group certificates issued before [January 1, 1997 or the effective date set in state regulations, whichever is later] shall be according to a table (but without use of selection factors) permitted by law for the valuation of whole life insurance issued on the same date as the health insurance contract. For long-term care insurance individual policies or group certificates issued on or after [January 1, 1997 or the effective date set in state regulations, whichever is later], the mortality basis used shall be the 1983 Group Annuity Mortality Table without projection. For long-term care insurance individual policies or group certificates issued on or after the effective date of Section 4B(1)(c)(iii), the mortality basis used shall be the 1994 Group Annuity Mortality Static Table.

B. Other mortality tables adopted by the NAIC and promulgated by the commissioner may be used in the calculation of the minimum reserves if appropriate for the type of benefits and if approved by the commissioner. The request for approval shall include the proposed mortality table and the reason that the standard specified in Subsection A is inappropriate.

C. For single premium credit insurance using the 85CIDA table, no separate mortality shall be assumed.

APPENDIX B. GLOSSARY OF TECHNICAL TERMS USED

As used in this valuation standard, the following terms have the following meaning:

ANNUAL-CLAIM COST. The net annual cost per unit of benefit before the addition of expenses, including claim settlement expenses, and a margin for profit or contingencies. For example, the annual claim cost for a $100 monthly disability benefit, for a maximum disability benefit period of one year, with an elimination period of one week, with respect to a male at age 35, in a certain occupation might be $12, while the gross premium for this benefit might be $18. The additional $6 would cover expenses and profit or contingencies.

CLAIMS ACCRUED. That portion of claims incurred on or prior to the valuation date which result in liability of the insurer for the payment of benefits for medical services which have been rendered on or prior to the valuation date, and for the payment of benefits for days of hospitalization and days of disability which have occurred on or prior to the valuation date, which the insurer has not paid as of the valuation date, but for which it is liable, and will have to pay after the valuation date. This liability is sometimes referred to as a liability for "accrued" benefits. A claim reserve, which represents an estimate of this accrued claim liability, must be established.

CLAIMS REPORTED. When an insurer has been informed that a claim has been incurred, if the date reported is on or prior to the valuation date, the claim is considered as a reported claim for annual statement purposes.

CLAIMS UNACCRUED. That portion of claims incurred on or prior to the valuation date which result in liability of the insurer for the payment of benefits for medical services expected to be rendered after the valuation date, and for benefits expected to be payable for days of hospitalization and days of disability occurring after the valuation date. This liability is sometimes referred to as a liability for unaccrued benefits. A claim reserve, which represents an estimate of the unaccrued claim payments expected to be made (which may or may not be discounted with interest), must be established.

CLAIMS UNREPORTED. When an insurer has not been informed, on or before the valuation date, concerning a claim that has been incurred on or prior to the valuation date, the claim is considered as an unreported claim for annual statement purposes.

DATE OF DISABLEMENT. The earliest date the insured is considered as being disabled under the definition of disability in the contract, based on a doctor's evaluation or other evidence. Normally this date will coincide with the start of any elimination period.

ELIMINATION PERIOD. A specified number of days, weeks, or months starting at the beginning of each period of loss, during which no benefits are payable.

GROSS PREMIUM. The amount of premium charged by the insurer. It includes the net premium (based on claim-cost) for the risk, together with any loading for expenses, profit or contingencies.

GROUP INSURANCE. The term group insurance includes blanket insurance and franchise insurance and any other forms of group insurance.

LEVEL PREMIUM. A premium calculated to remain unchanged throughout either the lifetime of the policy, or for some shorter projected period of years. The premium need not be guaranteed; in which case, although it is calculated to remain level, it may be changed if any of the assumptions on which it was based are revised at a later time.

Generally, the annual claim costs are expected to increase each year and the insurer, instead of charging premiums that correspondingly increase each year, charges a premium calculated to remain level for a period of years or for the lifetime of the contract. In this case the benefit portion of the premium is more than needed to provide for the cost of benefits during the earlier years of the policy and less than the actual cost in the later years. The building of a prospective contract reserve is a natural result of level premiums.

LONG-TERM CARE INSURANCE. Any insurance policy or rider advertised, marketed, offered or designed to provide coverage for not less than twelve (12) consecutive months for each covered person on an expense incurred, indemnity, prepaid or other basis; for one or more necessary or medically necessary diagnostic, preventive, therapeutic, rehabilitative, maintenance or personal care services, provided in a setting other than an acute care unit of a hospital. Such term also includes a policy or rider which provides for payment of benefits based upon cognitive impairment or the loss of functional capacity. Long-term care insurance may be issued by insurers; fraternal benefit societies; nonprofit health, hospital, and medical service corporations; prepaid health plans; health maintenance organizations or any similar organization to the extent they are otherwise authorized to issue life or health insurance. Long-term care insurance shall not include any insurance policy which is offered primarily to provide basic Medicare supplement coverage, basic hospital expense coverage, basic medical-surgical expense coverage, hospital confinement indemnity coverage, major medical expense coverage, disability income or related asset-protection coverage, accident only coverage, specified disease or specified accident coverage, or limited benefit health coverage.

MODAL PREMIUM. This refers to the premium paid on a contract based on a premium term which could be annual, semi-annual, quarterly, monthly, or weekly. Thus if the annual premium is $100 and if, instead, monthly premiums of $9 are paid then the modal premium is $9.

NEGATIVE RESERVE. Normally the terminal reserve is a positive value. However, if the values of the benefits are decreasing with advancing age or duration it could be a negative value, called a negative reserve.

PRELIMINARY TERM RESERVE METHOD. Under this method of valuation the valuation net premium for each year falling within the preliminary term period is exactly sufficient to cover the expected incurred claims of that year, so that the terminal reserves will be zero at the end of the year. As of the end of the preliminary term period, a new constant valuation net premium (or stream of changing valuation premiums) becomes applicable such that the present value of all such premiums is equal to the present value of all claims expected to be incurred following the end of the preliminary term period.

PRESENT VALUE OF AMOUNTS NOT YET DUE ON CLAIMS. The reserve for "claims unaccrued" (see definition), which may be discounted at interest.

RATING BLOCK. "Rating block" means a grouping of contracts determined by the valuation actuary based on common characteristics filed with the commissioner, such as a policy form or forms having similar benefit designs.

RESERVE. The term "reserve" is used to include all items of benefit liability, whether in the nature of incurred claim liability or in the nature of contract liability relating to future periods of coverage, and whether the liability is accrued or unaccrued.

Health Insurance Reserves Model Regulation

An insurer under its contracts promises benefits which result in:

(a) Claims which have been incurred, that is, for which the insurer has become obligated to make payment, on or prior to the valuation date. On these claims, payments expected to be made after the valuation date for accrued and unaccrued benefits are liabilities of the insurer which should be provided for by establishing claim reserves; or

(b) Claims which are expected to be incurred after the valuation date. Any present liability of the insurer for these future claims should be provided for by the establishment of contract reserves and unearned premium reserves.

TERMINAL RESERVE. This is the reserve at the end of a contract year, and is defined as the present value of benefits expected to be incurred after that contract year minus the present value of future valuation net premiums.

UNEARNED PREMIUM RESERVE. This reserve values that portion of the premium paid or due to the insurer which is applicable to the period of coverage extending beyond the valuation date. Thus if an annual premium of $120 was paid on November 1, $20 would be earned as of December 31 and the remaining $100 would be unearned. The unearned premium reserve could be on a gross basis as in this example, or on a valuation net premium basis.

VALUATION NET MODAL PREMIUM. This is the modal fraction of the valuation net annual premium that corresponds to the gross modal premium in effect on any contract to which contract reserves apply. Thus if the mode of payment in effect is quarterly, the valuation net modal premium is the quarterly equivalent of the valuation net annual premium.

APPENDIX C. RESERVES FOR WAIVER OF PREMIUM
(Supplementary explanatory material)

Waiver of premium reserves involve several special considerations. First, the disability valuation tables promulgated by the NAIC are based on exposures that include contracts on premium waiver as in-force contracts. Hence, contract reserves based on these tables are NOT reserves on "active lives" but rather reserves on contracts "in force." This is true for the 1964 CDT and for both the "1985 CIDA and CIDB tables.

Accordingly, tabular reserves using any of these tables should value reserves on the following basis:

> Claim reserves should include reserves for premiums expected to be waived, valuing as a minimum the valuation net premium being waived.

> Premium reserves should include contracts on premium waiver as in-force contracts, valuing as a minimum the unearned modal valuation net premium being waived.

> Contract reserves should include recognition of the waiver of premium benefit in addition to other contract benefits provided for, valuing as a minimum the valuation net premium to be waived.

If an insurer is, instead, valuing reserves on what is truly an active life table, or if a specific valuation table is not being used but the insurer's gross premiums are calculated on a basis that includes in the projected exposure only those contracts for which premiums are being paid, then it may not be necessary to provide specifically for waiver of premium reserves. Any insurer using such a true "active life" basis should carefully consider, however, whether or not additional liability should be recognized on account of premiums waived during periods of disability or during claim continuation.

Legislative History (all references are to the Proceedings of the NAIC).
1989 Proc. I 9, 23-25, 651 -658, 705 (adopted new model).
1989 Proc. II 13, 23-24, 467, 875 (adopted technical amendment).
1991 Proc. II 25, 58, 719, 1257-1264 (amended and reprinted).
1993 Proc. I 8, 136, 820, 1460-1462 (amended).
1993 Proc. 1st Quarter 3, 34, 266, 438-446 (amended and reprinted).
1996 Proc. 2nd Quarter 10, 30, 732, 960, 961-964 (amended).
1997 Proc. 4th Quarter 1175-1188 (model adopted later is printed here).
1998 Proc. 1st Quarter 15, 17, 770, 1000, 1 056-1 057 (amended).
2000 Proc. 2nd Quarter 21, 22, 163-164, 166-168, 1098, 1112 (amended).
2001 Proc. 2nd Quarter 12, 14, 112-113, 991, 1130, 1132-1137 (amended).
2003 Proc. 3rd Quarter 217, 1006, 1013, (amended, adopted by parent committee).
2003 Proc. 4th Quarter 16 (Adopted by Plenary).
2003 Proc. 4th Quarter 390, 2059, 2065, 2116-2121 (amended, further amendments adopted by parent committee).
2004 Proc. 1st Quarter Vol. I 53 (adopted by Plenary).

The following has been superseded by the model above: Reserve Standards for Individual Health Insurance Policies

1941 Proc. I 60-1 62 (adopted).
1957 Proc. I 75, 77, 78-85, 107 (amended).
1959 Proc. I 90 (reaffirmed).
1965 Proc. I 71, 73-86, 88 (adopted 1964 Commissioners Disability Table).
1981 Proc. II 27, 35, 558, 561, 778, 781, 823-826 (amended).
1985 Proc. II 11, 23, 564, 567-569, 609-612 (cancer tables added).
1986 Proc. I 601-605 (Contains amendments adopted in June 1985 but omitted from that Proceedings).
1986 Proc. I 9, 23, 547, 557-558, 666 (Appendix A amended).

The date in parentheses is the effective date of the legislation or regulation, with latest amendments. See KEY at end of listing for explanation of numbers in brackets.

HEALTH INSURANCE RESERVES MODEL REGULATION

NAIC MEMBER	MODEL/SIMILAR LEGIS.	RELATED LEGIS./REGS.
Alabama	ALA. ADMIN. CODE. ch. 482-1-134.01 to 482-1-134.06 (2005) [2].	ALA. CODE §§ 27-36-1 to 27-36-5 (1971).
Alaska	ALASKA STAT. §§ 21.18.082 to 21.18.084 (1997) (Similar to model).	
Arizona	NO ACTION TO DATE	
Arkansas	ARK. INS. RULE & REG. 22 (1976/1999) [2].	
California	CAL. ADMIN. CODE tit. 10 §§ 2310 to 2315 (1994) [2].	CAL. INS. CODE § 997 (1959/1984).
Colorado	COLO. ADMIN. INS. REG. 3-1-9 (1993) [2].	
Connecticut	CONN. GEN. STAT. §§ 38a-78-11 to 78-16 (1993/1998) [2].	
Delaware		DEL. CODE ANN. tit. 18 § 1108 (1953).
District of Columbia	NO ACTION TO DATE	
Florida	FLA. ADMIN. CODE §§ 69O-154.201 to 69O-154.210 (1999/2005).	
Georgia		GA. CODE ANN. § 33-10-8 (1960/1985).
Guam	NO ACTION TO DATE	
Hawaii		HAWAII REV. STAT. § 431:5-303 (1955/1987).
Idaho	IDAHO INS. REGS 68 [IDAPA 18.01.68] (1993) [2].	
Illinois	ILL. ADMIN. REG. tit. 50 §§ 2004.20 to 2004.30 (1965/2002) [1].	

HEALTH INSURANCE RESERVES MODEL REGULATION

NAIC MEMBER	MODEL/SIMILAR LEGIS.	RELATED LEGIS./REGS.
Indiana		IND. ADMIN. tit. 760 R.1-9-1 to 1-9-4 (1964) (Adopts some of NAIC explanations from 1957 model by reference) [1].
Iowa	NO ACTION TO DATE	
Kansas	KAN. ADMIN. REGS. § 40-4-2 1 (1968/1986)(Model adopted by reference) [1].	
Kentucky		KY. REV. STAT. § 304.6-070 (1970).
Louisiana		LA. REV. STAT. ANN. § 22:891: §22:893 (1968/1975).
Maine	ME. INS. REG. ch. 130 (1991) [2].	
Maryland		MD. ANN. CODE. INS. § 5-203 (1963/1997).
Massachusetts	NO ACTION TO DATE	
Michigan	MICH. COMP. LAWS §§ 500.701 to 500.737 (1994) [2].	
Minnesota	MINN. STAT. §§ 60A.70 to 60A.78 (2004) [2].	
Mississippi		MISS. CODE ANN. § 83-9-106 (1992) (Authority to adopt regulation).
Missouri	MO. ADMIN. CODE tit. 20 § 200-1.140(2)(A), (D) (1969/2001) [1].	
Montana		MONT. CODE ANN. § 33-2-514 (1959/19 95).
Nebraska		NEB. REV. STAT. § 44-409 (19 13/1985).

HEALTH INSURANCE RESERVES MODEL REGULATION

NAIC MEMBER	MODEL/SIMILAR LEGIS.	RELATED LEGIS./REGS.
Nevada		NEV. REV. STAT. § 681B.080 (1971).
New Hampshire	NO ACTION TO DATE	

Model Regulation Service—July 2006

HEALTH INSURANCE RESERVES MODEL REGULATION

NAIC MEMBER	MODEL/SIMILAR LEGIS.	RELATED LEGIS./REGS.
New Jersey	N.J. ADMIN. CODE §§ 11:4-6.1 to 11:4-6.8 (1965/2003) [1].	
New Mexico	N.M. ADMIN. CODE §§ 13.10.14.1 to 13.10.14.26 (1997/2003) [2].	
New York	N.Y. ADMIN. CODE tit. 11 §§ 94.1 to 94.12 (1971/2006) (Regulation 56) [1].	
North Carolina	N.C. ADMIN. CODE tit. 11 ch. 11F §§ 0201 to 0208 (1994/2004) [2].	
North Dakota	NO ACTION TO DATE	
Northern Marianas	NO ACTION TO DATE	
Ohio	OHIO ADMIN. CODE § 3901-3-13 (1996/2003) [2].	
Oklahoma		OKLA. STAT. tit. 36 § 1508 (1957).
Oregon	OR. ADMIN. R. 836-031-0200 to 836-031-0300 (1995) [2].	OR. REV. STAT. § 733.080 (1967/1971).
Pennsylvania	PA. ADMIN. CODE tit. 31 §§ 84a.1 to 84a.8 (1993/1999) [2].	
Puerto Rico		P.R. LAWS ANN. tit. 26 § 507 (1966).
Rhode Island	R.I. REGS. R27-86-001 to 27-86-007 (1996) [2].	

HEALTH INSURANCE RESERVES MODEL REGULATION

NAIC MEMBER	MODEL/SIMILAR LEGIS.	RELATED LEGIS./REGS.
South Carolina	S.C. INS. R 69-7 (1991/1997) [2].	
South Dakota		S.D. CODIFIED LAWS ANN. § 58-26-30 (1966).
Tennessee	TENN. ADMIN. COMP. ch. 0780-1-69 (1998).	
Texas	28 TEX. ADMIN. CODE §§ 3.7001 to 3.7010 (1992/2003) [2].	
Utah	NO ACTION TO DATE	
Vermont	NO ACTION TO DATE	
Virgin Islands	NO ACTION TO DATE	
Virginia	14 VA. ADMIN. CODE 5-320-10 to 5-320-70 (1979/1994) [2].	
Washington	WASH. ADMIN. CODE R. §§ 284-16-400 to 284-16-540 (1992) [2].	
West Virginia	W. VA. REGS. §§ 114-44-1 to 114-44-10 (1996) [2].	W. VA. CODE § 33-7-7 (1957/1969).
Wisconsin	WIS. ADMIN. CODE § INS. 3.17 (1989/1992) [2].	
Wyoming		WYO. STAT. § 26-6-107 (1967/1993).

KEY

[1] Old NAIC model, applying only to individual policies and first adopted in 1941; amended numerous times.

[2] Newer NAIC model adopted December 1988 and subsequently revised; shown on previous pages.

HEALTH INSURANCE RESERVES MODEL REGULATION

Case Law

The following cases are a sampling of court decisions on the subject.

NAIC MEMBER	STATUTE	CASE SUMMARY
Alabama	Ala. Code §27-36-5 (1975)	Old Southern Life Insurance Company v. State Dept. of Insurance, 537So.2d 30 (1988)
		Insurer assumed certain policies, which provided that a policyholder should receive each year a "surplus interest dividend." Insurer's practice had been to deduct policy loan indebtedness from the policy's cash value, arriving at a net cash value to which the dividend rate was applied to determine the dividend amount of the surplus interest dividend. The commissioner determined insurer improperly calculated dividends due because the term "cash value" as used in the policies refers to an amount free of indebtedness unless otherwise stated in the policy. After reviewing the record, the court affirmed the Commissioner's determination.
Nebraska	Neb. Rev. Stat. § 44-409 (1913/1985)	Western Life & Acc. Co. of Colorado v. State Ins. Board of Nebraska, 101 Neb. 152, 162 N.W. 530 (1917)
		District court upheld insurance board's decision to decline to issue a certificate to insurer on the ground that insurer refused to make any provision for the establishment of a reserve fund to meet the claims of persistent policyholders, as required by Rev. St. 1913, §§3139, 3275, 3235. Insurer appealed claiming they were organized under Colorado law, which regarded insurer as incorporated under an assessment plan. The court found that within the meaning of Nebraska insurance laws, insurer did not transact business on the assessment plan, and was not an assessment association. Insurer was, instead, a mutual company under Nebraska law, which is required under Rev. St. 1913 §3138 to maintain the same reserve as stock companies. The insurance board may compel a foreign insurer to provide a reserve fund required of a similar domestic insurer. The district court's holding was affirmed.

APPENDIX E

Model # 134

Guidelines for Filing of Rates for Individual Health Insurance Forms

National Association of Insurance Commissioners

© NAIC
Reprinted with permission from NAIC.
Further distribution is strictly prohibited.

© 2006 National Association of Insurance Commissioners
All rights reserved.

National Association of Insurance Commissioners
Insurance Products & Services Division
816-783-8300
Fax 816-460-7593
www.naic.org/insprod
prodserv@naic.org

Printed in the United States of America

No part of this book may be reproduced, stored in a retrieval system, or transmitted in any form or by any means, electronic or mechanical, including photocopying, recording, or any storage or retrieval system, without written permission from the NAIC.

Executive Headquarters
2301 McGee Street, Suite 800
Kansas City, MO 64108-2662
816-842-3600

Securities Valuation Office
48 Wall Street, 6th Floor
New York, NY 10005-2906
212-398-9000

Government Relations
Hall of States Bldg.
444 North Capitol NW, Suite 701
Washington, DC 20001-1509
202-624-7790

MODEL REGULATION SERVICE – JULY 2000 ✦ E-3

GUIDELINES FOR FILING OF RATES FOR INDIVIDUAL HEALTH INSURANCE FORMS

Table of Contents

Section 1. General
Section 2. Reasonableness of Benefits in Relation to Premiums
Appendix. Rate Filing Guidelines

Section 1. General

A. Every policy, rider or endorsement form affecting benefits that is submitted for approval shall be accompanied by a rate filing unless the rider or endorsement form does not require a change in the rate. Any subsequent addition to or change in rates applicable to the policy, rider or endorsement shall also be filed.

B. General Contents of All Rate Filings

The purpose of this guideline, including its Appendix, is to provide appropriate guidelines for the submission and the filing of individual health insurance rates and to establish standards for determining the reasonableness of the relationship of benefits to premiums. Each rate submission shall include an actuarial memorandum describing the basis on which rates were determined and shall indicate and describe the calculation of the ratio, hereinafter called "anticipated loss ratio," of the present value of the expected benefits to the present value of the expected premiums over the entire period for which rates are computed to provide coverage. Interest shall be used in the calculation of this loss ratio. Each rate submission must also include a certification by a qualified actuary that to the best of the actuary's knowledge and judgment the entire rate filing is in compliance with the applicable laws and regulations of the state to which it is submitted and that the benefits are reasonable in relation to premiums.

Drafting Note: Assumptions applying to the future "period for which rates are computed" should be reasonable in relation to the circumstances. For example, if future rates of inflation are a major factor, the period of projection of such rates normally should be short, such as three to five years only. Other assumptions, however, may still appropriately apply over the entire future policy renewal period, particularly in cases where the basic rate structure is one of level premiums based on original issue age.

C. Previously Approved Forms

Filings of rate revisions for a previously approved policy, rider or endorsement form shall also include the following:

(1) A statement of the scope and reason for the revision, and an estimate of the expected average effect on premiums, including the anticipated loss ratio for the form;

(2) A statement as to whether the filing applies only to new business, only to in force business, or both, and the reasons therefore;

(3) A history of the experience under existing rates, including at least the data indicated in Section 1D. The history may also include, if available and appropriate, the ratios of actual claims to the claims expected according to the assumptions underlying the existing rates.

Additional data might include: substitution of actual claim run-offs for claim reserves and liabilities, determination of loss ratios with the increase in policy reserves subtracted from premiums rather than added to benefits, accumulation of experience fund balances, substitution of net level policy reserves for preliminary term policy reserves, reserve adjustments arising because of select period loss experience, adjustment of premiums to an annual mode basis, or other adjustments or schedules suited to the form and to the records of the company. All additional data shall be reconciled, as appropriate, to the required data; and

(4) The date and magnitude of each previous rate change, if any.

D. Experience Records

(1) Insurers shall maintain records of earned premiums and incurred benefits for each calendar year for each policy form, including data for rider and endorsement forms that are used with the policy form, on the same basis, including all reserves, as required for the Accident and Health Policy Experience Exhibit. Separate data may be maintained for each rider of endorsement form to the extent appropriate. Subject to approval of the commissioner, experience under forms that provide substantially similar coverage and provisions that are issued to substantially similar risk classes and that are issued under similar underwriting standards, may be combined for purposes of evaluating experience data in relation to premium rates and rate revisions, particularly where statistical credibility would be materially improved by the combination. Once such a combining of forms is adopted, however, the insurer may not afterward again separate the experience, except with approval of the commissioner.

(2) The data shall be for all years of issue combined and for each calendar year of experience utilized in the rate determination process (but never less than the last three years). For example, for policies originally filed under this guideline, experience since inception would be required because of the utilization of the rule in Section 2B(2)(b)(ii). Here, it is permissible to combine experience for calendar years prior to the most recent five.

E. Evaluating Experience Data

In determining the credibility and appropriateness of experience data, due consideration must be given to all relevant factors, such as:

(1) Statistical credibility of premiums and benefits, e.g., low exposure, low loss frequency;

(2) Experienced and projected trends relative to the kind of coverage, e.g., inflation in medical expenses, economic cycles affecting disability income experience;

(3) The concentration of experience at early policy durations where select morbidity and preliminary term reserves are applicable and

where loss ratios are expected to be substantially lower than at later policy durations. Where this consideration is pertinent, ratios of actual to expected claims, on a select basis, will often be appropriate for an adequate evaluation; and

(4) The mix of business by risk classification.

Section 2. Reasonableness of Benefits in Relation to Premiums

A. New Forms

(1) With respect to a new form under which the average annual premium as defined in Paragraph (5) below, is expected to be at least as large as the maximum $X in Paragraph (3) below but not more than the minimum $X in Paragraph (4) below, benefits shall be deemed reasonable in relation to premiums provided the anticipated loss ratio is at least as great as shown in the following table:

Type of Coverage	Renewal Clause			
OR	CR	GR	NC	
Medical Expense	60%	55%	55%	50%
Loss of Income and Other	60%	55%	50%	45%

(2) Definitions of Renewal Clause

OR - Optionally Renewable: renewal is at the option of the insurance company.

CR - Conditionally Renewable: renewal can be declined by class, by geographic area or for stated reasons other than deterioration of health.

GR - Guaranteed Renewable: renewal cannot be declined by the insurance company for any reason, but the insurance company can revise rates on a class basis.

NC - Non-Cancelable: renewal cannot be declined nor can rates be revised by the insurance company.

(3) Low Average Premium Forms

For a policy form, including riders and endorsements, under which the expected average annual premium per policy is low (as defined below), the appropriate ratio from the table above should be adjusted downward by the following formula:

$$RN = R \times \frac{(I \times 500) + X}{(I \times 750)}$$

where: R is the table ratio

RN is the resulting guideline ratio

I is the consumer price index factor

X is the average annual premium up to a maximum of *I*.250.

The factor *I* is determined as follows:

$$I = \frac{CPI-U, \text{Year } (N-1)}{CPI-U, (1982)} = \frac{CIP-U, \text{Year } (N-1)}{293.3}$$

where:

(a) $(N-1)$ is the calendar year immediately preceding the calendar year (N) in which the rate filing is submitted in the state;

(a) $CPI-U$ is the consumer price index for all urban consumers, for all items, and for all regions of the U.S. combined, as determined by the U.S. Department of Labor, Bureau of Labor Statistics;

(b) The $CPI-U$ for any year $(N-1)$) is taken as the value of September. For 1982, this value was 293.3;

(c) Hence, for rate filings submitted during calendar year 1983, the value of *I* is 1.00.

(4) High Average Premium Forms

For a policy form, including riders and endorsements, under which the expected average annual premium per policy is high (as defined below), the appropriate ratio from the table above should be adjusted upward by the following formula:

$$RN = R \times \frac{(I \times 4000) + X}{(I \times 5500)}$$

Where: *R* is the table ratio

RN is the resulting guideline ratio

I is the consumer price index factor (as defined in Paragraph (3) above), or

X is an average annual premium exceeding *I* . 1500. In no event, however, shall *RN* exceed the lesser of:

(a) $R + 5R + 5$ percentage points, or
(b) 63%.

(5) Determination of Average Premium

The average annual premium per policy shall be estimated by the insurer based on an anticipated distribution of business by all significant criteria having a price difference, such as age, sex, amount, dependent status, rider frequency, etc., except assuming an annual mode for all policies (i.e., the fractional premium loading shall not affect the average annual premium or anticipated loss ratio calculation).

The value of X should be determined on the basis of the rates being filed. Thus, where this adjustment is applicable to a rate revision under Section 2B of these guidelines, rather than to a new form, X should be determined on the basis of anticipated average size premium immediately after the revised rates have fully taken effect.

(6) Medicare Supplement Forms

For Medicare supplement policies, benefits shall be deemed reasonable in relation to premiums provided the anticipated loss ratio is at least sixty percent (60%).

(7) Conflict with Specific Statutes or Regulations

The above anticipated loss ratio standards do not apply to a class of business where the standards are in conflict with specific statutes or regulations.

(8) Forms with Indexing of Benefits

Certain policy forms provide for automatic indexing of benefits in relation to some base that is not subject to control by the insurer or the insured. Medicare supplement plans under which benefits automatically adjust in response to changes in the Part A or Part B deductibles under federal Medicare are a common example. Other possibilities exist, under disability income, major medical and other forms of coverage.

In such cases, the insurer should be permitted to file rates on a basis that provides for automatic adjustment of premiums, on an actuarial basis appropriate in relation to the automatic adjustment in the benefits. While such premium adjustment would thus be considered "pre-filed," to apply "automatically," it should nevertheless be subject to ongoing monitoring of the continuing loss experience and there should be some agreement with the insurer that the commissioner may require, from time to time, renewed justification that the automatic premium adjustments remain appropriate and reasonable.

B. Rate Revisions

(1) With respect to filing of rate revisions for a previously approved form, or a group of previously approved forms combined for experience, benefits shall be deemed reasonable in relation to premiums, provided the revised rates meet the standards applicable to the prior rate filing for the form or forms.

In general, the rule that applies is that any rate revision is subject to the guideline basis under which the previous rates were filed (with consideration of all relevant rating factors: morbidity, expenses, persistency, interest, etc.), and to those regulatory guidelines, if any, that were in effect at the time of the filing. Where there was no written guideline applicable to the prior rate filing, the regulatory benchmark then generally recognized, such as the 1953 NAIC benchmark (1953 *Proceedings of the NAIC,* Vol. II, p. 542), will continue to govern rate revisions of the prior rate filings.

(2) With respect to filings of rate revisions for a form approved subject to these guidelines, benefits will be deemed reasonable in relation to premiums provided both the following loss ratios meet the standards in Section 2A of these guidelines:

(a) The anticipated loss ratio over the entire future period for which the revised rates are computed to provide coverage;

Drafting Note: Assumptions applying to the future "period for which rates are computed" should be reasonable in relation to the circumstances. For example, if future rates of inflation are a major factor, the period of projection of such rates normally should be short, such as three to five years only. Other assumptions, however, may still appropriately apply over the entire future policy renewal period, particularly in cases where the basic rate structure is one of level premiums based on original issue age.

(b) The lifetime anticipated loss ratio derived by dividing (i) by (ii) where (i) is the sum of the accumulated benefits from the original effective date of the form to the effective date of the revision, and the present value of future benefits, and (ii) is the sum of the accumulated premiums from the original effective date of the form to the effective date of the revision, and the present value of future premiums, such present values to be taken over the entire period for which the revised rates are computed to provide coverage, and the accumulated benefits and premiums to include an explicit estimate of the actual benefits and premiums from the last date as of which an accounting has been made to the effective date of the revision. Interest shall be used in the calculation of these accumulated benefits and premiums and present values only if it is a significant factor in the calculation of this loss ratio.

C. Anticipated loss ratios lower than those indicated in Subsection B(2)(a) and (2)(b) will require justification based on the special circumstances that may be applicable.

(1) Examples of coverages requiring special consideration are as follows:

(a) Accident only;
(b) Short term non-renewable, e.g., airline trip, student accident;
(c) Specified peril, e.g., cancer, common carrier;
(d) Other special risks.

(2) (a) Examples of other factors requiring special consideration are as follows:

   (i) Marketing methods, giving due consideration to acquisition and administration costs and to premium mode;
   (ii) Extraordinary expenses, or, in the case of a rate increase, expenses in excess of those expected under the previous rate filing;
   (iii) High risk of claim fluctuation because of the low loss frequency or the catastrophic, or experimental nature of the coverage;
   (iv) Product features such as long elimination periods, high deductibles and high maximum limits; and
   (v) The industrial or debit method of distribution.

   (b) Companies are urged to review their experience periodically and to file rate revisions, as appropriate, in a timely manner to avoid the necessity of later filing exceptionally large rate increases.

Appendix. Rate Filing Guidelines

A basic actuarial requirement in the establishment of a premium rate scale is that the benefits provided be reasonable in relation to premiums. This requirement has been incorporated in the statutes of many jurisdictions and in the regulations and operating rules, formal and informal, of the insurance departments of probably all jurisdictions.

One of the principal objectives of these guidelines is to establish a basis for assisting both those filing rates and those responsible for regulatory review of filings in deciding whether a premium rate filing meets this requirement.

The individuals who drafted these guidelines recognized that the guidelines would be applicable to the wide range of products marketed by a diversity of methods under the general title "Individual Health Insurance." For this reason, they decided it would be inappropriate to establish rigid rules or inflexible standards. It should be recognized, therefore, that the guidelines are intended to be only guidelines, and they must be interpreted and applied flexibly.

Section 2A of the guidelines includes a table of numerical values representing loss ratios that "shall be deemed reasonable in relation to premium." This "deemer level" of loss ratio is meant to be the initial guideline test for establishing the reasonableness of the premiums in relation to benefits. Satisfying this test establishes that the premiums are reasonable in relation to benefits. However, premium rates not meeting this test may still have benefits that are reasonable in relation to premiums based on further considerations.

Other parts of Section 2, and particularly Subsection C, give examples of situations where considerations beyond the initial test would be appropriate in determining the reasonableness of premiums in relation to benefits.

Although expenses are not addressed in detail in the guidelines, the variations in loss ratio benchmarks by average annual premiums per policy is clearly intended to provide for the fact that a substantial amount of general expense is not a function of premium but is flat per policy. Thus, the guidelines intend to make realistic provision for actual expenses as incurred. As inflation causes unit expenses to rise, despite the gains from improved productivity through greater mechanization, etc., the possibility of lower loss ratios may have to be confronted for some forms.

One of the purposes of Section 1 of the guidelines is to set the requirements for rate filings. The usefulness of this section is enhanced by showing herein the minimum requirements as to the documentation of these rate filings.

In developing the checklist below, consideration was merely given to pointing out some of the factors that may be involved in calculating the rates, e.g., interest, mortality, morbidity, selection, lapse, expenses, inflation, etc., and spell out how those factors might be used in such calculations. It was felt, however, that this approach would produce details not always necessary to justify or review the rate filing while leaving out possibly essential information.

The checklists are separate for filing of rates for a new product and filing of rate increases.

Checklist of Items to be included in Individual Health Insurance Rate Filing Submissions

Rates for a New Product

I. Policy Form, application, and endorsements required by State Law.

II. Rate Sheet

III. Actuarial Memorandum

    A. Brief description of the type of policy, benefits, renewability, general marketing method, and issue age limits.

    B. Brief description of how rates were determined, including the general description and source of each assumption used. For expenses, include percent of premium, dollars per policy or dollars per unit of benefit, or both.

    C. Estimated average annual premium per policy.

    D. Anticipated loss ratio, including a brief description of how it was calculated.

    E. Anticipated loss ratio presumed reasonable according to the guidelines.

    F. If Subsection D is less than Subsection E, supporting documentation for the use of the proposed premium rates.

    G. Certification by a qualified actuary that, to the best of the actuary's knowledge and judgment, the rate submission is in compliance with the applicable laws and regulations of the state and the benefits are reasonable in relation to the premiums.

[IV. A statement as to the status of this rate filing in the company's home state.]

Rate Increases for an Existing Product
for which Rates are Subject to this Guideline

I. New Rate Sheet

II. Actuarial Memorandum

   A. Brief description of the type of policy, benefits, renewability, general marketing method and issue age limits.

   B. Scope and reason for rate revision including a statement of whether the revision applies only to new business, only to in force business, or to both, and outline of all past rate increases on this form.

   C. Estimated average annual premium per policy, before and after rate increase. Descriptive relationship of proposed rate scale to current rate scale.

   D. Past experience, as specified in Section 2D of the guidelines, any other available data the insurer may wish to provide.

   E. Brief description of how revised rates were determined, including the general description and source of each assumption used. For expenses, include percent of premium, dollars per policy, or dollars per unit of benefit, or both.

   F. The anticipated future loss ratio and description of how it was calculated.

   G. The anticipated loss ratio that combines cumulative and future experience, and description of how it was calculated.

   H. Anticipated loss ratio presumed reasonable according to the guidelines.

   I. If Subsection F or G is less than Subsection H, supporting documentation for the use of such premium rates.

   J. Certification by a qualified actuary that, to the best of the actuary's knowledge and judgment, the rate submission is in compliance with the applicable laws and regulations of the state and the benefits are reasonable in relation to the premiums.

The test in Section 2B(2) is an innovation of these guidelines. It seems appropriate, therefore, that this appendix include an example of how it works.

The first test in Section 2B(2)(a) is the same for a new form, new business on an existing form, or experience on existing business following a rate revision. Suppose that we are talking about an OR form with an average annual premium exceeding $X, defined in the guidelines, and the new rates are originally set to provide the benchmark loss ratio of sixty percent (60%).

When the new rates are applied to existing business in force and we calculate the present value of future premiums and benefits, we obtain the following results.

Table 1 - Future Projection

	Present Value at Current Volume from next year anniversaries
Premiums	$30,000,000
Benefits	18,000,000
Loss Ratio	.60

Then we look at the accumulated experience for the past. Suppose it can be summarized as follows: The poor recent experience has prompted the need for the current increase request.

Table 2 - Accumulated Experience

	Prior to 3 years	Last 3 years	From last year end to next anniversary	Total
Premiums	$50,000,000	$10,000,000	$10,000,000	$70,000,000
Benefits	20,000,000	9,000,000	11,000,000	40,000,000
Loss Ratio	.400	.900	1.100	.571

When the accumulated and present value figures are combined, the following results appear.

Table 3 - Combined Experiences

	Accumulated	Present Value	Total
Premiums	$70,000,000	$30,000,000	$100,000,000
Benefits	40,000,000	18,000,000	58,000,000
Loss Ratio	.571	.600	.580

The test in Section 2B(2)(b) is not met.

With respect to future premiums on the existing volume, the rates proposed must be reduced so that the .58 result is increased to .60. Since the benefits are what they are and the present value is settled, we can work backwards to determine that the total premiums must be $96,666,667 ($58,000,000 ÷ .60). Thus the present value of future premiums must be $26,666,667 and the proposed rates, applicable to new business, must be reduced by one-ninth, with respect to the existing volume. The new table which meets the Section 2B(2)(b) test is as follows.

Table 4 - Revised Combined Experiences

	Accumulated	Present Value	Total
Premiums	$70,000,000	$26,666,667	$96,666,667
Benefits	40,000,000	18,000,000	58,000,000
Loss Ratio	.571	.675	.600

The next rate increase request will depend on how experience develops, if the company wishes to charge the same rates for new business and renewal, one way it could do so would be by reducing the rates otherwise proposed for new business. An alternative approach would be to combine the experience under new and existing business in a similar analysis to arrive at a single rate structure applying to both.

If the early experience under the form was poor, the losses would not be recoverable. Suppose, for instance, that only the last three years and the estimate for the last year-end to the next year's anniversary in the above example existed and the proposed new business rates applied. Then, the following test from Section 2B(2)(b) appears:

Table 5 - Alternate Combined Experiences

	Accumulated	Present Value	Total
Premiums	$20,000,000	$30,000,000	$50,000,000
Benefits	20,000,000	18,000,000	38,000,000
Loss Ratio	1.000	.600	.760

While the present value of future premiums could be increased under the Section 2B(2)(b) test to recover past losses and still meet the 60% benchmark, the test in Section 2B(2)(a) would preclude such an increase.

It is believed that this test will be rather simple to apply, in practice, from readily available records. It will be an effective tool in reviewing the reasonableness of rate increases.

Section 2B, as amended, is not intended to substitute new standards retroactively in place of standards in effect before the date of these guidelines. It is not intended that the rules be changed in the middle of the contract period. On the other hand, the principles of these guidelines may have been implicit in a state's former rules and guidelines.

It should be emphasized again that the tests in Section 2A and 2B have to do with benchmarks, not legal minimums. Section 2C mentions some situations in which lower loss ratios may be justifiable. If, however, a rate submission meets the benchmark standards and includes full documentation as described in the guidelines and this appendix, the requirement that benefits be reasonable in relation to premiums should be considered met.

Legislative history (all references are to the Proceedings of the NAIC)

1980 Proc. I 29, 38, 406, 410, 413, 416-425 (adopted).
1983 Proc. I 6, 35, 644, 652-659 (revised).
1983 Proc. II 16, 22, 638, 644, 646-655 (amended and reprinted).

The date in parentheses is the effective date of the legislation or regulation, with latest amendments.

GUIDELINES FOR FILING OF RATES FOR INDIVIDUAL HEALTH INSURANCE FORMS

NAIC MEMBER	MODEL/SIMILAR LEGIS.	RELATED LEGIS./REGS.
Alabama	NO ACTION TO DATE	
Alaska	NO ACTION TO DATE	
Arizona	ARIZ. ADMIN. COMP. R20-6-607 (1981) (Similar to NAIC model; the differences are explained in a circular letter dated 7/24/81).	
Arkansas		See BULLETIN 12-81 re loss ratios.
California		CAL. ADMIN. CODE tit. 10 R. 2219 to 2220.28 (1972) (Standards for review).
Colorado		COLO. ADMIN. INS. REG. 4-2-11 (1992/2001); Bulletin 07-01 (2001).
Connecticut		CONN. ADMIN. CODE tit. 38a §§ 481-1 to 481-4 (1990/2006) (amendments included in the Connecticut Law Journal).
Delaware		DEL. CODE ANN. tit. 18 §§ 2501 to 2531 (1953) § 3333 (1953) BULLETIN NOs. 79-1 (As amended), 7 1-15 (Filing procedures); DEL. ADMIN. CODE tit. 18 § 1305 (1991/2003).
District of Columbia	NO ACTION TO DATE	
Florida	FLA. ADMIN. CODE §§69O-149.002 to 69O-149.010 (1985/2005); 69O-149-022 (2005); 69O-149-205 to 69O-149-207 (2005/2006).	See Memorandum 2006-012.
Georgia	NO ACTION TO DATE	
Guam	NO ACTION TO DAT	

GUIDELINES FOR FILING OF RATES FOR
INDIVIDUAL HEALTH INSURANCE FORMS

NAIC MEMBER	MODEL/SIMILAR LEGIS.	RELATED LEGIS./REGS.
Hawaii		HAWAII REV. STAT. §§ 431:14F-101 to 431:14F-113 (2003/2006).
Idaho	NO ACTION TO DATE	
Illinois	NO ACTION TO DATE	
Indiana	NO ACTION TO DATE	
Iowa	IOWA ADMIN. CODE §§ 191-36.9 to 191-36. 12 (1982).	
Kansas	KAN. ADMIN. REGS. § 40-4-1 (1981/2003) (Adopted by reference subject to stated exceptions).	
Kentucky	806 KY. ADMIN. REGS. 17:070 (1982/1995).	
Louisiana	NO ACTION TO DATE	
Maine		ME. REV. STAT. ANN. tit. 24-A § 2736 (1979) (Rate filing required); ME. INS. REG. ch. 940 (2000).
Maryland		MD. ADMIN. CODE 31.10.01.02 (1965/1993) (Filing procedures).
Massachusetts		211 CODE OF MASS. REGS. 41.06 (1997/2002).
Michigan		MICH. ADMIN. CODE R. 500.801 to 500.806 (1974) (Includes standards for review).
Minnesota	NO ACTION TO DATE	
Mississippi		MISS. INS. REG. L. A. & H. 73-4 (1973) (Filing procedures).
Missouri	NO ACTION TO DATE	
Montana	NO ACTION TO DATE	

GUIDELINES FOR FILING OF RATES FOR INDIVIDUAL HEALTH INSURANCE FORMS

NAIC MEMBER	MODEL/SIMILAR LEGIS.	RELATED LEGIS./REGS.
Nebraska	NO ACTION TO DATE	
Nevada		NEV. BULLETIN 87-4 (1987) (Filing procedures).
New Hampshire	N.H. ADMIN. CODE INS. §401.01(c) (1982/1993) (Model will serve as guide for review).	N.H. ADMIN. CODE INS. §§401.02 to 401.03 (1982/1993) (Includes standards for review).
New Jersey		N.J. ADMIN. CODE §§ 11:4-18.1 to 11:4-18.10 (1980/1996) (Includes standards for review).
New Mexico	NO ACTION TO DATE	
New York		N.Y. ADMIN. CODE tit. 11 §§ 52.40 to 52.42 (Regulation 62) (1983/1996) (Filing procedures).
North Carolina	NO ACTION TO DATE	N.C. ADMIN. CODE tit. 11 ch. 16 § .0205 (1992/2005).
North Dakota	NO ACTION TO DATE	
Northern Marianas	NO ACTION TO DATE	
Ohio	NO ACTION TO DATE	
Oklahoma	NO ACTION TO DATE	
Oregon		OR. ADMIN. R. 836-010-0011 (1994/2002).
Pennsylvania		PA. ADMIN. CODE § 89.83 (1975) (Standards for review).
Puerto Rico	NO ACTION TO DATE	
Rhode Island		R.I. REGS. R27-23-1101 to 27-23-1107 (1979) (Filing procedures).
South Carolina	S.C. CODE ANN. § 38-71-310	

GUIDELINES FOR FILING OF RATES FOR
INDIVIDUAL HEALTH INSURANCE FORMS

NAIC MEMBER	MODEL/SIMILAR LEGIS.	RELATED LEGIS./REGS.
	(1988/1989) (Model adopted by reference).	
South Dakota	NO ACTION TO DATE	
Tennessee		TENN. ADMIN. COMP. ch. 0780-1-20 (1981/1994).

GUIDELINES FOR FILING OF RATES FOR
INDIVIDUAL HEALTH INSURANCE FORMS

NAIC MEMBER	MODEL/SIMILAR LEGIS.	RELATED LEGIS./REGS.
Texas	NO ACTION TO DATE	
Utah	UTAH INS. R590-85 (1980/2003)	*See also* Bulletin 96-2 (1996).
Vermont	NO ACTION TO DATE	
Virgin Islands	NO ACTION TO DATE	
Virginia	14 VA. ADMIN. CODE 5-130-10 to 5-130-100 (1981).	
Washington		WASH. ADMIN. CODE. R. §§ 284-60-010 to 284-60-100 (1983) (Standards for review).
West Virginia	NO ACTION TO DATE	
Wisconsin		WIS. ADMIN. CODE § INS. 3.13(6) (1958/1999) (Filing requirements).
Wyoming	NO ACTION TO DATE